£9.95 £3.95

D0545682

The Dukes

The Origins, Ennoblement and History of
26 Families

MULLER

BOOKS BY BRIAN MASTERS

Molière

Sartre

Saint-Exupéry

Rabelais

Dreams about H.M. The Queen

Wynyard Hall and the Londonderry Family

Camus: A Study

The Mistresses of Charles II

Now Barabbas was A Rotter: The Extraordinary Life of Marie Corelli

Georgiana, Duchess of Devonshire

Great Hostesses

*Killing for Company: the case
of Dennis Nilsen*

The Swinging Sixties

The Passion of John Aspinall

The Dukes

The Origins, Ennoblement and History
of 26 Families

Brian Masters

FREDERICK MULLER

London Sydney Auckland Johannesburg

For
CAROLINE
and for
FREDERICK

© Brian Masters 1975, 1977, 1980, 1988
All rights reserved
First published in Great Britain in 1975 by Blond & Briggs Ltd.
Second impression with additional material 1977
This revised and updated edition first published in Great Britain in 1988
by Frederick Muller, an imprint of

Century Hutchinson Ltd, Brookmount House, 62–65 Chandos Place,
London WC2N 4NW

Century Hutchinson Australia Pty Ltd
PO Box 496, 16–22 Church Street, Hawthorn, Victoria 3122, Australia

Century Hutchinson New Zealand Limited
PO Box 40–086, Glenfield, Auckland 10, New Zealand

Century Hutchinson South Africa (Pty) Ltd
PO Box 337, Bergvlei, 2021 South Africa

ISBN 0 09 173700 1

British Library Cataloguing in Publication Data
Masters, Brian, *1939–*
   The dukes: the origins, ennoblement
   and history of 26 families.——3rd ed.
   1. Great Britain. dukes to 1985
   I. Title
   305.5′223
   ISBN 0-09-173700-1

Contents

Acknowledgements

Mr E. K. Timings, M.A., F.S.A., Principal Assistant Keeper of the Public Record Office, has assiduously read every word of the MS and has made many helpful suggestions; I should like his contribution to the book which follows to be acknowledged first. Lady Camilla Osborne has substantially helped to track down some details of fact which have proved most useful, and undertook the task of proof-reading, for which I am deeply grateful. I wish particularly to mention Miss Stevenson of the Scottish National Portrait Gallery, Miss Evans and Miss Wimbush of the National Portrait Gallery, Miss Frankland of Ladbrokes Ltd, and Mr J. M. Keyworth of the Second Covent Garden Property Co. Ltd, all of whom have remained most helpful in spite of constant enquiries. The staff of the London Library are unfailingly obliging.

I am grateful to the Duke of Devonshire for permission to consult the papers in the Devonshire Collections, and to his librarian T. S. Wragg, M.B.E., T.D., for his guidance through them; also to the Duke of Atholl, who allowed me to consult his family papers at Blair Castle, to the Duke of Hamilton, for permission to see the Hamilton Papers currently being catalogued at the Scottish National Register of Archives, and to the Marquess of Londonderry, for permission to see the Londonderry Papers at Durham County Record Office. The Duke of Buccleuch and the Duke of Newcastle have both kindly involved themselves in lengthy correspondence with the author.

Those who have been personally very helpful with information include the Duchess of Devonshire, the Duke of Richmond, the Duke and Duchess of Somerset, the Duke of St Albans, the Duke of Bedford, the Duke of Hamilton, the Duke of Argyll, the Duke of Atholl, the Duke of Northumberland, K.G., the Marquess of Tavistock, the Marquess of Kildare, the Countess of Sutherland, and Mr Charles Janson. To all I should like here to express my gratitude.

For allowing me to take their time and plunder their knowledge I am indebted to Francis W. Steer, M.A., F.S.A., archivist to the Duke of Norfolk; J. N. R. James, Esq., Managing Trustee of the Grosvenor Estates; Michael Hanson, Esq.; and those descendants of the Duke of Somerset in the St Maur line – Mr Edward St Maur, Mr Joseph Hoare, and Mrs G. Kemmis-Betty.

Permission to use photographs of pictures in public collections and in private hands is gratefully acknowledged with each illustration, and due credit is likewise recorded to the photographers. I am also happy to record my thanks to various authors who have allowed me to quote from their works, specified in reference notes at the end of each chapter, and I trust they will accept this collective appreciation. Mrs Cecil Woodham-Smith in particular has been most generous in allowing me the freedom of her personal library.

The patience and industry of Mrs Diana Steer, who typed the manuscript, deserve to be recorded in rose-banks, and the generosity of the Marquess of Londonderry, who enabled me to write the final draft at his home in Co. Cleveland in the most peaceful conditions, is something for which gratitude seems woefully inadequate.

B.M.
Wynyard, 1975

Preface to 1988 Edition

In 1972 Anthony Blond made a bold suggestion. There had never, he said, been a book devoted to the history of all surviving dukedoms following each family from the date of creation to the present day in one volume. Many dukes were well known to history because they had been Prime Minister, or had won famous battles, or had distinguished themselves in some other way in the service of their country. A few were known for their slightly dotty personalities. There remained scores of other dukes whose lives languished unexamined in archive rooms and who perhaps deserved to be restored to their place in the genetic flow. Blond invited me to undertake the task of putting them all together and tracing family characteristics which persisted, sometimes obliquely, through many generations, and I spent the next three years in a gloriously eclectic ramble through five hundred years of history.

Though intended to be informative and entertaining, *The Dukes* has, since it first appeared in 1975, earned a gratifying reputation as a work of reference. It is for this reason that the reader might like to be acquainted with events which have occurred since the main text was published twelve years ago. The second edition of 1980 made some amendments in added footnotes; in some cases these too are out of date and have required revision. There are still twenty-six dukes (who will reduce to twenty-four in the next generation), but we now have a new Duke of Somerset, a new Duke of Beaufort, a new Duke of Portland, and a new Duke of Manchester. The young Duke of Roxburghe now has an infant son and heir (Marquess of Bowmont and Cessford), while his almost as young brother-in-law the Duke of Westminster still has not; until that day comes, he will remain potentially the last duke of the Grosvenor family. Furthermore, Elizabeth II's son Prince Andrew was created Duke of York one hour after his marriage to Sarah Ferguson in 1986. As a royal duke, he is without the scope of this book, although his grandson will fall within it when he inherits the title seventy or eighty years from now; even so, he has a tangential relevance in that he is reported to have proposed marriage to Miss Ferguson while staying at Floors Castle with the Duke and Duchess of Roxburghe. HRH The Duke of York may also justly be credited with an encouraging influence over the pages which follow, as the enthusiasm generated by his wedding kindled a whole new interest in the subject of dukes, their descent and their position in the land.

The twenty-six non-royal dukes are still working, ruminating, managing estates and avoiding attention much as before. They share, for the most part, an ineradicable shyness, of which there are many extravagant examples in the pages that follow, and prefer not to be noticed by any save their family, and dependants. Some succeed better than others. The Duke of Devonshire is constantly in the news, much to his chagrin, not only because he has embraced the responsibilities attendant upon his station by accepting onerous public duties, but because the Duchess's formidable family (the Mitfords) has been the subject of half a dozen books in the last twelve years as well as a musical stage version of their early years together. There is, of course, nothing a Duchess can do to deflect fame of this sort; it is the penalty of having a clutch of uncommon sisters. She has herself written a history of Chatsworth, called *The House*, which is quite the most entertaining account so far written, and incidentally has revealed her to be as gifted with words as her sisters Nancy, Jessica and Diana. For his part, the duke has achieved the impossible by securing the future of Chatsworth for generations to come in the face of mountains of legislation designed to prevent landowners passing on anything at all. That will be his enduring accomplishment, and one of which he will have every right to be proud.

The Duke of Rutland has won a long battle to deter prospectors from undermining Belvoir Castle and destroying one of the last oases of pristine beauty in the country, earning the gratitude of people who live there if not that of people who think progress a virtue whatever the cost. The Duke of St Albans, living in the south of France, has been gratified to watch his grandson Lord Vere, a student at Hertford College, Oxford, grow towards a sharing of his own conviction (supported by some academics) that the family is descended from the man who *really* wrote Shakespeare's plays – the last de Vere Earl of Oxford. We may expect to see a resurrection of this literary mystery when he eventually becomes Duke.

The heir to the Duke of Fife, Lord Macduff, has adopted the ducal style well ahead of time. Working in the City of London, he has been known to strike an assembled company of stockbrokers with awe at his approach. There is something still to be said for the view I first promulgated twelve years ago, that when one is in the presence of a duke one is aware that he is set apart from other members of the nobility – a giant in the magnificence of his ancestry, in the splendour of his genetic luggage, in the distinction of his manner. It is no accident that dukes take precedence over government ministers, envoys and bishops.

Brian Masters
London, 1988

Introduction

The title of duke is the rarest honour which the Crown may bestow on a person not of royal blood. It is next to the Crown itself in degree,* above every other subject in the realm, including those who hold dignities of much greater antiquity in the peerage, such as earls and barons, in existence long before the first duke was created 651 years ago. They are addressed officially by the monarch as "right trusty and entirely beloved cousins", and by everyone else as "Your Grace". They are the only peers whose title cannot be disguised by a generic style of address; whereas the Marquess of Anglesey, the Earl of Lichfield, Viscount Cowdray and Baron Teviot are levelled to the same degree in conversation as "Lord Anglesey", "Lord Lichfield", "Lord Cowdray", and "Lord Teviot", a duke is never a lord, always the "Duke of Such-and-such", and they would address each other, unless they were related or close, as "Duke". Their special status has allowed them to preserve an aura which even today can make the rest of us if not tremble at least defer with some inherited sense of hierarchy. The aura is now all that is left of the privileges attached to a dukedom, once so extensive as to paralyse the imagination. They are not even all aristocrats any more. None, it is true, can claim to have emerged from the working class; there have been no trade-union dukedoms created in the twentieth century, nor even any granted to the get-rich-quick boys in the property world. Some of the dukes, however, have a trickle of workmen's blood in their veins, due to some bizarre marriages in the past, and of the twenty-six still going, half a dozen are invincibly middle-class.

In common with other peers until the reforms of the nineteenth century, the dukes enjoyed privileges which seem scarcely credible. They were above the law. They could commit crime and escape the

---

* But not in precedence, see pages 15–16.

jurisdiction of the courts; no one could arrest them; they could run up debts to infinity without punishment; they had control of Parliament, many seats in the House of Commons being within the gift of a handful of noblemen, especially the dukes; they were the government of the land, in fact if not in appearance; they were England. "Flattered, adulated, deferred to, with incomes enormously increased by the Industrial Revolution, and as yet untaxed, all-powerful over a tenantry as yet unenfranchised, subject to no ordinary laws, holding the government of the country firmly in their hands and wielding through their closely-knit connections an unchallengeable social power, the milords of England were the astonishment and admiration of Europe."[1]

All this has thankfully gone. There is not a duke alive today who would wish for a return of such subservience or would attempt to justify such power. Gone, too, are some of the more absurd accoutrements of a ducal life – the personal trumpeter to announce one's presence, the retinue of personal servants, sometimes well over a hundred individuals, the pomposity of privilege. The modern dukes would not dare indulge in the antics of their forbears – requiring other people to wind their watches for them, or to hand them their dinner-plates wearing white kid gloves – for fear of being laughed to scorn. Yet some such habits have continued until within the last twenty years. The late Duke of Portland could talk of having bought a Rolls-Royce "off the peg" in Newcastle without the consciousness of humour. Many of the houses in which dukes live still have a personal staff of up to twenty persons, including cooks, butler, valet, "nanny", and chars, although such a staff no longer makes them singular – foreign ambassadors from communist countries can employ more.

Twenty of the dukes live in beautiful houses built at a time when the English aesthetic sense was at its most developed, houses far too big for them, in parks and grounds of ravishing beauty. One has chosen a nomadic life – the Duke of Bedford; two have exiled themselves to Africa – Manchester and Montrose; one lives in a flat in Monte Carlo – Duke of St Albans, and another in a house in Lymington – Duke of Newcastle; the late Duke of Leinster used to rent a room in Hove. Of the others, nine own more land than the Queen. The Crown estates have about 1,800,000 acres, which the Queen surrenders to the State in return for the Civil List, money she needs to run the royal households. As a private landowner, the Queen has only 40,000 acres at Balmoral and 7000 acres at Sandringham. In contrast, the Duke of Buccleuch has 250,000 acres, the Duke of Atholl 120,000, the Dukes of Northumberland and Argyll 80,000 each, and the Duke of Westminster owns a quarter of central London. The dukes have off-loaded thousands of acres since World War I, but what they have left is worth as much as it ever was, with the rise in agricultural land values. On paper at least, nearly all of them are millionaires in terms of their assets. As for cash in hand it is quite another story.

Before the beginning of the twentieth century the cost of being a duke, of maintaining the estate to the benefit of all tenants, of living in the lavish style which was expected of a duke, was prohibitive. The Marquess of Worcester, grandfather to the 1st Duke of Beaufort, wrote : "Since I was a Marquess I am worse by one hundred thousand pounds, and if I should be a duke, I should be an arrant beggar."[2] To obviate such noble penury, it was customary when creating a duke to give him money enough to live like one; the honour was hollow without the cash. Nowadays the running of an estate is so complex an affair, with farm economics and legislation, that it is above the heads of most dukes, who have therefore handed over the management of their affairs to a Board of Trustees, with expert advice from businessmen, and accept in return an allowance from the estate. The landowning duke can no longer afford to be a dilettante; he must be professional or sink. The most successful estates are those wherein the Duke has accepted his new role as Chairman of the Trustees. In the case of Bedford, the Duke made a success of the Woburn estates *in spite of* advice from the trustees; he proved himself, in effect, a better manager than they, though at the cost of methods not universally applauded.

Other shadows of privileges which they still retain include the likelihood of being considered for one of the great Offices of State. The Earl Marshalship has been hereditary in the House of Howard since 1672, but the office of Lord Steward, merged with the Crown since Henry IV, is appointed *pro hac vice* by the Sovereign. The current Steward is the Duke of Northumberland. The office originally consisted in placing the dishes on the lord's table at solemn feasts ("and cleaning out the fireplace, I think," said the Duke), but now it consists in announcing the Queen's guests on Great State Occasions. The Royal House of Stuart derived its name from the hereditary tenure of this office in Scotland, as the Butlers (Earls and Marquesses of Ormonde) were originally butlers to the monarch of Ireland.[3]

Dukes have always been high in the list of Knights of the Garter, the family of the Duke of Norfolk providing no less than twenty-four members (or thirty-five if you count the allied branches of Mowbray and Fitzalan as well as the Howards), closely followed by the family of Cavendish. Of the eleven Dukes of Devonshire in this family, the first ten all had the Garter. Today, three dukes are K.G. – Grafton, Northumberland, and Norfolk.

All dukes have the right to a coronet, on which are eight gold strawberry leaves, and a cape edged with stoat with black tails. Only on great State occasions, such as a Coronation, are these items now removed from the wardrobe, and a few of the dukes don't have them at all and are obliged to hire them. Even they may retain the favour of being addressed as "Your Grace", but some prefer to discourage it. A little boy was introduced to the Duke of Sutherland, whom he addressed as "Sir", to the consternation of his proud father, who dug him in the ribs and loudly whispered "Your Grace"; the boy looked the Duke in the eye and said, "For what we are about to receive may the Lord make us truly thankful."[4]

More often than not, while the privileges have been eroded, the responsibilities for which they were in some way a recompense have remained. Not that these responsibilities extend to an active involvement in governing the country; only Buccleuch, Portland, and Devonshire have held political office, the first two before they came to the title. There was a time when almost every duke was in politics; the Russells (Dukes of Bedford) have had a connection with the House of Commons for nearly 500 years, and the Cavendishes (Dukes of Devonshire) have always been political, from a sense of duty rather than predilection, as a natural return for the privilege of rank. The last duke to be Prime Minister was Wellington in 1828, but before him there were the Duke of Portland (1783 and 1807–9), the Duke of Grafton (1767–70), the Duke of Newcastle (1754–6 and 1757–62) and the Duke of Devonshire for eight months from November 1756 to July 1757.

The responsibilities that have remained are those of a landowner towards his tenantry, and towards the house in which he lives, often so beautiful as to be a national monument but to which the nation pays no contribution, towards the inheritance of which he is the guardian. A few have abnegated and abandoned their estate, not without reason, for they did not ask to be born to such responsibilities, and undeniably find life easier without them. They prefer to construct their own future. Most, however, hang on in the face of public misunderstanding and political prejudice, knowing that some dark force, as strong as the blood in their veins, commands them to do their best for the estate which they have been given. They are "men with few of the average man's opportunities, men who cannot rise but can only descend in the social scale, men condemned to eternal publicity, whose private lives are seldom their own. Men who may live only where their grandfathers have chosen and where the public expects. Men hamstrung by an inherited amateur status, to whom barely a profession is open. Men limited by the responsibilities of too large an income."[5] Some, like the Duke of Richmond, have successfully over-come the disadvantage of title by seeking the "average man's opportunities" as an average man : he worked on the factory floor to learn about engineering, then learned business techniques to make his Goodwood estate self-sufficient, with the result that his experience transcends all class divisions. Others, like the Duke of Somerset, have managed somehow to live a private life in a small country house without anyone appearing to realise that he exists.

Many dukes, however, like Sebastian in *The Edwardians,* have simply to face the limitations of their position : "Sebastian, condemned by the very circumstance of his situation to be nothing more, ever, than a commonplace young man; as commonplace as a king; for even his rebellions, were he to rebel, must be on ordained lines; there was nothing for him to rebel against, except his own good fortune, and that was a thing he could never evade . . . all these things were tied on to him like so many tin cans to the tail of a poor cat. With them went the romance of his whole make-up. Poor Sebastian, condemned to be romantic; condemned always to be romantically commonplace! What were the wild oats of such a young man? An inevitable crop, sown by his bad godmother at his christening. Not sown even by his own hand, but anticipated on his behalf. Poor Sebastian, his traditions were not only inherited, they were also prophetic. They stretched both ways. It was an unfair handicap."[6]

The large country estate, with the house as its pivot, was (and is) a peculiarly English affair. In many ways it was a perfect example in miniature of the welfare state, self-sufficient and self-protecting, with every member of the "family", from shepherds to carpenters to kitchen-maids, provided for from cradle to grave. Of course, it was capricious, depending as it did upon the personality of the Duke at its centre; should he choose to be mean (the nineteenth-century Duke of Newcastle springs to mind), the mini-welfare state collapsed. For the most part, however, people who lived on these estates had their births, clothes, education, health, weddings and funerals paid for.

Where, anyway, has this handful of families come from? What makes their status so special? In the first place, there have always been very few of them. The title of duke is granted the least often. Now there are twenty-six, but there have been times when there were only

two or three. The most there has been at one time was forty, at the
end of George I's reign, descending to thirty-one by 1930. Two or
three more are likely to be extinct by the end of the century, reducing
the total to twenty-three. There have been none (except royal)
created since 1900, and there are not likely to be any more.

The first dukedom in England was created in 1337, when Edward
III made his son the Black Prince Duke of Cornwall. This is now
hereditary in the heir to the throne. Shortly afterwards the dukedom
of Lancaster was also merged with the throne. The title of duke is not
indigenous in England. In the Roman Empire there had been the *dux*,
a leader or general, whence our word derives through the French *duc*,
which came to us with the Conquest. The Norman kings styled themselves Dukes of Normandy and Aquitaine in France, and were
understandably jealous of creating a title in England equal in rank
to one of their own. So 270 years had to pass before the first Englishman became a duke in 1337, and he was of royal blood. A dukedom
of Suffolk was twice created, in 1448 and 1514, and Richard II
created six dukes in one day, on 29th September 1397, but none
survived two years. The first non-royal duke to last was Norfolk in
1473, followed by Somerset, bestowed by Edward Seymour upon
himself in 1547 in the name of his ward, the infant King Edward VI.
Thereafter, the title was so rarely granted, and so regularly pruned by
beheadings and attainders, that there were no dukes at all in England
for thirty years after the execution of the Duke of Norfolk in 1572
(and no non-royal dukes for even longer).

Dukedoms proliferated in the seventeenth and eighteenth centuries,
dwindling to a handful of fresh creations in the nineteenth. The oldest
of these is Hamilton, created by Charles I in 1643, and the prize for
quantity must go to Charles II, who created twenty-six dukes,
including five nephews, two mistresses, and six bastard sons as well as
the unrelated Duke of Beaufort. Five of his creations survive. Of the
others which continue today, William and Mary are responsible for
Bedford (1694), Devonshire (1694) and Argyll (1701). Queen
Anne created Marlborough (1702), Rutland (1703), Atholl (1703),
Montrose (1707), Roxburghe (1707), and Brandon (1711);
George I created Portland (1716) and Manchester (1719); George
II, Newcastle (1756). The Dukes of Northumberland and Leinster
were both created in 1766 by George III, who honoured Wellington
in 1814. William IV created only one duke, Sutherland in 1833,
while Queen Victoria introduced four new creations, Abercorn
(1868), Westminster (1874), Gordon (1876) and Fife (1889), plus
two duplications in Argyll (1892) and Fife again (1900). It is

common knowledge that Winston Churchill was offered a dukedom by the present Queen, but respectfully declined.

In all, less than 500 individuals have had the right to call themselves Duke (or *suo jure* Duchess) in the 651 years since the first creation.[7]

The titles chosen do not always bear a close relation to the county or town where the grantee lives or holds land. The Duke of Devonshire, for example, has no landholding in Devon, but 72,000 acres in Derbyshire. The Duke of Norfolk has property in Sheffield and land in Sussex and Yorkshire, but precious little in Norfolk. The Duke of Richmond's land is in Sussex, and the Duke of Rutland's in Nottinghamshire. The Duke of St Albans had nothing to do with the town of that name, and the Duke of Sutherland owns not an acre in that county. The Duke of Manchester has hardly been near Manchester. On the other hand, the Dukes of Northumberland, Bedford, Argyll, Atholl, Roxburghe, are all firmly seated in the counties from which they take their titles, and Westminster in the City which his ancestors made so elegant.

Further complications arise when you consider that there is not *one* peerage system into which these twenty-six individuals fit, but *five*. There used to be just three separate peerages – of England, of Scotland, and of Ireland – until the union of England and Scotland in 1707, forming Great Britain and establishing peers of that new entity, and then the union of Great Britain and Ireland, forming the United Kingdom in 1801, giving us a fifth peerage. It may help to have a list showing how the dukes divide :

Dukes of England

Norfolk	(1483)
Somerset	(1547)
Richmond	(1675)
Grafton	(1675)
Beaufort	(1682)
St Albans	(1684)
Bedford	(1694)
Devonshire	(1694)
Marlborough	(1702)
Rutland	(1703)

Dukes of Scotland

Hamilton	(1643)
Buccleuch	(1663)

Argyll   (1701)
Atholl   (1703)
Montrose   (1707)
Roxburghe   (1707)
                    (*plus* Lennox, 1675, and Queensberry,
                    1684, held respectively by the
                    Dukes of Richmond and Buccleuch).

Dukes of Great Britain
    Portland   (1716)
    Manchester   (1719)
    Newcastle   (1756)
    Northumberland   (1766)
                    (*plus* Brandon, 1711, held by the
                    Duke of Hamilton).

Dukes of Ireland
    Leinster   (1766)
    Abercorn   (1868)

Dukes of the United Kingdom
    Wellington   (1814)
    Sutherland   (1833)
    Westminster   (1874)
    Fife   (1900)
                    (*plus* Gordon, 1876, held by the
                    Duke of Richmond, and Argyll, 1892,
                    held by the already Scottish
                    Duke of Argyll).

This list is also useful in so far as it reproduces the strict order of
precedence of the dukes, in the pyramid of hierarchy in England at
the peak of which sits the Queen. Above the dukes are only five male
members of the Royal Family in direct line of succession, the
Archbishops of Canterbury and York, the Prime Minister, Lord
High Chancellor, Lord President of the Council, Speaker of the
House of Commons, Lord Privy Seal, and High Commissioners and
ambassadors. The question of precedence has given much vexation to
the duchesses (most of the dukes could not give a damn), and, as we
shall see, has provided entertaining fun and games over the years. As
dukes of England take precedence above dukes of all four other
peerages, the Duke of Rutland goes before the Duke of Hamilton,
whose title is older and whose pride, in the last 200 years, has been

more easily injured. It also means that the Duke of Abercorn, whose family has not been particularly active, takes precedence above Wellington, the saviour of his country, and whose title is older by some fifty years, because Abercorn's dukedom is in the peerage of Ireland, and Wellington's only in the peerage of the United Kingdom.

It is a commonplace that dukes are boring. "How dull! Bless me! We are eleven of us, Dukes and Duchesses, and most dukefully dull we are," wrote Sarah Spencer when she accompanied Queen Victoria on a visit to Woburn Abbey in 1841.[8] That may have been true in the presence of the Queen, but they must all have been behaving *quite* out of character. Some of the dukes and duchesses who fill these pages are for the most part, supremely un-dull, they are bizarre, intransigent, naively selfish, eccentric, monumentally self-confident, and with a strong streak of delinquency in their natures. They are the kind of people who, placed on stage in a modern play, would have to be written down to be made credible. Of course there are exceptions – there have been and still are, shy dukes whose ancestors have used up all the self-confidence in the family genes and left none for them; there have been some who were malleable, ordinary – but it is tedious to qualify with exceptions all the time, and one is justified in attempting certain common characteristics, shared by most dukes at one time or another.

Their delinquency has enabled them to plunge indomitably through life with no regard for anything but the expression of their large personalities, with no need to question motives, and in the knowledge that no one will ask them to explain themselves. They do not look over their shoulders, nor even to the side, nor do they make allowances; they do not need to cultivate imagination – that is for others. With self-confidence as their shield, they can be rude, downright, rough, interfering, frank. They say what they mean and mean what they say. They can be sulky and critical, obedient to moods rather than opinions, moods of sweeping intensity and terrifying instability. They are easily irritated, and do not flinch from showing it. If they wanted to spit, they spat; duchesses could scratch their backs, and dukes their crutches, with impunity, because there was no one to tell them not to. This is not to say that dukes behave as boorishly as this paragraph suggests, but it does mean that the streak of impudence, of let's-see-what-we-can-get-away-with prankishness, and of sheer block-bustering obduracy, are strong enough in the inheritance for them to be tempted to respond in like manner, and for one to catch glimpses in them of ancestral arrogance.

What else? There is a rich vein of lunacy in many a ducal house.

I know that there is plenty of evidence of madness among dustmen or stockbrokers, and do not wish to labour the point, but when you consider that there have been mentally unstable people in the families of Howard (Dukes of Norfolk), Beauclerk (Dukes of St Albans), Hamilton (which affects the Dukes of Hamilton and Dukes of Abercorn), Murray (Dukes of Atholl), Fitzgerald (Dukes of Leinster), Cavendish-Bentinck (Dukes of Portland), Russell (Dukes of Bedford), and most recently Grosvenor (Dukes of Westminster), you see that over a third of the ducal families have borne the taint, and some descendants may still do. Of the other two-thirds, almost all have produced at least one duke whose eccentricities were so bizarre as to make his sanity questionable. I think it is safe to say that this is somewhat above the national average, and must bear some examination. The simplest explanation lies in persistent intermarriage, but I suspect there is a less demonstrable cause in that delinquency mentioned earlier, in the pure self-indulgence in which dukes have always been encouraged and which occasionally has toppled over the edge of civilised normality. Left to do as we please, we would all indulge those whimsical fantasies we privately nurture, and when we found that no one was there to contain us, we could with ease release ourselves totally from reality. This is what happened to the 5th Duke of Portland, and to many of the Dukes of Bedford. With others, however, the imbecility has been medical in character.

On the other hand, the mysteries of genetic inheritance are such that intermarriage between relations can often be beneficial, by preserving and repeating a strain of especial brilliance, or, even better, by combining two such strains which are themselves the product of four previous brilliant people. The result is that the number of remarkable men and women produced by ducal families is also far in excess of the national average. There are, for instance, no ordinary Russells; they have either been brilliant politicians, splendid speakers, stylish writers, or something has gone wrong and they have turned out bizarre and eccentric. The Cavendish family has produced scores of men with splendid intelligence and wisdom, with political sagacity, or simply with style. There is more than a fair share of great people among the Churchills, the Howards, the Grosvenors, and the Percys, while the family of the Duke of Richmond, producing one admirable person after another in almost unbroken succession, is practically an advertisement for the benefits of keeping marriage within a small circle of proven ability.

Reserve is another common characteristic of only recent evolution. Over the last 150 years it has become the norm for dukes decently to abstain from publicity. The rule has taken some hard knocks from the Duke of Bedford, the late Duke of Leinster, and the late Duke of Argyll, but otherwise a "low profile" is still generally observed.

Some dukes, while dispensing tremendous generosity to tenants and dependants, have been curiously mean to family and friends. For this I can find no explanation, but it occurs frequently enough, in up to half the ducal families, to warrant notice. No one can surpass the Dukes of Marlborough in this respect, while it has happened so often in the Dukes of Somerset that the present Duke has been left with only the bricks and mortar of his ancestral home, the rest of his inheritance having been hived off or dispersed by his ancestors. "What will you do with your money when you die?" a friend asked a miserly nobleman. "You have no children and you can't take it with you, and if you could it would melt."[9]

Heirs to a dukedom were generally educated to a spartan life, with appalling nursery food, and little, if any, parental affection. This was supposed to teach them self-reliance, but more often it had the effect of breeding those eccentricities which the adult developed in seeking to gratify all those desires denied him in infancy. One Duke of Manchester, for example, was fed on porridge for breakfast, bullock's heart and potatoes for lunch, bread and milk for tea.[10] Is it any wonder he should grow into a selfish luxuriant? The 1st Duke of Hamilton in adulthood slept every night in nightshirt, nightcap, bedsocks and night cravat, in a red damask bed heated by a warming-pan. "He slept on the suffocating softness of a feather mattress, between linen sheets, beneath anything from two to six pairs of blankets and two or three quilts. He slept in a propped-up position on bolsters and pillows, and of course he slept with the curtains of his bed pulled tightly shut."[11] There was also a coal fire burning in the bedroom, all of which might seem absurd until one remembers that the Duke was probably over-compensating for a childhood in which he all but froze to death.

Nor were the heirs told, in some cases, what lay in their future. The present Duke of Bedford had no idea he was related to the then Duke, let alone that he was his eventual heir, until a maid told him when he was sixteen. (He had never been to school, and so had escaped exposure to the teasing of friends, which would have revealed the truth of his position.) The present Duke of Newcastle admits that the fact he might one day be a duke was never discussed in the family and he never gave it a thought. In contrast, when the heir has been a distant cousin long since divorced from the main line of descent ("what we tactfully call a kinsman," says the Duke of Somerset), he and his family seem to have thought of little else. Such was the case with the Duke of St Albans, who had always been made conscious that he stood a chance of inheriting the dukedom, although a substantial genealogical detour was necessary for him to do so.

Two obsessions have united all ducal families without exception, at least up to World War I, and in some cases beyond II – marriage and rank, and the former was merely a way of ensuring that the latter was maintained. Marriage dominated the conversation of duchesses for two centuries. That the heir to a dukedom should marry went without saying; it would be fantasy to suggest otherwise. If he didn't care for women, *tant pis,* he must grit the stone between his teeth and get on with it. *Whom* he should marry was the abiding question. It ought to be the daughter of another duke, so that rank would not be diluted, and more often than not it was. The Duchess of Baden visited England in 1829 in order to find a husband for her daughter. She had eyes on the Duke of Buccleuch, but hesitated because he had only three dukedoms, which she erroneously supposed would go to the first three sons of the marriage, while the fourth would have no alternative but to go into the Church.[12] Occasionally an earl's daughter would insinuate herself into this private club and become a duchess, and even less frequently an untitled lady, or *buzz buzz,* a foreigner. The result of this vast incestuous dance, with dukes only marrying other dukes' daughters, to whom they were probably related in some way already, is that today all twenty-six dukes are related to each other. Some are now distant, but a quarter of them, even today, are close relatives, brothers-in-law, uncles, cousins to each other.

Of course, marriages were not made for love. Such a word was beneath their ducal consideration. When the Duke of Portland saw Miss Dallas-Yorke waiting for a train at Worksop station, fell in love with her on sight, and made her his duchess, he was not behaving very ducally. But then she was suitable anyway. Another lucky couple were the Duke and Duchess of Richmond in the eighteenth century, married in their adolescence to satisfy parental debts; they hated each other on sight, but re-met and fell in love two years afterwards. For the most part, marriage was like a move in a chess game, except that the partners were obliged, whether they liked it or not, to produce an heir somehow. Many would have been well advised to follow the example of John Spencer, who, presented with a list of eligible ladies drawn up by his grandmother Sarah, Duchess of Marlborough, in alphabetical order, simply pointed to the first on the list beginning with a C, and that was the end of the matter. Her name was

Cartaret, they were married, and it worked, in so far as such marketing can work. As long as rank was protected, and money was obtained in sufficient quantities to support that rank, infidelities after marriage were taken for granted. "What's that?" screamed the Duchess. "A painter? What painter? Who ever heard of such a thing? Sylvia Roehampton's daughter to marry a painter? But of course she won't. You marry Tony Wexford and we'll see what can be done about the painter afterwards."[13]

Double standards like this have protected the ducal families from total imbecility, for, indeed, had they continued to marry each other without the injection of some different blood, it is doubtful that any could have survived as sane humanity. In fact, there were many who were not their father's sons at all; this was tacitly known, accepted, and even applauded, as well it might be. Applauded or not, it is the inevitable result of marriage as a cold business proposition. It was gossip that some of the children of Violet, Duchess of Rutland, were fathered by different men. The Duke of Sutherland is possibly descended from an adulterous liaison which, if anyone cared to think about it or if it were true would deprive him in theory of the dukedom. Jane, Duchess of Gordon, who married three of her daughters to drunken dukes, married the fourth to the heir of Lord Cornwallis, but not without some difficulty. Cornwallis objected to the match because there was said to be madness in the Gordons. The Duchess reassured him: "I understand that you object to my daughter marrying your son on account of the insanity in the Gordon family: now I can solemnly assure you that there is not a single drop of Gordon blood in her veins."[14]

Lady Anne Foley wrote to her husband: "Dear Richard, I give you joy. I have just made you father of a beautiful boy. Yours etc. P.S. This is not a circular."[15]

The question of rank has bestirred dukes and duchesses more than anything else, and to a certain extent still does. In a way, they should be counted inferior to earls and barons, who represent much older English aristocracy. Only the marquesses are of more recent import than the dukes. But since the first duke (the Black Prince) was the son of the king, he naturally took precedence over the earls, who were hardly in a position to complain. When the first non-royal duke was created, and he too took precedence over the earls, there were some small stirrings of resentment, but the custom was already established and would have been difficult to overturn. Since then, the dukes have sometimes descended to absurd levels in order to let everyone know their precedence. The Duke of Devonshire thought himself bound to appear at the races with a coach-and-six and twelve outriders, and could scarce contain his fury when Lord Fitzwilliam, of inferior rank, appeared with two coaches and sixteen outriders.[16] There have been many arguments as to precedence, on which the House of Lords has been called to decide. The earliest known instance is a dispute between Baron Grey and Baron Beaumont (ancestor of the present Duke of Norfolk) in 1405. Coming up to the twentieth century, the Duke of Manchester displayed no signs that he was conscious of pleasantry when he challenged Prince Willie of Germany to a duel. "I offered to give him suitable reparation in Germany," he said "knowing that my own quarterings were sufficiently high to permit him to fight a duel without loss of prestige."[17]

In fairness to the dukes, it must be admitted that it was the duchesses, rather than they, who were most preoccupied with precedence. They developed the subtleties of rank to a fine art which, viewed from outside, had all the charm of a stately gavotte, yet all the absurdity of a farce. The Duke of Bedford remembers seeing the Duchess of Buccleuch and the Duchess of Northumberland sidling through the door together in their determination not to give precedence to the other.[18] The Duchess of Marlborough, who came from the United States as Consuelo Vanderbilt and had suddenly to learn the intricacies of precedence from one day to the next, said that she was always glad to know her own number in the order so that she would not make a mistake entering or leaving a room out of turn. She once waited at her own dining-room door to allow older women to pass through, and received a furious push from an irate marchioness who loudly claimed that it was just as vulgar to hang back as to leave before one's turn.[19] Lady Barrington said to Lady Sarah Lennox, daughter of the Duke of Richmond, when it was commonly expected that Lady Sarah would marry King George III, "Do, my dear Lady Sarah, let me take the lead and go in before you this once, for you will never have another opportunity of seeing my beautiful back."[20] The Duchess of Cleveland reproached an eager young man who tried to help by pulling her servant's bell for her to indicate that luncheon was over. "Sir, officiousness is not politeness," she said very slowly and forcibly.[21] Consuelo Vanderbilt attributed this ridiculous behaviour to an "enthroned fetish", and she was probably right, though I suspect boredom played a part. Duchesses had little else to worry about. After she had gained some confidence in this curious Lilliputian world, Consuelo enjoyed mischievously upsetting the applecart, ever so gently, when given the chance. She tells how she observed the Duchess of Buccleuch at a rehearsal in Westminster Abbey for a great

State occasion. The Duchess was "very much aware of the dignity of her rank and position. When our housekeeper, superb in black satin, was ushered to a seat beside her, I viewed with apprehension her surprised reaction; for never could she have supposed that anyone less than a Duchess would share her pew, and vainly did she try to place this new arrival among the twenty-seven ducal families she prided herself on knowing."[22]

A few years later, at the Coronation of Edward VII, four duchesses were chosen to hold the canopy above Queen Alexandra. Historically, this part of the ceremony was to shield the Queen from public gaze at a time when both King and Queen had to be stripped to the waist for the annointing. Like so much else that is traditional, the cause has gone and the symbol remains. The four ladies were Duchesses of Portland, Marlborough, Montrose and Sutherland, and to avoid complicated fuss, they were referred to in rehearsal as "1, 2, 3 and 4", with no nonsense about dignity.[23]

Isabella, Duchess of Manchester, took a non-ducal person for her second husband and so difficult did she find the adjustment to a lower rank that she actually petitioned the King to grant him a peerage dignity.[24]

That station has not entirely disappeared from our system of hierarchies was demonstrated as recently as 1963 when the Queen granted to Mr Grosvenor, *heir presumptive* to his brother the 4th Duke of Westminster, the rank, style and precedence of the son of a duke, although he was no such thing.

A secondary preoccupation for the dukes has been the antiquity of their ancestry, reaching a summit of caprice in the nineteenth century (although the Dukes of Norfolk were already getting into trouble for boasting about their ancestry some 400 years before). It became fashionable for all dukes to be descended from companions of the Conqueror, so they employed subservient genealogists to manufacture family trees which proved such descent. Unhappy with their English surnames, they sought to claim a romantic origin for which there was no real evidence. Thus the Duke of Bedford tried to show that his name Russell was derived from a Norman called "de Rosel", and Seymour, Duke of Somerset, demonstrated that his name was an anglicisation of "St Maur". The Duke of Leinster, whose family was old enough as it was, said a Florentine family called "Gherardini" was the origin of Fitzgerald, the Duke of Manchester that "Monte Acuto" was the ancestor of Montagu. This practice naturally brought genealogy into contempt, since deliberate invention was not excluded as a means to establishing these pedigrees. In fact, only a few of the English dukes can irrefutably trace their lines to the twelfth century, such as Westminster (the Grosvenors), Leinster (the Fitzgeralds), Beaufort (the Somersets), and, through two female digressions, Northumberland (the Percys). Some of the Scottish dukes, like Argyll (the Campbells) and Atholl (the Murrays), are undeniably older still, though shadowy. Nowadays, just as most dukes pay scant attention to who walks first into or out of a room, so many of them know no more about their ancestry than what they can find in Debrett or Burke.

All this is trivial compared with their real monument, achieved almost without trying, which has been to enrich the country's artistic heritage. Dukes have had taste, and the money with which to indulge it; if they lacked taste, they had the money to employ someone with taste to act on their behalf. They paid for the best architects to build their houses, the best painters to paint their portraits. By their patronage, they encouraged the development of the great British architects and painters; with their purchases, they brought to this country the best foreign works of art, from china to furniture to paintings and sculpture. One can argue for weeks whether they *should* have had so much money; most of them now would say they should not. The point is that they *did,* and the country as a whole is the beneficiary. At Boughton, Woburn, Chatsworth, Goodwood, and so on, there are incomparable treasures, which no other country can boast, because only here are such treasures used for the purpose for which they were bought, as décor to a home, instead of being ranged against the walls in a museum.

Since Lloyd George first began to bleed the rich, they have, as well as saving their own skins, tried to protect these collections from dispersal or disappearance abroad. The Dukes of Manchester and Newcastle sold everything and left, but they are not typical. The others have adjusted themselves to each new piece of legislation and so far have successfully kept the collections more or less intact. Until recently, it was possible to pass on to one's heir a tax-free inheritance, provided one lived for seven years after the date of the transfer. It has been said that one noble lord died a few weeks too soon, and his family had to leave him in a cold attic room until the time was opportune for them to announce his death officially. Now, with new laws coming into operation, even that ruse will no longer work. There is every possibility that Capital Transfer Tax and Wealth Tax will combine to break up the estates and send our artistic heritage abroad. No one in Britain will be tempted to buy a picture if he knows he will have to pay for it over and over again each year, and not even the dukes will be able to keep those that they have inherited. Perhaps there will soon come a day when there will be nothing left to see at Woburn Abbey and no point in visiting Goodwood. The dukes are not being acquiescent, however. In the van is Lord March, who will one day be Duke of Richmond, constantly emphasising to the public that it is not for himself that he wants the art treasures to remain at Goodwood (living in a remote wing of the house, he hardly sees them), but for the country. He once emptied one whole room to show visitors what might happen when everything was sold abroad.

We may be approaching the end of ducal estates. But not the end of dukes. While it is more or less certain that no new dukedoms will be created, only an Act of Parliament can remove those that already exist. Not even the Queen has the power to declare a dukedom extinct, except by attainder for high treason, and only one candidate, the Duke of Montrose, (see Chapter 14) has come anywhere near making himself so eligible. The crown is the fountain of all honour, and once a dukedom has been created, it can only descend according to limitation of the patent.

Before we embark upon an account of the separate ducal families, a word about the complexities of peerage law for those readers who, like myself, are not naturally familiar with such terms as *special remainder* or with the seemingly arbitrary use of courtesy titles.

When most titles were created, it was usually stipulated that the dignity would be inherited in *tail male*, that is with succession to the heirs male of the body of the grantee. This means in effect that the dukedom is inherited by a son, or nephew, or male cousin, or even uncle, as long as he can be traced back in male line to the first duke to hold the title, making him a male descendant of that duke's body. Sometimes the title is limited to *heirs general*, which means that it can descend through the female line. This is especially true of Scottish earldoms, and accounts for the separation of the dukedom and earldom of Sutherland in 1963, when the dukedom went to the *heir male*, and the earldom to the *heir general*, now Countess of Sutherland in her own right. She is still the heir "of the body" of the original Earl of Sutherland. Thirdly, a *special remainder* can be specified, enabling the title to pass not to a blood descendant, an heir "of the body", but to someone nominated by the grantee. Thus the 1st Duke of Newcastle named his son-in-law, Lord Lincoln, from whom the present Duke is descended, and the new Earl of Northumberland in the Seymour family named his son-in-law, Hugh Smithson, ancestor of the present Duke of Northumberland. *A special remainder* regulated the descent of the dukedom of Fife, enabling the 1st Duke's daughter to inherit the title in this century. In the case of the Duke of Marlborough, the patent is a most complicated document, listing the male descendants of each of his daughters in succession; the effect was to enable one of his daughters to succeed him, and the son of another daughter to succeed as 3rd Duke.

One more thing. The patent always rules that the heirs, whether *male*, *general*, or *special*, must be "lawfully begotten", two words which have barred many an illegitimate son from succession, and without which we should probably still have a Duke of Bolton now, and would definitely have a different Duke of Somerset from the man presently living at Maiden Bradley.

There is one very special case which is worth mentioning, although it impinges upon a dukedom only by implication.* The earldom of Devon was created for Edward Courtenay in 1553, with limitation to *heir male*, but not *of the body*. The title was extinct three years later, but in 1831 it was successfully claimed by a man whose descent was from an ancestor living 200 years *before* the creation of 1553, and who was, quite correctly, a male *heir* but not a *descendant* of the 1st Earl. The 17th Earl of Devon is alive today, and benefits from this unique entail.[25]

The reader will have to bear in mind the use of "courtesy titles" — the Duke of Beaufort may be referred to as Marquess of Worcester, or the Duke of Marlborough as Marquess of Blandford. A duke normally has many subsidiary titles; he is usually, in descending scale, Marquess of this, Earl of that, Viscount of another, and Baron of something else. His eldest son is allowed to use as his style of address the secondary title vested in his father, and *his* eldest son may take his grandfather's *third* title. Thus the Duke of Bedford's son is called Lord Tavistock, and his grandson Lord Howland. But neither son nor grandson are *in fact* peers; they cannot sit in the House of Lords, and there is nothing to prevent their standing for election to the House of Commons. The Duke of Buccleuch was in the House of Commons as an M.P. when he was known as Earl of Dalkeith in his father's lifetime. He was not *really* an earl, but was able to use his father's earldom "by courtesy" of the sovereign as a mere name.

Conversely, and here we go back to that fascinating topic of rank, the eldest son of a duke is *always* ranked as a marquess, whether or not his father holds a marquessate which he can use as his name. The son of the Duke of Grafton is called Earl of Euston, but is ranked as a marquess. And the son of the Duke of Somerset who, uniquely among

---

* i.e. *Dux Devon* is always known as the Duke of Devon*shire* to avoid confusion.

the dukes, has only one subsidiary title at the bottom of the scale –
Baron Seymour – is called Lord Seymour yet has the precedence of a
marquess above all 199 Earls, 132 Viscounts and 493 barons.

With such sketchy information I trust the tangle of names which
follows may be reduced to comparative simplicity.

REFERENCES

1. Cecil Woodham-Smith, *The Reason Why*, pp. 8–9.
2. Horatia Durant, *The Somerset Sequence*, p. 77.
3. *Complete Peerage*, II, App. D.
4. Duke of Sutherland, *Looking Back*, p. 101.
5. Lord Kinross, *The Dukes of England*, in *Life*, 15 November
   1943.
6. Vita Sackville-West, *The Edwardians*, p. 75.
7. *Complete Peerage*, VIII, App. A, by H. Pirie-Gordon and
   A. H. Doubleday.
8. *Correspondence* of Sarah Spencer, Lady Littelton (1912).
9. Nina Epton, *Milord and Milady*, p. 27.
10. Duke of Manchester, *My Candid Recollections*, p. 16.
11. Rosalind K. Marshall, *The Days of Duchess Anne*, p. 43.
12. *Lady Holland to Her Son*, p. 102.
13. Vita Sackville-West, *The Edwardians*, p. 159.
14. Augustus Hare, *In My Solitary Life*, p. 93.
15. Nina Epton, *Milord and Milady*, p. 208.
16. *Creevey Papers*, II, 129.
17. Duke of Manchester, *My Candid Recollections*, p. 233.
18. Duke of Bedford, *A Silver-plated Spoon*, p. 64.
19. Consuelo Vanderbilt Balsan, *The Glitter and the Gold*, p. 83.
20. *Life and Letters* of Lady Sarah Lennox, (1901), I, p. 92.
21. Augustus Hare, *In My Solitary Life*, p. 101.
22. Consuelo Vanderbilt Balsan, *op. cit.*, p. 98.
23. *ibid.*, 130, and Duke of Portland, *op. cit.*, 129.
24. *Complete Peerage*, VIII, 374 (d).
25. *Complete Peerage*, VII, App. E and F.

1. The Old Nobility

Duke of Norfolk; Duke of Somerset

From 1572 until the reign of James I there were no dukes in England. All the Dukes alive now derive their titles from creations well after this purge, except two, which descend from the violent years of pre-Elizabethan England. One survives from the Wars of the Roses – the dukedom of Norfolk, conferred upon the Howard family by Richard III in 1483, in suspicious circumstances which suggest at the very least connivance in the murder of the rightful heirs to the throne, the little princes in the Tower. The present Duke of Norfolk, 17th in line of descent from the alleged assassin, is therefore the Premier Duke and Earl in the peerage of England, with precedence over all other members of the nobility except the royal dukes. The second early dukedom survives from the Tudor period – the dukedom of Somerset, created in 1547 by the 1st Duke of Somerset and conferred upon himself (in the name of the child King Edward VI, whose uncle, Lord Protector, and virtual ruler he was). The present Duke of Somerset is the 19th in line of descent from this man, Edward Seymour, who seized power in the kingdom on the death of Henry VIII.

Together, they represent all that remains of the dukedoms existing when England was governed by gangsters, and when few of those who wielded power died a natural death. The titles of Norfolk and Somerset are owed to a bloody sword or to ruthlessness of a kind which we now only find in Sicily or New York. They were both dukes in the earliest sense of the word, leaders of men, military as well as political. Having risen to the summit of ambition and honours, they paid the price by sinking to the pit of disgrace, suffering numerous attainders under successive monarchs. It is a wonder either family survived at all. The 1st Duke of Norfolk died in battle, fighting alongside his friend Richard III; the 2nd Duke was three and a half years in the Tower of London, after being attainted by Henry VII's first parliament. He later rose once more to eminence; the 3rd Duke was found guilty of high treason, imprisoned in the Tower, and only escaped beheading by the timely death of Henry VIII; his son the Earl of Surrey (the famous poet) was imprisoned and beheaded; the 4th Duke of Norfolk, son to the Earl of Surrey, was imprisoned and beheaded for high treason in the reign of Elizabeth I; his son, Philip, Earl of Arundel, died in the Tower. And so on. As for the Seymours, Dukes of Somerset, the tale is similar. The 1st Duke was attainted, imprisoned, and beheaded; his great-grandson the 2nd Duke spent some time in the Tower. When his son, Lord Henry Seymour, was imprisoned there in 1651, the 2nd Duke commented, "I am very glad to hear that you have your health so well·in the Tower. It seems it is a place entailed upon our family, for we have now held it five generations, yet to speak the truth I·like not the place so well but that I could be very well contented the entail should be cut off."[1]

There are yet other circumstances which suggest similarities in the Howard and Seymour histories. Both families provided wives to Henry VIII, and attained their greatest power as a result. Queen Catherine Howard and Queen Anne Boleyn were grand-daughters of the 2nd Duke of Norfolk and nieces to the 3rd Duke. Queen Jane Seymour was sister to the Duke of Somerset. Thus both families were united by blood to the Crown, the Seymours to Edward VI and the Howards to Elizabeth I. Furthermore, both families have been bedevilled by the most overweening pride. The Seymours engendered a duke of such absurd pomposity that he is known to history as "The Proud Duke"; this is the 6th Duke of Somerset (1662–1748) whose extravagant conduct we shall see later. The pride of the Howards has been consistent through the centuries. More than 400 years ago they already regarded themselves as the sole representatives of the old nobility, and looked upon the newly ennobled Seymours as upstarts. The poet Earl of Surrey (1517–1547) was beheaded for having tried too hard to prove the superiority of his ancestry to that of the *parvenu* Seymours.

*   *   *

The Howards had every reason to brag of their antiquity. Although John Howard was not created Duke of Norfolk until 1483, he was descended through his mother from the Dukes of Norfolk of an earlier creation, vested in the Mowbray family (who turn up in Shakespeare's history plays); there had been a Mowbray Duke of Norfolk since 1397, descended from Thomas of Brotherton, a son of King Edward I. So the Howard connection ascends, in one way or another, to the very dawn of English history, and they have rarely been in danger of over-looking the fact.

The 1st Duke of Norfolk of the Howard line (1430–1485) was, as Sir John Howard, the son of a small landowner with ideas above·his station who married the Mowbray heiress. There was still a Mowbray

Duke of Norfolk at the time, and no reason to suppose that the title would not continue. But John Howard was nonetheless busy insinuating himself into the highest circles. The time was ripe for young men to advance themselves to the top if they happened to choose where to place their allegiance. John Howard was lucky. He chose the Yorkist side, became a close confidant of Edward IV, and, when he died, was the closest personal friend of his brother, Richard III. There is no doubt that John Howard and his son Thomas Howard were hand in glove with Richard both before and after his sordid machinations to occupy the throne of England. They were intimately acquainted with his plans; they may even have helped carry them out.

The sequence of events is as follows. The last Duke of Norfolk of the Mowbray line died in 1475. His daughter Anne was married at the age of five to Edward IV's second son, the infant Duke of York, who was then created Duke of Norfolk himself. They would eventually grow up, prosper, beget children, and continue the new line of Norfolks; they would also receive the Mowbray lands. If, however, Anne Mowbray were to die without heirs, the Mowbray lands would pass to two heirs by marriage, one of whom was John Howard.

In 1481 Anne Mowbray died, aged eight. John Howard could still not inherit the Mowbray lands, however, because the little Duke of York and Norfolk was still alive. All changed when Anne's father-in-law, King Edward IV, died in 1483. In his rush to usurp the throne, Richard Duke of Gloucester was aided and abetted by the willing Howard, who stood to gain almost as much by the removal of the two princes as Richard did himself. First, the elder prince, the new King Edward V, was conveyed to the Tower on 19th May.[2] The Constable of the Tower who received him was none other than John Howard. A month later, on 16th June, his brother, the little Duke of York, joined him. Again it was John Howard who persuaded the widowed Queen to hand over her second son into his (and Richard's) safe keeping.[3] Events moved quickly in the next few days. Hastings was eliminated with indecent speed, accused and executed, at Richard's behest, within a few hours; and it was Thomas Howard, John's son, who lured him into the trap which Richard had prepared.[4] On 25th June Richard was urged to take the throne, which he did without delay, supported at the right hand of the Chair of State in Westminster Hall by John Howard. Three days later, on 28th June 1483, John Howard was made Duke of Norfolk and Earl Marshal of England, and his son Thomas was created Earl of Surrey. At Richard's coronation on 8th July it was John Howard who carried the crown and filled the office of High Steward, while his son Thomas carried the Sword of State.

Those who deny the complicity of Richard III in the murder of the Princes in the Tower would do well to ponder this creation of the dukedom of Norfolk. If the princes were alive on 28th June, the creation could not have been made, as the younger prince, Duke of York, was also Duke of Norfolk. By elevating John Howard to this dignity, Richard tacitly admitted that the title was vacant and that the little prince was therefore dead. By this reckoning, the princes were murdered some time between 17th June and 28th June 1483.*

That Richard III was ultimately responsible for their deaths cannot reasonably be denied; it was essential to his purposes that they should both be eliminated. What is more interesting to us is that the Duke of Norfolk and his son were privy to the plans. There is no cast-iron evidence that Norfolk killed the boys, or personally ordered their murder. But the circumstantial evidence which implicates him is weighty. As Constable of the Tower he had the keys, and could achieve access at any time, without superior authority. As the intimate of Richard III over many years, and especially throughout these days in June 1483, it is inconceivable that he did not know what Richard was up to; indeed Richard relied on him to help realise his plans. As the envoy to the Queen, it was he who brought the little prince to the Tower. As heir to the Mowbray lands, he stood to gain more than anyone from the death of the boy. And he was rewarded for his fidelity by his elevation to the peerage so quickly that the corpses may not yet have been disposed of. The times were so violent that no man's life, be he ever so young, counted for much: power alone mattered. Richard III seized power with his henchmen John and Thomas Howard as wilful accomplices.

Fittingly, they were deprived of their power in the same violent manner. Richard had sat on the throne for only two years when the country was invaded by Henry Tudor, whom he went to meet with his forces at Bosworth. The King died at the battle of Bosworth Field in 1485, and by his side perished his faithful servant, John Duke of Norfolk, pierced by an arrow. His son Thomas Howard (who there-

* In fairness, it must be pointed out that many historians do not accept this line of argument. The Princes in the Tower had been declared bastards by an assembly of Lords and Commons who accepted that the marriage of their father Edward IV with Elizabeth Woodville was invalid under canon law. As bastards, they were automatically disinherited of titles or honours of any kind. Thus they were *legally* dead on 28 June 1483, though not necessarily *physically* dead, and the dukedom of Norfolk, held by young Richard of York, was vacant whether or not the boy was alive. This might be said to beg the question, for the dukedom of Norfolk had not been *inherited* by Richard of York, but was his by right of marriage to Anne Mowbray, the Norfolk heiress. Readers interested in pursuing the matter should consult P. M. Kendall, *Richard III*, Appendix I; Mancini's *Usurpation of Richard III*, ed. Armstrong; Jeremy Potter, *The Trail of Blood*. The author is indebted to Mr Jeremy Potter for these elucidations.

upon became 2nd Duke of Norfolk) survived the battle, but was taken prisoner by the invaders, and thrown into the Tower. The first Parliament of the new king, Henry VII, attainted Howard for High treason, confiscated his property (including the Mowbray lands), and deprived him of all titles and dignities. Technically, of course, he could not possibly be guilty of high treason, since Henry Tudor was neither *de facto* nor *de jure* King of England when Howard took arms against him, but this awkward point was side-stepped by making Henry's assumption of the crown retroactive by twenty-four hours, so that Howard's actions could be legally regarded as treasonable.[5]

Howard, stripped of all honours and influence, languished in the Tower for three and a half years. He used his time to demonstrate that solid Howard adaptability upon which his re-emergence was to be founded. He refused all opportunity to escape (a real chance presented itself in June 1487),[6] declaring that he was loyal to the Crown, whoever was wearing it. Before the dust had settled from the Battle of Bosworth he had told Henry, speaking of the slain Richard, "He was my crowned King, and if the parliamentary authority of England set the crown upon a stock, I will fight for that stock. And as I fought then for him, I will fight for you, when you are established by the said authority."[7] These are the words of a pragmatist and a wily politician. Firm loyalty to the Crown of England has been a quasi-religious duty of the Howards throughout the centuries, never more evident than today; it is certainly an attitude which allows of infinite flexibility. With the early Norfolks, it was simply a matter of survival; the Howards knew which side to butter their bread, and, like chameleons, they changed their colours according to whoever was in power. They may say that they were loyal to the Crown, not to the head beneath it, but they were far too canny really to believe such humbug. One of them, the 4th Duke (executed by Elizabeth I for having conspired with Mary Queen of Scots), backed the wrong horse and paid for it with his head. His protestations of loyalty to the Crown were then to no avail.

The 2nd Duke (1443–1524) was now biding his time in the Tower of London. Henry VII did not forget his words after Bosworth, observed his passivity in prison, and discerned his pragmatism. The King correctly judged that, given the opportunity, Howard would most likely serve faithfully. He released him in January 1489, and carefully measured the amount of favour shown. A small carrot it was to restore him to the earldom of Surrey; but the dukedom remained vacant, and most of his lands forfeited. There had to be the possibility of future preferment conditional on Howard's obedience, so the largest prizes were reserved. Howard then showed of what mettle he was made. Having served Edward IV and Richard III, he now served their enemy Henry VII with identical devotion, rising to become Chief General of England. After twenty years he was given back the lands which had been forfeited, and his total rehabilitation was confirmed by his being an executor of Henry VII's will. Adaptability brought its rewards.

Howard consolidated his position under Henry VIII, being the king's chief adviser and most influential member of the Privy Council. He was deeply resentful, however, of the influence wielded by Wolsey, who also had the ear of the King but did not, in Howard's view, deserve it. He was, after all, a commoner, a butcher's son. No amount of imprisonment, beheadings, attainders, would ever deflect a Howard from the opinion that his family was second to none in its nobility and ancestry, and by virtue of that inheritance, should take its place next to kings. Howard loathed Wolsey for mixing with the great, and secretly thought less of the King for deigning to confide in the upstart. It took very little to make the famous Howard pride bristle.

The Howard pride attained its finest expression at the Battle of Flodden Field in 1513. Whether it was strategy or luck, or, as the people thought, the intervention of divine aid, Howard led his troops to an astounding victory. Though nearly seventy years old, and though his troops were parched and their stomachs empty, he inspired them with such zeal that they routed the Scots, who lost 10,000 men against the English loss of barely 400. Insufficient attention has been paid to the contribution made by the Howard arrogance, which though unwelcome in society, is one of the most desirable qualities in battle.

Howard's reward was the restoration of his father's dukedom immediately after the battle in 1513. (There are some genealogical purists who claim that this was a new creation,[8] and that the dukedom of Norfolk should date from this year, but since he was the second Duke of the Howard line, and since he would have inherited in 1485 anyway, it is much simpler to maintain the creation of the dukedom in 1483.) He had travelled full circle back into the royal favour.

The old man was to show one more instance of pragmatism before his death. In 1521, aged nearly eighty, he was appointed Lord High Steward for the trial of Edward, Duke of Buckingham, on a charge of treason. Trials in the sixteenth century were mere formalities, of which the issue was decided beforehand. Buckingham was a personal friend of Norfolk, his daughter had married one of Norfolk's sons, and Norfolk was known to be in entire agreement with Buckingham's views. Yet Norfolk consented to preside at the trial of his friend, knowing full well that he would be required to pass a sentence of death. When the moment came there were tears streaming down his face.[9] However, he recovered sufficiently from his distress to accept some of the manors forfeited from Buckingham.

The 2nd Duke's most spectacular achievement was to lay the foundations of a family dynasty and to assure its continuance to the present day. Thirteen of his children survived, and all made astute marriages. His daughter Elizabeth was the mother of Anne Boleyn, Henry VIII's second wife; his son Edmund was the father of Catherine Howard, Henry's fifth wife; another grand-daughter married Henry's natural son, Henry Fitzroy; a daughter married into the family of de Vere, Earls of Oxford. The list is an impressive roll-call of sixteenth-century nobility, which spawned several distinct branches of Howards, many of which were ennobled. The Howard family holds or has held twenty-five different patents of creation to separate peerages, including the earldoms of Surrey, Suffolk, Northampton, Stafford and Carlisle. The Howards of Effingham, the Howards of Glossop, the Earls of Carlisle and of Suffolk, continue to the present day. In fact, the present Lord Howard of Glossop (also Lord Beaumont) inherited the dukedom of Norfolk in 1975. No family in the history of the country can boast such staying power or such success. The credit must go to the 2nd Duke of Norfolk, who, by skilful manipulation of his progeny, made certain that the name of Howard would not slide into oblivion.

He was succeeded by his eldest son, 3rd Duke of Norfolk (1473–1554), who resembled him in many ways. An excellent soldier, he fought with his father against the Scots and was ruthless and brutal in battle. Also like his father, he showed that his chief aim in life was the advancement of himself and his family, to which end he would acquiesce in whatever designs the King his master might cherish. He rose to become Henry VIII's Lord Treasurer (and, incidentally, the subject of one of Holbein's greatest portraits), signed the letter which threatened the Pope with loss of papal supremacy in England if he would not grant the King's divorce, and on the subsequent dissolution of the monasteries received extra lands as rewards for his loyalty. He even went so far as to preside at the trial of his niece Anne Boleyn, the disgraced Queen, and to make arrangements for her execution on the block. He followed this extraordinary cold-bloodedness by proposing another niece, Catherine Howard, as wife to the King, and only when she in turn lost her head were Norfolk and his family disgraced. There are not many examples in history of pragmatism pursued to such lengths.

Like his father, the 3rd Duke despised Wolsey for his low birth, revealing a depth of contempt which is only comprehensible in a dynastic family whose rightful place is undermined; "I will tear him with my teeth", he is reported to have said.[10] Similarly, he had no time for the up-and-coming Seymours. He marked out Edward Seymour, now Earl of Hertford, as his prime enemy, a disastrous mistake which backfired when Catherine Howard was beheaded; for Jane Seymour proved a better wife for the King than had the Howards, and she was the mother of the heir to the throne, Prince Edward. Gleefully, the Seymours pursued the Howards to their second downfall, and rose to eminence in their place.

The Seymours had been practically unknown until the King chose Jane Seymour as his third wife. The *paterfamilias,* Sir John Seymour, of Wolf Hall, Wiltshire, had been knighted by Henry VII in 1497 for his services against the Cornish rebels at Blackheath, but his subsequent career did not attract attention. It was his children who were to bring fame to the name of Seymour, notably Edward, Jane, and Thomas. As they rose in royal favour, so, in direct proportion, the Howards sank; the fortunes of the new family were directly related to the humiliation of the old, and the Seymours climbed to the highest rank by stamping on the slipping fingers of the Howards.

Jane Seymour, as the daughter of a country gentleman, was lady-in-waiting to Henry VIII's first two queens, Catherine of Aragon and Anne Boleyn. The King fell in love with her in 1535, and met her through a secret passage to her apartments at Greenwich. The fate of Queen Anne Boleyn was sealed; she was beheaded, and Jane married the King the very next day. Thus, from obscurity the Seymours were thrust into the headlines of English history, and, at the same time, the Howards suffered a set-back by the execution of the favoured niece Anne Boleyn. Jane secured the position of her family by giving birth to the much-needed son, the future King of England. Celebrations were ecstatic. At the christening, the Queen's brother, Edward Seymour, carried her stepdaughter Princess Elizabeth (the child of Anne Boleyn), and was elevated to the peerage as Earl of Hertford. (He had already been made Lord Beauchamp after the marriage.) Another brother, Thomas Seymour, was delivered from even deeper obscurity (he was a servant to Sir Francis Bryan) to take his place as a member of the Royal Family. Norfolk and his son the Earl of Surrey watched from the shadows in silent fury.

Jane died twelve days after the birth of her son, casting the King into genuine grief; he wore mourning for her, a consideration he did not show for his other wives. Her death consolidated the position at

Court of her brothers, to whom the King looked for consolation. There was no stopping them. Hertford became Captain-General in the north, revealing an unsuspected talent for battle when he raided Scotland in 1545 and within two weeks had burnt seven monasteries, sixteen castles, five towns, and 243 villages.[11] At the dissolution of the monasteries, he was granted lands which included Maiden Bradley in Wiltshire, where his descendant, the present Duke of Somerset, now lives.

The Howards grew restive. Another one of their number, Catherine Howard, had lost her head, while Edward and Thomas Seymour, who came from nowhere, continued to sit in the sunshine of royal favour. It was intolerable for Norfolk's son, the brilliant and impetuous Earl of Surrey. This man graces our anthologies with some of the loveliest poetry written in the English language, and introduced the Petrarchan sonnet to English literature. At the age of ten he had fallen in love with nine-year-old Lady Elizabeth Fitzgerald, daughter of the Earl of Kildare (and ancestor of the Dukes of Leinster), and had addressed to her some of his most beautiful sonnets expressing the ideal of Platonic love. He had then married Lady Frances de Vere, daughter of the Earl of Oxford. This man, whose poem *The Happy Life* recommends "no grudge nor strife . . . wisdom joined with simplicity", and exhorts the reader to be "contented with thine own estate", this man was before all else a Howard. He possessed the Howard vanity and arrogance in abundant measure, allied with a poetic sensibility which unleashed passions beyond rational control. Even for the sixteenth century, when birth and rank counted for far more than they do now, Surrey was unduly impressed with his ancestry. Jealous of the rise of the Seymours, he made a foolish move; he had his arms quartered with the arms of Edward the Confessor, thus claiming royal blood. He wanted to prove the superiority of his descent to that of the Seymours. In purely factual terms, Surrey was perfectly justified in quartering the royal arms, since he was descended through the Mowbray family from Thomas Brotherton, son of Edward I, and Richard I had permitted the Mowbrays the quartering. However, it was a dangerous gesture, knowing the antipathy of the Seymours and their power to express it. Surrey and his father were accused by the Seymours of treasonable designs, and were committed to the Tower.

There then followed the most unseemly squabble. The Howards' fate was not helped by dissension within the family. The Duke of Norfolk's private life had been the subject of gossip for some time. He and his wife had been forever quarrelling, and had eventually separated, as a result of the Duke's taking a mistress. What really rankled was that the mistress, Elizabeth Holland, was a washerwoman from the Duke's own household. The Duchess told Cromwell that Mistress Holland was "a churl's daughter, who was but a washer in my nursery eight years".[12] For a man from whom aristocratic snobbery came as fire from his nostrils, the Duke showed a remarkable lapse in taste. The affair rent the family asunder. The Duchess claimed she was afraid to enter the house. "He keeps that harlot Bess Holond and the residue of the harlots that bound me and pinnacled me and sat on my breast till I spat blood, and I reckon if I come home I shall be poisoned."[13] The affair is too distant now for us to judge whether she was being melodramatic, but the family appear to have believed it. Surrey took his father's side, but his wife, his daughter, and his mistress all testified against him to the Seymours. Matters were made worse by the daughter's statement that her brother (Surrey) had rigidly adhered to the old Catholic religion, an admission which cannot have pleased the King, and which further antagonised Seymour, who was a convinced Protestant. Father and son were attainted; their fall was absolute. The Earl of Surrey was beheaded on 21st January 1547, a martyr to vanity; he died for a trivial cause, which appears to the modern mind as mere "showing off", but which, in the nervous and agitated times of Henry VIII, was high treason. His father the Duke signed a confession, was about to lose his head, but was saved by the death of the King the night before the execution was due to take place.

It is odd how, in these early days, the fortunes of the Seymours continued to follow the demise of the Howards so closely. Only one week after the execution of Surrey, Henry VIII died (28th January 1547). Edward Seymour lost no time in seizing power; with the Howards out of the way, the "old nobility" could hinder him no longer with their petulant pride. He did not announce the king's death immediately, but first fetched the new King, Edward VI his nephew, who was now ten years old, and brought him to London. With the King's person in his custody, Seymour proclaimed himself Lord Protector of the Realm, releasing the secret of Henry's death and Edward's accession, and secured the right to act independently of the Privy Council's advice. Only one member of the Council strongly objected to this *coup d'état* – Wriothesley. A few days later Seymour created himself Baron Seymour, and on 16th February Duke of Somerset.

The warrant creating this dukedom is a unique document. It bears the signature of the boy king, "Edward", but it bears in addition a number of other signatures, among which can be seen "E. Somerset" who, in all logic, can hardly have existed, under *that name*, to put his signature to a document which would enable him *thenceforth*, to bear that name. The warrant may still be seen at the Public Record Office.

His brother Thomas was appointed Lord High Admiral of England and elevated as Lord Seymour of Sudeley (Sudeley Castle in Gloucestershire was where Thomas went to live with his new wife, Queen Catherine Parr, after being turned down by Princess Elizabeth). The Seymours had never imagined such heights of power; together the brothers ruled England, their nephew was king in theory, and the new Duke of Somerset was king in fact. The official designation by which he permitted himself to be called had a royal ring about it: "Edward, by the grace of God, Duke of Somerset".[14] He addressed the King of France as "brother".

The Lord Protector achieved much in the field of religious reform during his reign. He was, indeed, the first Protestant ruler of England. He allowed priests to marry, issued a proclamation against ceremonies, removed images, and enforced the use of English in church services, all measures regarded as extremely radical at the time; he was thought a "rank Calvinist",[15] and did openly correspond with Calvin. He was, however, intoxicated with the taste of power, and overstretched the forbearance of those about him. He was far too ready to line his own pocket, acquiring for himself vast properties from monastic lands, far more than might be regarded as reasonable, and a huge personal fortune. The high regard in which he obviously held himself was his undoing. He thought that he could proceed along the path of self-indulgence without hindrance, as long as the child king was at his bidding. He built a sumptuous palace in the Strand – Somerset House – and erected there a court of requests. The last straw was his making a stamp of the King's signature, which was an impudent admission that the power of the royal authority was entirely in his grasp.

Ironically, it was a family squabble which turned the tables against the Seymours, as it had against the Howards. The Duke of Somerset and his brother the Lord Admiral fell out almost as soon as they acquired power, and were virtually sworn enemies for the rest of their lives. As they were in control of the country, their strife did not make for harmonious government. Even their wives quarrelled over precedence, the Duchess claiming a higher status than the Queen Dowager. Thomas Seymour was jealous of his brother's supreme authority; he thought that the Lord Protectorship should have been shared equally

between them. Since Somerset had control of the King, Thomas
Seymour would have control of his sister the Princess Elizabeth.
When this failed, he turned his attentions to Lady Jane Grey (who
lived with him and his wife Catherine Parr at Sudeley). Then he
attempted to seduce the eleven-year-old boy king away from the Protector's authority by the most elementary ruse: he sent him secret
pocket-money. When he thought that he had the boy's confidence he
made a fatal miscalculation. He planned to kidnap him. With master
keys to the royal palaces, it was no trouble for Seymour to gain access
to his nephew. In the middle of a winter night, Seymour and some
confederates stole to the door of the King's bedroom. As he fumbled
with the lock, the King's pet spaniel barked, and Seymour ran the
dog through with his sword. But it was too late. The alarm was
raised, Seymour was arrested and conveyed to the Tower.

Lord Seymour of Sudeley was beheaded on his brother's orders on
Tower Hill in 1549, two years after the same fate had befallen
Thomas Howard, Earl of Surrey, for whose execution Seymour had
actively striven. It is a pity that history has no truck with the moral
principles of poetic justice, for here would be a splendid example of
the principle at work.

The following year, the Duke of Somerset himself began his decline.
He was deprived of his Protectorship (to which, anyway, he had had
no right in Henry VIII's will) and all other offices, was later imprisoned in the Tower, and finally found guilty of inciting the London
citizens to rebellion. The Duke's execution in 1552 provoked scenes of
unheard-of lamentation, for in spite of the man's rapaciousness and
unbridled ambition, he enjoyed considerable popularity with the
people. The period of his rule had been mercifully free from religious
persecution, and ordinary people slept more soundly in their beds
than they had done for a hundred years or more. They knew also
that he had a deeply felt concern and sympathy with the poorer
working classes, whose part he often took. Londoners always know in
their bones when they are ruled by someone with their interests at
heart, and they cherish him accordingly. They felt this for Charles II,
for Elizabeth I, for George VI, and for Lord Protector Somerset.

Orders had been given for the people to stay indoors until ten
o'clock, when the execution would already be over, but they were
wasted words. Tower Hill was crowded. The Duke addressed a few
words to the people before he placed his head on the block. He said
that he was glad to have advanced the cause of religion. Then he
was beheaded. The crowds rushed to dip their handkerchiefs in his
blood. At least one woman still had her handkerchief two years later.

When the Duke of Northumberland was led through the city in chains in 1554 for his opposition to Queen Mary, the woman shook her blood-stained handkerchief in front of him. "Behold the blood of that worthy man, that good uncle of that excellent King," she said, "which was shed by thy treacherous machinations, now, at this instant, begins to revenge itself upon thee."[16] Contemporary accounts have perhaps adorned the lady's prose a little, but that was no doubt the gist of what she said. The "excellent king" meanwhile, now fourteen years old, recorded his uncle's death in his diary in the manner of a dispassionate news item. "The Duke of Somerset had his head cut off upon Tower Hill between eight and nine o'clock in the morning."[17]

It was time for the Howards to re-emerge. The Seymour family, consigned to political oblivion, were never again to attain such heights. They now entered a century of comparative obscurity. The old Duke of Norfolk, 3rd of the Howard line, who had been saved from the scaffold by the perfect timing of Henry VIII's death, was reinstated by Mary Tudor, half-sister and successor of the child Edward VI, and allowed to die of old age, a rare privilege for the dukedom. His grandson the 4th Duke of Norfolk (1536–1572), son of the beheaded poet Surrey, succeeded in 1554 at the age of eighteen. He married Lady Mary Fitzalan, daughter and heiress of the Earl of Arundel, and she died in childbirth at the age of sixteen. The earldom of Arundel, one of the most ancient titles in the land, passed to her son Philip, and has been held by the Dukes of Norfolk ever since. This marriage marks the first alliance of the Howards and Fitzalans, the first joining of the titles of Norfolk and Arundel, an alliance commemorated in the family name of the present Duke, Miles Fitzalan-Howard.

Norfolk's career was tragic and tempestuous. He married three times, and was three times a widower. On each occasion his grief was hardly compensated by the wealth and lands he inherited from successive wives. By 1570, he was not only the richest man in England, and the loneliest, but the only duke in the realm, respected and revered as the head of English nobility, and living representative of an illustrious family whose past was already part of distant history. It was a virtually impregnable position, almost divine in its antiquity and in the veneration it inspired. The unique situation of the Howards was demonstrated at the coronation of Queen Elizabeth, when not only was Norfolk the Earl Marshal in charge of arrangements, but his father-in-law, Arundel, was Lord High Steward, his great-uncle, Lord Howard of Effingham, was Chamberlain of the royal household, and his wife the Duchess was one of the two principal ladies of honour. Elizabeth herself may have been the centre of attraction, but she was the only member of the Tudor family present, whereas around her, in front of her, and behind her were quantities of Howards who dominated the proceedings. She was even the daughter of a Howard.

All this was cast to the winds by the Duke's ineffaceable ambition and inexpungeable pride. He resented his role as stage manager of State ceremonial occasions, denied the high political office which his name deserved. Not satisfied with being a cousin of the Queen, he dreamed of the day when a Howard would sit on the throne of England.

The seed of his misfortune was once again the Howard arrogance. Just as his father and grandfather had despised Seymour on account of his low birth, and his great-grandfather the 2nd Duke of Norfolk had despised the butcher's son Wolsey, so the Elizabethan Duke turned his nose up at the Earl of Leicester, the Queen's favourite companion, lifelong friend, and flirtatious admirer. Norfolk was incapable of understanding that the Queen could possibly take Leicester's part against him. He had been eleven years old when his father was beheaded by the Seymours, who had thereby deprived his family of their rightful positions as protectors of the realm. He saw Leicester as the reincarnation of the perennial impudent upstart, and he smarted with indignation at the Queen's preference for him. He rebuked Leicester in a high-handed manner for behaving familiarly with the Queen, and for "kissing the Queen's majesty without being invited thereto".[18] Eventually, Norfolk was led to imagine that the only way of protecting the throne from the pernicious influence of such ne'er-do-wells was to look after the succession himself.

The Queen was not married, and showed no signs of remedying the situation. There was no obvious heir to the throne. The loudest claimant was Mary Queen of Scots, descended from Henry VII, and recognised by the French as the rightful Queen of England. But Elizabeth could not envisage such a claim. The two queens never met (to the eternal regret of biographers and dramatists), but they impinged upon each other's lives almost every day. Elizabeth was the obstacle to Mary's designs and the chief cause of her unhappiness; Mary was the sorest thorn in Elizabeth's flesh, and the one problem over which she prevaricated. Moreover, Elizabeth was Protestant, and Mary was Roman Catholic. The one man who might mediate between the two, it was suggested, was the Duke of Norfolk, nominally a Protestant, but belonging to an ancient Catholic family whom the Catholics still regarded as theirs. The question of the succession must be settled, but it could not be as long as the two women glowered at each other. Norfolk was the only man with the prestige to solve the issue. His mistake was to try to solve it without the Queen's knowledge or consent, and to allow himself to be talked into solving it by advancing himself. He would marry the Queen of the Scots.

On the face of it, this was not such a bad idea. Mary would succeed Elizabeth on the throne of England, and their offspring would assure the future of the crown. He was acceptable to both Protestants and Catholics. Nevertheless, it is astonishing that Norfolk should have considered for one moment either that Mary would have been acceptable to the English, or that she would have made a decent wife. The truth is that he hardly decided anything. He drifted with the tide, manipulated by his followers. For once, the famous Howard pragmatism, the ability to change allegiance according to the wind, was misjudged. Naturally, with her expert intelligence system and her wary First Minister Cecil, whose antennae were always alert, Elizabeth found him out. She asked him point blank if he intended to marry the Queen of Scots. Norfolk denied it. The Queen did not remind him that anyone with whom Mary contracted a marriage, or anyone who advised such a course, was *ipso facto* guilty of treason and would die as a matter of course. Had he forgotten? Typically, his reaction was to nurse a new resentment, this time against the career-conscious Cecil.

Whatever he said, Norfolk never relinquished his plan to marry Mary. For him, it was a question of families, of dynasties, of successions; it cannot have been love (although Mary sent him love letters) because they had never seen each other. It was a mixture of pride and politics, assuring the succession to the throne, and assuring that this succession would come to the Howards.[19] To this end, he was prepared to lie and dissemble. He wrote an abject letter to the Queen, protesting his loyalty, his love, his honour, and claiming that he had never entertained an intention of marrying the Scottish queen against Elizabeth's will; but he sent a draft of the letter to Mary for her approval before laying it before Queen Elizabeth.[20] Twice he promised that he had abandoned all plans of marriage, and twice he lied.

Eventually, Norfolk's amateur conspiracy was exposed; he was arrested, tried (one of his examiners was the Earl of Bedford, ancestor of the Duke of Bedford), and imprisoned. He was inevit-

ably condemned to death, but the Queen was a long time making up
her mind to sign the warrant. There had been no state executions
since her reign began fourteen years before, and she had a natural
aversion to the use of the scaffold upon which her mother and stepmother had died. Furthermore, Norfolk was her cousin in blood, and
the only Duke in her realm – the first man among her subjects. But
he was undeniably a traitor, and she was personally affronted that he
had misused her trust. For five long months she allowed him to
tremble within the Tower walls, before she finally signed the document in the spring of 1572. The scaffold had fallen apart with dis-
use, and a new one had to be constructed.[21] The Duke was beheaded
on 2nd June, but spared the indignity of having his bowels ripped
out and his head stuck on a spike on London Bridge. The Queen
was seen to be very downcast that day, and unapproachable.[22]

＊   ＊   ＊

A word must be said about the Howard religion. A chief singularity of the Dukes of Norfolk is that they are Roman Catholic. No
other ducal family survives from the Wars of the Roses, which
depleted the ranks of the English aristocracy to a disastrous degree,
so the Dukes of Norfolk may be said to have adhered to the "old"
religion by virtue of historical survival, or because they were of the
"old" nobility. It is misleading to think of them as *always* Roman
Catholic; for reasons of political expediency, there have been a
number of Protestants among them. The 4th Duke of Norfolk lived
as a Protestant, but was still regarded as a Catholic. In the months
before he was beheaded in 1572 he wrote a long letter to his children,
impressive in its dignity and honesty, but containing a disavowal of
the Catholic Church which does not quite ring true. "Upon my
blessing beware of blind Papistry, which brings nothing but bondage
to men's consciences", he wrote. "Perchance you have heretofore
heard, or perchance may hereafter hear, false bruits [rumours] that
I was a Papist. But trust unto it, I never since I knew what religion
meant, I thank God, was of other mind than now you shall hear that
I die in."[23] In view of Norfolk's support for the cause of Mary
Queen of Scots, and his tacit acquiescence in the proposed invasion
of Catholic armies which would rid the country of the Protestant
scourge and be welcomed with open arms by the populace (so they
thought), Norfolk's eleventh-hour rejection of papistry comes as a
surprise. Considering also that his wife and son (Philip, Earl of
Arundel) were almost fanatically Catholic, and that this same letter
contains exhortations to avoid pride, to eschew worldly gains, to

embrace modesty and self-denial, and not to be headstrong (advice he had spent a lifetime rejecting), the exercise appears more like a strategem to avoid reprisals against the Howards. It reads like a letter that is intended for publication. As a denial of the Catholic faith by a Howard, it must be regarded as an aberration.

Norfolk's son Philip Howard, Earl of Arundel (1557–1595), who could not claim the dukedom of Norfolk which now lay dormant owing to his father's attainder, was persecuted for his adherence to Catholicism, and imprisoned in the Tower for eleven years. He wasted and died there, but not before incurring more odium by openly praying for the success of the Spanish Armada. This man was eventually canonised by the Catholic Church in 1970, and is now known as St Philip Howard. Saint or not, his haughty insolent manner did not endear him to those who knew him casually. His son, too, Thomas Earl of Arundel (1585–1646), inherited that besetting vanity of rank which has plagued the Howards through centuries. He did not suffer himself to be addressed by any beneath him in status, and went so far as to be sent to the Tower for having insulted a fellow peer, Lord Spencer, in 1621. Spencer had made some reflection upon past events in their families. Arundel interrupted him rudely: "My Lord," he said, "when these things you speak of, were doing, your ancestors were keeping sheep!" to which Spencer replied, "When my ancestors, as you say, were keeping sheep, your ancestors were plotting treason." Arundel was not released from prison until he had made an apology.[24] Clarendon said that "he thought no other part of history considerable, but what related to his own family", and also that he was "without religion".

Owing to their more or less constant Catholicism, the Dukes of Norfolk henceforth retired from the political limelight. The first four dukes had played a leading part in the history of the country for nearly a hundred years, from 1473 until the 4th Duke went to the block in 1572, but thereafter their religion barred them from holding political office. Not for 250 years were the Norfolks allowed to take their seats in the Houses of Parliament. In 1829 the Roman Catholic Relief Bill repaired the injustice, and at last the 12th Duke of Norfolk (1765–1842), known as "Scroop" or "Twitch", or "Our Barney", took his seat in the House of Lords, while his son was the first Roman Catholic to sit in the Commons since the Reformation.

By then the damage of being in a back seat for so long had had its effect. Successive Dukes of Norfolk in the seventeenth and eighteenth centuries degenerated into a series of amiable eccentrics, obsessed with their own family history and living on the past.

The year 1572 might have marked the end of the dukedom were it not for the generosity of Charles II, who revived the title in 1660 by Act of Parliament, after it had lain dormant for nearly a hundred years. The man who was thus restored as 5th Duke of Norfolk (1626–1677) was a gibbering idiot who had suffered brain fever at the age of eighteen from which he never recovered. So dangerous a lunatic was he, that his next brother Lord Henry Howard had packed him off to Italy where he was kept in confinement and never allowed to set foot in England again. The titular Earl Marshal was "unapproachable . . . an incurable maniac".[25] Reresby saw him in exile and declared that "he laboured under all the Symptoms of Lunacy and Distraction". His younger brothers suspected that this madness was a fiction fostered by Henry Howard, who acted as Earl Marshal in the idiot's place, and they petitioned the House of Commons in 1676 to send for the Duke, saying that he was perfectly in command of his senses. The petition was not granted. Reresby and others, who had no axe to grind, were believed, and the risk of having a lunatic let loose on the country's ceremonial was not taken.[26] He died unmarried in Italy, his body brought back by laboursome journey, to England, where it was buried one whole year after death. His brother Henry Howard succeeded him as 6th Duke of Norfolk (1628–1684).

The 7th Duke of Norfolk (1655–1701) is remembered for a witty remark he is reputed to have made to James II,[27] and for the notorious affair his wife had with that handsome soldier of fortune, Sir John Germain. The Duchess's adultery was flaunted about town in a way which made a laughing-stock of the poor Duke. Germain would frequently stay at one of the Norfolks' country seats, where he was allocated a bedroom adjacent to the Duchess's own bedroom. The two rooms communicated by a false cupboard, which one walked into, then climbed over a wooden partition, and walked out of again into the next room. The partition inside the cupboard was six feet high, but did not reach the ceiling. One day the Duke came unexpectedly to his wife's bedroom, and finding the door locked, demanded entry. Germain was of course in bed with her. He had time only to leap out of bed, and on to the partition, where he sat perilously and uncomfortably, naked but for a shirt, not daring to drop down the other side for fear that he would be heard. To make matters worse, the Duchess's pet lap-dog followed him to the partition, and barked at him all the time, wagging his tail and thoroughly enjoying the fun. The Duke, strange to say, in spite of the racket, did not discover Germain hiding on his perch.[28]

The affair finally exploded in the courts in 1692. The Duke sued Germain for damages "for lying with the Duchess", claiming £100,000. He won his case, but the jury awarded him a miserable 100 marks only, presumably because they knew that he had a mistress himself and London was anyway bored with the spectacle of the Duke and Duchess fighting over lovers. The judge fulminated against him, telling the jury that "he was sorry the world should know how low virtue and chastity were held in England".[29] Anne Bagnalls wrote: "The town rings of the Duke of Norfolk's divorce, which will come to nothing but publishing each other's infamy."[30] How right she was.

The Duke died of apoplexy at the age of forty-six, and was succeeded by his nephews the 8th Duke (1683–1732) and the 9th Duke (1686–1777), who was a timid mouse of a man, married to a shrewish virago of a Duchess. It was she who gave the orders, he who obeyed. She was practically Duke of Norfolk herself, and was even called "My Lord Duchess" by those with a sense of humour. At a house-warming party she gave, which "all the earth" attended, Walpole says that "there was all the company afraid of the Duchess, and the Duke afraid of all the company".[31] Lady A. Irwin corroborates the impression of a Laurel and Hardy marriage. The Duchess, she says, "must act the man where talking is necessary".[32]

At all events, the marriage was childless, but so many Howards were about that there was no danger of the dukedom becoming extinct. It passed to his second cousin, son of Mr Charles Howard, who as 10th Duke of Norfolk (1720–1786) was another eccentric figure of the elegant eighteenth century, a "drunken old mad fellow" who "dressed like a Cardinal".[33] But his eccentricity was tame compared with the wild excesses of his son the 11th Duke, a theatrical, extravagant character who is one of those larger-than-life aristocrats, like the 4th Duke of Queensberry (Old Q), whose personality elbows all others off the pages of social history.

The 11th Duke of Norfolk (1746–1815) was corpulent, sweaty, muscle-bound, and graceless. He moved, dressed, and ate in a clumsy manner, was perpetually drunk, and never washed. "In cleanliness he was negligent to so great a degree", writes someone who knew him well, "that he rarely made use of water for purposes of bodily refreshment and comfort. He even carried the neglect of his person so far, that his servants were accustomed to avail themselves of his fits of intoxication, for the purpose of washing him." The servants would lay him out on the floor, undress him, and wash him head to toe while he was semi-conscious, or indeed out cold. He would otherwise presumably have smelt intolerably. He complained one day to

Dudley North that he suffered badly from rheumatism, and had tried every remedy without effect. "Pray, my Lord," said North, "did you ever try a clean shirt?"[34]

"Jockey of Norfolk" or "The Jockey", as the 11th Duke was called, surpassed all competitors in the consumption of wine. He was the most famous drunk of the eighteenth century. The Duke's capacity to drink anyone under the table, and then proceed to another party to start all over again, was well known. He could drink five or six times as much as anyone else before he would feel the effect. When finally the wine overcame him, after perhaps a whole night of debauchery to which drinking was only a prologue, he would collapse at dawn in the streets, where his harassed servants would find him sleeping peacefully in the gutter or on a bench.

His boon companion in these excesses was the Prince of Wales. Together, the Prince and the Duke were frequently seen, arms supporting each other, staggering up the street. Years later, the Prince and his royal brothers determined to make the Duke so drunk that he would forfeit his crown as champion imbiber. He was invited to a drinking party at the Pavilion in Brighton. He drove over from Arundel Castle, with his famous equipage of grey horses. Tumblers of wine were mixed with tumblers of brandy, the old man drinking one glass with everyone singly, so that he finished by consuming about ten times more than anyone else. The companions fell one by one like ninepins, and the Duke continued, unsteady but standing. Finally, he said he must go home, called for his carriage, and slumped within it. The royal princes, aching with merriment and swooning against the walls, waved him off, having instructed the coachman to drive him round in circles. The poor old Duke thought he was going home to Arundel, but he was driven around and around the Brighton Pavilion for half an hour, fell out at the end of the "journey", and into a bed, waking up the next morning to find he had been tricked into staying the night.[35]

Parallel with astonishing capacity for wine, Jockey possessed in equal measure an infinitely expandable stomach. He was the greatest gourmand of his time and the most venerated member of the Beefsteak Club, where he was always ceremoniously ushered to a Chair of State some steps higher than the rest of the diners. He would get through two or three steaks more quickly than they could be served up to him, and when it appeared that he could not possibly take any more, he would clean his plate ready for a fourth. Amazingly, his conversation seems not to have suffered from the onslaught. The strongest port failed to deaden his culture or wit.

It was the Duke of Norfolk and his royal chum who effected a revolution in eating habits in London society by establishing late hours. At the beginning of the eighteenth century it was customary to dine at four o'clock. By the 1770s this had advanced to seven o'clock for most people, or midnight for those who knew the habits of the Duke of Norfolk. It became fashionable to eat later and later, and to stay up all night. Walpole wrote: "The present folly is late hours. Everyone tried to be particular by being too late; and as everybody tries it, nobody is so. It is the fashion now to go to Ranelagh [where concerts were given at seven] two hours after it is over. You may not believe this, but it is literal. The music ends at ten; the company goes at twelve." People simply spent much less time sleeping than they do nowadays.[36]

It was while dining with the Prince at one of these late parties that the news was conveyed to Jockey that he had been deprived by the King of all his offices. A couple of days before he had proposed a toast at the Crown and Anchor "to the sovereign majesty of the people", a sentiment which was seditious to say the least, and not far short of treasonable. Of course, the Duke was drunk at the time, but nonetheless he had to be shown that he had gone too far. When he tried to strike up conversation with the King shortly afterwards, George cut him short in mid-sentence, saying, "*A propos*, my lord, have you seen 'Blue Beard'?"[37]

In order to hold office and to sit in Parliament (this was half a century before the Catholic Relief Bill), Jockey had renounced the Roman Catholic religion in 1780, but he remained a Catholic at heart for all that, especially when drunk, as everyone in the House knew. He was not always sober *there* either.

Another of Jockey's drinking companions was a Mr Huddlestone, who after one night of intoxication fell off his chair to the floor. A younger Howard went to assist the man to his feet, but the drunkard would have none of it. "Never shall it be said that the head of the house of Huddlestone was lifted from the ground by a younger branch of the house of Howard," he bellowed. The good-humoured Duke responded well. "The head of the house of Howard is too drunk to pick up the head of the house of Huddlestone," he said, "but he will lie down beside him with all the pleasure in the world." And he lay on the floor.[38]

Glimpses like this show that old Jockey was far more than the "dirty devil" that unkind Creevey called him, far more than a miserable drunkard, and it explains why, in spite of his eccentricities, he was enormously popular. He was never a violent drunk, never offensive, never really objectionable. He was essentially a good man whom life had treated badly. He had married twice, and his second wife, who survived him, had become a lunatic. Lady Holland put his case neatly. "The Duke of Norfolk is an extraordinary instance of the impossibility of *situation* being sufficient to secure happiness : he, however, finds in his own good temper an antidote to all the vexations of his life. He has all that rank, dignity, and wealth can give; he married a beautiful woman whose person he liked, possessed of £15,000 per annum. About eight years after she became mad, and from being intestate her immense possessions escheat to the Crown, there being no male heir to the Scudamores. It appears to be a hardship that the laws afford no relief to a person united to one insane, as no pretext can be more valid towards the dissolution of a marriage than an obstacle of that nature that impedes the fulfilling of every function belonging to the institution. He maintains with solid magnificence the splendour of his rank; everything about him bespeaks wealth and luxurious comfort. His servants are old domestics, fat, sleek, and happy; his table is profuse and exquisite. His taste is bad; he loves society, but has no selection, and swallows wine for quantity, not quality : he is gross in everything. The Duchess' madness has taken a sombre, *farouche* turn : she hates all mankind. The clergyman during a lucid interval advised her to read religious books, supplied her with some, and mingled his advice with pious exhortations. She acquiesced, and took the books. A few days after she returned them with scorn, saying, 'I wish I could believe your damned trumpery, as I should then be certain two-thirds of mankind would roast in Hell.' It was curious that in the Gospels she could find matter to gratify her malignity. The Duke behaves uncommonly well to her."[39]

We, in an age less obsequious towards revealed truth, might find it not so "curious" and if this be an example of the Duchess's ravings, they appear more akin to solid good sense. But in truth she was much further gone than this. Wraxall speaks of her "disordered intellect", and the Public Record Office contains pages of information about her insanity, as the records relating to the Scudamore inheritance reside there.

The Duke made up for the deprivation of "every function belonging to the institution" of marriage in his own beguiling manner. Driving through the village of Greystoke in Cumberland with his steward, he saw hordes of children waving at them from both sides of the road. "Whose are all these children?" he asked. The steward answered, "Some are mine, Your Grace, and some are yours."

In 1783, three centuries after the creation of the dukedom of

Norfolk in the Howard family, Jockey determined to hold a big party at Arundel Castle for "all the blood of all the Howards", to which every descendant of the 1st Duke would be invited to celebrate. He was forced to abandon the idea when calculations showed that over 6000 people would have to be included.

In old age, Jockey of Norfolk grew so large that he could hardly get through a door of ordinary proportions. But he was not fat in the belly – he was simply of huge girth all over, a living giant. His death in 1815 left a large gap, in bulk as much as in personality.[40]

The nineteenth-century Dukes of Norfolk are a much quieter collection of men. With the 15th Duke (1847–1917) we approach very close to the present day, for this devout, unwordly man is the father of the Duke who died recently. As he came to the title in 1860, only two men held that title for the 115 years until 1975.

The 15th Duke was the most religious of all the Howards, a deeply brooding ascetic who spent money building churches rather than buying clothes; he always dressed shabbily, was frequently mistaken for a tramp, and was often offered money, so poor did he look. Strangers whom he helped at railway stations would offer him tips. One woman visitor to the grounds of Arundel Castle told him to get off the grass, and a Salvation Army girl, when she saw his blue Garter ribbon, thought he was one of the Army.[41] The churches he built were St Philip Neri at Arundel and a church at Norwich which was one of the largest built since the Reformation. As the senior lay representative in England, he wielded much unseen power in the Church of Rome, as did his late son. It was owing to his influence that John Henry Newman was made a Cardinal.

The Duke was a saintly man, more so in fact than the ancestor Earl of Arundel who has since been canonised; he was a profoundly good and gentle soul. But, as so often happens with those whose goodness springs from conviction, he was not always an easy man to contend with. Devotion to the Catholic Church was the principle to which all else must needs be subordinated. Hence his support for Newman, who, though not an agreeable man, was a Catholic. The Duke's first wife was Lady Flora Hastings, a Protestant. Whether the Duke made it a condition of their marriage or not, she became a Catholic, much to the displeasure of her family, who would have nothing more to do with her.[41] The Duchess, too, was a saint of a kind, a wonderfully simple and good character. If any couple deserved to be happy, they did, yet it was upon them that catastrophe of the cruellest sort descended. Their son, heir to the highest dukedom of the realm, was mentally defective.

Philip Joseph Mary Fitzalan-Howard, Earl of Surrey and Arundel (1879–1902), who would in the normal course of events have been the next Duke of Norfolk, grew up an almost complete invalid. Practically blind, deaf and dumb, with the mind of an infant, there was never any hope that the boy would recover the use of his brain, although the Duke turned to his religion time and again for assistance, making the pilgrimage to Lourdes twenty-five times. The entire Catholic world prayed for him. As if this was not enough, the good Duchess died after ten years of marriage, leaving the Duke alone with his idiot son. He spent every possible hour as companion to the boy, lavishing care and attention with barely a flicker of intelligent response.

Philip died in 1902, at the age of twenty-three. He left £558 in his will. His father said, "After all, my boy has given more glory to God than any of us. Look at the Masses, novenas and pilgrimages of which he has been the occasion."[43] He endowed a piece of land in Yorkshire for the reception, maintenance, treatment and education of children suffering from physical disability or infirmity.

The Duke's life was, then, mostly private, devotional, and tragic. His forays into public life were, however, successful. Lady Warwick records the opinion that he was the best Postmaster-General ever;[44] it is to him that we owe the custom, now taken for granted, that letters which go astray may be re-addressed and re-delivered free of charge. His other contribution to public life was to restore the elaborate ceremonial for the coronation (in his capacity as Earl Marshal), which had fallen into neglect. He arranged the coronations of Edward VII in 1901 and George V in 1910.

Having no direct heir, the Duke was married again in 1904 to a woman thirty years younger than himself, Baroness Herries in her own right. The products of this union were three daughters and Bernard Marmaduke Fitzalan-Howard, who in 1917, at the age of nine, succeeded to a bewildering list of duties and titles as 16th Duke of Norfolk, Earl Marshal of England.

From the beginning, it was made clear to the little boy that he was very special. He was brought up by his uncle Lord Fitzalan of Derwent in the full consciousness of his unique position as Earl Marshal with precedence over almost every other subject in the kingdom, and trained by him to assume the rigorous duties of his office. It was the kind of upbringing that would have turned any other young man's head, but as he was a Howard, he knew in his blood that all this was his by right, and he was not at all perturbed by it. He was educated to think of himself almost as royalty.

The days when the Duke of Norfolk was preceded through the streets by trumpeters and followed by a retinue of a hundred men, when he was met five miles outside London by heralds who escorted him into the capital, and when crowds lined the street to see him pass, all that may be over;[45] but enough of the aura of the dukedom remains for him to be revered even in the twentieth century as folk-king of Sussex. Some of that mystical, quasi-divine quality clings yet to the Duke of Norfolk. On the late Duke's coming of age in 1929, there were celebrations lasting three days in the town of Arundel. The Duke made what amounted to a royal progress through the streets, crowded with the townspeople, his "subjects", who turned out symbolically to aver their allegiance. His Grace was received by the Mayor, who made an appropriate speech. Then he drove in an open carriage to Littlehampton (the greater part of the town belonged to him), while people lined the route to see him, the streets were decorated, and the town band gave him a rousing welcome. Shops in Arundel closed after midday, and a public holiday was declared. Schools were entertained at a fête in the grounds of the castle. A month later, 20,000 people joined in similar celebrations at Norfolk Park, Sheffield.[46] There was yet more public rejoicing at the Duke's marriage in 1937. The spirit of such occasions is medieval, even pagan in its unconscious ritual. Deep veneration was felt for the antiquity of the Duke's title and dignity, especially in Arundel where, as the Earl of Arundel, he possessed the charisma of a divine king which can only be explained by the people's innate, unconscious need for local mythology to be passed from generation to generation.

> *Since William rose and Harold fell*
> *There have been Earls of Arundel.*

It is the oldest earldom in the peerage of England, and until 1627 it was held as of right by anyone who owned Arundel Castle; in other words, it was a title independent of patents of creation. This is why, in 1572, the son of the attainted Duke of Norfolk was still known as Earl of Arundel, although all other titles had been forfeited. It was not within the power or jurisdiction of Parliament to withdraw the earldom, which was Philip Howard's right as long as he held Arundel Castle. Little wonder, then, that since the ancient earldom was allied to the ancient dukedom, successive incumbents have exerted unseen power upon the collective imagination of the local people.

The other singularity which sets Norfolk apart from all other dukes is his hereditary post as Earl Marshal of England. Unlike some other such positions (as, for example, the Duke of St Albans, who is Hereditary Grand Falconer, but never goes near a falcon), the Earl Marshal has a job to do, and a job of such complexity that there are only a handful of people who would have the knowledge to deputise for him. This is the work for which Bernard Norfolk was trained by his uncle, and which he performed to the sound of universal praise. The Earl Marshal is ultimate and alone in his responsibility to the Sovereign for all ceremonial occasions, for which onerous charge he is paid a fee of £20 per annum. The fee was fixed by Richard III in 1483 when he appointed the 1st Duke of Norfolk Earl Marshal, and fixed in perpetuity. The King also directed that the Earl Marshal should carry a staff with the royal arms in gold at one end, and at the other, the arms of the Duke of Norfolk. The Duke still carries this staff. The first Earl Marshal had been even earlier, in 1385, when the post was held by a Mowbray Duke of Norfolk; before that, they had been simply Marshals.

The late Duke's first duty was to arrange the funeral of George V, after which he was responsible for the proclamations of Edward VIII, George VI and Elizabeth II, the funerals of George VI, Queen Mary, and Sir Winston Churchill, and finally the investiture of Prince Charles as Prince of Wales. At the first of these, he was only twenty-seven years old. At all of them, he showed the same astonishing grasp of detail as his father had, and the same relentless pursuit of perfection. There was a time when the elaborate ceremonial of the coronation was understood by no one. When Queen Victoria was crowned, she was not told where to sit, what to say, when to get up, or what happened next. Her coronation was not far short of a shambles. Nowadays, thanks to the Duke, it is the most precise and splendid pageant in the world.

The Earl Marshal is not merely a stage-manager of state occasions. He is head of the College of Heralds, and as such exercises an authority independent of his titles. It is he who may ultimately decide what arms a newly created peer may bear, and by what title he may be known. He decides on matters of precedence. The staff at the College of Heralds is responsible to him.

The Duke was careful to avoid one embarrassing case of heraldry on which he might have been called to make a decision, since it affected his own coat of arms. The Norfolk coat bears an augmentation known as the Flodden augmentation, granted to the victor of that battle, along with restoration of the dukedom of Norfolk and regrant of some lands. The difficulty is that the Flodden augmentation was granted with remainder to *heirs general* of the grantee, while the dukedom was granted to *heirs male*. The result of this should be that only Lords Mowbray and Petre have the right to bear the augmentation, and *not* the Duke of Norfolk. (Other Howard descendants, the Earls of Carlisle and Suffolk for example, bear the augmentation on their arms.) We were denied, however, the cheerful spectacle of the Duke dragging himself before his own Court. It remains to be seen if the new Duke will allow the matter to be examined. (The *Complete Peerage*, Vol. X, Appendix N, says that this was all a mistake on the part of the King, and that the Flodden augmentation was intended to descend with the dukedom.)

The Earl Marshal was originally subordinate to the Constable (a military office), and the historical precedence of the Lord High Constable is marked to this day by his ranking on the *right* of the monarch at coronations, while the Earl Marshal is on the *left*.

The popular press has on occasion exaggerated the duties of the Earl Marshal in its desire to make of him a 'superstar' in accordance with the demands of modern public life. The late Duke was not infallible or omnipotent. When the funeral of the Duke of Windsor took place in London, for instance, many of the arrangements were undertaken by the Lord Chamberlain's office, while Fleet Street continued to assume that Norfolk was responsible for it all.

It is a curious tolerance, one likes to think peculiarly English, which allows the most solemn ritual in the Church of England, when the Head of the Church is crowned, to be within the total control of the senior Roman Catholic in the country. The evening before the coronation the keys of Westminster Abbey are handed to the Duke of Norfolk.

When Bernard Marmaduke became 16th Duke of Norfolk he inherited nearly 50,000 acres. The restrictions of twentieth-century life gradually encroached upon these holdings until he was left with 24,000 acres. In St James's Square stood Norfolk House, which had been the London residence of the family since 1684. This was sold in 1937, and pulled down; the furniture was auctioned. In 1931 the town of Littlehampton (or the half of it which belonged to the Duke) was sold, and part of the Arundel estate went in 1950. In 1959 the Duke moved out of Arundel Castle, which he had once said was to him "practically everything there is",[47] to a five-bedroomed house which he built in the park. The castle itself, with its 150 rooms, and forbidding aspect, had ceased to be an attractive or economical place to live, although, undaunted, the 17th Duke has announced his intention of living there. When Creevey saw it in the last century he wrote: "The devil himself could make nothing of the interior. Any-

thing so horrid and dark and frightful in all things I never beheld."[48]
It is open to the public.

The most lucrative portion of the estate is three and a quarter acres
just south of the Strand, which have been in the family since 1549.
Arundel Street, Norfolk Street, Maltravers Street, and Howard
Street all form part of this site. Now, of course, the new Duke of
Norfolk has added to the family holdings the extensive lands he owned
before he came to the dukedom.

Bernard Norfolk was a taciturn, withdrawn man, shy but sure of
himself. He had few opinions, but they were all unshakeable, and
mostly half a century behind those of his contemporaries. His right
to be right was unassailable. When he received criticism he was not
resentful but amazed; he could not comprehend that another view
might be possible. In this he was like the 4th Duke of Norfolk, who
antagonised Elizabeth I so much and eventually lost his head. He
failed to enter Oxford, but since it was Oxford's loss, he did not
mind. At the entrance examination he found himself sitting next to
an Asian student. "If they preferred his presence to mine at the
university, they were welcome to him," he said. The newspapers,
obsessed with trivia and saturated with wrong opinions, annoyed him.
"If I had my way," he said, "I'd shut down half the newspapers in
the country, and keep a tight censorship on the others, except *The
Times*."[49]

With his gruff manner, heavy-lidded eyes, and bluntness which was
just short of dismissive, he was one of the rare surviving noblemen
who managed to caricature themselves. At the investititure of the
Prince of Wales in 1970 the Duke had to deal with the Secretary of
State for Wales, George Thomas, son of a Rhondda miner. Thomas
offered him a cup of tea. "Never touch the stuff," replied Norfolk.
The Welshman then went to the cupboard to get some alcoholic
drinks. "Wrong time of day," said the Duke, and that was the end of
that. The two men later became friendly enough. The Duke said, "I
am going to call you George, and you will call me Bernard," and
Thomas says he felt it was an order.

He treated everyone with the same brisk laconic precision. Stories
of his behaviour at the coronation are legion. "If the bishops don't
learn to walk in step we shall be here all night" he is reported to have
said; and to the Archbishop of Canterbury, "No, no, Archbishop, that
won't do at all. Go back there and we'll do it all again."

He was not at all aware that his no-nonsense approach, shorn of
all unnecessary adornment, could be extremely funny. At dinner he
was heard to turn to a lady guest on his right and say, "Now; I have

only two topics of conversation – cricket and drains. Choose." He
claimed that he did not know when he was being amusing, and what's
more, he did not care.

The Howards have always been men of few words. On one occasion
Lord Carlisle and his brother travelled abroad together, and slept in
the same room at an inn in Germany. There was a third bed in
the room with the curtains drawn round it. Two days later, one
brother turned to the other and said, "Did you see what was in that
bed in our room the other night?" and the other answered, "Yes."
That was all the conversation they had on the matter, yet they had
both seen a dead body in the bed.[50]

Norfolk was also impatient of politicians with their meandering
style and clever evasions, being himself devastatingly direct and
monosyllabic. When in 1970 his trainer was fined £500 by the Jockey
Club for irregular practices, the Duke determined to have nothing
more to do with them. He would not enter into an argument, and
never forgave them. One of the reasons he got on so well with Richard
Dimbleby, for whom he wrote an obituary in *The Times*, was because
Dimbleby had a businesslike attitude similar to his own. He could not
bear fuss or delay.

Norfolk married Miss Lavinia Strutt, a Protestant, in 1937. They
had four daughters, and no son. The dukedom passed in 1975 to Lord
Beaumont, Baron Howard of Glossop, who is descended from the
13th Duke of Norfolk. In 1966 Bernard Marmaduke had settled a
million pounds on Lord Beaumont's son, Edward, born in 1956.

However austere, aloof and correct he may have appeared, Norfolk
enjoyed respect for his profound sense of duty and public service,
and affection for his obvious belief that the aristocracy must set an
example by getting down to the job in hand and doing it well. This
affection is something for which his training did not prepare him, and
it was the only aspect of his public life which troubled his calm. Just
before the coronation in 1953 he gave a press conference after which
the assembled journalists, many of radical persuasion, rose to their
feet in unison and gave him a spontaneous applause which visibly
surprised him. And at the coronation of George VI he found himself
mobbed by a Cockney crowd slapping him on the back and shouting
"Well done, Bernard!" He must have wondered what he had done
wrong.[51]

The man who succeeded as 17th Duke of Norfolk in 1975 is in a
different style altogether. Being a remote cousin, he has come to the
title by a "wavy line" which would not have veered in his direction at
all if one of the late Duke's children had been a boy. He is not over-

impressed by his luck. "Succeeding by death is a poor way of getting on," he says. "I am much prouder of having been a general."[52]

As Miles Fitzalan-Howard he graduated Bachelor of Arts at Christ Church, Oxford, then proceeded into the Grenadier Guards, with a thirty-year military career in front of him, rising to the rank of major-general, and collecting various distinctions along the way (Maltese Cross, C.B.E., C.B.). He was Director of Service Intelligence at the Ministry of Defence for a period, and Head of the British Military Mission to Russian Forces in Germany. He retired in 1967, and settled to a more peaceful life with his wife Anne Maxwell, two sons, and three daughters. Fitzalan-Howard then went into the City, as director of a merchant bank.

Within four years, from 1971 to 1975, a giddy succession of titles descended upon him. He succeeded his father as Baron Howard of Glossop (which is where one finds the Norfolk connection. The title of Howard of Glossop was created in 1869 for the second son of the 13th Duke of Norfolk as a "consolation peerage" to compensate for his failure to get elected M.P. for Preston; he had represented Arundel in the House of Commons for fourteen years from 1852 to 1868). The following year his mother died, passing on to him her own more ancient dignity, the barony of Beaumont, created in 1309 for the second cousin of Edward II. This title fell into abeyance in 1895, when the 10th Baron Beaumont killed himself accidentally with a shotgun when crossing a stile. This man, happily for his descendant, was converted to Roman Catholicism in 1880. The R.C. community in England would have been very shaken with a Protestant Duke of Norfolk. The barony was called out of abeyance in 1896 in favour of the present Duke's mother, then aged two.

As soon as the mantle of Norfolk fell upon him, he accepted the challenge ruefully, making no secret of his wish that the wavy line had taken another direction. Never before the centre of so much national attention, he takes publicity in his stride, with more of a desire to please than his predecessor, less impatience, less intolerance. The Howard bluntness, the cause of so much trouble in the past and source of so much endearment in more recent times, runs with undiminished vigour in Norfolk's veins. If he is embarrassed by the fuss, he will say so.

*   *   *

By an apt coincidence, the dukedom of Somerset was restored in the same year as the dukedom of Norfolk – 1660, 108 years after the execution of Edward Seymour, the 1st Duke, and eighty-eight years after the execution of Thomas Howard, 4th Duke of Norfolk. Thus were the descendants of the rival families, once bitter enemies, restored to their proper dignity at the same time. The man who then became 2nd Duke of Somerset for a month (he also died in 1660) was William Seymour, great-grandson of the 1st Duke, and Marquess of Hertford since 1641. He was a scholarly man, Chancellor of the University of Oxford 1643–1647 and again in 1660, a natural student. But it was for an adventure in love that the world knew his name.

When Master William Seymour was fifteen years old he was the object of passionate attentions from Lady Arabella Stuart, who was then twenty-seven. This would be no more than cause for amusing gossip were it not for the fact that Arabella was first cousin to James I, being descended from Henry VII through Margaret Tudor and therefore high in line of succession to the throne. No member of the Royal Family was allowed to fall in love without the Sovereign's approval, and James severely scolded his cousin, ordering her to break off the affair, which was quite unsuitable. Not only was William Seymour a pubescent boy, but he was not even *heir apparent* to his grandfather's title of Earl of Hertford, being a second son. The future revival of the dukedom of Somerset was not then even contemplated, and it would not have fallen upon him anyway. Arabella obeyed, but not without protesting that they were deeply and truly in love. Events were to prove her sincere.

The affair resumed in 1610, by which time he was twenty-two and she thirty-four. Their romance, more dramatic than any fiction, came to a head when they married clandestinely at Greenwich, without the King's consent, which, she being of royal blood, was essential. They were discovered and imprisoned, he in the Tower, she at Lambeth. They were treated with such leniency that he appears to have been allowed to visit her in prison while he was still nominally in chains himself. It was an easy matter for them to hatch a plot for escape.

Arabella escaped first, dressed as a man. Seymour was to follow her. He walked out of the Tower of London having changed clothes with his barber, and hastened to the continent in search of his wife. She, meanwhile, had been caught, and sent to the Tower. The young lovers never saw each other again. She was confined in the Tower for the rest of her short life, where she gradually lost her mind. She was quite insane when she died in 1615. Seymour eventually came back to England, married Frances Devereux, sister of the Earl of

Essex, in 1618, and led subsequently a more sedentary life. He died four weeks after being restored as 2nd Duke of Somerset in 1660.[53]

The Dukes of Somerset then went into a decline more absolute and more hedged in obscurity than the Dukes of Norfolk. The 3rd Duke inherited at the age of eight, and died at the age of nineteen of an unspecified "malignant fever" following a riotous libertine existence.[54] The 5th Duke (1658–1678) met his end in Italy at the age of twenty. He was with some French friends who foolishly insulted the wife of a Genovese gentleman called Horatio Botti. The touchy Italian knocked on the Duke's door, and when he answered, shot him dead on the spot.[55]

The 6th Duke of Somerset (1662–1748) was the brother of the dead man, and was descended from a younger son of the 1st Duke. He is the largest character in the Seymour gallery, an absurdly pompous eccentric who holds a place in the history of the family analogous to that held by Jockey of Norfolk in the Howard history. There is a difference, however. Jockey of Norfolk, though he drank too much, was loved. The "Proud Duke", 6th of Somerset, was loathed.

He was not without his abilities, but held them in higher regard than anyone else did. He came to the title at the age of sixteen, was Gentleman of the Bedchamber to both Charles II and James II, was made Knight of the Garter at twenty-one. Later distinctions included the Lord President of the Council and Master of the Horse. He made a spectacular marriage. His bride was Lady Elizabeth Percy, Countess of Ogle, daughter and sole heiress of the last Earl of Northumberland; she brought to the marriage and to the growing ego of the Duke of Somerset all the Percy estates and revenues, including Northumberland House in the Strand, Alnwick Castle, Petworth, and Syon House. Further, his bride held in her own right six of the oldest baronies in the kingdom, those of Percy, Lucy, Poynings, Fitz-Payne, Bryan, and Latimer. The Duke's self-importance henceforth knew no bounds, though it was all derived from his wife, as was almost all his money.

She, strange to say, at sixteen was already twice a widow. She had first married at the age of thirteen Henry Cavendish, Earl of Ogle. He died shortly afterwards, aged eighteen, and young Elizabeth was again on the market. She was pursued by Thomas Thynne of Longleat, a rogue and philanderer, and Count Koenigsmark, a hot-blooded continental nobleman. Being worth a considerable fortune the girl was under all kinds of pressures to place it somewhere, and Thynne was chosen as the most likely beneficiary. She married him in some secrecy, then promptly disappeared, having told her servants that she wanted to buy some plate, and instructed them to wait for her outside the Old Exchange, by her carriage. She did not return, but fled to seek the protection of Lady Temple, wife of the ambassador in Holland. Clearly, she was scared, as well she might be; her new husband was murdered in Pall Mall by hired assassins of his rival Koenigsmark.

The Duke of Somerset was this adolescent's third husband. As part of the marriage settlement, he was obliged to adopt the name Percy (which would otherwise disappear), but she later released him from this clause. The drama of her short history made her a fit object for lampoons. Swift wrote this impromptu piece, full of wicked implications (she had flaming red hair and was nicknamed "Carrots") :

Beware of *Carrots* from Northumberlond.
Carrots sown *Thyn* a deep root may get,
If so they are in *Sommer set*.
Their *Conyngs mark* them, for I have been told.
They assassine when young and poison when old.

Preening himself with pleasure, blossoming with the arrogance of rank, the Proud Duke loved nothing more than to put on his splendid robes. He relished ceremonies and grand occasions, anything which gave him an excuse to display his splendour. But he would only allow himself to be seen by those whose status in society made them worthy of such an honour. He never suffered the lower classes to set eyes upon him. He went so far as to build houses at strategic points between London and Petworth so that he would not be obliged, on making the journey between his properties, to stay at an inn. Courtiers were sent on ahead of him to clear the roads, so that his progress might proceed without obstruction. People were told to make themselves scarce, because His Grace did not deign to be seen by commoners. One man responded to this command in the only way merited, by thrusting a pig in the Duke's face. As Macaulay wrote, he was "a man in whom the pride of birth and rank amounted almost to a disease".[56]

Accounts of his stupid arrogance are abundant. On one occasion, his second wife tapped him lightly with her fan. "Madam," he said imperiously, "my first Duchess was a Percy, and she never took such a liberty." When his daughter Charlotte had the temerity to sit down in his presence, the Duke immediately deprived her of £20,000 of her inheritance.[57]

Stories such as these would be even more amusing were it not for the malignant cruelty which they conceal. For Somerset's pride was truly so grotesque that it made misery for his family. One laughed at him, and pitied those near him. Like Monsieur Jourdain in Molière's *Le Bourgeois Gentilhomme*, Somerset allowed his ridiculous obsessions to poison any natural filial love he may have felt. For example, he had a habit of dozing on his couch after dinner. It was the duty of his youngest daughter to sit and watch him while he slept. One day she left him, and he rolled off to the floor. When he woke up and found himself on the floor he was so furious that he forbade everyone in the house to speak to her, although they were to treat her with respect as *his* daughter. This torment went on for an entire year, the family and servants not daring to open their mouths to the poor girl, still less to approach His Grace to find out when or if the prohibition was to be lifted. So it was never known if he had forgiven her. "His whole stupid life was a series of pride and tyranny", said Walpole.[58]

His worst offence was to explode with anger against his son Lord Hertford because his grandson Lord Beauchamp died at the age of nineteen, thus depriving his line of an heir. Walpole tells the tale. "He has written the most shocking letter imaginable to poor Lord Hertford", he writes, "telling him that it is a judgement upon him for all his undutifulness, and that he must always look upon himself as the cause of his son's death. Lord Hertford is as good a man as lives, and has always been most unreasonably ill-used by that old tyrant. The title of Somerset will revert to Sir Edward Seymour."[59] Sir Edward was Speaker of the House of Commons, and is credited with having put the Proud Duke in his place in conversation with King William. The King said to him, "Sir Edward, I think you are of the Duke of Somerset's family?" to which he replied, "No, Sir; he is of mine."

To appreciate the import of Sir Edward Seymour's remark, we have to travel back to the beginning of the dukedom of Somerset and gingerly climb genealogical trees.

The Proud Duke, 6th in line, died in 1748, aged eighty-seven. His son succeeded as 7th Duke, was the following year created Earl of Northumberland, to perpetuate the title of his mother's family, the Percys, and since he had no sons after the death of Lord Beauchamp, special arrangements were made for the earldom to pass to the heirs of his son-in-law Hugh Smithson, who then became the ancestor of the present Duke of Northumberland.

A crisis occurred in the dukedom of Somerset, the first of several to beset this title, when the 7th Duke died the following year, 1750, bringing the line of descent to an abrupt end.

The 1st Duke of Somerset, Edward Seymour the Lord Protector (1500–1552) had married twice. The first marriage, to Katherine Fillol, was not an entire success. The paternity of their first son was suspect, and there was talk that Seymour was furious because the baby was born while he was absent for many months in France. When in 1547 he had himself created Duke of Somerset he had already been married again to Anne Stanhope, and he made the patent of creation specify an entail which placed the issue of this second marriage (the junior branch) in preference to the issue of the first marriage (the senior branch) by reason of Katherine Fillol's infidelity. The first son was cut out entirely. In order, the dukedom was to descend to

1. heirs male of himself and his second wife
2. heirs male by any future wife
3. to Edward, the second son by his first wife
4. to his brothers
5. to his heirs female

So, the first seven Dukes of Somerset were descended from Anne Stanhope. In 1750 the dignity reverted to the issue of the first marriage and Sir Edward Seymour, who claimed it, was a direct descendant of the second son by the first wife Katherine Fillol. (The first son, of dubious legitimacy, had conveniently died unmarried in 1552.) When Sir Edward Seymour the Speaker told King William that the Duke of Somerset belonged to *his* family rather than the other way round, he was not merely being funny. In the normal course his branch of the family would have had precedence from the very beginning, being heirs of the body of Edward Seymour, the Lord Protector's eldest surviving son.

The second branch of Seymours finally came to the title in 1750, with the 8th Duke of Somerset (1695–1757), a fifth cousin once removed of the 7th. The man who carries the title of Somerset now is descended from this 8th Duke, and therefore, through eleven generations, from the Lord Protector's first marriage.

The 10th Duke, Webb Seymour, was one of those strange hypochondriacs who frequently occur in ducal households; so terrified was he of catching smallpox that letters had to be hurled through a gingerly opened window. He may have been driven to excess by his wife, Anna Maria Bonnel – jealous, bigoted, and shrewish. Their eldest son, Edward Adolphus, succeeded as 11th Duke of Somerset

(1775–1855) and brought to the family its most intellectual member. A Fellow of the Royal Society, a Fellow of the Society of Antiquaries, and an author of learned treatises in scientific subjects, such as *Properties of the Ellipse,* the 11th Duke was a thinker. Diffident and cautious, trusting to his own reason but not in awe of it, he was a fine example of a son of the Age of Enlightenment, reflective, just, and temperate. He lived a retired existence in contemplation and contentment. His brother Lord Webb John Seymour (1777–1819) was also a man of intellect, with a heady reputation in the fields of science and mathematics. His closest friend was John Playfair (1748–1819), professor of mathematics and natural philosophy at the University of Edinburgh, and founder of the modern science of geology. Seymour and Playfair were quite inseparable; they would turn down an invitation to dine if they had not yet solved together an abstract problem which may have occupied their attentions for two or three days. So close were they that, according to Lord Cockburn, "they used to be called husband and wife, and in congeniality and affection no union could be more complete". Geology, he added, was their favourite pursuit.[60]

The studious 11th Duke fell in love with Lady Susan Hamilton, daughter of the 9th Duke of Hamilton, but her elder sister, Lady Charlotte, had eyes for him herself and, somehow or other, managed to woo him away to her own side. He was not the kind of man to put up much resistance, and one daughter was presumably as good as another. His bad-tempered mother objected to the match, probably on the grounds that Charlotte was much older than the Duke, but also possibly from spite; she was only the daughter of an esquire, whereas the Hamiltons were among the highest in the land. At all events, the wedding took place in 1800, and Lady Charlotte brought to the Seymour family many magnificent Hamilton heirlooms, paintings and furniture. There were Rembrandts, Rubens, Van Dycks, and plenty more, no doubt the cause of Creevey's acid comment about the new Duchess, that "false devil who robbed her brother Archie of his birthright",[61] brother Archie being Lord Archibald Hamilton. The treasures she filched from the dukedom of Hamilton and passed to the dukedom of Somerset were to be the cause of bitter family upheavals amongst the Seymours in the next generation, and to provoke a rift the effects of which are felt today. The Duchess was, incidentally, incredibly mean. The *Farington Diary* records her dinner table being decked with "nothing but a leg of mutton at the top and a dish of potatoes at the bottom".

The Duke adopted the name St Maur in the belief that his family

originated from Normandy, and in denial of his real origin from
Seymour, yet paradoxically he called both his daughters Jane. Vanity
of this kind was an unusual aberration for him. He married a second
time after Charlotte's death, and he and his second wife are buried
simply in a grave at Kensal Green cemetery, part of the tombstone
broken with neglect.

His son the 12th Duke of Somerset (1804–1885) rose to a more
elevated and responsible position in public life than any duke since
the Lord Protector, married one of the most beautiful women of the
day, and had five happy children. From every point of view, however,
his life was to develop tragically.

In the first place, the beautiful Duchess was not a popular choice.
She was one of the three celebrated grand-daughters of the playwright Richard Brinsley Sheridan and accordingly was always
known as the "Sheridan Duchess". That she was stunning there is
no question. Lord Dufferin saw her at the Eglinton tournament of
1839 and enthused about her "large deep blue or violet eyes, black
hair, black eyebrows and eyelashes, perfect features, and a complexion
of lilies and roses".[62] Disraeli wrote ecstatically, "anything so splendid
I never gazed upon . . . clusters of the darkest hair, the most brilliant
complexion, a contour of face perfectly ideal".[63]

This was all very well, but she was not an aristocrat. No amount
of beauty could make up for low birth. From the beginning, then,
the rest of the family were fiercely opposed to her. Her father-in-law
the 11th Duke (still alive at the time of the marriage), did all he
could to dissuade his impulsive son from embarking on such a union.
An eye for beauty was always a most powerful spur to any Seymour,
however, as his previous amours had shown. The principal seat of
the Seymours at this time was Stover Hall, in Devon, where the
Hamilton heirlooms were housed. That the Sheridan Duchess was
despised by other members of the family for her low birth is shown
by an extraordinary document signed by the 13th Duke, full of
vituperative contempt for her and her husband, which used to hang
for all to see at Maiden Bradley, and is now kept in a bottom drawer
there. In it, the Duke described her as a "low-born greedy beggar
woman", whose sole object was to get her hands on the property and
leave it away from the direct heirs. The Duchess of Hamilton commented acidly that she was not used to "novel splendours". The
Sheridan Duchess, who ate guinea-pigs and even produced a recipe
book to show dozens of ways in which guinea-pigs could be prepared,[64] was happy with her husband and children, and viewed with
patronising tolerance the rest of the Seymours.

As First Lord of the Admiralty, the 12th Duke was a man of distinction, remembered for having abolished flogging in the Navy. "There cannot be a more estimable and agreeable man", wrote Lady Holland,[65] and she was right. He inherited his father's quest for knowledge and evolved for himself the happy turn of phrase which marks a literary man. He published nothing of note, but some measure of the man may be inferred from a memorandum he wrote, from the Admiralty, recommending improvements in recreational facilities at Greenwich Hospital for Sailors. "This superb Palace", he said, "with its long Galleries and spacious Colonnades, must, from the Nature of the Institution, become intolerably wearisome to Men who are not totally incapable of taking part in any Occupation or Amusement." Leaving aside the nineteenth-century verbosity, this dry report shows a man with sensibilities which, in his private life, were to prove his undoing. "The Pensioners", he continued, "are necessarily shut out from all the wholesome Interests and Enjoyments of Life; they have no Employment; their material Wants are satisfied, and they are relieved from every care of providing for their own Comfort and Subsistence; they pass their Day in a state of listless Idleness and Mental Vacuity, until recalled at fixed Intervals to their Meals or their Beds. It is not surprising that Old Sailors so circumstanced should resort to the Alehouse or to worse Places . . . Greenwich Hospital has a monastic character, wanting everything that tends to enliven or endear a Home."[66]

Within a year of writing these sentences, the Duke's own home life was shattered by the most unforeseeable disaster.

There were five children of the marriage – Hermione, Ulrica, Guendolen, and two boys, Edward Adolphus Ferdinand known as 'Ferdy', who was the heir, and Lord Edward. Somerset had successfully petitioned for a new title, to commemorate the alleged St Maur origin of the family, and had been granted the title of Earl St Maur in the Peerage of the United Kingdom. Ferdy was henceforth known as Lord St Maur.

Father and sons were especially close. The Duke educated them personally for two hours every morning in his study. The elder boy revealed himself impatient of bookwork fairly soon; his was an adventurous spirit, eager for a life of action, which in time demanded to be set free, and though his wanderings caused his parents much anxious worry, no attempt was made to smother his desires. Young Edward, on the other hand, took to study with undisguised joy. "How cheerfully eager he looked, with a pen stuck behind his ear and a heap of books in his arms, piled up and balanced under his chin, as he turned into my father's study, dragging the door after him with his foot", wrote Lady Guendolen.[67] This picture relates to his thirteenth year. The Duke lavished devotion upon him.

The brothers kept in touch when St Maur began his obsessive travels about the world in search of military activity. "His love of soldering is almost a madness", wrote Mary Smith to the Duchess.[68] Martial ardour drove him to all parts of the globe, while his mother sat at home wondering where on earth he was, and his father sat in the Admiralty trying to conceal his embarrassment. He was arrested in Naples for bodily harm against someone he had picked an argument with, sued for damages, and settled out of court.[69] He turned up in the Far East, chasing a war, quite unperturbed by the perils of a strange climate. "You will make yourself miserable about dangers which in reality do not exist", he wrote in a vain attempt to placate the Duchess.[70] The Duke let it be known he was "vexed", and wanted his son to return home. It fell upon the sixteen-year-old Lord Edward to speak sense to his older brother. "Gadding about the world", wrote Edward, "is nothing but a kind of intellectual dissipation which must end in intellectual sea-sickness and headache."[71]

St Maur, restless and headstrong, would not be restrained. He wanted to cultivate experience, expose himself to foreign ways and views, fight battles. Glory was not his aim; it was far more complex than that. "Fame is the result of good fortune, not of real merit", he told Edward, "and no man of sense or independence should make that the object of his ambition."[72] In time, having spent so much time in the east, St Maur was seduced by the eastern ways of thought, and began to write urging the contemplative life. Young Edward was scornful. He told his brother he "wrapped himself in cerulean clouds of aspirations, and thinks that 'wishing' is the highest action of the mind".[73] So the boys grew steadily apart, St Maur becoming a friendless searcher after "the truth", shunning society, mixing with difficulty, a trifle *farouche*, and frankly admitting that he avoided English people abroad; Edward more gregarious, congenial, friendly, showing great promise of a bright future on sensible lines. He had wit, tenderness, and a highly gifted mind. At the age of eighteen, he was attaché at the British Embassy in Vienna, and at nineteen in Madrid. He was in America during the Civil War, on which he wrote an article for *Blackwood's Magazine*.

St Maur, meanwhile, found his way to India and volunteered to fight there in the relief of Lucknow. Headstrong as ever, he had to be restrained from throwing his life away. He was mentioned in despatches for "a daring gallantry at a most critical moment", corroborated by eyewitnesses who said he was as brave as a lion. This did little to comfort his parents, wondering where he would appear next. Under the name of Richard Sarsfield, he then joined Garibaldi's English volunteers in Italy, causing intense vexation to his father, still First Lord of the Admiralty. The *Daily News* was the first to spill the beans, with an eulogistic account of St Maur's courage and zeal. St Maur hastily wrote assuring his parents he did not wish to cause embarrassment. "My reason for not telling yourself or my mother of my intentions in coming here has been misunderstood. To leave you in complete ignorance of my movements was necessary in order to render you entirely irresponsible for my conduct."[74]

Lord Edward's travels brought him to India (was he pursuing his brother?) and to the climax of this sad family rift. On 18th December 1865 Edward was attacked by a bear in the Indian jungle. The bear had been wounded by an unexploded shell, and was crazed with pain. It seized Edward by the knee, the two rolled over and over together, until Edward managed to stab it. He was dragged to a jungle hospital, where he immediately wrote: "My dear Father, I write to you that you may tell my mother without startling her, that I have been bitten by a wounded bear. I hope the consequences may not be serious, but things do not look altogether well." An hour later he underwent an operation. The surgeons said that the only chance of saving his life was to amputate above the knee. Just before, weakening, he dictated a letter to his brother: "I have just decided to let them amputate this afternoon . . . I shall return perforce to a purely literary life . . . Do marry, is the advice from your affectionate cripple."

The following day, Lord Edward died from the effects of amputation, in a state of delirium. He was twenty-four. The Duchess received a telegram at the Admiralty when the Duke had retired to bed. After waking and telling him, she wrote to St Maur. "Oh, Ferdy, don't *quit the country* or you'll kill me – I am keeping up for your sake . . . Your Father is terribly cast down and says he will never recover it, and I believe him poor man." The Duke's reaction to shock grew worse the next morning. The Duchess again wrote to her remaining son: "My only boy, my darling Ferdy, your Father is terribly depressed, all his plans, all his future utterly cast away . . . He seems doubtful of being able to keep with the Government, I should be sorry he had not some political duties to keep his mind occupied, as I think private life, when he is so depressed, will depress him still further . . . he walks up and down."

In fact the Duke never did recover. The tragedy squashed his personality, flattened his vigour. He retired from public life, never to return. The Seymour family might well have all joined him in despair had they known that this was only the beginning of their troubles.

Lord St Maur, now the Duke's only son, escaped to Tangier, where he could indulge his brooding views on men and the world without giving offence. He set about learning Russian and Turkish, to add to the French, Spanish and German which he already spoke with fluency. He was more and more withdrawn from the society of men. "I think it is a pity", wrote Sir John Hay to the Duchess, "that a clever, vigorous mind like his should be lost in this wilderness."[75] His health was not good, however, due probably to the variety of odd diseases to which he had been exposed for years in the Far East, and he was obliged to return to England, where on 30th September 1869, he died suddenly of heart disease, with his mother beside him, at the age of thirty-four.

The Duke of Somerset retreated into dumb grief. He had always been a gentle, pliant man, but now he was quite unable to resist the overwhelming distortion of character that wretchedness brings. For the rest of his life he was sullen and embittered. The dukedom would pass in turn to his two brothers and then to his nephew; this he could not prevent. But he made sure that precious little else went to them. His will was regarded as so infamous a document by the rest of the family that the memory of it is still fresh. To his daughter Hermoine (who married Sir Frederick Graham) he left the London house at 40 Park Lane with all contents; to his daughter Guendolen (who married Sir John Ramsden) he left Bulstrode Park, Bucks, with all contents; to his daughter Ulrica (who wed a Thynne) he left estates in Lincolnshire, Cambridge, and Norfolk, together with all books and linen to be found at the Duke of Somerset's ancestral home, Maiden Bradley. Estates in Wiltshire and Somerset he left to his sons-in-law. The clause of the will which caused most uproar was the bequest of all household linen, furniture, china, glass, household objects, prints, ornaments, books and manuscripts from Stover, the family home, on trust for two infants who were not even Symours. The names were Harold St Maur and Ruth St Maur, and they were to receive Stover and its contents, including the Hamilton treasures, when they grew up. Meanwhile, they were held in trust by the sons-in-law Lord Henry Thynne and Sir John Ramsden. The next Duke of Somerset received the title, the shell of property at Berry Pomeroy, the estate entailed with the title at Maiden Bradley, and its fixtures and fittings, and that was all. No wonder he appended his signature to that petulant document which hung on the wall while he was Duke. It reads:

"The will of the 12th Duke of Somerset is misleading, in some cases untruthful, in others it appears to be an attempt to conceal the truth. He did not leave the Berry Pomeroy and Maiden Bradley estates to the 13th Duke, he has scraped and plundered both estates for many years. He sold part of the Maiden Bradley property, and he left various charges amounting to £50,000 on the remainder. The house has since been rebuilt. He left it a filthy ruin. The law enabled him to put aside his father's will; he barred the entail and when his sons died he claimed everything. But the pictures given to his mother for the Seymour family by his grandfather the 9th Duke of Hamilton, if legally, could not morally, could not honourably, belong to him.

"The estates mentioned above have belonged to the Seymours some four hundred years. Besides the Hamilton there are other family pictures, presents from Kings and Princes, to the first wife of the 11th Duke [i.e. Charlotte Hamilton]. Where are these pictures now? Who retains them? Or who has made away with them? The Duchess his mother said they would remain for ever treasures in the Seymour family. To gratify the low-born greedy beggar woman he would marry in opposition to his father, the 12th Duke has seized and made away with the land, the pictures, the miniatures, the plate, the prints, the linen, and the books. He was unable to make away with the title and he has left his successors his Will; his Will remains, and must remain, a lasting monument of infamy."

Archibald Seymour, 13th Duke of Somerset

The Sheridan Duchess, however "greedy" a beggar woman, was likewise thwarted by her husband's will, which left everything at Stover to these mysterious unknowns, Harold and Ruth. She caused a fraudulent photograph to be taken, showing her and her three daughters supposedly looking at the Hamilton pictures (the four figures have quite clearly been superimposed on the orginal photograph), and saying:

I have worked hard for you, my dears, and I have succeeded. The Duke will seize, will claim everything, not a picture, not a print, not a book, not even a teaspoon will he leave to the Seymour family.

Who were Harold and Ruth St Maur, who together with the sons-in-law, received the greater part of the Somerset inheritance? There is no mention of them in any of the peerage reference books. Yet the entire family knew very well who they were. The proverbial skeleton rattled so loudly in the cupboard that his bones can be heard tinkling today.

Harold and Ruth were the illegitimate offspring of Lord St Maur, the 12th Duke's elder son and heir. St Maur was not one to toe the line where women and suitable marriages were concerned. He scorned such matters. But it was well known he had a roving eye. "You may rest assured I shall not marry and settle here", he had written to his sister from India. The truth was, he had already met and "married" in his own lights an illiterate girl from Gazely, Suffolk, called Rosa Elizabeth Swann. His Mohammedan beliefs would have scant regard for the Christian idea of marriage, so that there was probably no legal Christian ceremony. Rosa's father was a bricklayer, her mother the daughter of another bricklayer, and both had marked a cross for a signature on *their* marriage certificate. They were gypsies only so far as they moved wherever work was available. As for Rosa, sometimes called Rosina, very little is known, except that the Duke of Somerset's family kept her existence very dark. She was a pretty girl, even beautiful, with a continental sultriness quite unlike an English rose. St Maur dressed her up as a boy and took her to Italy with him when he fought for Garibaldi. Otherwise he kept her in Brighton. She bore him two children, Harold and Ruth, and after his death was set up secretly by the Somersets at a house at 74 Camberwell New Road, in South London. In the same house lived a French tutor, the son of a wine merchant, called François Tournier, who was in all probability provided by the Somersets as well. In due course Rosa and Tournier were married, on 14th September 1872.

What happened to the infant love children, Harold and Ruth? They stood ultimately to gain more by their grandfather's will than anyone, which made them suddenly objects of interest. One of their father's sisters, Ulrica, at first took them in. She, however, was now married to a Svengali of a man, Lord Henry Thynne, son of the Marquess of Bath, a powerful man with a strong will and a hypnotic ability to impose it. Little inoffensive Ulrica went in some fear of him. Thynne saw the advantages of keeping control over the heirs. He was thwarted for a while. The Duke and Duchess took the infants out of his care and insisted on looking after them themselves. The Duke had completely retired into a sombre country existence, brooding in his library, with thought only for the children of his beloved son. Thynne bided his time.

When the Duke died, the children were still minors, and by the terms of the will, still under the care of official guardians, one of whom was Henry Thynne. He promptly began to sell off the children's heritage.

In 1890 there was a sale of paintings and other objects from the Stover collection, including Rubens, Lawrences, and Reynolds. These were what the Duke regarded as his "private" collection, in so far as they were not for the most part Seymour possessions, but Hamilton possessions inherited from his mother. It was his desire to consider them personal property to do with as he liked which caused all the rumpus with successive dukes and occasioned that bitter accusation from his brother that he had "made away" with the heirlooms. Anyway, Thynne now decided to sell the greater part of them, and to sell part of the Stover estate at the same time. Nobody has ever been able to discover why. Or where the proceeds of the sale went.*

Harold St Maur came of age and began to wonder about his parents. Could they have been married? He spent much of his fortune and a good deal of time trying to track down a marriage certificate. Years passed without success, until one day a man turned up who said, yes, the Earl St Maur and Rosa Swann had been married, and he had moreover been a witness. Henry Thynne was alarmed. It would not serve his interest that Harold St Maur should be proved the rightful Duke of Somerset. The mysterious gentleman was hustled away, and later that year opened a shop in Torquay with money he did not have; it was all very suspect. Word got about that Thynne had seen to it the marriage certificate should be destroyed.

Many years later there was another tantalising clue. As he lay dying in Algeria, François Tournier sent word to Harold that he had something of huge importance to tell him before it was too late. Harold did not go. Tournier, as Rosa's husband, no doubt knew everything there was to know about her. She herself had died at the age of twenty-three of tuberculosis in a French sanatorium (paid for by the Somersets). She had been allowed to wave goodbye to her children, but not to touch them. She would surely have confided in him, and may even have explained the mystery of her first "marriage".

Harold St Maur lived handsomely at Stover while the then Duke and Duchess of Somerset scrambled around at Maiden Bradley for a knife and fork to eat with, sitting in a house stripped bare but for straw on the floor. Augustus Hare visited them there in 1897. "You know it is almost the only remnant the title possesses from the once vast Somerset estates. The 12th Duke left everything he possibly could away, and when the present Duke and Duchess succeeded, they

---

* Relations now think it more likely that Thynne was protecting Harold's interests. Harold squandered most of his money.

were pictureless, bookless, almost spoonless. Still they were determined
to make the best of it . . . 'Algie and Susie', as they always speak of
each other, have had a most delightful life, enjoying and giving
enjoyment. No one ever looked more ducal than this genial, hearty,
handsome Duke : no one brighter or pleasanter than his Duchess."[76]
    Harold St Maur, who wrote the family history, *Annals of the Seymours*,
tactfully avoiding all mention of his parents' drama, had three sons.
Stover was sold and is now a girls' school. Harold moved to Kenya and
died there. He has one surviving grandson, Edward St Maur, a photographer in Chepstow, Gwent, who is the last person able to bear that
surname; he has three daughters. Were circumstances slightly
different, as his grandfather was never declared illegitimate by the
lords, he could, in theory, apply for a writ of summons to Parliament
as Earl St Maur. But the implication would be that he was also
the rightful Duke of Somerset, which is a nest better left undisturbed.
As it is, he has the sword with which Lord Edward killed the bear,
and the Stover inventory. Ruth St Maur has a son and nephew
living in London.*
and in 1891 to Algernon, 14th Duke, both brothers of the 12th. He
then died in 1894 and was succeeded by his son, whom Hare called
"Algie"; there had been four Dukes of Somerset in nine years.
    When Algie, the 15th Duke, died in 1923, yet another crisis threat-
ened the family. All that was left of the legitimate family were his
three nieces, Helen, Lettys, and Lucy, known collectively as "Hell let
loose". There was no direct heir, and the mantle was assumed by a
distant relation, Brigadier-General Sir Edward Hamilton Seymour, K.B.E., who could claim descent from only two of the previous
fifteen Dukes of Somerset, the 8th and of course the 1st; but he was
the senior *heir male of the body* of the Lord Protector, even if it
required considerable genealogical dexterity to see how. At least that
was his firm belief, until the Marquess of Hertford, also a Seymour,
challenged his right to the dukedom and claimed it for himself. It
was 1750 all over again. The matter had to be referred to the House
of Lords, and it was not until two years later that a final decision
was made.
    Sir Edward Hamilton Seymour was the great-grandson of Colonel
Francis Compton Seymour, a son of the 8th Duke of Somerset. This
Francis Compton in 1787 made a most unusual marriage, choosing
as his bride the daughter of an East End publican. Her name was

---

* In 1887 Ruth married William Cavendish-Bentinck. Their son, born 1897, is the
present Duke of Portland, having inherited the dukedom from his brother in 1980. So
Ferdy St Maur is after all the ancestor of a duke, though of the wrong duke.

Leonora Perkins, widow of a sailor called John Hudson, and the marriage took place at St Michael's, Crooked Lane, Woolwich. Their son, born 21st September 1788, leads directly to the new Duke. Hertford's case was that this boy was a bastard, as Leonora's first marriage to John Hudson was still valid. Why? Because Hudson was not dead at all.

In 1786, a year before the marriage with Seymour, there was a John Hudson who died in Calcutta and was buried there. He and Leonora had lived together at 9 Paddington Street since 1780. Lord Hertford, whose agents had resorted to a minute examination of local rate-books and other municipal records in order to get him the dukedom, pointed out that there was a John Hudson on the rate-book in 1790, and a John Hudson who died in Middlesex Hospital in 1791. Surely, he said, this is the man; he had deserted, returned to England, found his wife Leonora living with another man at 9 Paddington Street (our Seymour), and moved out. His name subsequently appears on the rate-book as residing at 28 Marylebone High Street. As for the John Hudson buried in Calcutta, that must be another man. Someone called Francis Seamore [sic] does not appear on the rate-book for 9 Paddington Street until 1791, the same year that a John Hudson died in Middlesex Hospital.

It was a pretty strong case. Hertford was, of course, the next legitimate heir if the then Duke of Somerset's descent could be successfully impugned, and there was something attractive about the idea of the two titles of Somerset and Hertford being joined again as they were in the sixteenth century. The Duke's reply was that all Hertford's "evidence" rested on conjecture, petty scandal, and supposition; he further claimed that the public baptism of Seymour's children by Leonora was inconceivable if Hudson were still alive; they lived openly as man and wife.

Before the House of Lords could make their decision, two more would-be dukes entered the fray. A man called Henry Seymour, descended from Leonora's third son by Francis Compton Seymour, said that their marriage did not take place until after the first two sons were born. As there was not a shred of documentary evidence to support the claim, he withdrew pretty quickly. The other claimant was Harold St Maur, who may well have been justified, but who could produce no marriage certificate to back him up.

The Committee of Privileges met to declare on 25th March 1925. They said that Lord Hertford asked them to believe that Hudson would accept that his wife should live in *his* house with another man, and move to another house round the corner, while still meeting the bills. That would require, said their lordships, a degree of self-sacrifice beyond credence. It is more likely that he would have turfed them both on to the street. More precisely, they had examined the hospital register and found that the John Hudson who died there was forty-four, whereas Leonora's husband would by then have been fifty-three had he lived. They therefore found that Hudson was dead, the marriage valid, and Sir Edward Hamilton Seymour rightfully 16th Duke of Somerset.[77]

So life at Maiden Bradley resumed. The Duke's son followed an almost identical military career, won the D.S.O., and the O.B.E., was mentioned in despatches, and bore the sceptre at the coronation of George VI. It was the first time any Duke of Somerset had been involved in a public occasion for over half a century. Apart from this one show of publicity, and his sporadic duties at Lord Lieutenant of Wiltshire, he led a quiet life. He was the only duke to have been adept at tapestry, knitting and conjuring, in which he was so accomplished that he was for many years President of the Magic Circle.

He married Miss Edith Parker, and their first two sons died in infancy. The late duke was their third son. Percy Hamilton Seymour, 18th Duke of Somerset, born in 1910, was educated at Clare College, Cambridge, then went into the army where he rose to the rank of major. He married the daughter of another major, and they had three children, two boys and a girl. So quietly did they live at Maiden Bradley, the only constant heirloom in this troubled descent, that few people seemed to know there *was* a Duke of Somerset. He rarely took his seat in the House of Lords, didn't like politicians ("no military man likes politicians") and visited London only when he had to. Not much is left of the house at Maiden Bradley, following successive demolishings in the nineteenth century. What is left, however, makes a comfortable country house, with six bedrooms, a kitchen garden, and dogs eddying around wherever you step. It is much more easy to manage than a Chatsworth or a Woburn. From the illustrations past there is only a mirror belonging to Mary Queen of Scots, which the vandals must have missed when the 12th Duke died, and a dusty ceremonial coach, which was spruced up and used when his daughter married. The village around the house used to belong to them, but that went in 1953. The present Duke still has about 5000 acres, and some of Totnes in Devon, which he has to nibble at occasionally by selling a house or two when necessity demands.

The dangerous days when Lord Protector Somerset and the Duke of Norfolk were dire enemies is a dim and distant echo of little consequence now in this peaceful Wiltshire house. The Duke of Somerset has not even met the Duke of Norfolk.

John Seymour, 19th Duke of Somerset, was born in 1952 and succeeded to the dukedom in 1984. He is markedly more interested in his ancestry than was his late father, has a house in Fulham and took his seat in the Lords in 1985. He made his maiden speech in 1987, and welcomes any debate on agriculture or forestry, as he feels passionately about the disastrous destruction of the rain forests over the globe. As this is a subject which will dominate attention in the closing years of the twentieth century, and moreover is arguably more important to the future of mankind in peacetime than the nuclear bomb, it is encouraging to think that the House of Lords, that great *bouillabaisse* of surprisingly democratic opinion, may produce a spokesman on the subject.

The Duke of Somerset is the first of the Seymours for many generations to take an active interest in the ruined castle of Berry Pomeroy, near Totnes, the only surviving house of four built by Lord Protector Somerset after 1547. Described by its historian Harry Gordon Slade as "an impossibly large and hideously inconvenient house", it is probably no wonder that it was already neglected and well on the way to ruin by 1688. Nonetheless, it remains in the ownership of the Duke of Somerset, who was considerably pleased to have it recognised by the Department of the Environment, which administers it, as the most important monument in the West of England. Similarly, the Duke was present at the 450th anniversary of the Yeomen of the Guard in Armoury Hall, representing the blood and spirit of the man who founded them and gave them their uniform, the Lord Protector 1st Duke, his direct ancestor. There is every sign that the dukedom of Somerset may once more emerge, if not into the limelight, at least into acknowledged visibility.

The Duke has a job, representing Sotheby's in Wiltshire, as well as a wife, whom he married in 1978, before he came to the title. The Duchess of Somerset, *née* Judith-Rose Hull, is the daughter of the deputy chairman of Shroders, John Folliott Charles Hull. They have a son and heir, Lord Seymour, born in 1982. (As the eldest son of a duke, by the way, this little boy has precedence over all earls, viscounts and barons in the country).

REFERENCES

1. *Hist. MSS Comm.*, 12th Rep., App. ix, p. 47.
2. Melvyn Tucker, *Thomas Howard*, p. 39.
3. D.N.B.
4. Tucker, *op. cit.*, 40.
5. Collins *Peerage*, I, 63; Tucker, *op. cit.*, 47.
6. D.N.B.
7. Camden *Remains*, 1605, p. 217, quoted in Tucker, *op. cit.*, 46n.
8. J. H. Round, *Studies in the Peerage*, p. 109.
9. D.N.B.
10. *Complete Peerage*, IX, 617 (d).
11. *Letters and Papers Henry VIII*, Vol. XX, Part 1, p. 846.
12. *Complete Peerage*, ex: Nott, *Works of Henry Howard*, App. xxvii.
13. *Letters and Papers Henry VIII*, Vol. XIV, Part 1, p. 160.
14. D.N.B.
15. D.N.B.
16. Collins, I, 70.
17. *Lit. Rem. of Edward VI*, II, 390.
18. Elizabeth Jenkins, *Elizabeth the Great*, p. 141.
19. Neville Williams, *Thomas Howard Fourth Duke of Norfolk*, pp. 139, 145.
20. Williams, *op. cit.*, 193.
21. Jenkins, *op. cit.*, 182.
22. *Ibid.*, 200.
23. Williams, 242.
24. Collins, I, 115.
25. *Complete Peerage*, IX, 626 (c).
26. Reresby *Memoirs* (1735), p. 41.
27. See D.N.B.
28. Wraxall, *Historical Memoirs*, p. 576.
29. *Hist. MSS. Comm., Portland MSS*, III, 508.
30. *Hist. MSS. Comm.*, VII, 429.
31. Walpole, Yale edition, XVII, 338.
32. *Hist. M S. Comm., Carlisle MSS.* p. 916.
33. Walpole, XXIII, 194.
34. Wraxall, *Posthumous Memoirs*, I, 31.
35. W. M. Thackeray, *The Four Georges*, pp. 131–2.
36. *History Today*, May 1974.
37. Wraxall, *Posthumous Memoirs*, I, 35.

38. *Old and New London*, IV, 186.
39. *Journal* of Elizabeth, Lady Holland, II, 9–10.
40. Wraxall, *Hist. Mem.*, 35–6.
41. *A Duke of Norfolk Notebook*, p. 68.
42. *ibid.*, 38.
43. *ibid.*, 124.
44. Frances, Countess of Warwick, *Afterthoughts.*
45. Williams, *op. cit.*, 48.
46. *The Times*, 27th May 1929, 31st May 1929.
47. *The News Chronicle*, 23rd May 1953.
48. Creevy, *Papers*, II, 162.
49. *The News Chronicle*, 23rd May 1953.
50. Augustus Hare, *In My Solitary Life*, p. 35.
51. *Sunday Mirror*, 6th September 1970.
52. *The Observer*, 2nd February 1975.
53. D.N.B.
54. *Hist. MSS. Comm.*, 6th Report, p. 368.
55. Collins, I, 184.
56. Macaulay, *History of England*, II, 271.
57. D.N.B.
58. Walpole, XX, 18.
59. *ibid.*, XVIII, 522–3.
60. Cockburn *Memorials*, in *Journal* of Lady Elizabeth Holland, II, 22.
61. Creevey, *Papers*, II, 64.
62. *Complete Peerage*, XII, Part 1, p. 86 (g).
63. Moneypenny, *Life of Disraeli*, I, 231.
64. *Leaves from the Notebooks* of Lady Dorothy Nevill, p. 14.
65. *Lady Holland to Her Son*, p. 201.
66. *House of Lords, Accounts and Papers*, 1864, Vol. XXIII.
67. *Letters and Memoirs of 12th Duke of Somerset*, ed. Lady Guendolen Ramsden, p. 292.
68. *Letters of Lord St Maur and Lord Edward St Maur*, p. 36.
69. *Complete Peerage.*
70. *Letters of Lord St Maur etc.*, 26th August 1857.
71. *ibid.*, 12th October 1862.
72. *ibid.*, 14th August 1857.
73. *ibid.*, 31st October 1862.
74. *ibid.*, 11th November 1860.
75. *ibid.*, 30th November 1867.
76. Augustus Hare, *op. cit.*, p. 283.
77. *The Times*, 19th February, 26th March 1925.

2. Bright Sons of Sublime Prostitution

Duke of Buccleuch; Duke of Grafton; Duke of Richmond;
Duke of St Albans

"Bright sons of sublime prostitution,
 You are made of the mire of the street,
 Where your grandmothers walked in pollution
 Till a coronet shone at their feet ...
 Graces by grace of such mothers
 As brightened the bed of King Charles."

Swinburne, *A Word for the Country*

King Charles II was one of the most popular monarchs ever to sit
on the English throne. He was also quite blatantly and publicly one
of the most sensual. It is by no means certain how many mistresses
he had, but a quick count shows at least fifteen. By these various
women, the King produced an illegitimate offspring of some fourteen children, many of whom he elevated to the peerage. No
monarch created more dukedoms than Charles, and six of them were
conferred on his own bastard sons. Of these, no less than four still
exist.

The Duke of Buccleuch is descended from the hapless Duke of
Monmouth, Charles's son by Lucy Walter; the Duke of Grafton from
a son the King fathered with Barbara Villiers; the Duke of Richmond
was the son of the French mistress, Louise de Kérouaille; and the
Duke of St Albans was Nell Gwynn's son. Buckingham is reputed to
have said that the King was "father of his people", and to have then
added, *sotto voce*, "of a good many of them".

Charles was not alone in his licentiousness, though he set the
tone for the whole country. Freedom of sexual experience was the
order of the day. Relieved to be rid of the Civil War, and frankly
glad to be alive, the people congratulated themselves in an orgy of

self-indulgence. It was a bold, lusty, ribald, amusing, drink-sodden, smelly, dangerous time, when people lived life to the hilt, fought duels, took mistresses, and urinated in the gutter. Pepys admitted to having never taken a bath in his life, and he was not exceptional. Sanitation did not matter in the hedonistic, epicurean London of 1660.

It was against this background that the King was seen to be sporting with one woman after another. The people preferred the royal mistresses to be English and honest, rather than foreign and haughty, hence they took Nell Gwynn to their hearts while they treated Louise de Kérouaille with scorn. But they did not object to the principle of the King having mistresses, nor did they mind the swift succession of bastards whom he acknowledged as his own. Only a Puritan like the diarist John Evelyn professed to be shocked to witness the King sitting and "toying with his concubines", but what Evelyn did not notice and what made the people tolerate the King's amours was his kindness towards them, his constancy in affection.[1] Of the three women watched by Evelyn, one was a current mistress, and the other two had been rival mistresses twenty years before. But the King was loyal to them all. He visited them all regularly, long after the initial passions had worn off, gave them titles, money, houses, and doted upon his numerous illegitimate children. He was no selfish sensualist, but a man capable of enduring love as well as sudden passion. His reputed last words on his death-bed were "Don't let poor Nelly starve", a remark which speaks volumes for his sentimental nature. The people discerned these qualities, and forgave him. They also knew that he was deeply loyal to his wife, Queen Catherine of Braganza, who could give him no children. He would never allow her place to be usurped nor respect towards her to be withheld. He was a model husband as well as an ardent adulterer; such paradoxes were possible in the seventeenth century, while in a more hypocritical age they would be unimaginable. Parliament was not happy with the amounts of money lavished on the royal mistresses when the Exchequer was down to its last halfpenny, but that the King should have mistresses there was no question.

During his years of exile Charles gained his first experience in the pursuit of love. He was only eighteen when he met Lucy Walter, the mother of the 1st Duke of Buccleuch, but she was not by any means the first woman to share his bed. Charles was probably a father at the age of sixteen, when he was in Jersey, but no proof is readily available; certainly, he was no virgin when he met Lucy. Lucy, too, was an experienced girl, a Welsh beauty of about eighteen, whom

Evelyn described as "brown, beautiful, bold, but insipid".[2] The two adolescents spent the summer of 1648 together and were so obviously awash with passion that many supposed them to have been secretly married. Lucy once claimed to be Charles's wife, and he often addressed her as such. Gossip about Lucy's marriage to Charles crops up again and again throughout his reign, and persists to this day. If it were true, it would have huge repercussions for the monarchical succession in England, and for Lucy's descendant, the present Duke of Buccleuch. For it would mean that the Duke had a better right to sit on the throne than does Queen Elizabeth II.

On 9th April 1649, in Rotterdam, Lucy gave birth to a boy, whom they called James, after his great-grandfather, James I. Scurrilous gossips said that Lucy was so promiscuous, she could not have been sure that the boy was fathered by Charles, and that he bore a far closer resemblance to Robert Sidney, who had also bedded Lucy at about the same time; the child had the same mole on his upper lip that Sidney had, they said. The possibility that the Buccleuch line is founded in part not only on an illegitimate birth, but on the *wrong* illegitimate birth, is alluring, to say the least. However, it does not stand up to scrutiny. There is no real evidence that Lucy was all that promiscuous, and Sidney, who was ugly (not handsome, as traditional versions have it), had no mole. Charles himself was in no doubt. He acknowledged the boy as his natural son, and held for him a tremendous affection all his life.[3]

The little boy spent his infancy with his mother in Paris, then came to London in 1656, when mother and son were swiftly clapped in the Tower by Cromwell. Vainly did Lucy proclaim that her boy was the son of "King Charles". She was expelled from England, and died in Paris at the age of twenty-eight, probably from syphilis.[4] It was then that the boy was placed in the charge of Lord Crofts, and was henceforth known as "James Crofts".

When he came to England again in 1662, and was presented at Court, his father now restored as King Charles II, the thirteen-year-old "James Crofts" caused a sensation by his ravishing good looks. Grammont described him as a dazzling, astonishing beauty. All contemporary accounts agree. He had his mother's sensuous seductiveness and his father's sweetness of nature.[5] His popularity was further increased by the sterility of the King's marriage, beside which he presented a radiant contrast. Rumours again multiplied that the King would ultimately recognise him as his lawful son, and heir to the throne of England, as there seemed little chance of his producing an heir with his queen. The notorious Barbara Villiers, the King's new mistress (and mother of another of the dukes we shall deal with in this chapter), is even said to have slept with the boy. She was certainly a nymphomaniac, and the scandalous tale is not improbable.[6] At all events, it was decided that the boy should be betrothed and married as soon as possible, and a wife was found for him in the twelve-year-old heir to the mighty house of Buccleuch, Anna, Countess of Buccleuch in her own right. She was rich, she was noble, she was pretty, and she was sole heiress since the death of her father and sister. The Scotts of Buccleuch were an ancient and respected family of Scottish chieftains well established before this marriage was contemplated. But they had only an earldom; the dukedom of Buccleuch was created in celebration of the marriage.

Legally, it was doubtful whether Anna should have succeeded to the earldom, which had been created in 1619 with remainder to heirs male; it ought to have become extinct with the death of the 2nd Earl, Anna's father, and she would have been simply Lady Anna Scott. But everyone has assumed that the succession must have been amended by patent or charter at a later date to allow remainder to heirs general. No such patent has ever been found; there is no record or trace of it.[7]

However, the little girl in question was accepted and known, whether rightly or wrongly, as the Countess of Buccleuch. Any son by James Crofts would eventually succeed as Earl of Buccleuch. But the King was not satisfied. Intoxicated with the success, beauty, the very existence of his son, he determined that he should bring Anna new titles, in return for all the estate which she was bringing to the marriage. She had vast estates in seven counties, plus four domaines and an income of £10,000 a year. Accordingly, the boy assumed the surname "Scott" in anticipation of his entering that family and continuing it (the Scotts of Buccleuch would otherwise have come to an end with the death of Anna in 1731). He was made a Knight of the Garter. Then, on 14th February 1663, he was created Baron Scott of Tyndale, Earl of Doncaster, and Duke of Monmouth, with precedence over all other dukes not of royal blood. Henceforth, he was to be fourth man in the realm, after the King, the Duke of York, and Prince Rupert. A few weeks later, on 20th April he was married to the little Countess of Buccleuch, and the same day they were created Duke and Duchess of Buccleuch, and Earl and Countess of Dalkeith. It is as the Duke of Monmouth that he is generally known to history. The King wrote to his sister: "This is Jameses marriage day, and I am goeing to sup with them, where we intend to dance and see them a bed together, but the ceremony shall stop there, for they are both too young to lye all night together."[8]

The King described his son in the marriage contract as *"Filio nostro naturali et illegitimo"*.[9] Honours were heaped upon him in dizzy sequence. It was a happy time. Pepys noted that the King continued to dote upon his son.

All this over-indulgence and flattery in childhood bore ill fruit as the young Duke of Monmouth grew up. In 1666, when he was seventeen, Pepys wrote that he was vicious and idle and would never be fit for anything. As his personality developed, he was seen to be a weak character, feeble in moral principle, easily swayed, of little intelligence, dilatory, volatile, a procrastinator. With his inability to make a decision and adhere to it, he was to be an easy tool in the hands of unscrupulous politicians. His chief recommendation continued to be grace and personal beauty. But being the acknowledged favourite son of the King (who by this time had other progeny by successive mistresses) he thought he could commit any act with impunity. He cannot escape responsibility for the sorry tale of Sir John Coventry, who was disfigured for life on Monmouth's orders. Sir John had made a slighting reference in the House of Commons to the King's consorting with actresses. Monmouth's response was vengeful in the extreme; he set a gang of thugs upon Sir John, who attacked him in the street, pinning him against the wall, and cut off his nose to the bone. Even allowing for nose-slitting as a fairly common method of revenge in those brutal times, this was not the action of a man of responsibility. He was only twenty-one at the time, and his reputation suffered.

The remainder of Monmouth's life belongs to the history of England, and there is no room here to rehearse all the vicissitudes of that sad story. Briefly, the impressionable and malleable Monmouth fell victim to the Machiavellian plans of Lord Shaftesbury and his faction, who sought to establish the bastard on the throne and rule England through him. Charles was bitterly disappointed in him, loving him as he did above all his other children, and the history of their relationship shows the conflict between political wisdom and filial love which beset the astute King. Time and again, Monmouth was banished and disgraced, then favoured with the King's goodwill when he showed remorse or contrition. Charles knew what a weak man his son had become and was always ready to forgive his shortcomings. But his patience was tried too often. Involved in the plot to assassinate his father, the "Rye House Plot", Monmouth confessed, was forgiven, and the following day retracted his confession and asked for his letter back. The King told him to go to hell. Monmouth said he was afraid that his confession would implicate others, but his changes of mind were always prompted by simple indecision rather than nobleness of motive.

Monmouth could be seriously entertained as a possible King of England only as long as rumours supporting his legitimacy persisted. It was such a romantic notion, and Monmouth such a handsome, dashing man, that the people *wanted* to believe that Charles II had married Lucy Walter. So strong was the belief that the King had twice to swear solemnly before the Privy Council that he had never married any woman but the Queen. Still the rumours were rife, and just as they encouraged Monmouth to believe that he was the rightful heir, so his supporters increased, and the rumours multiplied proportionately. They gave rise to Monmouth's disloyalty, and were in turn fostered by it. There was even a story that the marriage contract or proof of its existence, lay in a black box in the safe keeping of the Bishop of Durham, who passed it on to his son-in-law Sir Gilbert Gerard. But Gerard, summoned before the Privy Council, denied all knowledge of it, and to this day no proof has been produced that the black box or its contents ever existed.[10] Nevertheless, the legend will not die; subsequent events have given it a more intriguing weight. In the first place, the relevant page in the marriage register at the Church where the King is supposed to have married Lucy Walter was found, years later, to have been torn out. Secondly, there is a story that when the 5th Duke of Buccleuch, a direct descendant of Monmouth, was looking through old papers at Dalkeith House in the time of Queen Victoria, he came across the black box and the marriage certificate. He summoned his son and heir to his presence, and said, "I am now going to do something which should have been done a long time ago. The publication of this document in my right hand might have severe repercussions. It is something no loyal subject should possess." He then threw it into the fire.[11]

Charles II, whatever his faults, was a man of principle and truth. He was deeply loyal to the institution of monarchy, and would envisage nothing which might weaken it or place the lawful right of succession into disrepute. The heir to the throne was the Duke of York, his brother (later James II), who was politically and personally unpopular. He was, however, the heir and Charles would not compromise with his right to inherit the throne. Steadfastly, he refused to consider for a moment the legitimising of his son the Duke of Monmouth, to whom, in spite of everything, he remained devoted as only a loving father can be. When the King died, Monmouth was abroad, hatching plots. They both had cause to regret the gulf that had been erected between them by the easy ambitions of a spoilt child.

With the accession of James II, Monmouth and his followers (the compliant Duke doing most of the following) prepared to invade. On 20th June 1685 he was proclaimed King of England at Taunton, with the designation "King Monmouth" to avoid confusion with the James already on the throne, who was at the same time declared a traitor, and his parliament at Westminster a traitorous convention. Meanwhile, there was naturally a price on Monmouth's head, and he had been stripped of all his English dignities and titles. His rebellion was as feeble and irresolute as his character. His troops were routed at a battle on 5th July, and he himself fled. Disguised as a farmer, with two of his henchmen, he wandered the countryside for three days until he was discovered by a search party, hiding in a ditch. The "cowardly and self-seeking traitor"[12] was taken directly to the Tower.

With characteristic remorse, the Duke declared that it was never his idea to be proclaimed King. He signed a document which was meant to settle once and for all the question of his birth, but he may have been coerced, and we know that he was an easy prey to persuasion. He wrote :

"I declare yt ye Title of King was forct upon mee, & yt it was very much contrary to my opinion when I was proclaimed. For ye Satis-faction of the world, I doe declare that ye late King told me that hee was never married to my Mother."

No doubt with this act of contrition Monmouth saved his sons from the vengeance of the King and thus protected the line of the Dukes of Buccleuch from extinction. But the wording of the declaration is curious; he does not disavow his own belief in his legitimacy, by pointing out that his father had assured him of the contrary. To a certain extent, the question was left open.[13]

Hours after signing this document, Monmouth was dead. His end was harrowing. Pressed by the bishops to repent publicly of his rebellion, he would not employ the word, implying tacitly that it could not legally be considered "rebellion", but stated that he was sorry to have invaded the kingdom, and sorry to have caused blood-shed. In spite of their pestering, he would give no more. "I will make no speeches," he said, "I come to die . . . I shall die like a lamb."

No one can deny his courage. He refused to be blindfolded or tied, but of his own will placed his head on the block. He turned and asked to see the axe, then ran his thumb along the edge. "It is not sharp enough," he said, but the executioner reassured him, and he placed his head ready.

The first stroke of the axe did not sever his head. Monmouth turned and looked at his executioner, but said nothing. The second stroke wounded again, but the unfortunate man was still alive. He crossed his legs. At the third stroke, the deed was still not done, and the axeman lost his nerve and threw down the axe. The crowd was furious, and would have torn him to pieces had they been able to reach him. Finally, Monmouth's head was cut off with a knife.[14]

*   *   *

We must now travel back a few years from 1685, when Monmouth died, to 1663, when the next duke who concerns us, Grafton, was born. The ancestress of the Grafton line was the infamous seductress Barbara Villiers, later Countess of Castlemaine, still later Duchess of Cleveland, "the finest Woman of her age".[15] Charles II was already the father of three other illegitimate children besides James Crofts before he encountered Barbara Villiers, but none of his previous mistresses exerted such influence over him as she was destined to. She came from a single-minded ambitious family of courtiers with the determination to see their ambitions realised. They were expert flatterers, endowed with a beauty of body which they did not hesitate to use in the pursuit of their aims. The proof of their success lies in the enormous number of prominent and resourceful people who were or are descended from them. Barbara's cousin was George Villiers, 2nd Duke of Buckingham, a favourite with the King; his father, the 1st Duke, was lover and master of James I. The Dukes of Marlborough and Sir Winston Churchill are descended from Sir George Villiers (Barbara's great-grandfather) through his daughter Elizabeth Villiers. The Dukes of Atholl and Hamilton are descended from another daughter, Susan Villiers. There is Villiers blood in the Cecil family (Marquis of Salisbury), and in Lord John Russell and his grandson Bertrand Russell. Even our present Queen Elizabeth II is descended from Sir George Villiers through his son Edward. As for Barbara Villiers herself, she bore the King six children (at least he acknowledged six of them, though the paternity of some is open to doubt), and made herself the ancestress of not only the Duke of Grafton, but of Lord Castlereagh, Lord Melbourne, and Sir Anthony Eden (Lord Avon). No less than thirteen Prime Ministers trace their ancestry back to the seventeenth-century Villiers family. With such dynamic genes coursing through her veins, Barbara Villiers fell upon the sweet good-natured King as a praying mantis pounces on and gobbles up its victim.[16]

Even at the tender age of fifteen, Barbara had learnt to use her body to seduce and obtain what she wanted. With rich auburn hair and blue eyes and a flirtatious manner, she was not easily resistible; neither the King nor her countless other lovers, both before and after, can be blamed for succumbing to such obvious charms. In 1659, aged eighteen, she married an obscure person called Roger Palmer, who is only remembered for having been her husband. He was one of nature's cuckolds. Palmer was the father of not one of his wife's numerous offspring.

In the spring of 1660 the King met Mrs Palmer and took a fancy to her. It took no time at all for them to become lovers. Samuel Pepys was audibly moved by the sight of her. "I sat before Mrs Palmer, the King's mistress, and filled my eyes with her, which much pleased me."[17] In February of the following year, a daughter was born to her; Palmer said he was the father, everybody else said Lord Chesterfield was, but in time the King claimed that *he* was, and Palmer dutifully climbed down. Barbara then began to ask for, and get, the benefits of her royal liaison. Her quiet and obedient husband was made Earl of Castlemaine, so that she could proudly bear a title, and special arrangements were made in the patent of creation so that the title should pass to *her* male heirs, not his; this was tantamount to an explicit avowal that the affair was well and truly launched, and that Barbara intended to bear other royal children.

Two years later, Catherine of Braganza arrived in England to become Queen. Such an inconvenience was not allowed to interrupt the King's uproarious love affair with Barbara. He stayed with his mistress one whole week, every night and day, notes Pepys,[18] and went so far as to spend his intended bride's first night in England with the infamous Lady Castlemaine. Everybody knew, no attempt was made to conceal either the affair or the insult to the innocent Catherine, and Barbara was henceforth the object of public scorn and reproach.

Barbara was again pregnant, and she brazenly proposed that she should spend her confinement at Hampton Court, while the King and Queen were spending their honeymoon there. The King managed to resist this indelicate suggestion, but resistance to the lady's demands was becoming daily more difficult. She had a furious temper, could shout and scream, thump and rant, and burst into tears at will. If there was one thing the King could not abide, it was to see a woman crying; he would grant almost any favour to ease her distress, hardly stopping to reflect how simply a determined woman could (and can) manufacture a tearful crisis. So Barbara nearly always got her way.

Her second child and first son was born in June 1662. Poor Charles was torn again between his natural good manners towards his bride and the powerful spell this pretty hot-tempered passionate woman cast upon him. She begged him to make her a Lady of the Queen's Bedchamber, unaware of or unconcerned by the inappropriateness of such a suggestion. Charles agreed. When the Queen saw her name upon the list she struck it off in hurtful anger; she knew enough by now to realise that Barbara was her rival and that Barbara was winning. The Queen hardly spoke a word of English and did not understand the curious way in which this libertine Court operated. She had to capitulate. Charles insisted on keeping his word to Barbara, and the mistress was duly appointed to serve the wife.

Once Catherine had surrendered, she burdened Barbara with marks of affection and esteem. Her change of attitude is easy to comprehend when one remembers that she was deeply in love with her husband and wanted above all things to please him. If treating his loathsome and selfish mistress with respect would please him, then that is what she would do. Charles, who hated difficulties, squabbles, and tears, was delighted. He wanted everyone to be happy together without creating problems. At Somerset House in September, only a few weeks after the royal wedding, the King attended a party with his wife Queen Catherine, his mistress Lady Castlemaine, and his bastard son James Crofts by a previous mistress Lucy Walter, all in the same carriage. Charles was content.[19]

It was about this time that the unscrupulous and over-sexed Barbara reputedly made a play for the beautiful thirteen-year-old Mr Crofts, who was a kind of unofficial stepson to her. Pepys observed that she was "always" hanging on him. Sensing danger, the King married him off and created him Duke of Monmouth and Duke of Buccleuch only a few months later, in order, it was said, to rescue him from Barbara's attentions.[20] The boy had been flattered, and was too much in her company.

Barbara's reputation suffered more when it was noticed that in addition to her other sins, she was a cruel and heartless mother. She treated the new baby with such contemptuous irritation that the poor boy was permanently damaged, and grew up mentally deranged.[21]

Her temper grew more and more fierce. She was frequently heard shouting at the King. She called him a fool in public. Pepys was present on one occasion among many. He wrote in his diary:

"how imperious this woman is, and hectors the King to whatever she will. It seems she is with child, and the Kings says he did not get it; with that she made a slighting 'puh' with her mouth, and went out of the house."[22]

Since she was openly having an affair with Henry Jermyn, and sleeping with him more often than with the King, the latter's suspicions can hardly be said to be unjustified. Her second son, Henry, was born on 20th September 1663; this is the boy later to be created Duke of Grafton, whose descendant is the 11th and present Duke. The King refused to acknowledge the infant as his own. She badgered, screamed, fought with extreme violence, until in the end he relented. "God damn me, but you shall own it!" she shouted. But the circumstances of the infant Duke's birth remain questionable. Again in 1667, another quarrel erupted over the birth of her third son. She threatened that unless the King acknowledged the new child, she would take it to Whitehall and dash out its brains.[23] Pepys says, "She did threaten to bring all his bastards to his closet-door, and hath nearly hectored him out of his wits."[24]

Meanwhile, Lord Castlemaine (Mr Palmer that was) found himself paterfamilias of an ever-increasing brood with whose birth he had nothing whatever to do. The French Ambassador wrote of the Earl's worried look at finding two unexpected additions to his family.

When Barbara was converted to Roman Catholicism, Stillingfleet remarked, "If the Church of Rome has got no more by her than the Church of England has lost, the matter will not be much."[25] The diarist John Evelyn was yet more laconic. She was "the curse of our nation".[26]

At this distance, it is difficult to see what her attraction was, unless it be the wild, impassioned, impulsive and unpredictable nature which some men find compelling. There was also, of course, her sexual athleticism; Charles is reported to have said that she knew more positions than Aretino.[27] Charles was beginning to tire of her; he was weary of the constant scenes and quarrels, which were not at all to his taste. He was loyal to the extent that he would still see her regularly, dine with her, receive her at Court, but her influence and magic faded. It was easier now to give in to her material demands, causing only financial problems, which were nothing compared to the emotional problems her earlier antics created. Besides, they kept her quiet. She was given a residence in London, furnished at vast expense to suit her lavish taste; she was given an annual grant of £4700 from the Post Office, a lump sum in ready cash of £30,000, jewels and priceless plate from the royal collection, and the beautiful palace of Nonesuch near Epsom. This palace, standing in its own handsome park, was built by Henry VIII and was a favourite house of his daughter, Elizabeth I. Barbara received it as a gift, and characteristically, she plundered it, sold its contents, and gambled away the proceeds. She allowed the house to fall into such decay that it completely disappeared, and its foundations were only recently discovered by archaeologists. Although Barbara received thousands and thousands of pounds for her charms, she never kept a penny. She was seen one day wearing £40,000 worth of jewellery; on another, she lost nearly £20,000 at gambling. She insisted that her station required a coach drawn by eight horses, which Londoners rushed in crowds to see pass in the street, and she even took money from the royal purse to support her successive lovers.

In 1670 she was created Duchess of Cleveland. The normally sedate *Complete Peerage* is aroused to a passionate footnote by this title which was, it says, "conferred as actual wages of her prostitution and one which had stunk in the nostrils of the nation during the forty years she enjoyed it; one, too, which had not been redeemed from the slur thus attached to it by any merit of her successors, of whom the one was a fool and the other a nonentity".[28]

By the time Barbara was made Duchess, the King had already diverted his favours to other mistresses, especially the actresses Moll Davis and Nell Gwynn. Money and honours were lavished on Barbara to compensate for her demotion from the royal bed. Her subsequent history is no less rapacious. She had about ten other lovers, including the playwright Wycherley, John Churchill (later Duke of Marlborough), Ralph Montagu (later Duke of Montagu), and a fashionable rope-dancer called Jacob Hall. The King on his death-bed asked his brother to be kind to her. In old age she was trapped into a second marriage for which only lust can have been the motive. She chose her male counterpart, the notorious rake "Beau" Feilding, who "had only to give the lady a sight of his handsome person he designed to lay at her feet".[29] Alas, Feilding had married another lady, Mary Wadsworth, only *two weeks* before the marriage with Barbara, and had ditched her when he discovered she had no fortune. He was tried for bigamy in 1706, when the Old Bailey heard such evidence of lechery as it seldom suspects. Letters written by the Duchess are now in the British Museum, and are said to be among the most indecent which that mausoleum of dusty pornography possesses.[30] She moved to a house in Chiswick Mall (now called Walpole House) where she died of dropsy in 1709.

Her second son, Henry, is the one who concerns us. Just as Monmouth, the King's son by Lucy Walter, had been married off at a tender age to the rich heiress of the Buccleuchs, so this infant was wedded, at the age of nine, to Isabella, five-year-old daughter and heiress of the Earl of Arlington, and owner of Euston Hall, a splendid estate near Thetford in Norfolk. Through her, the boy would have estate and income; for her part, she would gain title and status : it was precisely the same arrangement for the same reasons that the Monmouth/Buccleuch marriage took place. According to the marriage laws prevailing, the marriage was void if either party be under the age of seven years, but perfectly valid if they be aged between seven years and fourteen years, with this condition : at fourteen in the boy's case, or at twelve in the girl's, either of them might withdraw their consent and the marriage was automatically voided. But if they both agreed to continue, the original ceremony was still valid.[31] It is as well to bear these laws in mind when we read of so many infant weddings; it explains why a good number of children elect to remarry when they are older and understand what they are doing. In Restoration England, fourteen for a boy and twelve for a girl was quite old enough in a matter such as this.

So, the son of Barbara Villiers, Duchess of Cleveland, was married in August 1672; two weeks later he was created Earl of Euston, the title taken from the country seat of his wife's family, where his descendants still live and still bear this title. In 1675 he was created Duke of Grafton, at the age of twelve. In 1679 the children went through a second marriage ceremony. He was now sixteen, and she was twelve, the minimum legal age to marry with consent.

The subsequent career of the 1st Duke of Grafton was short, but laudable. Evelyn wrote that he was "exceedingly handsome, by far surpassing any of the King's other natural issue", but he had reservations about his manners, and thought he had been "rudely bred". "Were he polished . . . he would be a tolerable person."[32] He was the opposite of a dandy. He loved the sea, and rose to be vice-admiral of England. He was also, not surprisingly considering his parentage, short-tempered and impulsive. He fought a duel with the brother of the Earl of Shrewsbury, for which he was pronounced guilty of manslaughter. But when he died at the siege of Cork, aged only twenty-seven, he was much lamented as a fine soldier and a rugged, honest man.

*　　　　*　　　　*

The Duke of Grafton was only five years old (and not yet ennobled) when the King began to taste the earthy charms of his most famous mistress, Nell Gwynn. She is one of the most enduring popular heroines of England, her irrepressible spirit, impudence, good humour, and Cockney frankness as alive in folklore now as they were in 1668. She is also the ancestress of the Duke of St Albans.

Nell was born probably in London (some say Hereford); she was a Cockney, working-class character, bold, uninhibited, friendly, and amusing. She was completely illiterate; the most she could bring herself to write was E.G. (for "Eleanor Gwynn") at the foot of a letter written for her by someone else. It is perfectly true that her career began at the Theatre Royal, Drury Lane, selling oranges. In the popular mind this is assigned to tradition but it is fact.

By virtue of an affair with one of the actors, she progressed from the pit to the stage, where she eventually became one of the most celebrated actresses of her day. Our knowledge of her career we owe largely to Samuel Pepys, who found her delightful and called her "pretty witty Nell". She was apparently an excellent comedienne, but embarrassingly bad when she tried heavy drama. It was at this point in her life, sometime in 1668, that the King "asked for" her; in other words, he knew her as an actress, not as an orange-girl. More accurately still, he knew her as a whore; all the theatres were as Burnet says, "nests of prostitution". Nell never made any attempt to disguise this bald truth, and the people loved her for it. She was rough, candid, honest. She could so easily have had her head turned by the royal favour. She could have assumed airs and graces, tried to make herself a "lady" with fine clothes. She could have softened her Cockney accent, pruned her rough speech of its worst swear-words, tried to compete with the ladies at Court. Charles would have grown bored. He could have any number of grand ladies; what he wanted was a change. And Nell's vitality, wit, honesty, her lack of pretence were intoxicating to him. Nell forever remained the rough diamond that she was, teasing the King, amusing him, shocking the other ladies with their noses in the air, irresistibly impertinent and iconoclastic. Evelyn spoke for the Court when he called her "an impudent comedian". It was a happy love affair, which gave the King years of pleasure and relaxed enjoyment. It could not have been more pointedly contrasted with the tempestuous affair with Barbara.

It should never be forgotten that Charles II had spent years in exile, away from the glitter of the Court and the forced chatter of aristocracy. He already knew the people, and recognised in Nell the qualities which he had previously valued. He was the most approachable King England has ever had. He liked to walk in the park for hours every day, feeding the ducks, talking with anyone who was about, strolling and telling stories. There was nothing pompous or remote about him. Nelly responded to that cheeky side of his nature which was amused to see the haughty and pretentious discomfited. He was at heart always a rascal, and Nell became his playmate.

Nell cost much less than Barbara, too. Of course, she had an allowance, it was part of the bargain that she should be paid, and Charles was not the kind of man to refuse. But she did not pester for vast sums merely to satisfy her vanity. She never forgot that she was a woman of the people, who had learnt in a harsh school the lessons of survival, and was used to being satisfied with life. The King gave her a residence and an income, and she did not ask for more.

Above all, her uninhibited teasing of the King was to the merry monarch a constant joy. She would give boisterous parties at her house at 79 Pall Mall, where the King and the Duke of York mixed with friends from the theatre and prostitutes from Drury Lane. They would all get drunk, and singing would go on well into the night. Once, Nell asked a singer called Bowman and his crew to entertain the royal guests. When they had finished, the King said how much he had enjoyed it. "Then, Sir," said Nell, "to show that you do not speak like a courtier, I hope you will make the performers a handsome present." The King rummaged in his pocket but had no money with him. The Duke of York did not have enough either. Nell turned to her friends and, feigning surprise, she said, "Odd's fish, what company am I got into."[33]

She was wonderfully indiscreet, and total without respect for her successor Louise de Kérouaille, who did assume the dignities she thought were due to a royal mistress. When once she was mobbed at Oxford, the crowd believing that her carriage contained Louise (whom they loathed and distrusted), Nell put her head out and said, "Pray, good people, be civil; I am the *Protestant* whore."

For the first two years of her royal liaison, Nelly had no serious rival. In 1670 she bore the King a son, Charles, who would one day found the line of the dukes of St Albans. By a dramatic coincidence, as we shall see, on the very night that Nelly was in labour, the King was on his way to Dover to meet his beloved sister Henrietta ("Minette") who was sailing from France. One of her entourage was a pretty baby-faced beauty called Louise de Kérouaille. Charles was captivated by his new mistress as his son by Nelly was being born.

The rivalry between the pretentious French intruder and the

down-to-earth Cockney actress entertained London for years. Nelly was a merciless tease, and would not allow the newcomer to get away with any *folies de grandeur*. Louise simply could not understand why the King should want to spend any time at all with such a low person as Nell; she stifled with rage to find herself competing with a common whore, a "noisy ill-mannered creature from the London slums",[34] whom she would rather not be obliged to look at. She was haughty, disdainful. The London people were naturally whole-heartedly on Nelly's side. They thought Louise was a French spy (and in that they were not far wrong); they distrusted her; they could not pronounce her name, so she became known as "Mrs Carwell", which further infuriated her.

When the Chevalier de Rohan was executed in France, Louise appeared at Court in deepest black, to signify that she was in mourning for a dear and close relation. The next day, Nelly turned up in black also. Louise asked her why, and Nell said she was in mourning for the Cham of Tartary, who was just about as closely related to her as was the Chevalier de Rohan to Louise. Louise swept off in a sulk, while Nell and the King laughed.[35] Madame de Sévigné reported a statement of Nell's in one of her famous letters. "This Duchess," said Nell (Louise was by now Duchess of Portsmouth), "acts the fine lady; she says she is related to everyone in France; as soon as any great nobleman dies she goes into deep mourning. Right, if she is of such nobility, why is she a whore? She ought to die of shame. As for me, it's my trade, I don't set myself up as anything better."[36]

In the same letter, Madame de Sévigné gives us this vivid portrait of Louise's mortifications at the hands of Nell. "But she did not foresee that a young actress was to cross her path, and to bewitch the King. She is powerless to detach him from this actress. He divides his money, his time, and his health between the pair. The actress is as proud as the Duchess of Portsmouth, whom she jeers at, mimics, and makes fun of. She braves her to her face, and often takes the King away from her, and boasts that she is the better-loved of the two. She is young, wild, bold, lewd, and ready-witted. She sings and dances and frankly makes love her business." [37]

By 1673, the new French mistress had been created Duchess of Portsmouth. The King's second son by Barbara Villiers had been given the titles Duke of Grafton and Earl of Euston, and was safely married, though still a child, to a rich heiress. Barbara herself had become Duchess of Cleveland, and another of her sons had been created Duke of Southampton. Meanwhile, the faithful and amusing

Nell was still plain Nell Gwynn, and her sons (there were now two) still nameless. They remained so for another three years.

There are two stories which tell how Nell's eldest son eventually received his title; one is traditional, but unverifiable, the other more likely. According to the first, Nell grew so impatient with the King that she grabbed hold of his six-year-old son, held him out of the window, and threatened to drop him if the King would not give him a name. "Stop, Nelly," shouted the King. "God save the Earl of Burford." The second story originates with the historian Granger and is more credible. Nelly said to her son, "Come here, you little bastard, and say hello to your father." The King remonstrated with her: "Don't call him that, Nelly," to which she replied, "Your Majesty has given me no other name to call him by."[38] So the child was created Earl of Burford and Baron Heddington on 27th December 1676. In 1683, when he was not yet thirteen, he was created Duke of St Albans, and the following year, Hereditary Grand Falconer of England. This office, which entails looking after the King's hawks, still belongs by right to the Duke of St Albans.

Nell herself received no title. There was a rumour that she was to be created Countess of Greenwich in 1685, but the King died before he could put his intention into effect. It is just as well that he did not. A title would not have suited her – perhaps she would not have accepted it – and would have offended the aristocracy. She may have made the King happy, but she was still an illiterate girl from the slums, and it would not have been considered fitting that she should be elevated to the peerage.

A far more appropriate memorial to her is the erection of Chelsea Royal Hospital, which tradition asserts was Nell's idea.[39] There is no proof that she had anything to do with it, but the tradition is too solid to collapse beneath the scepticism of historians. She was known to be kindly, warm-hearted, charitable and benevolent. The most one can say is that it would have been entirely characteristic of her to be involved in such a scheme. It accords with the temper and tone of her will, to which there was a codicil asking her son to "lay out twenty pounds yearly for the releasing of poor debtors out of prison every Christmas day" (a request which, like the others, he honoured).[40] Her own father had died in a debtors' gaol in Oxford.

Another instance of Nell's generosity and kindness is witnessed by a letter, one of the few we have, and written in another hand of course, which bears the date 14th April 1684.[41] It is addressed to Mrs Jennings (probably the mother of Frances and Sarah Jennings, who later became Duchesses of Tyrconnel and Marlborough),[42] and one sentence says, "Good madam, speak to Mr Beaver to come down too, that I may bespeak a ring for the Duke of Grafton, before he goes into France." The Duke of Grafton was now twenty-one years old, but the important point is that he was the son of Charles II by a former mistress, Barbara Villiers, and that Nell Gwynn wanted to give him a going-away present.

The King had granted Nell a house called Bestwood Park, which stayed in the family of St Albans until 1940. When she died in 1687 she left her estate to "my dear natural son, His Grace the Duke of St Albans", with specific codicils benefiting her servants, her nurses, and has already been noted, the poor.

The most telling indication of the goodness and character of Nell Gwynn is that no writer seems to have been able to bring himself to refer to her as anything but "Nell" or "Nelly". She is not called Miss or Mrs Gwynn or Eleanor Gwynn; to do so would be to distort her personality. It is nearly 300 years since she died, but the warmth and affection which this disarming jovial prostitute inspired is strong yet.

Besides the Duke of St Albans, some hundreds of people alive now can trace their ancestry back to Nell, through the 1st Duke. In 1901 there were 311 descendants, and there must now be considerably more. Sixty-seven of them were titled 'Honourable'; they included Beauclerks, Loders, Cavendishes, Capells, the Earl of Essex, the Countess of Warwick, the Duchess of Sutherland, the Countess of Westmorland, and so on. One woman, Ivy Gordon-Lennox, who in 1915 became the Duchess of Portland, was descended three times from Charles II, once through Nell Gwynn, once through Barbara Villiers, and once through Louise de Kérouaille.[43] The present Duke of Buccleuch also traces his ancestry to Nell through the 10th Duke of St Albans.

As for her son, the 1st Duke, who had counted among his tutors Thomas Otway, the author of Venice Preserved and The Soldier's Fortune, he developed into a fine and popular young man and a gallant soldier. He was a favourite with the Dowager Queen Catherine, Charles's widow, who gave him an allowance of £2000 a year. When he was still a boy he was betrothed to Lady Diana Vere, the daughter and sole heiress of the 20th and last Earl of Oxford. She was the last of the Veres, a family founded in England by Aubrey de Vere, who had come over with the Conqueror in 1066 and been ennobled as Earl of Oxford. He lived in a manor house marked by the area of London now called "Earl's Court", where he grew vines. His family is also recalled in De Vere Gardens, Kensington, and naturally in the surname of his descendant the Duke of St Albans, which is de Vere Beauclerk.

King Charles clearly made a habit of choosing wealthy females from grand families where there was no male heir to carry on the name, rescued that name from oblivion, and took in return the estate for one of his bastard sons. He went seriously wrong in St Albans' case. The de Veres were penniless, their fortune squandered; Diana brought practically nothing with her into the marriage. Perhaps it was Nell's easygoing nature which prevented her insisting that her boy should be provided with a rich bride. Anyway, the St Albans' descendants have always been relatively poor in consequence. The marriage took place in 1694.

When the Duke was thirty-four years old he was, according to Macky, "very like King Charles" (there was, at least, no doubt about *his* paternity), and that he had a "black complexion", by which he meant swarthy. He was, in addition, "well-bred, doth not love business, is well affected to the constitution of his country".[14] After that, we lose sight of him. Despite his having been a notable soldier, his career was not very public, or full of achievement. He seems to have preferred a quiet life with his wife Diana, who was a celebrated beauty and bore him eight sons. He died in 1726, aged fifty-six.

*   *   *

While Nelly was giving birth to the future Duke of St Albans at her house in Lincoln's Inn Fields, the King's sister, Henrietta, Duchess of Orléans, was sailing towards Dover to persuade her adoring brother to link England with France in an alliance, the result of which was the Treaty of Dover of 22nd May 1670. The King went out on the waters to meet her. Among her suite of 237 persons was a pretty little Maid of Honour called Louise Renée de Penencöet de Kérouaille. The King noticed her, and a different kind of alliance suggested itself to his heart. Louise was from a poor but noble Breton family. She was small, dark, refined, and thoroughly desirable. She deeply resented her place as Maid of Honour to an Englishwoman, believing that she was destined to take her rank among the most noble in France and England. More than anything, she wanted wealth – vast quantities of it. Politicians noticed the attraction which the King manifested, and determined that it should be made serviceable; meanwhile, Louise returned to France.

Weeks later, Henrietta was dead, suddenly and unexpectedly. The King was utterly heartbroken. The French King, Louis XIV, at once despatched Louise back to England, for consolation perhaps, and Charles sent a royal yacht to meet her at Calais. Within a very short time she was established at Court, and her influence assured. The French intended to use her as a lever to prise compliance from Charles and make English policy subservient to French designs. The French had noticed (who had not?) that King Charles II would subordinate almost any consideration to the satisfaction of his pleasure, and had wisely determined that they could put this dalliance to use. Louise was sent to England as a spy, a courtesan who would conduct international negotiations between the sheets. It took her a little time to adapt to the role, but with encouragement from Louis XIV and the French Ambassador, she not only succeeded, but surpassed expectations.

Plans for the consummation of the King's desire were well laid by the French Ambassador. The Ambassador would take Louise to stay at Euston Hall, the home of Lady Arlington, and future seat of the Dukes of Grafton. The King would no doubt avail himself of the opportunity to visit. He did, and there he spent his first night with his charming new mistress. Evelyn was also at Euston Hall, and professed to be shocked by the goings-on, which lasted a full fortnight. He can hardly bring himself to set down on paper that "she was for the most part in her undress all day, and that there was fondness and toying with that young wanton".[45] All the guests in the house knew that Louise had pleasured the King, for it was joyfully announced to the gathering the following morning. Nine months later, on 29th July 1672, Louise gave birth to a son, who was to be the ancestor of the line of Dukes of Richmond. It is a delicious irony in this profligate age that the 1st Duke of Richmond, illegitimate son of Charles II, was conceived at Euston Hall, home of the 1st Duke of Grafton, another illegitimate son of Charles II by a different mistress.

Disarmingly gentle, but sly and intriguing, Louise became the most successful of all the King's mistresses. She obtained honours for herself far more quickly than any of her predecessors. In 1673 she was created Duchess of Portsmouth, for which dignity she had to become a naturalised Englishwoman, and in 1675 her son was created Duke of Richmond, when he was only three years old – the youngest person ever to be so honoured in the history of the country. "Alone among Charles's mistresses, she had a conception of *la haute politique*: she alone in that ignoble Court could command the respect and co-operation of statesmen and ambassadors. She met the vulgar furies of the Duchess of Cleveland and the banter of Nell Gwynn with quiet disdain; she held her own with a certain dignity against the anger of the Commons, the hatred of the people, the attacks of politicians, and the waywardness of Charles, and for many years she was virtually Queen of England."[46]

The way in which she secured the title for her son is indicative of her determined ambition. The Duchess of Cleveland wanted her son to be created Duke of Grafton; Louise wanted hers to be Duke of Richmond. But Barbara made a fuss about precedence; she said that her son should have his title before the son of a French Maid of Honour, and should take his place at the head of the King's bastards. The King, who hated arguments, and felt besieged by the two women, determined that the patents of creation should be dated the same day, so that Grafton and Richmond would be equal. Louise was far too clever for that. With the connivance of Danby (later Duke of Leeds) with whom she is supposed to have had an affair, Louise presented her patents to the Lord Treasurer at midnight, just as he was stepping into his coach to go to Bath, and had them signed. When Barbara turned up with her lawyers in the morning she was told that the Lord Treasurer was out of town. Louise had achieved her aim of precedence, and her son was already the Duke of Richmond.[47] *

Nell Gwynn commented, "Even Barbara's brats were not made dukes until they were twelve or thirteen, but this French spy's son is ennobled when little more than an infant in arms."[48]

Louise was profoundly unpopular with the aristocracy and with the people. The aristocracy could not stomach a foreigner being given the highest honour in the English peerage merely because she was good in bed. The Marchioness of Worcester slighted her at Tunbridge Wells, when Louise demanded that her rank entitled her to precedence, with the remark that the English did not respect a duchy gained through prostitution. (This is not exactly true; the English respect a duchy gained by any means.) Aristocracy and people united to deplore her airs; she was a mistress in the grand manner, and she succeeded in irritating the profound English distrust of pretension and pomposity.

Her extravagance was gargantuan. She depleted the privy purse of more money even than Barbara Villiers. In December 1674 an annuity of £10,000 was settled on her, in addition to which she received *ad hoc* gifts from the King of staggering liberality. Her income varied, but in 1681 it amounted to £136,668.[49] Barbara had been expensive in a vulgar way, with her coach-and-eight, but Louise had a refinement of taste which could be satisfied only by the most

---

* In fact, the dukedom of Grafton did not receive the seal until a month later.

expensive and *recherché* items from Paris. She never lost sight of her aim to be rich, and to hold her head up high with the French aristocracy, in whose company she had been of low rank. Evelyn relates, "I was casually shown the Duchess of Portsmouth's splendid apartment at Whitehall. It is luxuriously furnished, and has ten times the richness and glory of the Queen's – such massy pieces of plate; whole tables and stands of incredible value."[50] Evelyn also said that the whole apartment was two or three times pulled down and rebuilt to satisfy her prodigal tastes. She was ostentatious, throwing money from her window in the hope that gossip might reach France and teach her compatriots how rich she had become to be able to indulge such extravagance.[51] The House of Commons was not at all happy. While he was paying out vast sums to gratify the vanity of Louise, he was also supporting Barbara, Nell, Moll Davis, and others, including indirectly lovers of Barbara. Louise exceeded all reason. She would receive visitors while an unnecessary number of maids were combing out her beautiful hair in a room hung with Gobelin tapestries.[52]

When her sister returned to France, having married the Earl of Pembroke, Louise chartered (and the King paid for) several ships to transport her across the Channel. There were chests filled with silver and silk; a hundred pounds in weight of pins and needles; five pounds in weight of iris-root scent; seventeen dozen gloves, pearls, ear-rings, diamonds, and money.[53]

On the face of it, the lady had achieved much in a very short time. She was an English duchess, countess and baroness, her infant son was an English duke, her sister was married to an English earl. She had money and influence. But she was not satisfied. In her heart she valued these English honours as trifles compared to the *real* honour of a French title. France was the most civilised land in the world, her king the most powerful, her Court and literature the most brilliant. Next to all this, the English were barbarians. She pestered Charles to persuade Louis XIV to give her a French duchy. At first the French King was reluctant. He gave Louise the duchy of Aubigny (which Charles's ancestors, the Stuarts, had previously held since 1422), on the curious condition that the estate should revert on her death to any one of Charles's natural sons whom he should appoint to succeed her. It was assumed that Charles would choose as successor her own son, Richmond, and that he and his descendants could then enjoy the estate without Louis XIV having to give him a separate French title, which was not desirable. The French Court, after all, was more select. So, Louise found herself possessor of a ducal estate in France, but without the title of *duchesse*. This was not what she wanted at all.

She pestered and pestered for years, until Louis XIV relented, and made her Duchesse d'Aubigny in January 1684.[54] The next year, her son the Duke of Richmond was naturalised a Frenchman, so that he could succeed her to the estate and title. To this day, the Duke of Richmond is also Duc d'Aubigny in France, one of only two British Dukes to hold a French dukedom as well.

Her son, the 1st Duke of Richmond, suffered from the same lavish distribution of honours as had destroyed the character of his half-brother the Duke of Monmouth. Most probably it was the snobbishness of Louise which insisted that her son should be created Duke of Richmond in the peerage of England at the age of three, Duke of Lennox in the peerage of Scotland four weeks later, that he should be granted a perpetual charge on every ton of coal exported from the Tyne, when he was only four years old, and that he should be installed as a Knight of the Garter at the age of nine. She further secured for him a position as High Steward of York, the second city of the realm, when he was eleven, and the appointment as Master of the Horse when he was not yet ten. There was even talk of his being made heir to the throne.[55] In short, he had little chance of growing into a responsible adult.

As an infant, he promised well. Evelyn has described the scene on Easter Day 1684, when the King went to chapel in Whitehall with three of his natural sons, the nineteen-year-old Duke of Northumberland, Barbara's son,* the Duke of St Albans, Nell's son, nearly fourteen, and the little Duke of Richmond, aged twelve, whom Evelyn said was "a very pretty boy".[56]

There is also the endearing story which relates to his investiture as a Knight of the Garter when he was nine. He was required to wear the blue ribbon round his neck, with the medallion of St George hanging in front. But, whether his mother had advised him differently or whether the child was just confused and mistaken, he wore the ribbon across the left shoulder. The King was so delighted he ordered that this should be henceforth the custom, which it still is.[57]

Richmond's star began to sink with the death of Charles II in 1685. The dying King had asked his brother, now James II, to look after the boy, but James hated the Duchess of Portsmouth, and was unlikely to arrange matters to suit her pleasure. One of his first actions was to deprive Richmond of his position as Master of the Horse, on the grounds that he was too young to discharge his duties properly; Louise was furious.[58] Richmond was, like his mother, given to petulance.

* No relation to the present line of dukes of Northumberland.

From his father, the 1st Duke inherited good looks, easy manners, grace and charm. From his mother he gained the fatal flaw of self-indulgence, which eventually ruined him. As a young man he was popular, but then he descended to such an abysmal level of drunken-ness and debauchery that he forfeited all the good opinions he had enjoyed. Saint-Simon wrote, with his usual clarity, that Richmond had been the most beautiful creature one could hope to cast eyes upon, and had become the most hideous. Swift was less harsh when he called him, simply, a "shallow Coxcomb"

One recognises his mother also in his unrelenting ambition. He enjoyed hunting, and fighting, was accounted a good soldier, but changed his allegiance whenever prompted by self-advancement. He fought for the French and for the English; he was a confirmed Protestant, and a convinced Catholic, and a Protestant again. In 1692 he married Anne, Lady Bellasis, by whom he had three children. Although he had by right of his titles lands in Scotland, England, and France, he took a liking to the Goodwood estate in Sussex, because it was near hunting land, and bought it from the Compton family in 1720. Here his descendants have lived ever since. He enjoyed the house for barely three years, dying in 1723 an unlamented grotesque old rake. His mother retained her beauty (Voltaire admired her in old age), and died in Paris in 1734.

*　　　*　　　*

Of the four ducal houses descended from Charles II, Buccleuch is the most distinguished and has been by far the most successful, if the accumulation of wealth be the measure of success. By exercising care and wisdom in the choice of wives over the generations, always from aristocratic families, and nearly always bringing property with them, the Buccleuchs watched their lands expand until they covered nearly half a million acres in the nineteenth century. Of course, they have not just sat by idly totting up figures; they are a far from indolent race, and are well known for having managed their vast estates with exemplary acumen and devotion. When one of Gladstone's daughters, staying at Drumlanrig Castle, a Buccleuch estate in Dumfriesshire, asked the 5th Duke, "Where are the park walls?" he replied by pointing to the distant mountains.[59]

The possessions are now greater by far than any private land-owner not only in Britain, but in Europe.

They started with Scottish estates derived from Buccleuch ancestors long before Charles II was born. To this they added the estates given by Charles to his errant son the Duke of Monmouth, who married into the Buccleuch family. When Monmouth was attainted for high treason in 1685 his dignities were naturally forefeited, but his Scottish peerages were regranted to his widow. The King then gave her the Monmouth property in England (though not the titles) which she promptly settled on the children. The 2nd Duke (1694–1751), Monmouth's grandson, lost ducal dignity by displaying an inappropriate taste for women of the lower classes. He plunged into the meanest company and became an object of contempt to his peers. Lady Louisa Stuart wrote that he was "a man of mean understanding and meaner habits",[60] by which she meant that he liked unkempt and uneducated women. He went so far as to marry one, a charwoman from Windsor called Alice Powell, who thereupon found herself a most incongruous Duchess of Buccleuch. But they had no children, and the curious Duke had already been married once before (to the Duke of Queensberry's daughter), from which union sprung his descendants in the Buccleuch and Queensberry line. His strange behaviour did, therefore, no lasting damage. His washerwoman duchess is buried in Wandsworth. He was also a spendthrift, recklessly chopping down his forests to make money from the sale of timber which he could spend on his "low amours". All in all, a quirky aberration in an otherwise regular descent.

Far more dangerous was the epidemic of smallpox which carried off many members of the family in 1750, almost threatening to wipe them out entirely. "Lord Dalkeith is dead of the smallpox in three days", wrote Walpole to Horace Mann. "It is so dreadfully fatal in his family, that besides several uncles and aunts, his eldest boy died of it last year; and his other brother, who was ill but two days, putrified so fast, that his limbs fell off, as they lifted the body into the coffin."[61] The title had to pass to a grandson.

The 3rd Duke of Buccleuch (1746–1812) consolidated the family fortune in three ways: he inherited from his mother, a daughter and heiress of the Duke of Argyll, lands in Scotland; he inherited the Queensberry lands in 1810 on the death of his cousin the 4th Duke of Queensberry, with considerable estates in Dumfriesshire (including Drumlanrig Castle); he also, incidentally, became 5th Duke of Queensberry at the same time; and finally he married a daughter of the Duke of Montagu, through whom his family inherited Montagu lands, including the sumptuous Boughton House.

So, the estates of three different families have become united in the family of Buccleuch, namely those of Scott, Dukes of Buccleuch, Douglas, Dukes of Queensberry, and Montagu, Dukes of Montagu.

This triple inheritance is reflected in the family surname of Montagu-Douglas-Scott.

His predecessor in the dukedom of Queensberry was the notorious old lecher the 4th Duke, known as "Old Q" (1724–1810). He was a famous figure in Regency London by virtue of his easily observable libido where young ladies were concerned. His house stood at the top of Piccadilly, Nos. 138 and 139, between Hamilton Place and Park Lane, sadly demolished in 1973. In sunny weather, Old Q would sit on his first-floor balcony, perched on a little cane chair and dressed in a blue coat and yellow breeches, a parasol over his head, ogling the ladies who walked beneath. He was a familiar sight to passersby. He built an exterior flight of stairs from the balcony to street level, so that when he gave the nod to his messenger at the door below, a man called Jack Radford, Jack could fetch the pretty victims to the Duke's company without their having to pass through the house. Stories were told of orgies going on inside the house, and he is known, on one occasion, to have re-enacted in his drawing-room, with three beautiful London girls, the scene in Homer where the goddesses revealed themselves to Paris and desired him to choose which was the most beautiful.

Old Q pursued pleasure under every shape, "and with as much ardour at fourscore as he had done at twenty", wrote Wraxall. It was said that the old *roué* took a prominent part in the orgies, and went to extraordinary lengths to stimulate his flagging sexual powers.[62] Love seems to have but rarely entered his life. He had as a young man a passion for Pelham's daughter, but they did not marry, perhaps because his dissipated habits made him an unsuitable match. In fact, neither Old Q nor Miss Pelham ever married. He fathered a natural daughter, to whom he showed little affection. "I wish I could make him feel as he ought, but one may as well wash a brick", wrote Warner to Selwyn. Lady Louisa Stuart was yet harsher. "What or whom did he ever love?" she asked.

When age had made a ruin of his body, with sight in only one eye, hearing in only one ear, practically toothless and full of aches and pains, a man whom Thackerary called "a wrinkled, palsied, toothless old Don Juan",[63] his mind remained alert, his memory clear, his judgement sound. Wraxall averred that Old Q had more common sense than anybody he knew. Raikes described him as a "little, sharp-looking man, very irritable, and swore like ten thousand troopers".[64] He also said he was mean, which does discredit to Raikes, for Old Q was always generous to his friends, to a degree rare in any age.

One instance of craftiness rather than meanness was the terms on which he paid his doctor, who slept at his bedside every night for the last six years of the Duke's life. He was paid a handsome daily rate while he lived, on the understanding that the doctor would receive not a penny when he died; Old Q loved life so much, he thought this a sensible insurance to prolong it. He also bathed in milk.

He could not bear to be bored. "What is there to make so much of in the Thames," he said, "I am quite tired of it. There it goes, flow, flow, flow, always the same."[65]

As his end approached in 1810 (an end which he unwittingly hastened by eating too much fruit), letters flooded in from women of every class and description, begging his favour. At least seventy letters littered his bed, unopened. Everyone panted to know how he would distribute his fortune. With little strength remaining, he muttered that he wanted to alter his will, since he decided it was foolish to leave legacies; everything belonged to Bonaparte, he rambled on, and therefore all distribution was idle. He died before he was able to put this intention into effect. The will gave away most of his fortune of £900,000 in twenty-five codicils leaving specific bequests, including £600 a year to the cashier at his bank. The male servants were provided for, but not one of the female, not even his housekeeper. And the doctor, Mr Fuller, was omitted according to the bargain.[66]

Old Q was one of the last aristocrats to keep up the practice of having a running footman beside his coach. Any candidate for the post would be made to dress up in full livery, then run up and down Piccadilly, while the Duke observed and timed him from his balcony. One such man, after his trial run, came before the balcony, panting. "You will do very well for me," said Old Q from above, imperiously. "And your livery will do very well for me," replied the man, who promptly ran off with it.[67]

The other Buccleuch ancestor, the Duke of Montagu, was eccentric in quite a different way. He was given to excesses of generosity. He once met an unkempt man on a walk in the Mall, dressed in rags, and invited him to dine the following Sunday. He learnt that the man's wife and family lived in penury in Yorkshire. When the man arrived for dinner, the Duke told him he had some pleasant people for him to meet, opened the door of the dining-room, and there revealed wife and children brought down by the Duke from Yorkshire. He called his lawyer, and there and then settled an annuity of £200 upon the astonished man.[68]

By the time the 5th Duke of Buccleuch (1806–1884) came into his titles at the age of thirteen, nine years after Queensberry's death, his various estates had swollen to a phenomenal size, and the self-assured youth was accounted important enough to be able to entertain George IV at Dalkeith House in Edinburgh for two weeks, when he was only sixteen years old. In adult life he was Lord Privy Seal and Lord President of the Council, but his brief foray into politics was not successful. Greville unkindly called him "worse than useless" in Peel's government, though he acknowledged that Buccleuch was good-humoured. Like all his family he was most successful as a landowner, wearing his shepherd's trousers and his peaked cap.[69] He was immensely popular with his tenants, and easy to get on with, equally at home with the peasant as with the prince, and had only one form of address for both. (One of his descendants is Lord Montagu of Beaulieu, whose surname is Douglas-Scott-Montagu.)

This duke, obviously an endearing character, kept all his houses ready for occupation by their owner at any moment (and there were nine of them, plus three others which he did not use). But he and his duchess felt very keenly that it was a matter of social duty to share these vast inheritances. So they literally kept open house. For three months every year Drumlanrig Castle in Scotland was a home for anyone who wanted to invite himself. He could bring his entire family, and retinue if he had one, and stay as long as he wanted. No one was ever refused or turned away as long as there was an empty bedroom in the house. This custom naturally encouraged an army of opportunists, but the family rule was to welcome everyone, notwithstanding their motives or the degree of their acquaintance with the Duke. All you had to do was write to him and tell him you were coming.[70]

The ease of manner, so characteristic of the Buccleuchs, survives into the twentieth century. The 8th Duke, who died in 1973, found it peculiarly distasteful to be treated according to rank. He was happiest entertaining people on any one of his huge estates, managing his farms, or hunting. The expertly bred Buccleuch hounds are one of the few remaining family packs, founded by the 5th Duke. He was one of the country's experts on forestry, and planted more than a million trees every year on his own lands. But his real genius lay in preserving his family possessions. Other twentieth-century dukes have been forced by overwhelming death duties and other burdensome taxes which come with the egalitarian age to sell much of their land, in some cases all of it, or to open their homes to the public. Buccleuch never had to sell an acre, and still managed to run three vast private homes, with a considerable domestic staff. In 1923 he formed a private company, Buccleuch Estates Ltd, which owns and runs all his property, and in the early 1950s he settled the major part of his personal shareholding on his son the Earl of Dalkeith (the present Duke), in consideration of his marriage, thus neatly avoiding an estimated £10,000,000 in death duties. Whenever he did sell, it was a painting or two, never land, and there is still an art collection left in his private hands worth millions. This is perhaps why the Duke of Buccleuch's wealth continued while other ducal houses were handed over to trustees and their owners struggled to keep going. A senior member of the Royal Household once observed that if the possessions of the Queen and the Duke of Buccleuch were offered to auction he would not care to say which would fetch the higher price.[71] And the Director of the Louvre Museum in Paris was heard to apologise to the Duke that the French furniture on display could not hope to match the Duke's private collection.

The most famous of the Buccleuch houses is Boughton House, near Kettering in Northamptonshire, with its seventy miles of avenues, and 100 acres of garden, modelled after Versailles. The estate covers 11,000 acres. When Chips Channon saw it in 1945 he was aghast with wonder; he wrote in his diary :

> "It is a dream house with a strange, sleepy quality, but its richness, its beauty and possessions are stupefying. Everything belonged to Charles I, or Marie de Medici, or was given by Louis XIV to the Duke of Monmouth. Every 'enfilade' is elegantly arranged with Buhl chests, important pictures, Caffieri clocks, and the whole house is crammed with tapestries and marvellous objects . . . It has hardly been lived in for 200 years. There is a writing-table which belonged to Cardinal Mazarin and 14 small Van Dyks in Walter Buccleuch's 'loo'. Over all this splendour Mollie reigns delightfully and effortlessly."[72]

Mollie was the Duchess, mother of the present Duke; elsewhere Channon says she has difficulty deciding which of her five tiaras to wear. Her predecessor was the Duchess of Buccleuch, whom the Duchess of Marlborough shocked by seating her housekeeper next to her in the pew of Westminster Abbey. Lady Warwick said that "Society for her consisted only of those upon whom she permitted herself to smile. The unfavoured were all of the outer darkness."[73]

Boughton House came to the Buccleuchs through the Duke of Montagu, who built it. Through the Duke of Queensberry came the other impressive property, already mentioned, Drumlanrig Castle in Dumfriesshire. If Boughton is the most beautiful house in England, then Drumlanrig is the most romantic in Scotland. It stands on a lofty hill, alone and dominant, and is built in local pink sandstone which glows in the sunset. Above the main entrance, clustered with turrets and towers, is a huge ducal coronet in stone. It is a breath-taking sight. It has been described as standing on a teacup inverted in a washbasin, the rim of which is the ring of mountains which the 5th Duke told Miss Gladstone were his park walls.

Then there is Eildon Hall in Roxburghshire, and Bowhill in Selkirk. Dalkeith House in Edinburgh is let to International Computers. The other houses are lived in.

The man who has recently succeeded to this daunting inheritance, currently amounting to a quarter of a million acres, is the 9th Duke of Buccleuch (born 1923), an unassuming cheerful former M.P. known to the House of Commons as "Johnny Dalkeith". While styled as the Earl of Dalkeith during his father's lifetime, he repre-sented Edinburgh North in the Commons, where he was warmly regarded. He was the first of his family for generations to marry out-side the aristocracy, choosing a pretty and enchanting model then known as Miss Jane McNeil. (His aunt Alice, daughter of the 7th Duke, married into the Royal Family, and is now H.R.H. Princess Alice, Dowager Duchess of Gloucester.)

Dalkeith's political career was interrupted by a serious riding accident which occurred in 1971, and which left him completely paralysed from the chest down. The horse fell on him and broke his spine. He did not lose consciousness, and remembers clearly his imme-diate thoughts. "The moment the horse fell on me, I knew my back was broken. I realised quite clearly that I was paralysed from the chest down and that I would have to learn to adjust to a completely new way of life. It was five minutes before anyone reached me. By this time I had weighed up the situation and was ready to start the process of recovery."[74] After convalescence, Dalkeith returned to the House of Commons in a wheelchair.

He might well have been able to continue service in the House for many years, but the decision not to was made for him by his father's death in 1973, when he became 9th Duke of Buccleuch and 11th Duke of Queensberry, as well as succeeding to ten other titles, with such romantic Scottish names as Earl of Drumlanrig and Sanquhar, Viscount of Nith, Torthorwald and Ross, and Lord Douglas of Kin-mount, Middlebie and Dornock. His English titles are Earl of Don-caster and Baron Scott of Tindal.

There is no reason in law or logic why he should not also be Duke of Monmouth, but only the 1st Duke held that title. When he was beheaded for high treason in 1685 all Monmouth's English titles were forfeited. His grandson, the 2nd Duke of Buccleuch, was restored by Act of Parliament in 1742 to the English peerages of Doncaster and Tindal, but not to the dukedom of Monmouth. The reason was presumably that there was already then living an Earl of Monmouth; this earldom became extinct in 1814, since when the way has been open for the Duke of Buccleuch to be restored as Duke of Monmouth. It is still within the Queen's power to reverse the attainder and resurrect this historic title.

One other distinction the Duke enjoys is Lord of the Manor of the Hundred of Knightlow in Warwickshire. In this capacity he is entitled to claim payment of the "Wroth Silver" on 11th November (Martinmas Day) every year. The ceremony has been faithfully conducted for about 1000 years. There are twenty-eight parishes involved, and each one sends a representative to drop his contribution to the silver in the hollow of Knightlow Cross. They usually drop mere pennies. But the whole procedure becomes potentially interesting if anyone defaults in payment. He then has to pay £1 for every penny that his contribution is short, or provide and give to the Duke a white bull with a red nose and red ears. When the ceremony is completed, they all repair to the Dun Cow at Stretton to celebrate with hot rum and milk.

*   *   *

The descendants of the Duke of Grafton have been chiefly remarkable for their indolence and their longevity. The 2nd Duke was "almost a slobberer, without one good quality" according to Dean Swift,[75] while Lord Waldegrave said he was "totally illiterate; yet from long observation and great natural sagacity he became the courtier of his time. . . . He was a great teazer; had an established right of saying whatever he pleased."[76] Lord Hervey thought him a "booby" and wrote an unkind verse about him :

"So your friend, booby Grafton, I'll e'en let you keep,
Awake he can't hurt, and he's still half asleep.
Nor ever was dangerous but to womankind,
And his body's as impotent now as his mind."

However, he was Lord Chamberlain to George II, and an influential man. And he built Euston Road. Walpole tells an amusing story about Grafton when he was old and ill, covered in sores. The Duke

of Newcastle was forever "popping in", and had a disconcerting habit
of throwing his arms around men and kissing them repeatedly and
passionately. Grafton's doctors thought Newcastle a nuisance and a
pest, and ordered that he should not be allowed in the house. But he
forced his way in, and

> "The Duke's gentleman would not admit him to the bedchamber,
> saying His Grace was asleep. Newcastle protested he would go in
> on tiptoe and only look at him – he rushed in, clattered his heels
> to waken him, then fell upon the bed, kissing and hugging him.
> Grafton waked; 'God, what's here?' 'Only I, my dear Lord' –
> Buss, buss, buss, buss! – 'God! How can you be such a beast to
> kiss such a creature as I am, all over plasters! Get along, get
> along!' and turned about and went to sleep."[77]

Grafton and Newcastle had both been, at various times, lovers of
George II's daughter, the Princess Amelia. According to some sources,
Grafton had spent time with another royal daughter, Princess Caro-
line.

The real torment of the 2nd Duke's life was his son and heir Lord
Euston, who by every account was a wicked and repellent creature.
The facts are few, and his contemporaries seem too horrified to enter
into details when they refer to him, but his evil reputation rests upon
his disgraceful treatment of his wife.

Lord Euston married Lady Dorothy Boyle on 10th October, 1741.
Within seven months, she was dead, and everyone appeared to be
glad for her. Lady Dorothy was the daughter of the Earl of Burlington (whose house was where the Royal Academy now stands in
Piccadilly, and after whom Burlington Arcade is named). She was
pretty, good-natured, gentle and quiet, and she had the misfortune
when only sixteen to fall in love with Lord Euston. She adored him,
fawned upon him, worshipped his every word. She seemed blind to
what everyone else knew, which was that he was boorish and cruel,
with a fearful temper, inherited no doubt from his great-grandmother
Barbara Villiers. At a ball at the Duke of Norfolk's in October 1740
(a year before they married) Euston was seen to treat his fiancée
with public contempt. On another occasion, at dinner, in front of
assembled guests, he shouted at her across the table, "Lady Dorothy,
how greedily you eat! It is no wonder that you are so fat." The poor
girl blushed and began to cry. Her mother, Lady Burlington, came
to her defence. "It is true, my lord, that she is fat, and I hope she
will always be so, for it is her constitution, and she will never be lean

until she is less happy than we have always tried to make her, which I shall endeavour to prevent her being." It is not recorded how the bullish Earl reacted to that humiliating riposte, but he was too insensitive for it to affect him. Lady Hertford, who was present, said that were the young lady *her* daughter, she would sooner prepare for her funeral than for such a marriage.[78]

Horace Mann recalls another instance when Lord Euston "gave a specimen of himself many years ago here, when he was so rude as to make the mild little Lady Essex say that she would hit him a slap in the face".[79] His behaviour must indeed have been unusually provocative to splinter the calm of aristocratic reserve to this extent.

Nothing was able to prevent Lady Dorothy's rush into disaster. After the marriage, Lord Euston forbade his mother-in-law to enter his house. Scandal exploded immediately. Walpole wrote in a tizzy only a fortnight after the wedding,

"I wrote you word that Lord Euston is married: in a week more I believe I shall write you word that he is divorced. He is brutal enough; and has forbid Lady Burlington his house, and that in very ungentle terms. The whole family is in confusion; the Duke of Grafton half dead, and Lord Burlington half mad. The latter has challenged Lord Euston, who accepted the challenge, but they were prevented . . . in short, one cannot go into a room but you hear something of it. Do you not pity the poor girl? of softest temper, vast beauty, birth, and fortune, to be so sacrificed!"[80]

There is total obscurity about what happened in those seven months of marriage. Hanbury Williams asserted that the marriage was never consummated.[81] Euston had had another bride in view, and we do not know what made him switch to Dorothy Boyle. Certainly, all the love was on her side. Walpole says above that Euston was "brutal . . . ungentle". Lady Orrery says that Dorothy "died from his ill-treatment of her", but does not specify in what way his treatment was ill.[82] Another writer can only bring himself to say that Lord Euston's behaviour was "almost too revolting to be believed", without telling us what it was so that we may be given the chance to believe it or not.

In fairness, Lady Dorothy's health had never been vigorous. When she was twelve years old she wrote to her mother

"This is to let you know that I was took with a swimming in my head last Saturday and they told me on Sunday that I had a sort of fit in the night but I was asleep and knew nothing of it and they sent to Mr Terry to come and he went next morning to consult Dr Mead who ordered Mr Dickens to come and bleed me which he did and at night Mr Terry gave me a vomit."[83]

It might well be that the "swimming" in her head was old-fashioned intoxication, to judge by the liquid nourishment she was served. "Pray mama send me word what you would have me drink with my dinner", she wrote, "for the Barrel Beer is so thick and so bitter that I cannot drink it."[84]

Medically, her death was caused by smallpox, for which Euston cannot in all justice be blamed. Yet contemporaries were in no doubt that he had contributed in some way.

After her death, her mother painted a portrait of her from memory, and placed beneath it this telling inscription :

LADY DOROTHY BOYLE

born May the 14th 1724

She was the comfort and Joy of her parents, the delight of all who knew her angelick temper, and the admiration of all who saw her beauty. She was married October the 10th, 1741, and delivered (by death) from misery

May the 2nd, 1742

The portrait is in the possession of the Duke of Devonshire.

A print was also published of Lady Dorothy, beneath which was appended this fulsome poem :

"View here ye Fair the boast of Female life,
  The faultless virgin, and the faithful wife;
  Once her fond parents' comfort, joy and pride,
  Who never gave them pang, till made a bride;
  In virtue, as in Beauty, she excelled,
  Yet Nature equally the balance held;
  When seen, all hearts her willing slaves became;
  When known, that knowledge damp'd each kindling flame :
  The wish of every noble Youth she shone,
  Till Love and Honour gave her all to One;
  To one – alas ! – unworthy such a prize,
  His soul to virtue deaf, to beauty blind his Eyes"[85]

There is evidence that the lamentable Euston terrorised his tenants as well as his wife. Walpole told his correspondent "a new exploit of his barbarity". A tenant brought his rent to Lord Euston, who said it was 3s. 6d. short. The tenant protested that he thought he was correct, but he would examine the account again, and meanwhile was quite happy to give His Lordship the additional 3s. 6d. if he so wished. Euston flew into a rage and threatened to have the man removed from his job on the estate forthwith. "The poor man, who has six children, and knew nothing of my Lord's being on no terms of power with his father, went home and shot himself."[86]

Relief more than sorrow greeted the news of Euston's death in 1747, thus removing the threat that this monster might become Duke of Grafton. The 2nd Duke died ten years later, and was succeeded in the title by his grandson, Augustus Henry, who belongs to history for his period in office as Prime Minister, between 1767 and 1770, and for his scandalous affair with Nancy Parsons.

Augustus Henry, 3rd Duke of Grafton (1735–1811) was not meant for high office. He was full of good intentions and generous motives, but he possessed in abundance the inherited traits of sloth and venery. He was lazy and pleasure-seeking, timid in decision, weak in resolve. He became Prime Minister because the then Prime Minister, Chatham, suffered a serious breakdown in health (from which he later recovered to rescue Grafton from the concentrated attacks which made his years in office a nightmare). As Massey has written, "unsteady, capricious, and indolent, he had hardly any quality for a statesman . . . he owed his elevation partly to accident, partly to his great rank and fortune".[87] *The Spectator* echoed this judgement: "a man of weak will, admirable purpose, and common intellect . . . for politics he had not the smallest talent".[88] Sir George Trevelyan has described him as "a most unlucky figure in history". Although much esteemed by some contemporaries, he was simply not equal to the tasks which were thrust upon him, and he suffered more than anyone from the cruel satire of Junius, whose *Letters* contain merciless attacks, in remorseless succession, made all the more deadly by the sharp purity of their style. I shall quote just one reference out of dozens :

"It is not that you do wrong by design, but that you should never do right by mistake. It is not that your indolence and your activity have been equally misapplied, but that the first uniform principle, or, if I may call it the genius of your life, should have carried you through every possible change and contradiction of conduct, without the momentary imputation or colour of a virtue . . . [the ancestors] of your grace, for instance, left no distressing examples of virtue, even to their legitimate posterity, and you may look back with pleasure to an illustrious pedigree, in which heraldry has not left a single good quality upon record to insult or upbraid you. You have better proofs of your descent, my lord, than the register of a marriage, or any troublesome inheritance or reputation. There are some hereditary strokes of character by which a family may be as clearly distinguished as by the blackest features of the human face."[89]

Junius also pointed the finger at Grafton, with bitterest jest, for his affair with Nancy Parsons, which made him, while still Prime Minister, the laughing-stock of London.

Nancy Parsons was the daughter of a Bond Street tailor, who married a man called Horton, but had affairs with a goodly section of London's nobility. She is described as "the Duke of Grafton's Mrs Horton, the Duke of Dorset's Mrs Horton, everybody's Mrs Horton". She also had a relationship with the Duke of Bedford, who installed her for a time at Woburn Abbey. She eventually married Lord Maynard, not that that made any difference to her habits. Foolishly, Grafton escorted her quite blatantly in public, making no allowance for good taste or piety. Junius then wrote some unpublishable obscene verses on the affair, called *Harry and Nan*, which, together with the sustained invective of the letters, upset the Prime Minister deeply. He was thrown into agonies of embarrassment and indecision, the verses preyed on his mind, so that he was incapacitated for whole days and neglected the duties of office.[90]

He took the earliest opportunity to resign, when Chatham was well enough to resume work in 1770. No one was more relieved than he. But he had been, to say the least, indiscreet, and he deserved reproach. The blood of Barbara Villiers pulsed through his veins, making him liable to drop everything for an indulgence of passion, which, with the influence of John Wesley just then being felt in the country, managed to outrage even those easygoing times. In the words of Walpole, he thought "the world should be postponed to a whore and a horse-race", and he "insulted the virtue and decency of mankind by the most unblushing violation of both". *Town and Country* was no less accusing; while Grafton was still Prime Minister, it published an issue condemning him as "a gamester who squandered the treasures of the nation upon horses and women, and who, left to guide the helm of fate, would soon plunge it into inevitable destruction".[91]

"His fall was universally ascribed to his pusillanimity [wrote Walpole], but whether betrayed by his fears or his friends, he had certainly been the chief author of his own disgrace. His haughtiness, indolence, reserve, and improvidence, had conjured up the storm; but his obstinacy and fickleness always relaying each other, and always *mal à propos*, were the radical causes of all the numerous absurdities that discoloured his conduct and exposed him to deserved reproaches; nor had he the depth of understanding to counterbalance the effects of his temper."[92]

The 3rd Duke of Grafton married twice, and had fourteen children, to whom he added an illegitimate offspring of a further eighteen according to one estimate.

Since then, successive Dukes of Grafton have settled down to less publicised lives, without high political office, but without too the constant calumnies on their name. In the nineteenth and twentieth centuries they have successfully thrown off the reputation of their ancestry to emerge modestly in their military careers. Only once did a brief flurry of publicity bring their name to general attention, and then it was quickly quashed. It was in connection with the Cleveland Street scandal of 1889 (see also Chapter 5). The Earl of Euston's name was mentioned by the *North London Press* as being a frequent visitor to the male brothel there, upon which he immediately brought an action for criminal libel against the newspaper. The editor and publisher were tried on 15th January 1890, bringing as their only substantial witness to show that the libel was true a dreadful young prostitute called John Saul, who gloried in the fuss. Saul testified that he had taken Lord Euston to 19 Cleveland Street and committed acts of indecency with him. Euston said he went there once, innocent of the purpose of the house, and had left immediately when he discovered that it was a brothel. Saul, who admitted that he was a professional "Mary-Anne" and earned £8 or £9 a week in this way, went into some sordid details about his craft, specifying the sort of pleasure that he alleged Euston enjoyed. But Saul was a loathsome creature, and his evidence was easily discredited. In the end, Euston won his case, cleared his name, and was given an apology by the *North London Press*, who nevertheless maintained that they had other evidence they were not at liberty to divulge. Saul, who ought logically to have been prosecuted for immorality or perjury, went scot free.

And no mention was made during the trial of a statement made to the police by another boy, Newlove, who also, independently of John Saul, had mentioned Euston's name.[93]

Euston was the son of the 7th Duke of Grafton, who outlived him. The 8th Duke, Euston's brother, had a son who was killed in an air crash in 1918, thus passing the dukedom directly to his grandson, the 9th Duke, at the age of sixteen. He, too, died in tragic circumstances at the wheel of his racing car at the age of twenty-two. He was succeeded by his cousin as 10th Duke in 1936.

The family still lives at Euston Hall, the property secured by marrying the infant 1st Duke to its owner. The house has undergone some changes in recent years. Evelyn described it in 1671 (before the 1st Duke of Grafton was born) as "a very noble pile . . . magnificent and commodious, as well within as without . . . but the soil dry, barren, and miserably sandy, which flies in drifts as the wind sits". The 10th Duke, who died in 1970, sold part of the Euston estate to meet death duties, leaving 11,000 acres which remain today; in 1950 he demolished two-thirds of Euston Hall itself with a view to economy, to save on running expenses and to modernise. At approximately the same time, he bought 24,000 acres in Rhodesia.

His son, the 11th Duke, born in 1919, lives at Euston in seclusion and deep privacy. Only in 1975 did he decide to open his house to the public, in celebration of European Architectural Heritage Year. Quite unlike his forbears, however, he is one of the most active of the twenty-six dukes alive today. A trustee of the London Museum, of the National Portrait Gallery, and of the Sir John Soane Museum, his first attentions go to the Society for Protection of Ancient Buildings, of which he is chairman. He is also connected with the Historic Churches Preservation Trust. The Duke's knowledge in these fields is immense; nobody knows more about Victorian building than he, and few care more passionately. He is also one of the half-dozen dukes who regularly appear in the House of Lords, where he speaks on his subject of conservation and preservation. He does not dabble in politics, but there are not many in his position who are so hard-working, or who have such a keen desire to contribute to national life.

The Duchess of Grafton, D.C.V.O., has been Mistress of the Robes to the Queen since 1967.

The streets surrounding Euston Station to the north of Bloomsbury all bear names which testify to the Grafton past. The 1st Duke's wife inherited not only the Euston estate, but the manor of Tottenham Court (hence Tottenham Court Road). Fitzroy Square

reminds us that the family surname is Fitzroy (*fils du roi*), of royal
descent.

*   *   *

The Dukes of St Albans have not been, for the most part, illustrious or accomplished, though they have been well placed; the 4th Duke was a close friend of George III and sat next to him, by royal command, at the Jockey Club dinner, but he was only Duke for a year. Historical memoirs have some scattered remarks about the rest, usually disparaging. Lord Hervey said of the 2nd Duke that he was "one of the weakest men either of the legitimate or spurious brood of the Stuarts";[94] he was grandson of Charles II and Nell Gwynn, both amenable and agreeable people, but not strong-willed.

The 3rd Duke was called by Walpole "the simple Duke of St Albans".[95] Simple or not, he managed to pack his life with, in the words of the biographers of the family, "a glittering crescendo of feats of incompetence quite unparalleled in the lives of any other dukes in the eighteenth century".[96] The soft sensuality of Charles II re-emerged in the 3rd Duke of St Albans, who began well by apparently fathering a child while he himself was still a schoolboy. Thereafter, he had several children (the number is not precise) scattered in Paris, Brussels and Venice, whither he had fled to escape his creditors. According to Walpole, he gave his kitchen-maid a child, then gave it a sumptuous funeral in defiance of his debts. Returning to England, he was thrown into a debtors' gaol.[97] By the time he died in 1786, the St Albans finances were chaotic. A contemporary epitaph had this to say about him :

"Immersed in Dissipation, knew not an Inclination
Which he forebore to gratify.
Contempt and Wretchedness
Closed the train of Dishonour, Riot and Sensuality.
He lamented his Mistakes, without reforming his Conduct;
And having lived a tyrannical Husband and an Insincere Friend,
Died an Exile, and a Mendicant."[98]

The 4th Duke was second cousin to the 3rd. He died unmarried at twenty-eight, and was succeeded as 5th Duke by his first cousin once removed, whose son, 6th Duke of St Albans, was "the most hideous, disagreeable little animal that I ever met with", in the words of Lady Harriet Cavendish.[99] He in turn was succeeded by his only son, aged four months. Or was he?

The child was born after twelve years of marriage, and during the course of a hectic affair the Duchess was having with one "Sinclair", who may have been Sir George Sinclair. The lovers were meeting again while the body of the late Duke was scarce cold, and in the next room, which gave rise, not unnaturally, to some comment. The Duchess announced another pregnancy after her husband's death, which was more than the family could take. Delicate investigations were made to prove that the foetus could not possibly belong to the late Duke. The whole business was resolved by fate in the end, as the little boy lived only ten months, to be succeeded by his Uncle William, who had been making all the fuss about his paternity.

There is one sophisticated exception to this sorry list – Topham Beauclerk, friend of Dr Johnson, and grandson of the 1st Duke of St Albans. His name derived from the outrageous character of his father, Lord Sidney Beauclerk, a pursuer of elderly rich ladies, and a handsome bounder, who persuaded Mr Topham of Windsor to leave him his fortune. Topham Beauclerk was dissolute, but cultured, intelligent, and enlightened. Johnson told him, "Thy body is all vice, and thy mind all virtue." He was good company, entertaining, well informed, and very well read. When he died, his library was sold at public auction, and fetched £5011 in 1781. Johnson wrote: "Poor dear Beauclerk – *nec, ut soles, debis joca.* His wit and folly, his acuteness and maliciousness, his merriment and reasoning, are now over. Such another will not often be found among mankind."

He had another, less savoury, reputation for lice, which flourished under his wig. He freely admitted that he had enough to stock a parish.

The most famous in the St Albans line, however, is one of the duchesses. Harriot Mellon, later Harriot Coutts, and finally Duchess of St Albans, was born penniless, and died one of the richest women in England. Like Nell Gwynn, she was working-class, an actress, and with wealthy admirers. Her marriage to the Duke caused quite a stir, as she was then fifty years old, stout, and a widow, while he was a mere simple-minded youth of twenty-six, who refused to grow up. They suited each other at the time. The St Albans purse needed replenishing (as always), and Harriot needed to be accepted in society; she married for rank, he for money. They were to be nicknamed "Lord Noodle and Queen Dollabella".

Harriot Mellon was born in or near 1777, the daughter of an Irish peasant woman and a mysterious soldier, whom no one has ever been able to trace. Mother and daughter lived by their wits, from day to day, and joined a travelling group of actors. Harriot was on stage before the age of ten, though she and her mother subsisted on a beggar's income never far from abject poverty, until she was noticed by the playwright Sheridan, when she was about sixteen, and promised advancement. Sheridan had to be pestered to keep his promise, but eventually arranged for Harriot to appear as Lydia Languish at Drury Lane. Her career progressed, including parts in *Twelfth Night* and *The Merry Wives of Windsor,* but her most famous role was Mrs Candour in *The School for Scandal.* She also played, unsuccessfully it appears, as Ophelia in *Hamlet,* Rosalind in *As You Like It* and Miranda in *The Tempest.* Her salary advanced to two guineas a week.

Two fortuitous events in 1806 or 1807 overturned Harriot's life. She won £10,000 (or a portion of it) in a raffle, and was able to buy a house in Highgate called Holly Lodge, which was later famous for her extravagant parties. The second stroke of fortune came when Thomas Coutts, the banker and the richest man of his day, fell hopelessly in love with her. He lavished expensive gifts upon her, and lifted her and her mother to the dizzy heights of sumptuous living. It was common knowledge that they were soon living together.[101] Two circumstances made the liaison particularly distasteful : Mr Coutts was still married, and he was nearly eighty years old. Harriot was in her early thirties. Her reputation never recovered from the malicious gossip which began to circulate. "Society", which consisted of about 300 people in London in those days, looked down its nose at this cheap adventure, and would never, but never, accept Harriot into their hallowed circles, however much money she might have. It has since become clear that the raffle she won was a discreet fiction; the money for Holly Lodge was put up by Coutts.

Mr Coutts's first wife died in 1815, and a few months later he secretly married Harriot. When the news became known, "decent" people felt outraged, though she cared little, for life was pleasant, money was abundant, and she had servants, style, and sequins. Mr Coutts was not a lascivious old man, but a kindly gentleman infatuated with Harriot's theatrical presence; he may even have been stage-struck. One day a jeweller called Mr Hamlet happened to show him a beautiful diamond cross. "How happy I should be with such a splendid specimen of jewellery," said Harriot, now Mrs Coutts, with as much subtlety as she could muster. Mr Coutts asked the jeweller how much it was worth. "I could not part with it for under £15,000," he said. "Bring me pen and ink," said Coutts, who simply wrote out a cheque.[102]

Thomas Coutts was over ninety when he finally died in 1822 (perhaps later than Harriot might reasonably have expected). His will left the whole of his fortune, about £900,000, to Harriot "for her sole use and benefit, and at her absolute disposal, without the deduction of a single legacy to any other person", although he had three daughters by his first marriage. Again, tongues wagged, but this was not so heartless as it seemed; all three daughters married well, and were comfortable, whereas Harriot had only what he could give her; besides, he trusted her not to forget them, and his trust was proven to be justified.

Three years later the romance with the Duke of St Albans began. To her credit, she did everything to discourage the young man, whose father had been courting her as well. She was a portly middle-aged woman, but with the high spirits and vivacity which in our own day has turned the head of many a young man beguiled by the theatrical manner. Besides, St Albans, who had only recently succeeded to the title, had not much money, and she now had plenty. He proposed in 1826, and she refused him, telling him to ask her again in twelve months' time if he still wanted her. When the year was up, he proposed a second time. She refused, sending her letter with a messenger on horseback. Then she thought better of it, and sent another messenger to catch up with the first and get the letter back.[103] The engagement was duly announced.

"The Duke of St Albans is to be married to Mother Coutts on Saturday", wrote Creevey, sardonically.[104] In another place he referred to her as "the old Dowager Coutts" and said "a more disgusting, frowsy, hairy old B. could not have been found in the Seven Dials".[185] Nevertheless, London society nodded knowingly and looked askance. Broughton said, "There are all sorts of ridiculous stories about the Duke and his marriage, but the baseness is more prominent than the folly of such a transaction",[106] and Sir Walter Scott wrote: "If the Duke marries her, he ensures an immense fortune; if she marries him, she has the first rank. The disparity of ages concerns no one but themselves; so they have my consent to marry, if they can get each other's."[107] Her stepson-in-law, Sir Francis Burdett, sat up all night before the wedding trying to persuade her not to go through with it.[108]

Before the ceremony, Harriot's servants wore the Coutts livery. Immediately afterwards they appeared in the St Albans yellow and black stockings.[109] He received, as a result of the union, £30,000, plus an estate in Essex valued at £26,000; all his unsettled property was answerable to the Coutts bank for any claims upon it. Lady Holland reflected on the appearance of the couple. The Duke, she wrote, "is rather melancholy . . . a handsome face with features quite immoveable, no sort of expression. A large, handsome, dark, fixed, glazed eye. She affected to be very joyous, but I think her gaiety all assumed. It is a strange alliance."[110]

Strange indeed. The new Duchess took into the marriage the pillow on which old Mr Coutts had expired. She travelled with it everywhere. The pillow and her favourite bible (which had belonged to Coutts) were always in a plain case by her side wherever she went.[111]

Still she was not accepted in society. She gave marvellous parties in Highgate, at which she hired all the birds from all the bird-dealers in London, and hung them in the grounds of her house, in keeping with her husband's office as Grand Falconer;[112] there were similarly extrovert parties at St Albans House in Brighton. But Lady Holland noticed that she was treated with spite. "The ladies did not behave prettily or at all like *grandes dames* to the Duchess of St Albans. They really *shouldered* her on their bench. How can women behave so to one another!"[113] Creevey professed to be appalled at her squandering of wealth while poor people were starving, and called her "a prodigal fool and devil", but again he was unjust. She was well known to be profusely generous and benevolent, and her kindness to the poor in Highgate is legendary. She never forgot her origins. She once heard that a woman was living in poverty in Brighton, disguised herself and visited her, leaving behind an envelope containing £300.[114] If she was cold-shouldered by the nobility, she remained vastly popular with the people. She felt her isolation. "All is coldness, reserve, and universal ennui", she wrote.[115] The Queen pointedly omitted her from an invitation to a ball at the Brighton Pavilion at which 830 persons were present; there was hardly anyone of substance left in Brighton who was not invited.[116]

When she fell ill she subsisted for the last two months on arrowroot and a little brandy, and nothing more. She clutched Mr Coutts' pillow to her, and expired on 6th August 1837.[117] The English nobility lost a colourful and unlikely member of their ranks. When her will was published those who had scorned and mocked had cause to show remorse. She left to the Duke of St Albans an annuity of £10,000, and two houses (including Holly Lodge). The rest of her vast fortune, now £1,800,000, she left to Miss Angela Burdett, Mr Coutt's grand-daughter. The newspapers gleefully pointed out that this fortune in gold weighed more than thirteen tons, that it would require 107 men to carry it, if each one carried 298 lb. equivalent to a sack of flour, or in sovereigns it would cover more than twenty-four miles and take more than ten weeks to count.[118] Angela grew into the Baroness Burdett-Coutts, the philanthropist.

The 9th Duke of St Albans, having first seduced a servant-girl, took as his second wife an Irishwoman called Elizabeth Gubbins. The marriage was a disaster as far as the descendants were (and are) concerned, for it is Miss Gubbins who is suspected of having brought insanity into the family. Her brother Charles Gubbins was mad.

For the time being, however, nothing was untoward. They had a son and heir, who succeeded as 10th Duke in 1849, and married Sybil Grey. With the next generation, the wayward seed was apparent. The 11th Duke of St Albans (1870–1934) went irretrievably mad, spending the last thirty years of his life locked up in a Sussex clinic. His brother William set fire to a building at Eton and then succumbed to total insanity. It is difficult to say whether this weakness must be traced *only* to Elizabeth Gubbins; after all, her husband the 9th Duke himself died of an epileptic fit at the age of forty-eight, and, further back, the 6th Duke died of apoplexy of the brain in 1815.

The next Duke was 'Obby', Osborne de Vere Beauclerk, 12th Duke of St Albans, half brother to the 11th, and grandson of Elizabeth Gubbins. Though he was always said to be "mad as a hatter" by nearly everyone who knew him, Obby's eccentricities did not make him certifiable. He never lost sight of the madness which afflicted both his brothers and was apt to be melancholy at times. Those who remember him (he died in 1964, nearly ninety years old) have a clearer impression of his colourful nonconformity. He proposed appearing at the coronation of 1953, for example, with a live falcon to remind everyone that he was Hereditary Grand Falconer, and when permission was not granted he elected not to go at all. He was a familiar sight in the church near where he lived in Ireland, snoring with a handkerchief over his face, only waking up to contradict the preacher with shouts of "Rubbish!" On a visit to Lord Dunraven, he arrived with a brown paper bag containing pyjamas and a toothbrush.[119] And he was known to ask the hall porter at his club to wind his watch for him. There was one occasion when he sat impassively in a hotel restaurant when a fire alarm disturbed him. He refused to move. As waiters tried to get him to escape, he said "Nonsense! Bring me some more toast." "But your Grace's clothes!" exclaimed the manager. "Throw them out of the window," said Obby.

The Duke married but had no children, which was a relief to him, for he feared passing on the hereditary madness. The fear did not extend to illegitimate offspring, of which he mischievously claimed a far greater number than could have been true. He had no time for his successor, the present Duke, whom he invited only once. He used to ask other members of the family to "do something about the heir". When he died it was realised that he had done precious little to protect what remained of the St Albans inheritance, and so passed on to the next duke nothing but death duties. "Bury me where I drop," he used to say.[120]

The man who succeeded as 13th Duke of St Albans in 1964 was Mr Charles de Vere Beauclerk, a descendant of the 8th Duke who died in 1825, before Miss Gubbins came into the picture. He had a Cambridge M.A. degree, and was decorated for his work in the Intelligence Division during the war with the O.B.E. After that he had a distinguished career in the Civil Service, in the Central Office of Information. He was still there when he became Duke, and did not in fact resign until six months later. He presented the unusual spectacle of a middle-class duke, descended from the coupling of King and Cockney girl, without a landed estate and dependent on a salaried position. He then went into the City, with a variety of companies whose interests include property, travel, advertising and finance. He had the acumen to make himself a millionaire, though he has not escaped some criticism.

The Duke had been married twice, has four sons and a daughter. His duchess is a slightly bohemian figure, born in Malaya and brought up in France, who for many years ran the Upper Grosvenor Art Galleries. The couple lived in a leasehold house in Chelsea, overlooking the Albert Bridge, with four bedrooms. They built on to it an art gallery, which housed the Duke's fine collection of family pictures, assembled mostly by his own efforts, and beautifully lit. They now live in an apartment in Monte Carlo.

What of the St Albans heirlooms? There is the Bishop Juxon ring, given by Charles I just before his execution; some miniatures and jewellery belonging to Nell Gwynn; and an exquisite seal of ivory, in the shape of a falcon, which most probably belonged to the 9th Duke.

The property has all disappeared. Bestwood Park, which had been given to Nell Gwynn and on which had been constructed a house resembling St Pancras Station, was sold in 1940. Holly Lodge, scene of Harriot's parties, was sold by auction in 1906 after the death of Baroness Burdett-Coutts, and since demolished. At one time the Duke tried to buy from Richmond Borough Council the house at Hampton Court which had associations with Nell Gwynn and which was popularly thought to be haunted by her ghost. But the Council demolished it. There is perhaps injustice in all this, as Nell was, after all, the most loyal of Charles's mistresses. She was far too sensible a girl ever to expect justice; she would not have been surprised.

St Albans has inherited from Charles II a jovial nature, easy to laugh and anxious for life to proceed smoothly and happily. If it does not, he is bewildered rather than bitter. He is discomfited by strangers, only at ease when they show they do not expect any special kind of behaviour. He does not take his seat in the Lords, nor possess the coronet and robes to which his rank entitles him. Embarrassment prevents him more than anything else. "I don't enjoy dressing up," he says, and one must agree that the ducal robes would sit uncomfortably on his shoulders. He has a passionate interest in his family and an inalienable fondness for Charles II. The Duke also believes that one of his ancestors, the de Vere Earl of Oxford, was Shakespeare, or part of him. He says that Shakespeare must have been a composite man, a team of lawyers, doctors, soldiers, and men of letters, and that Oxford was part of the team. A portrait of the Earl has pride of place in the Chelsea home.

This genial man is still Grand Falconer of England. But the right to drive down Birdcage Walk,* previously shared by the monarch and the Duke, has gone. The rootlessness of the dukedom, deprived of any inherited lands, is a sadness for which the Duke once made symbolic compensation: above the front door of his house in Chelsea, in thick black letters, was the word ST ALBANS.

*   *   *

It is splendidly apt that the descendants of Louise de Kérouaille – the Dukes of Richmond – should be more closely involved with the political life of the country than any of the other offspring of Charles II, for Louise was the most politically minded of his mistresses, and the very affair which gave birth to the 1st Duke was a successful exercise in political strategy. Not only that, but it is refreshing to find a line which has been universally popular, instead of a clutch of historical references which are derogatory or contemptuous. One welcomes the opportunity to celebrate an exceptional family.

Hervey, whose pen was usually dipped in poison, said of the 2nd Duke that he was "friendly, benevolent, generous, honourable, and

* The road which runs along the west side of St James's Park. Both James I and Charles II kept large numbers of exotic birds. The road was opened to the public in 1828.

thoroughly noble in his way of acting, talking, and thinking".[121] Praise from such a quarter is not to be taken for granted.

The story of the 2nd Duke's marriage is one of the strangest recorded. The Duke (1701–1750) was eighteen years old when he married Lady Sarah Cadogan, daughter of the 1st Earl of Cadogan; she was thirteen. The marriage had been arranged to settle a gambling debt between their parents. Immediately after the ceremony the girl was sent back to school and the young man was packed off to the continent with his tutor; he did not set foot in England again for three years. When he did return, he had such an unpleasant memory of his wife that, to avoid her, he spent his first evening at the theatre. There he was captivated on sight by a beautiful girl whom he determined to get to know. He asked who she was, and could he be introduced. "The reigning toast," he was told, "the beautiful Lady March" – his wife. One might say they fell in love at second sight.

From that moment they had an idyllic marriage, sustaining the comfort and excitement of first love all their lives. Long after their children were grown, Walpole saw them at a ball, and wrote: "The Duke sat by his wife all night, kissing her hand."[122] She bore him twelve children, most of whom enjoyed the famous Richmond good looks, and was pregnant twenty-seven times. "She has a belly up to her chin", wrote Hervey, "and looks mighty well. His Grace is in great anxiety for her welfare, and a boy."[123] At the same ball as that referred to above, "the two beauties were the Duke of Richmond's two daughters, and their mother, still handsomer than they". The daughters continued the romantic traditions of their parents; Lady Caroline Lennox eloped with Henry Fox (later Lord Holland), and Lady Emily married, against advice, the future 1st Duke of Leinster. George III was in love with a third daughter, Lady Sarah, and used to blush whenever he saw her.

The Duke was a member of Parliament (as Lord March), a Knight of the Garter, and a soldier, a fellow of the Royal Society, and President of the Society of Antiquaries. As much as 250 years before the safari park obsession took hold of some noble houses, Richmond established a private zoo at Goodwood, which contained five wolves, two tigers, one lion, two leopards, three bears, monkeys, eagles, and "a woman Tyger" and a "new animal he is very fond of which he calls a mangoose".[124] He was free of any snobbery about rank and status which, while not worthy of comment nowadays, was rare enough in the eighteenth century and was carried almost to revolutionary pitch by his son the 3rd Duke.

When he died he was genuinely lamented. Fielding called him "the late excellent Duke of Richmond". His wife died of grief not long afterwards.

The 3rd Duke of Richmond (1735–1806) was, like his father, of "an amorous disposition" and "a charming fine boy". He was deeply affectionate, and impetuously generous. "His person, manners, and address were full of dignity, and the personal beauty which distinguished Mlle de Kérouaille was not become extinct in him." He was "easy and accommodating in his manners and society".[125] Yet he is chiefly remembered for his effect on public life. One might almost call him a Socialist, so far in advance of his time were his extremely radical views. He introduced a Bill for Parliamentary Reform which even at the beginning of the twentieth century would have been considered intemperate. In 1730 only one person in six was entitled to vote, and most of the important seats in the House of Commons were within the gift of private landowners. Richmond's Bill proposed that there should be universal suffrage above the age of eighteen (which did not happen until the election of 1970), that elections should be held every June, and that the country should be divided into 558 equally populous districts. The Bill was rejected without a division.

He was a tireless campaigner for the reform of abuses in government, always ferretting, always posing awkward questions. He wanted the Civil List, which he thought wasteful and lavish to a shameful degree, to be severely cut. That proposal, too, was defeated.

On the matter of American independence, Richmond was again more to the left than any other nobleman. He said that the resistance of the colonists was "neither treason nor rebellion, but is perfectly justifiable in every possible political and moral sense". It is no wonder that he terrified his political colleagues with such pronouncements, and alienated public opinion. One M.P. said that if there were two Dukes of Richmond in the country he would not live in it.[126] George III is reported to have said "there was no man in his dominions by whom he had been so much offended, and no man to whom he was so much indebted, as the Duke of Richmond".[127]

His personal integrity and high-minded fight against abuses were so far beyond question that he retained the guarded affection of even those who could not stomach his views. He was not a man to bear grudges, though his austerity and tactlessness sometimes gave the opposite impression.[128] His one fault was to be pompously pleased with his own rectitude. Still, Walpole trumpeted his unequalled honour, said he was one of the virtuous few, and incapable of an unworthy action. "I worship his thousand virtues beyond any man's", he wrote.

"He is intrepid and tender, inflexible and humane beyond example. I do not know which is most amiable, his heart or his conscience. He ought too to be the great model to all our factions. No difference in sentiments between him and his friends makes the slightest impression upon his attachment to them."[129]

One other achievement was to open the first ever School of Antique Sculpture in England, financed by the Duke and housed in his Whitehall home, as early as 1758, some ten years before the foundation of the Royal Academy.

Richmond married Lady Mary Bruce, a descendant of Robert Bruce, but she died without issue. By his housekeeper, Mrs Bennett, he had three daughters, to whom he left £50,000 each, and another daughter by a Miss Le Clerc.

His successor, the 4th Duke (1764–1819), was his nephew. Once more, whatever references one can find testify to the inherent good nature of this agreeable family. Sir Robert Peel wrote : "I never knew a man of whom it could be said with so much justice that he was always anxious to find an excuse for the misconduct of his friends, and to put the most charitable construction on the acts of every human being."[130] It is probably true to say that Charles II is more faithfully represented in the Dukes of Richmond than in any of his other descendants. They carry the King's happy disposition in their posterity, his good companionship, his soft nature.

The 4th Duke inherited the family's good looks ("the finest formed man in England"),[131] and married Charlotte, daughter of the Duke of Gordon. This was the Duchess who gave the most famous party in history, the so-called "Waterloo Ball" on 15th June 1815, at a coach-maker's depot decorated to look like a ballroom, in the rue de la Blanchisserie in Brussels. It was the night before the Battle of Waterloo, and is remembered for having been a psychological weapon against Napoleon; Wellington received the news of the French attack at Charleroi while he was at the ball, and calmly proceeded with his dinner. Princess Alice, Countess of Athlone, grand-daughter of Queen Victoria, met someone in her youth who had been present at the Waterloo Ball, and was still telling the story in the 1970s.

The 'Waterloo' Duchess brought the Gordon estates into the Richmond family, and eventually the re-creation of the Gordon dukedom, bestowed on her grandson. The Duke died in Canada of an agonising disease. He was infected by hydrophobia by a rabid fox, and the only way in which he could secure medical attention (not that that could have saved him) was to sail up the St Lawrence. The sight of that vast expanse of water brought on successive violent fits, yet he fought his impulses and made the journey which must have been a slow thumbscrew of pain to him. Eventually, he could take it no longer. He begged to be rowed to dry land, then ran full pelt as far from water as possible. He died in a forest barn.

The 5th Duke, his son, had a distinguished political career, was a cabinet minister, and was tipped as Prime Minister after Wellington. He was, yet again, much liked, frank and open, and adored by his tenantry, but Greville left us a picture of political blundering which is far from flattering. Greville allows that he was a very good debater, good-humoured, a "good fellow" and an excellent friend, and readily admits that his colleagues held him in high regard, but adds that in his view he was "utterly incapable". He goes on : "He has, in fact, that weight which a man can derive from being positive, obstinate, pertinacious, and busy, but his understanding lies in a nutshell, and his information in a pin's head." In one of the most consummate portraits of character, at which Greville is so singularly adept, he brings to life this amiable man in a few telling but impolite words : "He happens to have his wits, such as they are, about him . . . is prejudiced, narrow-minded, illiterate, and ignorant, good-looking, good-humoured, unaffected, tedious, prolix, unassuming, and a Duke."[132]

The 6th Duke (1818–1903) was a personal favourite with Queen Victoria, who created him Duke of Gordon in 1876 (only one other fresh dukedom has been created since that date, the dukedom of Fife). This means that the present holder of the title has more dukedoms than any of his colleagues in that dignity. He is a duke four times over, being Duke of Lennox, Duke of Gordon, and Duke of Aubigny as well as Duke of Richmond. Another distinction is the number of Knights of the Garter there have been in the family; out of only nine Dukes, the first seven were invested K.G.

The present Duke of Richmond, born in 1904, might with justice be called 'the reluctant Duke'. He was not meant to inherit the titles, being the third son of the 8th Duke, but his eldest brother died in infancy, and the second brother, who was destined to be the heir, was killed in Russia in 1919. So Frederick Gordon-Lennox found himself prospective landlord of 280,000 acres, when in truth he would have been perfectly happy as a garage mechanic.

Both he and his brother were fascinated by machines. It was the age when both the motor-car and the aeroplane were young and dangerous. Their grandfather, the old 7th Duke, was very disapproving and thought them little short of revolutionary to show interest in such unsuitable subjects. But "Freddie", on coming down from Oxford, worked in a car factory, on the shop floor, as plain "Mr Settrington". "It was the happiest time of my life," he says.

"Freddie March" was famous in the early thirties as a racing-car driver. Probably no one person did more to foster British amateur car-racing than he, who converted a wartime airfield at Goodwood into the only permanent racing-track in England. It was "permanent" until 1966, when the risks to spectators as speeds became greater forced him to abandon it.

The Duke was one of the first landed aristocrats to foresee the necessity of adapting to a more restricted life-style. The familiar story of successive death duties changed the prospects of Goodwood over a few years, with the 7th Duke dying in 1928, and the 8th Duke soon after in 1935. Gordon Castle in Scotland was sold, with thousands of acres, another Scottish estate of 45,000 acres in Banffshire was sold to the Crown in 1937; pictures, rare books, went under the hammer. All that was left was the estate at Goodwood, and even that had to be compressed after the war, when the Duke had to face the ultimate decision how to carry on living at Goodwood in changed circumstances. In common with his reforming ancestors, he solved the problem in a characteristically social-minded way. (He says, incidentally, that the social conscience of the Richmonds lay in abeyance for 100 years, and that he was brought up strictly to think of "us and them".)

The Duke established various industries at Goodwood, to bring income to the estate and employment to tenants. A thriving wood turnery, making anything from chair legs upwards, was started with one circular saw. Private companies were formed, of which Goodwood Estates Ltd is the chief, to run the industries, the racecourse, and the house. The Duke and his son, Lord March, are now both tenants of this company, in which neither has a major shareholding. One whole wing of Goodwood, containing thirty bedrooms, was converted into five well-appointed flats, and let to workers and staff at peppercorn rents; some other rooms were made into a working-man's club. The Duke established a private pension scheme for all tenants at his own expense.

In 1950 "Glorious Goodwood", which Greville thought combined everything that was enjoyable in life, was opened to the public (it had been open once a week since 1912). In 1958 the Duke moved out of Goodwood House to a small cottage on the estate, with six rooms, where he now lives with his wife and a staff of two old-age pensioners. His son, Lord March, lives in one wing of Goodwood House, and runs the family businesses, which continue to grow and diversify. It is a long journey from the coal tax, which gave the first Duke and his descendants an income from every ton of coal exported from the Tyne. This was sold to the government in 1800 for £728,333, and was finally abolished in 1831. There are, however, the Goodwood races (horses, not cars) which have been among the most celebrated since 1802. Goodwood has one of the only two privately owned racecourses in the country, the other being Ascot, which belongs to the Queen.

The Duke of Richmond has managed, in a quiet and unheralded way, to straddle the chasm between the aristocratic life to which he was born and the society of middle-class and working-class people with whom he has spent much of his life. He has worked in a factory, and has run a car business in London. In this he is not alone in the twentieth century, but he has been more successful, because it is in his blood. He does not see the difficulty, nor the incongruity, of entertaining the Queen and Prince Philip at Goodwood, and personally waiting upon one's charwoman when she is ill. His grandfather would have shuddered, and there are other ducal incumbents now who would shudder still. Richmond is an unpretentious man, of easy manners, amiable, charming, good company, with a sense of humour sometimes at his own expense, and helpful. Hervey's remark on the 2nd Duke, his ancestor, could be applied with equal felicity to him. He has inherited not only four dukedoms, but something more precious – the genes of a family of decent and benevolent people.

The Duke's mother, Dowager Duchess of Richmond, died in 1971, aged ninety-nine years and six months, probably another record. In 1928 the Duke married Miss Elizabeth Hudson, a vicar's daughter from Wendover, a choice which met with blank incomprehension from his grandfather, who suspected they would have to live 'over the shop'. While they live in Carne's Seat, the small cottage with a big view, their son and heir, Lord March, lives at Goodwood, where he has been more energetic than anyone else in his efforts to show the public what would be the effects of currently proposed legislation on beautiful country houses, and to convince them that he and other landowners are there not because it is nice to live in a grand house while other people live in slums, but because he feels he is a guardian of part of the country's heritage. Duty, not choice, impels him to protect Goodwood, in the knowledge that if he doesn't, nobody else will.

REFERENCES

1. John Evelyn, *Diary*, 4th February 1685.
2. *ibid*, August 1649.
3. Elizabeth D'Oyley, *James Duke of Monmouth*, p. 10; Lord George Scott, *Lucy Walter, Wife or Mistress*, pp. 27, 74.
4. D.N.B.
5. D'Oyley, 27.
6. D.N.B.
7. *Complete Peerage*.
8. Hartmann, *Charles II and Madame*, p. 73.
9. D'Oyley, 33.
10. D'Oyley, 266; Arthur Bryant, *King Charles II*, pp. 161, 283, 301.
11. Scott, 105–1.1; Baronne D'Aulnoy, *Memoirs of the Court of England in 1675*, p. 379; Lord Mersey, *A Picture of Life 1872–1940*, p. 236.
12. *Complete Peerage*, I, App. E, p. 478.
13. D'Oyley, 316.
14. D'Oyley, 316–21, and Verney MSS.
15. Reresby, *Memoirs* (1735), p. 10.
16. Paul Bloomfield, *Uncommon People, passim*.
17. Pepys *Diary*, ed. Wheatley, Vol. II, p. 69.
18. Pepys, II, 239.
19. Arthur Bryant, *Charles II*, pp. 146–152.
20. D.N.B.
21. D.N.B.
22. Pepys, VII, 50.
23. Coxe MSS, quoted in *Complete Peerage*.
24. Pepys, VII, 59.
25. *Complete Peerage*
26. Evelyn, 1st March 1671.
27. H. Montgomery Hyde, *History of Pornography*, p. 76.
28. *Complete Peerage*, III, 284 (c).
29. Howell's *State Trials* (1816), Vol. XIV, pp. 1327 *et seq*.
30. Jeanine Delpech, *Duchess of Portsmouth*, p. 194.
31. *Notes and Queries*, 6th Series, Vol. VIII, p. 176
32. Evelyn, ed. Bray (1850), II, 135.
33. H. Noel Williams, *Rival Sultanas*, p. 169.
34. *ibid.*, 173.
35. *ibid.*, 174.

36. Delpech, 89.
37. *ibid.*, 88, H. Forneron, *Louise de Kérouaille*, pp. 115–17.
38. Granger's *History* (1779), Vol. III, p. 211.
39. Peter Cunningham, *The Story of Nell Gwynn*, pp. 121, 202.
40. *ibid.*, 152.
41. *ibid.*, 135.
42. *ibid.*, 206.
43. *Genealogical Magazine*, January 1901.
44. Macky, *Characters*, (1704), p. 50.
45. Evelyn, 9th October 1671.
46. Osmund Airy, *Charles II*.
47. Forneron, 118; Williams, 166.
48. Donald Adamson and Peter Beauclerk Dewar, *The House of Nell Gwynn*, p. 6.
49. D.N.B.
50. Evelyn, 10th September 1675.
51. Delpech, 71–2.
52. Forneron, 277.
53. *ibid.*, 280.
54. Williams, 148; Delpech, 175; D.N.B.
55. Delpech, 137.
56. Evelyn, II, 195, 199.
57. Delpech, 160; Collins *Peerage*, I, 206.
58. *Hist. MSS. Comm.*, Frankland-Russell-Astley MSS, p. 58.
59. Mary Gladstone, *Diaries and Letters*, 21st September 1865.
60. *Complete Peerage*.
61. Walpole, XX, 137–8.
62. Roger Mortimer, *The Jockey Club*, p. 24.
63. W. M. Thackeray, *The Four Georges*, p. 85.
64. T. Raikes, *Journal*.
65. *The Life of William Wilberforce*, p. 303, quoted in *Complete Peerage*.
66. *Old and New London*, IV, 286; *Journal* of Elizabeth Lady Holland, II, 281; Burke, *Romantic Records of the Aristocracy*, II, 42; Wraxall, *Posthumous Memoirs*, II, 175.
67. *Old and New London*, IV, 334.
68. *ibid.*, IV, 54.
69. Greville I, 298; V. 202.
70. Lord Ernest Hamilton, *Forty Years On*, p. 130.
71. *Daily Telegraph*, 5th October 1973.
72. Chips Channon, *Diaries*, ed. Robert Rhodes James, p. 428.
73. Frances, Countess of Warwick, *Afterthoughts*, p. 49.

74. *Daily Express*, 20th October 1971.
75. *Complete Peerage*.
76. Waldegrave, *Memoirs*, p. 114.
77. Walpole, XXI, 78–9.
78. *Correspondence* between Frances, Countess of Hertford and the Countess of Pomfret (1805), Vol. II, pp. 98–101.
79. Walpole, XVIII, 273.
80. *ibid.*, XVII, 174.
81. Sir Charles Hanbury Williams, *Works* (1822), Vol. I, p. 252.
82. *The Orrery Papers*, ed. Countess of Cork and Orrery (1903), Vol. II, p. 294.
83. *Chatsworth Collections*, 228.9 (23rd November 1736).
84. *ibid.*, 228.2 (18th September 1735).
85. *ibid.*, 228.14.
86. Walpole, XVIII, 255.
87. Massey, *History of England*, I, 189.
88. *The Spectator*, 12th November 1898.
89. *Letters of Junius* (1797), Vol. I, pp. 77–9.
90. Wraxall, *Historical Memoirs*, p. 273.
91. *Town and Country* (1769), Vol. I, p. 114.
92. Walpole, *Memoirs of the Reign of George III*, Vol. IV, p. 47.
93. Public Record Office, DPP 1, 95/4, 95/5.
94. *Complete Peerage*.
95. Walpole, XXI, 172.
96. Adamson and Dewar, *The House of Nell Gwynn*, p. 49.
97. *ibid.*, 54.
98. Sir Percy Croft, *The Abbey of Kilkhampton*, quoted in *Complete Peerage*.
99. Lady Harriet Cavendish, *Letters*, p. 36.
100. Adamson and Dewar, *op. cit.*, pp. 97–9.
101. *The Times*, 8th August 1837.
102. *Old and New London*, IV, 280.
103. Mrs Barron-Wilson, *Memoirs of Miss Mellon* (1886), Vol. II, p. 171.
104. Creevey *Papers*, II, 120.
105. Creevy, *Life and Times*, p. 266.
106. Broughton, *Recollections of a Long Life*, Vol. III, p. 203.
107. Lockhart, *Life of Sir Walter Scott*, Vol. VIII, p. 116.
108. Adamson and Dewar, *op. cit.*, p. 135.
109. *Lady Holland to Her Son*, p. 65.
110. *ibid.*, p. 71.
111. Barron-Wilson, *op. cit.*, p. 175.

112. *Old and New London*, V, 398.
113. *Lady Holland to Her Son*, 116.
114. Adamson and Dewar, *op. cit.*, 144.
115. Barron-Wilson, *op. cit.*, 184.
116. Creevey *Papers*, II, 217.
117. *The Times*, 8th August 1837.
118. *Old and New London*, IV, 281.
119. Adamson and Dewar, *op.cit.*, 189.
120. *ibid.*, 190.
121. Hervey, *Memoirs*, I, 252.
122. Walpole, XVII, 184.
123. *Lord Hervey and His Friends*, p. 100.
124. Earl of March, *A Duke and His Friends* (1911); *Lord Hervey and His Friends*, p. 137.
125. Walpole, *George III*, I, 20; Wraxall, *Hist. Mem.*, 371.
126. *Hist. MSS. Comm.*, Abergavenny MSS, p. 31.
127. *Correspondence of Charles James Fox*, Vol. I, p. 455.
128. Alison Olson, *The Radical Duke*.
129. Walpole, XXIX, 54.
130. *Private Letters of Sir Robert Peel*, p. 34.
131. Mrs Trench, *Remains*, p. 406.
132. Greville, I, 284; II, 399.

3. The Maverick

Duke of Bedford

John Russell, 13th Duke of Bedford, known to family and friends as Ian, is undoubtedly the maverick among dukes of the realm. Without apology and with entire success, he has exploited his title for the sake of his home, and has been seen to do so with unabashed relish. Bedford is now a world-famous showman who enjoys the kind of popularity usually accorded only to film stars. He has, indeed, appeared in several films, made countless television appearances, and pays his dues to Equity, the actors' union. Visitors to Woburn Abbey, his magnificent seat in Bedfordshire (pronounced "Wooburn", by the way), would receive the Duke's autograph whether they asked for it or not, and often were allowed, not to say encouraged, to shake the ducal hand. Such relentless exhibitionism has made Bedford the best known of the dukes, allowed him to live comfortably at Woburn, and rescued him from the parallel scourges of a cold manner and an obsessive shyness which are characteristic of his family.

Lord William Russell, brother to the 7th Duke and to Lord John Russell, the Prime Minister, wrote these words in his diary: "I think if all the hearts of all the Russells were put together, they would not yet make one good heart. Good God, how the Duke freezes one. I envy him not his possessions, and would not accept them, were I obliged to take his character with them."[1] And that was his own brother. The other brother, Lord John, suffered from the same freezing manner. Often ungracious, and sometimes offensive, he was involved in squabbles which were provoked by the Russell inability to make friends, and their tendency to sulk when thwarted. Queen Victoria developed a powerful aversion to him, and Greville wrote: "He is not conciliatory, and he sometimes gives grievous offence . . . he is miserably wanting in amenity, and in the small arts of acquiring popularity."[2] The same could not be said of the present Duke, who must have had to hold his ground against a tidal wave of inherited reticence and coldness surging within him to achieve the popularity that he now enjoys. His father, Hastings the 12th Duke, was the only son of the 11th Duke and his duchess, yet he was never invited, as a child, to join his parents for breakfast. He would appear in the dining-room where they breakfasted in silence (the Duke hardly uttered a word all his life, and the Duchess was stone-deaf so would not have heard him if he had), and would stand in the corner, until his father dismissed him with the words, "Tavistock, you may leave now." (The eldest son of the Duke of Bedford carries the title by courtesy of Marquess of Tavistock.) This same Duke was visited by his grandson, the present Duke, when his wife died in 1937. It was an attempt by the boy to show compassionate affection for the old man in his bereavement. But he was not expected; no appointment had been made, and the "audience" was suitably brief – five minutes. The boy was not invited to stay for lunch, so he returned by train to London.[3] Generations of Russells have clumsily repelled affectionate approaches, not only from outside the family, but from each other. There never was a more unhappy succession of hostilities between fathers and sons. The present Duke had all filial attachment severed by a monstrously impersonal childhood; he grew intensely to dislike his father, who in his turn heartily despised Ian. For years there was no contact between them at all, the 12th Duke preferring to pretend that his lamentable son did not exist. The 12th Duke, Hastings, did not speak to his father Herbrand, the 11th Duke, for more than twenty years; Herbrand professed to be disgusted by his son's militant pacifism, which he thought was a disgrace to the family, but the real reason for their estrangement was the congenital Russell coldness. Hastings had been naturally fond of his father in infancy, but this incipient affection was atrophied by the touch of ice, and it ruined his whole life.

The 9th Duke, also called Hastings, son of the Lord William Russell whose reflections above on Russell coldness introduced the topic, shows in his heart-rending letters an eager love for his father and a desperate adolescent desire to please him. As Mrs Blakiston has noted, "the battering his affectionate nature received from both his parents wrings the heart".[4] He grew into such a stiff, formal, loveless old man that he ended his life a morose and sullen hypochondriac. (He and his duchess were commonly called "The Icebergs".) The Duke gradually withdrew into dark misanthropy, unwilling to believe anything good of anyone; his only pleasure lay in congratulating himself that he had seen through the evils of mankind while everyone else remained unenlightened – a prophet of doom, in other words. Disraeli told Queen Victoria that Bedford was "a strange character. He enjoys his power and prosperity, and yet seems to hold a lower opinion of human nature than any man . . . a joyous cynic."[5] Hardly joyous; he ended by killing himself.

No less strange was his predecessor, the 8th Duke (cousin to the 9th and son of the 7th), whom Lord Grey found "the most impenetrable person I ever met with. More silent even than a Russell, it is impossible to get a word out of him."[6] He was then twenty-five years old. The poor young man sank deeper and deeper into his protective silence until he became a total recluse. For years, nobody so much as caught a glimpse of him, as the rare excursions he made from his London house were inside a completely dark carriage with the shutters down so that no light could penetrate.[7] "Let me live always among the chimney-pots," he used to say.[8]

Cold, abnormally shy and diffident, with a tendency to hypochondria and a deeply suspicious nature, the Russells have not been the easiest family to know. They have not been able to see others except as threats to their trembling personalities, as underminers of their cherished opinions, or as a danger to their precious health. This has made them obstinate in debate to the point of pig-headedness. The 7th Duke, in yet another example of endemic fraternal disloyalty, told Greville that his brother Lord John Russell was "very obstinate and unmanageable, and does not like to be found fault with or told things which run counter to his own ideas".[9] These precise words would fittingly describe Herbrand, 11th Duke; William Lord Russell ("the patriot"), whose obstinacy led to his execution; the 9th Duke, who thought himself unloved; the 8th who was terrified of meeting people; the 5th, of whom Sydney Smith said, "a peculiarity of the Russells is that they never alter their opinions".[10] Even the present Duke, whose stubbornness allowed him to retain Woburn as his home against all the advice of his trustees (who would have given it to the National Trust), may be said to inherit the Russell persistence. But the distillation of a dozen generations of Russells was achieved in that fascinating character the 12th Duke (1888–1953), father to the now Duke of Bedford, who was, like his son, the maverick of his time, though in an entirely different fashion.

Hastings Russell made an inauspicious entry into the world. His mother and father were walking across the windy Scottish moors when Lady Herbrand Russell (as she then was, her husband succeeding his brother as Duke much later) suddenly realised that her baby was about to be born. There was no time to reach home. The couple made for a derelict shepherd's cottage where, with no assistance save for the inexpert attention of two farmhands, the future Duke was born on a rough bed of heather.[11] His mother never recovered from the experience, remaining resolute in her refusal to have more children. She resented the trouble that he had given her, and was a neglectful "busy" mother whose energies were channelled into her cherished hospital work and, later, her flying, leaving none for the lonely son who stood in the corner at breakfast, waiting to be dismissed. He did not see another child until he was packed off to Eton at the age of thirteen. Inevitably, Hastings developed an odd, unorthodox personality. With all the disadvantages of the withdrawn Russell temperament in his blood, and the bonus of a deaf mother who did not pay him any attention and did not hear his plaintive questions, there was little chance of his being normal and healthy.

All his life, Hastings was consumed with self-loathing. Having been told as a child that he was a bother and a nuisance, he quickly assented, and spent the rest of his life considering that he was of little worth. Morbidly sensitive, and easily hurt, his instinct was to deflect attention away from himself, his personality, his intimate concerns, and direct it on to some other object. Hence his absorption in committee work, his active support of all manner of societies and associations for the underprivileged, the neglected, the minorities such as the Discharged Prisoners' Aid Society. His blind dedication to causes carried the implication that they were all more worthy of attention than he. His whole life was an exercise in self-effacement and self-abasement. As a conscientious objector, he would take no part in military tasks during the war, preferring to indulge his masochistic delight in menial work. He felt keenly his responsibility to do something for the war effort, and was happiest scrubbing floors or washing up in Y.M.C.A. canteens, which he did anonymously.[12] Secretly, he thought that was all he deserved.

Such deep, dark sourness and self-deprecation as this led very easily to an intensely religious turn of mind. He did not go to church, and went so far as to withdraw the Bedford obligations to finance the church at Woburn (a scandal since redressed by his son), but he embraced unorthodox sects which preached the very values his life most conspicuously lacked – friendliness, brotherhood, trust – and of course the supreme virtue of self-sacrifice. He was an active Quaker for more than twenty years.

The first indication that "Spinach", to give him his nickname, was destined to be rebellious was his pacifist activities in World War I, an example of quixotic thinking which exasperated his traditionalist and orthodox father, and led to a complete severance of relations between them. Duke Herbrand considered that "Spinach" had brought shame to the Bedford name, and never forgave him. He deigned to have contact with him once, when the time came, some twenty-five years later, for the old Duke and his son to conspire together to deprive the grandson, Ian, whom neither of them liked, of his inheritance.[13] The filial distrust of the Russells can be broken only by a yet stronger filial distrust.

"Spinach" held that the participation of Christian people in war was immoral. But the real motive for his pacifism sprang from a Russell trait which he inherited and of which his life was the supreme expression, a profound distrust of human nature. He thought that people, left to their own devices, were more bad than good, and that it was in the natural order of things that they should treat each other badly, and eventually make war upon each other. This feeling, for it was that rather than a belief – it ran in the blood – was not much more than an extension of his feeling that he himself was essentially "bad" unless spiritually guided. With such an underlying misanthropy, it is no wonder that he distrusted everyone with whom he came into contact. Like all his predecessors, he was always on the alert for someone to put him down, trick him, or betray his weakness. He was intensely suspicious. Those who knew him reasonably well affirm that he was the saddest man they ever met.

The Duke was often accused, by his son among others, of being opinionated. Like Lord John Russell, he could not listen to any view that did not agree with his own. But this was his only protection against the humiliation which he always feared was imminent and crushing. He would make speeches in the House of Lords setting forth a usually outrageous point of view, guaranteed at least to be against the majority, and then would leave the chamber without listening for any riposte from his fellow peers; timidity drove him out, not rudeness. The Lords were generally so offended by the Duke's views that they passed resolutions that "the Duke of Bedford be no longer heard", which had little effect, as he had already left by then. On one occasion there were cries of "Lock him up" in the Commons when his name was mentioned.[14] He would have liked nothing better, of course. He was continually disappointed in his desire for martyrdom.

He was labelled a Fascist and a Communist, neither of which was accurate, and there is a dim memory of him now as an eccentric who had to be kept quiet and out of trouble. Yet the views which the 12th Duke expressed were eccentric only because they were not held by the majority. There was little in them that was truly revolutionary. He brushed the sleeve of socialism, but never seized its hand. He was sincere and honest at a time when hypocrites abounded. He raised the matter (in the Lords), for example, of conscientious objectors and their unjustified persecution, with particular reference to an ex-miner who had been sent to a military hospital although he was perfectly sane. "As long as this persecution is allowed to continue it is nonsense for the Prime Minister to say that victimisation and man-hunting are odious to the British people. It is all too obvious that they are extremely agreeable to a section of the British people, including members of the tribunals and members of Parliament."[15] Such views seemed grossly unpatriotic, even treacherous, when the country was staggering from four and a half years of war, but they were not the less sensible for that. Most people accept the evils of war with a shrug; Bedford would not accept them. Sometimes he was led by his frustration into sheer folly. He maintained that Hitler would behave himself if we were to treat him with friendliness. The Lord Chancellor said that he was mad, and that he had "a capacity to swallow any yarn which supported his jaundiced views".[16] But the Duke of Westminster thought that he was the bravest man in England to stand up and express views which he knew excited the hostility of everyone in the Chamber.[17]

The Duke would have agreed with his ancestor Lord William Russell, who in 1839 wrote: "I sometimes see much weakness and hypocrisy in those who are honoured, and such firmness and goodness in those who are reviled, that I lose all respect for human judgement."[18] Hastings was reviled, and he certainly had no respect for human judgement. He knew that he was considered a heretic and a crank, but took comfort in the knowledge that he was right and everyone else was wrong. It is a comfort which has sustained the Russells for centuries, making political leaders of some, and martyrs of others.

His deep suspicion of human motives and his fear that everyone was intent upon his humiliation ultimately·led Duke Hastings into the very humiliation which he wanted most to avoid. Obstinacy, stubbornness, vanity and self-righteousness were to blame for his distasteful court case in 1935, when his estranged wife petitioned him for restitution of conjugal rights. She claimed that he had deserted her. He admitted that he had left her, but maintained that he was justified in refusing to cohabit with her, as she had displayed an "intimate and clandestine affection" for the children's tutor, Mr Cecil Squire. (There were three children.) It was typical of Hastings that he accused his wife not of adultery, but, in effect, of being disloyal and unkind to him. He and his wife, who were Marquess and Marchioness of Tavistock at this time, had lived in the same house with Mr Squire for some years. Their eldest son, Ian, was now a teenager. Squire had been an old acquaintance of the Marquess, and it was he who had introduced him into the family home. At first, they lived together quite well, but then Squire's influence over Lady Tavistock began to irk Lord Tavistock, and aroused his jealousy. Lady Tavistock was converted by Squire to Anglo-Catholicism, in direct opposition to her husband's wishes. Struggling hard to be reasonable, he accepted this as an expression of justifiable religious independence. Then Squire objected to some of Tavistock's weird friends (and he was surrounded by the most unscrupulous sycophants who exploited his shortcomings and flattered his misanthropy by loudly asserting that he was right and wise to distrust human duplicity; they told him what he most wanted to hear). Squire had gone so far as to refuse entry to the house to some of these objectionable people, who had been invited by Tavistock himself. Tavistock never smoked or drank, and would not allow tobacco or alcohol into the house; Squire introduced them both, further irritating the long-suffering Marquess.

Poor Hastings was certainly difficult to handle. His colossal sense of Christian duty, his piety and self-pity, were like the rock of Sisyphus to his family. His wife was not allowed pretty clothes because they were "worldly". To have a meal with him was an ordeal : as he would not allow smoke or drink, could not indulge in small talk, had no sense of humour, the hours dragged by in long silences interrupted by pious utterances. It is little wonder that Mr Squire took pity on the deprived Marchioness and strove to usher some more human lightness and cheerfulness into the house. But it is also no surprise that the deeply vulnerable Hastings should become more and more tetchy as his once adoring wife was taken from him to obey the counsel of another. He felt hurt and betrayed. Life between them became impossible. He received anonymous letters suggesting that his wife was having an affair with Squire, and that he was being made a fool of. He said in court that she refused him intercourse. Eventually, he left her.

Letters from Lord Tavistock to his wife and to Squire were read out in court. He conquered his jealousy when writing to Squire, and forced himself to be rational and calm. He enjoyed self-sacrifice. But his letter to his wife was less well controlled; he was obviously very hurt, lonely, and abandoned. It is a pathetic letter, crying out for gentleness. In court, Lady Tavistock refused to cease her friendship with Squire, a condition for the return of her husband, and her petition was dismissed. Hastings had won, but at what cost to his emotions. He was thereafter embittered and disillusioned. The black despair which ran through all his public speeches and led ultimately to his death was fuelled by this public betrayal, itself made inevitable by his quirky personality. The hearing had taken six days.[19]

Much later, his son wrote to him : "Underneath your Christian cloak lies a small, narrow, mean mind, incapable of forgiveness, generosity or feeling."[20] This is itself an ungenerous assessment. Poor "Spinach" was a tortured introspective misfit. His grandson, the present Lord Tavistock, has fond memories of his impulsive, impressive generosity towards children.

The Russells' desire to protect themselves from enemies, usually near rather than far, has engendered a family propensity towards hypochondria. When trouble brews, the first remedy of a Russell is to fall ill. The 7th Duke (1788–1861) was doing it all the time. His brother wrote in 1823 : ". . . as for Tavistock it is shocking to see him, he is a perfect skeleton, I never saw a man so altered in my life," and then adds, significantly, "Yeats thinks it is disordered functions – nothing organic."[21] Nowadays, we might make the same diagnosis with a different word – psychosomatic.

His son, the 8th Duke (1809–1872), was such a hypochondriac that he cloistered himself away from the world, refusing all contact, and hardly ever went out of the house. It has already been noted that the last years of his life were so heavily protected that no one saw him. His cousin, Hastings 9th Duke of Bedford (1819–1891), actually shot himself in a fit of depression over a bout of pneumonia; the inquest recorded a verdict that he killed himself while "temporarily insane".[22]

His namesake, Hastings 12th Duke of Bedford, once again represents the extreme point to which this obsession with disease may lead. Woburn Abbey was permanently sprayed with a germ-killer during his dukedom, so that it smelled antiseptic. His fear of contamination by germs had some risible results. He changed his underclothes three times a day, and carried a huge bottle of T.C.P. tablets in his pocket; whenever anyone coughed or sneezed he immediately sucked a lozenge.[23] His mother, Mary Duchess of Bedford, was so fascinated by disease that she became nurse and surgeon, and founded a hospital at Woburn, where she spent most of her waking hours. She would eagerly take visitors to see her latest "case".

So withdrawn have the Russells been from affectionate human contact that they have tended to look to animals for a more trustworthy response. Animals do not let you down, they do not betray or use you, they are not responsible for the evil which pervades the world, they will not tell you your faults or find you wanting; in short, they are safer. Duke Hastings was constantly writing letters to newspapers on such abstruse subjects as the house fly, the caterpillar, moles, or pigeons; he collected spiders; he was said to recognise by sight every one of the 300 deer at Woburn with whom he communed on long solitary walks, and he formed close ties with the golden carp whom he amused regularly.[24] When disgusted with human treachery, or what he saw as blind human adhesion to mistaken concepts, Hastings would repair to his animals; he would trust any creature more readily than he would a man. Nor was this a mere dilettante interest; he was an accomplished writer in the fields of animal and insect welfare. His father, Duke Herbrand, loved and cherished his herd of rare deer at Woburn, and was President of the Royal Zoological Society. Meetings of the Society were the only events which would tempt him to leave Woburn, where he, too, lived secluded and remote from the hustle and danger of human contact. The present Duke has made Woburn into one of the country's most famous safari parks, in which he shows an interest which cannot be merely commercial. He, too, is a Russell.

After the war, Hastings the 12th Duke withdrew more and more from the public eye, whose gaze he never enjoyed anyway, and betook himself to his lonely retreat at Endsleigh, the family property in Devon. There he communed with his animals and insects, and occasionally went for an early-morning shoot. "Spinach" had been fond from childhood of shooting, as had all his ancestors, and the paradox of killing creatures whom he professed to love did not appear to trouble him. He was an expert shot. One autumn morning in 1953 he went for his usual shoot and did not return. The next day he was found dead, lying in thick undergrowth with a 12-bore shotgun across his chest. The safety-catch was in the firing position, and the right barrel had been fired. At the inquest, the family solicitor, Connolly Gage, suggested that the Duke must have been sitting cross-legged waiting for something, have pulled the gun towards him, caught the trigger on some branches and been unable to prevent its firing. This hypothesis was heard, and a verdict of accidental death was returned. It is, to say the very least, improbable, and few people would now accept it.

The Duke was known to be depressed. The few friends in whom he had placed his trust, against the vociferous advice of everyone else, were revealed to be unworthy. His life had been a succession of disillusionments, as the fundamental duplicity of human kind impressed itself upon his sensitive soul. His marriage had been a disaster, his son a disappointment. In true Russell style, he had severed all connection with this son, save for the occasional distant letter. Even his religion ceased to be a solace. He was not the sort of man to shoot himself by accident, even supposing he could have done so in a sitting position. Suicide must remain the most logical and likely verdict.

Had he lived another eleven weeks, the seven-year term necessary to prevent prohibitive death duties devolving upon his unfortunate son would have expired. He cannot have been ignorant of this important fact, though his son thinks he simply miscalculated and got his dates wrong; he killed himself thinking that all arrangements were in order. He was vague about such matters anyway. On the other hand, I have heard it said in other ducal families that he left a note indicating spite as his motive.

The 12th Duke of Bedford was the last in the family to meet with a violent end, although the family history is not wanting in precedents. His daughter-in-law, the Marchioness of Tavistock (first wife of the present Duke before he succeeded to the dukedom), died as the result of an overdose of sodium amatol tablets, self-administered, in 1945. Her husband testified that she had not slept properly for ten days. An open verdict was recorded.[25]

The 12th Duke's mother, Mary Duchess of Bedford, also died in mysterious circumstances. She was an unconventional duchess, discarding the family jewels early in her married life to plunge into a life of active nursing. She established, staffed and ran a cottage hospital at Woburn, and turned it into a war hospital in 1914, with the grudging financial support of her strange and brooding husband. She became a skilled radiologist and sometimes surgeon as well as nurse, noting with satisfaction in her diary: "I here place on record that I today amputated a toe and excised a painful scar in the sole of the foot for Leslie Coop, of Handsworth, Birmingham."[26] The present Duchess is quoted on the subject of her pioneering predecessor – "Anyone 'ave a leetle pain, she open 'im up and 'ave a leetle look. Very medical."[27]

The Duchess suffered from the most appalling buzzing in the ears which rendered her almost totally deaf. She attributed this affliction to a youthful attack of typhoid fever in India. Whatever the cause, her deafness accounted for her loud, clear and commanding voice, which made her lonely son tremble so, and for her apparent indifference to his existence; what he thought was remoteness derived simply from her inability to hear him when he spoke to her. It was not until her husband told their son that he never wanted to see him again that she showed him how much she loved him by bursting into tears; he was shocked and dismayed, having thought such emotion utterly foreign to her.[28]

One day, the Duchess discovered that high altitudes in aeroplanes brought relief to the buzzing pain in her head which she described as "like railway trains rushing through stations";[29] that was the beginning of a new passion which was to make her famous throughout the land. Already in her sixties, the Duchess of Bedford became, of all things, a pilot. Duke Herbrand did not approve; this was worse, if possible, than cutting people up in hospital. But he acquiesced under protest, reserving the right to cut out every account of an air disaster from his newspaper, which he would place silently on her desk. His gentle remonstrance was not effective, however, and she flung herself with joy into her new pursuit. She built runways at Woburn, she flew with a co-pilot to South Africa and back, her adventures were avidly collected by the newspapers. She was something of a folk-heroine. She belonged to the British public, while her isolated son grew further and further away.

In 1937 Duke Herbrand told her that he could no longer afford to finance the hospital which was so dear to her heart. (He could, of course, have afforded a hundred hospitals, with wealth which would now appear fabulous.) The news depressed her terribly. It is not known what conversations passed between them, but she was seen to be unhappy for days afterwards. She was seventy-one years old, and still deaf. Her only son was a stranger to her, and an enemy to his father. When she took off in her de Havilland Gipsy from the hangar at Woburn on 22nd March she waved goodbye to her flight lieutenant and to her rigger, a gesture she had never before made, and which was not customary among flyers. She was not seen again.

The Duchess was no amateur pilot. She had experience of flying in all kinds of weathers, and had completed almost 200 hours of solo flying. There was no reason why an accident should occur.

There had been an occasion three years earlier when she and her flight lieutenant had come close to death in Morocco. She afterwards recorded in her diary: "I am persuaded that, when faced with apparently certain death in this way, one does not experience the terror which those who do not live to tell are supposed to feel . . . I thought it quite an agreeable way of finishing up compared with most ends which are the lot of man, and certainly the one I had most desired; for, with not a boat in sight and a very rough sea, the process could not have lasted long."[30]

The Duchess's suicide is by no means unlikely. Four days later parts of the aircraft were washed up, but her body was never found. A Captain Riley sighted the decomposed remains of an airwoman floating in the sea eleven miles off Cromer on 28th June; this was more than three months after her disappearance. He thought she was dressed in khaki flying kit, but since the family said she was not wearing khaki that day, it was concluded that the body could not have been that of the Duchess.[31]

The country mourned a colourful extravagant character. She must have been one of the first women to motor alone along the roads of Bedfordshire, an outrageous display of noncomformity in the early part of this century, and she was quite capable of carrying out her own repairs to motor-car or aircraft. Her starchy husband, whose feet were still held fast in the nineteenth century, pretended not to notice his wife's antics. She was adventurous and courageous, and possessed the blissful resources of a sense of humour, so helpful in her dealings with the dour family into which she had married. Here is her quiet diary entry for 8th August 1929, when she and her co-pilot were offered some unappetising food in a dingy dismal room in Aleppo. "He broke open a roll and I saw him looking very closely at his plate, and to my horror discovered that all the rolls were swarming with black ants inside. However, though I cannot say I felt 'none the worse', the black ants did not actively disagree with our digestion, and I only suffered mentally."[32]

We have already seen that the 9th Duke of Bedford (1819–1891) took his own life in a fit of depression arising from ill-health. Briefly to trace his progress from enthusiastic childhood to miserable old age is to see how each Russell generation smothers and stifles the brightness and gaiety of the one that follows. The 9th Duke was born Hastings Russell, first son of Lord and Lady William Russell. He was called Hastings after the Marquess of Hastings, a relation on his mother's side. (He must not be confused with the other Hastings in the family, the pacifist and enigmatic 12th Duke, about whom we have already said much.) His grandfather was the 6th Duke, his uncle became the 7th Duke, and his cousin was the 8th.

Young Hastings was something of a prodigy – intelligent, entertaining, as bright as a button. When he was seven years old, Lady Holland wrote: "As to Hastings he is without exception the most pleasing, promising child I ever saw, full of *sense* beside his acquirements, with all his father's courage, manliness and gentleness; not in the least spoiled, well-behaved and tractable." His father wrote proudly of him, "Lord Holland will not be able to say (as he does of the Russells) that he is like an otter, or that he never speaks, for he is handsome and jabbers like a magpie – he has all the quickness & *esprit* of his mother, & is quite a little prodigy . . . he is master of little Lieven & thumps him till he cries." His mother was no less lyrical in describing the charms of her first-born : "he speaks French like d'Alembert & English like Johnson – neither lisps, stammers, nor mispronounces, is quick, gay, passionate, good-hearted, gentle, ingenious, ruddy, bright-eyed, blue-eyed – fat, strong & healthy . . . if Lord Chesterfield had had such a son he need not have written his book."

Hastings grew up on the continent, with his mother and two brothers, to whom he was very close, and where he was very popular. He became in his adolescence an unusually good shot. He was liked and admired. What, then, went wrong? His parents grew apart from each other and quarrelled frequently by letter. All their own failings were heaped on to the young man's shoulders in their arguments – each parent saw him as living proof of the shortcomings of the other. His mother, Lady William, wrote to her brother-in-law Lord John, when Hastings was twenty-seven years old : "You must repress his excessive arrogance . . . He has erroneous notions of being heir apparent and is overbearing to a degree quite painful . . . He is quite altered, exceedingly insolent . . . compromised both by ill-temper and covetousness." The young man received letters in this vein from his mother, which quite dismayed and bewildered him. He wrote to his father : "I want encouragement & not rebuffs. Without a little vanity [self-esteem] nothing would be done in this world and to be constantly told by one's own Mother that one is an Idiot, a coward & liar is very disheartening."[33] One hundred years later, Mary Duchess of Bedford was writing of her pacifist son, the other Hastings : "I never thought I should be the mother of a coward."[34]

Discouraged and rejected by his mother, whom he adored, Hastings's naturally affectionate and bubbling personality withered and withdrew. He was no longer talkative in adulthood, but uncomfortably shy and retiring. He settled into the Russell mould of an obstinate, self-protecting recluse, obsessed by health. On 14th January 1891 he shot himself through the heart in an access of bad temper, delirium or insanity (no one is sure which) in his house at 81 Eaton Square; he was suffering from pneumonia at the time.

Hastings had married Lady Elizabeth Sackville-West, daughter of Lord de la Warr, and was father of both the 10th and 11th Dukes of Bedford, and grandfather of Hastings 12th Duke. One of his daughters, Lady Ela Russell, who died in 1936, was apt to talk to herself. Guests who overstayed their welcome at her house would hear her exclaim, in a loud whisper, "I wish they'd go! I wish they'd go!"[35]

Two members of the family have been murdered, one judicially and the other for money, and both were called William Russell. Lord William Russell (1767–1840) will have to be called "old" Lord William to avoid confusion with the other Lord William who was father to Hastings the 9th Duke. He was a son of the 4th Duke, and both the 5th and 6th Dukes were his brothers. "Old" Lord William was murdered by his Swiss valet, François Courvoisier, on 5th May 1840. The murder caused a commotion among the aristocracy. Greville wrote : "The extraordinary murder of Lord Wm. Russell . . . has excited a prodigious interest, and frightened all London out of its wits . . . half the world go to sleep expecting to have their throats cut before morning."[36] Greville doubted that the evidence was conclusive, but Courvoisier was found guilty on 20th June and two days later confessed to the crime. At his execution on 6th July there was a crowd of over 20,000 people.

On 21st July 1683 there took place the public execution at Lincoln's Inn Fields of William, Lord Russell, son of the 5th Earl of Bedford. His name was William Russell, but being the son of an earl and not of a duke (the dukedom was not created until later), he had no right to the appellation "Lord William". He did, however, inherit the courtesy title of "Lord Russell" on the death of his brother Francis (yet another hypochondriac) in 1678. Hence he is known to history as "William, Lord Russell" and must not be mistaken for the two "Lord William Russells" that we have so far considered. William, Lord Russell, was one of the most illustrious members of the family. He lived at a time when the Russells were closely involved in the political destiny of the country, and had been so for 150 years. He is commonly known to posterity as "the patriot", yet it was for high treason that he was executed.

William was a nonconformist in the Russell tradition. A fervent Protestant, he feared most that the King, Charles II, would fall under the influence of the "papists"; the King's brother and heir, the Duke of York, was openly suspected of being a Roman Catholic, which, to a Russell, meant that he had just stepped up from Hell. Something of a Puritan, Russell was also disgusted with the dissoluteness and extravagance of the Court. He proposed in the House of Commons that there should be a committee to consider "the sad and deplorable condition we are in, and the apprehensions we are under of popery and a standing army". He later proposed that the House should pass legislation to prevent a popish successor, and was the loudest supporter of the Exclusion Bill, which sought to disable the Duke of York from inheriting the crown. Lord Russell and the Duke of York were henceforth locked in a bitter fight, which had perforce to end with the downfall of one of them.

Lord Russell was supported by his intelligent and beautiful wife Rachel, one of the most engaging and important of the Russell wives, and as anti-papist as her husband. It was one of the few Russell marriages which worked. She had been born Rachel Wriothesley, daughter of the 4th Earl of Southampton, and therefore granddaughter of the Earl of Southampton who was Shakespeare's patron. (It is interesting to reflect that the present Duke of Bedford is descended in part from the friend to whom Shakespeare addressed most of his sonnets.) Rachel and her sisters were co-heirs to the Southampton estates, and Rachel received as her portion the lucrative Bloomsbury property which she had brought into the Bedford family. It is often said that all Bedfords are ruled by their wives, and this wife was certainly the driving-force behind William, who had integrity rather than initiative.

William and Rachel Russell held political meetings at Southampton House in London (later called Bedford House and now demolished) at which the early Whigs devised their strategy. The Russells earned a reputation for political extremism, which prejudiced the public against them when the time came for William's integrity to be tested.

Some of his political allies were responsible for a plan to assassinate the King and his brother the Duke of York as they drove past the Rye House on their way from Newmarket to Westminster. This became known as the "Rye House Plot", and the name of William, Lord Russell, was implicated by an informer. As a result, he was arrested (on 26th June 1683) and sent to the Tower pending his trial for high treason, although according to Macaulay the plot had been carefully kept from him. The trial took place on 13th July at the Old Bailey. That same morning one of Russell's most intimate friends and a political ally, the Earl of Essex, was found dead in the Tower. The suspicion of suicide did nothing to help the tense, susspenseful atmosphere in court, at what has since become one of the most famous trials ever to be held at the Old Bailey. There were nine judges, and amongst the counsel for the Crown was the up-and-coming, notorious Jeffries.

Russell pleaded "not guilty", maintained that he had not been present at the meeting which hatched the Rye House Plot, and stood firm on the principle that it should sometimes be permissible to resist a sovereign for the greater good of the people. Wiffen describes the scene in the florid prose fashionable among historians of the nineteenth century :

"With a serenity that excited the highest admiration, Lord Russell appeared at the bar of the Old Bailey. Every hardship that could be inflicted by angry and vindictive enemies, the steady patriot was doomed that day to bear. Even before he opened his lips in his defence, he was treated by Sawyer, the attorney-general, like a guilty felon. His request for the delay of a few hours, till his witnesses might arrive in town, though twice pleaded for by the chief justice, with a shew of compassion, was absolutely negatived. His right to the challenge of such jurors as possessed no freehold, was questioned, was impugned, was over-ruled. The death of his friend, Lord Essex . . . was tortured into an incontestable proof of guilt, and made . . . to press upon him with its extraneous and cumulative weight. He at length requested pens and an amanuensis. To prevent his having the aid of counsel, Sawyer said he might employ a *servant.* 'Any of your servants', said Pemberton, 'shall assist in writing for you.' '*Two*,' said the generous Jeffries, 'he may have *two* !' 'My wife,' said Lord Russell, the heart of the husband and the father rising to his tongue, 'my wife is here, my Lord, to do it !' The by-standers turned, and saw the daughter of the most virtuous minister whom Charles had ever possessed or disregarded, take her station at the table; and pity, shame and sorrow, and holy reverence, and thrilling indignation, touched by turns the soul of everyone who had a heart to feel for his country or himself, for wounded virtue or for violated freedom."[37]

Amongst hubbub and disorder and protest, William was found guilty and sentenced to death. The King later commuted this to simple beheading, a cleaner death more befitting a nobleman. The Duke of York wanted the execution to take place outside Lord Russell's own front door, but this sadistic vengeance was not granted.

In the few days before he was due to be executed, Russell, his family and friends, made frantic efforts to save him. Russell wrote to the King, and to the Duke of York; his wife Rachel herself delivered this letter to the Duchess of York. His father, the old Earl of Bedford, was distraught and desperate. He offered £100,000 for a pardon for his son. The Earl also wrote to the King, saying that he would be content with bread and water if only the life of his son were spared. It was all to no avail. When Lord Russell recognised there was no hope he wrote once more to the King pleading for consideration for his wife and children after his death. Rachel brought the three children, two girls and a little boy, to bid farewell to him at Newgate.

The execution took place on 21st July. It was a messy and unpleasant business, as the axeman did not despatch his victim at the first stroke. Evelyn describes the scene : "On the 21st was the Lord Russell decapitated in Lincoln's Inn Fields, the executioner giving him three butcherly strokes. The speech he made and the paper he gave the Sheriff declared his innocence and the nobleness of his family. And the piety and worthiness of this unhappy gentleman wrought effects of much pity, and various discourses on the plot."[38] Russell's head was sewn back on his body, and the remains buried in the family vault at Chenies. Fortunately for his descendants, the King announced that he did not intend to profit by the forfeiture of Russell's personal estate.

Six years later, when William and Mary were on the throne, their first Parliament passed an Act to reverse the attainder of William, Lord Russell, who was now lauded as "the ornament of his age". Scenes in the House of Commons that day were emotional and intense. One Whig member broke down as soon as he started speaking. "I cannot name my Lord Russell without disorder," he said. "It is enough to name him. I am not able to say more." His condemnation was declared null and void, and an injunction was passed to cancel and take off the file all record of the trial. The Earl of Bedford was created 1st Duke of Bedford and Marquess of Tavistock, by way of apology for the loss of his son, whom Macaulay called "the most virtuous of all the martyrs of English liberty".

The patent of creation has an interesting preamble which shows just how great a national hero William Russell was in the years after the Stuart débâcle. The preamble begins : "Since in human societies there are some men so far excelling others, that they may be truely said to embellish those very titles of Honour they wear, and to shed back upon them no less lustre, than others borrow from them", and continues in such laudatory terms that there is no doubt it is William Russell who is being honoured with the dukedom posthumously rather than his father the Earl of Bedford. Bedford's greatest honour, it said, was that

"from his loins issued the ornament of our Age, William the late Lord RUSSELL, whose superlative merits we think it not sufficient should be transmitted to all future generations upon the credit of Public Annals, but will have them inserted in these our Royal Letters Patents, as a monument consecrated to the most accomplish'd and consummate virtue in the said family . . . Know ye therefore etc."[39]

William Russell suffered the unseemly death of a martyr, but his descendants benefited from his life, and his death, more than from any other member of the family after the 1st Earl, who founded the family fortunes. William brought into the family, by marriage, the estates of the Earl of Southampton in Bloomsbury, which still yield a handsome revenue; his son married another heiress, Elizabeth Howland of Streatham, who brought yet more estates to the Bedford purse. And if it were not for his death there would be no dukedom of Bedford at all. The three little children who were brought to their father in prison at the moment of his deepest disgrace grew up to be 2nd Duke of Bedford, Duchess of Devonshire and Duchess of Rutland. And the radical meetings held in his London home laid the foundation for one of England's greatest political parties – the Whigs.

Mention should be made of another Russell distinguished by his nonconformity. Bertrand Russell, whose work in mathematics and logical positivism earned him a permanent place in the history of Western philosophy, was grandson of Lord John Russell and great-grandson of the 6th Duke of Bedford. He was therefore in direct line of descent from William, Lord Russell, whose quarrel with the establishment ended on the scaffold. The two men have in common their indomitable opposition to political deceit, and Bertrand Russell, like his ancestors, was more than once put in the pillory for his ruthless honesty, and twice imprisoned. In all his ninety-six years, he never once accepted the established view. (He carried, by the way, the title of Earl Russell, conferred on his grandfather, a title quite separate from the Earldom of Bedford, which is carried by the Duke.)

It is time to step backwards and examine the origins of the Russells, one of the greatest of Whig families. Wiffen, who had been commissioned by the 6th Duke to do precisely this, produced a family tree which showed descent from someone called Olaf the Sharp-eyed, King of Rerik, who lived at an unspecified date. One of his descendants was a certain Hugh de Rozel (in which we recognise the name Russell), who came with the Norman conquerors in 1066. Sad to say, all this is so much romantic invention.[40] The truth is more prosaic.

The Russells were traders and merchants from Weymouth, dealing in wine. It was John Russell, born about 1486, who raised the family to the giddy heights of vast wealth and title by a combination of chance and opportunism. The first chance occurred when Archduke Philip landed in England, close to Weymouth, in 1506. He was met by Sir Thomas Trenchard, who knew Russell, and sought the latter's help as an interpreter. Russell could speak several European languages fluently. Thus he accompanied the Archduke to Windsor, and proved himself such a lively and useful companion that the King, Henry VII, employed him as a gentleman of the Privy Chamber. From that moment, it is a story of rapid advance politically, socially, and financially, as John rose in the esteem of his monarch, and of his successor, Henry VIII, and held one important post after another. He was diplomat, soldier, counsellor, and trusted friend of the King. Apart from Wolsey, there was, for a while, no more important or influential man in the land. He married Anne, daughter of Sir Guy Sapcote, who brought the property of Chenies to the Russells in 1526 (where it remained until 1956, and where all the Earls and Dukes are buried). He was created Baron Russell of Chenies in 1539.

At the dissolution of the monasteries, the most lavish redistribution of wealth and land since the Conquest, Henry VIII and his son Edward VI simply gave to Russell vast lands which had been confiscated from the monks, including the lands of Woburn Abbey in Bedfordshire, thirty manors in Cornwall, Somerset and Devon, formerly belonging to the abbey of Tavistock, several thousands of acres formerly belonging to the abbey of Thorney in Cambridgeshire, and, in 1552, the Covent Garden "lying in the parish of St Martin's-in-the-fields next Charing Cross, with seven acres called Long Acre, of the yearly value of six pounds six shillings and eightpence" (there is to this day a street which bears the name Long Acre). On these acquisitions are founded the colossal wealth and territorial power of the family, who were "gorged with ecclesiastical spoils".[41] Covent Garden remained the personal property of the Russells for nearly 400 years.

When Henry VIII died, Russell was one of the executors, and in a position naturally to influence the boy king Edward VI. It was this monarch who conferred upon him the Earldom of Bedford in 1549. John Russell and his four immediate descendants were henceforth styled 'Lord Bedford'.

The 2nd Earl served Elizabeth I as his father had served the three previous monarchs, and was godfather to Sir Francis Drake. He was succeeded by his dissolute grandson, the 3rd Earl, who, with his spendthrift wife Lucy Harrington, proceeded to work his way through the inheritance with conscious abandon. On his death in 1627 the

title passed to his cousin, the 4th Earl, who was the first Russell to
make his home at Woburn. He fled there with his wife and ten
children to escape one of the sporadic plagues which clutched the
throat of London throughout the seventeenth century. He rescued the
family fortunes and commissioned Inigo Jones to build in Covent
Garden and Woburn; St Paul's Church in Covent Garden was one
result of this collaboration. Then, having survived the plague, he
succumbed to smallpox, and was succeeded by his son, the 5th Earl.
This is the one who was father of William, Lord Russell, "the patriot",
the political martyr beheaded in 1683, and who consequently became
the 1st Duke of Bedford. He had married Lady Anne Carr, who had
been born in the Tower of London, where her mother, the Countess
of Somerset, was imprisoned for the murder by poisoning of Sir
Thomas Overbury. Apparently, the truth was successfully kept from
Anne Carr that her mother had been a wicked murderess. After she
became Duchess of Bedford, and was told her parents' true history,
she collapsed in a fit.[42]

The 2nd Duke was grandson of the first, and son of the unfortunate
William, Lord Russell. He was called Wriothesley after his mother's
family, the Earls of Southampton, and this ambitious mother, whom
we know as Rachel, Lady Russell, arranged for him to marry a
wealthy heiress from Streatham, Elizabeth Howland. It was an
astute commercial venture, bringing another £100,000 to the
Bedford coffers, and yet more estates. Wriothesley had little choice in
the matter, which he had to accept as his destiny, trusting to his
mother's wisdom. He was fourteen and a half at the time of the
marriage, and his bride was thirteen. The wedding took place on
23rd May 1695 in a chapel of the Howland family mansion at
Streatham. Immediately afterwards, the King conferred upon the
bridegroom's family the new title Baron Howland of Streatham (in
order to preserve the bride's name), a title which to this day is given
by courtesy to the grandson of the Duke of Bedford; the present
Lord Howland was born in 1962.

The Duke's mother, Rachel, was in a position to request royal
favours, as her late husband was now a national hero, and his
execution recognised to have been a miscarriage of justice. She
squeezed every advantage from this circumstance.

The 3rd Duke, son of the 2nd, was also called Wriothesley. He was
one of the most notorious gamblers of his age. Had he been given his
way, he would have gambled with the entire Bloomsbury estate, but
his wife's grandmother, Sarah Duchess of Marlborough, intervened to
prevent the disaster. As it was, the Duke managed to lose every

available penny he could lay his hands on. In one evening he lost
nearly a quarter of a million pounds to the infamous gambler Jansen,
an occasion recorded by Pope in the line : *"Or when a duke to Jansen
punts at White's."* Not for more than forty years was this sum
surpassed as a gambling loss.[43] The Duke was "so intellectually weak
and easily imposed upon that he was the dupe of all the disreputable
men about town and the laughing-stock of Society".[44]

He was succeeded by his brother as 4th Duke, who had also married
a grand-daughter of the Duchess of Marlborough, so that the Duchess
was grandmother to two Duchesses of Bedford. To complicate
matters further, his daughter married the Duke of Marlborough of
the next generation, great-grandson of the redoubtable Duchess.

The 4th Duke rescued the family fortunes, once again, from the
ravages caused by his disastrous brother, and eventually was said to
be the richest man in England.[45] Certainly he was among the four
wealthiest individuals in the land.* Unlike his humourless descendants, the 4th Duke had a reputation for mirth and light-heartedness,
a reputation which did him little good. Pelham complained that
with him it was "all jollity, boyishness and vanity", and Walpole has
nothing but diminutive, hardly affectionate, epithets to describe him.
He is "little Aeolus", "the paramount little Duke of Bedford", "this
bustling little Duke", or simply the "merry little Duke".[46] When he
went into battle Walpole had this to say : "The Duke of Bedford
goes in his little round person with his regiment; he now takes
to the land, and says he is tired of being a pen and ink man."[47] The
celebrated satirist who wrote under the name of Junius was far less
gentle in his mockery. He wrote a savage letter to Bedford which
begins :

"My Lord,
    You are so little accustomed to receive any marks of respect or
esteem from the public, that if, in the following lines a compliment
or expression of applause should escape me, I fear you would
consider it as a mockery to your established character, and perhaps
an insult to your understanding. You have nice feelings, my Lord,
if we may judge from your resentments ...
    "You are indeed a very considerable man. The highest rank; a
splendid fortune; and a name, glorious till it was yours, were
sufficient to have supported you with meaner abilities than I think

---

* The others were the Dukes of Devonshire, Northumberland, and Bridgwater.
Fifty years later they were overtaken by the colossus Duke of Sutherland.

you possess. . . . Consider the character of an independent virtuous Duke of Bedford; imagine what he might be in this country, then reflect one moment upon what you are . . ."

It is a splendid piece of vitriolic prose, but it would be folly to regard it as representing the truth. The "bustling little Duke" was not the monster that Junius paints; even Walpole, who was not excessively fond of him by any means, believed that he was an honest man.[48] While we can recognise much of the Russell personality in Junius's portrait – obstinacy, a tendency to meanness, opportunism, and an inability to judge character, all traits which will surface again and and again in the next 150 years – the 4th Duke was neither an unprincipled nor a stupid man, and he did more than any other to make Woburn beautiful.

There are manifold other references to the fact that the Russells have long been held in high public esteem. "All the Russells are excellent", wrote Creevey, "and in my opinion there is nothing in the aristocracy to compare with this family." In spite of eccentricities, they have been one of the most intelligent families in all Europe.

One matter about which there can be no dispute is the extent of the Bedford fortune which, already a source of wonder in the eighteenth century, grew still greater in the nineteenth, even surviving the extravagances of the 5th and 6th Dukes. "The Duke of Bedford is every day making his colossal fortune greater and greater", mused the envious Greville.[49] By 1883, the combined estate covered 86,335 acres, with land in Bedfordshire, Devon, Cambridgeshire, Northampton-shire, Dorset, Buckinghamshire, Huntingdonshire, Cornwall, and, of course, the huge adjacent chunks of Covent Garden and Bloomsbury in London.[50] (There had in addition been great estates in Hampshire and Surrey.) It was one of the three or four largest family fortunes in England. So vast was it, that the management of the estates was a burden which successive Dukes deplored; it seems they paid for their riches by the sweat of long hours and constant worry. For example, the 7th Duke (brother to Lord John Russell, the Prime Minister) would rise at five o'clock every morning and spend the day grappling with the problems of his inheritance. He wrote that he considered himself "a well-paid agent with an income of £12,000 working for those who had mortgages and settlements on the estates". To his brother William he confided the terror he felt when confronted with his responsibilities: "You are little aware of the cares and worries and plagues I have had to go through in the course of the last year, and were it not that it would be wicked to complain of my lot, and not to be grateful for it, I should say that a man with fewer of these cares and responsibilities is a happier man . . . If I could put you in my place, and take your income in place of my own, I am sure I should not be a less happy man."[51] Not for the first time does a great landowner realise that one is better off with one acre than with one thousand. (His wife Duchess Anne, by the way, is credited with having invented the five o'clock tea.)[52]

In addition to the Bedford estates, various dukes have had small private properties scattered over the country, to which they have liked to escape. Duke Herbrand had a favourite house in Scotland. His Duchess (the "flying Duchess") paid £2 a year for a cottage between Orkney and Shetland where she indulged her bird-watching. She also had a house near Midhurst, where she constructed a runway for her aircraft, but she never lived there. There was a house on Chiswick Mall in London, which still bears the name "Bedford House", and which the present Duke once vainly attempted to buy back into the family.

The most sumptuous jewel in the Bedford crown was (and is) Woburn Abbey and its park, over 3000 acres surrounded by eleven and a half miles of brick walls. The house itself, built at different stages by Inigo Jones, Henry Holland, and Henry Flitcroft, is an elegant, reticent masterpiece, and was the scene of some of the most gracious living in the eighteenth and nineteenth centuries. Walpole, who spent a week there in 1751, said that he admired rather than liked it,[53] but Greville was ecstatic in his praise on several occasions. Whenever he could pause from writing disparaging remarks about the Bedfords he sprang into lyrical effusions about their home : "a house abounding in every sort of luxury and comfort, with inexhaustible resources for every taste . . . the house, place, establishment, and manner of living are the most magnificent I have seen. There is no place which gives so splendid an example of a Great English Lord as this. The chasse was brilliant; in five days we killed 835 pheasants, 645 hares, 59 rabbits, 10 partridges, and 5 woodcocks . . . I never saw such an abode of luxury and enjoyment . . . the management of the estates is like the administration of a little Kingdom. He has 450 people in his employment on the Bedfordshire property alone, not counting domestic servants . . . There is order, economy, comfort, and general content."[54] Greville liked to be spoiled. He chose well, for at this time (1820-40) hospitality at Woburn was the most luxurious in England. Lady William Russell described it as "the most jolly life in Christendom".[55]

Some of this style of living, less "jolly" perhaps but almost as sumptuous, continued until the death of the 11th Duke, Herbrand, in 1940. Herbrand had a staff of well over 200, most of whom he never saw. Workpeople and gardeners used to station themselves at strategic intervals in the park so that they could pass signals to each other to disappear from view whenever the Duke was approaching; this was to spare him the unpleasant sight of a workman.[56] He thought it not remotely odd that he should have fifty footmen with powdered hair, one of whom would stand behind the chair of each guest at dinner. Nor did it seem unduly extravagant to give each guest an individual gold tea-pot for breakfast. He never used the telephone in his life; that was part of modern living of which he preferred to remain ignorant.

Although Duke Herbrand visited London barely once a year, he kept two fully-staffed establishments in Belgrave Square, and eight chauffeurs. A guest to Woburn would be taken in one car, with chauffeur and private footman, while his luggage would travel with its own chauffeur and footman in another car. On the outskirts of London both cars would be met by two more, sent from Woburn, and passenger and luggage would transfer from one vehicle to another, with yet more uniformed footmen in attendance.[57] There were more servants employed whose sole task was to polish the vast silver collection, and who were required to sleep in the room with it.[58] The pages were clothed and fed, but were not paid.

Duke Herbrand did not regard his style of living as ostentatious; it would simply be silly for a nobleman to live in any other fashion. The realisation that many of his predecessors had earned a reputation for ostentation did not bother him (or did not occur to him). The worst offender was the 5th Duke, who succeeded in 1771 at the age of six, and never married. Like many a self-indulgent bachelor, he enjoyed making a display of himself. The waspish Walpole saw him on the occasion of the King's birthday, and wrote : "The Duke of Bedford eclipsed the whole birthday by his clothes, equipage, and servants : six of the latter walked on the side of the coach to keep off the crowd . . . their liveries are worth an argosie."[59] He it was who sold the family estates in Hampshire and Surrey, to pay for more ostentation of his person, and an even grander style of living. He was not popular. Walpole makes an unkind reference to him when he came of age, and ordered the estate manager to have all his palaces ready for him. Until then, the Dowager Duchess, his grandmother, had been living in them in the style of a reigning monarch. The peacock young Duke would have none of this, and wanted to show off in his own glorious possessions. Besides, he had a mistress, the notorious Nancy Parsons

(Lady Maynard), who had already been mistress to two dukes, their Graces of Grafton and Dorset, and who was now in her fifties. Bedford wanted to establish her at Woburn, and not unnaturally met with some hard opposition from his grandmother. Walpole wrote:

"If it is only to make room for another antique old woman for old woman, I should think one's own grandmother might be preferable to one that, for many reasons, might be grandmother of half London."[60]

In the end, both the old women, one his grandmother, the other his mistress, lived there, glowering at each other from opposite wings.

This grandmother, by the way, the 4th Duke's duchess, was not without her own penchant for showing off. At George III's coronation in 1761 the Duchess of Queensberry said that the Duchess of Bedford looked "like an orange-peach, half red and half yellow".[61]

The 5th Duke died in 1801, aged only thirty-seven, and was succeeded by his brother as 6th Duke. This man, whom we have come across earlier in the chapter, was also, according to Greville, a sybarite who relished the display of his wealth; but Greville may well have mixed some ungenerous envy with his harsh remarks:

"A more uninteresting, weak-minded, selfish character does not exist than the Duke of Bedford. He is a good-natured, plausible man without enemies, and really (though he does not think so) without friends; and naturally enough he does not think so, because there are many who pretend, like Brougham, a strong affection for him, and some who imagine they feel it. Vast property, rank, influence, and station always attract a sentiment which is dignified with the name of friendship, which assumes all its outward appearance, complies with its conditions, but which is really hollow and unsubstantial. The Duke of Bedford is a complete sensualist and thinks of nothing but his own personal enjoyments, and it has long been a part of his system not to allow himself to be disturbed by the necessities of others, or be ruffled by the slightest self-denials. He is affable, bland, and of easy intercouse, making rather a favourable impression on superficial observers; caring little (if at all) for the wants and wishes of others, but grudging nobody anything which does not interfere with his own enjoyments, and seeing with complacency those who surround him lap up the superfluities which may by chance bubble over from his cap of pleasure and happiness. It is a farce to talk of friendship with such a man, on whom, if he were not Duke of Bedford, Brougham would never waste a thought."[62]

Some of the dukes have swung to the very opposite point, and been positively mean. The 7th Duke, who had all the income from his estates, begrudged making an allowance to his brother, Lord John Russell, who had only what he earned, on which he had to support a wife and family, run a house suitable to a politician holding high office, entertain in a manner which his position demanded. Lord John regularly sent his bills to the Duke, who regularly settled them, but the younger brother suffered from the humiliation of this proceeding. A substantial annuity to Lord John would not have made the difference of a comma to the Duke's riches, but he would not make one. ". . . his love of money is so great that he cannot bring himself . . . to do a generous thing on a great scale", wrote one of his best friends. "His colossal fortune, which goes on increasing every day, and for which he has no use, might well be employed in making his brother easy, and in buying golden opinions for himself; but the passion of avarice and the pleasure of accumulation outweigh all such considerations."[63]

Again, "he thinks nothing but rolling up enormous savings which he cannot take with him and which he does not care to distribute".[64] Disraeli told Queen Victoria that Bedford considered accumulation the only pleasure of life, and that "he never retired to rest satisfied, unless he could trace that he had saved, that day, at least a five pound note".[65]

Similarly, the 12th Duke, Hastings, would not even allow his wife money to buy some presentable clothes, and his son and heir was expected to live on under £100 a year, and to find shirts that cost less than £3.

There is a story which relates to one Duchess of Bedford, wife to the 4th Duke, John. She gave a great ball at Woburn, but did not heat the grand house properly. Great houses were often cold and damp because it was the extraordinary habit in the eighteenth century to wash down the walls before giving a party. Some of the guests were uncomfortably cold. Three of them, Lord Lorn, George Selwyn and Horace Walpole (who, of course, tells the story), retired into a little room where there was a fire, and huddled round. The Duchess saw them, and said nothing, but minutes later a workman appeared with tools ready to take the door off the hinges.[66]

While Woburn glittered with resplendent dances, the money to pay for them came from the London properties. At one time the Duke of

Bedford personally owned the whole of Bloomsbury from Tottenham Court Road in the west to Russell Square and Southampton Row in the east, from New Oxford Street in the south almost to Euston Road in the north, plus the whole of Covent Garden from Drury Lane westwards to St Martin's Lane and from the Strand north to Long Acre. Covent Garden was sold before World War I, but a sizeable portion of Bloomsbury still belongs to the Bedford Estates.

When the Covent Garden of St Peter's, Westminster, was given to John Russell, Earl of Bedford, in 1551, it was undeveloped pasture land and orchard, and for many years it offered an interrupted rural view from the rear of the Earl's London house in the Strand. It was the 4th Earl (father of the 1st Duke) who commissioned Inigo Jones to develop the land and make in the centre of it a splendid piazza in the Italian Renaissance style, the first in London. The Earl's old house was demolished, and a sumptuous new residence erected to harmonise with the general scheme. Houses on the piazza were let at high rents to noblemen and rich merchants. Later, permission was granted for dealers in fruit and vegetables to sell their wares along the back garden wall of Bedford House, thus taking the first step in a process which was to evolve into London's most famous fruit market. Eventually, the traders dominated the square, obliterating the elegance of its architecture. Of Inigo Jones's grand design, only St Paul's Church remains, and some of the arcades around the square which suggest former dignity. The rest has been demolished, or smothered in the surrounding maze of little streets.

Towards the end of the nineteenth century, Covent Garden had degenerated into a slum, and the Duke became the object of a sustained campaign to persuade him to clean it up. *Punch* led the attack, calling him "Duke of Mudford" and his estates "Mud-Salad Market" and "Gloomsbury". It was *Punch*'s contention that Covent Garden was a disgrace to London; he compared His Grace of Mudford's negligence to the philanthropy of the Duke of Westminster, eventually goading Bedford into offering the site to the municipal authorities, who would not take it. There were cartoons showing the Duke lifting his robes above the squalid puddles of his streets.[67] This was the 9th Duke, Hastings, the unhappy sour hypochondriac, who regarded the attacks as yet another indication of the depths to which mankind may sink. Besides, what was the point of having lucrative property if you had to spend money maintaining it? It was not thus that the parsimonious Russells made their millions. "If one hadn't a few acres in London in these times of agricultural depression, I don't know what one would do," he said.[68]

The Russell connection with Covent Garden was finally severed in 1914, when Duke Herbrand sold almost the entire estate to Sir Joseph Beecham (of Beecham's Pills, and father to Sir Thomas, the conductor). The price was £2 million, and there was sensational publicity at the time. War and the death of Sir Joseph complicated the sale, the estate passing from the Beecham family to a publicly owned property company after the Great War. The Duke retained his private box at the Royal Opera House until 1940. It had been his of right since the lease of 1793, and it had its own lobby, lavatory, fireplace dominated by the Russell arms, chimney stack, staircase, and entrance from the street. It is said that one could happily live in the Bedford box. It now belongs to Covent Garden Properties Ltd, and is used by them in total independence of the Opera House. Also exempt from the sale was 26 James Street, which final link was sold by the 12th Duke in 1945.[69]

Like Covent Garden, Bloomsbury was monastic land confiscated at the Dissolution, and awarded to a deserving nobleman. In this case, the land consisted of an unexciting manor-house, some farm buildings, and acres of grazing land, and the nobleman was the 1st Earl of Southampton. His descendant, the 4th Earl, developed the land and built a splendid piazza which rivalled the Covent Garden Piazza of his neighbour the Earl of Bedford, to the south. He built a mansion for himself and his family – Southampton House. When he died in 1667 his estates were divided between his three daughters (there was no son), and the portion containing Bloomsbury and Southampton House was allotted to Rachel. She subsequently married William, Lord Russell, son of the Earl of Bedford, and her property automatically passed into his ownership. The couple lived in Southampton House. William was beheaded, but his son, as 2nd Duke of Bedford, was the first to inherit the combined estates of Covent Garden and Bloomsbury, the first from his grandfather, 5th Earl and 1st Duke, the second from his parents and maternal grandfather, the Earl of Southampton. He owned both Bedford House and Southampton House, two London palaces within walking distance of each other. As he had married the Howland heiress at the age of fourteen, he owned other substantial houses and estates in Streatham and Tooting Bec as well.

Today, the Russell connection with Bloomsbury is commemorated in over seventy street names which bear their family names, titles or houses. There is a Bedford Square, a Bedford Avenue, a Bedford Place, a Bedford Way, a Bedford Row, a Bedford Street and a Bedford Passage. In Streatham there is a Bedford Park. There is

Woburn Place and Woburn Walk, and again in Streatham, Woburn Road. There is Russell Square, and Great Russell Street, Chenies Street (named after the Buckinghamshire property), Tavistock Square, and Endsleigh Place and Endsleigh Street, named after the house on the Tavistock estate in Devon. Byng Place and Gordon Square are named after the two duchesses of John, 6th Duke of Bedford – the Hon. Georgiana Byng and Lady Georgiana Gordon – while Torrington Street recalls Georgiana's father, Viscount Torrington. Gower Street is an echo of an even earlier duchess, the Hon. Gertrude Leveson Gower, who married the 4th Duke. Even Eversholt Street is a Bedford name. The 2nd Duke, Wriothesley, bought the property of Eversholt in Bedfordshire, and this name was given to the street which linked the Bloomsbury estate with more Bedford lands in Camden Town. The Earl of Southampton, is remembered in Southampton Row.

The course of the twentieth century has seen the gradual, then rapid erosion of this vast inheritance. Covent Garden and the Thorney Estate in Cambridgeshire were both sold before World War I. (The Thorney estate had been with the family since the dissolution of the monasteries, and had increased in value phenomenally as a result of the Russells' pioneer work in draining the Fens and quite literally changing the map of England in consequence. The estate covered 20,000 acres. Duke Herbrand sold it to the tenants in 1909.)

The disaster which fragmented the remaining Russell properties was the death within fifteen years of the 11th and 12th Dukes. Owing largely to family squabbles, with successive dukes refusing to talk to each other, sufficient provision had not been made to protect the estate when Duke Herbrand died in 1940, leaving a liability for death duties over £3,000,000. The only way in which this could be paid was to sell chunks of the estates. The tax bill had still not been fully met when the 12th Duke died, a few weeks too early, in 1953, adding another £4,600,000 to the death duty assessment. Hence Chenies had to be sold in 1954. Endsleigh House and the 9000-acre estate in Devon went little by little, finally disappearing in 1962; the Bloomsbury estate has been nibbled at, the most recent sale being thirteen houses in Bedford Square in 1970. Only Woburn Abbey and the surrounding park remain intact.[70]

Even Woburn no longer *belongs* to the Duke of Bedford. The owners are the Bedford Estates, whose trustees have absolute discretion over what should be done with it and who should live there. Under the terms of the trusteeship, the Duke could have been tenant at Woburn for life, but his father and grandfather conspired to prevent that. The trustees wanted to give the house and park to the National Trust, but they met with such fierce opposition from the Duke that they allowed themselves to be persuaded by him to give him a limited tenancy while he would rescue Woburn from neglect, and take steps to see that it paid for itself. This is what he has done, with conspicuous success. (The tenancy was later extended to life, but the Duke chose to hand over Woburn to his son.) But it is important to remember that the opening of Woburn Abbey to paying visitors has contributed in no way to the settlement of death duties, nor was it ever intended to. The death duties were far too huge to be settled in any other way but by selling property. The Duke's entrance fee to Woburn goes towards keeping the house running, with its twenty-two sitting-rooms and twelve dining-rooms, its miles of corridors, maintenance and re-decoration, insurance, heating. It enables him to protect a home which would otherwise quickly succumb to old age, and towards which he feels a remarkably fierce territorial urge (this in spite of his not seeing Woburn until he was sixteen years old, at which point he learnt for the first time that he was related to the Duke of Bedford and would one day inherit that title himself). The Duke has a limited income from the estate, as do his son and grandson, but neither he nor they have any personal property on the Russell estates whatever. The famous Canalettos in the dining-room, worth an incalculable sum, do not belong to him.

The Duke has himself told the story of how he and his second wife set about clearing the junk which had accumulated while his father had been Duke, themselves cleaning, scrubbing, polishing, and arranging the rooms at Woburn so that they might be worth visiting. They went on to make it the most popular ducal residence in England, with an average of nearly 1,600,000 visitors a year, many on second or third visits. The name of Woburn is now known all over the world, the Duke's face recognised more readily than that of many a politician. So successful has he been in attracting tourists to Woburn that the Israeli government is said to have sought his advice on how to increase their tourist trade.[71] There was no end to the tricks and inventions he would entertain in order to lure more people to the park. He accepted paying guests, mostly American tourists, who paid large sums for the privilege of dining with a duke and duchess, and he professed to enjoy meeting them. If a farmhouse was derelict and needed to be demolished, he would advertise the fact, and charge a fee for watching the farmhouse go up in flames.[72] He was once on a visit to Blenheim Palace, residence of the Duke of Marlborough when he was recognised and his autograph was sought. He wrote astutely in the Blenheim guide-book that he hoped to see the tourists at Woburn.[73] More cleverly still, he exploited English snobbery by admitting visitors to Woburn by cheque, made payable to "His Grace the Duke of Bedford".[74] He frankly admits that he enjoys being a duke, and he quite clearly derives much pleasure from meeting a great variety of people.

None of this would be quite so remarkable were it not that Ian, 13th Duke of Bedford, is a Russell. He is deeply sensitive, naturally shy, preferably solitary. Although his third marriage, to Nicole, has been very happy, he must inevitably retain that essential Russell reserve. He has fought against the additional disadvantage of an eccentric upbringing, with tutors, nannies, nurses, maids, but never a relation, and a self-righteous father who, it must be admitted, treated him with malice. He has striven hard to save Woburn, and has found in the process an exhibitionist trait which must have lain dormant within the tight breasts of generations of Russells. "Having been brought up with servants, I have a servant's mind," he says. It is an enthusiastic success story, rare in the British aristocracy.

Bedford is unique among dukes for all these reasons and more. He is a charming and gentle man, with a quiet sense of humour and a gift for making easy conversation. He is also no fool. Disinherited by his father and grandfather, with a miserable allowance of £98 a year to live on, the young Lord Howland had to learn the value of endeavour. The family disapproved of his proposed first marriage (he now speaks himself of marriage as a "perilous enterprise", and tried to dissuade his son, Lord Tavistock, from marrying Henrietta Tiarks), so he supplemented his income by working as a reporter. With his second wife he emigrated to South Africa, where he learnt farming, and grew apricots. It was there that he was told he had become Duke of Bedford in 1953. He sometimes regrets the peace and simplicity of those years.

In 1974 he decided to leave Woburn for good, not because he does not still love the place, but because he wanted his son, Lord Tavistock, to take over while he was young enough to develop an interest. The Duke and Duchess are now nomadic, addressing conventions, appearing on television the world over, turning up in Portugal, Switzerland, Rome, Paris; they are "of no fixed abode". Lord Tavistock is by profession a stockbroker, with a quite different style from his father. The indications are that he resembles some of his less flamboyant ancestors. He would have preferred to remain in the City, where he was happy and relaxed, and where he had made his own way. He does not find it easy to adapt to the role of a public curiosity to be gazed upon and to have his hand shaken by strangers, but he recognises that personal appearances are part of the job, and he has turned Woburn into a thriving business enterprise. His wife is the former Henrietta Tiarks, and they have three sons, of whom the youngest is the first Russell to be born at Woburn for 100 years.

REFERENCES

1. Georgiana Blakiston, *Lord William Russell and His Wife,* p. 485.
2. Greville, V. 459.
3. Duke of Bedford, *Silver-Plated Spoon,* 73.
4. Blakiston, 28.
5. Buckle, *Life of Disraeli,* Vol. VI, p. 189.
6. Blakiston, 25
7. Greville, IV, 152 n.
8. Buckle, IV, 421.
9. Greville, VI, 51.
10. Bedford, 113
11. Bedford, 17.
12. *The Times,* 12th October 1953.
13. Bedford, 44.
14. *The Times,* 21st October 1941.
15. *The Times,* 19th January 1944.
16. *The Times,* 26th January 1944.
17. *The Times,* 16th October 1953.
18. Blakiston, 424.
19. *The Times,* 14th November 1935.
20. Bedford, 140.
21. Blakiston, 82.
22. *The Times,* 15th January 1891.
23. Bedford, 191.
24. Bedford, 212.
25. *The Times,* 3rd September 1945.
26. Duke of Bedford, *The Flying Duchess,* p. 59.
27. *The Observer,* 15th May 1966.
28. *Flying Duchess,* 66.
29. *ibid.,* 155.
30. *ibid.,* 143.
31. *The Times,* 29th June 1937.
32. *The Flying Duchess,* 92.
33. Blakiston, 32, 55, 66, 78, 526, 539.
34. *The Flying Duchess,* 63.

35. 12th Duke of Bedford, *The Years of Transition.*
36. Greville, IV, 261.
37. J. H. Wiffen, *Memoirs of the House of Russell*, Vol. II, p. 271.
38. John Evelyn's Diary, entry for 1683.
39. Chatsworth Collections, 27.4.
40. Wiffen, I, 17.
41. Greville, IV, 90.
42. Collins *Peerage*, I, 285.
43. Walpole, XVIII, 124.
44. *Great Governing Families in England*, II, 48.
45. Walpole, XXIII, 274; Blakiston, 433.
46. Walpole, ed. Cunningham, II, 22, 148, 191.
47. Walpole, XIX, 160.
48. Walpole, XX, 203.
49. Greville, V, 347.
50. Bateman's *Great Landowners.*
51. Blakiston, 442.
52. *Collections and Recollections of One who has Kept a Diary,*
    p. 107.
53. Walpole, XX, 281.
54. Greville, I, 86; V, 39; IV, 417.
55. Blakiston, 108.
56. Duke of Bedford, *A Book of Snobs*, p.31.
57. Bedford, 8.
58. *The Guardian*, 16th June 1971.
59. Walpole, ed. Cunningham, IX, 2332.
60. Walpole, XXIII, 344.
61. Walpole, ed. Cunningham, III, 438.
62. Greville, IV, 209.
63. *ibid.*, VIII, 26.
64. *The Stanleys of Alderley*, p. 303.
65. Buckle, *Life of Disraeli*, VI, p. 385.
66. Walpole, ed. Cunningham, IV, 203.
67. R. G. G. Price, *Mr Punch's History of Modern England,*
    pp. 182–5.
68. E. F. Benson, *As We Were*, p. 96.
69. *Survey of London*, Vol. XXXV, pp. 77, 84.
70. Christopher Trent, *The Russells*, pp. 163–7, 173–4, 294.
71. *Daily Express*, 13th October 1961.
72. *Daily Mail*, 28th May 1962.
73. *Daily Express*, 31st July 1962.
74. *The Sun*, 16th April 1968.

4. The Noble Houses of Cavendish

Duke of Devonshire; Duke of Portland

A Cavendish should always be pictured in his library. He is essentially a bookworm, studious, calm, cool, unflustered. His judgement is reflective, his actions well considered. The Cavendishes have a long and glorious tradition of political service, second to none, but they have tended to guide events from behind; the shouting and the banner-waving they have left to others. They have always been marked by an acute literary intelligence. Not that they have produced anyone as remarkable as Bertrand Russell in the Bedford family, but they share with the Russells this distinguishing feature of intelligence, and have occasionally produced playwrights, essayists, memoirists, and at least one original scientist. On the whole, however, their intelligence does not publicise itself, because a Cavendish does not have much energy. He likes to be left in peace. Also like the Russells, the Cavendishes boast a whole gallery of eccentrics, but on the other hand, they have a strong strain of earthiness. In common with the Russells and the Seymours, this family laid the foundation of its immense wealth on their share of confiscated monastery lands; they were advanced by Henry VIII and eventually spawned two separate dukedoms. The dukedom of Devonshire continues in unbroken line to the present day; the dukedom of Newcastle became extinct (and has nothing whatever to do with the present Duke of Newcastle), but the Cavendish family hopped by a series of marriages into the dukedom of Portland. So it is that Andrew Cavendish, Duke of Devonshire, and Sir William Cavendish-Bentinck, Duke of Portland, represent different branches of the same family, though in the latter's case the Bentinck connection is dominant.

The common ancestress of both Devonshire and Portland is that greatest of all Elizabethan women, making exception only for Queen Elizabeth herself – Bess of Hardwick. Elizabeth Hardwick, of Hardwick in Derbyshire, married four times, and was four times a widow. All her husbands were rich, they all adored her, and they all left her every penny they had. The last of the quartet was the Earl of Shrewsbury, and it was as Countess of Shrewsbury that Bess held Mary Queen of Scots prisoner in her house for seventeen years, on command of the Queen. It was only when Bess grew jealous of her husband's too-solicitous attentions to the Queen of Scots that she asked Elizabeth to remove her. It is also as Countess of Shrewsbury that Bess should be remembered by posterity, but history persists in calling her 'Bess of Hardwick', the familiar term by which she was known to her contemporaries, and which has remained her sobriquet for 400 years.

The second of Bess's husbands was Sir William Cavendish, close adviser to Henry VIII, and one of the architects of the dissolution of the monasteries. Fortunately for the subsequent comfort of the Cavendishes, this was the only marriage of the four which produced any children, so that all the booty which Bess had accumulated from four widowhoods went to the children of Sir William Cavendish.

Bess had a passion for building. It amounted almost to an illness. All her life she was surrounded by masons, carpenters, brick-dust. She could not cease building, and her workmen were still busy when she died. It was said that she believed a prediction that she could not die as long as she was building. We have reason to be grateful to the rogue who made such a promise, for Bess built three of the finest houses in the country, including Hardwick Hall, the most elegant of all surviving Elizabethan houses. To her second son, who became the 1st Earl of Devonshire and is the ancestor of the dukes of Devonshire, she left Hardwick, Chatsworth, and Oldcotes. To her third son, father of the Duke of Newcastle in the Cavendish line, and ancestor of the Duke of Portland she left Welbeck Abbey. Today the Duke of Devonshire still lives at Chatsworth, and the Duke of Portland at Welbeck, while the passionate woman who built their houses lies buried at All Hallows Church in Derby.

The first master of Chatsworth was William Cavendish, (1552–1625), son of Sir William and Bess, and nephew of George Cavendish, who wrote the *Life of Wolsey*. He was uncle to the 1st Duke of Newcastle of Welbeck Abbey (grandson of Sir William), and to Lady Arabella Stuart (grand-daughter of Sir William), whose romantic story is part of the history of the dukedom of Somerset. Thomas Cavendish, the navigator, was also distantly related.

Chatsworth had been built by Sir William at a cost of £80,000 and, with Hardwick Hall, it established William Cavendish as a person of consequence in the country. His importance was recognised by his elevation to the peerage as Earl of Devonshire, a title for which he is said to have paid £10,000.

All the Cavendish lands being in Derbyshire, and not an acre in Devonshire, the story got about that a scribe had made a mistake, and that "Devonshire" was written on the patent in error. In fact, the patent of 1618 quite clearly says "*Comes Devon*" (*comes* means "earl") and that of 1694 equally clearly says "*Dux Devon*"; the "shire" was added to the end by common consent to avoid confusion with the other earldom of Devon.

His son the 2nd Earl (1590–1628) was educated by Thomas Hobbes, who later became his secretary. Hobbes paid tribute to the Cavendish brilliance of intellect and incorruptible integrity, characteristics which recur often over the centuries, in a long eulogy of praise which he appended to his translation of Thucydides. Hobbes dedicated the book to his former pupil, "whom no man was able either to draw or jostle out of the straight path of justice". However bright he was, financial acumen was not among his attributes. He lived so well that he was obliged to sell some of the estates, and eventually died of over-indulgence at the age of thirty-eight. His son the 3rd Earl of Devonshire (1617–1684) continued the intellectual traditions of the family by being one of the first Fellows of the Royal Society in 1663. He also introduced the Cedar of Lebanon to England.[1]

It is with the next Earl (1640–1707) that the dukedom of Devonshire begins. Cavendish was one of the first Whigs, a close friend of the martyred William, Lord Russell, and a member of the exclusive radical set which hatched the Whig party at Southampton House. He tried to secure Russell's escape by proposing that they should change clothes when Cavendish was visiting him in his cell. Russell declined, and they parted company with embraces and floods of tears.[2] He supported the Exclusion Bill, which sought to deny the crown to James II, and was one of the seven signatories inviting the Prince of Orange to assume the crown of England. At the coronation of William and Mary in 1689, Cavendish was Lord High Steward, bearing the crown, while his daughter bore the Queen's train. Furthermore, it was he who had argued against Clarendon and Rochester in favour of James's deposition, saying that the country wanted a king, not merely a regent. No wonder, then, that King William III bestowed grateful favours upon Cavendish, one of his staunchest supporters, culminating in his highest honours as Marquess of Hartington and Duke of Devonshire in 1694, on the same day that his colleague and political ally Russell's father was made Duke of Bedford.

The Duke was not, however, bought by these favours. Unlike some ducal families, the Cavendishes may with justice claim to be above bribery. When the King showed signs of an immoderate religious bias, the Duke reminded him that he had come to England to protect Protestants, not to persecute Papists. He also made it quite clear that he thought the Sovereign should be subordinate to the will of the people.

If the Duke in political life was a man of sense, his private life was rather less well controlled. He had a reputation for lewdness, and an insatiable desire for the company of pretty women. Such amorousness has remained a characteristic of his descendants, hand in hand with their probity and their intelligence. When he died, an anonymous admirer recorded his charms in verse :

> "Whose awful sweetness challenged our esteem,
> Our sex's wonder and our sex's theme;
> Whose soft commanding looks our breasts assailed;
> He came and saw and at first sight prevailed."

The Duke of Devonshire was a bookworm. A student of Homer, Horace and Plutarch, he was extremely well-read, and even wrote an ode himself, on the death of Queen Mary, which received exaggerated praise from the flatterer John Dryden.

His son the 2nd Duke (1673–1729), who held many great offices in his career, married Rachel, the daughter of William, Lord Russell, and sister of the 2nd Duke of Bedford. Their son, 3rd Duke of Devonshire (1698–1755), gained his Oxford degree at the age of sixteen, married, and disappeared to the country, "for the unaccountable reason and unenvied pleasure of shutting himself up at Chatsworth with his ugly mad Duchess".[3] The next Duke (1720–1764) was Prime Minister for six months in 1756–7, but only in a caretaker capacity, because Pitt refused to serve under the outgoing Prime Minister, the Duke of Newcastle; Devonshire went into the job without much enthusiasm. He married one of the daughters of the Earl of Burlington, sister of that pathetic Dorothy Boyle who married Lord Euston, the Duke of Grafton's son, and who died after seven months of his ill-treatment. She brought yet more property to the Cavendish list, including Burlington House in Piccadilly (now the Royal Academy), Chiswick House, and lands in Yorkshire and Derbyshire.

Successive Dukes of Devonshire have never been particularly impressed with the extent of their property. One nineteenth-century duke was unaware that a certain grand house belonged to him, until someone told him. The 4th Duke was no exception. A Knight of the Garter, a Fellow of the Royal Society, and a Fellow of the Society of Antiquaries, he was happiest in his library, and content to leave politics to his brother Lord John Cavendish (Chancellor of the Exchequer 1782 and 1783). He began a Devonshire habit which perplexes historians, and can appear endearing to some, or stupid to others, of calling his offspring exclusively by nickname. His children were known as "Mrs Tiddle, Mrs Hopeful, Puss, Cat and Toe". The next generation was to immortalise the nicknames of that peculiar trio "Canis", "the Rat" and "Racky".

A contemporary of both the 4th and 5th Dukes of Devonshire, but unknown to either of them, was that odd and brilliant character Henry Cavendish (1731–1810), a grandson of the 2nd Duke. He brought much glory to the Cavendish name by his work in natural philosophy, and it was the sort of intellectual accomplishment which the Cavendishes revered above more worldly success. His demonstration of the composition of water in 1781 earned him a permanent place in the history of scientific discovery, in addition to which he was an excellent mathematician, astronomer, and geologist. Had Cavendish been a more normal man, more interested in self-advertisement, no doubt his discoveries would have been known beyond the confines of the Royal Society. But his blazing intelligence was yoked to a furtive, secretive, mistrustful nature, which kept him apart from the world, and gave rise to many eccentricities of behaviour.

Henry Cavendish lived alone in a villa overlooking Clapham Common. He ordered his dinner by leaving a note for his cook on the hall table. (It was the same every day – a leg of mutton.) An incorrigible misogynist, he never saw any of his servants, and was never seen by them. If any unlucky maid showed herself, she was instantly dismissed. To prevent accidents of this sort he had a second staircase built in his home. He abhorred all human contact, venturing out of his laboratories only to visit the Royal Society, and even there he barely uttered a word. If he saw anyone approach to talk to him, he would slink away in fear. To be looked at or addressed by a stranger seemed to give him positive pain, when he would dart away as if hurt.[4] Lord Brougham wrote that "he uttered fewer words in the course of his life than any man who ever lived to fourscore years, not at all excepting the monks of La Trappe".[5] Any attempt to draw him into conversation was almost certain to fail. Dr Wollaston said, "The way to talk to Cavendish is, never to look at him, but to talk as if it were into a vacancy, and then it is not unlikely you may set him going."[6] Then, when he did speak, it was with a frail, high-pitched squeak, which made it more understandable why he should avoid con-versation. He was never known to express an opinion on matters of the day, being completely indifferent to all but scientific knowledge. He went to the Royal Society with only money enough to pay for his dinner, and not a penny more. He picked his teeth with a fork, invariably hung his hat upon the same peg, and stuck his cane in his right boot. He never changed the cut of his clothes, so that when he died in 1810 he was still wearing the fashion of half a century earlier, thereby attracting the very attention which gave him so much distress.

Cavendish was one of the richest men of his day, but could not be bothered to do anything about it. He behaved as if he were a pauper, not through meanness, but indifference to the subject. The income was allowed to accumulate without attention. The bankers, discover-ing one day that they held £80,000 of his money, sent a messenger to apprise him of the fact. "What do you come here for? What do you want with me?" squeaked the nervous philosopher to a probably terrified bank clerk.

"Sir, I thought it proper to wait upon you," he said, "as we have a very large balance in hand of yours, and we wish your orders respecting it."

"If it is any trouble to you, I will take it out of your hands. Don't come here to plague me."

"Not the least trouble to us, sir, not the least. But we thought you might like some of it to be invested."

'Do so, do so, and don't come here to trouble me, or I'll remove it." And he showed the poor man the door.

The result of this academic indifference to money was that when he died Cavendish was the largest holder of bank-stock in England, with a fortune amounting to £1,175,000. His heir was his cousin, Lord George Cavendish, who had been allowed to visit the old man for half an hour each year, and who was grandfather of the 7th Duke of Devonshire. So the mad scientist's wealth found its way eventually back into the Devonshire pocket.

Dr George Wilson remembers Cavendish as "an intellectual head, thinking; a pair of wonderful acute eyes, observing; a pair of very skilful hands, experimenting or recording".[7]

The day he died, he ordered his servants not to come near him, and sat alone all day, sinking into death. The doctor found him too late, and Cavendish permitted himself an uncharacteristic but revealing comment with his last breath. "Any prolongation of life would only prolong its miseries," he said.

Meanwhile, his cousin, the 5th Duke of Devonshire (1748–1811), was leading a life devoted to prove the opposite, that pleasure was the principle which made the world go round. He had succeeded to the title at the age of sixteen and had early tasted the agreeable fruits of an inactive life. He need not have been so lethargic, being endowed with the Cavendish intelligence, and a sound judgement, but he saw no reason to exert himself, and so he didn't. He chatted pleasantly to friends, gambled constantly, and married two of the most engaging women of the day. In his time Devonshire House became the most famous house in London, and his domestic life the most talked about. For within those walls there occurred an amazing triangular relationship. The Duke, his duchess, and his mistress all living together, in defiance of public gossip, the offspring from both women sharing the nursery, and both women protesting the most undying affection for each other, a bond as strong between them as between each of them and the man they both loved.

Devonshire House entered the period of its greatest splendour in 1774, when the Duke married Georgiana Spencer, one of the two fascinating daughters of Lady Spencer. For the last quarter of the eighteenth century this house occupying the entire block between Berkeley Street and Stratton Street, with imposing forecourt and wrought-iron gates, "those gates that seemed to open but for kindness or to gaiety",[8] was the pivot of London society, the best known house in town. Through those gates passed the most famous men and women of the day – the Prince Regent, Sheridan, Fox, Lady Bessborough (Harriet, Georgiana's sister). Lady Caroline Lamb was growing up in the nursery, with a clutch of the Duke's legitimate and illegitimate children, and no doubt learning lessons in quiet observation which were to form her headstrong character. The lights were on all night, as Devonshire House parties would continue until dawn, gambling, dancing, gossiping, intriguing.

In the centre of this "vertiginous glitter"[9] sat the amiable Duke, holding court, scarcely bothering to move, a man able to make indolence appear attractive and inevitable. People eddied around him, eager to hear his opinion or ask his advice, which was always sound, but his qualities were known only to his friends. Not tempted to seek public office, he remained to the rest of the world an idle, nebulous character, overshadowed by his wife and his mistress.

A contemporary describes him as "a nobleman whose constitutional apathy formed his distinguishing characteristic. His figure was tall and manly, though not animated or graceful; his manners always calm and unruffled. He seemed to be incapable of any strong emotion, and destitute of all energy or activity of mind. As play became indispensable in order to rouse him from his lethargic habit, and to awaken his torpid faculties, he passed his evenings usually at Brook's engaged at whist or faro. Yet, beneath so quiet an exterior, he possessed a highly improved understanding; and on all disputes that occasionally arose among the members of the club, relative to passages of the Roman poets or historians, I know that appeal was commonly made to the duke, and his decision or opinion was regarded as final."[10] Someone else commented, "All his ideas arose in his mind with very gradual progress."

If the public knew little about the Duke, they knew everything about Duchess Georgiana. With impulsive joyful abandon, she exposed every facet of her character to public scrutiny, and seemed not to care what anyone thought.

Georgiana Spencer was descended from the ubiquitous Villiers family (see Chapter 2), which had included Charles II's mistress Barbara Villiers, through one of the Duke of Marlborough's daughters; she descended also, in another line, from Lettice Knollys, wife of Queen Elizabeth's Leicester, and mother of the same Queen's Essex. There was in her blood more than one gene of feminine fascination, and they all fused in her to create a creature who was undeniably the most irresistible woman of her age.

She was not particularly beautiful, but her personality was seductive to a degree. Everyone fell in love with her, everyone wanted to know her, everyone felt better for having met her. Walpole says, "The Duchess of Devonshire effaces all without being a beauty; but her youth, figure, flowing good nature, sense, and lively modesty, and modest familiarity make her a phenomenon."[11] Wraxall, another contemporary witness, agrees: ". . . the Duchess of Devonshire, one of the most distinguished females of high rank whom the last century produced. Her personal charms constituted her smallest pretension to universal admiration; nor did her beauty consist, like that of the Gunnings, in regularity of features and faultless formation of limbs and shape; it lay in the amenity and graces of her deportment, in her irresistible manners, and the seduction of her society."[12]

The charm of Georgiana's company lay in her impish spontaneity, and the genuine kindness of her heart. She was wild, loving, reckless, intoxicating. She jostled, bustled, winked her way through life, her days packed with feverish activity about nothing in particular, leaving a trail of men prostrate with admiration. She had above all the gift of enthusiasm, which she imparted to all who came her way.

Typical of her was the way in which she attacked the problem of canvassing for Fox in 1784. The Devonshires were a famous Whig family, Fox was a Whig candidate. It was essential that enough votes be cast to elect him. If the votes had to come from the working-class slums of London, then Georgiana and her sister Harriet, the Duchess and the Countess, would do their canvassing in those slums. They took the matter very seriously, a list of names and addresses in their hands. The story is justly famous, for the picture of incongruity it suggests is irresistible, and the portrait of Georgiana's unconventional character is vivid. The two ladies, from the pinnacle of London society, immaculately, expensively and exquisitely dressed, bubbling over with good nature and sparkle, walked into the pubs and shops of the East End and persuaded the locals to give their votes to Fox. Such ladies had never been seen in those parts. Georgiana and Harriet were triumphant; they caused a sensation. Georgiana gave a butcher a kiss (the most celebrated kiss in parliamentary history) for the promise of his vote, and an Irish sweep said that if he were God he would make her Queen of Heaven.[13] Georgiana now had half working-class London in her pocket, as well as the Prince of Wales and the whole of the smart set. Fox was elected.

The extravagance of this behaviour, while it might win admirers of her *élan*, did not win friends. Tongues began to wag, the newspapers to make unpleasant inferences. Malicious gossip, to which Georgiana was serenely indifferent, followed her everywhere, and caused her mother much anguish. Year after year Lady Spencer wrote letters of gentle remonstrance to her wild daughter, begging her to have a care of her reputation. "You must learn, my dearest Georgiana," she wrote in 1775 (nine years before the votes-for-kisses incident had marked her for posterity), "to respect yourself, and the world will soon follow your example, but while you herd only with the vicious and the pro- fligate you will be like them, pert, familiar, noisy, and indelicate, not to say indecent in your language and behaviour, and if you once copy them in their contempt for the censures of the grave, and their total disregard for the opinion of the world in general, you will be lost indeed past recovery."[14] This was when Georgiana had been Duchess of Devonshire for only a year. Ten years later, the mother is worried about the killing pace of her daughter's life, and the injury to her health which must result. It is clear from this letter, one among many, that the Duchess was taking tranquillisers to calm her down, and laudanum (*i.e.* opium, a common enough remedy at the time) to keep her going. "For God's sake try to compose yourself. I am terrified lest the perpetual hurry of your spirits, and the medicine you take, to obtain a false tranquillity, should injure you . . . Nothing is so bad for you as continual fretting. Why will you not say fairly: I have led a wild and scrambling life that disagrees with me. I have lost more money than I can afford. I will turn over a new leaf and lead a quiet sober life from this moment . . ."[15] The Duchess did not, of course, heed her mother's advice; she never heeded a moment's advice in her life. It was not that she was too stupid to understand that everyone was right. She knew that her mode of life was harmful, spoke herself of her "giddyness", and begged her children not to follow her example. But she was a creature of impulse and joy, who could assent to the force of rational argument, and immediately act in total disregard of it. The power of pleasure was paramount in her, so strong that it carried its own conviction.

Georgiana's greatest single fault was gambling. She lived in a gambling age, when almost the whole of the nobility loved to play, but she was the worst kind of gambler, one who lost, and who didn't know when to stop. She borrowed money, and went on as before, with the result that she accumulated enormous debts. The Duke gambled too, so did Old Q (the Duke of Queensbery), and Charles Fox, who once lost £20,000 at play. Gibbon tells us that Fox once played for twenty-two hours without pause, losing £500 an hour. And we already know of the Duke of Bedford's disastrous losses. People laid bets on anything, and when not laying bets they were amusing themselves at some other game. Most of the games have now been forgotten, and only some street names remain (such as The Mall) to remind us of the elegant times when the Court played at Mall. In old prints of St James's Park you can see the marks on the wall to note the balls. Thackeray says, "I have calculated the manner in which statesmen and persons of condition passed their time – and what with drinking, and dining, and supping, and cards, wonder how they got through their business at all."[16]

To such temptations, Georgiana was an easy prey. She threw herself into the dissipation of play with sublime disregard for the consequences, and without so much as a word to her husband (who does not seem to have cared what she did when she was not with him). In 1797 her sister Lady Bessborough was arrested and fined for gaming at the house of Lady Buckingham. Though Georgiana was never arrested, her addiction would have ruined her were it not for the help, understanding, and patience of her mother, her husband, and friends who willingly advanced her money. She was in debt all her life. She lied about the amounts she owed, and lied to herself about their importance. If she admitted to owing £6000, it was likely the true total of her debt was £26,000. She would borrow another few thousand, and then banish the matter from her mind.

By the end, she owed well over £120,000 to a variety of creditors, including the Duke of Bedford, and Coutts the banker. She kept the revelation of her sins from the Duke until the last possible moment. He appeared not to know what the rest of London knew, that his wife was a compulsive loser, and remained in ignorance of the truth for years. It is quite clear from her letters that she was terrified of telling him, and equally clear that he reacted like an angel, albeit a lethargic angel.

The dismal story of self-deceit is told in letters from poor Thomas Coutts (who later married Harriot Mellon, the actress who became Duchess of St Albans; see Chapter 2). Flattered that the most famous lady of London should come to him for help, the banker offered avuncular advice with one hand, and money with the other. The Duchess listened to the first in order to get hold of the second. In 1787 he wrote: ". . . how much it shocks me to think what your Grace puts into hazard by indulging a passion for play . . . I should be happy beyond expression if I could think I had even the smallest share in saving your Grace from the dreadful consequences I foresee. It is presumptuous, I confess, to suppose I can have any such power, and impertinent perhaps to obtrude my opinion, or to suppose any such advices at all requisite. From all this I can only take shelter in the purity of my intentions, and your Grace's goodness to see them in the true light."[17] Two years later, when the Duchess, far from repaying the debt, as she naively assumed it would somehow be repaid, had actually asked for more, Coutts is beginning to get anxious. "It is really *romance* what I have done with money already, and how to reconcile to any bounds of discretion (with my little means) to do more, I know not. Besides, tho' you say it will *save* you, how does it appear that the second £6000 will succeed (in this charming purpose) better than the first." After warning the Duchess again of the precipice on which she stands, of the danger to which she is exposed, the faithful Coutts promises to advance another £6000, at the same time suggesting that she ought perhaps to tell the Duke all. By 1792, five years after the first loan, and without any sign that a penny will be repaid, Coutts is disenchanted. "I have never yet refused a draft of yours," he says with conspicuous irritation, "perhaps it would have been quite as well for you, and much better for me, I had never *paid one.*" And ten months later: "But in money matters ninety-nine favours granted are annihilated by the hundredth when refused."[18] Well might he regard the fascinating Duchess as a kind of Circe.

Duchess Georgiana was fittingly a leader of fashion. The skirts worn at this time achieved an enormous circumference. Georgiana, in order to counterbalance this, took her powdered hair higher and higher above her head, until it could be piled up some two feet. Above this, she wore huge ostrich plumes, and the rest of fashionable London followed suit. So significant an innovation was it that even the *Dictionary of National Biography* mentions the Duchess's contribution to fashion.

Though not a learned woman, Georgiana was intelligent. She counted among her friends people like Johnson, who would never suffer a fool and was not a snob, and Sheridan. The stream of visitors to Devonshire House and Chatsworth included many men of culture as well as men of fashion or politics. She wrote a novel herself, published anonymously in 1779, called *The Sylph*. She never bothered to deny the attribution of authorship to her.

When Georgiana Spencer married in 1772 she captured the prize of the year in the Duke of Devonshire. Wealthy and undemanding, he was the perfect spouse. The marriage date had to be kept secret even from the bride, to avoid crowds and publicity which would have been inevitable had she blurted it out; she was told one morning after breakfast that she was to be married that day. Only the immediate family was present, including the Duke's sister, the Duchess of Portland. On that happy day in June she could not have known that she was to embark on a very strange alliance, involving three people instead of two. But had she known, she would not have been afraid.

Lady Elizabeth Foster first appeared on the scene in 1782 when the Devonshires had been married for eight years and were yet childless. Born in 1758, she was the daughter of the Earl of Bristol (the "Earl-Bishop") and had been married very unhappily to John Thomas Foster, M.P., in obedience to her parents. The marriage was a misery, Foster being a parsimonious tyrant. Two sons were born, but shortly afterwards Lady Elizabeth ceased to live with her husband. She was much admired by contemporaries, wooed by the Duke of Richmond and by Gibbon, amongst others, and was much more beautiful than Georgiana. To her friends she was known as "Bess". Gibbon writes of her, comparing her with the Duchess: "Bess is much nearer the level of a mortal, but a mortal for whom the wisest man, historic or medical, would throw away two or three worlds if he had them in possession." He also said that "if she chose to beckon the lord chancellor from his woolsack in full sight of the world, he could not resist obedience".[19]

In short, Lady Elizabeth was the second most fascinating woman of the day. It is curious that she and the Duchess should have been drawn to each other; one would have expected them, with more reason, to be rivals. The mysterious chemistry of friendship occurred at their first meeting, and they established a firm and ardent fellowship which lasted all their lives. Georgiana wanted so much for her husband the Duke to like her new friend. She could not have asked for better, as Lady Elizabeth became his mistress within a very short time, and all three lived more or less happily ever after. More or less, because although the three-sided affair did not threaten to overturn the love or friendship which each member felt for the other two, it did, perhaps naturally, cause some concern to other members of the family. Georgiana's mother, Lady Spencer, refused to meet Lady Elizabeth, so that the Duchess had tactfully to arrange her mother's visits to Chatsworth or Devonshire House while Lady Elizabeth was away. The imperturbable Duke did not waste energy in pondering the suitability or otherwise of the arrangement. He merely enjoyed it and went about his agreeable life as before. Nobody dared ask him about his domestic understandings, though everyone knew. Before long, he was fathering children by both ladies.

In July 1785 both wife and mistress gave birth, within a few weeks of each other. The Duchess's little girl was called Harriet and was born in the comfort of Devonshire House. (There was a previous daughter called Georgiana, born in 1783.) Lady Elizabeth's *accouchement* was squalid by comparison. Even the Devonshire House set could not risk the obloquy of the world by allowing the Duke's illegitimate daughter, as well as his legitimate one, to be born in his house in the same month. So Lady Elizabeth was packed off to Italy, where her little girl was brought into the world by a back-street amateur. She describes the scene in her diary: "Imagine a little staircase, dark and dirty, leading to the apartments of these people. The family consisted of the *Archi-Prêtre des Amoureux*; his woman-servant, a coarse, ugly and filthy creature, the doctor and his wife . . . everything that one can imagine of wicked, vulgar and horrible . . . I had to dine with him, and to endure the odious company of these people; I had to live in a house which was little better than a house of ill fame."[20] The girl was called Caroline St Jules, and when she came to London with her mother to take up her place in the nursery at Devonshire House she was passed off as the daughter of a French nobleman whom Lady Elizabeth and the Duchess had agreed to look after. One cannot be sure how many people were fooled, but the story grew increasingly thin with time, and with further additions to that strange nursery. Caroline grew up to marry George Lamb, brother of William Lamb, so that she too, was "Lady Caroline Lamb" as well as Lady Bessborough's daughter, who had married William Lamb. To differentiate the two, they were known as "Caro William" and "Caro George".

Three years later, Lady Elizabeth again went on her travels, this time to Rouen, to give birth to the Duke's son, whom they called Augustus Clifford (Clifford had been a title borne by the Duke's mother). Lady Elizabeth had what appears to us the cool effrontery to write to her dear friend the Duchess with the wish that she, Georgiana, may have a boy too. "Erring as I have been," she writes, "yet my heart can feel nothing but tenderness and joy at the sight of this dear child – I only wish now that my dear friend had a son also."[21]

Georgiana gave birth to a son and heir in 1790, the Marquess of Hartington, known as "Hart", who as a young man was desperately in love with his cousin Lady Caroline Lamb (i.e. Caro William); he was subsequently the 6th Duke of Devonshire. To make the matter even more complex, the Duke had another daughter by a third woman, and this girl was called Charlotte. Georgiana, too, had her obligatory visit to the continent, to give birth to her daughter by Charles Grey in 1791, a girl who was given the name Eliza Courtney. The Duchess was banished from England for two years as a result of this indiscretion (or "scrape", as she would call it), but was welcomed home by the Duke in 1793 to resume the round of pleasurable living. Half a century later, Greville wrote that "the private (for secret it never was) history of Devonshire House would be very curious and amusing as a scandalous chronicle, an exhibition of vice in its most refined and attractive form, full of grace, dignity and splendour, but I fancy full of misery and sorrow also".[22]

Greville was writing at a time in the social history of England when a moral stance took the place of decent behaviour, and when it was no longer possible to understand the curious morality which allowed the Devonshire House arrangement to work. He may well think that such debauchery must bring misery and sorrow, but he would be wrong. However freely they bestowed their emotions, the Devonshire trio were honourable towards each other, and far more "moral" in their behaviour to each other and to other human beings than the constrained, frustrated Victorians could ever hope to be. It was moral, for example, that the various children of these liaisons should each receive the parental affection that was their due. Jealousy, envy, hatred, were unknown to them. Their instincts were decent.

Greville was also denied the perusal of letters which passed between wife and mistress, and which would have made his eyes blink in incomprehension. Georgiana called her husband's mistress "my dearest, dearest, dearest Bess, my lovely friend . . . my angel love", and she signs herself, "your idolizing G". In January 1784 she wrotes: "I am gulchy, gulchy when I reflect at the length of time that is elapsed since we first knew one another here, at the length of time since I have lost you and at the distance to our meeting, but I comfort myself by thinking what a sacredness all this gives to our friendship. Thank God, we have now been long enough united not to blush at the short period of our friendship. Dr Dr Dr Bess, you grow every day more and more Canis's* sister and yr Georgine's friend . . . you my love, are Canis's child's guardian angel, his and my benefactress." When she confesses to Bess that she is deep in shameful debt, she begs her: "My angel Bess, write to me, tell me you don't hate me for this confession, oh, love, love, love me ever."[23]

Before anyone should wonder, in this age when our sensibilities are smothered by psycho-analysis, I suppose one ought to point out that there was no trace of a lesbian relationship between the two women. It was common form to address one's friend as "dearest love"; people were less ashamed of emotion than they are now, and they valued attachments. Brothers used terms of affection when addressing their sisters that would now seem excessive. Bess was no doubt right to say that the friendship she had with the Duchess was stronger "than perhaps ever united two people".[24] It certainly survived all the minor infidelities of love-making, and both Georgiana and Bess loved the Duke without feeling that they had therefore to hate each other.

Georgiana's decline into middle age was rapid, owing to the pace of her life, and the pills which she took to sustain her in it. Lady Holland described her in 1799, when she was only forty-two, as "painful to see; scarcely has she a vestige of those charms that once attracted all hearts. Her figure is corpulent, her complexion coarse, one eye gone, and her neck immense."[25] She had suffered torments with an infection of the eye, for which the medical attentions of the day were inadequate. She was prescribed an application of three spoonfuls of water mixed with two of brandy and one of vinegar, which all but ruined her sight completely. A handkerchief was tied around her neck to force all the blood into her head, and then leeches were applied to her eye to bleed it. Not surprisingly (to us) the eye became ulcerated and grew to the size of a grapefruit. She then changed to bathing it in warm milk, but it was too late. She fell back on laudanum to relieve the pain.

* "Canis" was the Duke. "Racky" was Bess, and "The Rat" was Georgiana.

Georgiana Duchess of Devonshire died in 1806 aged forty-eight, and with her died a brilliant epoch. Her friend Bess was distraught with grief. Her sister Lady Bessborough wrote : "Anything so horrible, so killing as her three days' agony no human being ever witnessed. I saw it all, held her thro' all her struggles, saw her expire, and since have again and again kiss'd her cold lips and press'd her lifeless body to my heart, and yet I am alive."[26] Not having known her, we cannot judge how given to exaggeration her obituarists might have been, but one of them writes with the ring of conviction when he says, "never, we will venture to say, was the death of any human being more universally lamented than hers will be."[27]

With her died also that wonderful gift of affection possessed by the whole Devonshire House set. The next generation was much less generous of heart. Georgiana's children turned on Bess, who continued to live with the Duke and grow old with him, and one of them, Harriet, known as Harryo, nursed an implacable hatred of her. When, three years later, the Duke took the only honourable and logical course by making Bess his second duchess, the children, now grown-up, were outraged. But the Duke first wrote a warm and eloquent letter to his mother-in-law Lady Spencer advising her of his intention.[28]

The marriage lasted only two years, for the Duke died in 1811, though Bess's love for him continued beyond the grave. The children were quite insensitive, and Hart, now the new duke, ordered her to leave Devonshire House a week later. She spent her last years in exile in Rome, where she gathered around her a coterie of eminent people of culture, and where she died in 1824. Hart, by this time reconciled, had her body brought back to England, where it lay in state at Devonshire House, before being buried in the Cavendish vault at Derby, alongside her beloved duke and her beloved friend, Georgiana.

Georgiana's son, Hart, the 6th Duke of Devonshire (1790–1858), led a life which was supremely characteristic of a Cavendish – undemonstrative, unnoticed, and comfortable. In common with his ancestors, he was a man of much ability, which he never used. His talents lay neglected, for want of the energy to make them blossom. In his case, the habits of timidity and reserve were compounded by an incurable deafness, which showed itself in childhood and persisted throughout his life. As a result of this, he never spoke in the House of Lords, though he conscientiously sat there and gave his vote. His tastes were literary, being a member of the Roxburghe Club, and he devoted much attention to his library at Chatsworth, to which he added many volumes bought from the Duke of Roxburghe's collection. A true Cavendish, his library was his home. Also like a Cavendish, his hospitality was lavish. Though he may have preferred solitude, he saw it as his duty to entertain and to share his various homes. In his lights, it would have been immoral to live alone in a grand house, so he suffered what must have been torment for him, to be surrounded by forty people at dinner every day, talking in a cacophony of sound which he could not unscramble into words.

Though he took no active part in political life, he was powerful enough by virtue of his name and possessions to be indifferent to status. He was known to decline a royal command, almost an unheard-of snub, because he had a party that evening at Chiswick which had been arranged long before.[29] Hart would not regard this as anything but simple truth. It was not within him to be insulting or calculating.

The one passion of his life, conceived in childhood and subdued in maturity, was his affection for his bewitching cousin, Lady Caroline Lamb, to whom he signed himself "Devilshire". Theirs was a puppy love grown into devotion, the letters between them full of eloquent endearments. The Duke did not marry, however; he was sometimes called the Bachelor Duke. No doubt his deafness made him uncertain in female company. His *affaires amoureuses* were reserved for Paris.

His fame rests not on an achievement of his, but on the achievements of his protégé, Sir Joseph Paxton. Were it not for Devonshire, Paxton may not have been discovered. Mr Paxton, a young man in his early twenties, was employed on the Duke's estate at Chatsworth as a gardener. The Duke recognised his special talents, and encouraged him to give them expression; he commissioned Paxton to build at Chatsworth a giant conservatory, 300 feet long by 145 feet wide, by 60 feet high, covering in all one acre. This unique construction soon attracted the world's notice to the young gardener, whose career culminated in the Crystal Palace built for the Exhibition of 1851, a vast glass building placed in Hyde Park, modelled to an extent on the conservatory at Chatsworth, and which now has a suburb of London named after it. Paxton and the Duke remained close friends all their lives, the one a brilliant worldly success, the other a disappointed and unhappy man. "I had rather all those plants were dead than have you ill", the Duke wrote to Paxton in 1835. "He is more kind to me than you can possibly imagine", said Paxton.[30] In a way, the Duke enjoyed Paxton's achievements by proxy.

He was succeeded by a distant cousin, the 7th Duke of Devonshire (1808–1891), who had been a member of Parliament for the University of Cambridge, a clever scholar with a scientific bent, and was subsequently Chancellor of the Universities of London and Cambridge. He liked being at Hardwick Hall because he could lead a more private life there. He married a grand-daughter of the 5th Duke, thus knitting the family together again, and was succeeded by his son Spencer Compton Cavendish (the first in the line not to be called William Cavendish after the founder of the family fortune), 8th Duke of Devonshire (1833–1908). For most of his life this man was Marquess of Hartington, coming to the dukedom at the age of fifty-eight, so it is by his nickname of "Harty-tarty" that the memory of him lingers.

Harty-tarty holds a place in the history of nineteenth-century politics far in excess of his achievements, by virtue of his solid common sense. He held many political offices, but grew to dislike them, and three times he refused to be Prime Minister. For forty years he was in and out of the Cabinet. He distrusted rhetoric and insincerity, of which he found all too much evidence in political life. His own mind worked slowly. He was not quick-witted, not eloquent, not amusing, not engaging, but he was a first-rate administrator, and had deep convictions, which he never compromised. Harty-tarty was boring, but right. Members would put up with his interminable factual speeches, delivered without a glint of humour or relief of phrase, because they knew he was more conscientious than anyone else, and had better judgement. Margot Asquith said that his speaking "was the finest example of pile-driving the world has ever seen". He himself knew how boring and laborious he was. He once yawned in the middle of a speech in the House, and apologised by explaining that what he was saying was "so damned dull".[31] Dutifully, Harty-tarty invited large numbers of house-guests to Chatsworth, but could rarely remember who they were. More than once there were nearly 500 people, including servants, staying in the house. He was a casual, easy-going man, impossible to impress. One of his guests wandered over to Pevensey Castle, a romantic ruin which belonged to the Duke.* At dinner, the Duke asked him where he had been, and the guest said how impressed he had been with Pevensey Castle. "Pevensey?" said the Duke, to whom the name rang a bell. "Whose is Pevensey?"[32]

Such a casual attitude to wealth and possessions carried its own charm. Just as it was impossible to impress the Duke, so he never

---

* Near Eastbourne, on the Duke's Compton Place estate.

sought to impress anyone else. Status-seeking was trivial to him, but if you had status already, it was equally trivial not to use it. One of his father's agents was disquieted by the amount of money which Harty-tarty was spending, and conveyed his concern to the Duke who could not understand what all the fuss was about. "Well," he said, "isn't there plenty of it?"

Harty-tarty was not ambitious; he had nothing to be ambitious for. He did not know the feeling of enthusiasm in anything. He was reported to have said that the happiest moment in his life was when his pig took first prize at an agricultural show. Whatever he said or did was based on principle, not gain or expediency. He had more probity and common sense, and was known to have them, than any of his contemporaries. Hence his enormous influence. "I don't know why it is," he said, "but whenever a man is caught cheating at cards the case is referred to me." However lightweight the remark, it shows that the Duke was reputed incorruptible, because he was above reward.

Margot Asquith has left us the best pen-portrait of this Duke. He was, she wrote, "a man whose like we shall never see again; he stood by himself and could have come from no country in the world but England. He had the figure and appearance of an artisan, with the brevity of a peasant, the courtesy of a king and the noisy sense of humour of a Falstaff . . . possessed of endless wisdom. He was perfectly disengaged from himself, fearlessly truthful, and without pettiness of any kind."[33]

As he grew older, Harty-tarty's constitutional somnolence became worse. He would fall asleep at dinner, during a speech, or at the top of the stairs. He fell asleep once in the House of Lords, woke up with a start, looked at the clock, and said, "Good heavens! What a bore! I shan't be in bed for another seven hours." On another occasion, he said, "I had a horrid nightmare. I dreamed I was making a speech in the House of Lords, and I woke up and found I was actually doing so."[34] His last remark, as he lay dying, was typical of the man. "Well," he said, "the game is over, and I'm not sorry."[35]

A game, indeed, it had been, and played with a finesse which only the Victorians could master. For this upright, thoughtful and straightforward man had for thirty years been having a discreet, but not secret, affair with the Duchess of Manchester.

The Duchess of Manchester, afterwards Duchess of Devonshire, was a German aristocrat by birth – Countess Louise von Alten. It was said that nobody could understand how beautiful a woman could be unless they had seen the Duchess of Manchester at thirty. She quickly became the leader of the "fast set" in London (as opposed to the more sedentary "Victorian" set), gambled and danced the days and nights away. She bore the Duke of Manchester five children but her one true love was Harty-tarty, to whom she was devoted. They always addressed each other formally in public, by their titles. No whisper of scandal was allowed to follow them; they were scrupulously correct.

Louise was a remorseless lady of ambition. It was she who pushed Hartington into the position of influence which he held. She wanted desperately for him to be Prime Minister, and he, of course, did not give it a thought. They made an odd couple of conflicting elements, he sluggish and contented, she powerfully imperious. She had something of the "unswerving relentlessness of a steam-roller about her, neither kindly nor unkindly, but crushing its way on, and flattening out the unevennesses of the road it intended to traverse". She prodded and drove him. Fortunately, he was possessed of such a large measure of common sense, that he did not allow himself to be influenced by her. As E. F. Benson has put it, "It was largely she who made him use his weight; he could use it equally well sitting down."[36]

When the Duke of Manchester died, Louise became the "Double Duchess' by marring Devonshire, and when he died she shuffled into an awesome old age, her looks gone, but her imperiousness augmented. Consuelo Vanderbilt (Duchess of Marlborough) described her as "a raddled old woman, covering her wrinkles with paint, and her pate with a brown wig. Her mouth was a red gash, and from it, when she saw me, issued a stream of abuse."[37] With her wigs, and her diamonds and her rouge, surrounded by minions, she was "rather like the half-ruinous shell of some castellated keep, with flower-boxes in full bloom on the crumbling sills . . . almost a piece of still life, expressionless, speechless, and motionless".[38] She died after a stroke at Sandown races in 1911.

For all that, Louise the Double Duchess was a faithful friend and wife. From the day they formed their romantic attachment to the day the Duke died, not once were they tempted elsewhere. Her love for him was touching; it alone was able to relax the features of her statuesque face, which generally showed no emotion at all in public. One who caught a glimpse of this love was Daisy Warwick, who wrote : "To all outward appearance both the Duke and Duchess of Devonshire were devoid of the normal human sympathies, but there was no other man in the world for her, and there was no other woman for him. They were not prepossessing people, but their love for one another was a very beautiful thing."[39]

She used to say that when Devonshire died he would go straight to Heaven (pointing her first finger high above her head), but Lord Salisbury, on the other hand . . . (her finger dived to the floor).[40] Little did she know that Salisbury's grand-daughter would herself become Duchess of Devonshire in time.

The 8th Duke died in 1908, and was succeeded by his nephew as 9th Duke (1868–1938), who continued the family's political traditions: he was Secretary of State for the Colonies, and Governor-General of Canada. His second son married Adele Astaire (Fred Astaire's sister), and his daughter Dorothy married Harold Macmillan, the Prime Minister.

The 10th Duke of Devonshire (1895–1950), who was deaf like the 6th Duke (Georgiana's son), suffered a period of family tragedies which made it seem that the Cavendishes were being pursued by a particularly malignant Fate. The son and heir, Marquess of Hartington, married a daughter of the American Ambassador, Joseph Kennedy, whose second son, Jack, would one day be President of the United States. She was Kathleen Kennedy, by every account the sweetest and most good-natured girl in the family. There was, however, one major difficulty. The Cavendishes, as one of the founding Whig families, had always been fiercely Protestant, and the Kennedys were as passionately Catholic.

Opposition to the marriage from the Kennedy side continued for years. The Kennedys would not countenance the idea of future grandchildren being educated in the Protestant tradition, and while the Duke's family was fond of Kathleen (or "Kick") personally, her religion did present an obstacle. "It amuses me to see how worried they all are," wrote Kick. Added to which, of course, the war had started, and Joe Kennedy was spending much of his time disparaging the British.

The marriage eventually took place in 1944, six years after permission had first been sought. Four months later, Hartington was killed in action, and the new Marchioness was herself killed in an air crash in 1948. Chips Channon wrote: "Billy Hartington killed; my adorable Charlie Cavendish [that's Adele Astaire's husband, who also died in 1944]. And now Eddie [the 10th Duke] dead at fifty-five. What dread score has destiny to pay off against the Devonshires? . . . Is it the end of Chatsworth and of Hardwick?"[41]

If one were superstitious, it would be impossible to resist the inference that the association with the Kennedy family had been fatal; it is well known that tragedy has consistently stalked the Kennedys. Lord Hartington was no ordinary loss – he was an extremely clever man with a promising future. His death made his brother, Andrew Robert Buxton Cavendish (born 1920), heir to the dukedom; he succeeded as 11th Duke in 1950.

In keeping with the family tradition of public service, the Duke of Devonshire has held political office. In fact, he is the only duke of the present generation to have done so after succeeding to his title. He was Minister of State for Commonwealth Relations from 1962 to 1964, then for Colonial Affairs for a year afterwards. Since leaving political life, he has devoted himself to other cherished duties, especially his association with Manchester University. He is Vice-Lieutenant of Derbyshire, a Trustee of the National Gallery, President of the Royal Hospital and of the Home for Incurables, and sometime President of the Lawn Tennis Association. He was a major in the Coldstream Guards, with whom he served in World War II.

To meet Devonshire is to have an uncanny feeling that one is in the presence of his formidable great-uncle the 8th Duke. A man of obvious ability and stature, he has authority in his style, and commands respect simply by his presence. Frivolity he abhors, flattery he would detest. He is not a man to receive or pay compliments easily. A certain diffidence allied to profound inherent probity make him a man of few words – abrupt and laconic. From his mother (a daughter of Lord Salisbury) he has inherited the Cecil voice with its rapid speech. (It has been said that a Cecil can get through more words in a minute than other people can in five.) Everything else about him is pure Cavendish, down to his impeccable suits.

The Duchess of Devonshire is one of the famous Mitford sisters, daughters of the 2nd Lord Redesdale. It is odd how all the fascinating aristocratic women whose fame has endured over the centuries have come in clutches. In the seventeenth century there were the Jennings sisters, one of whom became Duchess of Tyrconnel, and the other was the redoubtable Sarah Duchess of Marlborough. In the eighteenth century there were the two Gunnings girls – Elizabeth was in turn Duchess of Hamilton and Duchess of Argyll, while her sister was Countess of Coventry – followed by the Spencer girls, Georgiana Duchess of Devonshire and her sister Lady Bessborough. Proceeding into the nineteenth century, we have the three granddaughters of Richard Brinsley Sheridan (one of whom became Duchess of Somerset), all the seven Pattle girls – whose descendants include Virginia Woolf and the next Duke of Beaufort – and right at the end of the century, the Tennant sisters from Scotland, including Margot Asquith and two still alive, Baroness Elliot of Harewood, D.B.E., and Lady Wakehurst, D.B.E. The present-day representatives of this pattern are a hectic group of brilliant beautiful sisters, the Mitfords.

The unorthodox upbringing of the Mitford girls in a household dominated by an explosive reactionary father and a vague compliant mother has been vividly narrated by two of the sisters: the nursery managed to produce a family of strong individuals, including one Communist, one Fascist, and eventually one duchess. The late Nancy Mitford made her name as novelist and biographer. Jessica Mitford emigrated to the United States, and has written a number of successful books. Unity was a personal friend of Hitler, and Diana married Sir Oswald Mosley. The fifth, "Debo", is Duchess of Devonshire.

"Debo" decided at the age of eleven, according to sister Jessica's account, that she would marry a duke. While the other girls prayed that "Mr Right" would come along, she reserved her prayers for the "Duke of Right".* Thanks to Nancy, who clearly used her as a model for Linda in *The Pursuit of Love*, the Duchess is better known than almost any of her rank alive today. We know that she is sentimental and romantic. She is astonishingly beautiful, with cornflower-blue eyes that bewitch the least impressionable.

The Devonshires have a son and two daughters (one of whom has married into the ubiquitous Tennant family), and they live at Chatsworth, now a much quieter house. Seven gamekeepers are still employed there, and a domestic staff of fifteen, but over three-quarters of the house, a magnificent seventeenth-century mansion, is left alone for the public to enjoy. We tend to think of the "Stately Home business" as a twentieth-century necessity, but Chatsworth has been open to the public consistently since the eighteenth century. The archives are among the best kept in the country, and accommodate an endless stream of students. The Duke and Duchess have a floor to themselves, including two small but exquisite sitting-rooms in which they have kept alive the spirit of Georgiana. The rooms are decorated in precisely the style Georgiana would recognise, and, apart from a Domenichino cartoon and a Poussin, are hung with pictures of her and her contemporaries. Georgiana spent more time in London than at Chatsworth, but no matter, it is at Chatsworth that her presence is still felt.

At the coronation of 1953 "Debo" Devonshire wore Duchess Georgiana's eighteenth-century robes.

*   *   *

* It is fair to point out that when she married Captain Lord Andrew Cavendish he was the second son, and was not expected to inherit the titles.

The Duke of Devonshire is descended from the second son of Bess of Hardwick by Sir William Cavendish. Their third son, Charles, went to Welbeck Abbey and was the father of the Duke of Newcastle in the Cavendish family.*

The brother of the 1st Duke of Newcastle was the famous mathematician Sir Charles Cavendish, of Welbeck Abbey, and the wife of the 2nd Duke was an even more famous writer – Margaret Cavendish, Duchess of Newcastle (1624–1674). Sneered at by Walpole, who dismissed her as a "fertile pedant", the Duchess was highly regarded in her own time, and objective critics consider that her biography of her husband is very fine. Her output was enormous, including poetry, plays, and prose works, and most of her books are now extremely rare. She had an additional reputation for madness, fostered by her penchant for appearing in theatrical costume at the least appropriate time, and by her outrageously affected manners. Saner than many of her detractors, the Duchess was guilty of little more than a flair for display. There was no son and heir, so that the dukedom became extinct, but her daughter Henrietta married Edward Harley, Earl of Oxford, and this marriage also produced a female heir, Margaret, who in 1734 married the 2nd Duke of Portland. Thus it was that the Dukes of Portland became owners of Welbeck Abbey, and of the Harley properties in London, which span an area of Marylebone now spattered with street names which recall this complicated past – Harley Street, Welbeck Street, Cavendish Square, Portland Place, Great Titchfield Street (the Duke of Portland's second title is Marquess of Titchfield). Not only that, but it means the blood of Margaret Cavendish, Duchess of Newcastle, flows in the veins of the Duke of Portland.

The dukedom of Portland had been conferred upon the Bentinck family in 1716 in recognition of the capital role played by the 1st Duke's father, Hans Wilhelm Bentinck, in post-Stuart England. The story of the close friendship between William III and his protégé Hans Bentinck provides an intriguing chapter in the history of the British monarchy.

Hans Bentinck (1649–1709) was the son of a Dutch nobleman (the family continues in Holland today), who first came to the attention of the Prince of Orange in 1664, when he was fourteen years

* The seventeenth-century Duke of Newcastle was a Cavendish; the modern Duke of Newcastle is a Pelham-Clinton-Hope, and belongs to another chapter. They have nothing to do with one another. The first was Duke of Newcastle-upon-Tyne, the second is Duke of Newcastle-under-Lyme; the first line came to an end nearly 300 years ago, the second was not created until 1756 and continues into modern times.

old and the Prince was fifteen. The Prince made Hans his personal Page of Honour, and later a Nobleman of the Chamber. Bentinck was ravishingly beautiful, and possessed the rare virtue of constancy. The friendship thus begun in adolescence lasted an entire lifetime, surviving the onslaughts of jealousy, the competition of marriage, and the resentment of the House of Commons.

When they were both young men there occurred a critical event which was to secure the importance of their relationship. The Prince of Orange nearly died of smallpox, and were it not for the selfless attentions of Hans Bentinck he would almost certainly have succumbed. Hans slept with the Prince for sixteen days and nights, not daring to leave his side, in an attempt to absorb into his own body some of the fever which threatened his friend's life. It was an act of courage and devotion, and it worked. Hans did catch the fever, but both men survived, and the affection which bound them grew stronger as a result.

Hans was frequently sent to the Court of St James as William's personal envoy. It was he who negotiated William's marriage to Princess Mary of York, he who was instrumental in having the throne of England offered to William, he who was the Prince's most intimate counsellor. When William became King of England in 1689, Hans came to England with him, and established here the noble family of Bentinck.

The King had manifest reasons to be thankful, and was lavish in his demonstrations of gratitude. A few days before his coronation he created his friend Earl of Portland in the peerage of England, and granted him lands too numerous to count. The flow of gifts to Bentinck hardly abated in the years to come, so that he was in time the richest subject in Europe. Unfortunately, Bentinck had neither the grace nor tact to acknowledge that the massive bestowal of gifts in his receptive lap might legitimately arouse the jealousy of the English, no matter how much he may have deserved them. He was, after all, a foreigner, yet he came into possession of more English lands than any Englishman. He showed none of the deferential politeness that one might expect from a guest in the country, but on the contrary flaunted his new wealth, exploited his closeness to the King, and treated the English with lofty disdain. He did not care for the English, and made no attempt to ingratiate himself. Consequently, they did not care for him. Everyone recognised and applauded his integrity, his devotion to the King, his pellucid honesty, but the English wished that he would learn to flatter (an art which they had been busy perfecting through centuries of Court life), and would try a little harder to dissemble. He did not dissemble at all, and was profoundly unpopular. Even in his native Holland he was considered a foreigner now; he conspicuously lacked the dexterity to appear sympathetic.

There was a rumour that the King intended to create Bentinck Duke of Buckingham, which would have been asking for trouble. Already singularly disliked by the House of Commons, he would have exacerbated their mistrust by bearing the title created by James I for his lover George Villiers, and the plan was mercifully dropped. The Bentinck family had to wait until the second generation for their dukedom, conferred by George I in 1716.

Surprisingly for one with such feeling for friendship, Bentinck showed few discernible signs of emotion. Marlborough called him "a wooden fellow", and subsequent cartoons of his descendants have depicted them as blocks of Portland stone. Swift said unkindly that he was "as great a Dunce as ever I knew", but Swift was most likely venting spleen; for Bentinck was no fool.

At least his beauty was acknowledged by all, and his devotion to the King hardly in question. He was at the King's side on the death of Queen Mary, and with him at the disclosure of the assassination plot in 1696. His affection was real and not motivated by self-interest. It wavered only once, when William's attentions became engaged by a new favourite, Arnold van Keppel (created Earl of Albermarle).* Keppel's softer, more capricious nature captivated the King, who granted him favours which provoked a jealous rage in Bentinck of such ferocity that he seemed a different person. His customary cold control suddenly evaporated into a sulky sullenness. Quarrels erupted daily at Court, where Bentinck's naked nerves sparked scenes of lofty petulance, and the bluntness of hurt pride. He repelled William's attempts to make amends, refused to take his seat in the royal coach, and eventually resigned all his offices in a fit of umbrage. The King attempted to dissuade him, but he was firm. What really offended Bentinck were the shortcomings in his *own* character, cruelly highlighted by the contrast with Keppel's gentler graces, and about which he could do nothing. He deeply resented being passed over for being himself. He suffered the pain of rejection, in the knowledge that it was not for faults committed, but for transitory attractions with which he could not compete. Bentinck took refuge in an embassy in Paris, and William wrote him an affectionate letter promising that his feelings for him would continue until

---

* Walter Keppel, 9th Earl of Albermarle, is a direct descendant.

death. There are over 200 of these letters from the King, which amply testify to the generosity of their love.

The breach was not final. Bentinck was a close friend to the end of the King's life. On William's death-bed his last words were to ask for Portland, who came immediately, gave William his hand, and, as Luttrell tells us, the King "carried it to his heart with great tenderness".

Bentinck himself is buried in Westminster Abbey, as is his son, the 1st Duke of Portland (1682–1726). It was Bentinck's grandson, the 2nd Duke (1709–1762), who married the Cavendish and Harley heiress and moved his principal seat from Bulstrode Park, Bucks, to Welbeck Abbey, Notts. Like father and grandfather, he too was a conspicuously beautiful man, "reported to be the handsomest man in England". With Bentinck, Harley and Cavendish lands in his possession, he could afford the luxury of indifference to favours, and is said to have refused a position as Lord of the Bedchamber, because it was inconvenient; but he thanked the King nonetheless.[43]

His son the 3rd Duke of Portland (1738–1809) consolidated the Cavendish connection by marrying Dorothy Cavendish, daughter of the 4th Duke of Devonshire, in 1766, and by changing his own name to Cavendish-Bentinck in 1801. He was therefore the brother-in-law of the 5th Duke of Devonshire (Georgiana's husband), and while Devonshire lived in Devonshire House, Piccadilly, Portland lived down the road at Burlington House, another of his brother-in-law's properties.

The 3rd Duke was one of the best educated men in England, and the only member of the Bentinck family to assume high public office. He was Prime Minister in 1783 and 1807–9, and Home Secretary from 1794–1801. It is for his work as Home Secretary that his reputation should endure, for he belongs to the gallery of tolerant Englishmen who have helped establish the right to freedom of speech, not by noisy crusading, but by taking the principle for granted. As Home Secretary he had at his command vast arbitrary power which he refused to exert. He knew the value of leaving the expression of opinion untrammelled, and his achievement was quietly and stubbornly to show respect for it against the more vociferous will of angry men.

As Prime Minister he was less than successful. He had integrity and honour, but none of the rough ruthlessness that it takes to be a leader. His intentions were good, but weak his ability to push them. Consequently, he was regarded as a mere cypher. When he accepted the Premiership in 1807 it was with a reluctant heart, out of a sense of public duty. He was already old and gouty, feeble and unequal to the strain. The duel between Canning and Castlereagh on Wimbledon Common took place during his government, and the dishonour and scandal were too much for him. He resigned in October 1809 and died the same month.

Walpole was scornful of him. In 1782, before his first Premiership and when he was virtually unknown, Walpole wrote, "He has lived in Ducal dudgeon with half-a-dozen toad-eaters secluded from mankind behind the ramparts of Burlington wall. . . . It is very entertaining that two or three great families should persuade themselves that they have an hereditary and exclusive right of giving us a lead without a tongue."[44] Lady Elizabeth Holland was even less fair. "Of all the truly contemptible public characters in England among many", she wrote in her *Journal*, "surely his Grace of Portland stands the foremost; his friends even dare not say a word in his behalf."[45] While it is possible to accuse the 3rd Duke of lack of vigour, it is difficult to find anything contemptible in his career. Lady Elizabeth did not explain herself.

An interesting point is that his grandson, C. W. F. Bentinck, was grandfather to Queen Elizabeth the Queen Mother. The 3rd Duke of Portland is therefore an ancestor of Queen Elizabeth II.

The 4th Duke of Portland (1768–1854), who secretly bought Hughenden for Disraeli in 1847 so that the politician should have a house commensurate with his ambitions, had four sons. The heir died at the age of twenty-eight, leaving three confirmed bachelors. "None of the three Bentinck brothers was married, and none of them was likely to marry", wrote Lady Londonderry, without further comment. The three were Lord George Bentinck, Lord Henry Bentinck, and the strange man who was to succeed as 5th Duke of Portland.

Apart from a hopelessly romantic adoration conceived by Lord George Bentinck for the Duchess of Richmond, the three brothers showed themselves indifferent to marriage. The oddest of the three was the 5th Duke of Portland, who succeeded to the title at the age of fifty-four, by which time he was clearly established as a wild eccentric.

To begin with, the 5th Duke of Portland (1800–1879) dressed in a peculiar fashion. Whatever the weather, his trousers were secured a few inches above the ankle by a piece of old string, tied tight. In every season he carried an old umbrella, and a coat was always slung over his arm. The umbrella and coat were not intended to protect him from rain, but from the gaze of curious people. If anyone looked at him, he hid himself beneath the umbrella, and wrapped the huge coat around him. He was seen in sweltering summer wearing a heavy sable coat which touched the ground.[46] He bought three frock-coats at a time, of different sizes, so that he could wear one over the other. He habitually wore an old-fashioned wig. One of his rooms at Welbeck Abbey was lined with cupboards reaching floor to ceiling, and packed with green boxes, each containing a dark brown wig.[47] On top of the long wig he wore a hat, two feet high.

Thus attired, he would walk on his estates, avoiding everyone. He was never seen at Court, and never mingled in society. He appears to have been entirely friendless. Even his solicitors were not permitted an interview with him. None of his tenants, labourers, or servants was allowed to speak to him or acknowledge his presence in any way. The man who dared to touch his hat would be dismissed immediately. The same orders applied to the parson. Everyone at Welbeck had instructions that, if they chanced upon the Duke, they were to pass him by "as they would a tree".[48]

He inherited from his mother this peculiarity that he would not be seen by anyone. If he gave permission for anyone to visit Welbeck, he would always make a condition that "Mr So-and-So will be good enough not to *see* me". When he drove out, it was alone, in a black carriage, like a hearse, drawn by black horses, with all the blinds down. He had another carriage drawn by ponies, and driven by boys, but it also was draped in thick curtains. When he went to London, he did not leave his carriage; it was placed, with him inside, on a railway truck, unloaded at the London terminus, and driven to his house in Cavendish Square. The servants were naturally ordered out of the way, so that nobody saw him arrive or leave, and no one saw him while he was there. If he needed a doctor, the man would not be allowed to come any nearer than the door, where he could ask whatever questions he needed to ask of the valet, who then reported them to the Duke, and reported the Duke's answers to the doctor. Only the valet was allowed to feel the ducal pulse. If he went walking at night at Welbeck, it was with a woman companion, who had instructions never to speak to him, and to walk exactly forty yards ahead of him, carrying a lantern.

The Duke spent a great deal of money making Welbeck a splendid palace in which to entertain on a grand scale, but never invited anyone. He lived in a small suite of rooms tucked away in a corner of the vast house, and had a letter-box put in his bedroom door, so that he need never be disturbed. His daily meal was a chicken, killed in the morning. He ate half of it for lunch, and the other half for dinner. In the kitchen there was a chicken perpetually on a roasting-

spit, day after day for years, so that one would be ready for him whenever he rang for it.[49] The roast chicken would then be placed in a
lift, transported in a heated truck on rails along a tunnel 150 yards
to his rooms.

So obsessive did his need for privacy become that the Duke spent
the last years of his life, and a considerable part of his fortune, in
converting Welbeck Abbey in such a way that all rooms would be
underground. Like a shy mole, he burrowed deeper and deeper to
avoid the daylight. The subterranean rooms are still there. They were
approached by a single flight of stairs from the long tunnel which
formed part of fifteen miles of tunnelling. There was a huge library,
a billiard-room capable of holding half a dozen billiard tables, and
the largest ballroom in the country, capable of holding 2000 people
comfortably. This was approached from above, as a great lift
descended from the ceiling, and twenty people at a time could be thus
lowered into the ballroom (though one can hardly imagine anyone
wanting to be). Through a staircase in the ceiling of another room
was the riding-school, the second largest in the world, lit by 8000 jets
of gas, an exercising ground under glass, and a gallop of straw a
quarter of a mile long. Another tunnel, 200 yards long, led to a suite
of rooms covering four acres, and another to the stables, cow-houses
and dairies. The garden covered thirty acres, and required fifty-three
gardeners. There were eighty keepers in the dairies, and forty-five
grooms in the stables. When the Duke died, ninety-four horses were
in the underground stables.

There was even a private tunnel from the house to Worksop, one
and a quarter miles long, wide enough for two carriages. In short,
there was really no need for the Duke to be seen by anyone at any
time, and he succeeded in his passion for anonymity better than any
other ducal recluse.

For all this, however eccentric his behaviour, the 5th Duke of
Portland was one of the better landlords. He was generous to his
tenants and staff, providing always they took care *not* to treat him
with respect, and gave an enormous amount of his money to charity.
He built a skating-rink for the staff, and the poor maids were
obliged to skate from time to time whether they wanted to or not.
His one reprehensible act was to make a bonfire of some of his
pictures, worth several thousand pounds, because he deemed them
inadequate to the grandeur of the underground palace he was building. But he was clearly mentally unbalanced.

The work kept over 500 masons busy for years, and the end result
was quirky, dismal, impressive and cold. Augustus Hare wrote:

"All is vast, splendid and utterly comfortless: one could imagine no more awful and ghastly fate than waking up one day and finding oneself Duke of Portland and master of Welbeck."[50]

Unfortunately for the Portland family, there was one woman in England who dreamed precisely of waking up and finding herself mistress of Welbeck, and so powerful did her fantasy become that she grew to believe in it. Her persistence led to one of the most curious cases in the history of litigation, in which her family attempted to prove that the Duke of Portland had been leading a double life, that he had managed a shop in Baker Street for years, and that he had a son and heir living in Baker Street who should succeed to the dukedom. The lady who initiated this extravagant farce was a Mrs Druce.

In 1896 the Home Secretary received a curious application from one Mrs Anna Maria Druce, of 68 Baker Street, London, asking for permission to open a coffin at Highgate Cemetery. Mrs Druce claimed that the coffin, which was supposed to contain the body of her husband, T. C. Druce, was in fact empty, that the funeral of T. C. Druce in 1864 had been an elaborate pretence, and that her husband had continued to live until 1879 in his "other role" as the Duke of Portland. Consequently, she was in truth the Duchess of Portland, and her son should now be restored to his rightful inheritance as the Duke. The revelation of the empty coffin would show that T. C. Druce and the Duke of Portland were one and the same man.

More than ten years were to elapse before Mrs Druce's wish was granted, by which time she had been swept off the stage by the rush of events, and her place taken by more resourceful men. At the beginning, she was a lone crusader, appealing to the House of Lords, battling resolutely against all the obstacles which bureaucracy could hurl in her path. Her case was given impetus by the discovery that, when another member of the Druce family had been buried in 1893 in the family vault, the coffin containing T. C. Druce was seen to have caved in under the weight of the coffin above it, strongly suggesting that it might be empty. The newspapers relished the chance to celebrate the lonely fight of a poor downtrodden old woman against the mighty millions of a landed aristocrat, and the case was discussed for so many years before it reached the courts that there was barely a literate person in the country who did not know about the Druce-Portland case. By constant repetition, the lady's claims gathered support, while the 6th Duke kept a careful silence.

The case would never have gone so far were it not for the fact that the 5th Duke of Portland's habits were so odd, his secrecy so total.

It was perfectly possible that he had been leading a double life. He had no friends, so there was no one to say exactly what he looked like. He was not seen, so there were few to say exactly where he was. When his carriage was taken off the train in London and driven, with blinds drawn, to his London house, no one actually saw him get in it, travel in it, or get out of it. What was there to prevent his sneaking out of the railway station and walking down to Baker Street to assume his other identity as a shop-owner? If anyone wanted to lead a double life, nobody was better placed to achieve it than the 5th Duke of Portland. And the Duke was precisely that kind of eccentric to whom such an idea might appeal. Rumours had been flying around London for years that the Duke had something to hide, and it was common gossip in Baker Street that Mr Druce's funeral in 1864 had been false, long before Mrs Druce thought she was the Duchess of Portland. She merely gathered the rumours together and made use of them, not without a touch of genius.

The mass of circumstantial evidence which strongly suggested that the Duke and the shopkeeper were the same person was set out in a pamphlet called *Claim to the Portland Millions: Was Druce the Duke?* In it, the list of similarities of habit which linked the two men was striking. They were both secretive, both travelled in a closed carriage, and both made their coachman swear not to reveal where they went. They both had a passion for building underground. They both wore a great variety of wigs. They were both profoundly anti-social. They were fastidious, methodical, cautious and suspicious. They both had a skin complaint, and avoided the sunlight as a result. (This was another reason for the Duke's perpetual umbrella.) They both loathed to be acknowledged or saluted.

Furthermore, there were astonishing coincidences of timing in the events of their lives. In the first place, the Duke had not been present at the funeral of his father, the 4th Duke, in 1854; every male relation had been present but his successor. Was he in Baker Street at the time? Between 1816 and 1820 there were no records of the activities of the Duke, but plenty of evidence relating to T. C. Druce. Between 1820 and 1835, T. C. Druce disappears from view, but the Duke's activities are recorded. From 1835 to 1864 the process is again reversed, with the Duke in oblivion, and T. C. Druce on record. T. C. Druce was alleged to have died in 1864; from 1864 to 1879 there is the frantic building at Welbeck for which the Duke is famous, and everyone knows where he is.

With these subtle coincidences, Mrs Druce had nothing to do. She knew only that she was the Duchess, and that no one would believe her. Under the strain of constant complicated litigation over a number of years, her mind lost its balance. She would go to Highgate Cemetery every day, accompanied by a mining engineer, because she suspected that one of her opponents was about to remove the coffin surreptitiously. Her delusions multiplied, until she was removed, in 1903, to a mental home, after which nothing more is heard of her. There was now someone else to take control of the torrent she had unleashed.

Mr G. H. Druce came to London from Australia (where news of the fascinating case had filled pages of newsprint, as it had in all parts of the world) to reveal that he was the son of T. C. Druce by an earlier marriage, and that he was therefore the rightful Duke of Portland. He went into the fray with style; he formed companies, including G. H. Druce Ltd, the Druce–Portland Company and the New Druce–Portland Company, in which he invited the public to buy shares, pointing out that each investor would receive a profit of 6,400 per cent when Druce came into the Portland fortune. Subscriptions flowed in daily. Eventually, G. H. Druce brought a charge of perjury against another member of the Druce family (who steadfastly maintained that his father *had* died in 1864, and *was* buried at Highgate, and who objected to all the fuss), and the whole matter finally reached trial in the autumn of 1907.

The trial was a compulsive drug. Half the aristocratic ladies of London were present, and the Duke of Portland sat silently throughout. The public wanted the "underdog" to win, and the evidence clearly implied that he might.

His chief witness was a Mr Caldwell, who came from the United States to testify. Mr Caldwell had suffered from a skin disease, and had come to London to be treated by the late Sir Morell Mackenzie, who had introduced him to the Duke of Portland. The Duke suffered from a similar complaint, which Caldwell was able to cure for him. In consequence of this, an intimacy grew between them, and the Duke had confided to Caldwell that he led a dual existence. Caldwell had accompanied him to the Baker Street Bazaar, where he assumed his Druce identity, and had also seen him frequently at Welbeck. In 1864 the Duke had said that he was tired of the game, and wanted to devote himself full-time to his building at Welbeck. He therefore determined that T. C. Druce should "die", and asked Caldwell to help him stage a mock funeral. Caldwell had helped weigh the coffin down with lead. Afterwards the Duke returned to Welbeck, and T. C. Druce was forgotten (though some people claimed to have seen "T. C. Druce" in London after 1864).

The second key witness was Miss Robinson, who had been a "friend and typist" to the Duke, alias Druce, and was privy to the secret of the double identity. She had recorded the whole story, day by day, in her diary. Unfortunately, a few months before the trial, when the news of her diary and the definitive proof it contained had reached the newspapers, a man had snatched her handbag in the street, and stolen the diary. Since her arrival from New Zealand she had already been robbed five times, and had lost in this way some private letters from the Duke. It was strongly implied that someone was frightened enough to go to great lengths to destroy the evidence. But she had made a copy of the diary before the theft, and that was what she proposed to use in court. It later came out, and caused a sensation, that the Duke of Portland and his agents had indeed employed private investigators to track down information, and that these sleuths had on occasion exceeded their instructions. This was tantamount to an admission that Miss Robinson's diary had been snatched by agents of the 6th Duke of Portland, who risked losing his title and his fortune if the case were proven in favour of G. H. Druce.

The trial was not only momentous, but hilarious. The judge's dry wit would not allow the proceedings to assume the gravity that Druce's counsel wished to impose, and hardly a day passed by without the court erupting into laughter. Many hours were spent discussing the late Duke's skin complaint, which was a bulbous nose with two warts upon it, and every attempt to get Mr Caldwell to release the secret of his treatment to the nose was a failure. He would not reveal the secret to the medical faculty. He had been paid, he said, £10,000 for the cure, which the Duke gave him in £500 notes. Why was there no trace of them in his bank? Because he had pinned them to his shirt! If the Duke had wanted to pay by cheque, Caldwell would have refused to accept it. Caldwell testified that he had visited Welbeck through a tunnel from Worksop over a mile long, but counsel successfully pointed out that the tunnel had not been built until years afterwards, which made Caldwell's claim impossible to substantiate. There was a great deal more of Caldwell's evidence which was questionable, and his counsel, at the end of the case for the prosecution, provided a sensation by disowning him. It transpired that Caldwell had made a habit of appearing at such trials, and had lied his way through them all. He was described in court as "the most noxious perjurer that ever polluted the fountain of justice", at which florid prose more laughter ensued. He was later certified insane, and died in an asylum in 1911.[51]

Miss Robinson was demolished by ridicule. Everyone knew that all her documents had been "lost" or "stolen", and the judge would not admit the "copy" of her diary as evidence. She showed the court gifts which were presented to her by the Duke *alias* Druce, and much fun was had by counsel over their safety.

- Have you the brooch you spoke of the Duke giving you?
- Yes, I am wearing it, but I am not going to take it off. I have had several things stolen already (*Laughter*).
- Have you any objection to showing it to the magistrate?
The witness then stood up for the magistrate, and eventually took it off for him to see.
- Did he give you a ring?
- Yes.
- You will not trust my friend with the brooch?
- No (*Laughter*).
- Will you let Mr Avory see it? I will be surety for him.[52]

The ring and the brooch were discovered to be cheap rubbish that one might find at a fairground, and Miss Robinson further admitted under cross-examination that she had been paid £250 to give her evidence. One of the biggest laughs of the trial occurred when another witness recalled having seen Miss Robinson's famous diary; she had shown it to her on the boat coming from New Zealand. Witness said that it was odd-looking, and that it looked as if it had come out of the Ark. "That would account for the watermark," ventured the judge.[53]

On 30th December 1907 the coffin was eventually opened, and T. C. Druce's remains found to be in it. Thus eleven years of legal wrestling and speculation collapsed like a broken biscuit. Several of the witnesses (we have only mentioned the two principal here) were subsequently tried for perjury, and imprisoned. The 6th Duke of Portland continued to live at Welbeck, and the Druce descendants in Baker Street. The judge in his summing-up commented, "Sufficient to say that this case is an illustration of that love of the marvellous which is so deeply ingrained in human nature, and is likely to be remembered in legal annals as affording one more striking proof of the unfathomable depths of human credulity."[54]

Nevertheless, one mystery remained, and was the subject of some correspondence in *The Times*. In 1864, when T. C. Druce died, he was alleged to be seventy-one years old, and such is the record on the tombstone. The Duke of Portland was then sixty-four. According to the census returns, T. C. Druce in 1861 was sixty-two years old, which would make him sixty-four or sixty-five at death, not seventy-one.

The eccentric invisible old Duke died in 1879, and was buried, according to his wish, in Kensal Green Cemetery in North London, as anonymously as possible. No fuss, no parade, no crowds. Now, the tomb is completely obliterated by shrubs which he ordered to be planted there. He is as mysterious in death as he was in life. As he died childless, the London properties of Marylebone (Harley Street, Welbeck Street, etc.) devolved upon his sisters, one of whom married the Baron Howard de Walden, whose descendant is the present owner.

The 6th Duke of Portland (1857–1943) was a cousin of his predecessor, whom he had never met. He distinguished himself in politics, in literature, and in the army. One of his books, *Men, Women and Things,* though lacking the discipline of selection, is written in a chaste pleasing style. He had a firmly sensible attitude towards the changing times; he decided to move out of Welbeck Abbey long before many of his ducal cousins had abandoned their albatrosses, and built for himself a smaller comfortable house on the estate. The subterranean palace did not appeal to him anyway. His attitude towards his tenants, kindly and charming, was however feudal in its condescension. His duchess, who had been a real beauty and who survived until 1954, once lost her way in London and had to ask a policeman where she was. When he told her, she said, "The City? I have only been here in processions."[55]

Rather better known than the Duke, and quite a different character, was his bizarre, flamboyant sister, born Ottoline Cavendish-Bentinck but always known as Lady Ottoline Morrell, the feathered centre of the Bloomsbury set.

The Duke died in 1943 and was succeeded by his son, the 7th Duke of Portland, whom the Duke of Bedford has described as "a pompous-looking man with a moustache".[56] He sat in the House of Commons for twenty years as Lord Titchfield, and was twice a junior minister. He was a Knight of the Garter, Lord Lieutenant of Nottingham, and Chairman of the Royal Society for the Prevention of Cruelty to Children. His brother, Lord Morven Cavendish-Bentinck, was quite a well-known concert pianist.

'Chopper' Portland died in 1978. His widow, *née* Ivy Gordon-Lennox, is descended from Charles II through three different lines, by Nell Gwynn, by Louis de Kéroualle, and by Barbara Villiers (see Chapter 2). The Portlands had two daughters, but no sons, which meant that the dukedom passed to a kinsman who traced his descent from the 3rd Duke. Ferdinand Cavendish-Bentinck, 8th Duke of Portland, lived in East Africa from 1925 and was Speaker of the Legislative Assembly in Kenya before Independence. When Member for Agriculture in the Legislative Council he was responsible for the establishment of the glorious game parks there.

The present Duke is his brother, William Cavendish-Bentinck, who joined the Foreign Service in 1919. After serving in various posts, he was Chairman of the Joint Intelligence Sub-Committee of the Chiefs of Staff and Foreign Office Adviser to the Directors of Plans from 1939 to 1945, and then Ambassador to Poland in the difficult years after 1945. Since 1947 he has been Director of various companies in the U.K. and abroad and is now Chairman of Bayer UK Limited, also President of the British Nuclear Forum.

By the financial arrangements which 'Chopper' Portland made he stripped the title of all assets, and specifically excluded the present Duke and his brother from all benefit; they did not receive, and can never receive, a penny from the ducal estates, nor enjoy any of the heirlooms which have passed down from their common ancestor.

As the Duke's son predeceased him, the dukedom will end with the present generation. The Portland title, however, can continue under a different rank. The 1st Duke was the son of Hans Bentinck, created Earl of Portland by his friend, William of Orange. By his second marriage, Hans Bentinck had another son, whose direct descendant is Count Henry Bentinck, a Count of the Holy Roman Empire who was wounded and taken prisoner in the Second World War. Count Henry Bentinck now lives quietly in Devon. His son is an actor. The day will come when he can claim the earldom of Portland.

REFERENCES

1. *Complete Peerage.*
2. White Kennet, *Sermon at the Funeral of William Duke of Devonshire* (1707), p. 47.
3. Walpole, XX, 66.
4. John Timbs, *English Eccentrics and Eccentricities* (1866), Vol. I, p. 142
5. Brougham, *Lives of Philosophers of the Time of George III* (1846).
6. Timbs, p. 143.
7. *ibid.,* p. 146.
8. Dorothy Stuart, *Dearest Bess,* p. 143.
9. Elizabeth Jenkins, *Lady Caroline Lamb.*

10. Wraxall, *Posthumous Memoirs,* Vol. i, p. 9.

11. Walpole, XXV, 411.

12. Wraxall, *op. cit.,* p. 7.

13. Jenkins, *op. cit.,* p. 12.

14. ed. The Earl of Ilchester, *Georgiana,* p. 23.

15. *ibid.,* p. 97.

16. W. M. Thackeray, *The Four Georges,* p. 60.

17. *Georgiana,* p. 120. 18. *ibid.,* p. 189, 196.

19. D.N.B.

20. *Dearest Bess,* pp. 32–3. 21. *ibid.,* p. 44.

22. Greville, V, 308.

23. *Georgiana,* pp. 59, 63, 69, 77.

24. *Dearest Bess,* p. 12.

25. *Journal* of Elizabeth Lady Holland, Vol. I, p. 244.

26. *Georgiana,* p. 281. 27. *ibid.,* p. 10.

28. *Dearest Bess,* p. 169.

29. *Lady Holland to Her Son,* p. 18.

30. Devonshire Collections, *Paxton Letters,* 5, 19.

31. E. F. Benson, *As We Were,* p. 177. 32. *ibid.,* p. 176.

33. Margaret Asquith, *Autobiography,* p. 94.

34. Duke of Portland, *Men, Women and Things,* p. 187.

35. Anita Leslie, *Edwardians in Love,* p. 314.

36. E. F. Benson, *op. cit.,* pp. 174, 175.

37. Consuelo Vanderbilt Balsan, *The Glitter and the Gold,* p. 107.

38. E. F. Benson, *op. cit.,* p. 177.

39. Countess of Warwick, *Afterthoughts,* p. 77.

40. Margot Asquith, *Autobiography,* p. 93.

41. Chips Channon, *Diaries,* p. 450.

42. Jessica Mitford, *Hons and Rebels,* p. 104.

43. *Lord Hervey and His Friends,* p. 216.

44. Walpole (ed. Cunningham), Vol. VIII, p. 253.

45. *Journal* of Elizabeth Lady Holland, Vol. I, p. 182.

46. William Day, *Reminiscences of the Turf,* p. 136.

47. Duke of Portland, *Men, Women and Things,* p. 36.

48. *Daily Chronicle,* 15 March 1898; *The Times,* 8 December 1879.

49. Duke of Portland, *op. cit.,* p. 34.

50. Augustus Hare, *In My Solitary Life,* p. 178.

51. Theodore Besterman, *The Druce-Portland Case,* pp. 78–9, 204, 216, 272.

52. *ibid.,* 133. 53. *ibid.,* 100. 54. *ibid.,* 268.

55. Chips Channon, *Diaries,* p. 468.

56. Duke of Bedford, *A Silver-plated Spoon,* p. 119.

5. The Master

Duke of Beaufort

"I say that if these Bills are passed and the sound of the horn and the cry of the hounds are not again to be heard, it will be the worst thing ever to happen in this country." So spoke the distinctive hyperbolic voice of Sir Henry FitzRoy Somerset, 10th Duke of Beaufort, K.G., P.C., G.C.V.O., Master of the Queen's Horse, and the greatest fox-hunter of the twentieth century.

Foxhunting is not to the dukes of Beaufort a hobby, a pastime, a sport; it is a way of life, it is the very colour and sound of life itself. For more than 200 years successive dukes of Beaufort have hunted six days a week during the season. They have established the hunt which bears their name, the Beaufort Hunt, as the best, with the best pack of hounds in the world. It is an achievement of which they can with just cause be proud, an achievement symbolised by the registration number on the late Duke's car – MFH 1; he was beyond question the foremost Master of Fox Hounds in the country. In Gloucestershire, where his estate, Badminton, dominates the surrounding country, the Duke was known to everyone, family, friends, tenants, and strangers, not as "Your Grace" or "Duke", but as "Master". Even Queen Mary would call him nothing else. So one can well understand that the sound of the horn was music to his ears, and the excitement of the chase food for his blood; a life without foxhunting would not have been an unimaginable catastrophe to him; it did not bear contemplation.

The Duke of Beaufort was known also to the public as a close friend of the Royal Family. The Queen and other members of the Royal Family habitually stay at Badminton for the world-famous three-day event, the Badminton Horse Trials, initiated by the late Duke in 1949, and since risen to become the most highly esteemed horse event of the calendar. The Queen is known to have said that she is never happier than when she can stay at Badminton, and Queen Mary stayed there for the whole of World War II, descend-

ing upon the house in full convoy in 1939, and living there for the next
five years. Queen Mary was the Duchess of Beaufort's aunt who was
therefore descended directly from George III, and a member of the
"old" Royal Family, as opposed to the "new" Royal Family
represented by Queen Victoria, from whom Elizabeth II is descended.

But Beaufort's connection with royalty goes back much farther
than that, as he represents the only direct Plantagenet line left today,
though from illegitimate stock. (The last legitimate Plantagenet was
the Earl of Warwick who was executed in 1499.) The Duke's ancestor
is John of Gaunt, son of King Edward III, the same John of Gaunt
to whom Shakespeare gave one of his most rousing patriotic orations,
in *Richard II*.[2] What Shakespeare's play does not tell us is that John
of Gaunt had four illegitimate children by Katherine Swynford, his
mistress for twenty years, and to all four he gave the surname
"Beaufort", after a castle which his family had owned in the Cham-
pagne region of France for generations. One of these, John Beaufort,
born in 1372 or 1373, is the founder of the Beaufort family we know.
By the time he was twenty-four years old, his father had finally taken
Katherine Swynford as his third wife, and in 1396 Pope Boniface IX
ratified the marriage retroactively, in order to legitimise the offspring.
Parliament assented to the legitimising of the four Beaufort children
on the strict condition that none of them or their descendants should
ever lay claim to the throne; they were, of course, perilously close to it.
The usurper King Henry IV (Bolingbroke), another son of John of
Gaunt, was their half-brother. With this parliamentary caution in
mind one writer has pointed out the irony that obtained in 1914,
when all the crowned heads in Europe, with the exception of the
King of Spain, were descended from John of Gaunt and Katherine
Swynford.[3]

John Beaufort was soon afterwards created Earl of Somerset, in
which title he was succeeded by his brother Henry, who died at
seventeen. A third brother assumed the mantle, and was advanced to
the rank of Duke of Somerset in 1443, with precedence above the
Duke of Norfolk (of the Mowbray family; the first Howard Duke of
Norfolk was not for another forty years).

That a man with the surname of Somerset and the title of Beaufort
may be descended from men with the surname of Beaufort and the
title of Somerset obviously requires explanation, especially since the
dukedom of Somerset is now held by a man with the surname of
Seymour, who is no relation whatever to the present David Somerset,
Duke of Beaufort. The answer lies in another illegitimacy and yet
another invented surname.

The third Duke of Somerset, grandson of John of Gaunt, was attainted and beheaded in 1464. That was the end of the dukedom of Somerset in the Beaufort family; the title was recreated in 1547 for Edward Seymour, and it has stayed with the Seymours ever since. Meanwhile, the last Beaufort Duke of Somerset had fathered a bastard son called Charles, who adopted his father's title as a surname, and is therefore the founder of the Somerset family; when his uncle Edmund Beaufort died in 1471 the Beaufort family as such was extinct, and the new Somerset family began. Charles Somerset was a 2nd cousin of Henry VII, which may account for his being advanced in rank, in spite of his bastardy, to the title of Earl of Worcester. He married Elizabeth Herbert, daughter of the Earl of Huntingdon, by which he acquired Raglan Castle in Monmouthshire, still in the possession of his descendants.

The 3rd Earl of Worcester, William Somerset, played a key role in events which form the substance of another chapter, for he was present at the trials of both Protector Somerset and the 4th Duke of Norfolk, those implacable rivals, and one of the small ironies which delight the amateur historian is that he was the first peer to cast his vote in 1551 for the condemnation of the Protector, who had usurped a title which had previously belonged to his family. He also founded the family tradition of unswerving loyalty to the Crown, which has been observed with more or less fidelity by his descendants. He had his own company of actors, but there is no evidence that this taste has been inherited by subsequent generations. (The late Duke of Beaufort celebrated his fortieth wedding anniversary in 1964 by taking a coach-load to a Whitehall farce.)

The 4th Earl of Worcester (1553–1628), Edward Somerset, consolidated the tradition of loyalty to the Crown with astonishing success. Though a Catholic, he was an especial favourite with Elizabeth I, who trusted him above many others, and with James I and Charles I. His other contribution to family traditions was his love for horses. He was the best horseman and tilter of his generation,[4] and his supremacy was recognised by the Queen when she made him Master of the Horse, a post previously held by her two loves, Lord Leicester and Lord Essex. The Master of the Horse is one of the oldest offices under the Crown, and its holder is required to ride in attendance at every state procession. He is in charge of the royal stables and kennels, and has the privilege of borrowing any of the monarch's horses, grooms, or footmen, at his desire. The late Duke of Beaufort, like his ancestor 400 years ago, was Master of the Horse, and no more appropriate person could there have been for this office.

It was his love for horses that endeared Worcester to the new King, James I, who loved hunting, and who took Worcester with him on his expeditions. The King's reward for his companionship was to grant him in 1607 ferry rights over the River Severn from Aust to Chepstow, a right still possessed by his descendant. Until 1964, the Duke leased this right to a ferry company, for a handsome fee. There was some fuss about compensation to the Duke when the Severn Bridge was opened, making his ferry rights obsolete, which is worth mentioning only to correct a misapprehension held at the time. Leo Abse, M.P., objected to the principle of paying any compensation, on the grounds that "the country paid a heavy enough price at the time to James I for the favours he lavished on a series of handsome male favourites".[5] This, of course, is crass nonsense. Worcester was no "handsome male favourite". He was fifty years old when James came to the throne, and the king a mere twenty-seven. It is hardly likely that he took a fancy to old Worcester. Their relationship was professional and friendly; Worcester acted as the King's private secretary, and hunted with him regularly. The famous lovers, Robert Carr and George Villiers, came later.

The Earl was in favour with Charles I, who pushed him a step further up the ladder by making him Marquess of Worcester for having contributed a considerable sum of money to the royal purse. With his son, Edward Somerset, 2nd Marquess of Worcester (1601–1667), the dukedoms of Somerset and Beaufort collide for the last time, to be sorted out and sent their separate ways once and for all.

In 1644 Charles I sent to Worcester a remarkable document purporting to create him Duke of Somerset (the title had lain in abeyance since the death of Protector Somerset), with power to create his own peerages, from a baronet to a marquess, and confer them upon persons of his choice. He was to be Generalissimo of three armies, and Admiral of the Fleet at sea, and he was promised the hand of the King's daughter in marriage. The full text of this document, now at Badminton, can be read in Collins's *Peerage of England*, Vol. I, pages 206–7. It is now recognised to be a forgery,[6] but in the seventeenth century it was taken seriously enough for a Committee of the House of Lords to be convened to consider the matter. In 1660 both Edward Somerset and William Seymour laid claim to the dukedom of Somerset, held by ancestors of them both at different times. Edward Somerset's claim was based on this irregular patent, which had never received the seal, and was little more than a private promise of the King's which was never ratified. The House of Lords decided against Edward Somerset for this reason, and also because he was a Papist, and obnoxious to the people by virtue of that alone. It was concluded that a far better claim to the title was possessed by William Seymour, who was thereupon recognised as 2nd Duke of Somerset, while Edward Somerset, Marquess of Worcester, withdrew his claim. Twenty-two years later, his son would be created Duke of Beaufort, and the dispute would not again be revived.

Before we leave the Marquess, mention must be made of his book *A Century of Inventions*, at one time highly regarded, in which he tells of scores of machines he has constructed to perform impossible tasks, while neglecting to tell us how to construct the machines. One invention, the "hydraulic machine", was the subject of much speculation; it has often been claimed that Worcester anticipated the steam-engine with this machine by a couple of centuries, but this claim is not entertained by those who should know.

The man who was to become the 1st Duke of Beaufort, taking his title from the surname his forbears had carried, was Henry Somerset (1629–1700). It is to him that the family owes Badminton, which he inherited from his first cousin Elizabeth, grand-daughter of that 4th Earl of Worcester who had been the best horseman of his day, and who had bought Badminton from the Boteler family in 1608. The dukedom was created in 1682 "in consideration of noble descent from Edward III through John de Beaufort, son of John of Gaunt", conveniently ignoring the two illegitimacies on the way. The 1st Duke was a splendid man, and a circumspect diplomatist. He managed prudently to survive the Cromwellian period with honour, a period during which, under Cromwell's influence, he dropped his courtesy title and was known as plain Mister. The two men achieved some degree of compromise. In 1660, however, he was one of the twelve commoners deputed to invite Charles II to return to the throne, and thereafter Beaufort's loyalty to the legitimate crown was firm. He was the first of the family to plunge headlong into Tory principles so solid as to make it impossible for himself and all the dukes who followed him to think clearly about any alternative point of view. Mercifully, their Toryism has never collapsed into fantasy, as with the 4th Duke of Newcastle for example, but it has been rigid. The 1st Duke supported James II against the Monmouth rebellion in 1685, and was one of the two chief mourners at Charles II's funeral (along with, oddly enough, the Duke of Somerset). He then was consistently loyal to James II, opposing the faction which wanted to force abdication. He voted for a regency rather than for offering the crown to William of Orange, which he thought un-English. This did not go unnoticed by William who, once on the throne, received him coldly and kept him waiting an hour in an ante-room. Beaufort was unperturbed. He simply refused to give his oath of allegiance to King William, who in *his* view had no right to the throne of England. Later, the Duke and the King seem to have come to an understanding, though it is recorded that on one occasion when the King was a house-guest at Badminton, the domestic chaplain toasted the health of the King omitting to mention which one.[7] Politically the Duke of Beaufort was the very opposite of the Cavendishes, the Russells, and the Manners, all of whom founded ducal families. He was the highest of high Tories, and his political predilection seems to have been absorbed in the genes of the family, for all the Dukes of Beaufort have been uncompromising Tories from childhood to the grave. It is a natural consequence of their being country-bred foxhunters, and an inheritance from their Jacobite forefathers. The 2nd Duke is said to have been so Tory that he refused to have anything to do with the Court until 1710, when the Tories were returned to power, at which point he loftily announced to the Queen that he could now call her Queen "in reality".[8]

From this point on, the Dukes of Beaufort retired to the country and their hounds, steering clear of politics and the metropolis, which they considered irretrievably stained by the corruption of Whiggery and radicalism. They sought no power, no place in history. It was as if they considered political life beneath their level, too sordid to warrant their interest. A typical political comment is that of the 9th Duke, grandfather to the present Duke, who said he wished to see Winston Churchill torn to pieces by his hounds.[9]

Divorced from the mainstream of events, denying themselves the stimulation of town life, their intellectual development was stifled, and they inevitably became stuffy, puritanical, dull. Writing in 1787, Walpole said that "there never was a Duke of Beaufort that made it worth knowing which Duke it was",[10] and Lady Granville in the next century found life at Badminton intolerably boring. "So *borné* a set of minds I never met with", she wrote, "all the *élans* are kept for the hedges and ditches."[11] Examples of wit are as rare at Badminton as a Marxist tract. One joke has been recorded, attributed to Lord Charles Somerset (1767–1831), Governor of the Cape of Good Hope. He told a story about the naturalist Sir Joseph Banks, who went round the world with Captain Cook. Banks was being polite to an Irish merchant seaman, asking him where he had served. "In the East, sir." "Then doubtless, sir, you must have seen a variety of very curious objects," said Banks. "Pray do allow me to ask you if you ever happened to see a black cockatoo?" "A black cockatoo, no Sir Joseph, I never happened to see a black cockatoo," said the seaman, "but I'll tell you what, Sir Joseph, I have very frequently seen, a black cock or two."[12]

Some members of the family have embraced military careers, but their intellectual limitations have prevented their rising to positions of eminence or power. One disastrous exception achieved an unenviable place in history – Lord Fitzroy Somerset, youngest son of the 5th Duke of Beaufort, who was ennobled in his own right as Lord Raglan (1788–1855). This was the man who gave the order for one of the most lamentable episodes in our military annals, the Charge of the Light Brigade.

A picture has emerged in the course of these pages of a courteous Tory family of high principles, far removed from the rough and tumble of London life in which their political enemies, the Cavendishes and the Russells, gloried. While Georgiana Duchess of Devonshire presided over a decadent city, giggling headlong into amoral intrigues, the Beaufort family remained aloof and untainted in the pure Gloucestershire air. That at least is the popular impression. But it is by no means the whole truth. The Beauforts were not only Tories of probity, foxhunters of genius, loyal subjects of the realm. Some have been voluptuaries of distinction.

Long before the Devonshire House set established its eccentric code upon London life, there was a Duchess of Beaufort involved in the most unseemly scandal which culminated in unpleasant divorce proceedings. She was the Scudamore heiress, eventually mother (by a later marriage) of the mad Scudamore Duchess of Norfolk who drove the poor amiable 11th Duke of Norfolk to distraction. She married the 3rd Duke of Beaufort (1707–1745), about whom we know little save that he made Badminton what it is now, employing the architect William Kent to enlarge and improve the house, and that he died at the age of thirty-seven.

The Duke and Duchess of Beaufort did not have a happy marriage. The Duchess wasted no time before taking a lover, choosing as her paramour another married man, Lord Talbot. The couple were singularly open about their intrigue, and the Duke, at first, unusually taciturn. He said that he pitied Lord Talbot to have met with two such tempers as their two wives.[13] When the Duchess produced a child, which the world would regard as the Duke's, then was he obliged to take action. The divorce was heard in Doctors' Commons, and the details revealed were such as to delight the gossips. Walpole relished the case. "There is everything proved to your heart's content", he wrote, "to the birth of the child, and much delectable reading."[14]

The Duchess appears to have been totally abandoned. It was stated that she and Lord Talbot "knew each other beside every green hedge, and under every green tree".[15] When the verdict was quite clearly edging towards her conviction, she took a bold step. She said that the Duke was impotent.

It would have been easy for the Duke simply to deny the imputation, which would have left the matter unresolved, and presumably would not have affected the fact of his wife's adultery. But he was a brave man. He determined to prove her wrong. With no apparent consciousness of the high comedy of the situation, the Duke agreed to demonstrate his potency before a panel of medical men, including a Dr Meade, another physician, three surgeons (though why their presence was required is mysterious), and the Dean of the Arches. The six eminent gentlemen proposed to inspect the Duke's abilities in any place of public resort of his choosing, but at this he demurred. He said he would perform at Dr Meade's house, behind a screen, and that they were to come behind the screen when he would knock to indicate that he was ready. Let the invaluable Walpole take up the story. "He was some time behind the scenes : at last he knocked, and the good old folks saw what amazed them – what they had not seen many a day ! Cibber says, 'His Grace's—— is in everybody's mouth'. Now he is upon his mettle, and will sue Lord Talbot for fourscore thousand pounds damages."[16]

One need hardly say that the divorce was granted. There were no children from the marriage, fortunately for the Beaufort family, as the Duchess's mad daughter probably inherited the excesses of her conduct from her mother. The Duke was succeeded by his brother.

Nearly a hundred years later, the man who was to become 7th Duke of Beaufort (1792–1853) brought the Beaufort name once more to the centre of public attention. While still a very young man, and still as heir to the dukedom known as the Marquess of Worcester, he was "so open and free from every species of conceit, perhaps too humble in his own opinion". Moreover, and more to the point, he was of "such an amiable nature that he is sure of winning the affections of all".[17] It was the young man's misfortune to win the affection of a prostitute.

Harriette Wilson (1789–1846) is a shadowy character, euphemistically described as a "lady of fashion", who had a monopoly in aristocratic clients. She clearly had extraordinary fascination, as her lovers fell over each other's feet in their rush for her favours. "She was far from beautiful, but a smart, saucy girl, with good eyes, hair, and the manners of a wild schoolboy."[18] She would have

passed easily into oblivion, along with the scores of other ladies of her
kind about whom we know nothing, were it not that she had a
wonderful gift for recalling dialogue. In 1825 she published her
Memoirs and caused an immediate sensation. "I hold everything
which is not love, to be mere dull intervals in life", she wrote.[19] Queues
formed outside the publishing house, and barriers had to be set up to
control the crowds. Thirty editions appeared in the first year.
Harriette Wilson had drawn the veil away from the discreet amours
of the aristocracy, for her lovers were all named. Among them were
the subjects of two other chapters – the Duke of Argyll and the Duke
of Leinster – and a man three years younger than herself and under
the age of majority – the besotted Lord Worcester.

Lord Worcester was still an Oxford undergraduate, "a long, thin,
pale fellow, with straight hair",[20] when he was introduced to Harriette
by (such is the irony which infuses human relations) the man
whose rival he was to become, the Duke of Leinster. Worcester began
to pay her visits on his own initiative, and Harriette found herself
having to time entrances and exits so that Leinster and Worcester did
not meet; often one would arrive seconds after the other had left.
The Duke, of course, found out that his young friend was paying
court, and grew jealous. Harriette professed to be exasperated. "I am
to condole all the morning with one fool," she said, "and sympathise
the blessed long evening with another; neither can I be tender and true
to a dozen of you at a time."[21] But Worcester could not be deflected by
insults. He swore that he would never love another woman for the
rest of his life, that he would make Harriette Marchioness of Worcester, and eventually Duchess of Beaufort. She had only to say the
word. His daily protestations worked and before long he was never
out of her company. London began to notice that they were virtually living together. Worcester refused every invitation from any other
quarter, declaring that he would be miserable in any society without
Harriette. He even found excuses to decline an invitation from the
Prince of Wales, feigning lameness. His uncle Lord Charles Somerset supposed that they had been secretly married, so openly were
they living a conjugal life.

Word reached the 6th Duke of Beaufort and his duchess at
Badminton. They were furious. They rained letters upon their errant
son. In Harriette's admittedly biased account, "the Duke of Beaufort
did nothing but write and torment Lord Worcester to leave me, while
Worcester's love seemed to increase on the receipt of every scolding
letter. He daily swore to make me his wife. . . ." The Duchess did
not waste time trying to be tactful or persuasive; she came right to

the point. "This absurd attachment of yours for this vile profligate woman", she wrote, "does but prove the total subjugation of your understanding." To this Harriette's comment was, "he never possessed any".[22]

Harriette claimed that she kept Worcester out of mischief, prevented him from gambling, and steadfastly refused to be his wife, out of consideration for his parents, who would faint at the news. It is difficult to see why else she would refuse his importunate demands, but the Duke and Duchess would allow her no credit whatever. Their opposition naturally strengthened his determination and lent to the love story that element of romanticism which it would otherwise have lacked.

The Duke of Beaufort then sent an emissary to Harriette, one Mr Robinson, asking her to surrender all the letters which Worcester had sent her. She requested time to think about it, time which she used to consult solicitors, who advised her that the promises of marriage contained in the letters would win her in a court of law some £2000. The Beauforts wanted at all costs to avoid a public airing of their domestic troubles. The Duchess tried another approach, feeling sorry for herself, provoking hysterical scenes with her son, who had deserted her, forsaken her, abandoned her, and so on. She literally begged him to leave Harriette. But he would not budge. Meanwhile, Harriette handed over the letters.

Harriette wrote to the Duke, pointing out that she could not abandon Worcester now, so dependent was he on her affection (and this was demonstrably true), and that it was only his perseverance which had broken down her resistance in the first place. To this the Duke did not deign to reply, from which Harriette concluded that there was a difference between "high-bred" and "well-bred".

As a last resort, the Duke of Beaufort arranged for his son to leave his regiment and join the Duke of Wellington, fighting the Peninsular War in Spain. Worcester was appointed Wellington's A.D.C. It was to be an enforced separation from the wicked Harriette. Harriette was desperate. She thought it quite likely that Worcester would die in Spain, and the fault would have been hers. She determined to plead with the Duke in person to change his mind, and promise that she herself would go abroad and never again contact the Marquess. The Duke was due in London for one day. She went and knocked on his door in Grosvenor Square, and sent up a note. It was the first time they had met.

The interview passed stiffly. The Duke said she was a fool ever to have supposed that she could marry Worcester. Harriette replied, "I am naturally good, but you will, among you, harden my heart till it becomes cold and vicious. Since nothing generous, and no sacrifice on my part, is understood or felt, even when I would serve others, and while I only think of them you will not, or you cannot understand me. Allow me, then, to tell you, the fault is in your own character; I will not say in your heart but in your want of heart." The Duke was shamed into an apology. "I only wanted to observe to you that such unequal marriages are seldom if ever attended with happiness to either party," he said. When Harriette left, she asked, "Will your Grace shake hands with me?" to which the Duke replied, "With great pleasure."²³ He obviously thought the matter was at an end.

Worcester wrenched from his father a promise to pay Harriette a quarterly allowance during his absence in Spain, a promise which the Duke did not honour. "In this amiable conduct", wrote Harriette, "I take it for granted he was upheld and encouraged by his most interesting duchess."²⁴ Meanwhile, Worcester himself had embarked for Spain, having been dragged in floods of tears from Harriette's doorstep.

The only way in which Harriette could make the Duke pay was to threaten to join his son in Spain. Then the money arrived on time. When, however the Duke discovered that Miss Wilson had written a letter to Worcester, contrary to the terms of the bargain, he asked for the money back. Eventually Harriette Wilson had to take proceedings against the Duke of Beaufort to make him honour his bond. It is unlikely that she would have won the case, as she had indeed broken her side of the agreement by writing one letter, but Beaufort would have been shamed to insist on such treatment. A settlement was made out of court, and Harriette received £1200 as a lump sum. That was the end of the affair.

Harriette Wilson faded from the scene afterwards. She married a Mr Rochfort and settled in Paris, returning to England a pious widow. She died in 1846. The 6th Duke and Duchess of Beaufort buried their shabby behaviour in the decency of oblivion. He died in 1835.

As for Worcester, now 7th Duke of Beaufort, he recovered in due course, and, deprived of Harriette's restraining influence, indulged his passion for spending money. Greville noted that the family was "going to the dogs"²⁵ as fast as its good-natured head could drive it. He founded Pratt's Club, established in the kitchen of his personal steward, Pratt; was a Tory, a hunter, did all the usual Beaufort things. His emotional life, however, continued along lines which were out of the ordinary. His first wife was a niece of the Duke of Wellington, and his second wife was his first wife's half-sister. This was not a relationship which was regarded as respectable, falling as it did within the prohibited degrees of affinity. He admitted the unwisdom of the match by marrying in quasi-secrecy. The wedding took place at St George's, Hanover Square, with the bridegroom listed as "Henry Somerset, widower".[26] The marriage was legal, but was voidable in an ecclesiastical court. The law was changed in due course to oblige the Duke, and render his second marriage respectable. The Deceased Wife's Sister Bill passed in 1835 ratified all such marriages already celebrated, while forbidding any future such alliances. The law remained on the Statute Book until 1907.

Two of Beaufort's daughters inherited his romantic fancies. One of them, Lady Rose Somerset, eloped with one Mr Francis Lovell, an "amazingly good-looking" Life Guard, when she was but seventeen.[27] Another, Lady Augusta Somerset, conceived a flirtatious romance with Prince George of Cambridge, which erupted into yet another scandal. A story spread that Lady Augusta was pregnant by the Prince, that the Duke of Beaufort her father wanted him to marry her, which he was naturally prepared to do, but couldn't, owing to the Royal Marriages Act which stood in the way. The monarch was obliged, according to this Act, to give her approval before any member of the Royal Family could marry. (The Act still applies.) Queen Victoria was not disposed to give her consent.

Such were the bare bones of the rumour, which spread like a forest fire throughout Europe and screeched in all the newspapers. There was never any real truth to support it, except the flirtation, which was real enough, "such as is continually going on without any serious result between half the youths and girls in London".[28] The Duke of Beaufort, forgetting the dramatic proportions of his own youthful passion for Miss Wilson, was indignant; he caused a formal contraction of the story to appear in *The Times*, but it was too late. The damage was done. "There is such a disposition to believe such stories and such a reluctance to renounce such a belief once entertained . . . this calumny will affect the lady more or less as long as she lives." She was not pregnant, but "it is probably true enough that she behaved with very little prudence, delicacy, or reserve, for she is a very ill-behaved girl, ready for anything that her caprice or passions excite her to do". Like father, like daughter.

The worst of it was that the Queen herself believed the entire story. One would have thought that she would have known better, after the recent unpopularity she had incurred by her shameful treatment of poor Lady Flora Hastings, who had died partly as a result

of the scandal the Queen provoked. But no. She forbade the Court
to speak to or acknowledge Lady Augusta. When the Duchess of
Cambridge (Prince George's mother) took Lady Augusta to Windsor,
all the young ladies at court turned their heads to the wall. The
Queen exploded in a violent temper. How dare the Duchess attempt
to bring respectability to Lady Augusta by having her appear at
Windsor! It was scandalous that she should even be in the castle!
The Queen knew that the stories were true, she said. The Duchess
strode out, seething, and the Queen returned to her prudish husband.
Prince George gave his word that there was no truth in the matter,
to which Prince Albert grudgingly replied that he and the Queen
"supposed they must believe that it was so". Neither Cambridge nor
Beaufort was satisfied with this. Beaufort approached Peel, who was
scared of the Queen and dared not raise the subject. Finally, he summoned his courage, and the Queen allowed that she was entirely
satisfied and wanted to hear no more about it.[29] Beaufort boiled with
rage and indignation for months afterwards. When Prince Albert suggested his son Lord Worcester as Lord-in-Waiting, Beaufort sent a
peremptory refusal. As for Lady Augusta, she married the Austrian
Ambassador, Baron Neumann, the following year (1844); foreigners
were less touchy about scandal, and Neumann, being the son of
Metternich's father's gardener, was in no position to assume a holier-
than-thou attitude. (Metternich's father had also sported with the
gardener's wife.) Augusta died in 1850. Three years later the Duke
himself, a founder member of the Garrick Club, died, and the
dukedom passed to his son, 8th Duke of Beaufort (1824–1899),
whom we know as "The Blue Duke". (The Beaufort Hunt wears
blue instead of the usual red).

Like his grandson, the Blue Duke was before all else the best known
sporting figure in England. Not only a Master of Foxhounds, but
a first-class shot, angler, racing man. He edited the *Badminton
Library of Sports and Pastimes*, a collection of handbooks covering
everything from archery to dancing, and the game we know as
"Badminton" was invented at his house. He possessed the same
romantic energies as his sisters and father, and was well-known for
the number of his mistresses. His duchess, moreover, accepted their
existence with exemplary calm. A fine example of this marble reserve
at work is given in E. F. Benson's book *As We Were*. "The Duke of
Beaufort was away, but there was a party in the house, and one day
the butler told the Duchess as they went into lunch that a case had
arrived for His Grace, which he had unpacked: it contained a
picture, and he wanted to know where he was to hang it. So the

whole party went into the corridor, when lunch was over, to see the picture, and there they found the portrait of a very pretty young lady whom everybody knew to be the Duke's mistress. Was that an awkward situation? Not in the least. The Duchess with complete self-possession looked admiringly at it, and said, 'Is it not charming? A fancy portrait, I suppose,' and without a grin or a wink or a whisper, they all looked at the fancy portrait, and liked it immensely. It would do very well, thought the Duchess, just where it was, hung on the wall there. Then as they moved quietly on, she changed her mind. 'His Grace might like it in his own room perhaps,' she said to her butler. 'You had better hang it there.' That was all. Reticence and dignity had perfectly solved the method of dealing with this awkwardness, and when the Duke came home there was the fancy portrait hanging in his room as a pleasant surprise for him."[30]

The Duke, it appears, had far less self-control than the Duchess, and would turn blubbering to his sons when the mistress ditched him for someone else.[31] Perhaps the spectacle of father's heaving shoulders and mother's stately reserve influenced the next generation of Beaufort children more than they knew; two of the 8th Duke's sons were deeply involved in the one kind of emotional attachment which the Victorians icily forbade – the homosexual kind.

Lord Henry Somerset (1849–1932) was the Duke's second son. His career was conventional enough to begin with: member of Parliament for Monmouthshire in 1871, married in 1872, appointed Comptroller of the Royal Household in 1874. His wife was Isabel, whose mother Lady Somers was one of the fabulous Pattle sisters. Virginia Pattle had been so beautiful that she was mobbed and followed the way film-stars are a century later. Her every move was noted by the Press. The same family were to give us Virginia Woolf and Vanessa Bell, the former being named after her great-aunt Virginia Pattle, Lady Somers. Of Lady Somers's two daughters, one became Adeline Duchess of Bedford, and the other married Lord Henry Somerset. Presumably the pressures of convention made Lord Henry enter the alliance, for there can be no doubt that his inclinations lay elsewhere. What he did not bargain for was a mother-in-law who, in addition to being an astonishing beauty, was a meddlesome, domineering, frightful busybody. At the wedding, people noticed how the bride clung to her mother when it was time to leave for the honeymoon.[32] This did not augur well. Lord Henry did his duty by his wife, producing the required offspring to satisfy public (and family) morals, but his tenderest love was reserved for men. One in particular, a commoner called Harry Smith, who was seventeen when his relationship with Lord Henry began, provoked a disastrous response. Of course, Lady Henry knew what her husband was up to, and she was not made to suffer thereby; had she kept quiet, there is no reason why she should not have remained comfortable and reasonably content for the rest of her life; more than that no Victorian lady had a right to hope. But she made the mistake of revealing all to mother, who sparked off like a catherine-wheel. "Lady Somers descended on the situation, in a whirlwind of French horror and dramatic tableau, and persuaded her daughter not to spend another night in her husband's house."[33] Naturally, a public scandal ensued, out of which nobody emerged triumphant. The London clubs began to whisper about the "foul charges" which Isabel and her mother were spreading about London against Lord Henry. Isabel claimed in public that her husband was guilty of a crime mentioned only in the Bible, and the Victorian drawing-rooms fell hushed in mute horror. She sued for a separation, stating the reasons, and she won her case. Lord Henry was denied custody of his child. He resigned his post as Comptroller of the Royal House, and took the only course open to him; he fled the country in 1879. His wife was ostracised by society, much to her amazement, because, though she was the "innocent" party, she had sinned against the unwritten law, "thou must not admit the truth". She had mentioned the unmentionable and brought disrepute upon the head of the Beaufort house, when all could have been kept quiet. She would have done better to copy her mother-in-law, the imperturbable Duchess, rather than her excitable mother. From now on, she received no further invitations, was no longer welcomed in polite society, and, of course, could never marry again. She retired to the country, where she devoted herself to looking after drunkards.

Meanwhile, Lord Henry took refuge in Italy, and there wrote some beautiful poems celebrating his love for Harry Smith, who he admitted quite candidly was "dearer to me than my life".[34] He was never to see Harry again after the scandal, but his poems were published in London by Chatto & Windus under the title Songs of Adieu ten years later (1889), and in them he expresses the poignancy of a desperate affection which though killed by events yet refuses to die. He pleaded with Harry to join him :

"I cannot live without thee – oh, come back !
    Come back to him that, weeping, waits for thee;
For life is death without thee – oh, come back !
    Dear love, thou art the very life of me.

The 11th Duke of Norfolk,
"Jockey", from an engraving by
Thomas Williamson (*National
Portrait Gallery Archive*)

The 16th Duke of Norfolk at the State Opening of Parliament in 1923 (*Radio Times Hulton
Picture Library*)

The 6th Duke of Somerset, "The Proud Duke", from a painting attributed to Michael Dahl (*by courtesy of the Somerset International Finance Co. Ltd.*)

(above) The "Sheridan" Duchess of Somerset. From an engraving by W. H. Mote after Hayter (*National Portrait Gallery Archive*)

(left) The 12th Duke of Somerset in *Vanity Fair* cartoon (*Radio Times Hulton Picture Library*)

Rosa Swann, known as "Lady Seymour" (*by courtesy of Mr Edward St Maur*)

Earl St Maur (*by courtesy of Mr Edward St Maur*)

e Duke of Mon-
uth's head
ered with a
fe, 15 July 1685
itish Museum)

Drumlanrig Castle, Dumfriesshire (*Country Life*)

Alice Powell, Duchess of Buccleuch, 2nd
wife of 2nd Duke. From the painting
attributed to Thomas Hudson. (*By
courtesy of His Grace the Duke of Buccleuch*)

"Old Q" on his balcony in Piccadi
The 4th Duke of Queensberry (*Nat
Portrait Gallery Archive*)

The 1st Duke of St Albans and Lord James Beauclerk, sons of Nell Gwynn and Charles II

Harriet Mellon, later Mrs
Thomas Coutts and later
Duchess of St Albans (*Coutts
& Co*) from the painting by
George Clint

THE DUKE OF RICHMOND AND GORDON.

The 9th Duke of Richmond. From the cartoon by "The Tout" (*by permission of Ladbrokes*)

The 9th Duke of Bedford in Covent
Garden (*Punch*)

A HOLIDAY TASK.

Scene—*Mud-Salad Market.*

Duke of Mudford. "SWEET PRETTY PLACE, AIN'T IT?"
Mr. P. (*Inspector of Nuisances*). "NO, MY LORD DUKE, IT ISN'T PRETTY, AND IT ISN'T SWEET! HERE,
TAKE THIS BROOM, AND MAKE A CLEAN SWEEP OF IT!!"

e 13th Duke of Bedford at Woburn
bey (*Camera Press photograph by
n Seymour*)

Bess of Hardwick. Elizabeth Hardwick, Countess of Shrewsbury, ancestress of both the Duke of Devonshire and the Duke of Portland (*by permission of the National Trust, Ickworth*)

The 8th Duke of Devonshire (*Radio Times Hulton Picture Library*)

Louise von Alten, Duchess of Manchester and Duchess of Devonshire. From the painting by R. Thorburn (*Devonshire Collection Chatsworth. Reproduced by permission of the Trustees of the Chatsworth Settlement*)

The Duchess of Devonshire. From the painting by Pietro Annigoni (*Devonshir Collection, Chatsworth. Reproduced by permission of Her Grace the Duchess of Devonshire and the Trustees of the Chatswo Settlement*)

The 5th Duke of Portland
(*Radio Times Hulton Picture
Library*)

low) The 3rd Duke of
aufort. From the painting by
evisani and Wootton (*By
rtesy of His Grace the Duke of
aufort*)

The Funeral of the Duke of Wellington (*Guildhall Museum*)

Northumberland House, Strand. (*British Museum*)

(above) Lady Elizabeth Percy, "Carrots".
From the painting by Mary Beale, after Lely

(left) The 7th Duke of Leinster (*Radio Times Hulton Picture Library*)

The 8th Duke of Argyll. From the
painting by J. P. J. Hood (*By courtesy
of His Grace the Duke of Argyll*)

The 5th Duke of Atholl. Artist unknown.
(*By courtesy of His Grace the Duke of Atholl*)

The 6th Duke of Argyll. From the
drawing by H. Edridge (*By courtesy of
His Grace the Duke of Argyll*)

The 10th Duke of Atholl. From a
cartoon by David Langton (*By permission
of Ladbrokes*)

The 2nd Earl of Arran, ancestor of both the Dukes of Abercorn and the Dukes of Hamilton. From the painting by Cornelius Ketel. (*By courtesy of His Grace the Duke of Hamilton*)

The Murder of the Duke of Hamilton in Hyde Park (*British Museum*)

The 10th Duke of Hamilton. From the painting by Sir Daniel McNee. (*By courtesy of His Grace the Duke of Hamilton*)

The Duchess of Sutherland, formerly Mrs Blair. From the photograph by Downey. (*Radio Times Hulton Picture Library*)

The marriage of The Duke of Fife. (*Illustrated London News*)

Violet, Duchess of Rutland. (*Radio Times Hulton Picture Library*)

The 11th Duke of Leeds (*By courtesy of Lady Camilla Osborne*)

"Hast thou no care that, ebbing all too fast,
  My youth is scorched and scarred with burning tears?
Hath thy hard heart no memories of the past,
  No longings for the love of happier years?

"Come back! Come back! I beg thee from this boon –
  Oh, turn thine ear and hearken to my cry –
Come back! come back! and come, dear love, full soon,
  For if thou come not soon I needs must die."[35]

Harry did not, could not, come back. The cruel hypocrisy of the time
had despatched him as far away as possible from polite gaze, to New
Zealand, where he died in 1902. Lord Henry, now exiled for nearly
twenty-five years, thought England might be ready to receive him
again, and chose to come for Edward VII's coronation. He did not
reckon with his mother-in-law's vindictiveness. She set private detec-
tives upon him, who watched his every move, and she informed
Scotland Yard that the monster was again at large.[36] Presumably, his
own family at Badminton was not ready to forgive him either,
for he appears to have stayed in London only a few days, to return
once more to Florence, a saddened man.

Lord Henry's younger brother was Lord Arthur Somerset, born in
1851, a former Guards officer, and Assistant Equerry to the Prince
of Wales (Edward VII). In 1889 there erupted the scandal already
mentioned in a previous chapter, concerning a male brothel in Cleveland Street, frequented on the one hand by adolescent telegraph boys,
who were paid for their services, and on the other by members of the
aristocracy, who did the paying. The case would not have reached
the proportions it did were it not for the assiduous probing of the
North London Press, an organ since retreated into obscurity. The
newspaper named some clients of the establishment, among them
Lord Euston (son of the Duke of Grafton), who successfully sued;
by implication the Duke of Clarence, eldest son of the Prince of
Wales, and heir to the throne (he died in time, and was succeeded
as heir by his brother, George V); and Lord Arthur Somerset, who
was known in Cleveland Street as "Mr Brown".

A police constable called Sladden observed "Mr Brown" call at 19
Cleveland Street on 9th July and on 13th July 1889. Two weeks
later, on 25th July, P.C. Sladden went with two of the boys, Swins-
cow (aged fifteen) and, incredibly, Thickbroom (aged seventeen) to
Piccadilly, where they identified "Mr Brown" in the street as the man
they had both been to bed with at Cleveland Street. P.C. Sladden

then followed the suspect to Knightsbridge barracks, where he was identified as Lord Arthur Somerset.[37]

The same day, the papers were sent to the Director of Public Prosecutions, in whose opinion the evidence was sufficient to prosecute Lord Arthur for gross indecency. Another boy called Newlove had testified to the police that Lord Arthur "had to do with me on several occasions there"[38] and a fourth, a "good-looking curly-headed youth" of fifteen called Algernon Alleys, had been kept by Somerset for the past two years. There were a number of compromising letters to Alleys, which were hurriedly destroyed, but the police did have two of the postal orders which Lord Arthur had sent him, as well as sworn statements. The Prime Minister was informed, and he sent to the Lord Chancellor for an opinion; Lord Arthur should not be prosecuted, came the reply.

Meanwhile, the Prince of Wales, who was a personal friend to Lord Arthur, heard the rumours and refused to believe them. "I won't believe it," he said, "any more than I should if they accused the Archbishop of Canterbury", an unfortunate comparison since the Archbishop's sons were every one of them brothers in inclination. The Prince thought any man capable of such behaviour "an unfortunate lunatic".[39] Whatever his reasons (and his own son's name had also been whispered), the Prince of Wales brought some pressure to bear, and Lord Arthur Somerset was permitted to escape. The Chief Commissioner of Police suspected that this would happen. On 19th September he wrote to the Director of Public Prosecutions, "my impression is that it is by no means certain we shall be authorised to prosecute L.A.S. Steps will certainly be taken to remove him from the country and consequently 'Society'."[40] That is in fact what occurred. Lord Arthur exiled himself to Boulogne on 17th or 18th October, with the connivance of authority higher placed than the Director of Public Prosecutions, and remained beyond the jurisdiction of English courts. The warrant for his arrest was not issued until 12th November. Only once did he return to England, when he was smartly told to make himself scarce again. The man who ran the brothel, Hammond, also escaped abroad. Two who had acted as procurers for the others, Veck and Newlove, were prosecuted, found guilty, and sentenced to nine months' and four months' hard labour respectively, but not before Lord Arthur had tried to get them out of the country too, through the mediacy of his solicitor, leading to another trial. Newlove was eighteen years old. What the Duke of Beaufort made of all this, we are not told.

The 9th Duke of Beaufort (1847–1924), elder brother of Lords

Henry and Arthur, succeeded his father in 1899. Of him it is recorded that he strongly objected to the Gloucestershire Hussars (of which he was Colonel) being encamped in undignified fashion on Salisbury Plain and having to wear khaki; the Boer War had just finished, and austerity was the order of the day. "Because there has been a war in South Africa," proclaimed the Duke, "I do not see why we should be condemned to spend our time in wet tents and convicts' dress."[41]

His son was the 10th Duke of Beaufort, 1900–1984, the "Master". He also had half a dozen other titles, decorations from Norway, Sweden, Portugal, France, Belgium, Rumania, Ethiopia, and presided over that sub-county of Gloucestershire commonly known as "Beaufortshire". Beaufortshire is distinguished by a membership totally committed to the country life, with mud on their boots and hot air puffing from their nostrils, gentlemen farmers and retired military men, eligible daughters in expensive twin-sets giving all their attention to eldest sons and ignoring everyone else, and the whole community speaking with an unmistakable clipped nasal twang. They move about in large cars built for comfort not speed, never raise their voices except in the hunt, and return to elegant comfortable homes, full of old rugs, log fires, and house-dogs (The Duke himself had about a dozen house-dogs, and was President of the Battersea Dogs' Home).

The Duke's day was a strenuous one, as befitted a man grown to strength in the healthy country air. He was often called "as tough as nails".[42] His routine involved getting up at seven o'clock, and riding round the estate before breakfast to see what was going on. He knew the 120 men who worked on his estate far better than any factory boss knows his staff. No decision concerning the estate was taken without the Duke's active authority. He answered all his own letters. He was President of the Federation of Boys' Clubs, of the Outward Bound School, and of every society that has anything to do with horses. The only one that he had no time for is the Royal Society for the Prevention of Cruelty to Animals, which had the cheek to ask His Grace to treat with care the horses that were to draw the coronation coach in 1953. He replied that he knew how to treat horses, thank you. The Duke was Chancellor of the University of Bristol from 1966 to 1970, an appointment which provoked violent opposition from the students; clashes with the police marred the installation, and decorated the front page of all newspapers. Even *The Times* joined in the attack, and declared that it did not think the appointment was a wise choice.[43] However, the Duke rode it out, and was finally a very popular Chancellor indeed. He was not a man to succumb to pressures of any sort.

Anyone who travelled on an express train from London to South Wales, as I have had to do, might have been astonished that the train stopped briefly at a tiny station called Badminton, where usually no one would get off or on, and only two houses were in view. I always wondered by what anomaly this situation occurred. I now discover that the station was built in 1903 to oblige the then Duke of Beaufort in fair exchange for the Duke's permission to lay tracks across his land. Beaufort said to the Great Western Railway, in effect, you can run your railway track across my land if you guarantee that four trains per day will stop there. The Duke had the additional right to stop any other train that he wished, if he or his guests wanted to travel to London. The station was built just one mile from Badminton House, with the Duke's crest on the wall, and the stationmaster's office carpeted in red; the Queen used this as a waiting-room. With the demise of the train in favour of the motorcar as a popular means of transport, the railways lost money, and had to economise. In the face of severe financial need, the old promise to the Duke of Beaufort had to go the way of all privilege; Badminton station was closed in 1968.

The Duke was one of the foremost sportsmen in England. He had been President of the M.C.C., of Bristol Rovers Football Club, and of the British Olympic Association. But of course it is as the Master of Foxhounds that he is best remembered. Until he retired to the rear of the pack in 1966, the sight of the Duke of Beaufort at the head of the hunt was one of the greatest spectacles to be seen in England. He devoted an extraordinary amount of time and energy to keeping his hounds the finest pack in the land. His ancestors were largely responsible (though not solely) for the establishment of foxhunting in this country in the mid-eighteenth century, as a replacement to stag-hunting. (When James I and the Earl of Worcester hunted, it was stags they were after.) Two hunts soon had a reputation above the others, and they were both ducal; the Duke of Rutland's Belvoir Hunt, and the Duke of Beaufort's Badminton Hunt. Beaufort has the edge now because his hounds have rather more stamina and more bone, and also because the reigning Duke has always been Master of the hunt which bears his name. The Beauforts have a rare uncanny feeling for the hunt. It was said of the 8th Duke that he "had an intuitive perception, more animal than human, of what may be called the line of chase".[44]

The Duke naturally found himself the centre of controversy as

the twentieth century has moved slowly towards a different view of
foxhunting. Objections have been raised against it first on the
grounds that it is a sport for the "idle rich", and secondly because it
is cruel. The first objection holds no water at all. The hunt is
enjoyed by members of all classes, but since they are not all dukes,
they are not attacked for it. The Dowager Duchess of Beaufort rode
with the Banwen Miners' Hunt, and invited the miners to hunt with
the Beaufort.[45] The other objection is, however, more uncomfortable.
One cannot help feeling uneasy that people should derive pleasure
from seeing a living creature made dead; even the words used
in hunting terminology smack of violence. The hounds do not
kill a fox, they "break him up". A former Master of Foxhounds
has described the hunt as "a carnival, with men and women paying
money to take part in the slaughter",[46] and another correspondent
voiced the feelings of the Duke's critics when he wrote of "callousness
to animal suffering which is an affront to the civilised conscience".[47]
The Bishop of Southwark claimed that bloodsports were contrary
to Christian teaching, a charge that the Duke felt obliged to
answer, but which he avoided; he said the alternatives were worse,
which may well be true, but does not invalidate the Bishop's point.[48]
Some neighbouring farmers, tired of reasoning with a man who
could not bring reason to bear in a matter which was the fibre
of his soul, took from time to time to more strenuous methods.
There was one gentleman who threatened legal action against the
Beaufort Hunt if it continued to cross his land and do damage:
he said the hunters were boorish, and insulted him if he remonstrated
with them.[49] Another farmer shot the fox to put it out of its misery,
then ordered the Duke off his land. The Duke is reported to have
said, "Don't be silly", which is usually the incredulous reaction
of those who hunt foxes, and do not understand that it may be
offensive to others.[50]

The terrain of the Beaufort hunt was badly scissored by the M4,
cutting off the Dauntsey Vale, where a famous hunt in 1871 had
lasted for fifty miles, and the Duke had exhausted three mounts in
the chase. Horses and hounds are not allowed to cross motorways.
There is the occasional glimpse of humour amid all the earnestness.
Mr H. P. Forder, of Samuel Fox & Co., learning that the Duke of
Beaufort rode in a car marked MFH 1, wrote to *The Times*. "At these
works we travel in FOX 1", he said. "May I be assured that, should
we happen to meet His Grace upon the road, no unseemly incident
will occur?"[51] In his reply the Duke pointed out that his hunt went
nowhere near the works of Samuel Fox & Co.

Throughout World War II, Badminton played host, at the suggestion of the Government, to Queen Mary, who was the Duchess of Beaufort's aunt. Strict secrecy was imposed with the result that hardly anyone knew where she was all this time. Badminton certainly knew, however. The Duchess viewed with some apprehension Queen Mary's convoy of vans arrive in October 1939, with her seventy pieces of personal luggage, and retinue of fifty-five fastidious servants. The arrangement was that she should take over the whole house, or as much of it as she wanted, with the exception of the Duke's bedrooms and sitting-rooms. The Beauforts in effect were guests in their own home. The Duchess wrote: "Pandemonium was the least it could be called! The servants revolted, and scorned our humble home [Badminton *humble*!]. They refused to use the excellent rooms assigned to them. Fearful rows and battles royal were fought over my body. . . . The Queen, quite unconscious of the stir, has settled in well, and is busy cutting down trees and tearing down ivy." (Queen Mary hated ivy and attacked it wherever she saw it.)[52] She kept three suitcases ready packed throughout the war with which to escape in the event that the Nazis should attempt to kidnap her.[53]

As "Master" and his wife had no children, the dukedom passed in 1984 to Mr David Somerset, a cousin, and a connoisseur of Fine Art, whose wife, *née* Lady Caroline Thynne, is a daughter of the Marquess of Bath. It would be attractive to think that as Mr Somerset was not the son of his predecessor, he suddenly found himself transported at the age of fifty-six to a grandeur of style and a burden of responsibility for which he was not prepared, but such was not the case. He had been aware of what might befall him since the age of eighteen, when Master had told him on a visit to Badminton, "You must treat this place as your own." From then on, the 10th Duke effectively behaved as if David *were* his son, gradually involving him in decisions relating to Badminton and the estate, always consulting him, and in the last thirty years, more or less leaving plans for the future in his control. He has always lived on the estate and has been in and out of the house all his adult life.

The 11th Duke of Beaufort, therefore, carried on much as he did before. He is still Chairman of Marlborough Fine Art (UK) Ltd and has no intention of abandoning his life's work. He is resolutely apolitical, with no burning ambition to take his seat in the Lords. And he is not Master of the Queen's Horse; though the public mind long associated this position with the dukedom of Beaufort, it is not inherited with the title and is now held by the Earl of Westmoreland.

His descent is interesting, for his ancestor on one side is the poet

Lord Henry Somerset, who was banished into exile in 1879, while his grandmother was a daughter of the 10th Duke of St Albans, son of the mad Miss Gubbins. And of course, through Henry Somerset's wife, and in common with Virginia Woolf, he has the legacy of handsome looks from the Pattle sisters. The Duke's son and heir, Lord Worcester, was born in 1952. As there are two younger sons (and a daughter), the dukedom seems destined to continue henceforth in a straight line.

REFERENCES

1. *Daily Express*, 16th February, 1949.
2. William Shakespeare, *Richard II*, Act II, Sc. 1.
3. Osbert Sitwell, Preface to *The Somerset Sequence*, p. 9.
4. Collins, *Peerage*, Vol. I.
5. *Evening Standard*, 12th December 1964.
6. J. H. Round, *Studies in the Peerage*.
7. *Ailesbury Memoirs*, quoted in *Somerset Sequence*, p. 144.
8. Collins, I, 210.
9. Anita Leslie, *Edwardians in Love*, p. 248.
10. Walpole, ed. Cunningham, IX, p. 92.
11. *Letters* of Lady Granville, quoted in *Somerset Sequence*, p. 174.
12. Greville, I, 102.
13. Walpole, XVII, 486.
14. *ibid.*, XVIII, 185.
15. *ibid.*, XVII, 452–3.
16. *ibid.*, XVIII, 185.
17. *Lady Holland to Her Son*, p. 27.
18. Lockhart, *Life*, p. 585.
19. Harriette Wilson, *Memoirs*, p. 316.
20. *ibid.*, 273.
21. *ibid.*, 315.
22. *ibid.*, 391.
23. *ibid.*, 454–5.
24. *ibid.*, 497.
25. Greville, VI, 141.
26. *Somerset Sequence*, 183.
27. *ibid.*, 187.
28. Greville, VI, 49.
29. *ibid.*, and pp. 77–9.
30. E. F. Benson, *As We Were*, pp. 89–90.
31. *ibid.*, 90.

32. Kathleen Fitzpatrick, *Lady Henry Somerset,* p. 92.
33. E. F. Benson, *As We Were,* p. 91.
34. Timothy D'Arch Smith, *Love in Earnest,* p. 26.
35. *Songs of Adieu,* pp. 5–6.
36. Timothy D'Arch Smith, *op. cit.,* p. 27.
37. Public Record Office, DPP 1 95/5.
38. *ibid.*
39. Sir Philip Magnus, *King Edward VIII,* p. 214.
40. Public Record Office, DPP 1 95/1.
41. Ralph Nevill, *English Country House Life,* p. 156.
42. *Evening News,* 20th July 1951.
43. *The Times,* 20th May 1966.
44. T. F. Dale, *Eighth Duke of Beaufort and the Badminton Hunt,* p. 98.
45. *Daily Express,* 12th April, 1962.
46. *The People,* 8th November 1959.
47. Michael Peel, letter to *The Times,* 31st December 1969.
48. *The Times,* 29th December 1969.
49. *Daily Express,* 15th February 1962.
50. *Daily Express,* 12th April 1962.
51. *The Times,* 11th November 1960.
52. Osbert Sitwell, *Queen Mary and Others,* p. 34.
53. *ibid.,* 49.

6. For King and Country

Duke of Marlborough; Duke of Wellington

By an appropriate coincidence, the present Dukes of Marlborough and Wellington were introduced to the House of Lords on the same day – 20th July 1972. They are descended from men who had in common military genius, cool grasp and judgement, and a capacity for bold and quick decision. Away from the battlefield, however, where their personalities could be observed in less theatrical circumstances, the 1st Duke of Marlborough (1650–1722) and the 1st Duke of Wellington (1769–1852) were as different as two men ever could be.

In the first place, the fundamental principle which separated them was ambition. Marlborough was a man "on the make", who would not scruple to subordinate many a consideration to his own interest. He was quick to see where his advantage lay, and resolute in pursuing it. His ambition led him to desert his monarch, James II, when he saw that he had more to gain by supporting William of Orange, and to cover himself by giving clandestine support to James while holding positions of trust from William. "Marlborough was not the man to shrink from any means which would lead to his end, and apparently regarded a treasonable action as not less admissible than a stratagem in war."[1] Thackeray had this to say about him: "Here is my lord Duke of Marlborough kneeling too, the greatest warrior of all times; he who betrayed King William – betrayed King James II – betrayed Queen Anne – betrayed England to the French, the Elector to the Pretender, the Pretender to the Elector . . . and you, my lord Duke of Marlborough, you would sell me or any man else, if you found your advantage in it."[2]

Wellington, on the other hand, was completely devoid of vanity or personal ambition. Where Marlborough sought fame and greatness (and had to wait until he was over fifty before the opportunity came), Wellington had greatness thrust upon him in his thirties. He had none of the conceit, the guile, the deviousness of the other man. He was genuinely humble, his most highly developed motive being a sense of duty. He was unflinchingly loyal to each of the four monarchs he served, whatever he may have thought of them personally. His greatest victories and his most humble services were alike motivated by an equal degree of obligation towards his country, his superiors, or his fellows. He seems never to have been tempted to follow a course of action which would advance himself. He responded to patriotism, not to ambition, because he was essentially a man of great simplicity, straightforward, direct and truthful, who would find personal aggrandisement both distasteful and complex. Something of this attitude is in his remark that the difference between the English and the French was that "with the French, glory is the cause; with us, the result".[3] This also neatly defines the difference between Marlborough and Wellington.

It is simply not good enough to say, as Marlborough's apologists do, that they were the product of different ages. On the contrary, they helped to define what we now regard, with hindsight, as the characteristics of the times in which they lived. The explanations are more personal. Marlborough, the son of an already famous man, had fame as his object from the beginning. With good looks and a charming manner, he was naturally gregarious and social. It was perfectly normal that he should want to do well for himself. Wellington, on the other hand, was from a comparatively obscure family. At school he had been unsocial and alone, with a pet terrier as his closest companion. All his life he remained virtually friendless, in that he did not confide his deepest thoughts to anyone (probably not even to Arbuthnot). Unsure of his personal charm, he protected himself from having it exposed by making himself an intensely private individual. He never told anyone where he was going, and, of course, no one ever dared ask him. Answerable only to himself for his psychology, he thereby gained the strength to be strangely indifferent to public acclaim. "He held popularity in great contempt, and never seemed touched or pleased at the manifestations of popular admiration and attachment of which he was the object."[4] "Trust nothing to the enthusiasm of the people," he said,[5] and although most reports picture him as unfailingly courteous, there are occasions on which he is said to have been brusque with flatterers.[6] While Marlborough would measure his success by the effect he produced, in trivial as well as major issues, Wellington was true to himself, to his conscience, and to his duty. He had nerves of steel. No wonder he was nicknamed the "Iron" Duke.

Hardness and self-reliance may have assisted Wellington in his public duties, but they were hostile influences on his private life. His personality lacked tenderness, warmth and affection, the imaginative leap which enables a friend or a lover to take account of the sensibilities of another. He may not have had a cold heart, but he effectively barred anyone from finding out, so that only the coldness was visible.* Consequently, he never knew domestic happiness. He married Catherine Pakenham, Lord Longford's daughter, in 1806, and had two sons by her, but their fundamental incompatibility made them live apart after a few years, and he grew to dislike her. She was perhaps a lightweight compared to her husband, and unequal to the demands made by the scale of his personality, but she cannot be expected to bear all the blame for failing to make a success of living with such a secretive man. His relations with his son were likewise forbidding and terrifyingly formal. He one day refused to acknowledge a greeting from the young man, who was in civilian clothes, but curtly ignored him. Anxious to please, Douro rushed home to change into his uniform, whereupon his father, a quarter of an hour later, said, "Hello, Douro, I have not seen you for a long time."[7] Wellington was a renowned womaniser, yet none of his relationships were productive. He is said to have sat on the bed reading the Gospel of St John to a "woman of the streets". Harriette Wilson claims to have been one of his amours. The way in which she relates their conversations, with his harsh, staccato sentences, polite and accurate, but spare and giving nothing away, which was so typical of the man, testifies to the fact that she knew him. She says that he was unfeeling, with "fine nerves", and pays due tribute to his generosity. Incidentally, a further insight to his character as well as a now cliché phrase is afforded by the story of Harriette's publisher attempting to blackmail the Duke by suggesting that the book might be injurious to his reputation and could still be stopped on certain considerations. Wellington sent back the letter, having scrawled across it, "Publish and be damned".[8]

With Marlborough, it was quite otherwise. A deeply affectionate man, he was genuinely grief-stricken when his son and heir, Lord Blandford, died of smallpox at the age of seventeen in 1703. The signs are that he was a far more emotional man than Wellington. There were two strong love affairs in his life, one with the infamous Duchess of Cleveland (Charles II's mistress and mother of the Duke of Grafton), and one with the woman who became his wife, Sarah

* The letters he addressed to Miss A. M. Jenkins, published in 1899, were avuncular rather than tender.

Jennings. He was only twenty years old (and still a plain mister) when his affair with *la Cleveland* began in 1671; she was twenty-nine, and known to have a *penchant* for youngsters. The relationship lasted three years, producing a daughter on 16th July 1672. Fortunately, the King was already tiring of his bad-tempered mistress by this time, and had turned his attentions to Nell Gwynn. There is a story that he nevertheless surprised the young man in the Duchess's bedroom, giving him just sufficient time to escape through the window, at quite a height, to save what crumbs of honour she had left. For this timely gallantry she paid him £5000. Another version has it that Charles came face to face with the boy, and said to him, "Go, you are a rascal, but I forgive you because you do it to get your bread."[9] The inference is nasty, and time was to prove it justified. Whatever his relations with the Duchess of Cleveland, there is no doubt that Marlborough's marriage to Sarah Jennings was a most successful love match, the excitement of which lasted until death. One has only to read a handful of letters between them. "It is impossible to express with what a heavy heart I parted with you when I was at the waterside. I could have given my life to have come back," he wrote to her, adding a touch of pure romance: "I did for a great while have a perspective glass looking upon the cliffs in hopes I might have had one sight of you." Sarah, separated from her husband, thought of him constantly. She wrote, "Wherever you are whilst I have life my soul shall follow you, my ever dear Lord Marl, and wherever I am I shall only kill the time, wish for night, that I may sleep, and hope the next day to hear from you." More revealing than all is the letter which Sarah wrote to the Duke of Somerset (the so-called "Proud" Duke) who had graciously permitted himself to consider making her his wife, after Marlborough's death. Her reply is dignified, crushing, and touching. "If I were young and handsome as I was", she wrote, "instead of old and faded as I am, and you could lay the empire of the world at my feet, you should never share the heart and hand that once belonged to John, Duke of Marlborough."[10]

Other minor characteristics separate the two men. Marlborough was peevish, painfully aware of any slight; Wellington remained serenely unaffected by such matters. "There is no part of his great character more admirable or more rare than his temper and fortitude under great disappointments arising from the weakness or neglect of others", wrote Lord Mulgrave.[11] Marlborough was vain, Wellington modest, the former liked display, the latter abhorred it. When he was made Marquess of Wellington in 1812 he objected to the Union Jack being included in his coat of arms on the grounds that it was pretentious. He was also noted for extraordinary generosity, of which examples are manifold. Most interesting of all, perhaps, is the fact that when the Parliamentary Commissioners bought the estate of Stratfield Saye in 1817, for £263,000, and presented it to the Duke from a grateful nation, he spent every penny of income from the estate on improving it; not a *sou* did he spend on himself.[12] The reputation that Marlborough had for stinginess dies hard. If it is too strong to call him a miser (there are those who would say it is not), then he was certainly niggardly, giving rise to some amusing stories of his penny-pinching habits. Having devoted his life to *acquiring* money, he was not easily going to *lose* it. He was forever speculating how to add to it. As an old man, walking with difficulty, he would still walk home rather than pay sixpence for a chair to take him. His descendant Sir Winston Churchill, anxious to defend him against the charge of greed, nevertheless relates in his biography the story of his playing cards with General Pulteney. Marlborough asked Pulteney if he could borrow sixpence to pay for his chair-hire. Pulteney obliged, and the Duke left. Lord Bath, who was there, said, "I would venture any sum now, that the Duke goes home on foot. Do pray follow him out." Pulteney went to see, and there, sure enough, was the old man trudging to his lodgings.[13]

Lord Peterborough was once mistaken for the Duke of Marlborough by the London crowd, who surged around his chair shouting "God bless the Duke of Marlborough". Peterborough insisted that he was *not* the Duke, but the crowd would not be moved. He then got out of his chair, stood before them, and said, "I will give you two convincing proofs that I am not : one is, that I have but a single guinea," and he turned his pockets inside out, "the other is, that I give it to you."[14]

Much of Marlborough's unpleasant reputation in this regard can be assigned to Macaulay. Sarah Marlborough asserted that the Duke had never taken a bribe, and Sir Winston says that there is no evidence to contradict her. He goes so far as to call Macaulay a liar, and points out that at forty-five Marlborough was the poorest duke in England. For once, Churchill erred. First, at forty-five Marlborough was yet only an earl, being raised to the rank of duke at the age of fifty-two. Secondly, his great period of accumulating wealth was still in the future, when Queen Anne came to the throne; Anne was influenced to an extraordinary degree by her friends the Marlboroughs, John and Sarah.

From another point of view, it matters little that Marlborough was covetous. It is important only that he was a great general. As

Trevelyan wrote, "If he loved money, he gave England better value for every guinea he received than any other of her servants."

Sarah apparently shared this mean streak with her husband. She is said never to have put dots over her i's to save ink.[15] Another source, Prince Eugene, attributes the same habit to the Duke.

Much of the Duke's personality was public knowledge, which alone can account for his eventual unpopularity. In spite of his great achievements. "He had probably less public sympathy than any successful general." Wellington's massive popularity could not be more vividly contrasted with this. In 1814 his journey from Dover to London was a triumphal progress (this was even before Waterloo). The people themselves took over and drew his carriage from Westminster Bridge to Hamilton Place. Years later, at the Great Exhibition of 1851, his attraction had not dimmed; thousands stared at him instead of at the exhibition. At his funeral in 1852 one and a half million people lined the route. (The population of London was then 2,362,236.) "No man ever lived or died in the possession of more unanimous love, respect, and esteem from his countrymen," said Palmerston. Only once did this love turn sour. The Duke was a high Tory and a passionate opponent of the Reform Bill. The people stormed his London home, Apsley House, and threw stones at the windows. The Duchess was lying dead within. One stone passed over the Duke's head as he was writing, and cracked a picture on the opposite wall of the room.[16] He did not flinch. Characteristically, he did not deign to repair the broken windows, but boarded them up.

That apart, Wellington was revered almost as a god. He was thought to be omnipotent, his advice sought in every crisis. From Queen Victoria, who wrote in her journal, "The Duke is the best friend we have", to the Government, who pressed him against his will to be Prime Minister, to the thousands who doffed their hats to him, all had faith in his powers, and respect for his person. It is a pity he allowed himself to be persuaded into the Premiership, for he did not distinguish himself in politics. Even that, however, could not dim the magic of his especial position. Greville said he was midway between the Royal Family and other subjects; he was treated with greater respect than any other person not of royal birth. One amusing instance serves to show the awe which the Duke inspired. The Great Exhibition was due to be opened in Hyde Park, in Paxton's glorious crystal palace, when a potential disaster threatened. Within the glass building were three large elms, and they were so loaded with London sparrows that the birds might well soil and spoil all the goods on show, not to mention the people. Lord John Russell suggested that a regiment of Guards should go in and shoot all the sparrows, until the Prince of Wales pointed out that the glass would be shattered. Lord Palmerston then said that bird lime should be put on the branches; but the sparrows had by this time taken to nesting on the iron girders of the building, so that would not do. In desperation, the Queen said, "Send for the Duke of Wellington." The Duke said that he was no bird-catcher, but nonetheless presented himself at Buckingham Palace as bidden. A consultation was held. The Duke, always a man of few words, went up to the Queen and said simply, "Sparrow hawks, ma'am." In due course the sparrows flew out of the crystal building in a body, never to be seen again.[17]

Nothing can better illustrate the exceptional position of the Duke of Wellington than the occasion of his death, on 14th September 1852, which gave rise to unparalleled national grief. His corpse was brought from Walmer Castle to London on 10th November. As it started its journey, a most unusual thing happened – there was an earthquake in England. The shock was mild, but it was certainly felt, more strongly in Liverpool and Birkenhead than anywhere else. Some people thought there were robbers under the bed, others that it was the cat! Clocks were stopped, and crockery slid from dressers all over the area. Only the animals seem to have recognised instinctively that something more serious was afoot; dogs howled and trembled, cattle lowed and ran amok.[18] When the Duke's body arrived in London the earthquake had ceased.

On the first day of the lying-in-state there were scenes of terrifying confusion. A huge multitude surged forward to see the body, and soon found themselves trapped in panic. Children were held aloft to escape suffocation, there were frightful shrieks and screams of agony. Three people were crushed to death, followed by two more on the last day.

The funeral itself was the most impressive ever held, though Greville found it "tawdry, cumbrous, and vulgar".[19] The funeral car was drawn by twelve black horses (only six horses drew the Queen's carriage). It weighed eighteen tons, and had been made from the metal of guns captured at Waterloo. One hundred men had taken eighteen days to build the carriage, which can still be seen in the crypt of St Paul's. Behind there followed the Duke's own horse, led by his own groom. In St Paul's there were fifty-four candlesticks, seven feet high, and twelve silver candelabra in front of the bier.[20] It was as if the nation could not extend itself far enough to demonstrate its loss. *The Times* wrote: "It was impossible to convey any idea of the emotion felt by the nation, nothing like it had ever been manifested before."[21] The French Ambassador, Count Walewski, a natural son of Napoleon I, was reluctant to attend the funeral, and had to be ordered to do so by Louis Napoleon. Baron Brunnow commented : "If this ceremony were intended to bring the Duke to life again, I can conceive your reluctance to appear at it; but as it is only to bury him, I don't see you have anything to complain of."[22]

When the drums rolled, Queen Victoria burst into tears.

Indeed, not the least astonishing aspect of a remarkable career is the reverence shown by the French towards the man who defeated them. The Duke was never vindictive towards a defeated enemy, a generous quality which he shared with Marlborough. The period of his rule in Paris was even remembered with affection. On one occasion, not long after Waterloo, Wellington was spotted in civilian clothes at the Paris Opéra with Lord and Lady Castlereagh. The cry went up, *"Vive Wellington!"* and the conqueror was mobbed on his way out of the theatre. One Frenchman was heard saying to another, *"Mais pourquoi l'applaudissez-vous tant? Il nous a toujours battus."* *"Oui,"* said the other, *"mais il nous a battus en gentilhomme."*[23]

The French also admired, and envied, and were exasperated by, his imperturbable English phlegm. The Marquise d'Assche wrote : "I would willingly have throttled him from the impatience which his phlegm caused me and the ease of his conversation." There is no better instance of nonchalance than his famous appearance at the Duchess of Richmond's ball, the eve of Waterloo, when the French were threatening, and he put his phlegm to strategic use in showing them that they caused him no particular concern and would not prevent his enjoying his dinner. After eating, Wellington turned to Richmond and whispered a priceless remark. "Have you got a good map in the house ?"[24]

The man known simply to posterity as "The Duke" had been born Arthur Wellesley (or Wesley). The title of Wellington was selected for him by his brother William, "after ransacking the Peerage and examining the map". There was a place in Somerset called Welleslie, and not far away a town called Wellington. "I trust that you will not think there is anything unpleasant or trifling in the name of Wellington," wrote William. "I think you have chosen most fortunately," said Arthur Wellesley.[25] It is now recalled by the capital of New Zealand, by a mountain in Tasmania, by the Wellington boot, the Wellington apple, the Wellington barracks, and a giant Californian sequoia tree, not to mention nearly forty London streets called Wellington, seventeen called Wellesley, and over thirty pubs.

Queen Victoria opened Wellington College as his memorial in 1859, while he himself had been present at the opening of Waterloo Bridge in 1817. He had risen through the peerage to Duke in the space of only five years (Viscount 1809, Earl 1812, Marquess 1812, Duke 1814): a unique example. He was also awarded a Spanish dukedom, a Portuguese dukedom, Prince of Waterloo in the Netherlands, and twenty-three separate knighthoods from various countries.

Marlborough's name before elevation to the peerage had been John Churchill, the son of Sir Winston Churchill, M.P., an historian and intense royalist as well as a politician. Sir Winston's parents were John Churchill and Sarah Winston, and his wife was the daughter of Elizabeth Villiers, sister to the Duke of Buckingham, thus bringing a strain of Villiers blood to all succeeding Churchills.

The Churchills had originally come from Dorsetshire, though the claim of descent from one Roger de Courcil, Comrade-in-Arms of William the Conqueror, is probably fanciful. It was Sir Winston who first made the name Churchill a household word, as did his descendant and namesake, our own Sir Winston, 300 years later. The fortunes of the Churchills lay in their close relationship with the Stuarts. Sir Winston's daughter Arabella was mistress to the Duke of York, later James II. She bore him a son, the Duke of Berwick, who fought for the French against Marlborough; and several other children.

Arabella's brother, young John Churchill, was appointed a Page of Honour to the Duke of York. Later, his wife Sarah was made a Lady of the Bedchamber to Princess Anne, whose close friend she became (they called each other "Mrs Morley" and "Mrs Freeman") and over whom she wielded a singular influence. It was John and Sarah Churchill who persuaded Anne to accept William of Orange on the throne of England, as a direct reward for which John was made Earl of Marlborough. His titles were created in three different reigns; he was created Baron Churchill by James II in 1685, Earl of Marlborough by William and Mary in 1689, and Marquess of Blandford and Duke of Marlborough by Queen Anne in 1702, on the Queen's own initiative, without waiting for the recommendation of Parliament. The title of Marlborough was chosen, although he had no property there, because his mother had been distantly related to the Ley family, who had been Earls of Marlborough in the previous century. In 1704 he won his magnificent victory at Blenheim, with 22,000 acres and the building of Blenheim Palace as his reward.

Had he not been such a splendid general, Marlborough would most likely have been overshadowed by his tempestuous wife, Sarah; she it was who had the more dominant personality, sweeping not only her husband but Queen Anne herself into its power. It is interesting that Wellington should defend Marlborough, praise his sagacity, on the grounds that "his errors were due to his wife".[26] She has bequeathed some of her extravagant characteristics to generations of Churchills, most noticeably her pugnacity and her quarrelsome nature. The former emerged particularly in the late Sir Winston, who exuded so much pugnacity that the surplus was absorbed and assumed by his compatriots in time of crisis, while the latter has been the cause of constant bickerings, squabbles, feuds and ruptures among the Dukes of Marlborough through the ages.

Duchess Sarah quarrelled with everyone, with her family, her lawyers, her architect Vanbrugh. She was forever involved in one lawsuit or another. Hervey called her "Old Aetna" or "Vesuvius", always on the point of explosion, and when he saw her coming, looking "cross as the devil", he would make himself scarce. There are famous stories of Sarah's impulsive temper. Furious with her grand-daughter Lady Bateman, whom she suspected of encouraging the Marlborough heir in a disastrous marriage, she took some black paint and smeared it over a portrait of Lady Bateman on the wall, writing on the frame: "Now her face is as black as her heart." She had very beautiful long hair. In the midst of an argument with her husband, she cut it all off in front of him and threw it on the floor. (After his death the hair was found in one of his private drawers.) Lesser folk trembled at her approach. She went one day to consult her lawyer in his chambers, but had made no appointment. He was out to supper. She told his clerk she would wait, but at midnight she flew into a rage and left. The clerk said, "I don't know who she was, she wouldn't give a name, but she swore so much she must be a lady of quality."[27] Sarah gave a great dinner on her birthday to all her brood of children and grand-children. She compared the family to a great tree, with herself the root and all her branches flourishing about her. Her grandson John Spencer (who was her favourite) remarked that the branches would flourish more when the root was underground.[28] It took some courage to bait the formidable old woman thus.

Sir John Vanbrugh, the architect of Blenheim, had the devil's own job trying to extract payment from Sarah, whom he called "that wicked woman of Marlborough". "I have been forced into Chancery by that BBBB old B the Duchess of Marlborough", Vanbrugh wrote to his friend Tonson. "She has got an injunction on me by her friend the good Lord Chancellor, who declared that I was never employed by the Duke and therefore had no demand upon his estate for my services at Blenheim. I have prevailed with Sir Robert Walpole to help me in a scheme which I proposed to him by which I get my money in spite of the hussy's teeth."[29]

There is another side of Sarah Marlborough which has also been passed down to her posterity, and which generally receives less attention, and that is her gentle, epigrammatic wisdom, with a gift for well-structured, beguiling expression in words. She once wrote, "I am very fond of my three dogs, they have all of them gratitude, wit, and good sense : things very rare to be found in this country. They are fond of going out with me; but when I reason with them, and tell them it is not proper, they submit, and watch for my coming home, and meet me with as much joy as if I had never given them good advice."[30]

She also said she was not only sure of going to Heaven but of obtaining one of the best places.[31]

The Marlborough succession did not begin well. John and Sarah's only son died in 1703, depriving the dukedom of an heir. An Act of Parliament was passed in 1706 enabling the title to pass through the female line, which meant that the eldest daughter, Henrietta, became 2nd Duchess of Marlborough in her own right (1681–1733). Unfortunately, her son and heir was a reprobate who liked "low" company and had nothing to recommend him. He died at the age of thirty-one, probably after a drinking bout, a sad unlamented character. If we are to believe Hervey, his mother shed no tears; she said that "anybody who had any regard to *Papa*'s memory must be glad that the Duke of Marlborough was now not in danger of being represented in the next generation by one who must have brought any name he bore into contempt".[32] The title then passed to Henrietta's nephew, son of the great Duke's second daughter, who had married Charles Spencer, Earl of Sunderland. All subsequent Dukes are descended from this alliance of a male Spencer and a female Churchill (the family name is now Spencer-Churchill). The Spencers gave to future generations their least attractive characteristics. Spencer's father, 2nd Earl of Sunderland, was one of the most wicked, unprincipled villains in English public life. He was happy as long as he was at the centre of affairs, and would not scruple to betray allegiances in order to remain there.

The fruit of this alliance was the 3rd Duke of Marlborough (1706–1758), a sad and lonely character, of generous impulses, but no talent. Lord Landsdowne said he had "no force of character whatever"; it was more likely to have been smothered by his grandmother, old Sarah, who detested him. He seems to have embraced a military life simply because he was bored with staying at home and did not know what else to do with himself. When he became Duke, he took over Blenheim Palace and all the Churchill property, but surrendered (quite willingly) the Spencer property to his brother John. There were two causes for the explosive rupture between the new Duke and old Sarah. She wanted to lay claim to a portion of the 1st Duke's personal estate, a matter which could quite easily be settled amicably, as the new Duke was an obliging man. "But as a suit with her to go on *amicably* was a thing about as likely as for an oil-shop, set on fire, to be slow in burning",³³ the whole business ballooned into a full-scale family row. Then the Duke announced his intention of marrying a daughter of Lord Trevor (who had been a great enemy of his grandfather Marlborough), and Aetna erupted in a cloud of invective. She stormed and raged; the lady's father was a madman, she said, her mother a fool, her grandfather a rogue, and her grandmother a whore. Sarah wrote: "The woman herself (as they say, for I have never seen her) has been bred in a very low way and don't know how to behave herself upon any occasion; not at all pretty, and has a mean, ordinary look. As to the behaviour, if she has any sense, that may mend. But they say she has very bad teeth, which I think is an objection alone in a wife, and they will be sure to grow worse with time." The true objection did not edge its way into view until much more spite and spleen had been vented, and then, it was the familiar old obsession with money – "a contemptible family, the chief of which cheated his grandfather by a false mortgage of £10,000".³⁴ So that was it. She had not given him Marlborough's sword "lest he should pick out the diamonds and pawn them". It was at this point that, poisoned with acrimony, Sarah took a brush and disfigured her grand-daughter's portrait. The poor Duke put up with it all patiently, the whole world knowing that his grandmother loathed him, and George II had little time for him either. His wife did turn out to be coarse in time. After his death, she fell in love with her son's tutor, Dr Moore, and proposed marriage; he discreetly declined, but the connection served him well, for he was eventually Archbishop of Canterbury.

The 4th Duke of Marlborough (1739–1817), born in the midst of squabbles, was a nervous, highly strung man. Self-consciousness made him shy, an embarrassment which he covered by a sullen over-bearing manner. He was ill-at-ease, and made others feel so in his company, though they knew him to be a decent, hospitable man. His marriage to a daughter of the Duke of Bedford was extremely happy. Like his contemporary, the Duke of Queensberry (Old Q), Marlborough indulged the fashionable habit of employing a running footman. These men could run comfortably at about seven miles an hour, sometimes more, sustained by white wine and eggs. An amusing pastime was to stage a race between horse and carriage, and a running footman – it was something else to bet on in the eighteenth century. The last such race on record was between the Duke of Marlborough and his footman. The Duke was in a carriage and four, and started from Windsor at the same time as the footman, with London as their goal. The Duke won, but only just, and the footman died from the effects of overstrain.[35]

By one account, this duke did not pronounce a single word for three years, and was about to enter the fourth year of silence when it was announced that Madame de Staël, the French intellectual, was about to pay him a visit. "Take me away! Take me away!" he roared.[36]

His son the 5th Duke (1766–1840), who changed the family name from Spencer to Spencer-Churchill by royal licence, dated 26th May 1817, and who was the first man in England to abandon the foreign spelling of Marquess (*Marquis*), spent a fortune on books. He it was who bought the 1471 edition of Boccaccio from the Duke of Roxburghe's library in 1812, and founded the Roxburghe Club the same day. "He lived in utter retirement at one corner of his magnificent palace, a melancholy instance of the results of extravagance."[37]

The 6th Duke of Marlborough (1793–1857) was an entirely different proposition. In him seem to have fused the tough independent spirit of the Churchills and the intolerable amoral egoism of the Spencers. He had some of the qualities of a leader, and used them to base ends. Even as a boy he was first brought to notice for troublemaking. At Eton there was a headmaster called Keate, who took an inordinate pleasure in flogging boys. He boasted having flogged 200 in one day, and regretted not having flogged more. At last the boys rose in rebellion against the authoritarian rule, and ran amok in the "Keate riots"; one of the ringleaders was young Spencer-Churchill.

Lord Monson said that the boy was "one of the handsomest lads I ever saw". In later years he was to turn his good looks to full advantage in a disreputable escapade. In 1817, while he was still styled Lord Blandford, he began a liaison with a seventeen-year-old girl, Susan Adelaide Law, who lived with her parents in Seymour Place, Bryanston Square. She quite obviously was infatuated with him. Before long, he had made her pregnant, and she bore him a daughter. She must have begged to be made a respectable woman (and a Marchioness), for though they were living together as

Captain and Mrs Lawson and she received an allowance from Marl-borough funds, she was still only Miss Law. Blandford then staged a bogus marriage to satisfy her. The marriage took place in her father's house, with Blandford's brother as witness, and an officer in the army dressed up as a clergyman. Little Miss Law was completely deceived. She travelled with her "husband" to Scotland, where she said she was presented as the Marchioness of Blandford (though, predictably, neither of the lords she met on this occasion would corroborate her). She must have been the only person to be taken in by the farce, since it seems hardly likely her parents did not know the truth. However, the matter became public knowledge when, years later, the *Satirist* newspaper stated that Lord Blandford's subsequent marriage to Lord Galloway's daughter was bigamous, and that their children were bastards. The Blandfords had to take the matter to court, where the mock marriage was revealed, and it was also discovered the Duchess of Marlborough had been paying £400 a year to Miss Law (later reduced to £200), which went some way to redeem the Marl-borough name. For Blandford, the judge had some harsh words to say.[38]

With his son, the 7th Duke of Marlborough, we come close to the present day. The 7th Duke (1822–1883) married Fanny, daughter of Lord Londonderry, and their youngest son was Lord Randolph Churchill, father of Sir Winston. In fact, Winston Churchill was heir presumptive to the dukedom of Marlborough until he was eighteen; if his uncle had not had a son, Winston could have been a duke.

In the lifetime of the 7th Duke there erupted another family scandal, in which all the Spencer-Churchill foibles of arrogance, quarrelsomeness, pig-headedness, and tempestuous obstinacy were brought into play. It revolved around the Marquess of Blandford, the eldest son, Randolph's brother and Winston's uncle. He had mar-ried Bertha Hamilton, daughter of the Duke of Abercorn, a good-hearted but rather silly girl, known to her family as "Goosie". In an age which delighted in practical jokes, Goosie was the worst offender; she amused herself putting inkpots over the door when her husband walked in, placing a celluloid baby on his breakfast tray instead of a poached egg, as well as the full gamut of apple-pie beds and tied pyjamas. Aristocratic ladies were bored to death in the nineteenth century not knowing what to do with themselves between meals and decorous gossip. The mania for practical jokes sprang from that boredom (and persists to this day in some aristocratic descendants). Bertha Blandford drove her husband mad with her insufferable tricks and it is no wonder that he looked elsewhere for affection.

So started the Aylesford scandal, the details of which have often been related in print. Essentially, Blandford and Lady Aylesford decided to elope. That alone in mid-Victorian society was an inconceivable scandal, sinning against the law of do-as-you-will-so-long-as-you-do-not-admit-it. It was made worse by the involvement of the Prince of Wales. The Marlborough family and Lord and Lady Aylesford were in the Prince's "set", and Aylesford himself was with the Prince in India when the scandal broke. H.R.H. called Blandford a blackguard, whereupon Blandford's brother, irascible Lord Randolph, called upon the Princess of Wales and told her that the Prince himself had known Lady Aylesford well, and had addressed compromising letters to her, which he, Randolph, would publish so that the Prince would never sit on the throne of England. It was bald blackmail. In the turmoil which followed, the Prince escaped unscathed, the Aylesfords were ruined, and the Marlborough family was temporarily banished from the best circles. The old Duke was made bitterly unhappy, although it must be said he showed precious little understanding of his son's dilemma. Tempers were raw, no one stopped to reason calmly (except Blandford, who wrote his father some cogent literate letters which did no good at all but which revealed some of the Churchill power for expression in prose).

From this date, too, appears an unbreachable gulf between fathers and sons in the Marlborough sequence, reminiscent of the Russells, and most vividly shown in Winston's relations with his father. Bertha Blandford was herself the daughter of a Russell, the Duchess of Abercorn.

Bertha divorced her husband shortly before he became Duke, on the grounds of proven adultery with the Countess of Aylesford. The new Duke of Marlborough (1844–1892) married again, this time an American; the ceremony was performed by the Mayor of New York at the Tabernacle Baptists Church on 2nd Avenue.

We know something of the 9th Duke (1871–1934) through the memoirs of his wife, Consuelo Vanderbilt. Her story is particularly interesting because it represents one of the last instances of a purely arranged marriage, in which love played no part. English ducal families had taken such marriages in their stride as a necessary contribution towards maintaining rank, in itself far more important than happiness, and few women sacrificed in this way ever saw fit to complain. Consuelo was different. From sturdy independent American stock, she had no worship for the idea of family.

Consuelo Vanderbilt was the daughter of one of the handful of truly wealthy Americans. The Vanderbilt millions were legendary when the Duke of Marlborough began looking around. Consuelo's mother had everything that money could buy, ten times over, but one thing eluded her – status. Mrs Vanderbilt determined that her daughter would marry into the English aristocracy. Consuelo was a victim of material ambition, and of dwindling funds in ducal pockets. She lived at a time when it was more and more common for British dukes to protect their assets by marrying American heiresses – May Goelet married the Duke of Roxburghe in 1903 and Helena Zimmerman became Duchess of Manchester in 1900. Both women were friends of the Vanderbilts; indeed, Consuelo was named after a previous American Duchess of Manchester, her godmother – Consuelo Iznaga del Valle.

Mrs Vanderbilt was quite merciless in the pursuit of her aims. Once she had the Duke of Marlborough in her sights, no amount of tears or protests from her daughter would shift her. Consuelo was already in love with someone else, so she had to be imprisoned in her own house to make sure she would never meet him. She was not allowed out, her letters were intercepted and read, and her outgoing mail was censored. Cunningly, Mrs Vanderbilt let it be known that her daughter would consider an approach from the Duke. A meeting was arranged. They did not like each other at all, but that was not the point. He, too, was in love with someone else, who was not suitable. He was not slow to see the advantage, financially speaking, of such a union. For the sake of the continued wealth of the Marlboroughs, he was prepared to sacrifice himself. We do not know if he considered the sacrifice *she* was making; perhaps there was none, in his eyes. He was giving her the rank of a duchess and the privilege of belonging to the Churchill family. "When I broke the news of our engagement to my brothers," wrote Consuelo, "Harold observed, 'He is only marrying you for your money', and with this last slap to my pride I burst into tears."[39]

And so they were wed, in 1896. There was not the merest surge of love between the two from the beginning. They remained strangers to each other. They had children, including the 10th Duke, but their characters were irreconcilable. The Duchess tells how their meals together at Blenheim would be painfully silent, the Duke staring into space and she bored to desperation; mealtimes with Herbrand, 11th Duke of Bedford, and his wife were exactly the same.

Consuelo's first meeting with the Dowager Duchess, Fanny, was frightening. She was told she must keep up the prestige of the family at all costs, and she uttered a command which must serve as one of the highest ironies in British history. "Your first duty is to have a

child," she said, "and it must be a son, because it would be intolerable to have that little upstart Winston become Duke. Are you in the
family way?"[40]

The marriage settlement gave the Duke £20,000 a year out of the
Vanderbilt wealth, and income from a £500,000 fund. In the
present generation this has been augmented by the millions she in
herited from her father, and some of which she passed to her Marlborough heirs. From that point of view, the marriage was a success.
From the human view, however, it was disaster. From 1907, they
lived apart, finally divorcing in 1921. She then married Jacques
Balsan, and died in 1964. His second marriage was to another American, Gladys Deacon, who knew Marcel Proust for years. She used to
tell how Proust was fascinated by the sound of aristocratic names. He
was most excited by the name Duchess of Northumberland. "*Je vais
l'annoncer*," he said, got out of bed, opened wide the door, and
yelled, "*Madame la Duchesse de Northumberland.*"[41]

From Consuelo we also learn something of the Churchill character,
which we can recognise in the Duke's antecedents and kinsmen. He
had a passion for pageantry and magnificent spectacle (which Winston shared), but was otherwise a silent brooder. Many of the dukes
have had a morbid, pessimistic dark nature.

The 10th Duke of Marlborough (1897–1972), Consuelo's son, did
his best to retrieve Blenheim from the gloom in which his unhappy
father had plunged it. A great deal was spent on restoration in 1966
(the Ministry of Works contributing £55,000), and those great un-
welcoming rooms, built to impress rather than to be comfortable,
heard some laughter. He continued to live, however, in nineteenth-
century fashion, choosing to ignore the changing times around him.
He had wit, but a forbidding presence and gruff manner made those
who came into contact with him uncomfortable. On one occasion,
an American guest asked politely if he might try one of the Duke's
excellent cigars, and received the abrupt reply, "They don't grow on
trees, y'know." The 1st Duke would have understood. After a row
with Randolph Churchill he is supposed to have shouted, "Never
darken the doorstep of my palace again!"

The Duke died only two months after his second marriage, to
Laura Canfield, grand-daughter of the Earl of Wemyss, and was succeeded in the honours by his son, the present Duke of Marlborough,
born in 1926.

And what honours! Apart from being Marquess of Blandford, Earl
of Sunderland, Baron Spencer and Baron Churchill in this country,
he is a Prince of the Holy Roman Empire, and Prince of Mindelheim,

in Swabia, dignities which he holds by virtue of his descent from the 1st Duke of Marlborough. More impressive than any title is the surname he bears, for his ancestors and his kinsmen have elevated the name of Churchill above any peerage degree. From Sir Winston Churchill (1620–1688) to Sir Winston Churchill (1874–1965), the family strengths and weaknesses have produced with consistency either spectacular or lamentable personalities, but rarely an indifferent one. They are not the kind of people that can be ignored. Egotistical and explosive, they are fighters, who rise to a challenge and thrive on argument. They are not noted for their kindness. From the Sunderlands they inherit a passion for publicity, from Duchess Sarah a perverse delight in confrontation, and from the 1st Duke a warmth of heart which has made them time and again an easy prey to love. One feels that the Churchills long to be sweet and gentle, but cannot help being harsh and forbidding.

The 11th Duke of Marlborough was a captain in the Life Guards, then studied at an agricultural college. He has married three times, always with the din of public interest around his ears. At his first marriage, to Susan Hornby in 1951, the Queen (now Queen Mother), Queen Mary, and Princess Margaret were all present. The marriage was dissolved in 1960 on the grounds of his wife's adultery. A year later, in a chaotic Greek ceremony in Paris where newsgatherers were in greater number than guests, he married Athina Livanos, known to the world as "Tina" Onassis, as she had previously been married to Aristotle Onassis, the Greek shipowner. Tina's life was a pathetic study in malignant fate. Though beautiful, and enclosed on all sides by millionaires, tragedy stalked her. By her marriage to Onassis, she had two children, a boy and a girl. Their son died in an air-crash at the age of twenty-four, and the daughter, Christina, has attempted suicide. Tina's sister twice married another millionaire Greek, Stavros Niarchos, before she, too, killed herself. Tina herself divorced Lord Blandford (he was not yet Duke) in 1971, and married her brother-in-law, the same Niarchos. Within two years, Tina was dead.

Meanwhile, Blandford took as his third wife a Swedish countess, Rosita Douglas, who is the present Duchess of Marlborough. They have a son, born in 1974. Meanwhile, the heir, born in 1955, son of the first marriage to Susan Hornby, has had his indiscretions subjected to intense public scrutiny while his qualities go largely unnoticed. The Churchill saga seems likely to continue as colourfully as ever.

The renown of the Duke of Wellington has been like a heavy hand clapped over the mouth of his descendants. So powerful is his legend, so brilliant his reputation, that they have remained forever in his shadow, borrowing their existence from him, speaking only to pay tribute to him. Until very recently, successive Dukes of Wellington were virtually unnoticeable. The life of the Iron Duke's son, who succeeded as 2nd Duke (1807–1884), illustrates very clearly the emasculating effect of a father only one step short of a deity. He tried to enter public life, was Master of the Horse, a Knight of the Garter, and a Privy Councillor, but he did not make his mark. As he could not be as great as his father (who could?) he devoted himself to trying to please him. This was not so easy either. He was once asked whether his father had shown him any kindness, to which he replied, "No, he never even so much as patted me on the shoulder when I was a boy, but it was because he hated my mother."[42] In adult life, too, Douro was always endeavouring to merit the love of his eminent father. On another occasion, when the great Duke was at Walmer Castle, the officers of a neighbouring garrison called to pay their respects. The major at this garrison was Lord Douro, who thought it would be absurd to take part in the visit, as he saw his father every day in the normal course. Consequently, the Duke invited all the officers to dinner, except his own son, and during the meal said to the Colonel, "By the way, who is your major? for he has not called on me."[43]

In the end, the 2nd Duke of Wellington dedicated his life in the service of his father. He edited the Iron Duke's correspendence in twenty-three volumes, an undertaking of such immensity that it can only have been a labour of love. "No son ever erected a finer monument."[44] Augustus Hare met the Duke when he was aged, "dressed like a poor pensioner", living at Stratfield Saye amongst the relics of his father. This was in 1875. "It was touching to see the old man, who for the greater part of his lifetime existed in unloving awe of a father he had always feared and been little noticed by, now, in the evening of life, treasuring up every reminiscence of him and considering every memorial as sacred. In his close stuffy little room were the last pheasants the Duke had shot, the miniatures of his mother and aunt and of himself and his brother as children, his grandfather's portrait, a good one of Marshal Saxe, and the picture of the horse Copenhagen."[45] He died, without fanfare, at Brighton railway station.

The next two dukes were both his nephews, and the 5th Duke was his great-nephew. All three were inconspicuous, led military careers, and married modestly. In 1941 the 6th Duke of Wellington succeeded (1912–1943); he was killed in action in the landing at Salerno, and is buried in Italy. His death at the age of thirty-one unexpectedly diverted the dukedom to his uncle, a clever diplomat and architect called Lord Gerald Wellesley (1885–1972), who was a son of the 4th Duke. Wellesley was well known before he came to the title, more so than the nephew whom he succeeded, for he and his wife, Dorothy Wellesley, were near the centre of literary and artistic life in London. Dorothy Wellesley was herself a distinguished poet, much admired by W. B. Yeats, with many volumes of verse to her credit. They were at home with the Bells, Vanessa and Clive, or the Nicolsons, Harold and Vita, more than in society drawing-rooms. Dorothy was a close friend of Vita Sackville-West (who, of course, was a fellow poet) and it was she who first saw Sissinghurst Castle and brought it to Vita and Harold's attention; then they bought it and made it the famous romantic house and garden it is today. Wellesley served in the diplomatic service in Petrograd, spoke fluent Russian, and revisited Russia in later years. He served in World War II. The restoration of Castle Hill in North Devonshire was the best known of his architectural projects. In later years he earned much admiration as an historian; it is not generally acknowledged that the keepers of museums and archives throughout the country held the Duke in very high regard, for he was a gentleman intellectual, informed in all branches of the arts and accomplished in many of them. He wrote five books, four of which were on the subject of his illustrious ancestor. His most precious inheritance was the great archive at Apsley House and Stratfield Saye which he and his librarian Francis Needham both skilfully arranged and preserved. His wife died in 1956, after a lifetime's suffering from neuritis of the extremities, which made the tips of her fingers permanently tense. The Duke spent the rest of his life bringing to public attention more and more information about the 1st Duke of Wellington.

If anyone should not yet be convinced of the power of genetic inheritance, he might reflect for a moment on the Wellington line, and on the Marlborough characteristics. The word "duty" was never off the Iron Duke's lips from one day to the next; his despatches and correspondence are full of references to duty. It was the concept by which he ruled his life. His son burnt midnight oil editing the Duke's letters for public consumption, impelled by a sense of duty. Gerald Wellesley, the 7th Duke, gave his London home to the nation out of duty. In 1947 he made over to the country Apsley House at Hyde Park Corner, whose address has long been No. 1, London, converting it into a museum full of personal relics of Wellington, and retaining for himself a small flat on the top floor, free of rent and rates. Apsley House was the Duke's personal property, having been bought by the Iron Duke, rather than it having been given to him by the nation, as was the case with Stratfield Saye. It is now administered by the Victoria and Albert Museum. His son, the 8th and present Duke of Wellington (1915–), has spent more than £135,000 on converting part of the grounds at Stratfield Saye into a pleasure park for urban dwellers who need some pleasant rural surroundings, money that he can expect very little return on, since he eschews lions and funfairs. "I have a duty to provide land for recreation," he said, adding that it was for him "an opportunity to repay in some measure the debt of gratitude our family owes to the nation".[46] The house was opened to the public in 1974.*

Fittingly, the 8th Duke of Wellington has had a military career, serving in World War II, and at one time commanding the Household Cavalry. His duchess is the daughter of a major-general, and they have four sons and a daughter; the heir, Lord Douro, was born in 1945. Wellington holds a number of honours awarded to himself, instead of inherited, including the Légion d'Honneur from France, the M.V.O., the O.B.E. and the M.C. They cannot, of course, compare with the resplendent list he has inherited from the Iron Duke, whereby he is Duke of Ciudad Rodrigo in Spain, and a Grandee of the First Class in that country, Duke of Vittoria in Portugal, and Prince of Waterloo. He still receives £571 annually from the Belgian government in recognition of the victory of Waterloo.

Perhaps we are not meant to expect justice in genetic inheritance, but we cannot be reproached for observing its absence. The Wellesleys are a more preferable race of men and women than the Churchills; they have grace and tact, decent manners and an agreeable nature which makes for good company; they have, too, inherited a concept of honour which they would not (cannot) disgrace. None of this could be said of the Churchills, who have shown themselves time and again to be unkindly, rude, boorish, erratic, irascible, hot-tempered and egotistical. And yet it is the Churchills that continue to breed men of exceptional ability, men who have been in and out of the pages of our history for centuries, while the Wellesleys produced only one man, a giant, but a giant alone, in whose shadow all descendants shrink to human size.

* Neither Blenheim Palace nor Stratfield Saye may ever be sold.

REFERENCES

1. D.N.B.
2. W. M. Thackeray, *The Four Georges*, p. 33.
3. Elizabeth Longford, *Wellington*, Vol. II, p. 405.
4. Greville, VI, 364.
5. D.N.B.
6. Edith Marchioness of Londonderry, *Frances Anne*, p. 99.
7. Augustus Hare, *In My Solitary Life*, p. 162.
8. Longford, *op. cit.*, I, 166–7.
9. Winston S. Churchill, *Marlborough*, Vol. I, pp. 69–70.
10. *ibid.*, I, 143.
11. *Hist. MSS. Comm.*, Bathurst MSS, p. 216.
12. D.N.B.
13. Churchill, *op. cit.*, I, 470.
14. *Literary Gazette*, 1827, p. 121, from the Earl of Bridgewater's *Family Anecdotes*.
15. Walpole, XXV, 609.
16. Emma Lady Brownlow, *Slight Reminiscences of a Septuagenarian*, p. 144.
17. Cecil Woodham-Smith, *Queen Victoria*, Vol. I, p. 220.
18. *Annual Register*, 1852, p. 187.
19. Greville, VI, 370.
20. *Annual Register*, 1852, p. 485.
21. *The Times*, 18th November 1852.
22. Greville, VI, 372.
23. Lady Brownlow, *op. cit.*, p. 45.
24. Longford, *op. cit.*, I, 419.
25. *ibid.*, p. 198.
26. Greville, V, 125.
27. *Old and New London*, I, 176.
28. Greville, IV, 434.
29. quoted in Martin S. Briggs. *Men of Taste*.
30. Sarah, Duchess Dowager of Marlborough, *Opinions* (1788), p. 15.
31. Nina Epton, *Milord and Milady*, p. 93.
32. *Hervey and His Friends*, p. 83.
33. Lady Louisa Stuart, Introductory Anecdotes to *Life and Letters* of Lady Mary Wortley-Montagu.
34. *Lord Hervey and His Friends*, pp. 288, 295.
35. *Leaves from the Notebooks* of Lady Dorothy Nevill, p. 135.

36. Gronow, quoted in Epton, *op. cit.*, p. 114.
37. *Annual Register*, 1840.
38. *Annual Register*, 1838, pp. 294–6.
39. Consuelo Vanderbilt Balsan, *The Glitter and the Gold*, p. 40.
40. *ibid.*, p. 57.
41. Harold Nicolson, *Diaries*, Vol. I, p. 150.
42. Augustus Hare, *In My Solitary Life*, p. 149.
43. *ibid.*, p. 162.
44. *Complete Peerage.*
45. Augustus Hare, *op. cit.*, p. 81.
46. *Daily Telegraph*, 10th July, 1974.

7. What Happened to the Percys?

Duke of Northumberland

Hugh Algernon Percy is the uncrowned King of Northumberland. He lives in an impregnable, grey, austere medieval fortress, Alnwick Castle, which was built in 1100 and has been the home of his ancestors since 1309; his estate covers 98,000 acres with 3500 separate tenancies and is one of the best run in the country; he is Lord Steward of Her Majesty's Household, a post which still carries some duties (he announces the guests at State banquets); and he is himself a walking definition of ducal affinity – his brother-in-law is the Duke of Sutherland, his nephew is Duke of Hamilton, his father-in-law was the late Duke of Buccleuch, his grandfather was Duke of Richmond, and his great-grandfather Duke of Argyll. More than all this, he is the head of the Percys, a family which can trace its ancestry to the year 886, the Percys who gave us Hotspur, immortalised by Shakespeare, and Blessed Thomas Percy, beheaded by Elizabeth I.

Who were the Percys? The were a prominent Norman family, descended from Mainfred, a Danish chief who settled in Normandy in 886, before the time of Rollo. Their chief seat was at a place called Perci, and according to the custom they took their name from their property. The first member of the family to come to England was William de Percy (1030 1096), an intimate friend of William the Conqueror; he came in 1066 or 1067, and was known as William "*als gernons*" or "William with the Whiskers". The name Algernon has been persistently in the family ever since. This William de Percy "*als gernons*" established himself in the north of England immediately, and by the time Domesday Book was compiled, he was listed as being lord of over 100 manors. His descendants bore the title Baron Percy.

It is an illustrious pedigree, second to none. Only one thing is wrong : the Duke is not really a Percy at all. His name should be Smithson.

The Percy family came to an end in the twelfth century, when there was no male issue of the 3rd Baron Percy. The heiress was Agnes, the last representative of the family. But the *name* of Percy was preserved. Agnes married Josceline de Louvain (himself a man of some note, the son of the Duke of Brabant and a descendant of Charlemagne), making it a condition of the marriage that he should adopt the name of Percy. With all the property he was to obtain from her, it was an easy concession to make. His descendants founded the line of Earls of Northumberland which people the history plays of Shakespeare.

There was the 1st Earl (1342–1408), a friend of Richard II who turned traitor and was largely responsible for placing Henry IV (Bolingbroke) on the throne. There was his son, the tempestuous sabre-rattling Sir Henry Percy, nicknamed "Hotspur" by his enemies the Scots, who marvelled that he loved battles so much he could not keep out of them; Hotspur led the English forces at the Battle of Otterburn. There was the 4th Earl (1446–1489), who along with the 1st Duke of Norfolk was a close supporter of Richard III, though he did not fight at Bosworth; his son and successor was "Henry the Magnificent", who lived like a king, and his grandson was "Henry the Unthrifty" who all his life was in love with Anne Boleyn. He naturally made way for Henry VIII, but he might well have married her had not the King taken a liking to her. Anne's death undoubtedly shortened the Earl's own life; he was present at her trial, and was so overcome that he grew pale and had to leave. He died on the day of her execution.

His successor was his nephew, the 7th Earl of Northumberland, known as "Blessed Thomas Percy". An ardent Catholic, he led a rebellion against Elizabeth I in 1569, in company with the Earl of Westmorland. His purpose was to restore the Catholic religion in England, and to place Mary Queen of Scots on the English throne. He was captured and beheaded in the market-place at York in 1572, the same year in which the unfortunate 4th Duke of Norfolk lost his head for similar offences.

The next in line was Blessed Thomas's brother, who committed suicide in the Tower of London in 1585, and was succeeded by the 9th Earl, who spent sixteen years of his life imprisoned there. One of Guy Fawkes's accomplices in the Gunpowder Plot of 1605 was Thomas Percy, a cousin of the Earl of Northumberland. The Earl was suspected of being a party to the conspiracy, and of wanting to place himself at the head of the Papists in England. The charges were not proven, but his imprisonment was by way of keeping him out of mischief. He was a learned man, consorting with mathematicians and scientists in his cell, and writing some sensible *Advice to His Son* which was eventually published in 1930. The sundial on Martin Tower was placed there for Nothumberland's benefit.

Algernon Percy, 10th Earl of Northumberland (1602–1668), a moderate Parliamentarian, was entrusted with the care of Charles I's children in 1645, and played a prominent part in the Restoration of the monarchy. He married twice; first to a daughter of the Cecil family, in spite of his father's deep disapproval, who said that "the blood of Percy would not mix with the blood of Cecil if you poured it on a dish".[1] That may well have been, but the trouble was that there was very little of the Percy blood left, and something had to be done. The marriage produced five daughters, and the wife died. His second wife was a daughter of the Howards; through this marriage he and his descendants gained possession of Northampton House (built by Henry Howard, Earl of Northampton), subsequently known as Northumberland House, and occupying a prize position where Northumberland Avenue now runs, from the river to Trafalgar Square. This second marriage produced one son, the 11th Earl, who in turn had a son who died in infancy. With that child, the Percys came to an end, for the second time in their long history. All that was left was one daughter, the Lady Elizabeth Percy, who became the loneliest and richest heiress in the country when her father died in 1670, at the age of twenty-five. A mere infant of four years she carried a heavy burden; she was the owner of vast estates; the Earldom of Northumberland and the Barony of Percy were now extinct, and the ancient family of Percy would die with her. She was the most eligible heiress in England, and as a result the poor girl was married three times before she was sixteen.

To understand how the modern Duke of Northumberland can tell himself a Percy when the Percy line came to an end in 1670, one must examine the complicated series of accidents and designs which involved the descendants of Lady Elizabeth Percy. Elizabeth, nick-named "Carrots" because of her red hair, was pestered by suitors. Charles II wanted her as a wife for one of his bastard sons, but this time he was unlucky. At the age of twelve, she was made to marry the Earl of Ogle, who died six months later. Her second husband was Thomas Thynne of Longleat, who was murdered by hired assassins in Pall Mall at the behest of another jealous suitor, Count Köningsmark. Twice a widow at the age of sixteen, she finally married in 1682 that preposterous "Proud" Duke of Somerset (see Chapter 1). It is not even possible to say that she lived happily ever after, since life as the Duchess of Somerset, the consort of a mad overbearing tyrant, cannot have been pleasant. She died in 1722, and all her Percy estates became vested in the dukedom of Somerset. Immediately, their son, Algernon Seymour, was created Baron Percy to preserve his mother's name.

Algernon married and produced a son and daughter. The son was Lord Beauchamp, heir to the dukedom of Somerset and eventual heir to the Percy property; Alnwick Castle, would, in the normal course, pass down with the dukedom of Somerset. The daughter was Elizabeth Seymour, who in 1740 made a marriage of significance to our story.

Elizabeth Seymour's husband was a Yorkshire squire, Sir Hugh Smithson, Bart. She was thereupon known as Lady Betty Smithson, and for the next four years there was no reason to suppose that Sir Hugh and Lady Betty would change their status in life. He was heir to no title. Then, in 1744, Lady Betty's brother Lord Beauchamp suddenly died, an event which threw all the related families into disarray. It meant the eventual end of that line of Seymours, and it made Lady Betty sole heiress to some of the Seymour estates, and to all the Percy estates of her grandmother. It also made Sir Hugh Smithson a very important man indeed.

The fate of the Seymours, the Percys and the Smithsons was settled in a kaleidoscope of events between 1748 and 1750. First, the Proud Duke of Somerset died, and was succeeded as 7th Duke by his son Algernon, Betty's father. In 1749, the 7th Duke of Somerset was made 1st Earl of Northumberland of a new creation. And as he had no male heirs, a most unusual stipulation was included in the patent of creation, according to which the title and Percy estates (including Alnwick Castle) should pass at his death to his son-in-law Smithson, and subsequently to Smithson's heirs by the body of Lady Betty. In 1750 the 7th Duke of Somerset died. The dukedom passed to a very distant kinsman (ancestor of the present Duke of Somerset), and the new earldom of Northumberland passed to Sir Hugh Smithson, who promptly assumed the name and arms of Percy by Act of Parliament.

Almost a century had passed since the last Earl of Northumberland had died, well beyond the memory of those alive in 1750. Smithson had married, not a Percy, but a Seymour, great-granddaughter of the last Percy. That he should now become a Percy was altogether an amazing piece of invention.

The Smithsons were themselves a modest but ancient Yorkshire family. In Domesday Book there is listed a certain Malgrun de Smethton, from whom there is a clear descent to Sir Hugh. But this was little compared to the majesty of Alnwick Castle and the riches which came from ownership of several thousand acres. Unfortunately the signs are that Smithson's sudden elevation to the highest ranks went straight to his head.

His style of living became ostentatious, his manner overbearing. Honours and favours were heaped upon him, but they served only to fuel his vanity. Selwyn described him at dinner as "nothing but fur and diamonds", and Dr Johnson exclaimed that he "is only fit to succeed himself".[2] He paraded his status and flashed his money, both in gambling for unnecessarily high odds, and, fortunately, in renovating and improving all three of his great palaces. His wife made a tactless point of being attended by more footmen than the Queen, and travelling with a greater retinue of coaches.[3] She had "such a pyramid of baubles upon her head that she was exactly like the Princess of Babylon". The newspapers called her "Duchess of Charing Cross".[4] Walpole regarded him as mediocre, and wrote bitterly of his self-aggrandisement; Walpole was childishly jealous of Smithson's brilliant rise in rank and position, and allowed his spite to colour his judgement. He put about the story that Smithson's grandfather had been a coachman. Still, the measure of Smithson's character shows through Walpole's rancour. "The old nobility beheld his pride with envy and anger", he writes, "and thence were the less disposed to overlook the littleness of his temper, or the slender portion he possessed of abilities; for his expense was a mere sacrifice to vanity, as appeared by his sordid and illiberal behaviour at play. Nor were his talents more solid than his generosity. With mechanic application to every branch of knowledge, he possessed none beyond the surface; and having an unbounded propensity to discussion, he disgusted his hearers without informing them . . . Lord Northumberland's foibles ought to have passed almost for virtues in an age so destitute of intrinsic merit."[5]

Walpole's judgement was supported by the London crowd, which has always been a keen barometer of worth in a man. Londoners are not fooled by show or pretension; they are quick to deflate a man whose head has swollen. Northumberland was extremely unpopular with the crowd. He was once forced from his carriage and robbed of his watch and purse. He was suspected of being unscrupulous as well; his candidate was opposing Wilkes at the election in Brentford, Middlesex, when a riot took place at one election meeting, and two men were killed in the crush. Northumberland was accused of having hired the mob, and was almost prosecuted for murder. The crowds forced him and his wife to drink Wilkes's health in public.

To be Earl of Northumberland was not enough for his vanity, although it had satisfied generations of the real Percys. He was proposed as Lord Chamberlain, but the Marquess of Hertford was appointed instead. Northumberland demanded some sort of advancement by way of compensation, and when a marquessate was suggested, he insisted that he should have a dukedom. The ·King reluctantly agreed.

Another dukedom was to be created at the same time, and offered to the Earl of Cardigan, who had married Lady Mary Montagu. Both creations were subject to limitations; first, that both men should resign all their offices; second, that their heirs should be limited to those begotten on their present wives, excluding all other offspring. Cardigan refused these conditions, saying that he thought titles were honours and rewards, not punishments.[6] But Northumberland acquiesced, and obtained his precedence. He wanted the title Duke of Brabant, which had belonged to the ancestors of the earlier Earls of Northumberland through Josceline de Louvain, but this would not be appropriate, as it was not an English title. It is doubtful whether it would be in the King's power to grant it, without inventing it out of the blue. So he settled for Northumberland, and Hugh Percy (*né* Smithson) became 1st Duke of Northumberland and Earl Percy in 1766, and Viscount Lovaine of Alnwick in 1784. He is the direct ancestor of the present Duke.

The only inconvenience which might upset matters would be the sudden appearance of a genuine Percy heir. They were not wanting. One claimant, called James Percy, had pressed his rights persistently for twenty years, immediately after the death of the last Earl of Northumberland in 1670. He was a trunkmaker, and he wanted to be an Earl. He petitioned the House of Lords, claiming descent from one Percy after another, all of whom were proven to have died childless, or unmarried. There had been a story that during Queen Elizabeth's reign, when it was dangerous to be a Percy, some of the Percy children had been sent to Petworth in hampers. It was a romantic idea, but groundless in fact. James Percy claimed that his father had been one of the children hidden in the hamper. The passage of 100 years since the event, which would make his father fairly ancient, did not deter him. The Lords found against him, and sentenced him to be brought before the courts at Westminster Hall, wearing around his neck a placard, on which should be written: "The False and Impudent Pretender to the Earldom of Northumberland."

James Percy was no threat, as he had long since been dead. Other claimants were sprinkled about, though they were less vociferous, and did nothing to press their view. Dr Johnson knew a Dr Percy, who was said to "know" that he was the heir male of the Percys, and to have it proven by genealogists.[7]

The Duchess, who was described by Lady Harriet Spencer as "very fat and has a great beard almost like a man",[8] had been told that she would not live beyond her sixtieth birthday. So firmly did she believe the prediction, that she spent the last few days before that birthday taking leave of friends and staff, and making necessary arrangements. On the day, she was confined to bed, and was clearly ill. At six o'clock in the evening, she asked what time it was. "I have then still two hours to live," she said, "for I was born at eight o'clock." She died two hours later, having lived sixty years to the minute.[9]

The Duke survived her by ten years. Later dukes have not made any solid mark in history, though they have been very important in Northumberland. Their excursions into political life have been, on the whole, unsuccessful. They lack the patience and equilibrium necessary for a political career, and the desire to court popularity does not come easily to them. They are pious. The 6th Duke (1810–1899) read prayers every evening at ten o'clock in the family chapel. "It is the only time I have seen evening prayers in any country house for the last fifteen years", wrote Augustus Hare.[10] The 8th Duke (1880–1930) wrote some highly competent short stories, published posthumously, which have a religious theme. The first of them, *The Shadow on the Moor*, is a very disturbing ghost story, told with a tension in the narrative which many more famous writers would envy. Most of the dukes have shown a love of learning. The 4th Duke (1792–1865) went with Herschel to the Cape, collected Egyptian antiquities at Alnwick,* paid for the publication of the monumental *Arabic Lexicon*, and was F.R.S., F.S.A., F.G.S., and F.A.S. In our own day Lord Eustace Percy (1887–1958), son of the 7th Duke, in 1909 came first in the Foreign Office competition, the most rigorous examination in the country. He had a brilliant brain, smothered by the anonymity of Whitehall. He wrote an excellent life of John Knox. Lord Richard Percy, the present Duke's brother, is a lecturer in zoology at the University of Newcastle-upon-Tyne.

The Northumberlands have been noted for their generosity. The 2nd Duke (1742–1817) was particularly generous towards the actor Kemble. Covent Garden Theatre was burned to the ground in 1808, representing financial ruin for Kemble, who had recently invested

* Now at Durham University.

every penny he had in that theatre. The Duke gave him £10,000, which Kemble refused to accept as a gift, but considered a loan. Two months later the foundation stone of the new theatre was laid, and the Duke sent to Kemble the bond which Kemble had written promising to repay the £10,000. With it was a letter: "It being a day of rejoicing, he concluded there would be a bonfire, and he therefore requested that the enclosed obligation might be thrown in, to heighten the flames."[11] He was also friendly with Casanova, who visited him at Alnwick and apparently passed on to the Duke some of his conquests.

This Duke entertained twice a week at Alnwick, inviting tradesmen as well as aristocrats. When inflation reduced the value of money, he reduced his rents by twenty-five per cent. He was a compassionate and just man, who won the respect of the enemy when he fought at Boston and Concord in the American War of Independence; he had a secret sympathy with the American colonists, which matured as he examined their reasons. His life was scarred by an unfortunate marriage to Lady Anne Stuart, daughter of the Earl of Bute, who was little short of a nymphomaniac. She bestowed her favours on all and sundry, except that is for her husband, who divorced her in 1779, after fifteen years of fruitless marriage, and an unsavoury hearing before the House of Lords. The maid, Sarah Reekes, testified before their lordships that a young Cambridge gentleman, William Bird, Esq., was a frequent visitor to her mistress, and that she often found them "undressed together", and "the bed much tumbled".[12] Percy married again, this time to the daughter of a Customs officer who was later ennobled, Frances Burrell, by whom he had several children, including his successor, the 3rd Duke of Northumberland (1785–1847).

The 3rd Duke was the only one of the Northumberland line to make any sort of impact in public life, and that was not always for the best. He was enlightened, it was true; in 1807 he introduced a bill for the abolition of slavery in the colonies, which was counted out in the House and led to naught. He advised against the application of class distinction in the administration of criminal law, and always countered arguments of which he disapproved by the cool assessment of factual evidence. As the facts changed, so his opinion would change in accordance; he lacked the uncompromising nature of the true politician, being more of a political philosopher himself. He was, if a label were needed, a very moderate Tory, but he voted with the Whigs in the House of Commons, and with the Tories in the House of Lords. But how often can the most laudable of causes be jeopardised by unattractive advocates. The Duke of Northumberland was not an ally one would welcome. His philosophy was in the end quite shallow, the result of a half-educated man, and he possessed the weaknesses of his family – ostentation and an artless conversation. Lady Holland thought him a "weak, silly man . . . a poor creature, vain, ostentatious and null".[13] When he was appointed Ambassador Extraordinary at the coronation of Charles X in Paris, he took with him twenty carriages, and added £8000 of diamonds to the family necklace. His appointment as Lord Lieutenant of Ireland was extremely unpopular. Greville wrote of him : "He is a very good sort of man, with a very narrow understanding, an eternal talker, and a prodigious bore . . . he has no political opinions . . . an absolute nullity, a bore beyond all bores, and, in spite of his desire to spend money and be affable, very unpopular. The Duchess complains of it and can't imagine why, for they do all they can to be liked, but in vain." Greville concludes with a gesture of dismissal which makes one feel for the poor Duke in his medieval castle : "no one cares for such a man of straw".[14]

Of him it is recorded that he was pressed by his ambitious wife to petition for the Garter immediately upon his succession to the dukedom in 1817. Lord Granville demurred, politely but firmly. The Duke said, "Then your Lordship will agree that I am the first Percy who was ever refused the Garter," to which Granville replied, "And moreover the first Smithson that ever presumed to think of it."[15] (He got his Garter, as had his two predecessors. In point of fact, every Duke of Northumberland with the exception of the 5th has been K.G.)

His duchess, Charlotte Florentia, was governess to Princess Victoria between 1835 and 1837, until she resigned owing to differences with the Princess's mother, Duchess of Kent, and her Svengali, Conroy. The Duchess of Northumberland took her responsibilities seriously, actually drawing up a programme of study for Victoria. An educated princess was not what Conroy wanted, so the Duchess had to leave.[16]

The Northumberlands find a place in history for their involvement with a British heroine Grace Darling (1815–1842). Grace and her father lived in the Longstone lighthouse off Farne Islands. On 7th September 1838 a ship bound from Hull to Dundee was wrecked off the coast, and Grace and her father rowed out to rescue the survivors, in the full knowledge that their own lives were thereby at risk. In the public acclaim which followed, the Duke of Northumberland assumed the role of guardian to young Grace, in a ponderous but well-meaning way. The family have been associated with the Royal

National Lifeboat Institution ever since (the present Duke being Treasurer).

The 4th Duke, one of the kindest of men, is still known in the county as "Algernon the Benevolent", though he died as long ago as 1865, his tenants giving him a sumptuous funeral.

Thereafter, we lose sight of subsequent dukes, except in the pages of *Hansard*. They were always, of course, closely involved in local Northumberland affairs, and at Westminster they have held various political offices. But they have been austere; they do not appear to have come out in society very much. One of the 5th Duke's sons has the distinction of being the only member of a ducal family to have won the Victoria Cross.

When we come to the 8th Duke, Alan Ian Percy (1880–1930), we approach modern times, although he, apparently, did not. All contemporary accounts refer to him as an anachronism, entrenched in a feudal paternalism which expected deference due to a mini-monarch. *The Times* called him "a strong Tory, militant and uncompromising",[17] hinting as far as it dare at a certain narrow-mindedness. On 1st March 1921 the Duke addressed a meeting at the House of Commons. "There is overwhelming evidence," he said, "that an international conspiracy exists which aims at the destruction of all existing institutions of Government and society, of all religion, of all moral laws, and all property throughout the United Kingdom, India, our Colonies, France and America." The conspiracy had decided to attack us through India and Ireland, and the I.R.A. was a Bolshevist organisation directed from Moscow. "One purpose in starting the rebellion first in Ireland is to compel us to maintain so large a garrison in that country that the forces of Great Britain may be insufficient to deal with the Communist rising when it takes place."[18] The Duke of Northumberland made himself the spokesman of a intransigent, panicky pessimism which, in the end, did him a disservice, for it made his views appear to be grounded in emotion, whereas he had a crystal intelligence.

He also had considerable spirit. He once walked from Montreal to Ottawa in sub-zero temperatures, taking a day and a night in the journey.

His duchess was Helen Gordon-Lennox, daughter of the Duke of Richmond, and a very distinguished lady. At the coronation in 1953 she looked more regal and secure than any member of the Royal Family, and in a way she was – her husband a duke, her brother a duke, and eventually both her sons dukes and both her daughters duchesses : it is an impressive record.

The next duke (1912–1940) was killed in action during World War II, leading a platoon of the Grenadier Guards at Tournai. He was succeeded by his brother, the 10th and present Duke of Northumberland, K.G., T.D., F.R.S., born in 1914. The Duke is a taciturn man who talks to his boots and has the rare gift of being quite relaxed in any situation. He gives an impression of nonchalance which is perhaps deceptive. He is urbane, elegant and witty. He is something of a revolutionary in the Northumberland line for having sent his daughters to a council school.

Three-quarters of Alnwick Castle is now a Teachers' Training College, and the Duke's family uses the remainder, contriving somehow to make a forbidding edifice into a comfortable home. Their quarters look out to the Auditor's Tower, where the 6th Earl of Northumberland locked up his auditor until he would balance the books properly. In the library there are half a dozen drawings by Molly Bishop of the Duke's three beautiful daughters (one of whom married Count Pierre de Cabarrus in 1974). There are three sons. The heir, Lord Percy, was born in 1953 with the Queen as his godmother, only a month after her coronation.

The Duchess, a daughter of the late Duke of Buccleuch, is a woman of extraordinary energy. The Duke, too, is a far from idle man. He headed the Committee of Enquiry into the slaughter of horses, another committee into Foot and Mouth disease; he is President of the Royal Agricultural Society and of the British Show Jumping Association, and he is, naturally, Lord Lieutenant of Northumberland.

There was a time when the Northumberlands had a magnificent town house in London. Northumberland House, pulled down in 1874, was the last of the noblemen's palaces on the Strand. The demolition of this sumptuous palace marked the end of the Strand as it had been known, a long line of beautiful houses each with a garden down to the Thames; it was then a road from London to Westminster. When commerce flooded into the area, Northumberland House was eventually swamped by little shops. According to tradition, the Earl of Northampton (for whom the house was originally built) had been ridiculed for building at the village of Charing, so far from his town residence. With the passage of time, the house found itself in the centre of the hubbub of modern London, and had to make way for Northumberland Avenue. It was the oldest residential house in London, begun by a Howard, continued by a Percy, and completed by a Seymour, the home of the Northumberlands for two and a half centuries, but the Metropolitan Board of Works said that it must go. Compensation of £497,000 was paid to the then Duke for the compulsory purchase. The Duke removed the Percy lion which sat on the top of the house to his Middlesex property, Syon House, and he packaged many of the cornices and fireplaces which he wished to preserve. Some of them are still in their packaging.

As for Syon House, that was opened to the public in 1950 and the Duke lives there whenever he has to be in London. What of the rest of the Percy land? The Stanwick estate in Yorkshire was sold in 1920, and two years later there followed the Albury Park estate in Surrey (keeping, however, the mansion itself). The centre of the landholdings is still Alnwick.

It is ironic that the most famous member of the Northumberland family is remembered in America rather than in England. James Smithson (1765–1829) was the illegitimate son of the 1st Duke of Northumberland by Elizabeth Hungerford Keate. He was born in France (it was customary for pregnant mistresses to be sent to the continent so that they might resume a normal shape discreetly; the Duke of Devonshire did the same each time Lady Elizabeth Foster was expecting his offspring), and was known for a time as Louis Macie, then as James Lewis. He studied at Pembroke College, Oxford, where his brilliant scientific mind made him the leading chemist and mineralogist of his year. It was as mineralogist that he made his name, and a carbonite of zinc is named after him – *Smithsonite*. He travelled widely in the course of his work, and died at Genoa at the age of sixty-four.

Smithson held extremely radical views, as far to the left as his father's descendants would be to the right. He thought that monarchy was "a contemptible encumbrance". His republican sympathies account for his having left almost his entire wealth to the United States, in those days the bright hope of the left-wing reformers. He was a very rich man, with money derived from his mother, not his father, and the bequest he made was quite specific: "to the United States of America, to be found at Washington, under the name of the Smithsonian Institution, an establishment for the increase and diffusion of knowledge among men". Two years later, £104,000 was sent from London to the United States, after negotiations with a personal envoy of the President, and the Institution was established in 1846, the government of the U.S. agreeing to pay six per cent on the capital in perpetuity. The first Secretary of the Institute interpreted its functions as follows: "To assist men of science in making original researches, to publish them in a series of volumes, and to give a copy of them to every first-class library on the face of the earth." In addition, it has conducted scientific expeditions to all parts of the world. It is a source of information to private citizens, and has a museum housed in one of the most beautiful buildings in America.

While the Duke of Northumberland occupies the splendid ancestral home of the descendants of Agnes Percy, his own family is commemorated not in England, but in the name of a scientific institution in Washington, D.C.

REFERENCES

1. Fonblanque, *The House of Percy*, Vol. II, p. 370.
2. Boswell, *Life of Johnson*, p. 447.
3. Walpole, XXXIV, 23.
4. Walpole, XXXII, 211.
5. Walpole, *Memoirs of the Reign of George III*, Vol. I. p. 333.
6. *ibid.*, II, 260.
7. Boswell, *Life of Johnson*, p. 931.
8. *Lady Bessborough and Her Family Circle*, p. 19.
9. *Diaries of a Duchess*, ed. Grieg (1926) p. x.
10. Augustus Hare, *In My Solitary Life*, p. 222.
11. *Old and New London*, Vol. III, p. 321.
12. *House of Lords Journal*, 21st January 1779.
13. *Lady Holland to Her Son*, pp. 88, 94.
14. Greville, I, 240, 312, 305.
15. *Literary Gazette*, 1827, p. 154, from Earl of Bridgwater's *Family Anecdotes*.
16. Cecil Woodham-Smith, *Queen Victoria*, Vol. I pp. 97–9.
17. *The Times*, 25th August 1930.
18. *Conspiracy against the British Empire*, pamphlet, 1st March 1921.

8. The Geraldine Ape

Duke of Leinster

Sometime between 1260 and 1270 there was a disastrous fire at the castle of Woodstock, near Athy in County Kildare, Ireland. It happened so quickly that there was no time to organise a sensible evacuation of the building. In their panic, people ran in all directions to find a way out. They viewed the conflagration from safety, and when it had died down, they took stock. To their horror, they realised that in the confusion they had left behind the infant heir of the family, little John FitzThomas FitzGerald. The servants rushed back to the house, and found his room in ruins; there was no sign of him. Then someone heard a strange sound from the roof of one of the towers. Looking up, they saw a monkey, normally kept chained up as a bizarre pet, carefully holding the baby in its arms. It had taken him out of his swaddling clothes, licked and cleaned him, and wrapped him up again carefully. The baby grew up to become the 1st Earl of Kildare, and to found the illustrious family of the Kildare Geraldines (or FitzGeralds). In recognition of the extraordinary debt which the family.and all its descendants owe to that monkey, the Earl fashioned his family crest with two monkeys as supporters, and a third posing triumphant at the top. The Earls of Kildare continue in unbroken male succession to the present day, the 26th Earl of Kildare being Edward FitzGerald, Duke of Leinster, Premier Duke, Marquess and Earl of Ireland. All have acknowledged that their branch of the family would never have existed were it not for the quick thinking of the Geraldine Ape.

The ape has remained with the Geraldines in spirit throughout their history, and to him they are wont to ascribe their knack for survival. At least three more times they were on the brink of extinction. In 1537 Henry VIII tried systematically to wipe them all out by murdering the 10th Earl of Kildare and his five uncles. But he forgot the Earl's half-brother, who succeeded to the title and continued the line. When the 15th Earl died at the age of nine in 1620 and was succeeded by his seventeen-year-old cousin, this young man was the last surviving FitzGerald. "On his life alone depended the continuance of this race, once so widely spread."[1] And again in 1743, the 20th Earl of Kildare, later 1st Duke of Leinster, was the only male representative of the Kildare branch of the Geraldines.

By their title of Kildare, the family recall the county which was their home for seven centuries, and by their name of FitzGerald ("sons of Gerald") they recall their descent from Gerald of Windsor, a Norman baron who married Nesta, daughter of the King of South Wales – Rhys the Great – and whose son Maurice fitz Gerald conquered Ireland. The "Great Conquistador", as he is known, subdued the Irish and made Kildare his home, dying in 1176. Soon afterwards his son Thomas built Maynooth Castle and continued the family's service to the English king by defending it vigorously against the natives. He was Justiciar of Ireland, a position of great power held by many of his descendants. It is his grandson, John FitzThomas FitzGerald, who was rescued by the monkey.

The Geraldines eventually became Irish by adoption, rising to a pinnacle of popularity as the "good" family of Ireland,[2] by which time their conquering ancestor had long since been forgiven. They waited 500 years before reaching the status of a dukedom, and during this period their history was closely interwoven with the history of Ireland itself. John FitzThomas FitzGerald, "one of the most unruly even of the Irish barons",[3] controlled a large part of the country, and was created 1st Earl of Kildare in 1316 for having defended Ireland against Robert the Bruce. His descendants were warriors, famous for their war-cry "Crom a-boo" (or "Croom to victory", Croom being one of the castles belonging to the Earls of Kildare)[4] which became so associated with power and valour that an Act of Parliament under Henry VII was passed forbidding its use.[5] The cry of a rival family, the Butlers, was abolished at the same time. *Crom a Boo* is still the motto of the Dukes of Leinster.

There was another branch of the FitzGeralds, also descended from Maurice fitzGerald the Conqueror, and raised to the peerage as Earls of Desmond. (They too claimed to have been rescued by an ape, but bore no evidence in their crest.) When the 7th Earl of Kildare married a daughter of the Earl of Desmond, the two lines were united, and their son, 8th Earl of Kildare (1456–1513) had two FitzGerald grandfathers. He was known as the "Great Earl" of Kildare, and was the first of the family to be honoured with the Garter. The Earls of Desmond are now extinct, though there does survive another descent from the Conqueror of Ireland, represented by the present Marquess of Lansdowne, whose surname is Fitz-maurice.

In the Tudor period two members of the family made their mark in different ways. Lady Elizabeth FitzGerald (1528–1589), a daughter of the 9th Earl of Kildare, was the "Fair Geraldine" to whom Henry Howard, Earl of Surrey and son of the Duke of Nor-folk, addressed his love poems. She was twelve years old at the time of this Petrarchan romance, and at fifteen she married Sir Anthony Browne, a sixty-year-old widower. Surrey deplored this marriage in his later poems. A later marriage was to Edward Fiennes Clinton, Earl of Lincoln and ancestor of the present Duke of Newcastle.

Lady Elizabeth's brother was "Silken Thomas", the 10th Earl (1513–1537), so called because his horsemen wore silken fringes on their helmets. For having permitted the murder of the Archbishop of Dublin, the Pope excommunicated Silken Thomas, along with his associates, in terms of the most un-Christian curses. "O good Lord! send to them, and every of them, hunger and thirst", says the docu-ment (I have modernised the spelling), "and strike them and every of them, with pestilence, till they, and every of them be consumed, and their generation clean eradicated and delivered of this world, that there be no memory of them, strike them, and every of them, also with such leprosy, that from the highest part of the head to the sole of their foot, there be no whole place. Strike them also with madness, blindness, and woodenness of mind, etc."[8] Thomas's father, the 9th Earl, died of a broken heart on hearing of this curse in 1534.

Meanwhile, the English government set about trying to put the curse into practice. The Geraldine Rebellion, of which Silken Thomas was the head, had seriously threatened the English authority in Ireland. Thomas had formally declared war on England, a far more dangerous act than the killing of a trembling Archbishop. It was determined that these FitzGeralds should never more prove troublesome. Thomas was captured and imprisoned for sixteen months in the Tower (his name, scratched on the wall of Beauchamp Tower, can still be seen), while all other males of the family were rounded up. On 3rd February 1537 the 10th Earl of Kildare, aged twenty-four, and his five uncles were executed at Tyburn in the barbarous manner reserved for the most contemptible traitors. They were hanged, drawn and quartered, that is their bowels were removed before death, and their bodies chopped up. Two of the uncles were known to have had nothing whatever to do with the rebellion, but they were murdered because they were FitzGeralds. As we have seen, they missed one twelve-year-old boy, suffering from small-pox, who was rescued by the Bishop of Kildare and kept in hiding. Wrapped in a blanket, he was taken first to his sister, then to his aunt Lady Eleanor FitzGerald, and finally fled to Liège, pursued at every step by the King's agents. Henry VIII wanted desperately to get the fugitive child into his hands. The boy finally made his way to Rome, where he was protected by Pope Paul III, and lived to return to England after Henry's death. Mary Tudor annulled the attainder against his family and restored him to the earldom of Kildare. Strangely, we find that this 11th Earl had signed the letters patent for the succession of Lady Jane Grey to the throne in 1553; Mary was perhaps more expedient than forgiving.

The mighty race of little earls proceeded once more on its path towards the dukedom, continually rising in importance if not in size. Frequent references to the earls' diminutive stature put one in mind of a family of leprechauns. Maurice fitz Gerald's son, and founder of the Kildare line, was said to be "a man of small stature, but of no mean valour and integrity".[7] The 16th Earl (1603–1660) was actually known as "The Fairy Earl" because of his size. Lord Edward Fitz-Gerald (1763–1798), rebel son of the 1st Duke, was stated to be five feet and five inches tall.

They developed also in political sensibility. Their battle-cry silenced, they gradually substituted for a doctrine of victory to the strong, one that all power was a trust for the people, and that personal liberty as well as personal property was sacrosanct. It was a doctrine which evolved in England and was exported to France and to America, where it changed the destinies of both those countries. In England it founded the Whig party, and when its principles were applied to Ireland, it fomented rebellion. In England the Dukes of Bedford, Devonshire, and Rutland among others led the Whig movement, while in Ireland it was the future Duke of Leinster who fought to apply Whig policies. If the English non-landowner suffered from a discriminatory system, the Irishman was a virtual slave, with no voice in his own future, no freedom to live as he wanted, no existence outside his belonging to his landlord. The FitzGeralds "strove to make Irish parliament in Irish affairs what the English parliament was in English ones".[8] From this date, the middle of the eighteenth century, the FitzGeralds are invincibly popular in Ireland, and one of them, Lord Edward, was to be a national martyr.

The 20th Earl of Kildare came to the title in 1744, once more the solitary male representative of the Geraldines of Kildare. He remedied that by marrying a lady from a family noted for its fertility, and who gave him seventeen children (nine sons and eight daughters). The lady was Emily Lennox, daughter of those romantic lovers, the 2nd Duke and Duchess of Richmond, who fell wildly in love long after they married. The Duchess of Richmond had been pregnant twenty-seven times in twenty-nine years of marriage. At first, the Duke would not consent to his lovely daughter marrying Kildare, in spite of his wealth, because there was said to be scrofula (known as "king's evil") in the family.[9] But Richmond relented a few months later, and the marriage took place in February 1747, to celebrate which Kildare was given an English viscountcy. He was already an M.P., a Privy Councillor, a Lieutenant-General, and the Governor of County Kildare, as well as the most popular peer in Ireland. His support for the popular party did nothing to diminish his own ambition for peerage titles. The viscountcy did not satisfy him; he wanted to be a duke. "Did he mention the Irish dukedom to you?" wrote Richmond to the Duke of Newcastle, one week before the wedding. "I know it is what he has set his heart upon."[10]

He waited another twenty years. In 1761 he was created Earl of Offaly (he already had the barony of that name) and Marquess of Kildare, with the promise that whenever the King saw fit to create a new duke in the peerage of England, he would receive a dukedom in the peerage of Ireland. The promise was kept in 1766, four weeks after Hugh Smithson (Percy) became 1st Duke of Northumberland; Kildare chose the title of Leinster.

The new Duke's fifth son, Edward, was just three years old. He was to grow up in an atmosphere of quasi-revolution, his father and his father's friends espousing the new concept of the sovereignty of Parliament above the Crown, and equality under the law, and his cousin, the 3rd Duke of Richmond, hovering on the brink of socialism. Edward was the idol of his family, the most intelligent, the most thoughtful, and the most fervent. His enthusiasms proved fatal. When advised that he should keep cool and quiet on the subject of Irish politics for the time being, he said, "I keep my breath to cool my porridge."[11]

He early joined the Sussex militia and in 1781 was savagely wounded in the thigh, and left to die on the field. His survival was assured only by a negro called Tony, who took him to his hut and nursed him. From that day to the end of his life, FitzGerald kept Tony as his devoted servant. He travelled widely on the North American continent and was made an honorary member of the Bear tribe. In 1791, in the wake of the French Revolution (of which the Whigs approved), a "Society of United Irishmen" was established, with the avowed aim of abolishing religious discrimination in Ireland, expelling the English influence, and eventually declaring a Republic. Lord Edward did not join until 1796, but in 1792 he was in Paris, staying at the same hotel as Paine and eating meals with him; he joined in a famous toast for the abolition of all hereditary titles.[12]

By 1797 the United Irishmen numbered 280,000 conscripts, armed and eager to invade England. Edward FitzGerald was now one of the military leaders and a rabid reformist. He planned to invade at the side of French forces, and there was even a project to begin the rising by murdering eighty leading noblemen (though it is not certain that FitzGerald was privy to this intention). The government could not afford to tolerate this incipient insurrection for long. One Thomas Reynolds informed that a meeting of the conspirators would be held on a certain day, as a result of which many were arrested. Lord Edward, warned in advance, escaped into hiding, with an arrest warrant on his head. He remained in Dublin throughout his supposed exile, sometimes disguised as a woman, and actively planned a rising for 23rd May 1798. When, however, a reward was offered for his capture, Lord Edward was in real danger. The story of his end is the stuff of which martyrs are made.

The reward naturally induced Lord Edward's betrayal, as it was intended to do. An informer disclosed that he was hiding with one Murphy, a feather dealer, and on 19th May Swan and Ryan went there to arrest him. He had just had dinner, and was lying on his bed upstairs. Swan and Ryan burst into the room. There followed a scuffle, and accounts differ as to the details of what happened next. His friends claim that Ryan shot at him through the door, and wounded him, refusing to allow medical attention to the wounds for twenty-four hours. Less partial versions agree that FitzGerald fired the first shot, which killed Ryan, and that FitzGerald was subsequently shot in the right arm after a desperate struggle. He was given medical attention, and pronounced free from danger. But the wound festered, and he died on 4th June in Newgate prison.[13] Ireland had another of her beloved martyrs.

Lord Edward's loss was the most acutely felt because he was not merely a political fanatic, but a splendid man. As so often happens, his virtues endeared him even to those who detested his views. Lady Holland, admittedly a friend of the family, says, "Such was the winning character of poor Lord Edward that without patronage, wealth, no very superior abilities, he had the faculty of attaching men of all ranks to his person."[14] The modern vernacular has a less elegant shorthand for saying the same thing: he had the common touch.

His mother, the Dowager Duchess, had long since been widowed, and remarried, to an uncouth Scot called Ogilvie, whom she had engaged to tutor her younger children and fallen in love with. She had even produced a second family, of three daughters, making a total of twenty children. She shared her son Edward's passion for democratic ideals, and was a fervent admirer of Rousseau. So, too, was the 2nd Duke of Leinster (1749–1804), her second son, and thereby a great-great-grandson of Charles II through the Richmond offspring. Leinster was a voluble Whig, perpetually getting to his feet in the House of Lords to make one protest after another against the government. He supported the United Irishmen unswervingly, for which he was virtually deified in Ireland. One historian describes him as "an honest, undeviating friend of the Irish nation".[15] The same author says that Leinster was generally respected as a public man and universally beloved as a private one. Other views are not so complimentary. He does not appear to have been very intelligent, his talents were seriously limited. He was the first Knight of the Order of St Patrick (founded to parallel the Order of the Thistle in Scotland). His wife, than whom "there was never more loveable creature breathing",[16] died of grief in 1798, a few weeks after the death of her beloved brother-in-law Lord Edward. The Duke himself died of strangury. *Town and Country* had revealed, twenty years earlier, that he kept a secret mistress.[17]

His son, the 3rd Duke of Leinster (1791–1874) was again a Whig, again Lord Lieutenant of County Kildare, and again a Grand Master of Freemasons, like his father. He was Lord High Constable at the coronations of both William IV and Queen Victoria. He did not make much of a mark, and references to him are mostly inconsequential. Creevey talks of his kindness and good humour, "he would not have minded brushing my coat if I had wanted it",[18] and others agree that he was a good sort. Our prime source is the doubtful one of Harriette Wilson, who thought him charming, but a stupid fool and a bore. She introduces him to us with characteristic verve: "Now the said Duke of Leinster being a very stingy, stupid blockhead, whom nobody knows, I will describe him. His person was pretty good; straight, stout, and middle-sized, with a good, fair Irish allowance of leg . . . I never saw anything more decided in the shape of curls than those which adorned and distinguished Leinster's crop . . . I do not see how a man could be well handsomer, without a mind. His Grace was at that time in the constant habit of assenting to whatever anybody said, good or bad. He was all smiles and sweet good-humour." She allows him to be a man of honour, and he comes through the pages, in spite of her bitchiness and almost without her awareness, as a man worth knowing. She is impatient with him; "I am not going to sit down all my life to love this fool", she writes. "I must have something for the mind to feed on", and one can quite believe that Harriette was cleverer than he. She pays tribute once more to his easy-going nature, noticed by others, in her usual back-hand way: "he never had anything on earth to recommend him to my notice, save that excellent temper".[19] Leinster's behaviour when Harriette betrays him does more than anything to reveal the man's qualities as well as his weakness. It seems clear that she was never his mistress, if only because he could easily be kept an obedient suitor without ever being granted the prize for which he was suiting. It was he who introduced her to Lord Worcester, the future Duke of Beaufort, whereupon her attentions turned away from Leinster to plunge into a real love affair. Leinster was chagrined. His friend had stolen his lady-love. It was too much. He asked Harriette, with dignity and decorum, kindly to refrain from making her affair with Worcester obvious until such time as he could decently leave the country, but he wished her well.

Harriette Wilson is not always reliable. She is generally valued for the vividness of her dialogue, not the veracity of her portraits. She is, however, corroborated by another, independent source. In 1816, when the Duke was twenty-five (some four or five years after his liaison with Harriette), he paid his respects to a sixteen-year-old heiress, Frances Anne Vane-Tempest, with a view to assessing her possibilities as his duchess. What he thought of her we do not know, but the young girl confided to her diary exactly what she thought of him. He was "not ill-looking, very amiable, of the highest rank and immense fortune, in short he was an unexceptionable parti. I met him frequently in Bruton Street, and always thought him dull. He did not propose to me but his grandfather Mr Ogilvy [that same rough Scots tutor who married the 1st Duchess of Leinster] did to my guardians. Mrs Taylor [her aunt and guardian] said she had no objection to him but she thought it a mercenary marriage on his part and said I was too young to marry for a year. My mother tormented me extremely [this was her other guardian]. She said she could not object to one so unobjectionable, but she balanced against his rank and merits so many defects, stinginess, love of Ireland, etc., that had I liked the Duke I should have been puzzled."[20] Nothing came of the encounter. The Duke married a daughter of the Earl of Harrington two years later, and Frances Anne became the celebrated coal-owning Marchioness of Londonderry.

The 4th Duke of Leinster (1819–1887) had the unhappy experience of living at a time when the ideas promulgated by his reforming ancestors took root in Ireland and incited the long bloody struggle to evict the English influence altogether. Protests were loud against the absentee landlord who charged extortionate rents for very little, and spent all the proceeds on amusing himself in London. The Duke of Leinster could not be counted among such people. He lived all his life among his tenants, and did all he could to improve their welfare and meet their demands. He even offered to sell them their land under the terms of Lord Ashbourne's Act, which provided for the advance by the Land Commission of the full purchase money to a tenant who agreed with his landlord to buy his holding, but the offer was rejected.* The FitzGeralds showed the Irish how to stand up for themselves, and the Irish stood up against the FitzGeralds. In revolution there is no room for demanding fair play.

Leinster did not bother with politics. He wrote the history of his family, *Earls of Kildare*, an indispensable reference book, and had a happy marriage with one of the ubiquitous Leveson-Gowers, a daughter of the 2nd Duke of Sutherland. She died only a few months after him in 1887, when the title passed to his son, father of the 6th and 7th Dukes.

The 5th Duke of Leinster (1851–1893), who died of typhoid fever, also eschewed politics, leading a simple life with simple habits. The glamour of his existence derived from his wife Hermione, a daughter of the Earl of Faversham and, according to the Duke of Portland, one of the great beauties of the late Victorian era. Lady Londonderry has written of her "renowned beauty" and "strikingly brilliant complexion",[21] while a more recent author refers to her as "the beautiful tubercular Hermione".[22] She died in the south of France, where she had repaired for her health.

These two deaths mark the virtual end of the long and illustrious history of a remarkable family. After seven centuries of influence and distinction, the Geraldines of Kildare enter upon a sad decline with the coming of the twentieth century. The 5th Duke and Hermione had three sons, the eldest of whom naturally succeeded as 6th Duke. It is upon the youngest boy, however, that we must concetrate our attention.

Lord Edward FitzGerald, born in 1892, was only eighteen months old when his father died, thus depriving him of a restraining influence which might have made all the difference to events. With the law of *primo geniture* effectively releasing him from any of the restrictions

* The Land Purchase Act of 1885.

which accompany the responsibilities of a head of family, Lord
Edward threw himself into a carefree and joyful youth. He was
handsome, adventurous, and a lord; life was going to be fun. In 1913
he married, at Wandsworth Registry Office, an actress on the musical
comedy stage, May Etheridge, one of the singers and dancers who
are nowadays known under the generic name of "Gaiety Girls"
(although they did not all perform at the Gaiety Theatre). It was one
of the alliances between aristocracy and stage which was a part of life
in Edwardian London. In 1914 their only son was born, and by the
following year the marriage was at an end; they did not divorce until
seventeen years later, but they had ceased to live together in 1915. He
claimed later that he had never been in love with May Etheridge.

Lord Edward served with distinction in the Great War, as captain
in the Argyll and Sutherland Highlanders, and was wounded. The
war produced two events which were to shape his future. First, his
next older brother, Lord Desmond, was killed in action in France in
1916, which placed Edward next in line for the dukedom. (Desmond
died a hero's death. He threw himself on a bomb to save the lives of
his colleagues.) Secondly, his eldest brother, the Duke, was afflicted
with a tumour on the brain which rendered him a useless invalid,
incapable of managing family affairs. The Leinster fortune was in the
hands of trustees who, observing Lord Edward's style of living, did
not wish to make him a handsome regular allowance which he would
immediately waste. He, on the other hand, seeing that he would almost
certainly come into the dukedom one day, as his brother would not
marry and have children, saw no reason to cease enjoying life in his
fashion. The result was, he ran up enormous debts.

In 1919 a receiving order was made against him as a bankrupt. It
was then that he made the fateful decision to gamble away his
inheritance.

A wealthy business man called Sir Harry Mallaby-Deeley proposed
to advance Lord Edward £60,000 immediately, which would cancel
his debts, in return for the sale of his reversionary life interest in the
Leinster estates. In other words, for as long as he lived, any income
due to him from the estate would go instead to Mallaby-Deeley and
his heirs. To FitzGerald it seemed a reasonable chance to take. His
brother was still a young man, and as long as he was alive, his own
income from the estate was negligible or nil. The loan would get him
out of a scrape *now*; he could deal with the future when it happened.

Unfortunately for Edward FitzGerald, his invalid brother died in
1922, and he became 7th Duke of Leinster, entitled to an income
from the settled estates of £80,000 a year, but destined never to get a

penny. The contract he had signed with Mallaby-Deeley was legal and binding. None of the family property would belong to him as long as he lived. There was even a clause in the contract which gave Mallaby-Deeley the right to prevent the Duke from doing anything which might shorten his life and so reduce the period for which he would legally own the Duke's estate. He insured the Duke's life for £300,000. The trustees offered to buy back the inheritance for £250,000, but Mallaby-Deeley would have none of it. He asked £400,000. The most he would grant was a purely voluntary gift of £1000 a year to the Duke. The Duke of Leinster had ruined himself, and there was nothing that anyone could do about it.

He showed little sign of being chastened. Another receiving order was made against him in 1923, but still he lived as if he were a rich man. It was not entirely his fault that he was trapped in a vortex of publicity which laid bare his every indiscretion. Deprived of his own money, he tried other ways of getting it. In July 1922 he laid a bet for £3000 that he could drive from London to Aberdeen in fifteen hours. He made the journey in fourteen and a half hours, covering 557 miles, no small feat in 1922. Unfortunately, he was summonsed for failing to produce a driving licence. On 15th July he was fined £2 for speeding (at thirty-eight and a half miles per hour!) and four days later he paid £5 for speeding on Constitution Hill (at thirty-three miles per hour). It transpired that he had previous convictions dating back to 1914.

The 1923 bankruptcy hearing showed a total debt of £25,300 listed by creditors. The income from the Leinster estates was protected from the claims of creditors and left absolutely in the discretion of the trustees, who would not release it. For the Duke, therefore, it was a *personal* debt; he had no remunerative occupation and no capital, his only source still being £20 a week.

There was some furniture left to him by the terms of his father's will (the 5th Duke). He thought he would sell this. Said the Official Receiver, "Are any steps being taken to release the furniture in Ireland?" to which Mr Salaman, the Duke's harassed solicitor, had to reply, "I am told that if anyone from England attempts to release it they will be shot."

A few months later the Duke was found guilty of obtaining credit on false pretences, and had to suffer the humiliation of a stern rebuke from the judge, who told him, "We treat everyone alike in these courts."[23] He fled for a while to America. (Mallaby-Deeley later relented, and sold some of the Leinster property to pay off the creditors.)

The Duke retired to a life of comparative obscurity after these inauspicious beginnings, emerging to serve in World War II, and to marry three more times. May Etheridge died of an overdose of sleeping draught in 1935. He married, secondly, Raffaelle Kennedy. His third wife was also a musical comedy star, Denise Orme (real name Jessie Smithers), who had previously been twice married. The six children of her first marriage included the Duchess of Bedford (Lydia, the present Duke's second wife), Lady Cadogan, and Joan Aly Khan. The Duke of Bedford described her as "one of the most enchanting and fascinating characters I have ever met".

She could be as abrupt as anyone born to the style. If she found a bore amongst her guests, she would go to the chair in which he was comfortably installed, shake him by the hand, and say, "I'm sorry you're going. Do come again," pull him out of the chair and propel him backwards out of the door.[24] She died in 1960.

The Duke's last wife was Mrs Conner (*née* Felton), whom he married in 1965. She used to be the housekeeper at the block of service flatlets where the Duke lived, and she hailed from Streatham. The Duke lived in a succession of council flats or bedsitting-rooms all his life. For forty-five years he was an undischarged bankrupt, thereby forfeiting his right to sit in the House of Lords or to participate in the coronation ceremonies of 1937 and 1953. He was finally discharged from bankruptcies in 1964. For a while, he and his duchess ran a tea-shop in Rye. Leinster eventually took his seat in the Lords for the first time on 15 July 1975: he had been Duke for more than half a century.

Meanwhile, the Mallaby-Deeleys flourished, and the Leinster estate dribbled away. They sold Carton, the principal family seat in County Kildare, in 1951; the purchaser was Lord Brocket, the brewer. The heir, Lord Kildare (May Etheridge's son), had to give his permission for the sale, which he did in exchange for being allowed to live at another family property, Kilkea Castle, with enough cash to renovate it. He lived there from 1949 to 1960, and his children were born there. It then became an American hotel, specialising in "group tours", and is now a health farm. With the proceeds from the sale, Lord Kildare bought a comfortable house in Oxfordshire, which was not his to sell, but which he occupied by virtue of a smaller conditional settlement of the Leinster Trust. (It is furnished entirely with the contents of Carton, and hung with family pictures, which belonged, of course, like everything else, to the Mallaby-Deeleys.)

The 7th Duke of Leinster died in London in March, 1976, at the age of eighty-three. Even in death he was pursued by insatiable publicity.

Before he could be left in peace, and the errors of his life forgotten, his very title was challenged by a claimant living near San Francisco, California, whose name was Leonard Fitzgerald. (Murmurs had been heard from him earlier than this, but they now reached a crescendo.) Mr Fitzgerald's claim to be the rightful Duke was based upon an assertion that he was the son of the 6th Duke who was supposed to have died an invalid in Edinburgh in 1922, but who in fact emigrated and lived until 1967. According to this version of events, the 1922 death certificate referred to another brother, Frederick, whose existence had been kept quiet, and whose name was changed to 'Maurice' on the certificate, while the real Maurice had run away on a cattle boat to the New World. (Why this should happen, no one has seen fit to explain, and fanciful stories that the man in Edinburgh was an hermaphrodite do nothing to render it more plausible.) Were this true, then the genuine Duke of Leinster had been living in Wyoming, leaving the title and family problems of his younger brother. Throughout 1976, newspapers picked at the story repeatedly, while the new Duke kept silent, protecting his family as best he could from ill-informed gossip.

The final word was given in September 1976 when the Lord Chancellor instructed that a writ of summons to attend the House of Lords be issued to the 8th Duke of Leinster. The Duke took his seat on 21st October 1976. The Lord Chancellor is not known to behave frivolously in such matters, and one may well conclude that the San Francisco claimant will be lost in historical perspective.

During his father's lifetime, the 8th Duke was unable to settle part of the estate on other members of the family, but was obliged to watch it diminish to vanishing point, powerless to intervene. Now that he has inherited, the entire family estate has reverted to him, or what is left of it, and the Mallaby-Deeleys have no further interest. He has worked all his life, knowing that he was not entitled to a penny from the estate, and he continues to work now. He is Chairman of C.S.E. Aviation, at Oxford, the largest air training school in Europe. He has never borne resentment against the Mallaby-Deeley family. He recognised that his father made a bad deal, and Sir Harry a good one, and has never thought it a productive exercise to chastise anyone for a gamble which cost him the greater part of his inheritance.

REFERENCES

1. *Complete Peerage.*
2. Cecil Woodham-Smith, *The Great Hunger,* p. 42.
3. D.N.B.
4. *Complete Peerage.*
5. Duke of Leinster, *The Earl of Kildare,* p. 307.
6. *ibid.,* 309.
7. D.N.B.
8. Brian Fitzgerald, *Emily Duchess of Leinster,* p. 141.
9. Walpole, XIX, 241–2.
10. 13 February, 1747. British Museum Additional MSS, 32710, F. 201.
11. Fitzgerald, *op. cit.,* p. 204.
12. D.N.B.
13. *Journal* of Elizabeth Lady Holland, Vol. I, p. 187; D.N.B.
14. *ibid.,* p. 188.
15. Barrington's *Historic Memoirs,* quoted in Fitzgerald, *op. cit.,* p. 274.
16. *Complete Peerage.*
17. *Town and Country,* Vol. VIII, p. 569.
18. Creevey *Papers,* Vol. II, p. 191.
19. Harriette Wilson, *Memoirs,* Vol. I, pp. 211, 253, 282.
20. Edith Marchioness of Londonderry, *Frances Anne,* p. 24.
21. Edith Marchioness of Londonderry, *Retrospect,* p. 16.
22. Anita Leslie, *Edwardians in Love,* p. 263.
23. *The Times,* 23rd December 1922; 9th January, 23rd January, 16th March, 26th April, 9th, 15th, 16th and 29th May 1923.
24. Duke of Bedford, *A Silver-plated Spoon,* pp. 172–3.

9. Clash of the Clans

Duke of Argyll; Duke of Atholl; Duke of Roxburghe

Scottish dukes for the most part regard themselves as chieftains first, and as dukes only second. The flattery of a title cannot bend a man's vanity if he already carries an eminence among his own people far above that which could be bestowed by any monarch. Ian Campbell, for example (born 1937), though Duke of Argyll twice and a host of other dignities besides, is above all Mac Cailein Mhor ("Son of the great Colin"), a Celtic honour which his family has held since 1280, and by virtue of which he is chief of Clan Campbell.

The clans have a bloody history. That they have survived the slaughter at all is due to the fact that illegitimacy was no bar to membership; there were always more "Campbells" to take over. Added to which if a man lived on Campbell land he was obliged to become one of the family and adopt the Campbell name. ("Campbell" originally meant "the man with the crooked mouth".)

Clan Campbell gained ascendancy over the others by brute tenacity in the first place, reinforced by shrewd political cunning. The Campbells had quick brains, could turn every circumstance to their own advantage, probe every situation, and not hesitate at all to change skins, chameleon-like, when it suited them. By the fifteenth century they had immense authority in Scotland, and in the sixteenth were closely involved with Mary Queen of Scots. It was the time of their deepest ruthlessness. "The Scottish nobles from the fourteenth to the sixteenth century were probably the most turbulent, rapacious and ignorant in Europe . . . resolute champions of indefensible privileges."[1]

We have to jump a few hundred years and begin our story at the point where they came into contact with our other characters, Atholl and Roxburghe, at the beginning of the seventeenth century, when all three were ranged in the bitter quarrel over religion. Two-thirds of church plunder had fallen into the hands of Scots noblemen, which largely accounted for their rabid Protestantism; self-interest more than anything else was behind it. The events under Charles I finally led to dukedoms for them all. It started with a Prayer Book.

Foolishly unaware of the stern power of Scots dogmatism, Charles I attempted to impose upon Scotland a new Prayer Book which in tone sounded suspiciously close to the detested Popish liturgy. The first solemn reading took place in St Giles's Church in Edinburgh in July 1637, and the ceremony quickly turned into a riot. Footstools were hurled across the church amid a din of outraged religious pride. Within hours, a surge of feeling had swept through the capital that startled the King. He offered to amend certain passages, he insisted on his own hatred of Popery, he sought to placate and compromise. But the Scots would be satisfied with nothing less than the withdrawal of the new Prayer Book, and of that implacability was born the attitudes which were set towards inevitable collision.

In 1638 a solemn Covenant was drawn up, a bond by which the Scots would "adhere to and defend the aforesaid true religion, and forbear the practise of all novations in the matter of the worship of God till they be tried and allowed in free Assemblies or Parliaments". On 28th February the Covenant was read in the church of Blackfriars in Edinburgh, after which it was signed by masses of Scots, from the highest in the land to the frenzied crowd, some of whom cut a vein for their ink. The first to sign was the ancestor of another of our ducal families, the Earl of Sutherland. The signatories and supporters were henceforth known as the "Covenanters", and their opponents the "Royalists". Though they did not say so, and though they still pledged loyalty to the King (if he would mend his ways), the Covenanters were starting a revolution. In the ensuing Civil War, the Earl of Roxburghe was for the King, while his son and heir Harry joined the Covenanters (the Earl even had to take refuge in the Mayor's house in Newcastle to escape the murderous wrath of his own son). The Earl of Atholl was also Royalist. The Marquess of Hamilton was for the King, and the Earl of Montrose was first for the Covenanters, then for the King, for his loyalty to whom he suffered one of the most hideous deaths in Scottish history at the hands of Argyll and the Covenanters. As for Argyll, after some initial hesitation he became the leader of the rebellious faction. His father had warned the King that he was "a man of craft and subtlety and falsehood, and can love no man; and if he ever finds it in his power to do you a mischief he will be sure to do it".[2] Certainly his career supports his father's bad opinion of him, for he moved from one firmly held principle to another with the consistency of blancmange.

Argyll's first *prise de position* was at the General Assembly of 1638, which developed almost haphazardly into a revolutionary gathering. The King had sent a Royal Commissioner (Hamilton) to declare the Assembly dissolved, whereupon the delegates decided to take no notice, and to proceed as if nothing had happened. From that moment, of course, the Assembly was treasonable. Argyll came off his fence and declared himself by repudiating the Royal Commissioner. Since he had an army of thousands at his command, he was immediately adopted as the leader of the Covenanters.

By 1641 Argyll was made a Marquess to ensure his loyalty and in 1651 he placed the crown on Charles II's head at Scone. But he had acquiesced under Cromwell, his loyalties were, to say the least, in question, and Charles did not trust him. In 1660, at the Restoration, Argyll tried to seek conciliation with the King, but it was too late. Mindful perhaps of Argyll's remorseless, vengeful and savage treatment of his enemy Montrose, whose body had been hacked into little bits and whose withered hand had been nailed up outside the the King's window, Charles thought the only place for this barbarian was in prison. He had proved that his word was as substantial as the wind. His own explanation for his tergiversations was that he was a "distracted man in a distracted time", but such pleading was insufficient to save him. He was tried for High Treason, imprisoned in Edinburgh Castle, and executed at the Market Cross of Edinburgh in 1661. His behaviour as he went to his end was the most admirable episode of his life. He was calm, dignified, polite, totally without rancour, delivered a long lucid speech before he died, and afterwards it was found that his stomach had completely digested the partridge he had eaten not long before, a sure sign of an equable mood. His head was placed on a spike on the Tolbooth, the same spot where Montrose's head had previously been on display. It remained there for three years, the object of loathing by those who came to see it. Clarendon said he was "a person of extraordinary cunning". He was the only Scottish noble to be executed at the Restoration. With his death, Scotland heaved a sigh. As Churchill has written, "We may admire as polished flint the convictions and purposes of the Scots Government and its divines, but one must be thankful never to have been brought into contact with any of them."[3]

The 9th Earl of Argyll, restored to his father's earldom in 1663, though not to the marquessate, was in total opposition to his father most of his life. The Marquess had even had to ask for an English garrison to protect him from the ravages of his son's attacks on his lands (as Roxburghe had sought protection from *his* son). The new earl was personally in charge of Charles II in Scotland, and behaved very decently towards him (much to the annoyance of his father). He tried to effect the inconceivable by reconciling the House of Argyll with the House of Montrose; he was godfather to Montrose's son. But the age-old enmity with the House of Atholl continued.

James II resented the power wielded by Argyll in the Highlands, where he was nicknamed "King Campbell", and further loathed him for being the leader of the Protestant cause. There was no way in which the King and the Earl could be friends. James eventually secured his downfall by making an issue of his refusal to subscribe to the Test Act, which was insufficiently anti-Popish for him. He was accused, found guilty of High Treason, and sentenced to death. "I know nothing of the Scotch law, but this I know, that we should not hang a dog here, on the grounds on which my lord Argyle has been sentenced," said Halifax.[4] This was in 1681. He was imprisoned, and while awaiting execution, he escaped in the disguise of a page, with the help of his step-daughter. His last years were devoted to supporting the Monmouth rebellion, at first from exile in Holland, and later in Scotland. He was captured and beheaded in 1685, on the same spot as his father twenty-four years previously.

The next in line was created 1st Duke of Argyll in 1701, followed very shortly by the 1st Duke of Atholl and the 1st Duke of Roxburghe. The Atholls and the Roxburghes had been pursuing their own destinies while the House of Argyll had disgraced itself twice in two generations. The Marquess of Atholl, so created in 1676, together with a sonorous list of other titles which began the unrivalled collection of honours possessed by this family, was a firm Royalist. He took up arms in support of Charles II, rose to prominence after the Restoration, and was instrumental in tickling the wounds of Argyll's disgrace. It was he who had captured Argyll, plundered his lands, and captured his son Charles, who had sent round the fiery cross to raise the Clan Campbell; Atholl intended to hang him at his father's gate at Inveraray Castle, and was only prevented from this barbarous act by the intervention of the Privy Council. Contemporaries did not think highly of Atholl, who resembled the Argylls in being equivocal and unreliable. Macaulay called him "the falsest, the most fickle, the most pusillanimous of mankind". In fairness to Atholl, such qualities appear not to be unique among Scottish families; the more one reads of the chieftains and the earls, the more one is convinced that there is hardly a dependable or constant man among them. One brilliant exception was his son, the 1st Duke of Atholl (1660–1724), who at least was true to his word. "*Sa parole est inviolable*," said a contemporary. Most importantly, he was a powerful supporter of William of Orange.

The 1st Earl of Roxburghe had accompanied James I to England on his accession to the throne in 1603, and had been a Royalist in the Civil War. His son and heir Harry Ker was with the Covenanters. He, incidentally, died of a bout of heavy drinking, thus creating havoc in the Roxburghe succession, the complications of which are felt to this day. The 2nd, 3rd and 4th Earls of Roxburghe made no significant mark on the course of events, but the 5th Earl was a man of some eminence, and it was he who became 1st Duke of Roxburghe in 1707. He, too, was a powerful supporter of William of Orange.

These three men, then, had in common their commitment to William of Orange, their espousal of Whig principles, their descent from irascible tribal warriors. And they founded three ducal houses.

*　　　　*　　　　*

The 1st Duke of Argyll was closely identified with William of Orange. He joined him in The Hague and travelled with him to England. He administered the coronation oath to William and Mary. His father and grandfather had been executed for treason, and he was determined at all costs to avoid the same fate. He enjoyed himself, and saw no cause to diminish the sum of life's pleasures. Though married, he lived apart from his wife, and died "in the arms of his whore" after a riotous life. It should not be forgotten, however, that he was chief of Clan Campbell at the time of their most shameful hour. In 1692 thirty-eight members of the Clan Macdonald were murdered, some in their sleep, by Campbells who had accepted the Macdonald offer of hospitality for the night. It is the blackest of clan treacheries, and it has come to be known as the Massacre of Glencoe.

The 2nd Duke of Argyll (1678 or 1680 to 1743) possessed all the cunning of his wily ancestors, yet added some leavening of his own. He was a brilliant military man, serving under Marlborough from 1708 to 1710 with some distinction, and eventually rising to the position of Field Marshal. His military reputation at the beginning of the eighteenth century was second only to that of Marlborough himself. This, however, did not satisfy him. He considered that only the sole command of the army would be commensurate with the distinction his family deserved. Anything less was a slur. He consequently nursed a gnawing hatred for Marlborough, based on jealousy.

Argyll was in love with the military life, he envied Marlborough's exalted position, he saw him as a rival. No opportunity to do a disservice to his superior was ever missed. Marlborough was led to write: "I cannot have a worse opinion of anybody than of the Duke of Argyll."[5]

Obviously, the Duke was ruled by extremes of passion. Hottempered, proud, and impetuous, he was profoundly conscious of being the senior representative of a clan already 500 years old, and would not consider humility to be appropriate. Swift thought him ambitious and covetous, but such was only the surface. Family pride was his motive, more than personal ambition.

Argyll's own contribution to the family characteristic was an astonishing oratorical power, since when the Dukes of Argyll have more than once been among the most accomplished speakers of their time. The 2nd Duke's influence in state affairs was attributable in some measure to the power of his voice, which carried conviction as well as persuasion. His word (like the Duke of Atholl's) was sacred, altogether "free of the least share of dissimulation", said Lockhart. In this at least he departed from the traditions of his forbears.

The 3rd Duke of Argyll (1682–1761) took less after his brother the 2nd Duke than after his father the 1st Duke, who, it is remembered, died in the arms of his whore. This Argyll also had a mistress, to whom he left all his property in England, and by whom he fathered an illegitimate son. She was Mrs Ann Williams, and the boy was known as William Campbell. By his wife, the Duke had no children at all, so that his titles passed to a distant Campbell, and the bastard William had more common descendants who no doubt live in England now. The Duke was said to treat his wife badly, preferring the company of his cats, and there was even a rumour that he murdered her and buried her under the stairs. Talking of cats, Walpole says that it would be barbarous to send any to Argyll, "he will shut them up and starve them, and then bury them under the stairs with his wife".[6] There is no evidence whatever for this insinuation, and the Duchess was in fact interred in a perfectly regular manner; but for Walpole to repeat a rumour, it must have been in circulation already, and there must have been some reason to believe it. Walpole also said he had a "mysterious dingy nature", and that he lived darkly, like a wizard. The general belief in his strangeness, and in his wife's odd death, was strong enough to set tongues wagging again when he provoked a duel between Lord Coke and Henry Bellenden, both brothers-in-law, because one had been rash enough to voice the current suspicion. "I have no doubt but a man who would dispatch his wife would have no scruple at the assassination of a person that should reproach him with it," commented Walpole.[7]

It should be mentioned that the 3rd Duke assembled one of the most valuable private libraries in the country (when he died in 1761 the twenty-one-year-old Duke of Roxburghe was just beginning *his* collection, which would eclipse Argyll's, and remain celebrated among bibliophiles to the present day). He renovated and improved Inveraray Castle, and built Whitton Place at Twickenham, on the edge of Hounslow Heath,· where highway robbers were hung on gibbets. Bramston wrote a gently satirical epigram which suggested that when the Duke caught sight of a rogue on a gibbet,

> *He beheld it and wept, for it caused him to muse on*
> *Full many a Campbell, that died with his shoes on.*

The ducal coronet passed to a cousin, descended from the Earls of Argyll, who was the 4th Duke of Argyll (1693–1770). A military man, his duchess was famed for her wit and beauty, and was buried "with unusual honours" at St Anne's, Soho. Not such wit and beauty as was possessed, however, by the next duchess, wife of the 5th Duke (1723–1806), and before that the wife of the Duke of Hamilton – the legendary Elizabeth Gunning.

An account of the amazing Gunning story belongs to the Hamilton dukedom, but so riveting is her personal fascination that she can bear some repetition here. In 1750 it is true to say that there were no more famous women alive than Elizabeth and Maria Gunning, from Ireland, daughters of Mr John Gunning. They were mobbed in the streets by admirers anxious to catch a glimpse of them, or still better to touch them. They could not emerge from a carriage without causing a stampede. "These are two Irish girls," said Walpole, a note of wonder in his voice, "of no fortune, who are declared the handsomest women alive."[8] They even created a proverb. The kindest wish of good fortune you could receive in Dublin was "May the luck of the Gunnings attend you". Luck indeed. Maria became Countess of Coventry, and Elizabeth Duchess of Hamilton. She was then created Baroness Hamilton in her own right, with remainder to her heirs male, and she became Duchess again on her marriage with the Duke of Argyll. A third Duke, of Bridgwater, was also asking her to marry him, and even George III was among her admirers. When she settled for Argyll, however, society approved. "It is a match that would not disgrace Arcadia . . . her beauty has made sufficient noise, and in some people's eyes is even improved . . . exactly like antediluvian lovers, they reconcile contending clans."[9] (The Earl of Argyll, it will be remembered, had defied the Marquess of Hamilton in 1638, and become head of the anti-royalist Covenanters; the families had been hereditary enemies ever since). Again Walpole sounds breathless with astonishment: "What an extraordinary fate is attached to these two women! Who could have believed that a Gunning would unite the two great houses of Campbell and Hamilton?" Not only that, but of Elizabeth Gunning's children, four would become dukes, and one an earl. The present dukes of Hamilton and Argyll are both descended from her. To make the picture complete, she was not only beautiful, not only lucky, but so irreproachably *nice*. She had the most delightful, charming character, which gives strength to her legend; transient beauty is not enough to create the kind of reputation that the name Gunning evokes, 200 years later. Her beauty was very temporary; ill-health spoilt its bloom, making her dowdy. Her sister suffered a worse fate. She wore too much white paint on her face, and contracted a consumptive condition as a result, from which she died at the age of twenty-five. The Duke of Argyll has necessarily been smothered by the reputation of his wife. He rose to the rank of Field Marshal, collected another title in the peerage of Great Britain, and died a happy old man. His son, 6th Duke of Argyll (1768–1839), half-brother of the Duke of Hamilton, is known to us only through his affair with Harriette Wilson.

Harriette assures us that Argyll inherited all his mother's Gunning beauty. "For my part", she says, "I had never seen a countenance I had thought half so beautifully expressive."[10] Since she was something of a connoisseuse, we may take such praise as no light matter. Frederick Lamb had told her he was "the finest fellow on earth, and all the women adore him". Harriette later noticed the beautiful and voluptuous expression of Argyll's dark blue eyes. Resistance was vain. They made an assignation, on the turnpike. Harriette waited, and waited; Argyll failed to arrive. Stinging with humiliation, she wrote him a cold letter, which was intended to put an end to the friendship. She even believed the stories of his vanity, that he knew he could have any woman he wanted, that he was ravishingly beautiful, and that he would derive satisfaction from jilting a young lady. Whatever the case, Harriette seems to be unaware that she is, like all the others, obedient to his bidding. He made an excuse; she believed him; the affair got under way, at his pace and when he wanted. It was a passionate relationship, ending in Miss Wilson's being installed at the nobleman's London residence. Her comment at this time is that he was languishing in the self-neglect of bachelorhood, with some ragged shirts, a threadbare suit, "an old horse, an old groom, an old carriage, and an old château. It was to console himself for all this antiquity, I suppose, that he fixed upon so very young a mistress as myself. Thus, after having gone through all the routine of sighs, vows, and rural walks he at last saw me blooming and safe in his dismal *château* in Argyll Street."* This precedes in time the more protracted affair with the Duke of Beaufort's heir (see Chapter 5). Happiness was short-lived with Argyll. There were frequent jealous rows, occasioned by his apparently insatiable need to allow the rest of London to enjoy his beauty. In one of her very rare moments of prurient suggestiveness, Harriette relates one such row, and comments, "Our reconciliation was completed, in the usual way."[11]

But not for long. The jealousies she felt whenever his carriage was spied outside another woman's house were compounded with anger when he took to paying court to her sister, Amy. Suddenly, she noticed less how beautiful were his eyes, and more how old he was. Amy became pregnant by the Duke. Harriette threw a tantrum, and Argyll announced his engagement to Lady Paget, later Lady Anglesea, a woman with Villiers blood. And that was the end of that.

We lose track of the Duke, who retired to a quiet life at Inveraray Castle. Though he was said to have had a son by Lady Anglesea before marriage, there were no children born in wedlock, so he was succeeded in the titles by his brother (another son of Elizabeth Gunning), whose son eventually became 8th Duke of Argyll (1823–1900).

The 8th Duke is the giant of recent history in the Argyll sequence. A list of his positions and honours gives some impression of the stature of the man – Chancellor of the University of St Andrews, Rector of Glasgow, Postmaster-General, three times Lord Privy Seal, and so on – and a further list of nearly twenty books, beginning with *Letter to the Peers from a Peer's Son*, written when he was nineteen, indicates his intellectual ability. He was one of only four persons who have been allowed to retain their Knighthood of the Thistle after being appointed a Knight of the Garter, and he was created Duke of Argyll in the peerage of the United Kingdom by Queen Victoria in 1892. But none of this can reconstruct the presence of the man, which was entirely controlled by his voice. He was brilliant in speech, and ponderous in print. He was one of the great orators of the nineteenth century, but now that all those who heard him are dead, his oratory has died too. The great Ciceronian eloquence we must perforce believe on trust. There are plenty of impressions assigned to memoirs. His daughter, Lady Frances Balfour, says that her father had "a voice and intonation impossible to describe; I have heard it

* The London Palladium now stands on the site of Argyll House.

likened to a silver clarion, to memory it sounds more like the notes of a bell. The beauty of each portion was brought out, though there was never a trace of emphasis or unction."[12] The *Dictionary of National Biography* maintains that his oratory was second only to that of Gladstone and Bright. "He was the last survivor of the school which was careful of literary finish, and not afraid of emotion." He had a happy knack of exposing humbug, and revealing truth, with literary finesse and balance. When there was talk of "peace with honour" he called it "retreat with boasting". His position on the American Civil War was steadfast in support of the union. One of his speeches in the Lords is typically lucid, persuasive, and learned. "There is a curious animal in Loch Fynne," he said, "which I have sometimes dredged up from the bottom of the sea, and which performs the most extraordinary and unaccountable acts of suicide and self-destruction. It is a peculiar kind of star-fish, which, when brought up from the bottom of the water, immediately throws off all its arms; its very centre breaks up, and nothing remains of one of the most beautiful forms in nature but a thousand wriggling fragments. Such undoubtedly would have been the fate of the American union if its government had admitted what is called the right of secession. I think we ought to admit in fairness to the Americans, that there are some things worth fighting for, and that national existence is one of them."[13]

The Duke said he had a cross-bench mind. A Liberal in temperament, and natural leader of the Scottish Whigs, he nevertheless sat with the Conservatives in the House. From the Duke of Portland, we have a rare portrait of the man's appearance. He had, said Portland, a commanding presence. "He had a leonine head of hair, through which he occasionally passed his hand, emphasising his periods with repeated thumps of his stick."[14]

Argyll married three times, first a daughter of the Duke of Sutherland, by whom he had five sons and seven daughters. One of the daughters married the Duke of Northumberland, and was grandmother of the present Duke. When he died, Argyll was accorded four whole columns of obituary notice in *The Times*, a virtual essay of several thousand words. The writer paid tribute to Argyll's "telling and forcible controversial style", but regretted a certain tendency to preach. "He looked, as a matter of course, for an attitude of intellectual and moral submission on the part of his hearers and his followers, combined of that which the chief expects from his clansmen, the professor from his class, and the minister from his congregation." An old inn-keeper in Oban explained the Duke's predicament thus: "Well, ye see, the Duke is in a vara deeficult position; his pride o' birth prevents his associating with men of his ain intellect, and his pride o' intellect equally prevents his associating with men of his ain birth."[15]

His son, 9th Duke of Argyll (1845–1914) married one of Queen Victoria's daughters, Princess Louise, thereby becoming a member of the Royal Family. The Prince of Wales (Edward VII) objected to the marriage on the grounds that the heir to the House of Argyll was below rank.[16] The Duke and Duchess resided in Canada for five years (he was Governor-General), but otherwise led an uneventful life, as royals. When the Duke died there were two weeks of Court mourning; he was, after all, uncle to the reigning monarch. Should anyone have thought, or still think, that the clan system is dead in Scotland, he need only look at the list of pall-bearers at the Duke's funeral in 1914. Every one of them was a chief in the hierarchy of the Campbell clan. There was the Marquess of Breadalbane, Angus Campbell (Captain of Dunstaffnage Castle), Iain Campbell (Captain of Saddell Castle), Ronald Campbell (heir male of the House of Craignish) Archibald Campbell (Laird of Lochnell,) Colin Campbell (Laird of Jura), Iain Campbell (Laird of Kilberry), and more besides. They were burying not the Duke of Argyll, but Mac Caelein Mhor.

The 10th Duke was a nephew of the 9th. Born in 1872, he entered reluctantly into the twentieth century, grumbling and grunting the while. A crotchety old man, he despised every modern invention, abominated motor-cars, and he rode a bicycle. He refused to use the telephone, or have one in the house. He possessed in full measure the Campbell mastery of words, and any government official who dared to interfere with the adminstration of his estates was devastated with rich invective. One was threatened with being "clapped in the dungeon". He neglected Inveraray abominably, allowing trees to rot where they fell, thunderstorms to sweep untrammeled through the house, while he was busy in his study, writing or copying old letters, indulging his passion for genealogical research.* In many respects, he was a brother in spirit to the 11th Duke of Bedford, who died in 1940. The Duke of Argyll lived to 1949. Both

---

* James Lees-Milne describes him at length in *Ancestral Voices.* Short, with white hair and a white face, a shrill woman's voice, often hysterical, Lees-Milne thought he was 'very eunuchy' and Lady Victor Paget described him as an elderly hermaphrodite. Inveraray was awash with books on lepidoptera, numismatics, medieval liturgy, and other recondite subjects on all of which the Duke was an authority. He told how the male guests used to march out of the castle in file after breakfast, each with his own footman carrying an umbrella, to an outside lavatory where they sat facing each other ten in a row, and having finished marched back to the castle.

men belonged by temperament to the nineteenth century.

No sooner did the 11th Duke of Argyll (1903–1973) take possession of Inveraray Castle from his late cousin than he plunged headlong into a welter of publicity from which he never quite escaped. The cause of the immediate flurry of attention was his plan to dredge Tobermory Bay and raise the Spanish galleon which tradition held was sunk there. In 1588, after the defeat of the Spanish Armada, the "Greate Treasure Shippe of Spaine", called the *Duque di Florencia,* sailed northwards to the friendly Scottish coast, hoping for refuge. Although England and Spain were at war, the Scots were still well disposed towards Spain, which was then the richest country in the world. But Elizabeth's highly efficient secret service discovered the Spaniards' intent, and wrecked the ship on 11th September 1588, by having a spy set fire to the powder room. Spanish propaganda subsequently claimed that it was only a small hired transport, but Elizabeth's informers knew otherwise. The ship was said to contain £30 million worth of treasure.

The King of Spain had been certain of victory. He planned to divide England among his nobles, and the money he sent over with this ship was intended as wages for his invading forces. We all know that his plans were thwarted, but what meanwhile happened to the treasure? It rested on the silt at the bottom of Tobermory Bay, and has since resisted all attempts to recover it. Charles I gave up trying, and granted salvage rights to the 1st Duke of Argyll, who was thereby permitted to keep whatever booty the wreck might contain, supposing always that he would be able to lay his hands on it, with the sole condition that the royal coffers might receive one per cent of the treasure's value. The present Duke of Argyll still retains this unique right.

In 1950 the new Duke enlisted the help of the Royal Navy in a final attempt to locate the wreck. On nine occasions between 1661 and 1919 attempts had been made, and small pieces had been brought to the surface – candlesticks, doubloons, swords, compasses. By now, the wreck had sunk so deeply into the mud that it was completely invisible, and sophisticated devices were required to discover where it was. On 2nd April the experts announced that they had indeed discovered a galleon, and brought to the surface specimens of African oak, which is precisely what the ship would be made of. Sceptics kept their silence.

Having located the galleon, the Royal Navy's task was complete. It was for others to plunder the treasure. Four years later, the Duke financed another try. This time, more ship's timber was found, some scabbards, and a cannon. But no treasure. The dive had to be abandoned, as being both too dangerous and too expensive, but the Duke had established that the Tobermory Bay galleon was no legend; it was the only known galleon of the Spanish Armada, and it was still there. In all likelihood, if it did contain £30 million as Elizabeth I's spies maintained, then it contains as much now.

At all events, the search brought the Duke of Argyll to public notice. It was a romantic and exciting quest, and he as the questor was a popular figure, a folk hero. He was hardly out of the newspapers. But the publicity he received a few years later was of a far less welcome kind, and for a period of four years he eclipsed in public attention even the Duke of Bedford.

Argyll had not been brought up at Inveraray, being only a cousin of his predecessor. He had been educated in the United States, had fought in World War II, and been taken prisoner. The years from 1940 to 1945 were spent in a P.O.W. camp, an experience which broke his health. He had already married twice when he succeeded to the title. His first wife had been a daughter of Lord Beaverbrook, by whom he had a daughter, Lady Jeanne Louise Campbell, who later married the American writer Norman Mailer for a few months. His second wife, a divorcee called Louise Morris, gave him two sons, one of whom is the present Duke. In 1951 this marriage also ended in divorce, and Argyll married an old friend, Margaret Sweeney (born 1914).

The new Duchess had been a famous débutante of the 1930s, perhaps the most photographed woman in the inter-war years. She had been born Margaret Whigham, daughter of a poor Glasgow worker who made himself a very wealthy man, and left her his fortune. She was educated in the United States, and "came out" in London with the effect of a seismic shock. Among the men who sought her were the Earl of Warwick and the Aly Khan, the former of whom she was ready to marry, but withdrew not long before the ceremony. Her husband, in the end, was an American businessman called Charles Sweeney, by whom she had a daughter who is now the Duchess of Rutland.

It was as Margaret Sweeney that she married the Duke of Argyll in 1951. Whatever else may have happened, she devoted herself to the task of restoring Inveraray Castle with a passion for which the local inhabitants are still grateful. "Her Grace has come to Inveraray like a touch of spring," said one.[17] It was largely as the result of her work that the little town of Inveraray, a model of town planning, was recognised as worthy of protection as a national monument.

In August 1959 the marriage erupted into a public quarrel which bounced in and out of the courts for the next four years. The Duchess defended unsuccessfully, providing the newspapers with their best opportunity to be shocked, prurient, and snobbish all at the same time. Historians will find in the details of this case an interesting comment on the circular movement of social fashions; there had certainly not been as amazing a divorce case in high circles since the Duchess of Cleveland, mother to the dukes of Grafton had her marriage annulled in 1706.

The Duke was granted his divorce, and married for a fourth time not long afterwards. Both he and the Duchess wrote about their marriage in the Sunday newspapers, he in terms so private that she successfully brought an order compelling him to excise some sentences. The judge read to a silent court the offending passage. "How any man with any decent feelings," he said, "could seek to publish such a thing to the world for his pecuniary benefit passes comprehension." The principle that marital confidence should be protected was upheld, and occasioned much editorial comment. It contributed to the debate on the limits of privacy. As a direct result of this article, the Duke was asked politely to leave his club, White's.

In 1969 the Duke went to live in France, where he had spent much of his youth (he was bilingual), and where he felt happiest. He returned to Scotland an ill man in 1973, and died in hospital. The 11th Duke of Argyll had led a life pursued by newspapermen from the day he succeeded to the day he died. It was not always of his choosing. He preferred the quiet life at Inveraray. But his judgement sometimes failed him, and the press triumphantly relished his mistakes.

Very different from his father is Ian Campbell, 12th Duke of Argyll, who is handsome, responsible and happy. Born in 1937 and brought up in the United States, he married Iona Colquhoun of Liss in 1964, and they have two children, Torquhil and Louise. Before he succeeded in the title in 1973, Ian Campbell had tackled a dozen different jobs and had lived in many parts of the world. For four years he worked behind the Iron Curtain, in East Germany, Hungary and Romania, for Rank Xerox. He still has disparate business interests which have nothing to do with the Argyll estates, and has brought to the running of the estate the businessman's priorities of efficiency and profit. The result is that a dynamic pulse is felt at Inveraray which has been lacking for years. The Duke claims to be able to do any of the jobs which the estate requires of its employees, and has done them all at some stage in his life. He loves every acre at Inveraray, and accepts that the tasks he was born to undertake there involve hard work and responsibility. He does not feel that the treasures in the house (which include a magnificent library) are *his*, but that he is their custodian.

The Duchess is a quiet, sensible, disciplined woman, even-tempered and patient. She epitomises the Englishman's idea of a Scottish beauty.

The Duke and his heir together represent the continuation of a history which is awesome in its antiquity. Dunstaffnage Castle, of which Argyll is Hereditary Keeper, is where the early Scottish kings were crowned. The hereditary baton used by the dukes in their capacity as Keeper of the Royal Household in Scotland was stolen from Inveraray in 1952, and has never been found. The Duke has had a new one made to replace it.

On 5th November, 1975, fire broke out at Inveraray Castle, completely destroying the top floor and the roof in a conflagration which could be seen for miles. Two hundred paintings stored in the attic were all lost, including a Gainsborough, but damage to the rest of the house was caused by the millions of gallons of water which were pumped in to beat the flames. The entire house was saturated, and all the floors and ceilings had to be lifted and removed to prevent dry and wet rot. None of the furnishings and pictures normally on show to the public was damaged beyond repair, but the house was rendered uninhabitable, until the Duke of Argyll and his family were able to move into the basement rooms, formerly the old kitchens and laundries, in 1976. The roof was entirely rebuilt in one year, a formidable undertaking for such a large house, and the renovations were scheduled for completion by the end of 1977. The cost of restoration was estimated at £850,000, only 21% of it to be covered by insurance. The remainder was raised from private donations and receipts from a special Fire Exhibition held in the summer of 1976, which attracted 75,000 visitors. Cause of the fire was presumed to be electrical.

Perhaps the most impressive relic at Inveraray, more eloquent even than a ducal coronet, is a very simple sporran which belonged to Rob Roy.

*   *   *

Rob Roy takes us neatly back to the beginning of the eighteenth century, and to the beginning of another dukedom, for the man who captured Rob Roy in 1717 was that mortal enemy of the Campbells and staunch Hanoverian, the 1st Duke of Atholl (1660–1724). Poor Atholl was waging two wars, one on a national scale against the Jacobite rebellion, and one a private squabble with members of his own family. The House of Atholl was irretrievably divided over the rebellion, with Murrays on both sides. For the government there was the Duke, and his second son, Lord James Murray. For the Jacobites there were the three other sons, Lord Charles, Lord George, and the heir, Marquess of Tullibardine. These three were pledged to return the House of Stuart to the throne; they were uncompromising in their support, and if it meant schism within the family, so be it. Tullibardine actually took Blair Castle by force, with 500 men, from his own brother. He accompanied the Young Pretender into Scotland, and was intimately identified with his cause. Of the three Murrays involved in the Rising, perhaps the most significant, and the most illustrious leader, was Lord George Murray. But for the purposes of our story, the eldest son, Tullibardine, affects matters more closely.

The Marquess of Tullibardine brought disgrace upon the family (in his father's eyes, and in the eyes of the government, with which the Duke had busily ingratiated himself) by his Jacobite actions. He was in due course attainted for High Treason and imprisoned in the Tower. His father then procured an Act of Parliament to divert his titles and estates from the heir to his second son, Lord James Murray, who was ideologically safe. Tullibardine thus found himself, most irregularly, disinherited. He can hardly have been surprised. His friend and mentor, the Pretender, in 1717 re-clothed him with some suitable titles, including that of Duke of Rannoch, but of course this was only a nominal dignity, never ratified. (The present Duke of Atholl could lay claim to the dukedom of Rannoch, but it is doubtful whether any support in peerage law would be forthcoming.) When the 1st Duke of Atholl died in 1724, the Jacobites naturally recognised the imprisoned and shorn former Marquess as 2nd Duke, but the rest of the country, which is what mattered, recognised the other son, James. In the course of time, James became *de facto* Duke as well as parliamentary Duke, as Tullibardine died in prison in 1746, frustrated and unheeded.

However matters turned out, there is no doubt that the discredited Tullibardine was a much more colourful character than his insipid brother, who became Duke. Tullibardine was fiery, passionate, headstrong, a bright blazing man whose eyes shone with the convictions in his breast. The 2nd Duke of Atholl (1690–1764), though of the same blood, was quiet and dull. He was Lord Privy Seal, like his father, but little is recorded of any achievement in his long life. He married the widow of a Hammersmith merchant, by whom he had two sons, who died in infancy, and two daughters. The eldest girl,

Jean, was ordered in the family interest to marry cousin Johnny (who was in line to be 3rd Duke), but she refused, choosing instead to elope, at the age of seventeen, with the forty-five-year-old 20th Earl of Crawford. Little good did it do her, for she caught the plague on her honeymoon, and died. Her husband died two years later of an old battle-wound. The torch then passed to the only surviving daughter, Charlotte, who dutifully married cousin Johnny, the 3rd Duke of Atholl (1729–1774). The couple, who were sovereigns by inheritance of the Isle of Man, sold their sovereignty to the government in 1765 for £70,000, retaining, however, an ancient right to present the kings and queens of England with two falcons on the day of their coronation. The present Duke still has this right, but has yet to have an opportunity to exercise it.

The 3rd Duke died dramatically. He was seized with an apoplectic fit, then swallowed a teacup full of hartshorn (something like ammonia), after which he bled violently at the nose and mouth and complained of being so hot that the only cure would be to sit up to his chin in the River Tay. In fact, his reason had gone. At eight o'clock one evening he managed to slip out of the house unseen, and first leaving his hat on the bank of the river, he plunged in. His body was found eight miles downstream the next day.[18]

Excesses became more and more common with the Atholl family. The rebel Tullibardine is the archetype of a Murray who does not know where to draw the line. The 3rd Duke's brother, General Murray, was a recognised fanatic "with a deranged state of understanding".[19] His son Lord George Murray, who became Bishop of St David's, was pious in the extreme, while his namesake, the Jacobite Lord George, is said to have hidden in the Highlands reading the Bible for months on end. His grandson, the 5th Duke, was quite mad.

In the meantime, there was the 4th Duke, a forester who introduced larch into Scotland and planted millions of trees, to finance which he asked Parliament to vote him more money for the sale of the Isle of Man. They did.

His son and heir, Lord Tullibardine, was a good-looking bright young man, who began to give cause for concern as he was highly excitable one moment, and deeply reflective the next. When he reached the age of twenty, he was sent to Portugal with his regiment, and a personal physician to watch over him, Dr Alexander Menzies. No sooner had they arrived than Tullibardine began to show some alarming symptoms which could no longer be ascribed t. temperament. Something awful happened in Portugal, though exactly what it was cannot now be ascertained. The family have always thought he was struck on the head; Menzies thought it might be the heat of the sun. Whatever it was, Menzies felt obliged to write in strictest confidence to the family physician, Sir Walter Farquhar: "I think it my duty to inform you that on Friday last he discovered some appearances of mental derangement." This was on 13th April 1798. Menzies trembled at the prospect of having to tell the Duke his son was a lunatic, and asked Farquhar if he would do the job for him. Meanwhile, Menzies would endeavour to keep the matter as secret as possible, though "the attack was so violent and unexpected that in the circumstances in which he was placed in a garrison under military command, it was impossible to conceal it".[20] He would bring the Marquess back to England as soon as possible.

Back in London, Menzies again wrote to Farquhar on 22nd June, 1798, "He seems lost in thought and speaks to himself. He is subject to incoherency and false judgements and is even at times violent. One day he was allowed to walk out, but he was so desirous of making his escape that he applied to persons whom he met to rescue him. About eight days ago he fairly got over the garden wall and over the wall of another small enclosure, tho' pursued by the servant who got hold of him in the fields. He is at times so absent that he seems ill pleased at having the train of his thoughts interrupted by a question . . . one day recently he was convinced that he was then confined and punished for a mutiny he had been guilty of in Lisbon, and two days afterwards he wished to work for his bread and blamed the Duke of Atholl for allowing his son to be reduced to these circumstances. The work he wished for was to dig with a spade. When opposed in anything he eagerly wishes he will not hesitate to strike any person. . . . About ten days ago the person who attends him gave him a knife to eat his dinner, which I had seldom ventured to do. He started up from the table suddenly with the knife in his hand, and attacked the man who was obliged to defend himself with a chair."[21]

By the same date, Menzies wrote to the Duke and referred to his son's "indisposition".

The boy never recovered his senses. He became 5th Duke of Atholl in 1830, but it is doubtful whether he ever knew it. He was by that time in a padded room in St John's Wood, where there were no windows for him to break, and the tiny household of two male and one female servant kept him out of harm's way,[22] while family affairs were run by his younger brother, Lord Glenlyon. The Duke died unnoticed in 1846, and was succeeded by his nephew.

The wife of the 6th Duke was a close friend of Queen Victoria, and was chiefly remarkable for having travelled in a most unconventional way, in a boat-carriage, a kind of boat with wheels. Her son "Bardie" (a diminutive of Tullibardine) was the most notable Murray for some generations. The 8th Duke of Atholl (1871–1942), as he later became, was a military man. He fought at the Battle of Khartoum, and in the Boer War, always mentioned in despatches. He was decorated twice, with the D.S.O. and the M.V.O., and rose to the rank of brigadier-general. During World War II, when he was seventy years old, he joined the Home Guard, and took turns as sentry officer on duty in Whitehall. Between the wars, Bardie was involved in less laudable exploits. He was full of entrepreneurial ideas which seldom worked. One of them landed him in a court of law. The Duke hit upon the idea of selling cancelled sweepstake tickets at ten shillings a time without disclosing which charities the proceeds would benefit. It was called "The Duke of Atholl's Fund", and privately he referred to it as "my bit of fun".[23] The law did not find it funny; it arrested him for fraud and placed him on trial. The whole episode was simply a well-intentioned venture which misfired because the promoter lacked experience. *Truth* commented: "It is perhaps doubtful whether it is discreet of the Duke to talk about thickheadedness."[24]

Bardie's wife outshone him in fame. Katherine Ramsay, Duchess of Atholl (1874–1960), was a most remarkable woman, with so many achievements to her credit that it is difficult to know where to start. Called "The Begum of Blair" by the House of Commons, she exercised considerable influence in her day, owing to the fearless courage with which she expressed unpopular opinions, and to the prominence she achieved in public life, in spite of her sex and in spite of her title.

It may seem a paradox that the title of Duchess could prove a hindrance to one's career, but in Katherine Ramsay's case it certainly was. At a time when Duchesses were expected to glitter in comfortable vacuity, Katherine plunged into a professional career, an unheard-of vulgarity. She was nurse, musician, and eventually Member of Parliament. The only contemporary Duchess who scorned the conventions in this way, refusing to sit behind a tea-pot all her life, was the "Flying" Duchess of Bedford. The two ladies had much in common.

Katherine Ramsay was the daughter of the 10th Baronet of Banff, who had made the first ascent of Mont Blanc. After an education at Wimbledon High School for Girls, she won a scholarship to the Royal College of Music, which carried a fair amount of money with it. Katherine had no need of the money, so she gave it to an impecunious coloured student, whose career thereby flourished. His name was Coleridge Taylor.

In due time, of course, Katherine had to take her place, somewhat ruefully, in society. The tedium of weekends in the country, when she was introduced to one eldest son after another, and was required to manufacture stiff-backed small talk, almost too small to be visible, was anathema to her. She took a book of Beethoven quartets to occupy her mind while the other ladies exchanged platitudes. Or she would go for a ride on her bicycle. This was still the nineteenth century, and ladies did not ride bicycles.

Katherine Ramsay met the dashing "Bardie" in the closing months of the century, and married him in 1899. At Blair Castle, she was carried over the threshold, according to ancient family tradition, by the two oldest tenants on the estate.

Bardie cannot have known the extent to which Katherine's unconventionality would reach. Within a few years, she had devoted herself to a work of remarkable historical research, remarkable because it would normally engage the attentions of a man knee-deep in archive administration, a *Military History of the County of Perthshire from 1660 to 1902*. Her intellect could no longer be written off, and her rank could happily be ignored. From now on, the new Duchess of Atholl was taken very seriously. She was invited to sit upon various committees, her experience and erudition were valued, her hospital work at Blair during the Great War firmly appreciated. In 1918 she was created a Dame of the British Empire.

Even so, there were many in the country who were unaware of the singular qualities of the Duchess of Atholl. This was remedied in 1923 when she took the unprecedented step for a person of her rank, let alone a woman, and stood for Parliament. She was elected as Member of Parliament for West Perth by 150 votes, and made her maiden speech on her third day in the House. It was such an impressive performance that Lady Astor, Lloyd George, and Austen Chamberlain all crossed the floor of the House to congratulate her. The Duchess was launched upon a political career which would occupy her for the next quarter of a century, make her one of the first women to hold ministerial office in any government, and in some ways to make the name of Atholl notorious throughout the land.

The Duchess held manifold posts. She began as Parliamentary Secretary to the Board of Education, and was a substitute delegate to the League of Nations. Committee work followed, lectures, books. She wrote on political matters about which she felt deeply; the Duchess was no dilettante. She nursed an abiding hatred of all totalitarian régimes, of whatever colour, and threw herself into the cause of the oppressed with complete disregard as to whether such a cause was currently fashionable. One of her books, *Out of the Deep,* drew attention to the plight of Germans in Russia, who were starving as a result of eviction from their homes. *The Conscription of a People* dealt with Soviet Labour Laws and the labour camps. *Women and Politics* was more general.

The turning-point came with the eruption of the Spanish Civil War. All should have realised by now that the Duchess was a woman of uncompromising principle, but some professed to be shocked when she openly embraced the cause of the Republicans, and wrote to Prime Minister Chamberlain suggesting that the Spanish Republicans should be helped with arms to defend themselves. She thought the British Government morally weakened by the non-intervention policy, which was a tacit acquiescence in the crushing of the Spanish people. She told Chamberlain that the government ought to oppose all further aggression. His answer was to expel her from the government. A year later, after Munich, she was one of the handful of politicians who did not greet Chamberlain's capitulation with cheers. The first Conservative woman minister left the Tory party for good.

From now on, she was known as the "Red Duchess", because her support for the Spanish Republicans had identified her with the Communist cause. No one could have been more vociferous in her hatred of Communist oppression, but political reputations are made on shifting sands. She retired from public life, having devoted more energies to public work than any other duchess in our history. She held Honorary Doctorates at the universities of Oxford, Glasgow, Manchester, Durham, Columbia, Leeds, and MacGill. She was described as a "tiny, upright, hawk-like figure", and by that malicious snob Channon as "sour, sunken, and sallow". All who knew her agree that she was incapable of a mean thought, was utterly unselfish, kind and good, and was a total stranger to hypocrisy: rare qualities in political life.

Her brother-in-law, Bardie's younger brother, became the 9th Duke of Atholl (1879–1957), and he appears to have succumbed to some of her powerful influence. He spoke nine languages fluently and, like the Duchess, identified readily with oppressed people. He was so shocked by the Yalta settlement that he converted his Edinburgh house into a Polish hostel, and spent his every weekend with the exiles, caring for them, apologising to them for the perfidy of politicians. He was no mean authority on Perthshire history. The Duke never married, which meant that almost all his titles and estates went to a distant kinsman, Mr Iain Murray, whose connection with the Atholl line had to be traced back 200 years over six generations to the 3rd Duke.

In 1957 Mr Iain Murray was twenty-six years old, living comfortably with his mother in a large house in St John's Wood, London. The press saw the romantic side of his inheritance, and depicted him as assistant manager of a printing works in Uxbridge, earning £20 a week and commuting by underground train from a poky flat. They wanted him to suddenly come aglow with his fifteen titles, as spectacular lights warm over a bare Christmas tree.

The press did not mention that his family *owned* the printing works, which was subsidiary to much larger business concerns belonging to his mother. Neither did they mention that his mother was a daughter of Lord Cowdray, and that they had owned and lived at Blair Castle, the ancestral Atholl home, since 1932. Iain Murray's branch of the family had, in short, taken over long before he became 10th Duke of Atholl.

He is now chairman of Westminster Press, his mother's family firm, as well as being in charge of the Murray estate in Perthshire, covering 120,000 acres and employing over 100 people. There are twenty tenant farmers. The Duke attends the Lords regularly, speaking there on his own subject of forestry, upon which he is now expert. He is a man of friendly disposition, witty and well informed. His languid appearance belies the truth – he is in fact eternally busy and energetic. He has an old-fashioned habit, not common even in ducal circles these days, of changing for dinner, even if he dines alone. In one private corner of Blair Castle "Snape" the butler and his wife look after him, while the rest of the romantic white castle plays host to the public.

If the Duke does not marry, the title will pass to another very distant kinsman, already over seventy-five, and then to some Murrays who have been in South Africa for three generations, and are unlikely to want to leave. It seems possible, therefore, that, though Murrays will continue to live at Blair as they have done for 400 years, the Atholl title will disappear overseas.

The Duke has a curious distinction. He is the only man in the country who is permitted a private army. Queen Victoria and Prince Albert spent three weeks at Blair in 1844. So much did they enjoy the holiday that Her Majesty, perhaps mischievously, conferred upon the Duke and his heirs the unique right to summon an army, called the Atholl Highlanders. Enlistment is voluntary and unpaid. At the moment the army is about eighty strong, with twelve pipers and six drummers; they have their own uniform and parade twice a year. At

Blair Castle there is an old visitors' book which records not only the name, but the weight of each visitor.

*   *   *

While the Dukes of Argyll and Atholl have been indulging their oratory and enthusiasm, the House of Roxburghe has in the meantime progressed quietly, without fuss, producing a succession of pleasant men with a penchant for books, and one duke in particular who collected one of the best libraries ever. If they have been noticeable at all, it is because their line of descent is erratic and ridiculous, and genealogical experts have had from time to time to put their heads together to work out who should be the next duke in accordance with the instructions of the original patent, which cannot, to everyone's chagrin, be altered. It is necessary to give some attention to this descent, which has perplexed learned minds.

One has to start with the 1st Earl of Roxburghe, who died in 1650. Had his son and heir, Harry Ker, lived, the earldom and subsequent dukedom would doubtless have progressed in more or less orderly manner. But Harry Ker predeceased his father after a night of heavy drinking, leaving none but females to carry the name, which would mean the end of the Roxburghe title after only one generation. To avoid this, the Earl obtained a *novodamus* of his honours, which meant that he could resign them to the Crown, and then redirect them to heirs of his choosing. He therefore ignored the regular heir of line, and nominated precisely how the title was to pass from one relation to another, according to his own desire and whim, in perpetuity. The Roxburghe honours still pass (as they must) according to the directions laid down in 1646, though it is by no means simple to follow them.

Simplified, the revised patent provided for the title to pass to the eldest grandson of the 1st Earl, through his daughter, who had married a Drummond. There was a condition attached; the young Drummond would have to marry his first cousin Jean Ker (daughter of the dead Harry Ker), or the title would pass to another branch. Drummond dutifully obeyed. So, for the next hundred years, the holders of the Roxburghe title were the Drummond family, although they changed their name to Ker.

When the 4th Duke died in 1805, the Drummond line, descended from the 1st Earl's eldest daughter, died with him, and a grubby scramble followed to see who could legitimately grab the coronet.

There were four claimants to the dukedom – Lady Essex Ker,

daughter of the 2nd Duke, and *heir of line* to the 1st Earl of Roxburghe; Mr Walter Ker, *heir male* to the 1st Earl; John Bellenden Ker, *heir male* of the 2nd Earl (and second cousin to the Duke who had just died and who had fought for the succession to go to him, even entailing his estates upon him. Bellenden Ker was a noted botanist, wit and man of fashion); and Sir James Innes, who was descended from Margaret Ker, another daughter of the Harry Ker who caused all the confusion by dying too soon in the seventeenth century. There was another, less serious, claimant, a baker in Kingston, Jamaica, called Robert Hepburn Ker.[25]

The House of Lords discussed the problem for seven years, from 1805 to 1812, during which time the dukedom lay dormant. Thousands of pages of genealogical evidence were produced by the claimants, all carefully examined and weighed by their lordships. In the end, they had only to consult the original patent, which stated that if the heirs male of the 1st Earl's daughter (*i.e.* the Drummonds) should fail, as they did in 1805, then the honours should devolve upon the heirs male of his grand-daughter Margaret (his son Harry's daughter). By this rule, the heir was Sir James Innes, who thus became 5th Duke of Roxburghe in 1812, changed his name to Innes-Ker, and founded the branch of the family which flourishes today. He had spent £50,000 proving his right to inherit.

A word about the Innes family, which came into the picture for the first time in 1812. Sir James's father had been 28th Laird of Innes, the family having held Innes since Malcolm IV had conferred it upon their direct ancestor, Berowald Flandrensis, in 1160. But their fortunes had soured, and Sir James's father had been obliged to sell the ancient barony of Innes to his cousin in order to keep his family going. The dukedom of Roxburghe could not have come their way at a more opportune moment, with over 60,000 acres in Roxburghe-shire and a thriving household at Floors Castle, all of which came with the titles; the House of Lords had set aside the 4th Duke's entailing of the estates upon John Bellenden Ker, without which the new Duke would have been just as poorly off as before. As it happened, he thoroughly enjoyed his new status, spending his closing years in peaceful retirement at Floors, with his pretty young wife. As James Innes, he had married in 1769, and his wife had died in 1807, in the midst of the succession crisis. One week after her death, he married again, and was eighty-one years old when his son and heir was born in 1816. I know of no more impressive record than that. The old man lived on to 1823.

Guy David Innes-Ker, the 10th and present Duke of Roxburghe, is a direct descendant of this Sir James Innes, who won the case in 1812. He is, at the time of publication, only twenty-one years old, but if the succession were not assured by his offspring, or other male descendants of the 5th Duke, then the honours would have to be traced back again to the original patent, and would fall on whatever male heirs there may be of any of Harry Ker's three daughters. It would certainly require the House of Lords to unravel the mess again. The dukedom of Roxburghe was the last dignity to be created in the peerage of Scotland, one day after the dukedom of Montrose in 1707. A fresh patent, more sensibly organised, could have been issued to designate the inheritors of the dukedom, but Queen Anne foolishly allowed the same remainder as had applied to the earldom.

It is difficult to assess the personality of the Roxburghe family, as those characteristics shown by the first four dukes can have little relevance at all to the following six, to whom they are only very distantly related. The first four, up to 1805, were Drummonds, the succeeding six, from 1812, have been Innes.

The first four Dukes of Roxburghe must not go unrecorded simply because they are not ancestors of the present Duke. They were all eminent, admirable, delightful men, and deserve to be remembered. To read contemporary reports of the 1st Duke in particular, who lived from 1680 to 1741, is to wish that one had known him. In the first place, he was thoroughly well educated, speaking Latin and Greek fluently, and most modern European languages. He was "a young gentleman of great learning and virtue", said Macky, and Lockhart describes him as "the best accomplished young man of quality in Europe", which is no small compliment from a political opponent. Add to this that he was very good-looking, "brown-complexioned and handsome", according to Macky. Further, he had such charm as to bewitch even those who disagreed with him. Patten agrees: ". . . with the agreeable Looks of good Humour, that by all that are so happy to be acquainted with him, he gains their Affection and Applause". The Duke clearly had a beautiful personality. Politically, he was a Whig supporter of the Hanoverian succession, and was opposed to Walpole, who is the only man to tell a discreditable story of him. Sir Robert Walpole claimed that Roxburghe had persuaded the Duke of Montrose to resign his position as Secretary of State on some scruple of conscience, then promptly applied for it himself. (It is true that Montrose held the position from 1714 to 1715, and Roxburghe from 1716 to 1725.) All one can say is that such self-seeking is so totally out of character that it would require more than the word of a political opponent to establish it.

The Duke was a pall-bearer at the funeral of Newton in West-minster Abbey, 1727. His love of learning, his feel for books and for the knowledge they contained, were passed to his son (a friend of Fielding) and his grandson, the 3rd Duke and great book-collector.

The 3rd Duke of Roxburghe (1740–1804) was in some ways a sad man who took refuge from the injustice of life in his unique collection of books. As a young man, he had fallen in love with Christiana, the eldest daughter of the Duke of Mecklenburgh-Strelitz. It was a true match, so rare a thing in aristocratic marriages of the eighteenth and nineteenth centuries, and they would have made a supremely happy couple. They had every intention of marrying, but then her younger sister Charlotte became engaged to the English king, George III, and it was intimated to Roxburghe that it would be prudent of him to break off his courtship of Christiana. Presumably the King would have lost face if he could only catch a younger daughter when one of his Scottish noblemen could walk off with the prized eldest daughter. Whatever the case, Roxburghe obliged. Both he and Christiana never ceased to love each other, and neither of them married. The Duke smothered all his disappointments in bibliography. He became melancholy, retiring, spending hours and days at a stretch collating his rare editions. He and the King would compete even in that, and more than once Roxburghe would have the galling experi-ence of conceding to the royal preference a book he dearly wanted. But they were friendly enough, and it is said the King was very fond of him. The collection grew into the finest in the kingdom, housed at the Roxburghe residence in St James's Square, and assuming a fame which has become legendary. He had an unrivalled collection of books from Caxton's press, and a collection of ballads without parallel (these are now in the British Museum).

When the Duke died in 1804, there was no one to whom he could safely leave his collection. They passed by inheritance to his successor in the title, the 4th Duke of Roxburghe, but he was already an old man of seventy-six (a cousin of the book-collecting 3rd Duke), and had only months to live. He died in 1805, and as we have seen, the Drummonds, the Bellendens, the Kers and the Innes were thrown into turmoil by the question of the succession. Seven years later, Sir James Innes was called to Parliament as 5th Duke of Roxburghe, and one of his first actions was to sell off, by auction, the entire Roxburghe collection of rare boks. With hindsight, this appears to have been a monstrously philistine act, with which we can have little patience. We know the Innes family were on hard times, and the motive for the sale can only have been financial. The new Duke was impoverished by the cost of proving his claim. However, it was a great event, lasting forty-

five days, from 18th May to 8th July 1812. The singularly most glorious day was 24th June, when the gem of the collection, an edition of
Boccaccio dating from 1471, was sold to the Marquess of Blandford
(later Duke of Marlborough) for £2260. To mark the occasion, the
bibliographer Dibden assembled the greatest bibliophiles of the day at
dinner in St Albans Tavern, and there and then founded the
Roxburghe Club, limited to twenty-four members. It may well be that
Dibden and his friends did not want the old Duke's achievement to be
erased without trace by the new Duke's sale, in which event they
succeeded, for the Roxburghe Club is a famed monument to the zeal
of book-collectors.

The second line of Roxburghes have been quite a different breed.
From the 6th Duke (born in his father's eighty-first year) to the present
Duke, they have mostly been soldiers, austere and remote. They have
mixed in the highest circles, the 7th Duke marrying into the Churchill
family, and the 8th becoming one of the most intimate friends of
George V and Queen Mary. It was he who brought new wealth to
the family in time-honoured manner by marrying an American
multi-millionairess. Ogden Goelet was one of the richest men in New
York, and when his daughter May became the future Duchess of
Roxburghe he settled £5 million on her. The fortune was subsequently
inherited by her son, the late 9th Duke, and her grandson, who now
wears the coronet. Roxburghe is at the time of writing the youngest
of our dukes, born in 1954.

Like his father, grandfather, and great-grandfather, he served in
the army, and continued to do so after succeeding to the dukedom.
Roxburghe then learnt something of business to prepare himself
for the task of running Floors Castle, his magnificently impressive
seat at Kelso set in 53,000 acres. He has now turned it into one of the
prime attractions of the Border Country, in triumphant defiance of
its centuries of age. He has also opened a fine hotel on the estate
(somewhat like the Devonshires, who have built two, and the Richmonds, who have one at Goodwood), and is active with the local
Tourist Board and Wildlife Trust.

In September, 1976, the Duke of Roxburghe married a sister of the
present Duke of Westminster, thereby adding another strand to the
intricate web of family relationships which unite all ducal families to
each other. The Duke of Westminster, the Duke of Abercorn, and the
Duke of Roxburghe are brothers-in-law to one another. His son,
Marquess of Bowmont and Cessford, was born in 1981, while his
daughter, Lady Sophia Innes-Ker, enjoyed a moment of public
attention as a delectable bridesmaid at the wedding of Prince Andrew
to Sarah Ferguson in 1986.

REFERENCES

1. John Buchan, *Montrose*, p. 65.
2. *Complete Peerage.*
3. Winston S. Churchill, *History of the English-Speaking Peoples,* Vol. II, p. 234.
4. *Complete Peerage.*
5. D.N.B.
6. Walpole, XVII, 506.
7. *ibid.,* IX, 61.
8. *ibid.,* III, 59.
9. *ibid.,* XXI, 267.
10. Harriette Wilson, *Memoirs,* p. 13.
11. *ibid.,* pp. 32, 35.
12. Lady Frances Balfour, *Ne Oblifiscaris,* p. 14.
13. D.N.B.
14. Duke of Portland, *Men, Women and Things,* p. 190.
15. *The Times,* 25th April 1900.
16. J. Pope-Hennessey, *Queen Mary,* pp. 36, 518.
17. *Daily Mirror,* 6th June 1952.
18. *Hist. MSS. Comm.,* 11th Report, App. Part 5, p. 368.
19. Wraxall, *Hist. Memoirs,* p. 213.
20. Atholl Papers, 59 (5), 51.
21. Atholl Papers, 59 (5), 139.
22. Public Record Office, 1841 Census, H.O. 107/678, Section 10.
23. 8th Duke of Atholl to Hamish Murray, 1st August 1933.
24. *Truth,* 4th October 1933.
25. *Gentleman's Magazine,* June 1809.
26. Lockhart, Patten, Macky, all quoted in *Complete Peerage.*

10. *The Pride of the Hamiltons*

Duke of Hamilton; Duke of Abercorn

The rules governing descent in the peerage can produce some fascinating anomalies. Consider the family of Hamilton, which has spawned two separate dukedoms:

- the Duke of Abercorn represents the junior branch, lives in Ireland and has an Irish dukedom. Yet he is the *heir male* of the original Hamilton, and is therefore head of the House of Hamilton.
- the Duke of Hamilton carries the much older Scottish dukedom, and represents the *senior* branch of the family. Yet this branch forfeited the right to be head of the family because it descended through the female line. To make matters worse, he *is*, however, *heir male* of the House of Douglas and head of *that* family.
- they are *both* Duke of Châtelherault in France!

They have also produced along the way an almost unrivalled collection of odd preposterous characters. But first the genealogy needs to be unravelled, for which a brief excursion into Scottish history is necessary.

The common ancestor of both Hamilton and Abercorn was the 2nd Earl of Arran, who died in 1575. He was Governor of Scotland, and second only to the Crown in power. His grandfather had married Lady Mary Stewart, daughter of James II of Scotland, which made Arran *heir presumptive* to the throne of Scotland, a position held by the Hamiltons for the next hundred years. He was guardian to Mary Queen of Scots in her minority, and consequently much courted by the French who wished to secure his alliance against Elizabeth of England. It was for this reason that Henri II conferred upon him the dukedom of Châtelherault in Poitou in 1549; it was a bribe to buy his loyalty; later on we shall look at what happened, or should have happened, to this title.

The 2nd Earl of Arran* had five sons, of whom :

(1) died young
(2) succeeded as 3rd Earl of Arran, but was insane and locked up
(3) succeeded as 4th Earl, due to the incapacity of his brother, was made Marquess of Hamilton in 1599, and is the progenitor of the Dukes of Hamilton
(4) was made Lord Paisley in 1587, is the father of the 1st Earl of Abercorn, progenitor of the Dukes of Abercorn.

Henry VIII actually considered a marriage between his daughter, then Princess Elizabeth, with Arran's eldest surviving son and heir, because he was first in line to the Scottish throne after Mary. Nothing came of it, fortunately for England, as the boy was already well on the way towards lunacy.

Arran's second son did not wait for the death of his brother to assume control of the family. The mad Earl, who was, it seems, "crackbrained and fantastic" rather than a total lunatic, was kept out of harm's way, while his brother was created Marquess of Hamilton in 1599, and Earl of Arran. He was rigidly Protestant, separating from his more easy-going and tolerant brother Claud, Lord Paisley. His son was 2nd Marquess of Hamilton (1589–1625), also loyal to the Crown, but he died prematurely at the age of thirty-five, and it was suspected that he had been poisoned. If so, his wife might have had something to do with it; she was opposed to him politically, even raising an army to fight for the Covenanters against the King, and riding herself at the head of the troops. They had married when Hamilton was fourteen years old, and by the time he was sixteen, his son and heir had been born. This is the child who was to become 1st Duke of Hamilton (1606–1649). Like his father, he also married at fourteen, and his bride was a mere seven years old. It is worth pausing a moment to consider this child, for her mother was Susan Villiers, sister of the Duke of Buckingham and daughter of Sir George Villiers, whose offspring are to be found in so many of our noble families. Evidence of the dominant Villiers personality emerges in several of the dukes of Hamilton, particularly the 4th and the 6th. The 4th Duke reinforced the Villiers connection by fathering a natural son by Barbara Fitzroy, who was the daughter of Charles II and Barbara Villiers, Duchess of Cleveland.

As Marquess of Hamilton, the 1st Duke is already known to us as the opponent of Argyll at the time of the Covenant, for he was the

* He has nothing to do, by the way, with the journalist Earl of Arran of our own day, whose family name was Gore, and whose title was Irish.

luckless royal Commissioner whose task was to compel acceptance of the new Prayer Book in Edinburgh, and who failed dismally. In 1638 he suffered the humiliation of having declared, in the name of the King, the dissolution of the Scottish Assembly, and being wholly ignored by the Scots, who went on with their meeting as if he had not been there. The following year he led the King's army against the Covenanters, once more with disastrous results. Like his forbear Arran, he brought success to none of his undertakings, yet, also like Arran, he wielded an influence quite out of proportion to his talents. Clarendon says that he "had the greatest power over the affections of the King, of any man of that time", and that "no man had such an ascendant over him". The historian also states that Hamilton had more enemies than any man in the kingdom. In the *Dictionary of National Biography* he is reckoned "devoid of intellectual or moral strength, and he was therefore easily brought to fancy all future tasks easy and all present obstacles insuperable". With his limited understanding, he sought compromise as the solution to all problems, with the result that problems were simply shelved, while Hamilton felt pleased with himself.

The last years of his life were pathetically useless. Only weeks after he was created Duke, he found himself in prison, where he languished from 1644 to 1646. In 1648 he led the Scottish army for the relief of the King, with typical ineptitude, surrendering to Cromwell at Uttoxeter after the briefest display of resolution. Cromwell was not a ditherer like his victim. In 1649 Hamilton was indicted, tried, found guilty of treason, and beheaded in Palace Yard, Westminster, only weeks after the King to whom he had been so faithful.

A contemporary said, "There is one good quality in this man, *viz.* that he was born and that God made him : and another, *viz.* that he is dead, and we must speak nothing but good of the dead."

History has not flattered Hamilton. His pomposity, arrogance and wordiness have been noted (all qualities which were to occur again and again in his descendants), as well as his ineffectual deceits. The best portrait of him is by John Buchan, who describes him as "a vain, secret being, a diligent tramper of backstairs, and a master of incompetent intrigue, he is throughout his career a sheep in wolf's clothing . . . His life was one long pose, but the poses were many and contradictory, and the world came to regard as a knave one who was principally a fool."[1]

Hamilton's reward for his fidelity had been his elevation to the rank of Duke in 1643 (which makes this the third oldest dukedom in the Union, surpassed only by Norfolk and Somerset, and paramount in

Scotland). Having only two daughters, he arranged for a *special remainder* naming his brother William as heir to all titles and estates, assuming, one suspects, that William would beget healthy male heirs. It was to turn out differently.

William, 2nd Duke of Hamilton (1616–1651) emerges the more admirable in comparison with his brother. He had courage, intelligence, and honesty, and might have proceeded, after the Civil War, to a distinguished career. His courage, however, cut short his life. Leading the King's troops at the Battle of Worcester in 1651, he could not be restrained from fighting in the thick of carnage, his leg was shattered by a ball from a Cromwellian musket, and he died twelve days later. He was thirty-four years old, and had been Duke for two years.

In his will, made the previous year, he wrote: "Considering the extraordinary kindness my late dearest brother James, Duke of Hamilton, did express to me both in his life and at his death by preferring me even to his own children, I conceive myself in duty and gratitude bound to prefer his to mine, and therefore I do leave and nominate my dearest niece Lady Anna Hamilton, his eldest lawful daughter, as my sole executor . . . and freely give unto her all my jewels, silver, plate, hangings, pictures, beds and whatsoever goods else are mine."[2] As for the titles, they would be hers anyway, by the terms of the patent of 1643. Thus Anne became Duchess of Hamilton in her own right.

It is at this point, *anno* 1651, that the male heir of the Hamilton family ceases to be found in the senior branch. Henceforth, the head of the Hamiltons is the man who bears the title of Abercorn, descended from the Marquess of Hamilton's younger brother Claud. The implications of this situation were not lost on the Earl of Abercorn, who immediately set in motion a lawsuit claiming the right to all the Hamilton estates and titles. This was a fanciful claim, for he must have known that all previous entails had been cancelled by the 2nd Duke, as one can so easily redirect an inheritance in the Scottish peerage, and that his settlement of the estates on Anne had been legally recognised. However, Abercorn's anomalous position as male head of the family was tacitly recognised in 1661 when Duchess Anne named the Abercorn line as eventual heirs in the event of the failure of the Hamilton line. This has yet to occur, but the stipulation is still valid today.

Duchess Anne further complicated matters by marrying William Douglas, Earl of Selkirk, and petitioning the King to make him what we should now call a Life Peer, with the title of Duke of Hamilton.

Thus, she was Duchess of Hamilton twice over, once in her own right, and once by virtue of being married to the new Duke. Or, if you like, the 3rd Duke of Hamilton of the first creation (Anne) married the 1st (and last) Duke of Hamilton of the second creation. Their son, who became 4th Duke, inherited his mother's, not his father's, title.

This man, the 4th Duke of Hamilton (1658–1712) was a disaster. He has been accorded a lengthy footnote in history by the circumstances of his death, in the most notorious of all Hyde Park duels, but the fuss generated by the duel has obscured all previous mention of him. From the first, he was a bone-headed wastrel, using the Hamilton estate, even in the lifetime of his mother, as simply a bottomless source of revenue with which to amuse himself. Selfish, pleasure-seeking, indolent and arrogant, his squalid end might easily have been predicted by those who knew him. He had spent some time in prison on suspicion of Jacobite sympathies (and sent there on the advice of his own father), during which time he contrived to father a child by Barbara Fitzroy (daughter of Charles II and Barbara Villiers), to which he paid no attention whatever; the child was brought up in the household of its grandmother Villiers. Even those who have kind words to say about him do so, it is clear, under the pressure of wishing to be fair towards a man whom many thought had been murdered. There is a letter written within days of the duel in which the writer says, "I assure you he has more friends at present than ever he had while alive."[3] The taint of pride and vanity, never far below the surface in the Hamiltons, together with the absurdly hot-tempered habits of the day, was responsible for a duel which created more excitement than any other. In fairness, Hamilton's opponent, Lord Mohun, came to Hyde Park with an even more unsavoury reputation than the Duke.

Lord Mohun was an infamous profligate. Perpetually drunk, always seeking quarrels, he was no stranger to Hyde Park. He had frequently been engaged in duels, or midnight brawls, and had been twice tried for murder.[4] His connection with Hamilton was by marriage. They had both married nieces of the Earl of Macclesfield, who on his death-bed had named Mohun as his sole heir, to the exclusion of Hamilton. For eleven years the Duke fought this decision in the courts, and was eventually provoked to cast doubt upon the credibility of one of Mohun's witnesses, to which Mohun retorted that the witness had as much truth as His Grace. The following day the Duke was visited by General Maccartney, on behalf of Lord Mohun, challenging the Duke to meet his lordship in Hyde Park, the usual place for such assignations. The challenge was accepted, the appointment fixed for seven o'clock the next morning, Sunday, 15th November 1712.

Maccartney, who brought with him a similarly fierce and hot-tempered reputation, was Lord Mohun's second. The Duke was seconded by his illegitimate son, Colonel Hamilton. In short, there could hardly have been assembled four more dangerous, foolhardy men; the encounter was bound to be bloody. The Duke addressed Maccartney: "I am well assured, sir," he said, "that all this is by your contrivance, and therefore you shall have your share in the dance; my friend here, Colonel Hamilton, will entertain you." The fight then began with the fury of mad dogs, the seconds joining in, as was then sometimes the custom. No attempt was made at skill; such hatred and pride swelled their emotions that they fell upon each other with unbridled ferocity. It was less an affair of honour than of anger. Maccartney was the first to be disarmed, having wounded his opponent in the right leg. But Colonel Hamilton's attention was diverted by cries of pain from the Duke and, ignoring Maccartney, he rushed to his aid. The Duke had been wounded in both legs. Mohun had been struck through the groin, in the arm, and several times in the chest. Their swords were dripping with blood, their faces bathed in it, the grass around them stained. Still they fought on, in rage and fury, paying no thought whatever to self-defence. Some early morning strollers came upon the scene, stood and watched in awe. Then each man made a lunge at the other, simultaneously. The Duke's sword passed right through Lord Mohun's body, to the hilt. Being ambidextrous, he had been fighting with his left hand; Mohun with his dying gesture slashed the Duke's unprotected right arm, severing an artery.[5] The Duke fell against a tree, into the arms of Colonel Hamilton, who had dropped his sword. Maccartney then grabbed the sword, and plunged it into the dying Duke's breast, as he lay supported by his son. One of Mohun's footmen, according to contemporary rumour, also attacked the Duke. Mohun died on the spot, and Hamilton was dead before he could be conveyed to his house. The onlookers had made no move to help or intervene, but as soon as the Duke's body was carried off, they fell upon the tree and stripped away pieces of bark for souvenirs. Sightseers flocked there for days afterwards.

Comment excited by the affair lasted a long time, and divided London society along political lines. The Tories said that the Duke's death had been engineered by the Whigs, who had an army of thugs lurking in Hyde Park wating to finish off the job should Lord Mohun bungle it. There was of course no truth in this. But the role of Maccartney was sufficiently suspicious for the Privy Council to order an enquiry, at which Colonel Hamilton testified on oath that Maccartney had struck the Duke while he was holding him against the tree. Maccartney had already fled to Holland, so he must have thought there was some truth in the allegation himself. On the strength of Hamilton's evidence, a warrant was issued for Maccartney's arrest, and proclamation was made offering a reward by the Crown of £500 for his apprehension. The Duchess of Hamilton added a further £200. Foreign governments were approached with a view to extradition.

On the accession of George I Maccartney returned to England and was arrested for murder. He was tried in June 1716, when Hamilton's evidence was discredited by his admission of possible error. (Hamilton had himself been tried and acquitted.) Maccartney was found not guilty of murder, but guilty of manslaughter, and was burnt in the hand with a cold iron, according to the custom of the day.

Just before the duel, Hamilton had been appointed Ambassador to Paris, and had delayed his departure in order to settle the dispute with Mohun. Had he left in time, he would probably have disappeared into the fog of minor history, never to be remembered. He had recently been created Duke of Brandon in the peerage of Great Britain (by Queen Anne in 1711), being one of the first creations since the union with Scotland. But the House of Lords had voted that he should not be entitled to a seat under this name; he would be allowed to continue to sit as a representative peer for Scotland. The Lords did not object to the principle, but to its being applied in favour of the 4th Duke of Hamilton.

Of his son, the 5th Duke, little is known, save that he reflected family traits in finding it difficult to make up his mind whether he was a Jacobite or not. He married three times. His brother earns a mention for the simple distinction of being called Lord Anne Hamilton. He was named after his godmother, Queen Anne, an honour which he may have lived to regret. We have no record that he found his name embarrassing, but it is known that Lord Anne was kept by a wealthy older woman, Mary Edwards, with an income of £60,000 a year, until she grew tired of him. There is a possibility that they married secretly in 1731; he was already twice a widower by 1729, when he was twenty-six years old.

His first wife had died at the age of eighteen in giving birth to the son and heir, the 6th Duke of Hamilton and 3rd Duke of Brandon (1724–1758) whose fame rests on his having married one of the most beautiful women of the eighteenth century, Elizabeth Gunning.

Elizabeth and Maria Gunning were the daughters of an impoverished Irishman, John Gunning, of County Roscommon. They were so poor that they had to escape the bailiffs by handing their furniture out of a window after midnight.[6] They came to London while they were still under twenty, and somehow or other gained access to the Duchess of Bedford, after which they were presented at Court. From that moment there was no looking back for the Gunnings. Their qualities were beauty of face and body, and pleasant good nature. With such boons, their want of a dowry or a station in life was, for once, of small matter. Within months of their arrival they were the most famous ladies in London. At the presentation, says Walpole, "the crowd was so great, that even the noble mob in the Drawing-room clambered upon tables and chairs to look at her. There are mobs at their doors to see them get into their chairs; and people go early to get places at the theatres when it is known they will be there."[7]

One of those who were captivated by the beauty of Elizabeth Gunning was the "hot, debauched, extravagant" Duke of Hamilton, a well-known rake, hardly ever sober, and alarmingly over-sexed. So much did he want her, and so passionate were his imprecations, that when she said she would not submit to his desires before they were married, he married her within the hour. At Hyde Park Corner there was a church, St George's Chapel, where clandestine or hurried marriages often took place. The parson was summoned from his bed at 12.30 a.m., but even he would not perform the ceremony without, at least, a ring. So Elizabeth Gunning became Duchess of Hamilton with the ring from a bed-curtain. She was eighteen years old. Henry Fox described the marriage with euphemism : "I fancy he tried what he could without matrimony. But at one o'clock (not prevailing I suppose) sent for his friend Lord Hume out of bed . . . in consequence of which he was in bed with the lady soon after two, and carried her out of town the next morning."[8]

They journeyed northwards to the Duke's palace in Scotland and when it was known they would stop at an inn in Newcastle 700 people sat up all night, to catch a glimpse of her.[9] Maria Gunning became Countess of Coventry, and died of consumption in 1760. The Duke of Hamilton died in 1758, aged thirty-four, apparently of a cold, and the following year Elizabeth married Lord Lorne, eventually Duke of Argyll. In this way the ancient dispute between the Hamiltons and the Campbells, deadly enemies in the seventeenth century, was resolved by a poor but pretty Irish girl.

Her rise in rank was unique in peerage. From being Miss Gunning she accumulated five dukedoms, six marquessates, nine baronies, two viscountcies, six counties (earldoms) – twenty-eight titles in all. No one in the world beneath a crowned head possessed so many peerage dignities.

All four of her sons became dukes. Her eldest by Hamilton was 7th Duke of Hamilton, who died at the age of fourteen, and was succeeded by his brother as 8th Duke (1756–1799). From his mother he inherited commanding beauty of face, from his father an over-developed sexual appetite. He was convicted of adultery with the Countess of Eglinton in 1788, as a result of which the Earl was granted a divorce. He had an affair with one Mrs Esten, producing an illegitimate daughter, to whom he left as much as he could, obliging his successor in the dukedom to buy it all back. His legitimate wife was a commoner, one of the Burrell girls, daughters of a Customs officer; she divorced him sixteen years later. The Duke was never able to control his dissipated ways, his love for low company, his alcoholism, or the Hamilton quick temper. He died aged forty-four, from too much good living.

The 9th Duke was father to Lady Anne Hamilton, poor Queen Caroline's only friend, and supposed author of that scandalously revealing *Secret History of the Court of England*. Creevey saw her waiting upon the Queen, leaning on her brother Archy's arm, "though she is full six feet high, and bears a striking resemblance to one of Lord Derby's great red deer".[10] Another daughter was Charlotte, who married the 11th Duke of Somerset, taking with her many Hamilton heirlooms which were to cause irreconcilable rifts in the Somerset family a generation later.

For the next hundred years, the dukes of Hamilton were chiefly notable for the exaggerated importance they attached to their own rank and ancient birth. The 10th Duke of Hamilton (1767–1852) carried pride in family to risible extremes. He firmly believed, without a hint of tongue in cheek, that he was heir to the throne of Scotland, being descended from the regent Earl of Arran. Heaven knows what he would have done to anyone who pointed out that the Earl of Abercorn was the direct descendant in the male line. Strangely enough, both this Duke and his approximate contemporary, Marquess of Abercorn, were known as *magnifico*, for they rivalled each other in pomposity. For his part, the Duke decided that no nobleman of his extraordinary class should be without a hermit in the grounds of his palace; it was a fashionable ornament. So he advertised for one, stipulating that the hermit should shave his beard only once a

year, and only lightly.[11] It was, however, in his death that he surpassed himself. He had an Egyptian sarcophagus brought to Scotland from Thebes, which had been made for an ancient Egyptian
queen, and bore her sculpted and painted image on the outside.
He had bought it in open auction for £11,000, outbidding the
British Museum. To house the sarcophagus he built a colossal and
ridiculous mausoleum, with dome and marble and statues, in which
would lie himself and his nine predecessors, as well as all future heirs
to the throne of Scotland. "What a grand sight it will be," he used
to say, "when Twelve Dukes of Hamilton rise together here at the
Resurrection!" He frequently would go to his splendid tomb and lie
in it to see how it fitted. His last ride out was to buy spices for his
own embalming (and he *was* embalmed), and as he lay dying he
was haunted by the thought that he might not fit the sarcophagus,
which could not be altered being made of Egyptian syenite, the
hardest of all rocks. His last words were, "Double me up! Double
me up!", but no amount of doubling could squeeze his body into the
mummy-case, so his feet had to be chopped off, and placed in
separately.[12*]

The 11th Duke (1811–1863), son of the modern Pharaoh, had
his share of honest Hamilton excess. He married a German princess
and was friend and neighbour to the Duchess of Teck, who often
visited Baden. The Tecks' little daughter, Princess May of Teck,
remembered the Hamiltons in later life when she sat on the consort
throne of England as Queen Mary.[13] The 11th Duke never travelled
in France with a lesser retinue than 200 horses, carriages, and
servants. He used to drive down the Champs-Elysées in a carriage
drawn by twelve horses and six postilions, in contravention of the
law which forbade anyone but the Emperor Napoleon to drive with
more than eight horses and postilions (it was called the Sumptuary
Law). Hamilton, of course, considered himself at least the equal of
Napoleon, and far aloof from such petty legalities.[14]

The 12th Duke (1845–1895) married a daughter of Louise von
Alten, who was in turn Duchess of Manchester and Duchess of
Devonshire. On him we must linger a while, for he resurrected the
old quarrel over *who* should be the Duke of Châtelherault. Briefly,
we must go back and see what happened to this title, conferred on
James Hamilton, 2nd Earl of Arran, in 1549.

---

* Another example of an ostentatious departure was the funeral of the Duke of
Rothes, more elaborate and impressive than either Wellington's or Churchill's. The
cost of whole regiments of ceremonial guards, soldiers, banners, trumpets, heralds
and coaches effectively ruined the family finances forever.

The patent of Henri II creating the dignity specifically nominates Arran's heirs in perpetuity ("*pour lui, ses. hoirs et ayants cause, à perpétuité*"). But who were Arran's heirs? Certainly not the dukes of Hamilton. The heir male of Arran was Abercorn, and the *heir of line* was the Earl of Derby. According to an edict of Louis XIV, dated May 17,11, all French dukedoms could *only* descend through the direct male line, which would make Abercorn entitled to the dukedom of Châtelherault. The Hamiltons were not having any of this.

From 1651 (the death of the 2nd Duke of Hamilton) until 1799, the family made no attempt to claim the French title, although they had occasionally pocketed the income from the duchy while it lasted. Then, in 1818, the Marquess of Abercorn was recognised in France as Duc de Châtelherault. The 10th Duke of Hamilton (the one who died like an Egyptian Empress) was disdainful. He simply assumed the title the following year, 1819, as if the Abercorn line did not exist. He was acting illegally in so doing.

The squabble went on for the rest of the century, and fills two huge boxes of documents in the Hamilton archives. The Hamiltons had the upper hand, for they were in a position to pull strings – the 12th Duke's mother was a cousin of Napoleon! Accordingly, in 1864, he succeeded in being "confirmed" in the French title by the French Emperor, "*le Duc d'Hamilton a été maintenu et confirmé, par décret du avril 20, 1864 dans le titre héréditaire du Duc de Châtel-herault* etc."[15] Hamilton's case rested on his ancestor, the 2nd Duke and last in the male line of Hamiltons in *that* branch of the family, having entailed his French honours on 19th March 1650 upon Duchess Anne and *her* heirs.[16] Two things make this view of events untenable, (1) that the 2nd Duke *could not* have altered the entail of a French duchy, it was simply not in his power to do so, (2) that Napoleon *could not* "confirm" a title which the "holder" did not legally possess.

As one peerage lawyer wrote, "His Grace of Hamilton has as much right to it as he has to the throne of China."

The upshot of it all is that the present Duke of Abercorn is, whether he or anyone else likes it or not, the legal Duke of Châtelherault (1549), whereas the present Duke of Hamilton is *also* Duke of Châtelherault by a new Napoleonic creation of 1864. Neither of them is at all exercised by the problem.*

Now back to the 12th Duke of Hamilton, busy accumulating as many titles as he could. Another title he claimed, with justification

* Anyone wishing to enquire further should consult the Hamilton Papers at the Scottish National Register of Archives.

this time, and with success, was the even more complex earldom of
Selkirk. It is worth looking at, because it must be unique in the entire
peerage.

The 1st Earl of Selkirk was William Douglas, the man who married Anne, Duchess of Hamilton in her own right and was later
created Duke of Hamilton himself, for his lifetime only. (Incidentally,
this marriage united the Douglas and Hamilton lines that we find
reflected in the family surname.) He had been Earl of Selkirk in
1646, and Duke of Hamilton in 1660. On receiving the dukedom,
he *resigned* his earldom, surrendering it to the King's hands to do
with as His Majesty pleased. In fact, by surrendering a dignity to the
King, you give back what was only yours during the monarch's
pleasure, the monarch being the source and fountain of all peerage
dignities. So the King assumed the earldom of Selkirk himself for
a period. However, there was always the tacit understanding that it
should be reconferred, with a fresh patent, on the Duke's family, but
with a unique remainder. It was stipulated that this title should
belong to the *third* son of the Duke of Hamilton and *his* heirs male
and that, if the line failed, and if the lines of any younger sons
should fail, the title should revert to the Duke of Hamilton of the
day *until such time* as he had a younger son to start a new line of
earls of Selkirk. As long as the Duke of Hamilton had one son, the
earldom would be absorbed into his subsidiary titles; but it would
re-emerge as a title in its own right (*not* a courtesy title) when
there was a cadet branch of the family to assume it. Accordingly the
title was conferred upon the third son of the 1st Duke in 1688, and
remained with his descendants until 1886, when their line came to
an end and it was claimed by the 12th Duke of Hamilton. It
remained with the dukedom until the death of the 13th Duke in
1940, whereupon his dukedom and subsidiary titles passed to his
eldest son, while the independent earldom of Selkirk went to his
second son, Group Captain Lord Nigel Douglas-Hamilton (who was
on active service at the time and did not claim his title until
after the war). He, then, is the 7th and present Earl of Selkirk,
and his son, born in 1939, is the Master of Selkirk; a new line of
earls has begun, to exist in divergence from the senior line of
Hamiltons.

His brother, 14th Duke of Hamilton (1903–1973) was also a
group captain in the war, and a distinguished pilot. In 1933 he made
history as chief pilot of the Houston Everest Expedition by being the
first man ever to fly over the top of Mount Everest; he cleared it by
barely 100 feet. From that moment he was a national hero. Later, he
was President of the British Airline Pilots' Association, and started a

flying school at Prestwick which developed under his care into a world-famous airport; he was chairman of Scottish Aviation Ltd, which founded and owned the airport until its international status made it too busy to handle privately.

There were many facets of the Duke's character which would make him more interesting than most of his ancestors even without the headlines created by Rudolph Hess in the war. The 14th Duke was consciously at variance with his forbears' pompous inflexible Toryism. At Oxford he was captain of the University Boxing Team, and accounted the best amateur boxer of his year, a distinction which would have appalled the nineteenth-century Hamiltons, if, that is, they would have believed it. Worse still, he worked incognito at the coal face in one of the family mines, as "Mr Hamilton", and carried a trade-union card. He was probably the first Duke of Hamilton to be even distantly aware of working-class life, certainly the only one to experience it at first hand. Slightly younger than he, but still of the same generation and shaped by the same upheavals in aristocratic life in the first quarter of the century, is the present Duke of Richmond, who has worked on the factory floor.

The 14th Duke was also a Member of Parliament for ten years before he inherited in 1940, and Lord Steward of the Royal Household. He never smoked, and never drank. If his name springs to mind in the post-war era, it is not as a boxer, or pilot, or a coal-miner, but as the embarrassed central character in the Rudolph Hess drama of 1941.

In May 1941 a German parachutist calling himself Oberleutnant Alfred Horn landed on the Duke of Hamilton's estate in Scotland, having made a hazardous solo flight over enemy territory. When brought before the Duke, he made the astonishing claim to be in reality Rudolph Hess, Hitler's deputy, and to be engaged on a peace mission. He pointed out to the Duke that Germany did not wish to continue the war with England, preferring rather to conserve her forces the better to smash Russia, and would welcome the opportunity to initiate peace negotiations. The central condition which Hitler would make was that England should abandon her traditional position of always opposing the strongest power in Europe. Hess was clearly under the impression that England had been cowed by the blitz, and that the real power in the country was the handful of German sympathisers in the Conservative Party. Why had the Duke of Hamilton been selected to receive this explosive guest? Hess had discussed the possibility of peace overtures with one Albrecht Haushofer, who was known to the Duke, and Haushofer had suggested that Hamilton might be the man to approach, as he had the ear of everyone who mattered in England, including Churchill and the King. There was the tacit implication that he might be receptive to the idea.

The Duke always claimed that he had never met Hess. He had been present at the Olympic Games in Munich in 1936, and might have been seen by Hess there, and he remembered having mentioned to Haushofer that he would like to meet him. On the other hand, there was another Hamilton, Sir Ian, who was well known in Germany, and who had met Hess several times; he also had been mentioned as a possible contact by Haushofer. It now looks very likely that the deputy Fuehrer chose the wrong Hamilton.

The Duke flew straight to London to report to Churchill, who looked at him as if he were mad. "Do you mean to tell me that the Deputy Fuehrer of Germany is in our hands?" he said. Nevertheless, Churchill would not disrupt his plan to watch a Marx Brothers film.

Meanwhile, on the German side, Hitler was bursting with rage. He had previously not been consulted. Rudolph Hess, whose influence with Hitler had been waning, had made a desperate attempt to curry favour, and misread the Fuehrer's view of independent initiative as well as of the mood in England. With historical perspective, one now sees that the Hess episode was an insignificant interruption in the course of the war. Hess was imprisoned in the Tower of London, and sentenced to imprisonment for life at the Nuremberg trials. He languished in Spandau prison, a pathetic, not very intelligent, lonely old man, until his death in 1987. In view of the intent behind his flight – to make peace with England and concentrate on overcoming Russia – it is little wonder that the Russians insisted he should stay in prison literally until he died. As for the Duke of Hamilton, he was an unwilling participant in a bizarre affair, but by virtue of having been chosen by Hess, has been accorded a footnote in the history of the war which he would rather forgo. His own service in the war, as group captain in the Royal Air Force, is more deserving of recollection.

The map which Hess used to guide him over Scotland, with his own arrow marks on it, hangs on the wall in the family home.

The Duke died in 1973, and was succeeded by his son as 15th Duke of Hamilton (born 1938). He is the Premier Peer of Scotland, and Hereditary Keeper of Holyroodhouse Palace in Edinburgh, the Queen's official residence; the position entitles him to a suite of rooms to be kept always at his disposal in the Palace. His mother is sister to the present Duke of Northumberland. In 1972 he married Sarah, daughter of Sir Walter Scott.

Like his father, he was in the Royal Air Force, and before inheriting the titles was employed as a test pilot by Scottish Aviation. He

is one of the versatile, buccaneer, sporting dukes, as opposed to political dukes like Devonshire or businessmen like St Albans. It is not
without significance that his ancestor, the first Hamilton to be raised
to the peerage as Earl of Arran, was so rewarded for being an
excellent jouster. Hamilton is an accomplished sportsman in many
fields, including motor-racing and skin-diving. He frankly admits that
he would have much rather gone on being a test pilot, which he
enjoyed, than becoming a ducal landowner. He has had to learn a
great deal about estate management and farming. The estates are
now run by a limited company, of which he is chairman, and which
has such a fine record of efficiency that it actually farms more acres
than it owns : the arrangement is a complicated one.

The Duke and Duchess live in a house in East Lothian, while the
estate office is at the official ducal seat, Lennoxlove, at Haddington,
owned by the limited company and rented by it to the Dowager
Duchess. Lennoxlove was named after the Duchess of Lennox and
Richmond, better known as "la Belle Stuart", one of Charles II's
mistresses and the model for Britannia on our coins. But it has been
with dukes of Hamilton for less than thirty years. The original
seat was the magnificent Hamilton Palce, demolished in 1922 in what
the present Duke calls "one of the architectual crimes of the century".
The estate in those days was run by a board of trustees, one of
whom was the Chancellor of the Exchequer. They gave the worst
possible advice to the crippled 13th Duke, telling him that the Palace
would have to be destroyed (a) because of the danger of subsidence
due to mine-workings beneath, (b) because it was difficult to drain
efficiently, (c) because the country needed coal, and the Palace was
sitting on it. Patriotic fervour more than anything impelled the Duke
to get rid of one of the best houses in the country – the Great War
had ended four years before and emotions were still running high.
He took his seventeen-year-old son (the present Duke's father) to have
a last look at the place, and told him he could choose one single
object from amongst the treasures to keep for himself, before they all
disappeared. He chose a mirror, which is still in the family. They
also managed to save family portraits, and the death-mask of Mary
Queen of Scots, now at Lennoxlove.

The mausoleum in which the twelve Dukes of Hamilton lay stood
in the grounds of Hamilton Palace. When the Palace was demolished,
the mausoleum was left, but the bodies were removed and interred.
The grounds now belong to Strathclyde Park.

The present Duke has had the idea of digging up the Egyptian
sarcophagus, and placing it on show in the mausoleum. It would

lend greater interest to the mausoleum, and apart from anything else, it is an extremely rare and beautiful object.

Strathclyde Park was prepared to accept the sarcophagus as a gift, but could not afford to buy it. It is now worth anything up to £1 million, so rare an object it is. The Duke agreed. He has now been advised by his lawyers that once the coffin is dug up, it becomes an asset, and the Duke may have to pay heavy wealth tax every year he keeps it; if he gives it away he will pay Capital Transfer Tax; if he sells it, he will pay Capital Transfer Tax and Capital Gains Tax. All things considered, it is better to leave the old Duke where he lies.

*   *   *

Now to the House of Hamilton in Ireland. Lord Arran's second surviving son, Claud Lord Paisley, went mad. His son was created Earl of Abercorn in 1606, taking the title from land he held in Linlithgow. At the same time he was granted lands in County Tyrone, Ireland, and it was there that the family seat – Baron's Court – was built. His descendant was made Duke of Abercorn by Queen Victoria in 1868, but first, there are a pair of Georgian eccentrics to divert us.

The 8th Earl of Abercorn (1712–1789) never married, leaving himself free to indulge and aggravate that stony aloof fastidious nature which becomes obsessive with so many bachelors. Join to this a fair share of that Hamilton pride, and you have a crotchety, stiff and unsociable man. He is said to have made the tour of Europe in so perpendicular a stýle as never to have touched the back of his carriage.[18] He once received the Queen at his house, whereupon the King thanked him, saying that he was afraid Her Majesty's visit had given him a good deal of trouble. "A good deal indeed," replied Lord Abercorn.

He was highly offended if anyone should presume to pay him a visit without the formality of a card of invitation. This was an English habit, but not usual in Scotland, where it was assumed that a nobleman's house always had a welcome for callers. (The 5th Duke of Buccleuch played host at Drumlanrig to dozens of people whom he had never met.) The Earl of Abercorn was on a visit to his Scottish estate when a local historian called Robertson who, poor man, was unaware of the Earl's reputation for stiffness, called to pay his respects. He found Lord Abercorn by the shrubbery in the garden, went up to him, and commented on how well the shrubs had grown since his lordship's last visit. "They have nothing else to do," replied Abercorn, and walked away.

In fairness, it is also recorded that Lord Abercorn was kind to those around him, as long as they respected his exalted rank. Even he was surpassed in pomposity by his successor, his nephew, born Mr Hamilton but successively Earl and Marquess of Abercorn (1756–1818). While it may be said that the old Earl was prickly, the new Marquess was positively pretentious. Born a commoner, he grew into the most inflexible aristocrat, with a menacing, overpowering personality; even the King went in fear of him. He dined every day wearing the Blue Ribbon of the Knight of the Garter; he even hunted in it. The maids were not allowed to change the linen on his august bed unless they wore white kid gloves; more personal contact would be degrading to his rank. Footmen were required to dip their hands in a bowl of rose-water before handing him a dish. He travelled always with four carriages and ten outriders, and if he gave a party, it was not for a weekend, nor a week, but for an entire month. The moment any person became famous, he had to be invited to the Marquess of Abercorn's. The boy actor, Master Betty, was a frequent guest. Also, anyone who was beautiful (or *known* to be so) would receive an invitation. The guests could do as they wished, on the understanding that they were not to address Lord Abercorn except at table. Few would ever dare to open their mouths even there. When a very poor novel called *Thaddeus of Warsaw* by the young Jane Porter became the success of the moment, Abercorn said, "Gad! We must have these Porters. Write, my dear Lady Abercorn." (Jane had a novelist sister, Anna Maria Porter.) She wrote, and Jane replied that she could not afford the fare. A cheque was sent. They duly arrived, and the Marquess peered at them from behind a curtain. He was disappointed; they were not as good-looking as he had been led to believe. "Witches, my lady," he said, and disappeared, leaving Lady Abercorn to entertain them; they did not see him.[19]

Such peculiar conduct did not endear Abercorn to his contemporaries, who thought him a rather ridiculous figure, self-consciously grand, and vacuous at the centre. He was variously known as *il magnifico* (a sobriquet passed on to his kinsman, the 10th Duke of Hamilton), or *Don Whiskerandos* because he looked Spanish. There was no doubting that he was a marquess; he worked hard at the role. "An air of grace and dignity diffused over his whole person", says Wraxall, "he could not be mistaken for an ordinary man."[20] Pride informed his every remark. Even before he inherited the earldom, when he was plain Mr Hamilton, he had visiting cards which proclaimed him "D'Hamilton, Comte Héréditaire d'Aber-corn".[21] Once clothed with the accoutrements of nobility, he simply could not be restrained. Someone remarked upon the livery worn by his servants, which was identical to that worn by those serving younger members of the Royal Family, saying, "I suppose your family took it from them." The temerity! Abercorn raised his chin. "Sir," he said, "it was the livery of the Hamiltons before the House of Brunswick had a servant to put it on."[22] Lady Holland could scarcely believe her ears. She wrote : "He was always supposed to be a little cracked, and his pride is beyond belief."

Abercorn did nothing with his life. Politics bored him. He devoted his time to acting the part of a grandee, and entertaining the famous and the beautiful. It comes as a surprise, therefore, to see honours heaped upon him, first a marquessate, then the Garter, then a Privy Councillor, without any obvious merit. The answer is to be found in his friendship with the Prime Minister, Pitt, whom he had known when they were young men at Cambridge, and from whose acquaintance he now profited as much as he could. Pitt, it was even suggested, profited also; he was paid for persuading the King to look upon Abercorn with favour. This is how Wraxall tactfully puts it : "no honours or concession in the power of the Crown to bestow were above the pretensions of a man, who not only descended from the royal line of Scottish kings, but was himself the head and representative of the Dukes of Hamilton in male succession. . . . When, however, as a further augmentation to so many dignities and distinctions conferred on this nobleman, the Garter was finally added by Pitt some years later, there were not wanting individuals who sought for the solution of such extraordinary acts of predilection or friendship by recourse to more concealed causes."[23] Wraxall goes on to point out that Abercorn was wealthy and Pitt so poor that he could not pay his taxes or the butcher when he came to the door, and hints darkly that the Prime Minister received £1000 from Abercorn's purse.

He almost went too far, however, when he prevailed upon Pitt to grant the precedence of an earl's daughter to his intended bride. He had already been married once, to a Miss Copley, by whom he had several children. She died in 1791, when he announced his intention of marrying his first cousin, Cecil Hamilton, a parson's daughter. Now that he had a clearer vision of his place in life, there was one obstacle to his plans, namely that "he found it quite impossible to demean himself by marrying anyone who had not the distinction of a title".[24] He bullied Pitt and frightened the King into granting her the style "Lady Cecil Hamilton", although there was no way in which either she or her father could have come anywhere near the title, and in spite of her having four older sisters, who were still plain "Miss". Moreover, this story relates to the year 1789, when Abercorn's first wife was still alive. This implication is that he intended to marry Cecil as soon as his wife was removed from the living, and that he was already her lover. The King was made to ennoble an adulteress. As Wraxall remarks, even Charles II might have hesitated; as it was, the King and Queen showed "strong marks of repugnance" before relenting.

The marriage duly took place, but was not happy; seven years later it ended in divorce. With a touch of the farcical, Abercorn proved that even in distress his pride was paramount. When he heard that his wife intended to elope, he sent a message to her begging that she should elope in the family coach, "as it ought never to be said that Lady Abercorn left her husband's roof in a hack chaise".[25]

Within months, the whisper was heard in London drawing-rooms that the old Marquess intended to marry again. Nobody could quite believe it and he, well aware of the stir he would cause, determined that Lady Anne Hatton should become his wife in the utmost secrecy. The fiancée was sitting at tea with Lady Bessborough when a porter entered saying, that Lady Anne must hurry, for Lord Abercorn had just left word that she was to be married at four in the afternoon. "This intelligence so communicated surprised them, but compliance and punctuality are indispensable qualities where Lord A. is concerned, therefore they obeyed." After the ceremony, he bowed to the new Marchioness, then went off with a cavalcade of servants to dine with his own family, while she dined with hers.[26]

Quite apart from pride in rank, old Abercorn had a superabundance of normal human vanity. When he was quite aged, he was involved in an accident with the phaeton, which broke both his legs. His first worry was that his beauty and elegance might be impaired. He sought reassurances from the doctor, who unwisely remarked that Lord Abercorn could not hope to escape without some consequences at his advanced age. The following day he received his fee and an intimation that his services were no longer required. Bewildered, he turned to a London specialist, Dr Pemberton, for an explanation of the Marquess's conduct. "No one must ever suggest that he is not in his first youth," he said.[27]

Whatever his eccentricities, the Marquess of Abercorn was not an evil man. Lady Holland had the measure of him. "He is haughty and capricious," she wrote, "with enough of vanity to make him do a generous action, and with a dash of madness to make him do a lively one.' There were instances when he behaved with admirable public spirit. During the flour famine in the early nineteenth century, neither he nor any of his guests, no matter how exalted, were allowed to eat anything made with flour. There can be no excuse to rejoice in the series of disasters which befell him as he grew old. His first wife, Miss Copley, had died of consumption shortly after giving birth to her sixth child. In 1803, the eldest daughter, aged nineteen and engaged to be married, also died of consumption. In 1808 the second son, Lord Claud, died of the disease, followed by the second daughter, Lady Catherine, in 1812. There were two children left, the heir Lord Hamilton, and the youngest and prettiest Lady Maria. The old Marquess devoted all his love now to this last daughter, bringing her every medical attention. The doctors of the day thought, however, that night air was not healthy, and prescribed sleeping with closed windows and curtains drawn round four-poster beds. In such conditions, Maria could not fight against the hereditary curse, and she died at the age of eighteen. Four months later the last child, Lord Hamilton, died of consumption too. Abercorn could hold his head high no longer. Yet he still maintained enough pride to deny that any Hamilton could possibly die of consumption; it was thought to be a disease associated with poverty, with the working classes, and with undernourishment. He bullied the doctors to write a letter to *The Times* announcing that his eldest daughter did not succumb to consumption. But by the end, even he was bound to admit that the Copley curse had carried off his children. Fortunately none of it has passed down to subsequent generations. The present Duke of Abercorn is a direct descendant of the last child, Lord Hamilton, who died in 1814 at the age of twenty-seven, and whose eldest son was created 1st Duke of Abercorn by Queen Victoria.

None of the dukes of Abercorn has been eccentric, and none has been illustrious. They have tended to remain on the periphery of political life, reserving themselves for the job they do best, in which they are almost unsurpassed, which is to be the monarch's representative in Ireland. The first Duke was twice Lord Lieutenant of Ireland and the 3rd Duke, who died in 1953, held the post of Governor of Northern Ireland for twenty-four years. They have been popular in this role. They carry it off with style, dignity, and panache. Of course, the lowly have been required to keep their place, but they seem to have done so with joy. The first Duke, known as "Old Splendid", was practically worshipped by the locals. One of his sons wrote, "The veneration in which my father was held by the country people around him almost surpassed belief."[28] As for the paraphernalia of a governorship – the entertaining, the balls, the ritual, the glitter, the deference – they performed it as to the manner born (which, indeed, they were). In fact, it was for being so good at entertaining that they most probably received their dukedom. Lord and Lady Abercorn received the Prince and Princess of Wales at their home in Ireland in April 1868. "Bertie" and Alexandra enjoyed themselves so much that they returned to London full of praise for the work of the Lord Lieutenant; the patent creating the dukedom of Abercorn is dated 10th August of that year.

The Duke's wife was a daughter of the 6th Duke of Bedford. They had six sons and seven daughters. One daughter became Duchess of Buccleuch and another was Duchess of Marlborough (the idiotic Bertha, who drove her poor husband frantic with her infantile practical jokes). Two of the younger sons brought real literary distinction to the family. There have been dukes who have written books – the dukes of Argyll, Sutherland and Portland – and still more ducal younger sons, but they are for the most part pallid affairs. The books of Lord Ernest Hamilton, however, and to a lesser degree of his brother Lord Frederick, are works of true merit. The former's *Halycon Era* is a model of what a book of memoirs should be, and is mercifully free of Victorian affectation. There are half a dozen books by one brother or the other which are still read with pleasure. This is a unique accomplishment in ducal families.

The daughter who was later to be Duchess of Buccleuch, Lady Louise Hamilton, was received into the Church by the Archbishop of Canterbury when she was four years old. To keep her quiet and still, her mother had given her a sugared almond to suck. When, in the course of the ceremony, the Archbishop picked her up, she took the sweet from her mouth and popped it into his. With both hands occupied, he could not possibly remove it, and could not very well spit it out, so he patiently sucked it, while the congregation, made anxious by the silence, thought he had had a stroke.[29]

Of the 2nd Duke of Abercorn (1838–1913), *Vanity Fair* wrote: "He has not done much, but he has done nothing badly. . . . He has enjoyed the friendship of illustrious persons and, oddly enough, he has deserved it. He is full of tact, agreeable, and endowed with the good manners which oblige even Radicals to admit that blue blood has its advantages."

The present Duke, who inherited the title in 1979, is fifth in line. He is the only nobleman to have distinctions in the three peerages of Great Britain, Ireland *and* Scotland, as well as the French dukedom of Châtelherault. His mother, widow of the 4th Duke, has been Woman of the Bedchamber to Queen Elizabeth the Queen Mother since 1937. Abercorn is in every way a modern man, devoting himself to the promotion of industry and prosperity in Northern Ireland, passionately concerned with the reconciliation of opposing ideas in Ireland, but wise enough to demonstrate his concern quietly and unobtrusively, diffident in manner but firm in resolve. His 'family room' at the ancestral home, Baron's Court in County Tyrone, is the most overtly modern to be found in any ducal seat, delighting some visitors and appalling others, but leaving no one indifferent. The Duke takes his seat in the Lords regularly and made his maiden speech within days of being introduced. He is also the first of the Hamiltons to marry outside what he calls the 'charmed circle'; his Duchess is one of the beautiful grand-daughters of Sir Harold Wernher of Luton Hoo, née Alexandra Anastasia Phillips and known as 'Sasha'. Her sister, Natalia Ayesha, is the Duchess of Westminster. The complicated ties of relationship between the Dukes of Abercorn and Westminster illustrate yet again how the dukes leap-frog in and out of each other's families, for Abercorn is Westminster's godfather, second cousin, and brother-in-law.

The most celebrated member of the Abercorn line is the old Duchess, wife of the 1st Duke, who was still alive when the present Duke was born. In other words, she lived to see her grandchildren's grandchildren. When she died in 1905 she was ninety-two years old; her direct descendants, issued from her body and alive at the time, numbered 169 persons. In 1894 she had posed for a photograph with 101 of them. Nor was the accident of longevity the only distinction which makes this lady worth remembering. She was, by all accounts, a charming, genial, essentially good person. The Duke of Portland said that she was the most genial old lady he ever saw. Her son Lord Ernest said she refused to credit evil in anyone and shed sweetness and kindliness on all around her. She was perfectly happy for nearly a century, was never bored, and her marriage with the Duke was exemplary, romantic. Even after fifty years of marriage, the old couple would sing together the duets of their youth, and played chess together every evening.[30] Twice a week, well into old age, she would call at every house in the village. She remembered unfailingly the names of every cottager, the names of their children, whom they had married. She took with her a home-made drink, known as "Her Grace's Bottle", composed of iron-water, old whisky, sal volatile, red lavender, cardamoms, and ginger. Whisky, apparently, was the dominant ingredient. When she had passed eighty, she spent most of her day fishing, with a footman in attendance. He would bait the hook for her, and take the rod from her hand whenever she flicked a fish on to the grass beside her. He would then carefully unhook the fish and just as carefully place it back in the water, and the ritual would continue thus for hours.[31]. When she was eighty-six years old, the old Duchess got on stilts to demonstrate the art to a wobbly great-grandchild. The grand old Duchess of Abercorn appears in the photograph albums of more than a few families today. She was the "one golden link that held together some fifty families scattered here and there about the United Kingdom".[32]

REFERENCES

1. John Buchan, *Montrose,* p. 42.
2. Rosalind K. Marshall, *The Days of Duchess Anne,* p. 25.
3. Quoted in *Complete Peerage.*
4. *Old and New London,* IV, 392.
5. Marshall, *op. cit.,* p. 229.
6. Duchess of Bedford, *Now the Duchesses,* p. 60.
7. Walpole, XX, 311.
8. MSS of Sir Charles Hanbury Williams, quoted in Walpole, Vol. XX, p. 303 fn.
9. Walpole, XX, 317.
10. Creevey, *Papers,* Vol. I, p. 309.
11. Timbs, *English Eccentrics and Eccentricities,* Vol. I, p. 162.
12. Augustus Hare, *The Years With Mother,* p. 188.
13. James Pope-Hennessey, *Queen Mary,* p. 148.
14. Duke of Manchester, *My Candid Recollections,* p. 248.
15. *Complete Peerage,* Vol. I, App. B.
16. Hamilton Papers M8, (42, 47, 63, 2, 5, 20, 40).
17. Lord James Douglas-Hamilton, *Motive for a Mission, passim.*
18. *Gentleman's Magazine,* October 1789.
19. Timbs, *op. cit.,* II, 286.
20. Wraxall, *Posthumous Memoirs,* Vol. I, p. 61.
21. *Journal* of Lady Elizabeth Holland, Vol. II, p. 67.
22. *ibid.,* p. 70.
23. Wraxall, *op. cit.,* I, 65.
24. Lord Ernest Hamilton, *Old Days and New,* p. 26.
25. G. E. Russell, *Collections and Recollections* (1898).
26. *Journal* of Elizabeth Lady Holland, Vol. II, p. 69.
27. Lord Ernest Hamilton, *op. cit.,* p. 30.
28. Lord Ernest Hamilton, *Forty Years On,* p. 43.
29. Lord Frederic Hamilton, *Here, There and Everywhere,* p. 157.
30. Lord Frederic Hamilton, *Days Before Yesterday,* p. 325.
31. Duke of Portland, *Men, Women and Things,* p. 309.
32. Lord Ernest Hamilton, *Forty Years On,* p. 302.

11. A Talent for Absorbing Heiresses

Duke of Sutherland

At the northernmost tip of Scotland there lies the huge county of Sutherland, covering 1,298,000 acres of windswept, almost treeless highlands. Only Caithness and the Orkneys are more distant. Sutherland is battered by the sea on three sides, and dominated by wild outbursts of rock in the interior. Its inhabitants are descended from hardy Norsemen and rough independent Gaels. It is a forbidding but beautiful place, and it belonged in its entirety, as personal property, to one man in the nineteenth century, an Englishman – the Duke of Sutherland.

Now the Duke of Sutherland lives in Roxburghshire and Suffolk, with not an acre in Sutherland. His kinswoman, on the other hand, Elizabeth Countess of Sutherland in her own right, does still own 100,000 acres in the county, while the ancient family seat of Dunrobin Castle belongs to a Charitable Trust.

At first glance, it is not easy to see what these two people have to do with each other. They do not even have the same surname : the Duke is John Egerton, the Countess is Elizabeth Sutherland, Mrs Janson. These surnames, however, are very misleading. In fact, both the Duke and the Countess *should* bear the surname Leveson-Gower (pronounced Looson-Gore). Until 1963 the dukedom and the earldom were vested in one person, George Granville Sutherland-Leveson-Gower, 5th Duke and 23rd Earl of Sutherland. On his death, the dukedom went to a distant relation, while the earldom went to his niece. To find out why, we must go back 200 years and follow the fortunes of the Gower family.

The Gowers represent the single most illuminating example of how to advance in social status without talent or achievement, but by the unfailing method of marrying heiresses. They were by no means the only family to adopt this route to wealth (the Dukes of Buccleuch were another), but they did make the advance with more dazzling speed than anyone else. It was Disraeli who said they had a talent for "absorbing heiresses", a talent which was to bring them a million and a half acres, making them the largest private landowners in Europe.

Within the space of three generations, they rose from a baronetcy to a dukedom, and also, as it happened, from nonentity to notoriety. By the time they had finished, they could claim to be the "richest, most powerful, and most disliked family in England".[1]

Sir Thomas Gower, the 2nd baronet, married Frances Leveson, sole heiress of Sir John Leveson in Staffordshire. From being a small Yorkshire squire, he was suddenly owner of the Trentham estate in Staffordshire and the Lilleshall estate in Shropshire. His son Sir William Leveson-Gower married another heiress, Lady Jane Granville, daughter of the Earl of Bath. Their son John married Catherine Manners, daughter of the 1st Duke of Rutland, and was the first of the three generations to climb towards a dukedom. He was raised to the peerage as Baron Gower of Sittenham. His son was created Earl Gower and Viscount Trentham, and married three rich wives, each of whom added to the nicely accumulating wealth. His son also married three times, choosing as his second wife Lady Louisa Egerton, daughter and co-heiress of the 1st Duke of Bridgwater, and leaping up the ladder to a marquessate : he was created Marquess of Stafford in 1786. It is *his* son, the 2nd Marquess of Stafford, who begins the Sutherland story by marrying the greatest heiress of all, the Scottish Countess of Sutherland.

The earldom of Sutherland, like many a Scottish title, has had a turbulent, bloodthirsty history. Tradition held that the earls were descended from a Norse invader who, on landing at the coast of Sutherland, was set upon by a number of wild cats.[2] The battle which ensued was long and fierce, but he slew them all, and survived to found the Sutherland family. To this day, the Countess of Sutherland has a wild cat on her coat of arms, and the motto *Sans Peur* ("Fearless"). Be that as it may, the first of the family to own land was granted the district of Sutherland by William the Lion in 1196, and created earl about 1235.

Some of the stories involving his descendants are enough to freeze the spine. In 1395 the 6th Earl of Sutherland was parleying with the chief of the Mackays in an attempt to settle their inevitable differences by negotiation when he lost his temper and murdered Mackay and his son with his bare hands. In the sixteenth century Lady Isobel Sinclair, mother of the second in line to the earldom, decided to dispose of the 11th Earl and his son by poison. She invited them to dinner, served the poisoned ale to her guests, and was thwarted only by the Earl's timely realisation of what was going on. He fled from the house, as Lady Isobel's son entered and was himself served the ale by a servant who was not privy to the secret. A few days later, the Earl and Countess were both dead, as was Lady Isobel's son, for whose sake the plan was conceived. Lady Isobel was sent to Edinburgh prison, where she committed suicide, and the rightful heir, Alexander, the only one·not to touch the poison, succeeded as 11th Earl.[3]

The title passed through the heirs of line into different families, until in 1766 the 18th Earl died at the age of thirty-one, only two weeks after his wife had died, aged twenty-six. They left one surviving daughter, an infant barely one year old, who was 19th Countess of Sutherland in her own right (although her guardians had to fight for this recognition against two other claimants), and *Ban mhorair Chataibh*, a Celtic title meaning "Great Lady of Sutherland". It was she who married Granville Leveson-Gower when she was twenty, culminating the series of clever marriages in the Gower family, and founding what was to be the line of dukes of Sutherland.

But for the moment we are in 1785, when Leveson-Gower married the Countess. As dowry, she brought her husband 1735 square miles of land, or two-thirds of the county of Sutherland. The following year, his father was created Marquess of Stafford, and he himself inherited that title in 1803, together with the Shropshire, Staffordshire and Yorkshire estates. In the same year, his uncle the bachelor Duke of Bridgwater died, leaving him the finest private art collection in the country at that time, and a still greater fortune. Leveson-Gower had risen from comparative obscurity to an unassailable position, with tens of thousands of tenants and a colossal income of £300,000 a year; his nearest rivals, like the dukes of Devonshire and Bedford, were considered extremely rich with £50,000 a year. Greville rightly called him "a leviathan of wealth".[4] The pity was that neither he nor the Countess possessed the intelligence to know how best to use all this money. Neither subtlety nor sensitivity had been passed down by the Gowers. From 1803 to 1833, this couple were known as Marquess and Marchioness of Stafford, names which during that period were loathed in the shire of Sutherland, because the Marquess and his wife had decided in their wisdom to "improve" the land.

There can be no dispute that Sutherland needed improving. In 1812 there was not a single road in the whole county, and only one bridge. It was wild isolated country, rugged and barren, almost like a lunar landscape. Hardly anyone ventured into the interior, and those who did emerged weather-beaten and hungry, swearing never to go back. The Marquess of Stafford was not one of them. For twenty years he saw nothing of Sutherland save what was visible from Dunrobin Castle, and showed no inclination to explore.[5] But in 1811 Parliament offered to pay half the expense of building roads in Scotland, if landowners would bear the other half. First, Stafford bought off the Reay estate for £300,000 (only one year's income to him), so that he was master of almost the entire county, and then he set to work. By the time he had finished, twenty years later, he had built 450 miles of excellent roads, among the best in Great Britain, 134 bridges, and an iron bridge with a span of 150 feet, uniting Sutherland and Ross-shire at Bonar. He had opened up the county to the mail service, which now went as far as Thurso, and previously did not penetrate Sutherland at all. Improvements there had been, and great was the achievement. But in the process the lives of the people had been made a misery.

The trouble was, the Staffords had no imagination. They were not the kind of people to see that what they were doing could cause distress, because they could see no further than their noses and their inhuman statistics. Even his own grandson, the Victorian aesthete Lord Ronald Gower, had to admit that Stafford was a bottomlessly dull man. He never did or said anything that was worth remembering, said Gower, and what he wrote was boring beyond comprehension. He suffered from gout and myopia, and was conspicuous only by virtue of his huge hawk-like nose, bigger even than Wellington's, a nose, incidentally, that was bequeathed by his family to the Beauforts, and is still proudly worn by the present Duke of Beaufort (Stafford's sister married a Duke of Beaufort). He had only one ambition, to be a duke, and it drove him desperate;[6] it was the only rank he could be awarded, having inherited the others already. "He might have slipped into his grave and the *Dictionary of National Biography* without being remembered for anything more spectacular than his wealth and his art collection had it not been for his marriage and its consequences."[7]

As for his wife, she had been pretty as a young girl, and excited the admiration of Lady Bessborough, who thought her the most enviable person she knew, "with great cleverness, beauty, talents, and a thousand amiable qualities . . . a propriety of manner and conduct".[8] Her tenants saw another person. Though she was the Great Lady of Sutherland, she spoke no Gaelic (the only language of her people), and according to one writer actually despised the customs and manners of the Highland people whose chief she was. "She was as

English in mood and taste as the furniture of a London drawing-room."[9]

The folk over whom this cushioned couple ruled, and about whom they knew nothing, were a tough race of mountain-dwellers, completely insular (owing to the absence of roads) and fiercely independent. They lived in crude hovels scattered over the Highlands, grew potatoes, raised a few goats and cattle, and brewed raw whisky. Their standards were never far above famine level, and they lived in "conditions of penury and squalor that can only fairly be compared with those of a famine area in contemporary India, and were tolerable only because they were familiar and traditional".[10] There were about 25,000 of them, and they were as much a race of foreigners to the English (which includes the Marquess of Stafford) as the Red Indians of America or the Aborigines of Australia. They were said to be lamentably indolent, and only their bravery in war was acknowledged. The Countess thought of them as a burden, the Marquess didn't think of them at all.

So, when the government offered to share the cost of "improving" the land, it never entered Lord Stafford's head that the inhabitants might object to being forcibly moved from their homes, like a bothersome ant-hill. They were ignorant, illiterate, slothful. It was not their business to object. The Marquess's agents presented themselves at thousands of huts, with orders for the tenants to move to the coast. Not only were they to be evicted, but they were expected to pay four shillings each towards the cost of the road-building, which the Marquess would otherwise have to bear out of his own pocket. Those who went struggled to earn a new living on a notoriously inhospitable coast, rugged and stormy and rocky, perched precariously like leaves in autumn. They had spent their lives rearing goats and growing crops; now they were to fish – there was nothing else for them to do. The huts they left behind, where they had lived for generations, were burned to the ground before they had time to get over the horizon. Those who refused to leave saw their houses burned before their eyes, sometimes with their few belongings still inside. Others emigrated to Northern America. One way or another, the land was swept clear of people, to make way for roads, and to prepare the land for southern sheep-farmers, who were even then being invited to establish themselves in Sutherland. The county was divided into lots, and advertised in the south.

The Marquess and the Countess saw none of the evictions: they were not aware of any suffering, and if they were they would not have spared more than a moment's reflection; for these Highlanders were not *real* people; they were natives, and they were uneconomic. Lord Stafford was "seized as much as I am with the rage of improvements", wrote the Countess of Sutherland. "It was as if the whole population of Sutherland was being shaken in a great cup, thrown out, and allowed to fall where it would on the coast or blow away to the other side of the world", wrote the historian of the Great Improvement. There is no record of how many people were summarily removed in this way, but it was somewhere between 5000 and 15,000. The criminal insensitivity of Lord and Lady Stafford has not been forgotten in Sutherland. One of them, a stonemason, immortalised his people's plight in later years: "The country was darkened by the smoke of burnings", he wrote, "and the descendants were ruined, trampled upon, dispersed, and compelled to seek asylum across the sea". This man, Donald Macleod, was hounded by Stafford's men, and driven eventually into exile; his wife was driven into madness by the persecution she suffered.[11]

As the cruelty of the Sutherland evictions became known, fierce arguments raged as to whose fault it was, and inevitably some misconceptions have taken root in time. The most notorious sheep-farmer was Patrick Sellar, a sadist whose worst excesses have entered legend. When the Countess and her husband heard what had been going on in their names they were appalled.[12] Nor can their chief agent, the architect of the improvements, be entirely blamed. He was James Loch, a self-made man, enlightened and intelligent. He allowed his vision of a bright future for the county to overwhelm his humanity, perhaps, but only the best motives can be laid at his door.

The clearance policy did enormous good in the long run. It opened up the country, provided employment and mobility, spread educational standards, and conquered once and for all the threat of famine. The Staffords *personally* gained nothing from it. Their investment never made a return. The clearances took place between 1806 and 1820, and were meant to make way for southern sheep-farmers who would bring prosperity to the county. In fact, sheep-farming was a failure, and after 1820 the price of wool fell drastically. Local inhabitants were, in the end, triumphant.

Whatever the economic wisdom of the scheme, history has convicted the Staffords of criminal responsibility. It was "an economic policy that entailed the instant transformation of an ancient way of life . . . part of the internal colonisation of Britain".[13] A local man pointed out, "It is one thing thing to build a village, to which people may resort if they choose it, and another to drive them from the country into villages where they must starve, unless they change at once their manners, their habits, and their occupations."[14] Lord Stafford could not possibly have understood this, and must stand condemned for a decision of principle which was his – that for the sake of progress it was worth destroying the happiness of thousands of people.

Professor Checkland has called the clearances "one of the most tragic and emotive incidents in the long death of traditional peasant society in Britain",[15] and F. F. Darling went as far as to say they were "of the order of brutality expected of a Norse raid a thousand years earlier".[16] No wonder Karl Marx, with his curious blend of intellectual precision in the service of distorted dogma, should have written an entire article on Sutherland in the *People's Paper*.[17]

In 1833 Stafford achieved his ultimate aim of becoming a duke, and, though an Englishman, the title he was given was Duke of Sutherland. He lived to enjoy his new rank only six months. "I believe he is the richest individual who ever died", wrote Greville.[18] He had been Ambassador in France during the French Revolution, he had opened the Bridgwater Collection at Stafford House in London to the public, but nothing could brighten his memory. He has come to posterity as the dullard who threw out his wife's hereditary tenants.

The Duke's widow lived for another six years, during which time she was known to the world by a unique and curious title – the "Duchess-Countess". She lost her prettiness, and grew rather plump, which enabled Creevey to make one of his pitilessly precise observations. "It was as good as a play", he wrote, "to see old Sutherland moving her huge *derrière* by slow and dignified degrees about in her chair, so as to come into action if necessary."[19]

The Duchess-Countess died in 1839, and her two sons began the two separate lines of descent which bring us to 1963. From the first son were descended the next four dukes of Sutherland, and from the second son (see page 340) are descended the Earls of Ellesmere, the last of whom succeeded as 6th and present Duke of Sutherland in 1963.

The 2nd Duke of Sutherland (1786–1861) does not appear to have been very distinguished. Like his father, he said and did nothing which has been remembered. We do, however, know that he was bookish. He was an original member of the Roxburghe Club, a Trustee of the British Museum, and a Commissioner for the Fine Arts. It is also certain that he took a far greater interest in his tenants than his parents had done. The potato famine of 1846–8 caused him acute anxiety and real emotional stress, as he tried personally to deal with the hardships his people suffered. Apart from that, all that has come down to us is that he was stone-deaf, conceived a hopeless passion for the Queen of Prussia, so strong that he fell dangerously ill on hearing of her death, and that he married Harriet, a grand-daughter of Georgiana and the 5th Duke of Devonshire.

As so often happens, it was the Duchess who made more of a mark than the Duke. It was she who bestirred him to build Cliveden, the handsome country house in Buckinghamshire, which earned notice in World War II as the home of the Astors. Her friendship with Queen Victoria has made her name more than a footnote to history, surviving even the embarrassment of fainting away during dinner at the Palace.[20] She was the Queen's favourite Mistress of the Robes, and one of her closest friends. The only instance of discord between the two women occurred when the Duchess failed to persuade the Queen to give the Garter to the Duke of Sutherland. Victoria thought, justifiably, that he had quite enough already.[21] At all other times their intimacy was unassailable. On a visit to Stafford House, the Queen was wont to say, "I have come from my house to your palace." She was the Queen's only companion in the first years of the Queen's widowhood. Both women were widowed in the same year, 1861. When she herself died, her son Lord Ronald Gower was with her. Her last words were, "I think I shall sleep now; I am so tired."[22] Mother and son had a warm and close relationship, which gave him the comfort and strength to be one of the few homosexuals in the Victorian period who could hold his head high. It was known that he lived with a man called Frank Hird, whom he had adopted, and it was rumoured that he was the model for Lord Henry Wootten in Oscar Wilde's *The Picture of Dorian Gray*. But he was not driven into exile, perhaps because, unlike the Duke of Beaufort's sons and Wilde himself, Gower was discreet. Scandal never approached him. Duchess Harriet probably knew all there was to know of his life, and understood him. "She would enter into whatever one did or felt," he wrote later, "whether in sorrow or in joy."[23]

Her other son succeeded as 3rd Duke of Sutherland (1828–1892), who by this time possessed the entire county of Sutherland (by virtue of his *earldom*). He built his own private railway (called "The Duke of Sutherland's") which remained in the family until nationalisation in 1950, and even dug (unsuccessfully) for gold. One is bound to wonder what on earth he could possibly have done with it. He is otherwise chiefly remembered for having popularised the cigarette and flaunted the taboo which did not allow smoking in public places.[24]

He married twice. The first wife, Annie, was created Countess of Cromartie in her own right, and is the ancestress of the present

Earl of Cromartie. She was not an easy woman to live with. Lady Barker found her religious fervour and intense toadyism "horribly disgusting",[25] and her daughter-in-law recalled that she lived in two rooms of Stafford House, lying on a sofa under a red silk eiderdown, and surrounded by Minah birds and parrots, "which perched all over the room and on the head of the old retriever".[26] She dined alone every day, always on chicken. She was an angel compared with her successor.

Duchess Annie died in November 1888. The last ten years had not been happy. She viewed with apprehension the appearance of a Mrs Blair, who was spending far too much time in the Duke's company, and seemed to have gained control over his every intention. She feared that the Duke might marry Mrs Blair after her death, and intimated as much to her son, Lord Stafford. None of the family could stand Mrs Blair, a vulgar, malicious woman, with cunning bristling at her finger-tips. They could not have known that she would be their stepmother so soon.

The Duke married Mrs Blair in Florida only three months after Annie's death. Society turned its well-trained back. In the first place the "liaison" had been the subject of gossip for years, which was crime enough, and in the second they should have waited the customary twelve months before insulting the dead woman's memory. There was worse to come.

Duchess Annie had left her wardrobe to her daughter Lady Alexandra, with specific instructions that she and she only was to have the keys to boxes containing her clothes. Within two hours of the new Duchess's arrival at Stafford House on the Mall, she had taken charge of her predecessor's wardrobe, and thereafter went around in her clothes and underwear. She contrived to get her stepson Lord Stafford and his wife Millie out of Lilleshall, Staffordshire, where they were living, and to confiscate all their furniture. The Duke set in motion legal actions to disentail some of the Sutherland estate to be given to his new wife. With these and other schemes afoot, an impassable breach opened between the Duke on one side, and his son and daughter on the other. Lord Stafford refused to shake his step-mother's hand, Lady Alexandra refused to be under the same roof with her. The Duke could not be made to see that this "female" was a wicked woman.

Duchess Blair's intention was to be accepted by society; this could not happen so long as she was not accepted by her husband's family. Her other intention was grim and black – she set about gaining possession of all the Sutherland property for herself in the long term, at the expense of the rightful heirs, and in the short term, to lay her hands on as much of his money as she could. The second was the easier task. She persuaded the Duke that his son had too great an allowance; he obediently reduced it, and the son was forced to live elsewhere as a result. The difference was pocketed by herself. She then persuaded him that his servants were robbing him, that his household expenses were too high, and that she could save on them if he would let her. She said the expenses amounted to £18,000 a year, and she could run the households more efficiently on that herself. (In fact, the expenses were only £14,000 a year.) He gave her the money, she dismissed the servants, employed new ones of her own choosing, and ran the households personally, for about £10,000 a year. The other £8,000 went into her private bank account, without her husband's knowledge.

The long-term aims were more difficult. It was essential to Duchess Blair's plan that the Duke and his children should be estranged. She set about poisoning his mind against them, so that he would gradually agree to disinheriting them and giving her everything instead. She destroyed some of their letters, interpreted others in her own way. The result was that by the beginning of 1892, the Duke, entirely in her control, was his own son's mortal enemy, threatening to injure him as much as was in his power (and that was very much indeed). Lady Alexandra had meanwhile died from the strain of it all, while the Duke and his son squabbled as to who should pay her doctor's bills.

She went so far as to publish a pamphlet giving her jaundiced version of events over the previous two years, which her stepson was bound to answer. There is a copy with his pencilled comments in the margin, "infernal lie", "this is actionable" and so on. The Duke then decided to amend his will in his wife's favour. The letter of instruction to the solicitors was written in her hand, and the draft of the new will was also in her hand. It gave her all his personal estate, every item in the great houses of Trentham, Lilleshall, Tittensor, Stafford House and Dunrobin Castle, apart from the heirlooms which he could not leave away from his son, plus the exclusive right to use family jewels in her lifetime. He was about to disentail Lilleshall and leave that to her as well, but he died before he could put it into effect.[27]

The Duke's death in 1892 was followed by two years' litigation.* Mrs Blair, now Dowager Duchess, attempted to gain possession of one of the houses, with her two brothers, and said she would force entry; extra caretakers were employed to prevent her doing so. The

* The 12th Duke of Somerset had made a similar will just seven years before, but his successors did not contest it. See Chapter 1.

new Duke resisted the will on the grounds of her undue influence and fraud, claiming that she had instilled into the mind of his father an unreasonable hostility towards his children. She, in the presence of her solicitors, snatched a bundle of her late husband's papers and threw them into the fire. For this she was fined £250 and imprisoned in Holloway for six weeks.[28] She married again and lived until 1912.

"Strath", the 4th Duke of Sutherland (1851–1913), once a Liberal M.P., was a notorious gambler and member of the "fast set" which included the Duchess of Manchester. His wife Millicent Fanny, a woman of pellucid beauty, was contemporary with Lady London- derry and the Duchess of Atholl, the three of them riding bicycles down the Mall daily and often being chased by the police for it. Nevertheless, she was one of the most assiduous social workers of her day.

The 5th Duke (1888–1963) was the last of that line, for though married twice he had no children. He deserves mention for having proposed legislation to introduce Life Peers to the House of Lords, a measure adopted thirty-three years later. He off-loaded a considerable amount of his property after World War I, selling the Lilleshall estate and 144 square miles of Sutherland in 1919, and buying instead the "smaller" residence of Sutton Place. (This is now the home of J. Paul Getty.) His autobiography *Looking Back* serves no good to his memory, for it is the unwilling confession of a man whose greatest joy in life was the killing of wild animals. Of course, he was not alone in this, but there are few such self-satisfied chronicles of idle slaughter. The Duke admits that he shot his first stag when he was ten years old, and that he has shot well over a thousand altogether. His Grace enjoyed visiting his estate at Lilleshall, because "what I enjoyed best . . . were the pheasant shoots when, with seven to nine guns, we would bring down anything from 800 to 1000 birds in the day". He found the shooting of elephants, from a safe distance, "exciting", and boasts that he "got a bison and several tigers". A man in his shooting party, Montague Guest, fell dead during the shoot. The Duke's comment was, "Personally, I can imagine no pleasanter way to die."[29]

As it happened, he died without a gun in his hand. The succession to his titles was split between two families, and the dukedom was separated from the earldom of Sutherland for the first time in 124 years. The earldom, being able to pass through the female line, went to his niece Mrs Janson, who is now the 24th Countess of Sutherland, with Dunrobin Castle as her seat, a smaller house in Sutherland as her home, and a house in Edwardes Square, London. She has twin sons, one of whom is heir to the earldom and bears the name of Baron Strathnaver, a spurious title which has never been a peerage dignity and was never created by patent. It is merely a territorial style, not available to the heir apparent as a courtesy title. He is also Master of Sutherland, a peculiarly Scottish title which is born by legal right by the heir apparent or presumptive to a Scottish peerage title.[30] Thus the heir to the Duke of Argyll is Master of Campbell (though generally known as Marquess of Lorne), and the heir to Lord Lovat is Master of Lovat, and is known as such. Lord Strathnaver would have far more right to call himself Master of Sutherland, for this is not a courtesy title at all, but a peerage dignity vested in him. However, long usage has established the custom of the heir being referred to as Lord Strathnaver, and it offends no one. Lord Strathnaver, who has been a police constable, married twice. By his second wife he has a son and heir, Alexander.

So where does the new Duke of Sutherland come from? He was born the Hon. John Egerton, son of the Earl of Ellesmere. In 1939 he married Lady Diana Percy, daughter of the Duke of Northumberland (and sister to the present Duke), just before going to war, where he was captured and imprisoned by the enemy. In 1944 he succeeded to his father's title as Earl of Ellesmere, and in 1963 became Duke of Sutherland on the death of his distant relation. It is curious that the dukedom was created for the benefit of the Leveson-Gowers, yet the name of Leveson-Gower has now disappeared from the title. The present Duke, who has no children, has an heir presumptive, Cyril Egerton, born in 1905, who has a son. So the name of Egerton seems assured in the Sutherland descent. This is because the Duke is descended from the 1st Duke's *second* son, Lord Francis Leveson-Gower (1800–1857), who was created Earl of Ellesmere and assumed the surname Egerton to fulfil a condition which enabled him to inherit in 1845 the estates of his bachelor uncle the last Duke of Bridgwater (whose name *was* Egerton). Old Bridgwater would be delighted if he could know that his surname has survived at the expense of the Leveson-Gowers.

The Duke has a house in Roxburghshire, purchased by his father in 1912 and a house in Suffolk. The line of which he is representative has much more agreeable characteristics than that of the first five Dukes of Sutherland. His ancestor, Lord Francis, in no way resembled his insensitive father. Nothing but praise for his gentleness, his erudition, his charm, informs opinions of contemporaries. He was a member of the Roxburghe Club and himself wrote twenty-six books. He had no enemies, was always more considerate of others than of himself, pursued truth and virtue all his life. He was a perfect example of how to live. Even Creevey laid aside his acid quill to admit, "greater civility I defy anyone to receive than I have done from him".[31] And Greville, to whom he was related, penned the most splendid tribute. On inheriting the Bridgwater estate, he "found himself the possessor of vast wealth, and surrounded by a population sunk in ignorance and vice". He then spent the remainder of his life devoted to the welfare of the people in his charge. "He employed his wealth liberally in promoting the material comfort and raising the moral condition of those by whose labour that wealth was produced." He built churches, schools, libraries. He became "the object of general veneration and attachment". But, says Greville, only his family had the luck to know the excellence and charm of his character. "He regarded with indifference the ordinary objects of wordly ambition. He lived in and for his family, and he was their joy, their delight, and their pride."[32]

A final curiosity. Lord Francis Leveson-Gower may well not have been the son of the 1st Duke of Sutherland at all, which would explain why he resembled him so little. It was widely believed that his father was Lord Carlisle. His "official" father had anyway been advised by doctors to abstain from intercourse with his wife in the year that she became pregnant. If this is true, then the present Duke's connection with the ducal line is not by blood, but by adoption.

REFERENCES

1. Eric Richards, *The Leviathan of Wealth*, p. 4.
2. Duke of Sutherland, *Looking Back*, p. 20.
3. *ibid.*, p. 21; D.N.B.
4. Greville, II, 404.
5. John Prebble, *The Highland Clearances*, p. 63.
6. Creevey *Papers*, Vol. I, p. 216.
7. Prebble, *op. cit.*, p. 62.
8. Lord Granville Leveson-Gower, *Private Correspondence*, Vol. I, p. 118.
9. Prebble, 60.
10. P. Gaskell, *Morvern Transformed*, p. 9.
11. Prebble, 67–79, 85–91, 107, 111, 113, 118.
12. Richards, *op. cit.*, p. 284.
13. *ibid.*, 193.

14. *ibid.*, 168.
15. Professor Checkland, Foreword to Richards, *op. cit.*
16. F. F. Darling, *West Highland Survey*, p. 6.
17. *People's Paper*, 12 March 1853.
18. Greville, II, 404.
19. Creevey, *Life and Times*, p. 366.
20. *Lady Holland to Her Son*, p. 182.
21. Greville, V, 227.
22. Lord Ronald Gower, Vol. I, p. 317.
23. *ibid.*, I, 324.
24. *Leaves from the Notebooks* of Lady Dorothy Nevill, p. 127.
25. Augustus Hare, *In My Solitary Life*, p. 80.
26. Sutherland, *Looking Back*, p. 38.
27. Londonderry Papers, D/Lo/F 631
28. *Complete Peerage.*
29. Sutherland, *Looking Back*, pp. 55–6, 64.
30. Valentine Heywood, *British Titles*, pp. 103–5.
31. Creevey, *Life and Times*, p. 283.
32. Greville, VII, 271–2.

12. Contrasts in Fortune

Duke of Rutland; Duke of Newcastle; Duke of Fife

The three Dukes of this chapter are not connected in any way. One was a Whig who eluded fame, another a Tory who chased it, and the third an unknown Scot who had fame thrust upon him when he married into the Royal Family. They are united only by the hand of irony. For the descendants of the reluctant Duke of Rutland have gone from strength to strength, those of the eager Duke of Newcastle have suffered one catastrophe after another, and those of the Duke of Fife have withdrawn once more into the shadows.

*   *   *

When William III died in 1702, in his pocket was found a letter from Rachel Lady Russell, begging the King "in the most submissive manner imaginable" to make the Earl of Rutland a duke. What, one might ask, was it to do with Lady Russell? Further down in the letter, which is now at Chatsworth, she reveals her interest and at the same time her silken subtle blackmail. "Be pleased to allow me to answer for all those I am related to", she says, "they will look on themselves equally honoured with Lord Rutland by your favour to his family."[1]

And there you have it. Rachel was the widow of William Russell, martyred for his part in the Rye House Plot, and now a posthumous national hero under King William. Parliament and people were willing to do anything to please her. As compensation for her loss, Rachel already had two dukes in the family – her son was Duke of Bedford, and her son-in-law was Duke of Devonshire, both created in 1694. She had one other daughter, who had married Lord Roos, later, Earl of Rutland. Rachel wanted duchesses for daughters, a countess was not good enough. She pressed the case in spite of Rutland himself, who was really not very interested in being a duke and did nothing to promote his advancement. He was even a little embarrassed by it all.

The King died with the letter in his pocket, and Lady Russell took up the matter with his successor, Queen Anne, immediately. She persuaded her daughter to write to Rutland imploring him to accept the title when it was offered. Queen Anne prevaricated. She was well disposed towards Rutland, who had sheltered her at Belvoir Castle when her father, James II, was overthrown, but did not want to create jealousies among her peers. She was, she said, "determined not to create or promote any one single person, there are so many that ask, and whoever is refused may be angry". Lady Russell would not let the matter rest. "I shall continue to be as watchful as I can", she wrote to Rutland, "that we miss not what we think we have a certain assurance of. Courts are slippery places."[2]

Rachel eventually extracted from the Queen a promise that she would make good the late King's intention, but only after she had made John Churchill Duke of Marlborough. Rachel grudgingly conceded that this would be proper. Accordingly John Manners, Lord Roos's father, was created Duke of Rutland and Marquess of Granby on 29th March 1703, three months after Marlborough. The girl for whom all this was done, Catherine Russell, Lady Roos, died too soon to enjoy it. She was Duchess of Rutland for less than a year, dying in childbirth at her ninth pregnancy in 1711, when her husband had been Duke for nine months.

The Manners family took to their new distinction easily and without fuss. They had already been considerable landowners for over 600 years and were nicely settled in their grand style of country living. Their very name may testify to their significance. "Manners" could derive from Mesnières, the town near Rouen where the family lived before the Conquest, or it could be from Medieval Latin *manerium*, meaning "manor-house". The first to be mentioned in history is Robert de Maneriis in the eleventh century. Their two seats today are Belvoir Castle (pronounced "Beaver"), and romantic Haddon Hall in Derbyshire, next door to Chatsworth.

Belvoir Castle has belonged to the Manners since 1508, coming into the family by the customary route of marriage (it had previously been the home of the Barons de Ros). The other house, Haddon Hall, is, in the words of Nicholas Pevsner, "the English castle *par excellence*, not the forbidding fortress on an unassailable crag, but the large, rambling, safe, grey lovable home of knights and their ladies, the unreasonable dream-castle of those who think of the Middle Ages as a time of chivalry and valour and noble feelings".[3]

Haddon Hall came to the Manners through a romantic elopement, the archetypical tale of chivalry. John Manners, second son of the 1st Earl of Rutland, fell in love with one of the daughters at Haddon Hall – the beautiful auburn-haired Dorothy Vernon. Dorothy lived there with father, Sir George Vernon, stepmother, and sister. Sir George did not approve of young Manners, and forbade his daughter to entertain him. But such was the strength of their love that John Manners disguised himself as a forester and came to Haddon Hall to see Dorothy undetected. These clandestine interviews went on for a while, until Sir George got wind of them, and locked his daughter up. Father, stepmother and sister kept her virtually prisoner at Haddon. But they did not reckon on John's determination. The night that Dorothy's sister was married, while all and sundry were distracted by the festivities in the ballroom, Dorothy slipped out, through a door which still exists, down the steps that are still there, on to the bridge, where she found her shining white knight who whisked her off on galloping steed into the balmy night. They galloped all night long until they reached Aylston, in Leicestershire, where they were married. It is the best of all elopement stories, and the name of Dorothy Vernon justly reverberates through the centuries. Sir George died and John and Dorothy eventually returned to Haddon Hall, where it may be supposed they lived happily ever after. The love story is important, because their grandson became 8th Earl of Rutland, and his descendants continue in direct line to the present Duke of Rutland.[4]

The earldom was created in 1525, conferred by Henry VIII upon Thomas Manners (c. 1492–1543). Thomas was thus rewarded for his loyalty to the King, a loyalty which had taken Henry's side in the divorce question. He had pleaded with Pope Clement VII to accede to Henry's wishes,[5] and when his embassy was unsuccessful, had been one of the judges at the trial of Anne Boleyn. Thomas, who was also descended through the female line from a sister of Edward IV, was showered with lands at the dissolution of the monasteries by a grateful Henry.

Since then, the family has shown an abundant lack of ambition. They have remained in the country, minding their own business, and looking after their dependants in the best traditions of landowners' responsibility. Writing about the 5th Duke of Rutland (1778–1857), Greville calls him selfish, in the sense of self-indulgent, but acknowledges that his patrician approach is more beneficial than is often realised. "The Duke of Rutland is as selfish a man as any of his class, that is, he never does what he does not like, and spends his whole life in a round of such pleasures as suit his taste, but he is neither a foolish nor a bad man, and partly from a sense of duty, partly from inclination, he devotes time and labour to the interest and welfare of the people who live and labour on his estate." Greville points out that he attended all the meetings of the residents, invited anyone who had a complaint to see him privately, and was more a friend than "political quacks and adventurers who flatter and cajole them".[6] His second son, Lord John Manners, who was later 7th Duke of Rutland (1818–1906), founded a political group devoted to raising the condition of the people, called "Young England". Manners and Smythe and a few Cambridge friends were responsible for the movement. They were disciples of Disraeli, and they were Tories. They wanted to reconstruct Toryism on a popular basis, and thought the working classes could be trusted to follow them. They wanted the advancement of the people, but under the leadership of the aristocracy, who would have the experience necessary to construct sensible policies. Manners advocated public holidays and factory reform. The common enemy, in his view, of the aristocracy and the working classes was middle-class liberalism. Disraeli drew a portrait of the Duke when he was Lord John Manners in his novel *Coningsby*; the Duke is "Lord Henry Sydney", and of him Disraeli writes, "he devoted his time and thought, labour and life, to one vast and noble purpose, the elevation of the condition of the great body of the people".[7] The "Young England" group lasted only a few years.

Another example is afforded by the 4th Duke of Rutland (1754–1787) who spoke out against the punitive taxation imposed on the American colonies, his ally in this being once again the Duke of Richmond. He said that the taxation was "commenced in iniquity, is pursued with resentment, and can terminate in nothing but blood". He proposed a motion in the House of Lords "to cause the most speedy and effectual measures to be taken for restoring peace in America", which was defeated by 243 votes to 86. This duke's father was the famous Marquess of Granby, the General (1721–1770), son of the 3rd Duke who outlived him. Granby, though he waged war, wanted peace and, though an aristocrat, was loved by his soldiers. There are few examples in our history of a more popular soldier, a fact illustrated by the number of pubs and inns up and down the country which bear his name. Only the Duke of Wellington has more public houses named after him.

Granby was Colonel of the Leicester Blues, and Commander-in-Chief in Europe. The Battle of Minden is justly associated with his courage and wisdom. He married a daughter of the Proud Duke of Somerset, and was painted by Reynolds no less than twelve times.

He was a blazing hero, whose career should have ended in glory. Unwarranted attacks by the satirist Junius, who wanted to break the government of the Duke of Grafton and used Granby as a lever, spoilt the last years of his life. He still excited admiration everywhere, was revered by King and commoner alike; "George II respected and loved him; George III respected and feared him."[8] Politically motivated malice could not harm his reputation for long. When he died of stomach gout at the age of forty-nine, the whole country mourned. Wraxall wrote: "The celebrated Marquess of Granby, notwithstanding the attack made on him by Junius, and the greater misfortune that he underwent of being defended by Sir William Draper, left behind him a name dear to Englishmen."[9] William Pitt simply said, "The loss to England is, indeed, irreparable."[10]

Granby's son, the 4th Duke of Rutland, died even younger at the age of thirty-three. In his case, it was disease of the liver which carried him off, brought about by a gargantuan appetite. He began each day with a breakfast of six or seven turkey's eggs,[11] washed down all day long with port. He was not the only one, of course; the Georgian period was drowned in port, which explains why so many characters in this book died of gout. Drunkenness was so common that debates in the Houses of Parliament were frequently unintelligible because the assembled representatives of the people were too inebriated to know what they were saying. Old Jockey of Norfolk (the 11th Duke of Norfolk) was alive at this time, and the most celebrated drunk in England. Rutland certainly killed himself by gross overindulgence. He was "a victim of his irregularities", as a contemporary tactfully put it.[12] After death, his body was opened, and "his liver appeared so much decayed and wasted, as to render his recovery impossible". There is a touching story that he asked to see his wife shortly before he died, and, realising that she was then too far away, said, "In point of time, it will be impossible, I must therefore be content to die, with her image before my mind's eye."[13]

His wife was Lady Mary Somerset, a daughter of the 4th Duke of Beaufort. She was one of the celebrated beauties of the age, rivalling her contemporary Georgiana, Duchess of Devonshire. She was the very essence of femininity, magnetising the gaze of all who saw her. "Grace itself formed her limbs, and accompanied her movements . . . the Plantagenets could not have been represented by a more faultless sample of female loveliness."[14] The writer informs us that he is neither partial nor exaggerating in his description. But she fell far short of the formidable Georgiana in personality. While Georgiana seduced everyone with the sparkle of her conversation, the Duchess of Rutland was rather dull. She was to be seen and not heard. The Duke consoled himself by taking more lively mistresses, the most regular of which was a Mrs Billington. According to a saucy article among the *tête-à-tête* series, his grandfather the 3rd Duke (1696–1779) had been practically insatiable. "We shall not attempt", it says, "to enumerate all the grizettes Cornuto [the Duke] has successively enjoyed within these eight months, as the catalogue would swell this article far beyond its usual extent."[15]

Two more duchesses of Rutland have made their mark. The wife of the 5th Duke had a well-known affair with H.R.H. the Duke of York (uncle to Queen Victoria), and, more recently, the wife of the 8th Duke was an artist of no small distinction. This was Violet, Duchess of Rutland, *née* Violet Lindsay, mother of Lady Diana Cooper (born 1892). She began marriage as Mrs Manners, as her husband was then Mr Henry Manners, son of Lord John Manners; Lord John then became 7th Duke, and Mr Henry eventually 8th Duke of Rutland. Duchess Violet's work was pre-Raphaelite in style inspired particularly by Burne-Jones. Her portraits in pencil and water-colour show an extremely delicate and sensitive touch. If she was not taken as seriously as she deserved, she had her rank to blame which acted as a disavantage to her. But foreigners, not saddled with the tangle of confused emotions and prejudices which the English class-system breeds, have never doubted her worth as an artist. Her work hangs in the Louvre in Paris. Her most accomplished piece is not a drawing, but a sculpture, inspired by poetry and personal tragedy. It is a statue of her eldest son, who died at the age of nine in 1894, and it can now be seen at Haddon Hall.

Quite apart from her work as an artist, she was a considerable figure in Edwardian England, and into the 1920s and 1930s. She had limitless energy, and astonishing beauty. While she reigned at Belvoir, the castle, unknown to most of England, became famous. She was one of "The Souls", an intellectual group at the turn of the century which prided itself on unconventional behaviour and discussion long before the Bloomsbury set of Virginia Woolf and Lytton Strachey began to shock polite society. "The Souls", so called because that was one of their perennial subjects of conversation, were revolutionary in so far as they talked about matters which were supposed to be taboo for nice well-bred ladies. They were led by the Tennant sisters from Scotland, who had no time for such nonsense, and who virtually changed the tone of London society within a few years. One of them, Margot, married Prime Minister Asquith. Another Soul was the last of the great rakes, Harry Cust (of Lord

Brownlow's family), who appears to have gone to bed with every beautiful woman in London. One of his *amours* was Violet, Duchess of Rutland. She died in 1937, leaving "many devoted descendants".[16]

Her husband, the 8th Duke (1852–1925), was Principal Private Secretary to the Prime Minister Lord Salisbury, and was known by the sobriquet "Salisbury's Manners", a nice *double entendre*.

Belvoir Castle, with its terraces and towers, its boundless prospect, and its exterior "so grand as to sink criticism in admiration",[17] is heavy with historical associations, and knew its days of glitter and fame long before Duchess Violet made its name well-known in this century. James I was entertained there six times by Francis, 6th Earl of Rutland (1578–1632), whose daughter Catherine Manners married the King's lover George Villiers, Duke of Buckingham, in 1620. During the Civil War, Belvoir was first taken by the Royalists, then stormed by the Parliamentary party, who afterwards dismantled it brick by brick. The reigning Earl rebuilt it after the Restoration, completing the work in 1668. In the time of the 4th Duke, the chaplain of Belvoir was the poet George Crabbe. Then, in 1816, a second catastrophe befell the castle – a fire which caused £120,000 worth of damage. Over 200 paintings were lost that day, including twenty portraits by Reynolds, some Rubens, some Van Dycks. It was quickly rebuilt, and the old medieval ways re-established. Until comparatively recent times, into the twentieth century, the style of living at Belvoir was romantically archaic, with trumpeters in bright livery and powered wigs marching up and down the corridors and sounding a great blast when it was time for guests to get up; the watchman, who throughout the night shouted the time at each hour; the ballroom always ready for dancing; a private orchestra playing soft music in a room adjoining the dining-room – background noise from musicians who were never seen.[18]

Haddon Hall has had a quieter history. The last Duke to live there was the 3rd, in the eighteenth century, and he only sporadically. In 1700, more or less, it ceased to be inhabited, and remained so for more than 200 years. Until, that is, the 9th Duke of Rutland (1886–1940) achieved his childhood ambition and took up residence there in 1927, two years after he came to the title. This duke was a very learned man, a Fellow of the Society of Antiquaries, and a considerable historian, who cherished the Manners family archives when so many other great families were throwing them into an attic room (or the "muniment" room) and forgetting them. In 1939, the Duke offered Belvoir and Haddon as a wartime refuge for many of the Public

Records which, if they remained in Chancery Lane, stood risk of destruction by bombing. (Actually the Public Record Office suffered only superficial damage.) The offer was gladly accepted, and the Duke was made an (unpaid) Assistant Keeper in order that he could legally have custody of the records. He became quite an expert at making seals. He married a daughter of Frank Tennant, one of his mother's "Souls", and died in 1940. His son the present Duke continued his father's custodianship of the Public Records until the end of the war.

Though Belvoir and Haddon still belong to the Duke, much of the estates of both have been sold in this century to meet the costs of taxation. After World War I it has been estimated that a quarter of England changed hands as the great landowners off-loaded thousands of acres. Rutland was no exception. Some 14,000 acres of Haddon were sold in 1920 for £355,458, and another sale of 28,000 acres of Belvoir followed shortly afterwards for £1½ million. There are 18,000 acres left, managed by the present Duke, who also has business interests in the Midlands; the Rutland Development Company is concerned with hotels.

They are a pious family. One of them, Charles Manners-Sutton (1755–1828), who was a grandson of the 3rd Duke of Rutland, became Archibishop of Canterbury and baptised Queen Victoria. A number of the Manners have tried their hand at poetry, but usually with less happy results. The only one to achieve a measure of decency in the literary field was Lord John Manners (7th Duke of Rutland), Disraeli's friend and the "Young England" enthusiast, later to be Postmaster-General; he published several volumes of poetry. On the other hand, it has been seriously suggested that Roger Manners, 5th Earl of Rutland (1576–1612) was William Shakespeare. There is a heavy nineteenth-century German thesis, by one Carl E. Bleibtreu, which seeks to prove this identity.[19] Other foreign academics held the same conviction, though it has never been entertained in this country. Were it true, then *Venus and Adonis* was written while its author was barely fifteen years old, and half a dozen of his plays before he was twenty.

This same earl was involved in the Essex plot against Elizabeth I, and was imprisoned in the Tower with his brothers in 1600. His lands were restored by James I in 1603, so his disgrace did not last long.

One curious feature of the Rutland story is the number of early deaths they have suffered. Of course, familes were decimated by plague and epidemics in Elizabethan times, and the state of medical knowledge was so rudimentary that no one could reasonably expect to live long. But the Rutlands were exceptionally prone to short lives. The 2nd Earl was thirty-seven when he died, the 3rd Earl was thirty-eight: the 4th Earl died at thirty-six and the 5th Earl at thirty-five. (His wife, a daughter of Sir Philip Sidney, was so distraught that she died a few weeks later, using pills provided by Sir Walter Raleigh.)[20] The 6th Earl lived to fifty-four, but his sons died in infancy (about which more later). The 2nd Duke of Rutland was forty-five when he died, and the soldier Marquess of Granby forty-nine. His son the 4th Duke was only thirty-three. Catherine, daughter of the 2nd Duke, lost both her sons by an epidemic sore throat, then miscarried of twins. "It looks as if it was a plague fixed on the walls of their house", wrote Walpole.

The rest lived to a decent old age, it is true, but there have been tragedies in more recent times. The son and heir of the 8th Duke of Rutland and Violet died at the age of nine, in 1894, and the present Duke's second son, Lord Robert Manners, died of leukaemia at the age of two in 1964.

It would be natural to assign all this to coincidence, or even to point out that there are marginally more Manners who lived long than died young. This would be to ignore an interesting circumstance. In 1620 two servant-girls were executed at Lincoln for witchcraft; they had placed a curse on the Manners heirs.

The bald facts of the case are these: the 6th Earl and Countess of Rutland took pity upon a very poor foul-mouthed woman called Joan Flower. Gossips said she was a witch, because her eyes were "fiery and hollow, her speech fell and envious, her demeanour strange and exotic". She was heard to curse and swear on the slightest pretext. The Rutlands, decent folk, took no notice of such rumours, and employed Joan's two daughters at Belvoir Castle. They were Margaret and Philippa Flower. They were first engaged as occasional charwomen, and Margaret was later promoted as a permanent servant, in the wash-house.

The gossips got to work again when the other daughter, Philippa, took a local boy, Thomas Simpson, for her lover. He claimed that he was so besotted with her that he could not leave her, even when he wanted to. A common enough feeling, one would have thought, but Philippa was said to have bewitched him. She was "lewdly transported with the love of one Thomas Simpson".

Certain other indecencies, not specified, were imputed to Margaret Flower, upon which the Countess sacked her. Mother Joan was so furious that she placed a curse upon the whole Manners family. The Earl and Countess forthwith fell violently ill, vomiting abominably.

Their two sons, Henry and Francis, were also attacked, and succumbed. They died mere infants, depriving their bereaved parents of
a direct heir (the earldom passed to a brother).

The Flower girls were arrested and tried at Lincoln. The accusation was that they were the instruments of their mother's sorcery, and
that the devil worked through them. Joan made a melodramatic
gesture at the trial, which sealed her fate. She took some bread and
some butter, and declaimed "If I am guilty of witchcraft, may this
bread and butter never go through me." She ate it, and died immediately in terrible agony, confirming to the assembled judges that she
was indeed the devil's mistress. Her daughters then confessed, were
convicted of murder, and executed.[21]

At Bottesford Church there is a monument to the dead children,
erected by their father the Earl, on which is written the fact that they
died of sorcery. There was, then, in 1620 no doubt about the matter.
With hindsight and better knowledge, we can see how the mistake
could be made in an hysterical age, when the distinction between
religion and superstition was not understood, least of all by the
Church, and when incomprehensible disasters, like plagues, needed to
be answered for. The truth is quite likely that the girls were guilty
of murder, but that their powers were merely human. They probably
poisoned the children, goaded by the malicious revenge of their
unpopular mother, and attempted the same on the parents, whose
constitutions were better able to tolerate the attack. Also, they were
undoubted whores. It is possible that they were convinced themselves
that they must be witches to be capable of such evil intent. Still, the
case is on record for what it is worth. And it must not go unsaid
that many of the earls who died young existed up to a century before
Joan Flower uttered her supposed curse.

The Manners family have continued their little kingdom based on
benevolent paternalism for centuries, without looking over their
shoulder at any imprecations from witches. They have not made any
cymbals crash, they have not been Prime Ministers, but they have
one great soldier and one Postmaster-General. More than this, they
can comfortably congratulate themselves on having been decent men
who disarm enemies. Even Walpole, who was not really happy unless
he could bring the great down to a level where they could be
scrutinised to their detriment, could not be unkind to the 3rd Duke,
"a nobleman of great worth and goodness", he said.[22] The same was
true of the 4th, 5th and 6th Dukes. The 7th Duke (Lord John
Manners) was lamented even by Queen Victoria, who said she would
miss him very much;[23] he was, says the biographer of Disraeli, "of a

loyalty, purity, and kindness of nature, that amounted almost to genius".[24]

The 10th Duke of Rutland, C.B.E., was born in 1919. He was chairman of Leicester County Council 1974–77. He has been married twice. The first wife was a model, Anne Cumming-Bell, and the present Duchess is Frances Sweeney, daughter of Mr Sweeney, an American businessman, and Margaret Whigham (formerly Duchess of Argyll). The heir, Marquess of Granby, was born in 1959, and the Duchess Dowager lives in a small house on the Belvoir estate.

*   *   *   *

The dukes of Newcastle might have been invented as a sharp contrast to the dukes of Rutland, for their qualities could not be less alike. The Newcastle character has throughout been fickle, feckless, restless and irresolute, and in consequence their fortunes have been unstable. When the 6th Duke married Henrietta Adela Hope in the nineteenth century the foundations of the Newcastle estate were already showing cracks. He had been before the bankruptcy courts in 1870. Hence Miss Hope, though illegitimate and a *nouveau riche* (with the Hope Diamond in her pocket), and not therefore the most suitable duchess material, was welcomed as a salvation. "Lord Lincoln is to marry Miss Hope," wrote a contemporary (Lincoln is the courtesy title), "the daughter of ugly little Henry Hope with the big house in Piccadilly. She is illegitimate, but pretty. Her mother is a Frenchwoman. She will have all Hope's fortune, £50,000 a year. It is a great thing for the dukedom of Newcastle and will put it on its legs again."[25] Alas, not for long. The Hope collection of pictures, which included one of the most famous Vermeers in the world, plus thirty tons of sculpture and nine tons of books, were all disposed of by auction in various sales before 1917. The notorious 44½-carat blue diamond was sold for £120,000. All that remains of the Hope connection is its addition to Pelham and Clinton in the family surname. The Hope diamond was said to bring bad luck to whomever owned it.

It is not just bad luck. The Newcastles have suffered from an inability to make a decision and stick to it. Sometimes the results have been serious. The 5th Duke (1811–1864) was in charge of the War Office at the time of the Crimean campaign. Such a man in such a place at such a time could hardly have been more inopportune. He stayed up all night trying to grapple with the problem, and reached no conclusions at all. He lacked the resource necessary to deal with an emergency. He was slow, vacillating, and knew nothing of military affairs. He insisted on doing everything himself, caused himself much anxiety of mind by dwelling upon the Crimean catastrophe over which he presided, and died at fifty-three, a broken man. "I hear Newcastle is very low," wrote Greville, "as well he may be, for no man was ever placed in so painful a position, and it is one from which it is impossible for him to extricate himself."[26]

His achievement was to establish military bases for the protection of trade.

The 1st Duke of Newcastle of the present creation, Thomas Pelham-Holles (1693–1768), was in an even more exalted position, for he was Prime Minister for the best part of seven years from 1754 to 1762. (His younger and more famous brother, Henry Pelham, preceded him as Prime Minister.) The country has probably never had, before or since, a more universally ridiculed leader than Newcastle. He was a total buffoon. Hopelessly disorganised, and deeply ignorant, he seriously thought Hanover was north of England. He fussed and bothered and bustled and rushed and appeared all the time ever so important and busy, but his absurd posturings brought him laughter, not prestige. Hervey makes all kinds of disparaging remarks about him. The Duke is "light-headed", "a fidget, a fright and a bustle", he talks without thinking, and he has "limb-fever".[27] "Wealth, titles and power and honours can no more give sense to the Duke of Newcastle, than paint, patches and brocade can give beauty to the Duchess of Rutland."[28] Walpole said that it made him smile to watch Newcastle "frisking while his grave is digging".[29]

Nobody took him seriously. He was quite devoid of tact, insulting people through innocent foolishness and being deeply hurt and worried if ever he found out that he had done so (people made sure he did), for he wanted more than anything to get on well with everyone, and for everyone to think him a splendid fellow. Naturally, they did not; they thought him obsequious and silly.

Newcastle concluded that there was a conspiracy against him, which made him anxious, fretful, and finally jealous. "He personalised any political or family disagreement as a lack of love for him or lack of understanding of his predicament of the moment."[30] His vanity was injured; he had tried so hard to please, and his failure he ascribed to the faithlessness of those around him. Thereupon, he became distrustful and suspicious to the point of paranoia. He harboured grudges. He would burst into tears on the smallest pretext. "His nature and mind were warped, twisted and stunted, and his life must have been an agony, though perhaps he himself did not clearly realise how much he suffered. He was haunted by fears; every small incident was the portent of terrible things to come; every molehill a volcano. With an abundant substratum of intelligence and common sense, he looked a fool, and with an inexhaustible fund of warm human kindness and sincere goodwill, he acquired a reputation for dishonesty. . . . If he was vain, this was merely a craving for some compensation for the insults and humiliations, real and imaginary, which he daily suffered and which cut him to the heart.''[31]

Of this humiliation, there is ample evidence in his letters. In one outburst to the Bishop of Salisbury he is hurt "to see me deserted, and abandoned by almost everybody, by my own Family particularly, and my Enemies, by that alone, encouraged and enabled to treat me with the greatest Marks of Indignity and Contempt; when all I expect is Common Decency, and Common Respect".[32]

The best that can be said for the Duke of Newcastle is that his faults were forgivable, and his intentions good. But he was not a statesman. Among dukes, he was the chemical opposite of that solid imperturbable 8th Duke of Devonshire, who refused three times the office of Prime Minister, yet wielded more influence by sitting still than did all the ceaseless scurrying of Newcastle, "at least as much frightened of doing right as of doing wrong".

Newcastle had a habit of throwing his arms about people's necks and smothering them with kisses. He turned up on the Duke of Grafton's sickbed and almost caused him a relapse with his energetic demonstrations of affection.

The 2nd Duke (1720–1794), who was known as Lord Lincoln in his youth, had a very high opinion of his sexual powers, about which he boasted far and wide. He was famous for his bed-hopping. He was encouraged, it is true, by that licentious age to take advantage of his good looks; even the King acknowledged that in his view Lincoln was "the handsomest man in England".[33] The Earl was twenty-one years old when this remark relates, and already a lady-killer. Sir Charles Hanbury Williams addressed him a wickedly explicit Ode:

> "O Lincoln, joy of womankind,
> To you this humble ode's design'd;
>   Let —— inspire my song :
> Gods! with what pow'rs you are endu'd!
> Tiberius was not half so lewd,
>   Nor Hercules so strong."[34]

In 1743 he was appointed Lord of the Bedchamber, and Walpole played a joke on him. At a masquerade ball, he dressed as a Persian, and thus disguised approached Lord Lincoln, producing from his bosom a letter wrapped in Persian silk, saying it was from Kouli Kan. It was addressed to "Henry Clinton Earl of Lincoln, highly favoured among women". Here is a piece of it:

"We have heard prodigious things of thee: they say, thy vigour is nine times beyond that of our prophet; and that thou art more amorous than Solomon the son of David. Yet they tell us, that thou art not above the ordinary stature of the sons of men: are these things so?
. . . Adieu, happy young man! May thy days be as long as thy manhood, and may thy manhood continue more piercing than Zufager, that sword of Hali which had two points, etc." [35]

Lady W. Montagu's messenger-boy, who was barely sixteen years old, said that he was not such a child that he did not know what went on whenever Lord Lincoln paid a call. Her ladyship always instructed the staff to admit no one else, and then called for pen and ink, declaring that she and Lord Lincoln were engaged in writing history.

Lincoln subordinated everything to his amorous pursuits. He had no time for his uncle, the 1st Duke, who foolishly adored him, and in politics he was "as much of a nonentity as a duke can in England be . . . a nullity". [36]

His descendant, the 6th Duke of Newcastle (1834–1879), married on an impulse of the heart. He saw a beautiful girl walking down the street in Nice, followed her for a while, and determined to find out who she was. This was Henrietta Adela Hope, illegitimate daughter of Henry Hope, and she was in time Duchess of Newcastle. After her husband's death she became a Roman Catholic, and went to live in the slums of Whitechapel with two other ladies, devoting herself to social work. Like the "flying Duchess" of Bedford, who liked to show her guests the most "interesting" cases in her cottage hospital at Woburn, the Duchess of Newcastle loved the worst cases of social degradation in the East End. She is buried at St Patrick's Leytonstone.

The 8th Duke (1866–1941) married twice. His first wife was an actress, or more accurately a song-and-dance girl, called Mary Augusta Yohé, an American girl of Dutch extraction. They married at Hampstead Register Office in 1894. The marriage was a disaster, ending in divorce in 1902. The Duke chose for his second wife the daughter of an Australian banker. She was Olive Murial Thompson, and when she died in 1912 he retreated from public view as completely as he could. He had also lost a leg in a shooting accident by this time.

The son of the 8th Duke and Olive Muriel Thompson is the 9th and present Duke of Newcastle, born in 1907. He flew with the R.A.F. in World War II, and has been a squadron leader. He has been married three times. His first wife was Mrs Jean Banks Gimbernat, the adopted daughter of Mr Banks of New York. They were divorced in 1940. The Duke's second wife was Lady Mary Montagu-Stuart-Wortley, daughter of the Earl of Wharncliffe, in 1946. They had two daughters, then separated. Before he could marry his third wife, Sally Ann Wemyss, the Duke was cited in her divorce case amid a torrent of unaccustomed publicity. The episode was called by the Duchess "overpoweringly vulgar".[38] Two years later, the Duke was divorced, and he married the present Duchess in Jamaica in 1959. By that time he had broken every tangible link with England.

- The Duke's second daughter, Lady Kathleen Pelham-Clinton-Hope, in 1970 provided the newspapers with the most picturesque instance of impulsive affection in the history of her family. She met a London Transport Underground train guard at a party one evening, and married him the next day. His name was Edward Reynolds. Three days later they were separated. Lady Kathleen told the newspapers that it had all been a joke, "a gas" to use her own expression.[39]

Curiously, Lady Kathleen's sudden elopement in 1970 is almost exactly paralleled by that of her great-great-aunt Lady Susan Clinton in 1858. Lady Susan did not choose a railway guard, but her impulses were just as raw.

She was the only daughter of the 5th Duke of Newcastle (the Crimean one), and she fell in love with Lord Adolphus Vane, son of the 3rd Marquess of Londonderry. It was a *coup de foudre*. Unfortunately, the Duke withheld his consent. Three times she implored him, and three times he made her refuse Lord Adolphus. The reasons were not rank or money this time: the Londonderrys were wealthy enough. The real cause was sinister: Lord Adolphus was on the brink of madness, although none of the participants in the drama which ensued can bring themselves to say so.

The Duke wrote to Lady Londonderry (with a style fitting for one who had been the only duke ever to be President of the Oxford Union, in 1831),

". . . though I hope you will feel that I may rightly decline to enter into particulars or assign any reason, I must distinctly and positively refuse my consent to the marriage. Moreover I can hold out no hope of any change of my resolution in this respect. . . . I should add that I cannot allow any meeting in future, and therefore my daughter will leave town at once. Of course Lord Adolphus will feel that as a Gentleman he must not think of correspondence.[40]

Lady Londonderry wrote back appealing to the Duke's "kind heart", telling of her son "whose unhappiness I cannot witness without pain and anxiety", of his "intense misery", and of Lady Susan's sincere attachment to him, but failing to mention that he was off his head. The Duke was unmoved. Frustrated by inaction, the young lovers met clandestinely, and Newcastle was roused to write another starchy letter to her ladyship, telling darkly that "his behaviour afterwards was such as, in writing to you, I should not trust myself to characterise". More than this, "he subjected my daughter to an indignity which few girls ever had to submit to from a man aspiring to the position of husband".[41] Whatever could he have done?

Lady Susan was compelled to write a final letter of refusal to Adolphus, hinting that she would like to say more were she at liberty to speak her own mind. A year later, she did speak her own mind. On the day she came of age, 23rd April 1860, she walked out of her father's house, and met Lord Adolphus in Bryanston Square. They were married that day at St Mary's Church.[42]

She was given away by her brother Lord Lincoln (later 6th Duke). Her father was broken-hearted, and would have nothing more to do with her. Lady Londonderry tactfully stayed away from the church, but gave them a wedding breakfast at Londonderry House afterwards. The honeymoon took place in Brighton, where happiness lasted barely a week. Lord Adolphus had one of his attacks, went berserk, and frightened his wife out of her wits. A year later he was arrested for causing a disturbance in Coventry Street, the newspapers were full of his "serious illness", and doctors wrote alarming letters to his brother Lord Vane. Susan, Lady Adolphus as she now was, grew desperate with fear, leading a miserable life for four years during which she lived on opium. Adolphus died of his last attack in 1864. She lived on till 1875.

One of the 5th Duke's sons, Lord Arthur Clinton, made himself noticed by homosexual attachments. The Duke was decidedly unlucky.

He had also to live with the reputation of his extraordinary father the 4th Duke of Newcastle (1785–1851), whose rigid conservatism marked him out as a personality lacking the precious ingredient of equilibrium. His social attitudes and his political opinions were so far beyond the extremities of right-wing Toryism that he fell out with all and sundry. The *Illustrated London News* commented upon his "unbending consistency and determined hostility to the progress of liberal opinions".[43] He refused to vote against the Reform Bill, of which he disapproved; he said that he did not require evidence, that he would have no such Bill, and that he would not meddle with the discussion at all except to oppose it point-blank.[44] On another occasion he was so obdurate against Lord John Russell about the appointment of magistrates in his own county, where he deemed he had sole right to decisions of that nature, that Russell was bound to get the Queen to dismiss him from his post as Lord Lieutenant of Nottinghamshire. Russell wrote bluntly: "Her Majesty has no further occasion for your services", which bewildered the innocent Newcastle so much that he took the letter to the Duke of Wellington. "What shall I do?" he asked. "Do?" said Wellington. "Do nothing."[45]

The most celebrated row he unwittingly provoked was occasioned by his ejecting tenants from his property at Newark, without due regard for their welfare, it was thought. He was attacked by the *Morning Chronicle*, leaving him almost speechless with incomprehension. He summoned his reason to make the historic remark, "Is it not lawful for me to do what I please with my own?" upon which a storm broke about his ears. The crowds attacked him in the street, besieged his residences; one of his homes, Nottingham Castle, was burnt to the ground by a furious mob, at which the Duke had to reinforce his other properties as if in wartime. The Attorney General was on record as saying that the Duke's remark was "scandalous and wicked", whereupon the still ingenuous Duke, unaware that he had said or done anything wrong, took the matter to the House of Lords, and sought their lordships' support. He claimed that he had been abused and baited by the "vulgar multitude" and that the Attorney General had sided with his enemies. The House of Lords did not give him satisfaction. In the first place, they could not, since his personal popularity was not a matter for their consideration. Secondly, they disapproved of his attitude as much as the rest of the country. Thirdly, he added to his troubles by letting slip another opinion which confirmed his isolation. He said that he hoped no Englishman would consent to admit anything so revolting, so debasing to the character of the nation, as vote by ballot.[46] The Lord Chancellor elected to proceed with serious business, and the embattled Duke retired in high dudgeon to nurse his resentments.

Innocence informed the 4th Duke's arrogance, as it had fuelled the 1st Duke's insane comings-and-goings, and the 5th Duke's hopeless dealing with the Crimean tragedy. They have not been a mischievous or evil line; they simply did not know any better. They have been impulsive, impetuous, reaching decisions for emotional reasons and unable to reach them at all for rational ones.

Where have they come from, this erratic family? The most ancient part of their surname is Clinton, which ascends to the days of William the Conqueror. The family was founded by one Renebald de Clinton, who took his surname from the place in which he lived, Glympton in Oxfordshire. He was the ancestor of the Earls of Lincoln, created in 1572, of whom the most illustrious member (the *only* illustrious member) was the 1st Earl (1512–1585). He was Lord High Admiral, and is credited with the rare accomplishment of having served under Henry VIII, Edward VI, Mary Tudor, and Elizabeth I, and having been respected and revered by all four. He is buried at St George's Chapel, Windsor Castle, beneath an ornate alabaster monument. The 2nd Lord Lincoln was insane, and the 4th married a daughter of Lord Saye and Sele, adopting her surname of Fiennes (pronounced Fynes) in addition to his own. And so eventually we come to the 9th Earl of Lincoln, whose name was Fiennes-Clinton, and who was subsequently, by a curious route, 2nd Duke of Newcastle. (The name Fiennes was dropped by his descendants.).

The 1st Duke, the neurotic Prime Minister, was created Duke of Newcastle-upon-Tyne in 1715, because his mother, Grace Holles, had been a sister of a previous Duke of Newcastle, and he had inherited the Newcastle estate through her. Thus the 1st Duke of Newcastle of this creation is Thomas Pelham (or Pelham-Holles), who has nothing yet to do with Fiennes-Clinton, Earl of Lincoln. The Duke had a brother, Henry Pelham (also Prime Minister), and a sister, Lucy Pelham, who later married Lord Lincoln. Henry Pelham had a daughter, Catherine Pelham, but no sons, whereas Lord and Lady Lincoln (Lucy) had a son and heir, the 9th Earl of Lincoln. The Duke, meanwhile, had no offspring at all, no one to leave his estate to, and no one to inherit his dukedom. The patent of creation would not allow the dukedom to go to anyone but his son, and he had none. He would dearly have loved to leave the title to his nephew, the Earl of Lincoln. An ingenious solution was found.

In 1756 he was created Duke of Newcastle again, with special remainder to his nephew, but as he was already Duke of Newcastle-upon-Tyne, he would have a second dukedom, that of Newcastle-under-Lyme (or "under-Line", as the patent erroneously stated). Hence the dukedom of Newcastle-upon-Tyne was extinct with the

1st Duke's death in 1768, while the dukedom of Newcastle-under-Lyme is borne to this day by the Earls of Lincoln, descendants of the 1st Duke's nephew. Lincoln consolidated the affair by marrying his own cousin, Catherine Pelham; he was the son of Lucy Pelham, she the daughter of Henry Pelham, and to both the 1st Duke of Newcastle was uncle. Their descendants were henceforth known as Pelham-Clinton, until the present Duke's father added the name Hope by Royal Licence in 1887. Of the three surnames, only Clinton is strictly accurate, since both Pelham and Hope have been adopted as the result of marriage.

Now the dukedom seems bound for extinction. The 9th Duke of Newcastle has two daughters. His heir is a cousin, Edward Charles Pelham-Clinton, born in 1920, who is Assistant Keeper of the Royal Scottish Museum in Edinburgh, and a bachelor. In all likelihood he will succeed as 10th Duke, and the title will cease with him.

The earldom of Lincoln will continue. There are dozens of Clintons descended from the earls before they married into the Pelham family in 1744, who are ready to lay claim to the title.

Of the Newcastle estate, nothing tangible now remains. Their principal seat was Clumber, one of the four great houses collectively known as "The Dukeries"* near Worksop. From the beginning of World War I, Clumber was rarely inhabited. In 1929 the 8th Duke, a lonely unconventional man, decided on a process of liquidation which would get rid of the Newcastle estate as it then stood. He persuaded the trustees to agree, and Clumber was demolished in 1938. "It was before the era of 'Stately Homes'," says his son the present Duke. "No institution wanted it. Demolition was the only answer."

As the family did not intend to live in another house as big, it was equally evident that they would have to off-load the contents. It took a whole year of auctions to sell the books from the Clumber library, fetching £64,000. The other contents were disposed of in a series of sales over the next few years. A policy of re-investment and renewal followed. The Duke died in 1941. His son and successor has led a somewhat nomadic life. He left England for Rhodesia in 1948, bought a farm there, and settled down for a few years. He has also bought a house in Jamaica, and a house near Bath, both since sold. He has returned to England, having sold everything he held in Rhodesia, and now lives quietly in Lymington. He runs one farm; the trust owns three more.

* The other three were Welbeck (Duke of Portland), Worksop (Duke of Norfolk), and Thoresby (Duke of Kingston).

The Duke is not political, and rarely social. He has little connection with other dukes, or with the social zigzagging of London "society". He has never taken part in a coronation. He has no servants. "The fact that I might one day be Newcastle was never discussed," he says. "I never gave it a thought."

*   *   *

In the summer of 1889 Princess Louise, eldest daughter of the Prince of Wales and grand-daughter of Queen Victoria, became engaged to the Earl of Fife, an obscure Scottish laird. Her cousin, Princess May of Teck (later Queen Mary), thought it a little odd. "What do you say to Louise's engagement to Lord Fife?" she wrote to her Aunt Augusta. "We are very glad for her because she has liked him for some years, but for a future Royal Princess to marry a subject seems rather strange don't you think so?" Queen Victoria, who was both sentimental and had a keen eye for the advantages of any proposal, was thoroughly in favour. "It is a very brilliant marriage in a worldly point of view", she wrote, "as he is immensely rich."[47] Besides which, he was handsome and likeable. Princess Louise, an apathetic, sickly creature, much given to whining, was unlikely to do better. That Fife was not of royal blood was a mere inconvenience, which the old Queen knew well she could remedy by the simple expedient of elevating him to the highest rank among her subjects. So, on the very day of the marriage, 27th July 1889, Louise's husband became 1st Duke of Fife, holder of the last dukedom to be created. (He had been offered the dukedom of Inverness, but had refused.)[48]

The wedding was a splendid, glittering occasion. A royal romance was guaranteed to catch the public imagination, but this was something more. The Princess had not gone abroad to choose some German princeling whom nobody had ever heard of, but had chosen instead a Scot, whom she loved, and the Queen had given her blessing. It was certainly a departure from custom, and cause for wild enthusiasm. The wedding took place in the private chapel at Buckingham Palace, Louise still looking very pale, according to the Queen, who also disapproved of her dress. "She was too plainly dressed", she wrote, "and had her veil over her face, which *no Princess* ever has and which I think unbecoming and not right." The Queen was quite correct; today her rigid observance of royal practice is adhered to more strictly, as for example when Princess Anne married, with her face uncovered. The Fifes moved into a house in Richmond Park, called Sheen Lodge, where they led a very happy life, and where their two daughters were born.

The origins of the Fifes was by no means clear. They had extensive land in Scotland (none of it in Fife), were known to be pleasant and obliging, quite harmless, and small in build; one of them had been known as "Creely Duff" or "dwarf-like Duff". Duff was the family name. One theory averred descent from the Macduff Earls of Fife, one of whom is prominent in Shakespeare's *Macbeth*. But the connection has never successfully been traced. A second version claimed that the Duffs themselves were from a direct line dating from 1404. Unfortunately, a genealogical scholar showed that this theory rested on falsified evidence. In the mausoleum at Duff House, Banff, lay a stone effigy, purporting to be of the first Duff, and carrying the date 1404; the genealogist proved that the effigy had been removed from St Anne's Chapel in 1792, and that the inscription had been tampered with after its arrival at Duff House.[49] With the best will, one must conclude that the origin of the Fifes is mysterious. They have always been ardent Scots, which alone would endear them to Queen Victoria; one of them had earth and gravel brought down from Scotland to fill the garden and paths of Fife House in Whitehall, on the Thames, so that he would only need to tread on Scottish soil.[50]

Less than two years after their marriage, H.R.H. Princess Louise, Duchess of Fife, and the Duke of Fife, were presented with a sudden crisis of succession which promised to engulf them both. The heir presumptive to the throne of England, Prince Eddy, Duke of Clarence, caught influenza and pneumonia, and within a few days lay dead. At his bedside on 14th January 1891 were his mother, the Princess of Wales (soon to be Queen Alexandra), holding his hand for hours on end, his brother Prince George, and his sister and brother-in-law, the Fifes. The tragedy resided not only in the premature death of a handsome and popular prince, but in the doubt which his death cast upon the future. For the heir to the throne, after the Prince of Wales, was Prince George, unmarried and poor in health. Next in line was his sister Louise. His life and his alone separated the throne from the Duchess of Fife, who, highly strung and mouse-like, would scarcely make an ideal Queen. All efforts were now concentrated on getting Prince George married and with a family.

In the forefront of these endeavours were the Fifes, desperate to avoid the throne. They encouraged Prince George to pursue his dead brother's fiancée, the estimable and ideal Princess May of Teck. Their house at Richmond was especially well suited as a rendezvous, quiet, secluded, but very near London. Here the young couple met regularly, prodded by the anxious Fifes. One day the Duchess said to her brother, "Now, Georgie, don't you think you ought to take May into the garden to look at the frogs in the pond?" Beside the pond the future George V proposed to the future Queen Mary and was accepted. May noted in her diary that the Fifes were "delighted".[51]

In the meantime, something had to be done about the Fifes' own future. They had two daughters, and were unlikely to have more children, which meant that the dukedom would be extinct after only one generation. There was one solution. The dukedom would have to be created again, with special remainder allowing the title to descend through the female line. The Queen obliged, and in 1900 the Duke of Fife became duke a second time; it is this title which is borne by his descendant, the previous dukedom and all other earlier titles being extinct with his death in 1912.

In 1905, soon after her father became King, the Duchess was named Princess Royal, which entitled her daughters to carry the style of "Her Highness". They were not a family to be constantly in the public eye, although on one occasion there was no avoiding an avalanche of publicity. In December 1911 the family embarked on the P. & O. steamship *Delhi,* bound for Bombay. The Fifes were due to disembark in Egypt, whence they were repairing for the Duchess's health, always too fragile to withstand an English winter. On the night of 13th December a furious storm broke. Black clouds poured down torrents of rain, gales whipped up mountainous waves, and at 2 a.m. the ship began to go under. They were some miles off Cape Spartel, on the coast of Morocco. Signals soon brought other ships to the rescue, but the sea was too turbulent to attempt transferring passengers from one ship to another. The only hope was to get them into small craft and make as best one could for the shore. The Princess Royal and her husband refused to leave the *Delhi* until other women and children had been taken off, by which time the ship was filling fast. They had literally to be dropped from a height and caught in the small boats, wearing only nightclothes, as there had been no time to retrieve personal belongings. Their little boat was swamped by waves, in spite of frantic baling, obliging them to rely on lifebelts. Princess Alix disappeared under the water for a while. Louise tells the story herself in a letter to her brother King George. "We got on alright but waves were huge, they swept down on us and filled the boat, we baled, but not any good, water came up to our knees and she sank! flinging us all out! We floated in our belts – waves like iron walls tore over us, knocked us under, Admiral Cradock gripped my shoulder and *saved* me! – Thank God my Macduff and children both on beach but had been *under* too, it was an awful *moment,* our clothes so heavy, and we were breathless and shivery . . . It is an extraordinary nightmare, and we are indeed grateful to be *all* here and alive still."[52]

Once on shore the Fife family walked to the lighthouse, where they were given coffee and whatever assortment of clothing could be found. The Princess Royal sent a telegram: "S.S. Delhi to Queen Alexandra, London. All safe. Louise." They then mounted on mules and, still shivering and drenched, trod their way painfully across rugged country to Tangier. The journey took three hours.[53]

The Fifes continued afterwards to Egypt to resume their holiday, but tragedy struck belatedly when the Duke contracted pleurisy and pneumonia, as a result of which he died, on 29th January 1912. His daughter maintained that the illness had nothing to do with the ship-wreck, but medical opinion was not quick to agree with her.

In accordance with the terms of the fresh patent of 1900, the Duke was succeeded by his elder daughter as Duchess of Fife.* She married Prince Arthur of Connaught, which had the effect of submerging the Fife dukedom in her other, royal, honours; she was known to the world as H.R.H. Princess Arthur of Connaught. She was the first member of the Royal Family to be matron of a nursing-home, before which she had worked incognito as a nurse and a sister at both University College Hospital and Queen Charlotte's Hospital. Her one son predeceased her, thus spelling the end of the Connaught title, while the Fife dukedom passed on her death in 1959 to the son of her sister, Princess Maud, then Lord Carnegie, now the 3rd Duke of Fife.

The Duke, born in 1929, chairman of the Amateur Boxing Association, was pursued by newspapers in his twenties as one of the most likely husbands for Princess Margaret, whom he had known since childhood. (Another was Lord Dalkeith, now Duke of Buccleuch.) He, however, spent more time with a ballet dancer called Mary Drage, whose Catholic religion prevented any permanent alliance. As a descendant of George II he was subject to the Royal Marriages Act, which requires the Sovereign's consent to any engagement. In 1956 he married the Hon. Caroline Dewar, daughter of Lord Forteviot, who owned the Dewar Scotch whisky firm. Ten years later they were divorced, on grounds of her adultery. There are two children of the marriage, a boy and a girl. The son, Lord Macduff, born in 1961, is the solitary heir to this last of the dukedoms. He married in 1987.

* Only two other women have *inherited* a dukedom – the Duchess of Marl-borough in 1722, and the Duchess of Hamilton in 1651.

REFERENCES

1. Devonshire Collections, 28. 102.
2. *Hist. MSS. Comm.*, Rutland MSS, Vol. II, pp. 168–75.
3. Nicholas Pevsner, *Derbyshire*, p. 141.
4. Duchess of Rutland, *Haddon Hall* (pamphlet, 1890), p. 18.
5. *Letters and Papers Henry VIII*, Vol. IV, Part iii, p. 2929.
6. Greville, IV, 9.
7. Benjamin Disraeli, *Coningsby*, Book IX, Ch. 1.
8. D.N.B.
9. Wraxall, *Posthumous Memoirs*, Vol. II, p. 365.
10. William Pitt, *Correspondence,* Vol. III, p. 477.
11. Wraxall, *Historical Memoirs*, p. 367.
12. *ibid.*, p. 543.
13. *London Chronicle*, 24th October 1787.
14. Wraxall, *Hist. Mem.*, 370.
15. *Town and Country*, Vol. II, p. 401 (1770).
16. Chips Channon, *Diaries*, p. 142.
17. Greville, III, 1.
18. Augustus Hare, *In My Solitary Life*, p. 252.
19. Clark E. Bleibtreu, *Der Wahre Shakespeare* (Munich, 1907).
20. *Cal. S. P. Dom.*, 1611–18, p. 143.
21. Eller, pp. 62–6.
22. Walpole, *Memoirs of the Reign of George II*, Vol. II, p. 2.
23. *Letters of Queen Victoria*, quoted in *Complete Peerage*.
24. Moneypenny, *Life of Disraeli*, Vol. II, p. 163.
25. *The Stanleys of Alderley*, ed. Nancy Mitford.
26. Greville, VII, 94.
27. *Lord Hervey and His Friends*, p. 171.
28. *ibid.*, p. 140.
29. Walpole, XXII, p. 102.
30. R. A. Kelch, *Newcastle: A Duke without Money.*
31. L. B. Namier, *England in the Age of the American Revolution.*
32. Kelch, *op. cit.*, pp. 183–4.
33. Walpole, XVII, 210.
34. Sir Charles Hanbury Williams, *Works* (1822), Vol. II, p. 33.
35. Walpole, XVIII, 167.
36. Sanford and Townsend, *Great Governing Families of England,* Vol. I, p. 211.
37. Lady Paget, quoted in *Complete Peerage.*
38. *Sunday Express*, 15th December 1957.

39. *Daily Sketch*, 14th March 1970.
40. Londonderry Papers, D/Lo/C 234, Duke of Newcastle to Lady Londonderry, 13th July 1858.
41. *ibid.*, 8th September 1858.
42. Edith Marchioness of Londonderry, *Frances Anne*, pp. 291–4.
43. *Illustrated London News*, 18th January 1851, p. 37.
44. Greville, III, 231.
45. Greville, IV, 156.
46. Hansard, House of Lords, 3rd December 1830.
47. James Pope-Hennessey, *Queen Mary*, pp. 180–1.
48. *Annual Register*, 1889.
49. *Genealogist Magazine*, 1886.
50. *Old and New London*, Vol. III, p. 335.
51. Pope-Hennessey, op. cit., pp. 259–60.
52. *ibid.*, pp. 462–3.
53. *The Times*, 14th December 1911.

13. The Legacy of Mary Davies

Duke of Westminster

It is commonly supposed that Queen Victoria felt obliged to make Hugh Lupus Grosvenor a duke in 1874, because he was more wealthy than she was. With an income exceeding a £¼ million a year and the most desirable piece of real estate in London, extending over Belgravia and Mayfair, wealth was, for better or worse, the singular most noticeable thing about him. Granville was the first to suggest the elevation. "Has it ever crossed you to make your Cheshire neighbour a Duke?" he wrote to Gladstone on 8th February 1874. "Your suggestion about Westminster has often crossed my mind," Gladstone replied, "and I have every disposition to recommend it."[1] Accordingly, he took the opportunity to include Grosvenor's name on the list for dissolution honours occasioned by his resignation. On 17th February he wrote: "My dear Westminster [he was then Marquess of Westminster], I have received authority from the Queen to place a Dukedom at your disposal and I hope you may accept it, for both you and Lady Westminster will wear it right nobly. With my dying breath, Yours sincerely, W. E. Gladstone." The Marquess replied next day with his acceptance, adding a postscript: "May I venture to say that if we have any option in the matter we should like to retain the title of 'Westminster' and that of 'Earl Grosvenor' for the eldest son as at present."[2]

Barely 100 years old, the dukedom of Westminster is therefore a fledgling title; only that of Fife is more recent. Paradoxically, however, the family of Grosvenor in whom it is vested has ancestry stretching back in unbroken male line to the time of the Conqueror, with an authenticity that many a longer-established ducal house might envy. Gilbert le Gros Veneur, Chief Huntsman to William the Conqueror and nephew to Hugh Lupus, William's nephew, gave the family its surname. In 1160 Robert le Grosvenor received a grant of land from the Earl of Chester at Budworth, Co. Chester, where the family settled and has remained ever since. Familiar names in their early history presage a future which they could not have suspected; Sir Robert Grosvenor, who died in 1396, married the widow of one Thomas *Belgrave*, and in 1450 Raufe Grosvenor married the heiress Joan Eton (or *Eaton*) of Eaton, Co. Chester. By the late seventeenth century the Grosvenors were a family of great antiquity and considerable, though not ostentatious, fortune. They lacked one advantage – a London base. Their property was entirely provincial and they were not well-placed or well-known in the south. A suitable remedy was found in the marriage of Sir Thomas Grosvenor, 3rd Baronet, Member of Parliament for Chester and Mayor of Chester, with the twelve-year-old heiress Mary Davies, of Ebury, Middlesex, whose marriage portion included the manor of Ebury, comfortably close to London. The Ebury property was not particularly remarkable, being largely swamp and lagoon in the south, and poor pasture in the north. Indeed, it was Mary Davies who gained most by the marriage, since the Grosvenors were then far the richer family of the two. And they were shrewd. Sir Thomas knew that the Ebury lands, unexciting as they were, were well-situated and would be ripe for development one day. The date of the marriage was 8th October 1677. The Ebury property is now Belgravia and Mayfair, and it still belongs to Sir Thomas's descendants.

Ebury was bounded in the south by the river Thames, in the north by the Roman road from London to Bath (now Oxford Street and Bayswater Road), in the east by the Tybourne, and in the west by a stream called the Westbourne. In all, it covered 1090 acres, formerly belonging to the Abbey of Westminster, confiscated and redistributed in the time of Henry VIII. The King took what he thought was the best part of it for himself, in 1540, enclosed it and stocked it with deer; this is now Hyde Park. The southern part, sometimes submerged at high tide, with islands rising above the highwater mark (the isle of Chesil = Chels-ea; the isle of Bermond = Bermond's ea; Battersea was another), is now Pimlico and Belgravia. Between 1300 and 1700 the land underwent practically no change at all, being too clayey and waterlogged to permit building. As recently as the beginning of the nineteenth century, it was still meadow, an open and rural spot known as "Five Fields" and infested with robbers and footpads (highwaymen). All that had happened in 400 years was that the property had changed hands by purchase, gift and inheritance.

In 1626 the land was sold to Hugh Awdeley, or Audley (1577–1662) for £9400. Audley had a reputation for usury and double-dealing, which modern research has gone some way to redress. He was "careful, capable, covetous, but not corrupt".[3] Certain it is that he knew how to make money, having increased his own capital some 2000 per cent in his lifetime. He lived so long that he became a legendary figure, pointed at in public; he also succumbed to the whims of old age, changing his will and settlements several times a year. By the terms of the last settlement, dated 1st November 1662, he bequeathed his Middlesex property to his business clerk and nephew, Alexander Davies, and his brother Thomas Davies. Audley died that year, and Alexander bought out his brother's portion of the estate, leaving the whole, some 430 acres, to his infant daughter Mary, who married Sir Thomas Grosvenor. Alexander may have had plans for the land. He was, after all, an ambitious and clever young man, with ideas of his own. But the plague struck him down at the age of thirty, in July 1665, when little Mary was but five months old (she was born on 17th January 1665).

As visible proof that she was an heiress to be taken seriously, Mary was able to ride out in her own private coach, drawn by six horses, when she was still a child, and roughly contemporary with that other child heiress, Lady Elizabeth Percy, the last of the Percys, who took her estate into the Seymour family, whence some of it passed to the Smithsons. Little Mary Davies had nothing to compare with such an inheritance. There were problems from the beginning. The estate of Alexander Davies, her father, was weighed down in debt. An Act of Parliament was passed in 1675 to enable some of the estate to be sold on Mary's behalf to settle these debts. The part chosen for selling was Goring House and its grounds. This went to the Earl of Arlington, who left it to his daughter, the Duchess of Grafton, who sold it to the Duke of Buckingham, who demolished it and built a new house on the site in 1702, calling it Buckingham House, and then sold it to George III. It is now Buckingham Palace and has been Crown property ever since. In the grounds of the palace is a mulberry tree which traditionally dates from the time when this land belonged to Mary Davies.[4]

Mary was known as the "Maid of Ebury" because she was a mere twelve years old when she married Sir Thomas Grosvenor at St Clement Dane's, her grandfather the Reverend Richard Dukeson officiating. From this nickname has sprung the erroneous story that Grosvenor married a milkmaid.

She bore Sir Thomas five sons and three daughters, before she showed the first signs of losing her sanity. He died in 1700, at the age of forty-four, unable to make adequate provision for her protection in time. After her husband's death, Mary Davies nearly lost the entire Ebury property to an unscrupulous pair of brothers called Fenwick, who, had they succeeded, would have cast the Grosvenors forever into obscurity. One Lodowick Fenwick, a Jesuit priest, took advantage of her fragility of mind to gain control of her movements and her decisions. She had become absurdly religious and quite unpredictably crazy, locking people in cupboards and wearing feathers on her sleeves to help her fly. In this condition, she became a virtual prisoner of Fenwick when they went to the continent. The priest's brother, Edward Fenwick, later claimed that he had married Mary in France, and that consequently he was the legal owner of her property. He gave notice to all the Grosvenor tenants that rents should henceforth be paid to *him*. Mary's cause was taken up by her guardian, Charles Cholmondeley, and the resulting trial was a constant source of interest in the capital. Mary's defence rested on six points :

(1) that she had been disturbed in her mind since 1696
(2) that Father Fenwick had acquired complete mastery over her, on occasion by force
(3) that he sent home from France all her personal staff, and replaced them with his own relatives or appointees
(4) that she had been weakened by drugs and bleeding
(5) that she had no knowledge of any marriage with Edward Fenwick
(6) that if such a ceremony had taken place, it would be null and void in the eyes of the law

Amongst the body of evidence given as to her being drugged, there was testimony that opium had been placed in her poached eggs, and that she would throw hysterical scenes, hurling food at Fenwick and screaming that she was being poisoned.

In spite of all this, and allowing for the fact that the Fenwicks were unprincipled rogues, the jury of the Queen's Bench found that the marriage, though forced, was valid, and they declared in favour of Fenwick.

If we do not now refer to the Fenwick estates in Belgravia and Mayfair, it is because the matter was subsequently placed before the Court of Delegates of Sergeants Inn, who overturned the verdict. They found in favour of Lady Grosvenor, on the grounds that she was not *compos mentis* at the time of the alleged marriage, and imposed silence on Edward Fenwick for ever more. The Grosvenors were secure.[5]

Mary lived until 1730, a complete lunatic for the last few years. Exactly one year later her grandson was born, Richard Grosvenor, the first in the family to be raised to the peerage, on the recommendation of Pitt, as Earl Grosvenor (1731–1802). He and his descendants continued to add to the family property buying the manor of Eccleston and the hamlet of Belgrave, and to maintain their close connections with Chester, as mayors and Members of Parliament. His son, Robert Grosvenor (1767–1845), turned his attentions to the dreary tract of land inherited from Mary Davies, an area still unprepossessing, where clothes were hung out, bulls were baited, and dog-fights encouraged. Then, nearby Buckingham House was rebuilt as a royal palace in 1825, and Grosvenor saw his chance. To investigate what could be done to develop the site, he employed Thomas Cubitt who discovered that beneath the soggy clay was a stratum of gravel of some depth, which would support building. Grosvenor obtained an Act of Parliament in 1826 to permit him to drain the land and remove the topsoil of clay, which was burned into bricks, and Cubitt planned his elegant suburb to be built on the substratum of gravel. Five years later, "Belgravia" came into existence, while beneath its handsome exterior at high water in spring tides, the River Thames still flowed only a few feet below. Grosvenor was advanced one step further in the peerage as Marquess of Westminster.

The wealth of the Grosvenors was now approaching vast proportions. Grosvenor's son had married Lady Elizabeth Leveson-Gower in 1819; a dynastic merging without precedent, for the bride was the daughter of the Duke of Sutherland and the Duchess-Countess of Sutherland, reputed to be the richest couple in Europe. (Lady Elizabeth, by the way, lived to the age of ninety-four, almost elbowing her way into the twentieth century.) It was their son, Hugh Lupus Grosvenor (1825–1899), who was made 1st Duke of Westminster in 1874, having become so rich that he could not be ignored. He consolidated his status by marrying his daughter Margaret to Prince Adolphus of Teck, the future Queen Mary's brother. Queen Victoria, with her keen eye for a bargain, wrote, "It is a vy *good* connection – ... & she will doubtless be well off."[6]

The Duke further consolidated his wealth, by taking as his first wife his own cousin, a daughter of the 2nd Duke of Sutherland. His second wife, Catherine Cavendish, lived until 1941. We are brought closer to the modern age by the 2nd Duke, his grandson, who lived from 1879 to 1953, and was always known as "Bend Or". He presided over the diversification of the Grosvenor estates and its growth into an international business, with interests on four conti-

nents, superbly well managed, and large enough to compete with
many a public corporation. "Bend Or" used to send back his shirts
and linen from all over the world to his private laundry at Eaton
Hall.[7] The Duke's hydra-headed business was still a private family
concern, the various companies subordinate, in the end, to the
efficient running of his personal estate.

Of course, the jewel in the crown is those 300 acres in London,
100 in Mayfair, and 200 in Belgravia. This was all Bend Or's personal property, with which he could do as he pleased. One other man
was involved in policy decisions, the agent, Mr George Ridley. It
was a nineteenth-century system operating in the middle of the
twentieth, but it worked because Ridley's vision and sound good
sense inspired it. He had been with the family virtually all his life,
his only qualifications for his huge responsibilities being those of
experience and loyalty. Under Ridley's guidance, the Duke turned
his attention to the Reay estate in the extreme north-west of Scotland. This, which had been adjacent to the Sutherland property and
had been absorbed by the Duke of Sutherland, was bought from him
by the Duke of Westminster in 1870 (at the same time as he bought
Cliveden from the same man). Since then, the Grosvenors had kept
the estate together, supported it and maintained it, but done little to
change the prospects of the 100,000 acres. Consequently, the area
was gradually being deserted by its inhabitants, searching farther
afield for fruitful employment and abandoning their unproductive
land.

Ridley and the Duke determined to arrest this process. They
undertook to plant 2500 acres with pine, spruce and larch, to buy
the redundant sea-fishing business at Kinlochbervie, re-develop the
harbour and establish a transport system which would enable fish
landed one evening to be marketed the following morning. All this
was in 1951. Almost immediately, the scheme proved a glorious
success. By 1965, the fish landed on the Reay estate was the most
highly valued, and the quantity made this once abandoned port the
second busiest in Scotland. The area has become happy and pros-
perous, and is continually growing. A whole subdivision of the
Grosvenor estates is employed in its management. A school was built,
and given to the local council for a symbolic rental. The capital
expenditure involved in this development has been enormous, and
the return, or "profit", non-existent. It has been a perfect example
of the nineteenth-century ethic which governed some, if not all,
ducal estates, according to which the duke in residence has a deep-
rooted obligation, by virtue of his birth, towards people who live on

land which he owns, and a responsibility to use his wealth for their benefit as much as for his own.

This is not the place to list all the multifarious interests of the Grosvenor estates, but a few instances serve to illustrate why they have been so successful. A combination of wisdom and adventure has informed their actions.

After World War II, the Eaton Square property could no longer support large family houses; nobody was left who could afford them. The Grosvenor estates undertook, at vast expense, to convert the whole area into flats (there was, of course, profit in *this* scheme). The centre of Chester has been developed as a modern shopping area. Annacis Island, in the Fraser river in Canada, was bought in 1950, and a huge scheme of conversion into an industrial estate undertaken. Millions of tons of sand had to be dredged from the river and piled on to the 1700-acre island, to raise it above the level of flood risk. Eventually, over forty factories were established on the island, providing employment for thousands. This project was developed in partnership with John Laing & Son.

The Grosvenor Estates is no longer run personally by the Duke of Westminster, though it is still a settled estate, and his word is still ultimately law. There is now a board of trustees, under J. N. C. James, who trained with the Grosvenor branch in Canada, and an advisory panel of bankers and outside businessmen. They hope to avoid mistakes of the past. There was no real need for Grosvenor House to be pulled down in 1924 and replaced by an hotel; it was a beautiful house and should have been preserved. Similarly, financial motives alone permitted the southern face of Grosvenor Square to be demolished and replaced with a pseudo-Georgian façade behind which hides the Britannia Hotel. Other sales have been more mysterious. It is not clear why the Pimlico estate was sold in its entirety in 1950, nor why half the Eaton Hall estate in Chesire went in 1919; the family could certainly have afforded to keep them. It can only have been to release funds which could be used elsewhere. The revenue from the Pimlico sale was doubtless used to develop the Reay estate; Douglas Sutherland has said: "It is hard to imagine any modern bricks and mortar tycoon spending surplus profits or investing capital in the way that the Grosvenor Estates have in the north of Scotland, with no thought of ultimate gain." Nor can one imagine one of our tycoons *giving* land to Westminster City Council and Westminster Housing Association, as the 2nd Duke did, so that workpeople could be housed at reasonable rents near to their place of work. During the agricultural depression of the thirties, he handed back to his tenants fifty per cent of their rents.[8]

It is surprising that such a well-known family should be so secretive, and that they should have managed so well to retain their privacy. Little of any detail is known about the dukes of Westminster. Bend Or is perhaps the most familiar, as his reputation for womanising kept him in the public eye, and led him four times to the marriage register. His name, incidentally, derives initially from his grandfather's horse Bend Or, who won the Derby in the year in which the 2nd Duke was born – 1879. To discover why the racehorse had such a curious name, one must go beyond 1879 by nearly 500 years. Between 1386 and 1390 there was a bitter dispute between Sir Robert Grosvenor and Sir Richard Scrope as to which of the two families had the right to bear arms "azure, a bend or". Grosvenor had borne such arms since the time of Hugh Lupus, but Scrope challenged the right, and eventually won the day, with a decision of the King's in his favour. Grosvenor thereupon changed his arms to "azure, a garb or", which his descendant the Duke of Westminster keeps to this day, although the original "bend or" arms have not been forgotten; hence the Derby winner and the 2nd Duke's nickname.

According to a recent account Bend Or was trapped into his first marriage with Constance Cornwallis-West in 1901 by the mischievous character of the Prince of Wales, who told him that he could not avoid the honourable course of marriage, as he had been spied alone with the lady in the garden.[9] They were divorced in 1919. The following year he married Violet Nelson, divorcing her in 1926, and the Hon. Loelia Ponsonby in 1930. Of this marriage we have some record. They were divorced in 1947, when the Duke took his last bride, Anne Sullivan.

The picture of Bend Or's private character, as portrayed by his third wife, is not particularly endearing, but it rings true, as it accords with what little information we have as the character of his ancestors. Loelia Ponsonby was the grand-daughter of Grey, Queen Victoria's Private Secretary for the last twenty-five years of her life. Consequently, she had been brought up in a grace and favour apartment in St James's Palace, heavily protected by governesses and hardly allowed to be seen until she "came out". She had no preparation whatever for marriage to a difficult man like Bend Or.

He proposed in flamboyant fashion, indicating nonetheless a secret shyness. He sent Loelia a letter with a message to expect a present by special courier, and asking her to reply by the same courier. The present was a sapphire engagement ring. Thereafter he was constantly placing diamond necklaces under her pillow, in her handbag, by her breakfast plate. Only later did she realise that these gifts were as nothing when proffered by a man with "a most treacherous nature, filled with jealousy to a quite impossible degree". His jealousy hinged upon a terrible fear that Loelia would enjoy herself more with almost anyone else than with him; she was to him like a possession. He even told her that she must stop seeing her own mother, and must choose between them. He had been used to having his own way, selfishness had become the rule of his life. Accordingly, he would change plans, obey whims and fancies, with no one else to consider but himself. He was not prepared to amend these habits for his wife. On the other hand, he appears to have been surrounded by the most miserable kind of sycophants, who were thrilled to be near a man with so much money, and would never gainsay him. "He only liked what he called 'genuine people', and his only criterion for selecting these people seemed to be that they were complete nonentities."[10] The Duke took their side against his wife on many occasions, permitting them to treat her as an interloper in the marital home. Such a situation could not long continue. The 12th Duke of Bedford, Hastings the Pacifist, was similarly governed by selfishness and subservience to flattery, and his marriage suffered in like fashion.

The day that he died, Chips Channon wrote: "So Bend Or the great Duke of Westminster is dead at last; magnificent, courteous, a mixture of Henry VIII and Lorenzo il Magnifico, he lived for pleasure – and women – for seventy-four years. His wealth was incalculable; his charm overwhelming; but he was restless, spoilt, irritable, and rather splendid in a very English way. He was fair, handsome, lavish; yet his life was an empty failure; he did few kindnesses, leaves no monument."[11]

His life was not a failure if you count the achievements of the estate, but it was if you consider that he found it impossible to know anyone or have anyone know him in any really intimate way. If he did few kindnesses, it was because he didn't know how to; he hadn't the knack. Just as the Churchills and the Russells have been strangers to each other from one generation to the next, have made no effort to understand each other, with the result that they have been imprisoned and scared, locked up in their own personality. A different view is given by the Duke of Manchester, who found Bend Or "one of the most generous, kind-hearted fellows in the world . . . he has been a disappointed man".[12] But Manchester had not the equipment to understand him properly – he was obeying an instinct for solidarity.

The 1st Duke, Bend Or's grandfather, was uncommunicative in

precisely the same way. His own mother described him as "pinched and dry", or "Mr Poker", and one entry in her diary tells us that he was "more amiable than usual which does not mean much".[12] His sons found him awesome, stern and distant, and of them he had no good opinion. He thought them a bunch of weak dissipated characters, unworthy of the name they carried, and he did not try to know them better. If we go back a further generation, we find that the 1st Duke was, in his turn, harshly criticised and rebuked throughout his boyhood and youth by *his* father, the 2nd Marquess of Westminster, who held him in no great esteem or affection.[14] The Marquess suffered from precisely the same hereditary problems of being closed and cold, a perpetual solitary mystery, priggish and unapproachable, and totally humourless. His wife wrote to her mother, "I sometimes tell him he is not *demonstrative* enough and nobody would know if he is pleased or not."[15]

Another thread of personality which runs throughout the Grosvenor family is a passionate obsession with horses and horse-racing. The 1st Earl Grosvenor could not even spare the time to receive his title, so devoted was he to the turf: "yesterday when he should have kissed hands, he was gone to Newmarket to see the trial of a race horse".[16] He seems to have spent far too much time, and money by the turf altogether; his debts amounted to £180,000, which his heirs had to settle,[17] bearing in mind perhaps that it was worth it, for he had been the greatest breeder of racing-stock in his day. Racehorses were a passion to every subsequent generation, and the 1st Duke was the proud owner of four Derby winners.

It should not be forgotten, also, that they have uniformly been courageous, if a trifle unconventional, in wartime. Bend Or was mentioned in despatches in the Great War, and received the Légion d'Honneur and the D.S.O. for bravery.

When he died in 1953, the Grosvenor Estates were faced with an unprecedented bill for death duties, amounting to £20 million and requiring a whole sub-department of the Inland Revenue to be established to deal with it. As the 3rd Duke, Bend Or's cousin, was a permanent invalid unable to deal with the matter, all decisions were taken by George Ridley and the Trustees, including the plan to launch into a world-wide expansion which was so successful that it more than recovered the £20 million lost to the Exchequer. The 2nd Duke made provision before his death that no such disaster should occur again on such an extravagant scale. His two successors in the title were both elderly men, both childless, and both likely to bring upon the estate further intolerable tax bills in quick succession.

Even the resilient Grosvenor Estate could not easily have survived three such debts. The terms of Bend Or's will divided the family assets into a twenty-part trust fund, limiting as far as possible the amount of wealth which could be assigned to any one member of the family. The arrangement whereby the Duke was in sole possession of all assets, and had a personal income of £1 a minute, no longer applies, although the present Duke did very well out of the scheme; he had three parts of the trust by the terms of the will, to which another three parts were added on the death of the 3rd Duke, and a further three when the 4th Duke died. When only the heir, he owned nine-twentieths of the Grosvenor family assets, which in 1975 amounted to something over £70 million.

The 5th Duke of Westminster (born 1910) succeeded his brother in 1967. He was born plain Mr Grosvenor, the junior member of a junior branch of the family, thrust into prominence by the barren-ness of his predecessors. While still a commoner, he pursued a political career with some assiduity, as M.P. for Fermanagh and South Tyrone from 1955 to 1964, and then as Senator for Northern Ireland, which he had long considered home; his mother was born in Ireland. For two years he was Parliamentary Private Secretary to the Secretary of State for Foreign Affairs, Selwyn Lloyd; was a Freeman of the City of London and the City of Chester, and a frequent spokesman on Northern Ireland affairs, where he was a cautious supporter of reform, but by degrees and within the United Kingdom. "In this country you have to hurry very slowly," he once said.[18]

The 5th Duke, generally known as "Pud", undertook a fundamental reorganisation of the estate management almost as soon as he inherited. The cosy system of ducal head and chief agent, assisted by family trustees, could no longer cope with an empire of such size. He established a committee of four executive managers, each the head of his own department, and with his own staff. One was responsible for the London estate alone, another for the agricultural and forestry estates, a third was concerned with urban developments, and a fourth with various offshoot companies. Some superfluous properties were sold, such as the Bridgwater estate in Shropshire, bought in 1950 and sold for £2 million in 1972. A smaller concrete house was built at Eaton, with a sensible number of bedrooms. The Duke kept his house in Ireland, and naturally used a flat in his own Eaton Square when in London.

In 1946 Pud married the Hon. Viola Lyttelton, daughter of Lord Cobham and a Cavendish. They had two daughters, one of whom, Leonora, married the photographer Earl of Lichfield in 1975, and the other married the Duke of Roxburghe in 1977. Their son is the present Duke, born in 1951. On this young man alone rests the future of the coronet, for he is the last male descendant of the 1st Duke. Although the 1st Duke had seven sons by his first wife, and two more by his second, the heirs male of the body have dwindled by a series of misfortunes to one. The 1st Duke's heir, who was passionately fond of engineering (like the Duke of Richmond) and was often to be found in the railway workshops at Crewe, died at the age of thirty. He was an epileptic. Bend Or was his son, and Bend Or's son and heir died at the age of five in 1909. The title then swept over to a mysterious man, son of the 1st Duke's third son, whose history is kept very much secret. The 3rd Duke is variously described as "an invalid",[19] or as a man who "lived in retirement".[20] *The Times* obituary covers only three lines, less than has generally been accorded even to a footballer. Elsewhere he earns a reference as "a solitary old man who used to breed heavy-laying ducks".[12]

The fact is, the Duke was mad. He was hidden away in a small house with garage in Dittons Road, Polegate, in the rural district of Hailsham, near Eastbourne, where he led his anonymous and inoffensive life, while the great empire of which he was the titular head proceeded independently in London. He did not marry.

The 4th Duke married, but had no heir. He was badly wounded in World War II, and never fully recovered from his injuries. It behoves the 6th Duke, then, to save the title from extinction, although whatever may happen to the title, the name and fame of Grosvenor are assured of survival. Somehow it has always been understood that the name of Grosvenor is the important element, and that the title of Westminster is a mere appendage. This is not true of any other dukedom, where the title is always known at the expense of the surname.

A walk through the streets of central London tells the entire story of this chapter in microcosm. For in *Ebury* Street, and South *Audley* Street, and *Davies* Street, and in the grandiose beauty of *Grosvenor*, *Belgrave*, and *Eaton* Squares, is written the foresight of an astute family.

Legislation of the last quarter of the twentieth century threatened to erase the achievements of the Grosvenor family. By the terms of the Leasehold Reform Act of 1967, and the Housing Acts of 1969 and 1974, leaseholders were enabled to buy the freehold of their houses against the wishes of their landlords, providing the rateable

---

* For more detailed information, the reader is directed to Nigel Hague, *Leasehold Enfranchisement* (Sweet and Maxwell).

value did not exceed £1500 in London or £750 elsewhere. This posed a serious problem for the Grosvenor Estate, for it meant that many of the Belgravia and Mayfair properties became immediately liable for enfranchisement in this way. Horrid visions of beautiful Regency houses being painted red or black or purple, having their original windows removed and replaced by modern designs, or being substantially altered, presented themselves, with the Grosvenors, who had conceived and maintained Belgravia in its purity, powerless to object. The Estate did not accept the inevitability of such a prospect. After protracted negotiations, they succeeded in having incorporated into the Act a Section (19) which allows for the landlord to retain the right to continue a management policy for the whole estate, while in no way interfering with the leaseholder's right to buy the property. A landlord with an enlightened and cohesive management policy may apply to the Minister of Housing for a certificate to retain management powers. In the case of Belgravia, the High Court approved the granting of such a certificate in 1973. This means that the Estate reserves control over structural altera- tions, ensures that the architectural scale and design are maintained and requires all inhabitants, whether tenants or not, to carry out external painting every three years in the approved colour. It also controls the use of properties. Thus we are not, after all, the last generation to see the beauty of Belgravia; the foresight of the Grosvenor Estate ensures that it will be preserved.*

The Duke of Westminster, though the youngest but one of the twenty-six dukes alive now, is in many ways the most serious and im- pressive. Totally unlike Bend Or, who was a *bon viveur* above all else, he is actively concerned with the running of the Grosvenor Estates, where he is Chairman of the Board of Trustees and works full-time. Besides this, he is connected with no less than one hundred and thirty- nine other organisations which claim his attention, though he prefers to avoid public duties which are purely ceremonial. The Duke sits on the House of Lords European committee for rural policy, but does not take his seat in the chamber. A committed advocate of the democratic principle, he believes the second chamber should be made more effective by being composed of elected representatives whose opinions should be heeded, rather than tolerated. Nor is he a man to shoulder his huge responsibilities simply because they have been inherited; he embraces them with relish and energy. Naturally, he was trained in all aspects of the Grosvenor Estates from an early age, but his father wisely gave

* The author is indebted to J. Lindgren of the Grosvenor Office for information in this paragraph.

him a year off to do as he wished, during which time he was, amongst other things, a cowboy in Canada; he was not, in consequence, tempted to feel himself trapped or burdened by his fate.

The Duke is married to Natalia Ayesha Phillips ('Tally'), granddaughter of Sir Harold Wernher. Her sister, Alexandra Anastasia ('Sasha') is Duchess of Abercorn. The Duke of Westminster is not only the Duke of Abercorn's brother-in-law, but his godson and second cousin as well.

REFERENCES

1. *Complete Peerage.*
2. Gervas Huxley, *Victorian Duke,* pp. 100–1.
3. C. T. Gatty, *Mary Davies and the Manor of Ebury,* Vol. 1, p. 89.
4. *ibid.,* Vol. II, p. 181.
5. *ibid.,* II, 118–9, 129, 150.
6. James Pope-Hennessey, *Queen Mary,* p. 303.
7. Douglas Sutherland, *The Landowners,* p. 93.
8. *ibid.,* pp. 83, 96.
9. Anita Leslie, *Edwardians in Love,* p. 223.
10. Duchess of Bedford, *Now the Duchesses,* pp. 175, 177, 181.
11. Chips Channon, *Diaries,* p. 477.
12. Duke of Manchester, *My Candid Recollections,* p. 236.
13. Gervas Huxley, *op. cit.,* p. 103.
14. *ibid.,* p. 91.
15. Gervas Huxley, *Lady Elizabeth and the Grosvenors,* p. 15.
16. Walpole, XXI, 490.
17. F. M. L. Thompson, *English Landed Society in the Nineteenth Century,* p. 89.
18. *The Times,* 10th February 1969.
19. *Complete Peerage.*
20. *The Times,* 23rd February 1963.
21. Anthony Sampson, *Anatomy of Britain,* p. 12.

14. The Expatriates

Duke of Manchester; Duke of Montrose

The Duke of Manchester referred to in this chapter died in 1977 but has remained the central figure as he was the last of his line to make any mark. His son, the 11th Duke, died in 1985, whereupon the titles passed to a younger brother, born in 1938, who lives somewhere in England and attempts to keep the lowest of profiles.

There was a time when it was unthinkable that any peer of the realm, especially a duke, should live anywhere but on his land. It was his duty to do so. Some went abroad to escape creditors (like the eighteenth-century Duke of St Albans), or to side-step the scandal which their activities would provoke were they to remain in England (like the Duke of Beaufort's sons in the nineteenth century), and some because they were loose in the head and an embarrassment to their families. No one lived abroad through *choice*. The climate is different now. A number of peers have emigrated because taxation was bleeding them dry, or because they found that the atmosphere in Britain had become oppressive. The Duke of Bedford lived in South Africa before he came to the title (whereupon he returned immediately to England to assume his responsibilities at Woburn). The Duke of Newcastle also made his home in Africa for some years, though he now lives in quiet anonymity in Hampshire. Two dukes remained in Africa – their Graces of Manchester and of Montrose. The Duke of Manchester (1902–1977) lived in Kenya from 1946, and the Duke of Montrose (born 1907) in Rhodesia since 1931. They were virtual exiles, and they wanted to be – and Montrose, of course, still is.

A degree of disapproval is felt, rather vaguely perhaps, when mention of their name is made. There is a suspicion that they ought to have stayed when times were bad, their ancestors having reaped handsome rewards from the good times. Their departure does not accord with the principle of interdependent loyalty in which ducal estates have flourished. The tenants might well feel their lords have bolted.

(In fairness, it should be pointed out that in Montrose's case at least, the family estates are run by his son and heir Lord Graham.)

Manchester and Montrose had much in common which could explain why they, and not others, left the country. They both came from families which have long been prey to wanderlust. The 10th Duke of Manchester's mother and grandmother were both Americans, who brought to the blood a certain internationalism. The Duke soon displayed an urge to spread his wings. He was for many years a Commander in the Royal Navy. His father had been a lieutenant in the R.N.V.R. The Duke of Montrose, too, was in the R.N.V.R., and his father might even be described as obsessed with the sea. He devoted his entire life to the sea and sailors, giving long service to the Royal National Lifeboat Institution. Both with naval training, Montrose and Manchester were also both passionate farmers. Manchester inherited this from his grandmother's family, who were southern plantation people in the United States. His brother, Lord Edward Montagu, felt the draw before he did, and went to farm in Canada. His son Roderick lives in Edmonton, Alberta. The Montrose passion for farming derives from the long association of the family with the Scottish lowlands.

Other ties united the two. They both came from a long line of handsome men, and were distantly related. The Duke of Montrose is descended twice over from Manchester stock; his great-grandfather was the 7th Duke of Manchester, and his great-great-great-grandfather was the 4th Duke. It is no surprise that they should have shared certain family characteristics, then, which impelled them to choose exile.

Most prominent among these characteristics is an unabashed blunt conviction that the white races are inherently superior to all others. The Duke of Manchester's father published his memoirs in 1932. Under one illustration he wrote the caption, "some of the niggers employed on my grandparents' plantation". In the text he felt the need to explain the use of such a word. "As the modern jargon of equal rights for everybody had not then penetrated to their childlike minds thay had no objection to being called 'niggers', and would in fact have been surprised at any other description being given to them."[1] Some years later, in 1960, the Duke of Montrose was able to write, "It is common observation that the African child is a bright and promising little fellow up to the age of puberty, which he reaches in any case two years before the European. He then becomes hopelessly inadequate and disappointing and it is well known that this is due to his almost total obsession henceforth in matters of sex."[2] On other occasions Montrose has been heard to refer to the dark savage depths of the African mind, to "mongrelisation" for miscegenation, and to people who have ideas different from his own as "long-haired enthusiasts".[3]

The Duke of Manchester had a staff of 187 persons on his farm in

Kenya, with fourteen houseboys and twenty gardeners. There are no more than a couple of dukes in Britain who could match this. It is odd to think that the ducal style of life, more or less extinct in this country, should have continued to thrive in Africa. Another motive comes from a crusading nature. Both men believed that the African countries have reason to be grateful for their presence in their midst of representatives of a superior culture and European mentality. Montrose in particular is a religious man (his son, daughter and son-in-law are all actively engaged in the Moral Rearmament crusade) who sometimes betrays a belief in divine mission. He is on record as saying that Rhodesian territory is mentioned in the Bible and that Rhodesians were people of destiny charged with the task of being a blessing to mankind.[4]

Manchester and Montrose were made of the stuff of pioneers. They had the courage of the pioneer, the readiness to work hard, the determination and the ruthlessness. When Manchester went to Kenya in 1946, he lived in a mud hut. He drove the tractors to establish his own farm, and built his own magnificent house (not, of course, single-handed). He died with 11,000 acres in glorious country and reason to be proud of his achievement. The house contained some of the family treasures which he brought out of England, including Holbeins, Van Dycks, an Aubusson carpet, and a library of 13,000 books. The seat of the family in England, Kimbolton Castle in Huntingdonshire, was sold to Kimbolton Grammar School in 1950 for £12,500, and the entire contents were auctioned off the year before. Some paintings of huge dimensions, attributed to Rubens, Van Dyck, Tintoretto and Veronese, went for ten and eleven guineas apiece. The other seat, in Ireland – Tandaragee Castle, County Armagh – has been empty since the last duke's time. The Manchester estate possessed about 14,000 acres in England, but the 10th Duke himself broke all ties with this country and most of the estates were put up for sale. His heir, Lord Mandeville, farmed in Kenya, and his brother, we have seen, farms in Canada. The Duke was so identified with Kenya that he mastered several of the local languages, including Swahili. He married twice. His first wife was Nell Stead, an Australian, who died in 1966. The second wife was a native of California, formerly Mrs Crocker. Preceding duchesses of Manchester have been German, Cuban, American, Australian and American, the last English duchess being at the beginning of the nineteenth century.

The Duke of Montrose went to Rhodesia at the age of twenty-four, when he was heir apparent to the titles. He had no money, and worked from scratch to establish the 3000-acre farm he now manages. In 1925 there had been 130,000 acres on Montrose property in Scotland, shrinking within a few years, largely through the voracious demands of death duties, to 10,000 acres. It was at that point that young Lord Graham packed his bags and left. The family seat, Buchanan Castle, had proved too large for anyone to live in, so they had moved to a farm house, to which they added some rooms, called Auchmar. Here, not far from Glasgow, the Duke's son and heir, Marquess of Graham, now lives.

Montrose is an immensely impressive man, six feet and five inches tall (he weighed eleven and a quarter pounds at birth!), shambling and dominant. He has winning Celtic charm, courtesy and warmth, but when roused he can be gruff to a degree. His reputation for bluntness is well-deserved. He is not a man to waste words or to ingratiate.

The Duke of Manchester ceased to have any official function when his country became independent, whereas the Duke of Montrose continued his political interests in Rhodesia, presenting himself by the way with a curious and embarrassing ethical problem. In 1962 he was appointed Minister of Agriculture in Winston Field's government; his colleague at the Treasury was Ian Smith. Two years later Field resigned and provoked the crisis which produced Ian Smith's own government, the Unilateral Declaration of Independence, the abortive constitutional conferences, and the appeal from the Queen to her Rhodesian subjects to obey her Ministers at Westminster. Throughout this crisis, Montrose retained his post at the Ministry of Agriculture, transferring later to the Ministry of External Affairs and Defence. He was, therefore, part of a rebellious illegal government, guilty in constitutional law of treason. It is a beguiling irony which makes a traitor of the direct descendant of the Great Montrose, one of the most illustrious heroes in our history, who gave his life in the service of the Crown. The irony appears to be lost on the Duke, who wrote an article explaining that he did not feel himself bound by the oath of allegiance to remain loyal to ideals which he does not share, and which were not in his mind when he took the oath.[5] It is doubtful if the argument would hold up in law. He would, at least theoretically, be liable to prosecution under the Treason Act of 1351 for taking part in a treacherous assembly against the Queen's Majesty. Roger Casement and Lord Haw-Haw were both prosecuted under this Act. Since U.D.I. the Duke has not been back to Britain to test the matter. He holds a Rhodesian passport and considers himself a Rhodesian in all but birth. He recently applied for a British passport, which was refused.*

Willie Hamilton, tireless pursuer of the abusers of privilege, suggested that the noble Duke be banned henceforth from Westminster. The Prime Minister of the day, Harold Wilson, would not be pressed. "Those who have had a chance of observing this member of the illegal régime at close quarters will not treat him with quite so much seriousness as you do," he said. The Duke's constitutional position continues to be a peculiar unresolved anomaly.

As time progressed, Montrose was revealed to be too extreme even for Mr Smith. He had already broken with his old friend Humphrey Gibbs, H.M. Governor, as a result of the crisis, and in 1968 came the rupture with Smith, whose policy of gradualism exasperated the Duke. It was widely rumoured that Montrose had persuaded Smith to reverse his position and reject the agreement he had worked out with Wilson on H.M.S. *Tiger* in 1966.[6] This time Smith could not be pushed towards obstinacy, so Montrose resigned from his government. The resignation did not make the impression he might have expected. The *Daily Telegraph*, in a leader, called him "an insignificant person",[7] which must have hurt; word was passed round that he had not been a particularly effective minister anyway, and that his speeches as well as his understanding of the work were often less polished than those of the black men whose intelligence he so deplored.

Montrose remains passionately devoted to the idea of Commonwealth, and just as hotly antagonistic against the idea of Common Market. He is a man of strong emotions, intensely patriotic (though to which *patria* is sometimes confusing), outspoken, unmoved by compromise. If he were to meet his great ancestor at the pearly gates, they would hardly recognise one another. Sometimes his passion rouses him to an impressive rhetoric. "We shall soon know," he said in 1965, "whether our mother country will say to us 'My sons go in peace with my blessing', or whether she will throw us from her, spitefully, upon a rocky road, while she clutches to her bosom the cuckoos in her nest."[8]

He has not been in government now since 1968, but is still in Rhodesia, where he prefers to be known as Angus Graham. Even as

* The essence of the offence of Treason lies in the withdrawal of allegiance which is owed to the Sovereign by all British subjects wherever they may be. Those wishing to pursue the matter might with profit consult Halsbury's *Laws of England*, wherein grounds for the charge of Treason are listed, among which is the action of a person who 'levies war against the Sovereign in her realm, or gives them aid or comfort in the realm, or elsewhere.' The Treason Act of 1351 has been amended by Treason Act, 1795, Treason Act, 1817, Treason Felony Act, 1848, and the Statute Law Revision Act of 1948.

a minister he was never more than "Lord Graham", apparently to avoid embarrassing the Rhodesians who would not know how to address him. Also, he quite manifestly feels more easy as Angus Graham, the Rhodesian farmer.

Interestingly enough, the family name "Graham" is perhaps derived from a word "greim" meaning one who is (or looks) determined, one who holds hard,[9] as in the modern "grim-faced". If so, it would apply most aptly to the 7th Duke of Montrose, and to that part of the personality of his great ancestor, the great Marquess of Montrose. They have little else in common.

The Marquess of Montrose (1612–1650), great-grandfather of the dukedom is one of the giant figures of history, martyr, military genius, poet, democratic idealist, and hero of romance and chivalry. He is, in his way, as great a man as Wellington or Marlborough, and brings to the name of Montrose as much lustre and distinction. He died before his task could be completed, but he left behind him "an inspiration and a name which would outlast the ruin of his hopes".[10]

Montrose was descended from a line of earls, the first of whom was killed at Flodden Field on 9th September 1513, fighting in the opposite camp to Surrey, ancestor of the Duke of Norfolk. The story of Montrose runs parallel with that of Argyll and of Hamilton, ancestors of the dukes of that name, who have found their way into other chapters. Of the three, it is Montrose who has become legendary, while Argyll and Hamilton have difficulty retrieving any kind of reputation from the events.

We are in Covenanting times. Charles I had attempted to impose upon the Scots a new Prayer Book, or "Book of Public Service" to give it its full name, which was formal, elaborate, and smelt a little of Roman liturgy. It did not please the Scots, at that time seduced by the simplicity of Presbyterianism which preferred extempore prayers and eschewed ceremony, with the result that Charles's orders were greeted with riots in churches throughout Scotland and the beginning of a fatal schism had appeared. A week later, the National Covenant was drawn up, a large parchment promising to defend king and country against the impertinent power of the bishops and against the threat of Popery. The parchment was stretched out upon a tombstone, and "for three days, wet or fine, from morn to dusk, the scratching of the pen never ceased".[11] Those who signed the Covenant were henceforth known as Covenanters, and those who refused were the Royalists. Of the former, young Montrose, high-spirited, eager to serve and to make his mark, was foremost. Of the latter, it was Hamilton, the King's friend and adviser, who led, a pompous, strutting over-rated peacock of a man, who loved the luxurious Court of London, and visited Scotland with reluctance.

At the famous Assembly of 1638, over which presided Hamilton as the King's Commissioner, the third protagonist, Argyll, had not yet declared himself. Hamilton dissolved the Assembly, at which point it ceased to be legal, and stalked out without anyone paying him any attention. Argyll then stepped in and within minutes had established himself as the leader of the Covenanting Party; he was the wealthiest, the most powerful as chief of the Campbells, the most wily and shrewd man present.

Montrose was no match for either Hamilton, whose sycophancy he could not emulate, or Argyll, whose political wisdom was too mature for him, and both were shortly to be his enemy. He had a frank, honest nature, candour and youthful enthusiasm. He was certainly the most intelligent of the three and was to entertain a philosophy which the other two were incapable of understanding.

Montrose was above all a thinker. While other Scottish nobles were governed by fierce passions, fanatical convictions, the inflexibility of unreflective, over-confident youth, Montrose was governed by reason, by calm analysis. He was unique in the Scotland of that time. His ideals were democratic; he valued the conception of Sovereignty, but did not confuse it with Monarchy. For a stable government, sovereignty was essential, either the sovereignty of kings, as in Europe, or of a council of nobles, as in Venice, or of the representatives of the people, as in ancient Rome. He did not hold that the monarchical system was necessarily the best, simply because it was the system which obtained in Britain, but he did see that it was better to improve it than to overthrow it. His idea was a constitutional monarchy, a king circumscribed by duty towards his people and obedience to the law. What he feared most was the instability which led to anarchy, and the vilest of evils – oppression. Anarchy, he said, was "the oppression and tyranny of subjects, the most fierce, insatiable, and insufferable tyranny in the world".[12] Many of these ideas were generations ahead of their time, and inconceivable in a land where the divine right of kings to rule without question was the order of the day. When Argyll took over as the Covenanting leader, policies became extreme, stupid, and cruel; they threatened the stability which Montrose cherished, the rule of law, the precious legality upon which any charge must be based. He left them and joined the King, telling him frankly that he would cease to support His Majesty if he (the King) were to diverge from his duty of defending the religion and rights of his people. It was a bold declaration.

Initially, Hamilton was able to turn the King against the young man who suddenly offered his services. Hamilton was jealous of Montrose's popularity, beauty and dash, and was afraid that he might get too close to the King. Eventually, however, Charles learned to trust the convert, and sent him on a mission to bring Scotland to obedience.

Montrose had no army, no means of raising one, and would be imprisoned as soon as he entered Scotland, yet he must somehow subdue Scotland for the King. All he had was the King's order. It was a hopeless task. "As in most great adventures, there was no solid hope save in the soul of the adventurer. . . . He was to fling himself into the midst of a hostile country to improvise an army."[13] This is exactly what he achieved. In disguise, with only the power of his personality to defend him, Montrose made for the Highlands, and there he revealed his identity, captured the imagination of those sturdy Highlanders, and emerged from the darkness some weeks later to win a series of impossible battles, with a force of 1500 men against thousands. For a year, he won one battle after another – Inverlochy, Dundee, Aberdeen, Tippermuir, until he appeared invincible. That year, 1642, saw the birth of his legend.

As a strategist, he was without peer. Space will not allow an examination of his battles, but a brilliant lucid account is offered in John Buchan's book. This strategic cunning was in spite of the unfamiliarity of the Highlands; the Grahams were a lowland family. Not only was he a military genius, which would not alone be sufficient for a legend, but he was a leader of decency and humanity. In an age when it was routine for a conquering army to plunder, pillage, murder and rape, Montrose forbade his men any such vengeful act; they were allowed victuals, but not wanton destruction. The men were unpaid, yet they were loyal. They observed his ideals of succour to the wounded, avoidance of unnecessary bloodshed, and generosity to a defeated army. Within a year the name of Montrose rang around the Highlands with a power that made Argyll and Hamilton tremble. He had "kindled already a fire which the parliament of Edinburgh could not quench".[14]

He was finally defeated at the battle of Philiphaugh. Just before hostilities began, he took the Garter ribbon from around his neck and concealed it in the cleft of a holly tree, meaning to return and reclaim it later. Of course, he never did. Years later it was discovered there, and returned to the Montrose family, with whom it remains.[15]

The rest of an exciting career must be passed over rapidly. When Charles I was executed, Montrose fainted at the news. He then shut himself in his study for two days and two nights to think. He emerged determined to expiate the King's death, but knowing that the odds were against him. He declared his loyalty to Charles II, "as I never desired to live but for their Majesty's service, so shall I never shun to die for yours".[16] The new king in exile made a fatal error of judgement in negotiating with the Argyll faction in Edinburgh, whom he had officially to treat as the legitimate government there, while commissioning Montrose privately to go back to Scotland and fight against Argyll in the King's name. Argyll promptly placed a price of £30,000 on Montrose's head, declared him a traitor and called him "James Graham". Montrose wrote to the King that he would abandon his life for the King's interests, "with that integrity that you and all the world shall see that it is not your fortunes, but you, in whatsoever fortune, that I make sacred to serve".[17]

Montrose was betrayed by MacLeod of Assynt, who had offered him shelter. He was brought to Edinburgh. The people of the city had been told that the miserable traitor was about to be shown to them, and they were encouraged to line the streets for his entry. Some were hired to stone him. He was placed on a hangman's cart, his arms tied to his sides so that he would not be able to avoid the stones, and a fanfare was sounded when the exhibition was about to begin. The cart creaked slowly into the street called Canongate, packed tight with a jeering mob. Within seconds an amazing change overtook the crowd. The jeering ceased, the shouting died down, and soon there was nothing but an eerie respectful silence, stabbed occassionally with sobbing. For three hours the cart edged its way up the Canongate, and by the end of the journey the fame of Montrose was assured. Argyll was celebrating the wedding of his son on the same day and in the same street. He peered through a curtain at his vanquished foe, whose cart had come to a standstill so thick were the crowds, and hoping to see the degradation of a hero, saw instead a man whom he, Argyll, had helped to canonise.

Montrose approached the market cross where he was to hang on a gibbet thirty feet high (later known as "Argyll's altar" or the Ministers' altar), taunted and provoked by the clergy who wished him to repent. He remained cool and unfailingly courteous, impressing all with the dignity of his bearing. Only once did he raise his voice slightly. "Gentleman, let me die in peace," he said, and there was silence. He climbed the ladder, looked at the rope, and asked "How long must I hang there?" The hangman fixed the halter, tears streaming down his face, and Montrose, without flinching stepped off to his death. His body hung there for three hours, was then hacked to pieces, the head placed on a spike on the Tolbooth (where it remained for eleven years, until it was replaced by Argyll's), and the limbs distributed to Stirling, Glasgow, Perth, and Aberdeen. It was a death reserved for a criminal, not for a nobleman or a soldier. Montrose's only comment was that he was pleased the Scots should make sure his loyalty was proved throughout the country in so forceful and visible a way. His last words were, "God have mercy on this afflicted land."

So died a man whose sense of justice, mercy and truth shone in an age of vindictiveness, a man who insisted on treating his prisoners well, who allowed them to write to their family and friends, and entertained them at his own table, a man who retired from the battle to write a profession of faith remarkable for its style as for its content, or to write some beautiful verse. His equal has not been seen in Scotland. In John Buchan's phrase, it was "a career which must rank among the marvels of our history".

Montrose's son was the 2nd Marquess (1631–1669), known as "The Good Marquess", who effected a decent reconciliation between his house and the Argylls. He said that he could not vote at the trial of Argyll in 1661, because he was too closely involved to be impartial. In 1667 the two sons drank each other's health in public, and Argyll was appointed guardian to Montrose's son. When Montrose died, Argyll travelled from Inveraray to attend his funeral.[18]

The 1st Duke of Montrose (1682–1742) was elevated to the highest rank as a reward for his services in connection with the union with Scotland in 1707. He had been a strong supporter of the union, and of the Protestant succession, much to the annoyance of his father's side of the family. It was said that he was led by the nose and governed by his mother and her relations, which, in view of his sweet disposition and good nature, is more than likely. The influence of his name carried some weight when he allied himself against the Jacobite rebellion of 1715. There again, his mother seems to have made the decision as to what side he should take. A satirical verse of the time makes no bones about it :

> "Limner, proceed, conspicuously expose
> The chicken hearted narrow soul Montrose,
> Show how he doth debase his noble line
> Which heretofore illustriously did shine.
> Show how he makes himself a fool of State,
> A slave to avarice, to his friends ungrate."[19]

He also has a place in the history of Rob Roy, for it was owing to the failure of a speculation which Rob Roy shared with the Duke and the Duke's demand for repayment, that Roy had to resort to an outlaw's life, supporting himself by robbing the Duke's tenants.

Political life was a wasteland to the 2nd Duke of Montrose (1712–1790), for he was totally deaf, and for the last thirty years, quite blind as well. His life was miserably isolated, needing an interpreter to speak even to his wife. Their one joy was their son, Lord Graham. The deafness, incidentally, was to recur in the family four generations later.

His Duchess died very suddenly one day after dinner. They ate some minced veal, which she said she liked extremely well, then slumped back in her chair lifeless.

The 3rd Duke (1755–1836) resumed political life. He was in turn Master of the Horse, President of the Board of Trade, Postmaster-General, and Lord Chamberlain. His handling of these positions was not very distinguished, and he seems chiefly to be remembered for having effected a change in the law which enabled Highlanders to wear the kilt, long prohibited, prompting a wit to congratulate him thus :

> *Thy patriot zeal has bared their parts behind*
> *To the keen whistling of the wintry wind.*

He was handsome man, with "symmetry of external figure" and no fool; the general view was that the jobs given him taxed his undoubted abilities too far. Wraxall said that he "displayed various qualities calculated to compensate for the want of great ability; particuarly, the prudence, sagacity, and attention to his own interests, so characteristic of the Caledonian people".[20] Pitt, who made him Lord of the Treasury as well as much else besides, was thought to have overloaded him. The same Wraxall tetchily pointed out that Montrose was only given the Garter "after long hesitation", because the Duke of Norfolk had refused it.

His son was a man in much the same mould, reserved, not easily reachable, but with that strict Montrose honour which recurs. Also Postmaster-General (he actually *reduced* overseas postal charges), he introduced into the family bag of idiosyncrasies an overbalance towards the right-wing which has persisted into the twentieth century. His duchess·caused a stir in the wake of the Flora Hastings scandal by publicly hissing Queen Victoria. Lady Flora Hastings had been driven to illness and early death by a nasty campaign of gossip in which Queen Victoria had played an unworthy part. The substance of the tattle was that Lady Flora was unlawfully pregnant, and as a Lady of the Bedchamber to the Queen's mother, Duchess of Kent, her condition was indecent. The rumour was without any foundation, but the poor girl had to submit to medical examination and private torment; she died at Buckingham Palace in 1839, aged thirty-three, bringing a storm of vehement unpopularity about the Queen's head. The Duchess of Montrose made her one contribution to history by booing Victoria as she made her customary progress down the course at Ascot. The Duchess's companion was Lady Sarah Ingestre. The Queen wanted to have both women flogged,[21] and her defendants thought them foolish and vulgar.[22] The affair was shortly patched up, and the Duke, who died in 1874 at the age of seventy-five, was once more admitted at Court.

He was succeeded by his son as 5th Duke of Montrose (1852–1925), on whose death the family estates were decimated to meet taxation. His wife, Hermione, was a grand-daughter of the sad 12th Duke of Somerset, thus bringing into the Montrose genes the blood of that ill-fated man.

The 6th Duke of Montrose (1878–1954), A.D.C. to George V (as had been his father), was the sailor Duke, a Knight of the Thistle, and C.V.O. Among his more esoteric accomplishments was the first-ever film of a total eclipse of the sun, which he took in India in 1899, and the invention of the first aircraft carrier. More significantly, he demonstrated in bold lines the Graham political leanings by working as chairman of the Scottish Nationalist Party, although it is fair to say that the independence he wanted for Scotland was relative and limited, not absolute. He probably inherited his deafness from an ancestral propensity. He married a daughter of the 12th Duke of Hamilton, and their son is the present Rhodesian Duke.

Their grandson is heir to the titles, Marquess of Graham, married to a Canadian and living on Graham land in Scotland, of which about 10,000 acres remain. Lord Graham, enthusiastic in the Moral Rearmament movement, is caretaker of the relics of the Marquess of Montrose, that most tolerant and generous of men, to whom M.R.A. would have been anathema.

*   *   *

While the Marquess was fighting for the King in Scotland, with sensational success, the 2nd Earl of Manchester (1602–1671) was fighting somewhat half-heartedly for Cromwell in England, with no success to speak of. Despondency overwhelmed him, as he realised "if we beat the king ninety-nine times, he is king still, and so will his posterity be after him; but if the king beat us once, we shall all be hanged, and our posterity made slaves".[23] His personality was not made for the burden of war. Like Montrose, he most wanted a peaceful constitutional monarchy, yet he found himself on the opposite side to the Marquess. Meekness and a gentle nature fashioned his attitudes, and although he was a Puritan, he was no extreme ascetic. Softness of temper endeared him to all except Cromwell, who grew steadily exasperated with his mildness, and charged him with waging the war incompetently. Neglect and incapacity were levelled against him by the furious Cromwell, who, according to Clarendon, "hated him above all men, and desired to have taken away his life".[24] He even accused the earl of cowardice, which was not justified. In truth, Manchester was sick to death with the war, which he secretly realised was futile because it was not lawful. However reasonable might be the grievances of the Puritans, they were outside the law in rebellion against the King. Manchester was more principled than Cromwell, and he was, after all, from an illustrious family of lawyers; he knew what he was talking about.

From the beginning, Manchester had no stomach for rebellion. He was convinced that the King was in error, but he was brought into open opposition by one of Charles's grossest blunders, and one of the most direct causes of the Civil War. The King had entered the House of Commons and attempted to arrest five of the members, charging them with treason. The Earl of Manchester was one of the five. Clarendon tells the story vividly :

"On 3 January 1642 he accused Lord Mandeville (later Earl of Manchester) and five members of the House of Commons – including Pym, Hampden, Heselrige and Holles – of high treason. The next day he went himself to arrest them, taking with him a file of musketeers. But the news had gone before him, and as Charles entered the House of Commons the five members were already on their way by boat to a safe refuge in the City. When the king looked round the House and saw that his enemies had fled, he called on the Speaker to tell him where they had gone, but the Speaker fell on his knees and answered: 'May it please your Majesty, I have neither eyes to see, nor tongue to speak in this place but as the House is pleased to direct me, whose servant I am.' Charles knew that his coup had failed. 'Well,' he said, 'since I see all the birds are flown, I do expect from you that you shall send them unto me as soon as they return hither', and he left the House as abruptly as he had come."[25]

The next time Charles went to the Palace of Westminster, it was to stand trial.

Manchester was not suited by disposition to those tempestuous times; he could not call upon a reserve of hatred or ferocity to carry him through. Cromwell could stand it no longer, and got rid of him. "He was at last dismissed, and removed from any trust for no other reason, but because he was not wicked enough."[26]

He opposed the ordinance to place the King on trial with the strongest resolution of his career, and had no part in his execution. He was active in bringing about the Restoration, bearing the Sword of State at Charles II's coronation in 1661, and he was on the bench which tried the regicides. History has allowed him a decent repentance.

If anything proved that he preferred the fireside to the battlefront, it was the Earl of Manchester's marriages. He married no less than five times (the first four wives all died), three of them members of the same family. He was the husband in turn of the Earl of Warwick's daughter, the Earl of Warwick's sister, and the Earl of Warwick's wife.

Manchester, whose family name was Montagu, was descended from Sir Edward Montagu (1532–1602) of Boughton in Northamptonshire. Sir Edward's father, a Lord Chief Justice, had refused to recognise the patent which created Edward Seymour 1st Duke of Somerset (as it had been created by Seymour himself), and had recognised Lady Jane Grey as Queen (for which he later apologised). In both cases, he established the family tradition of strict legal probity on which this line of lawyers has prided itself. He bought Boughton House in 1528. The second Sir Edward Montagu had six sons, of whom the first was created Baron Montagu of Boughton and was ancestor to the Dukes of Montagu. The title is now extinct, but the Montagu lands, including Boughton House, passed by marriage into the Duke of Buccleuch's family; the Buccleuch of today lives at Boughton. The third son, Sydney Montagu, was ancestor of the earls of Sandwich, and the second son was Henry Montagu, Earl of Manchester and ancestor of the dukes of Manchester. The Montagu name survives today not only in the dukedom of Manchester and that of Buccleuch (Montagu-Douglas-Scott), but also in the family name of Lord Montagu of Beaulieu (Douglas-Scott-Montagu). All three men are descended from Sir Edward.

The Manchester family claims an ultimate descent from one Drogo de Monte Acuto, who came with the Conqueror, and all Dukes of Manchester since 1855 have borne the name "Drogo" in recognition of the fact. It is, however, entirely fanciful. They are actually descended from a man called Richard Ladde, who changed his name to "Montagu" about 1447. Nobody knows why.[27]

We shall see that the Manchesters have long accepted an erroneous version of the derivation of their principal title as well.

Henry Montagu was created Baron Kimbolton and Viscount Mandeville in 1620, and Earl of Manchester in 1626. He had shortly before, in 1619 or 1620, bought from the Wingfield family a handsome residence in Huntingdonshire called Kimbolton Castle, notable as a place where Catherine of Aragon had been imprisoned and spent the last ten years of her life. It had previously been the ancient seat of the Mendevils. Thus, when Henry Montagu bought the post of Lord High Treasurer of England for £20,000 from the Duke of Buckingham, who traded blatantly in political offices and peerage titles to fill the King's purse, he was told the position carried a peerage with it, so he chose as his titles the name of his new home, and the name of its previous owners – Kimbolton and Mandeville.* In effect, he bought himself into the peerage, as others did in different ways. Only ten months later, Mandeville had to relinquish this office, but the peerage titles were there to stay.

Five years after that, he was raised still higher as 1st Earl of Manchester. It has long been assumed, even by the dukes of Manchester themselves, that this title had nothing whatever to do with the cotton-spinning industrial city in the north of England. Ten miles from Kimbolton Castle is a little place called Godmanchester, which is supposed to have given its name to the Earl, who then shortened it. One only has to consult the patent roll of 1626 to see that this is wrong. Henry Montagu is quite clearly Earl of Manchester *in the county of Lancaster*, in spite of his never having been near the place. Godmanchester in Huntingdonshire is a red herring. The most that can be said is that the local village, by an association of ideas, suggested "Manchester" to his mind for want of any better alternative.

Montagu had first come to notice as a lawyer and a judge. In 1616 he had opened the case against Lord and Lady Somerset in their trial for the murder of Sir Thomas Overbury. He was an assiduous member of the Star Chamber, noted for his lawyer's impartiality, equal in condemnation of Puritan and Papist. He became one of Charles I's most trusted advisers, his probity unquestioned. Later he was Lord Privy Seal and Speaker of the House of Lords. Theologically deeply learned, Manchester published a Protestant treatise which he called *Contemplationes Mortis et Immortalitatis*, in dignified and persuasive prose. It first appeared in 1631 running into fifteen

---

* Just as, in 1933, the brewer Mr Nall-Cain bought Lord Melbourne's old house, Brocket Hall in Hertfordshire and took the name "Lord Brocket" for his peerage. He now lives at the Duke of Leinster's old seat, Carton.

editions by 1688. Hand in hand with piety, he was drunk with every meal.[28]

His son was the 2nd Earl, Cromwell's reluctant lieutenant, and his grandson 3rd Earl of Manchester fought as Captain in the Duke of Monmouth's regiment of 1666.

The 4th Earl was created 1st Duke of Manchester (1662–1722), though it is not at all easy to see why. He had been a lifelong supporter of William of Orange since the two met in Europe in 1685 (the Earl was then twenty-three years old), demonstrating his support by bearing St Edward's staff at the coronation of William and Mary in 1689. His life carries no surprises. In common with father, grandfather, and back to Sir Edward Montagu, he revered the constitution and loved the process of law. Nevertheless, as Ambassador to Venice and Paris successively, he does not appear to have done very well, meeting with rebuffs and evasions in his diplomacy, so that his dukedom, conferred by George I in 1719, can only have been a prize for trying.

Belle Montagu is remembered by those who wish to draw from her life a lesson in the duplicity and cunning of women. She was a daughter of the Duke of Montagu, and grand-daughter of the great Marlborough. She conceived a passion for the handsome twenty-three-year-old 2nd Duke of Manchester (1700–1739), to whom she was, of course, distantly related. "Belle is at this instant in the paradisal state of receiving visits every day from a passionate lover, who is her first love", wrote one lady. There was a story, unattested but fascinating, that the Duke was so insane with love that he shut himself into a room with a pair of loaded pistols and determined to kill himself if she would not have him. Unfortunately, his aim was not good. The first shot took away his right eye and some bone. The second shot shattered his jaw. He then tried to string himself from the ceiling. Servants came to his rescue, and Belle was so impressed she consented to marry him then and there. Certainly they were married very quickly, in April of that year, and certainly they were miserably unhappy within six months. Belle gave her husband a dreadful time. "The Duchess of Manchester frets, shrugs, and barks there as usual; but whether Her Grace has swallow'd or spit out again the tips of all the noses she has bit off since you left England, I am unable to inform you. The only reason why she has never deprived her dear Duke of his, I suppose, is that she hopes one time or other to lead him by it."[29] So wrote Lord Hervey to Henry Fox, eight years after the marriage. Elsewhere he refers to them as the she-tiger and the jackass.

Belle must have been a trying woman. Apart from her habit of coming down to breakfast with a parrot, a monkey and a lapdog,[30] she was pursued by enslaved men. She showed no remorse when her husband, to whom her indifference was now public knowledge, died at the age of thirty-nine, leaving her only the furniture of two upstairs rooms and everything else to his brother. Within a year the poor Earl of Scarborough was smitten with a passion for her which ended in his suicide. (Probably this story has become confused with the unsubstantiated account of the Duke's mania; Scarborough definitely *did* die.) He had apparently entrusted to her a state secret which she had foolishly divulged in gossip, leaving the man no choice but to kill himself.[31] Or he may have died for love of her. A few years afterwards she married an obscure Irishman called Hussey, for whom she obtained a suitable ennoblement. Charles Hanbury Williams drily noted : "How slight the difference is between The Duchess and the Hussey."

The Duke had meanwhile been succeeded by his brother as 3rd Duke of Manchester (1710–1762), whose son the 4th Duke (1737–1788) deserves attention for having given London one of its famous squares. He built himself a town house in 1776, called it Manchester House, and the square front Manchester Square. The house now holds the Wallace Collection and has changed its name; the square is still the same, however, as are Manchester Street, Mandeville Place, and now the Mandeville Hotel.

Politically, the 4th Duke was a Whig, and an estimable man, although Wraxall speaks disparagingly of him. He gave generous support to the colonists throughout the American War of Independence, being one of the few to agree wholeheartedly with the Duke of Richmond's progressive views in the matter. He voted for Richmond's motion of 5th March 1776 to suspend hostilities with the colonists, and again on 23rd March his motion requesting the withdrawal of troops from America. In 1779 he predicted that the same trouble would eventually occur in Ireland.

Manchester was appointed Lord Lieutenant for the county of Huntingdonshire and, intriguingly, High Steward of Godmanchester. It must surely be from this time that the confusion as to the origin of the title dates. He died from a violent three-day fever after catching a chill watching cricket at Brighton.

So did his son, the 5th Duke (1771–1843), who continued his father's enlightened policies, particularly as Governor of Jamaica for nearly twenty years (1808–1827). In the face of vigorous opposition from the sugar and coffee planters, the Duke of Manchester intro-

duced a number of reforms for the benefit of black slaves. To propose
that whips should not be carried in the streets, and that women
should be exempt from flogging may not now seem aggressively
socialist, but it was a brave man who would take the side of the
slaves even in a measured degree at the beginning of the nineteenth
century.

Another of the Duke's attitudes, of which there is also thankfully
no vestige today, was that extraordinary indifference to the affairs of
his own family, that impenetrable starchiness of the paterfamilias
which we so often find in the aristocracy of the eighteenth and
nineteenth centuries. A glimpse of it is afforded in 1822, when the
Duke's son and heir, Lord Mandeville, announced his engagement.
A lady approached the Duke and complimented him, making polite
phrases about young Mandeville's excellent character, talents, manners, etc., until the Duke interrupted her to say that he knew little
or nothing of the young man.[32] Perhaps his accident two years
before had had some effect; he had fallen out of his carriage and
fractured his skull. Or perhaps he simply was not interested in the
boy, who reminded him of his notorious wife and their unhappy
marriage. She had been a daughter of Jane, Duchess of Gordon, and
had become the archetype of the Duchess who really *did* elope with
her footman, some time before 1812. As for the Duke, he was widely
regarded as a splendid-looking man. One woman went so far as to
describe him as "the most beautiful statue-like person that ever was
seen in flesh and blood".[33]

With the coming of the Victorian and Edwardian eras, the Manchesters enter a period when they are leaders of the "fast set", taking
their cue from the Prince of Wales, and viewed askance by the
better-behaved ducal families. The Abercorns, their neighbours in
London, darkly instructed their children that the Manchesters were
"worldly".[34] None of this volatility within the social scale was achieved
by the dukes; the 7th Duke of Manchester (1823–1890) was "a
well-intentioned bore", and his laboursome book, *Court and Society,*
corroborates the judgement. But his wife was a different matter. It
was she who brought zest and sparkle to the Manchester set and
made it "fast", and who, with her driving ambition, lifted her dull
husband from the shadows. She was Louise von Alten, a German
countess, gloriously beautiful, and eventually to be known as the
"Double Duchess". We have already met her as the Duchess of
Devonshire. She married the Duke of Devonshire forty years after she
married the Duke of Manchester, but even before that she exerted a
powerful influence over her retiring protégé, who was far more intel-

ligent than her husband and far more worthy of her ambitions. Louise's spell has not yet quite evaporated in the last quarter of the twentieth century, while the two husbands, whom she made shine, have grown dim with time.

The death of Louise in 1911 really did mark the end of an era; for once the cliché is appropriate. Three years later the Great War smashed the aristocratic way of life with indiscriminate vengeance, and the like of Louise von Alten was not to be seen again. On a domestic scale, her death also marked a profound change in the Manchester family (although it is true to say the Devonshires have gone on much as before). In the last hundred years, the Dukes of Manchester have gradually divorced themselves from English life, have married colossally wealthy foreign heiresses and taken their money abroad. Kimbolton Castle, which gave them one of their titles, is now a grammar school. The 9th Duke of Manchester very neatly made the last flamboyant gesture of the old style at about the same date that Louise died; he challenged Crown Prince Willie of Germany to a duel, because the man had behaved like a cad.[35] Willie did not accept, but it must be one of the last such challenges seriously made in our history. Characteristically, Manchester was most concerned that the Crown Prince should not refuse simply because his rank as Duke was not sufficiently elevated for the German to accept with honour. Only ten or twenty years later, everyone would have laughed the man to scorn.

The 8th Duke (1853–1892) married Consuelo Iznaga del Valle, of Ravenswood, U.S.A., and of Cuba. She had wit and vivacity and was very popular. Besides a son and heir, she produced twin daughters, Alice and Mary, who as infants were presented to Queen Victoria, on whom they immediately pounced, without ceremony, almost choking her with embraces, and shouting "Nice Queen! Nice Queen!" They must have been charming, for the Queen was, this time, amused. Later at lunch, the little girls were appalled to see Her Majesty take up a chicken bone and pick it with her fingers. Pointing at her, they shouted in unison, "Piggy wiggy!!"[36] Alas, the girls had a much chastened future. They were both ill in their youth, and died of consumption, one aged sixteen, the other at twenty-one.

The 9th Duke (1877–1947) married the daughter of a railway director in Cincinnati, Ohio, Helena Zimmerman, and their son was the Kenyan duke, Alexander Drogo Montagu, o.b.e.

In 1967 the modern descent of those accomplished lawyer Montagus, who we are told love the constitution of their country and cherished the way in which its history was preserved in legal documents, removed the Manchester Papers from the Public Record Office, where they had been deposited for a century. The Keepers of the Office protested, pointing out that the collection was a valuable source for scholars and should reside in the P.R.O. if the Duke of Manchester was not prepared to house them himself. He offered them for sale to the Office, at a price of £1200 but there were no funds to meet such a demand. He then offered them to the British Museum, and they too could not afford to buy them. So the 10th Duke sold them at Sotheby's, and the precious collection was dispersed to all winds. Among the papers was found an unknown manuscript poem in the hand of John Donne.

REFERENCES

1. The Duke of Manchester, *My Candid Recollections*, p.30.
2. Submission to 1960 Monckton Commission, quoted in *The Times*, 13th September 1968.
3. *Sunday Mirror*, 17th October 1965.
4. *The Guardian*, 4th October 1965.
5. *The Scotsman*, 10th November 1964.
6. *The Observer*, 12th September 1968.
7. *Daily Telegraph*, 13th September 1968.
8. *The Guardian*, 4th October 1965.
9. Duke of Montrose, *My Ditty Box*, p. 11.
10. S. R. Gardiner, quoted in *Complete Peerage*.
11. C. V. Wedgwood, *Montrose*, p. 27.
12. John Buchan, *Montrose*, Appendix.
13. *ibid.*, pp. 168–9.
14. Clarendon, *History of the Rebellion*, Chapter XV.
15. Duke of Montrose, *My Ditty Box*, p. 13.
16. British Museum, Egerton MSS, 19399, f. 62, quoted in *Complete Peerage*.
17. *Cal. S. P. Dom., 1650*, p. 61.
18. *Hist. MSS. Comm.*, 6th Report, p. 609.
19. *Complete Peerage*.
20. Wraxall, *Posthumous Memoirs*, Vol. I, p. 59.

21. Cecil Woodham-Smith, *Queen Victoria*, Vol. I, p. 180.
22. Greville, IV, 81.
23. D.N.B.
24. Clarendon, *History of the Rebellion*, Chapter XXIV.
25. *ibid.*, Introduction.
26. *Characters of the Seventeenth Century*, ed. David Nichol Smith, p. 162.
27. *Complete Peerage*, Vol. IV, Appendix D.
28. Bernard Falk, *The Way of the Montagues*, p. 40.
29. *Lord Hervey and His Friends*, p. 121.
30. Falk, *op. cit.*, p. 282.
31. Duke of Manchester, *My Candid Recollections*, p. 27.
32. Creevey, *Life and Times*, p. 171.
33. *Complete Peerage*.
34. Lord Ernest Hamilton, *The Halycon Era*, p. 74.
35. Duke of Manchester, *My Candid Recollections*, p. 233.
36. *ibid.*, p. 56.

15. Distinctive Extinctions

Duke of Bridgwater; Duchess of Albemarle; Duchess of Bolton; Duchess of Kingston; Duchess of Cleveland; Duke of Berwick; Duke of Leeds

In the history of the realm, 162 separate ducal titles have been created (excluding the royal dukedoms), and only twenty-six remain today. It would be a pity to ignore some of the more interesting or colourful characters of the past, whose lines are now extinct. Some, like the Duke of Buckingham (of the Villiers family), would deserve, and have been accorded, a book to themselves; others, like the Duke of Ancaster, belong in oblivion. I would like, at this point, to select, in a totally arbitrary and personal way, a few of the personalities who were once the centre of attention but who now languish in neglect.

A name which has occurred more than once in these pages is the Duke of Bridgwater. He turns up in the Sutherland story, for they inherited his property and the present Duke of Sutherland bears his surname – Egerton; he is mentioned in the Hamilton and the Argyll accounts, for he was a suitor of the widowed Duchess of Hamilton (Elizabeth Gunning), who later accepted the Duke of Argyll; and some of his property was recently sold by the Duke of Westminster.

There were only three dukes of Bridgwater, a father and two sons. It is the 3rd Duke, Francis Egerton (1736–1803), who made the title famous by building the Bridgwater canals and so anticipating by over half a century the great revolution in transport brought about by the railways. So celebrated was this achievement that it is often supposed his title was chosen to represent "bridge over the water". The title in fact predated the canal system by many years, and is owed instead to a small town in County Somerset, which means "the burg of Walter" and should therefore always be spelt without the central "e".

Francis Egerton was the second son of the 1st Duke of Bridgwater

(Scroop Egerton) and Lady Rachel Russell,* daughter of the Duke of Bedford. As a child he was "not only sickly, but apparently of such feeble intellect that his exclusion from succession to the dukedom was actually contemplated". However, his elder brother died, which brought him the dukedom at the age of twelve. At seventeen he was still a disaster, ignorant and unruly. While still a very young man, he proposed to Elizabeth Gunning and was at first accepted. But he insisted that after the marriage she should have nothing further to do with her sister Lady Coventry, of whom he did not approve. She not surprisingly refused to comply with this condition, so he abruptly broke off the engagement, and retired in disgust to his country seat in Lancashire, at the age of twenty-three, resolved to have nothing more to do with "society".

Within weeks of his self-inflicted exile, he turned his attention to his canal scheme, which presumably he had been nurturing. He obtained authority by Act of Parliament to build a canal from Worsley to Salford, but James Brindley the contractor, who had undertaken similar but less ambitious work for Lord Stafford, the Duke's brother-in-law, persuaded him to build the canal as far as Manchester, with an aqueduct over the Irwell. We now take such matters so much for granted that it is difficult to imagine how absurdly futuristic it appeared to contemporaries, who ridiculed the whole idea. Fortunately Bridgwater was not one to be deflected by mockery, so he adopted the scheme with almost visible defiance. A second Act of Parliament was obtained in 1760, and so was built the first canal in England to be entirely independent of a natural stream throughout its course. The aqueduct attracted sightseers, and, more practically, the price of coal in Manchester was reduced by half as a result of cheap transport. The Duke of Bridgwater was called the founder of British inland navigation.

That is not the end of the story, however. The Duke and Brindley then proposed a canal from Manchester to Liverpool. They met with fierce opposition. It was a foolish undertaking, the idea of a madman, it would never be realised. Unperturbed, the Duke proceeded with his plan, gained the permission of Parliament, and built the canal, twenty-eight miles long, three times as long as the earlier one. It was an astonishing engineering feat, achieved at great personal cost to the Duke, who had not only to pay for the construction, but to compensate landowners whose land had been acquired by compulsory purchase. He reduced his own spending to that of a modest worker,

* Not to be confused with Rachel Lady Russell, her grandmother.

with enough to live and eat (he did not bother much with clothing), and Brindley accepted a fee of just one guinea a week. Nearly a quarter of a million pounds was spent on the construction, but ultimately the canals were so successful they yielded the Duke an income of £80,000 a year. The Bridgwater canal still serves the country; it was bought by the Manchester Ship Canal Co. in 1890 for £1,710,000.

Personally, the Duke was rather odd. He would talk about nothing but canals, and he never wrote a letter unless he absolutely had to. He paid no heed to what he was wearing, was utterly careless of his appearance, and despised those who were correspondingly careful. He had few friends. After the Gunning episode, he became a resolute misogynist, not even allowing a woman servant to wait on him. He accumulated a priceless collection of paintings, which passed to the Duke of Sutherland, his brother-in-law, and has since been dispersed. So much contempt did he have for any embellishment, for anything pretty and ornamental as opposed to merely useful, that one day, finding some flowers had been planted in his garden, he whipped off their heads with his stick and ordered them to be rooted up.[1]

The dukedom was extinct with his death in 1803, but the earldom passed to a nephew, who was even more eccentric than his uncle.

The 8th and last Earl of Bridgwater (1756–1829), also named Francis Egerton, lived alone in a house on the rue St Honoré in Paris, which he referred to as the Hotel Egerton. He was unmarried, but surrounded by friends, none of whom, however, did he select from the human species. The house was filled to overflowing with cats and dogs, which he picked up on the streets and invited to share his home. There were at least fifteen dogs, many of which were frequently observed driving through the streets of Paris in a carriage with four horses and attended by footmen. They shared his meals with him, at his dining-table, dressed up as people, with napkins round their necks, and each with a liveried footman standing behind. Bridgwater's bootmaker had a constant order to supply boots for the dogs, as well as for himself – he never wore the same pair twice in a year, there were never less than 365 pairs of boots ready for him. If any one of the dogs misbehaved himself at dinner, he was the next day banished to the servants' quarters, where he ate his meal dressed in livery until he repented. The garden was stocked with rabbits, and with pigeons and partridges whose wings were clipped to allow his lordship the sport of killing a few for his dinner. In his will, a strange document, he made a number of legacies to his servants with the instruction that such legacies were to be regarded as void if he should be "assassinated or poisoned".[2] The dogs inherited nothing.

When his dentist, Monsieur Chemans, happened to reveal that his little son had been stricken with scarlet fever, Bridgwater rushed out of the room, stripped naked, and threw his clothes on the fire to escape contamination. The servants were commanded to do the same.

Bridgwater spent his time writing dozens of eccentric books, now unavailable for the most part except in the British Museum. They show a learned man whose intelligence degenerated into whimsy. His name is remembered for one bequest in the will, an endowment of £8000 to be given to those authors who would write the most satisfactory essays on "the Power, Wisdom, and Goodness of God, as manifested in His Creation". These subsequently were known as the "Bridgwater Treatises".

Even more crazy than Bridgwater was the Mad Duchess of Albemarle (1654–1734), born Elizabeth Cavendish, a daughter of the Duke of Newcastle in the Cavendish line, and thereby descended from Bess of Hardwick and distantly related to both the Devonshires and the Portlands. She married first Christopher Monck, 2nd Duke of Albemarle on 30th December 1669, when she was fifteen years old, and her bridgegroom sixteen. At first her tantrums gave no serious cause for alarm, but her mind showed signs of being unhinged before she was thirty. She rarely seemed to know what she was saying or doing, with the result that an excursion with her into society was an embarrassment. There are some letters written by her at this young age, now among the Buccleuch papers, which make no sense whatever unless one considers them the ravings of a maniac. Poor Albemarle was driven to drink by the strain of it all, and died at the age of thirty-five in 1688, when his wife had been mad for about six years.

Demented though she was, the Duchess was still a prize to be sought. There was no heir to the Albemarle fortune, a fact not lost on noble suitors who lined up to make her happy, affecting to turn a blind eye to her goings-on. She was now living in seclusion, looked after by two ageing doctors and a pair of conniving sisters, Mary and Sarah Wright. She had moreover descended to such depths of insanity that she made it known she would not deign to consider any second husband unless he was a crowned head. Amazingly enough, there was a man whose greed was so much greater than his pride as to allow him to woo under these conditions. Ralph Montagu, a relation of the Manchester family, presented himself to the mad Duchess as the Emperor of China, was accepted by her to gratify the dying wish of her father Newcastle, and was married to her in a ceremony befitting her new rank. Everyone involved took part in the deception, and to her dying day she thought she was Empress of China and was served on the knee accordingly.

No sooner was Ralph established in the Empress's Palace (renamed Montagu House, which is now the British Museum), than he petitioned the King, William III, to grant him a dukedom in a truly grovelling letter. In due time, he was created Duke of Montagu, which incidentally, though she did not know it, made Elizabeth Cavendish a double duchess, the first of three women so distinguished in our peerage history (the other two being Elizabeth Gunning – Hamilton and Argyll, and Louise von Alten – Manchester and Devonshire).

The new marriage produced nothing but trouble for the Duke of Montagu. A less determined man might well have collapsed under the weight of endless lawsuits concerning the Albemarle property, but he simply bribed his witnesses to perjure themselves in order that he might hang on to the £7000 a year which was his due from the Duchess. Since no one had seen her for years, it was bruited that she had died and that Montagu was concealing her death from the world so that his ill-gotten gains might continue. He was eventually obliged by special Act of Parliament to produce her in public. Meanwhile, she was declared a lunatic, unable to manage her affairs, and removed to a house where she could be looked after more carefully. "Only by dint of the most cunning artifices was she induced to transfer the seat of her imperial throne from Bloomsbury to Clerkenwell."[3]

Not before having the last laugh, however. The Duke of Montagu, for all his cunning, was not clever enough to outlive her. He died in 1709, prompting a reflection which must have been shared by many. "For my part I'm apt to think he could have foreseen, or rather believed at what a distance this present world and he would soon have been, he for the honour sake of his family would discreetly have knock'd her Ladyship on the head in good time."[4]

She lived to the age of eighty, though she was popularly believed to be ninety-six when she died.

To go back one generation in the Albemarle line, one finds that the 1st Duke, General George Monck, also made a curious marriage. While he was a prisoner in the Tower of London in 1646, he made the acquaintance of a common slattern called Anne Clarges, who was occasionally employed at the prison as visiting sempstress. It was in such a capacity, no doubt, that she came into contact with the

Duke, and before long he made her his mistress as well. The daughter of a farrier in the Strand, sister of an apothecary, and wife of a milliner, Anne was engaged in the selling of perfumes and wash-balls. By all accounts, her sweet-smelling employment did little to alleviate the unwholesomeness of her person. She was popularly known as "Dirty Bess" and Pepys called her, in a relatively kind moment, a "plain, homely dowdy" or, less tolerantly, "the veryest slut and drudge and the foulest worde that can be spoken of a woman almost".[5]

After his release from prison, the Duke and Anne lived together as man and wife for about seven years, eventually marrying on 23rd January 1653, presumably because she was pregnant. She gave birth to Christopher Monck, the 2nd Duke of Albemarle, in an attic over a tailor's shop seven months later.

To say that she did not fit easily into the aristocratic life would be an understatement. Everyone was appalled. Clarendon wrote that the Duke was "cursed, after long familiarity, to marry a woman of the lowest extraction, the least wit, and less beauty". Pepys nicknamed her "the Monkey Duchess", and agreed that beauty was not among her attributes; she was "a damned ill-looked woman". After dining with the couple, he went home to write of "dirty dishes, and a nasty wife at table, and bad meat".[6] She was also commonly suspected of avarice and extortion. In short, Anne Clarges had positively nothing to recommend her; her vulgar habits and her ignorance brought derision upon the Duke.

Worse was to follow. Her first husband, the milliner, was a man called Thomas Radford, whom she married in 1633, when she was seventeen. It now appeared that there was no evidence whatever to indicate that he was dead, as she claimed. If this were true, then her marriage to Albemarle was null and void, and her son Christopher, the 2nd Duke, was a bastard. All this affected the Duke of Montagu rather closely, because if Christopher Monck was illegitimate, then his mad duchess wife would not be entitled to the Albermarle fortune, and Montagu's dreadful marriage would have been in vain. None of the questions had been raised until both dukes of Albermarle were safely dead, but eventually the whole matter had to be aired in a noisy trial before Lord Chief Justice Holt on the King's Bench. Several witnesses were brought forward to testify that they had seen Thomas Radford after his alleged death, but as no one could produce him in the flesh the jury decided that "Dirty Bess" had legally become Duchess of Albemarle after all.

The dukedom has been extinct since 1689; there is an earldom of

Albemarle, dating from 1696, which continues in the Keppel family, descendants of William III's friend who supplanted Bentinck.

Anne Clarges was by no means the only working-class girl to become a duchess. We have seen before that many a duke has felt an irresistible attraction towards ladies of what they would call "low birth", sometimes resulting in the most unlikely marriages. Often such wives have been chosen from among the ranks of actresses, such as Harriot Mellon, who became Duchess of St Albans in 1827, May Yohé in 1894, who would have become Duchess of Newcastle but for her divorce, May Etheridge – Duchess of Leinster in 1922 (married 1913), and Marianne de Malkhazouny – Duchess of Leeds in 1933 and living today. Rarely have these marriages proved successful but a romatic exception is offered by the example of Lavinia Fenton and the Duke of Bolton in the eighteenth century.

The 3rd Duke of Bolton (1685–1754) had been a single-minded turbulent youth even at school, disobedient of authority and eager to follow his own ideas and inclinations in the face of what was expected of him in the way of ducal behaviour. He did his duty in marrying a pleasant and virtuous woman, but he did not happen to like her, and was not about to pretend that he did. "My Lord made her an early confession of his aversion", wrote Lady Mary Montague in 1714. He then embarked on a life as a handsome libertine about town, until one day he went to see *The Beggar's Opera* and fell irrevocably in love with the leading actress, Lavinia Fenton.

Lavinia was a pretty little Cockney girl, the illegitimate daughter of Mrs Fenton by a man called Beswick, who disappeared from view. Her parents ran a coffee house at Charing Cross, frequented by *habitués* of the theatre, called "humming beaux", who were charmed by the ease with which Lavinia would entertain them singing songs from the shows they loved. Her beautiful voice and perfect pitch soon brought her to public attention and eventually on to the stage in 1726, in *The Beaux' Stratagem*. She was an immediate success. "She became the talk of the coffee houses, the most celebrated toast in town. Her face, her form, her grace, her voice, her archness, her simplicity, were lauded alike on all hands."[7] On 29th January 1728 she created the part of Polly Peachum in *The Beggar's Opera*, and was thereafter the rage. The theatre was crowded every night. Lavinia Fenton was more famous than the opera itself. Admirers guarded her nightly on her walk home from the theatre. Her portrait appeared on ladies' fans. It was not that her voice was particularly well-trained or operatically pure, but her style and charm caught the imagination. Known to her fans as "Pretty Polly", she played in

The Beggar's Opera sixty-two times, giving her final performance on 19th June 1728, after which she retired from the stage, at the age of twenty.

The reason for her sudden decision was no secret. She had been wooed and won by the forty-three-year-old gallant who watched her from his box night after night, the Duke of Bolton. That same year they ran away together, and she spent the next twenty-three years as his mistress, with an annual settlement from him of £400. They had three sons, none of whom could inherit the dukedom, being illegitimate, and they never ceased to be happy. Her conversation, wit, and discreet conduct were much admired. Four weeks after his estranged wife died in 1751, he made Lavinia Duchess of Bolton in a ceremony at Aix-de-Provence. He died in 1754, leaving everything to "my dear and well-beloved wife", having made generous settlements on his family during his lifetime. Lavinia died in 1760. The dukedom passed to his brothers and nephew, finally becoming extinct in 1794.

Much less fortunate was the marriage made by the Duke of Kingston with Elizabeth Chudleigh in 1796, eventually giving rise to the most notorious aristocratic scandal of the eighteenth century. Elizabeth Chudleigh started life in misfortune. The poor daughter of Colonel Thomas Chudleigh, Lieutenant-Governor of Chelsea Hospital, who died when she was six, she left London with no prospects of improvement. As she grew into adolescence, she became aware that her one capital was her beauty. Her first love affair is said to have occurred when she was fifteen years old. When she was twenty, she was noticed by the Earl of Bath, who took an interest in her and brought her back to London, securing for her an appointment as Maid of Honour to Augusta, Princess of Wales. An early instance of her impudence and wit is afforded by the story of her response to the Princess who saw fit to reproach Elizabeth for her flirting. As the Princess was at the time engaged in a clandestine affair with Lord Bute, Elizabeth Chudleigh was not ready to accept blandishments from that quarter. *"Votre Altesse Royale sait que chacune a son But,"* she said.

The lustful Duke of Hamilton, then nineteen, fell in love with her on sight, but had to leave almost immediately for the obligatory grand tour of Europe. He wrote to her regularly from the continent, intending to make her his duchess on his return, but his letters were intercepted and never delivered to her. Faced with what he thought was deliberate discouragement, his ardour cooled. He afterwards married Elizabeth Gunning.

She, meanwhile, thinking Hamilton had betrayed his word, married someone else in an attack of peevishness. At Winchester races, she had met Augustus Hervey, son of Lord Hervey and grandson of the Earl of Bristol, and on a sudden impulse they married secretly at Lainston chapel on 4th August 1744. The reason for the secrecy was simple : they were both poor, and she could not afford to lose her position as Maid of Honour. The cat was nearly out of the bag when she gave birth to a boy in 1746, baptised in Chelsea as Henry Augustus, son of Augustus Hervey; the child lived only a few weeks. Even this she contrived somehow to keep secret. Later that year, she and Augustus separated once and for all, both conveniently forgetting that they were husband and wife.

At the court of Princess Augusta, "Miss Chudleigh" continued to flaunt convention with lewd speech and frankly enticing behaviour. In a less permissive age she would have been quickly dismissed. She "concentrated her rhetoric into swearing, and dressed in a style next door to nakedness".[8] Not surprisingly, men clustered around her in a heat of aroused libido, to which her vulgar ways acted as a spur of extra spice. The Duke of Ancaster wanted to marry her, even George II made no bones about his love for her; the King made her mother housekeeper at Windsor, and gave her an allowance from his personal funds.

Suddenly, the whole farcical kaleidoscope made a desperate shift when Augustus Hervey came closer to inheriting the earldom of Bristol. Elizabeth thought it would be wise to protect her future by establishing the marriage in the registry at Lainston, without yet making it public knowledge. This she did in 1759, at the same time taking the Duke of Kingston as her lover. It was a notorious liaison, as her behaviour was becoming more and more objectionable, her language richer. She gave splendid balls, and fell down drunk as often as not in their midst. Her life was one of sordid dissipation.

Augustus Hervey was now wanting to marry again. Before he could divorce Elizabeth, however, he had to prove that he was married to her, in which endeavour she was by no means willing to cooperate. She was nevertheless in a quandary. She did not want the scandal of a divorce, but she *did* want to be free of Hervey so that she could marry the Duke of Kingston. The pair of them agreed therefore that she should bring a suit of jactitation against him, to which he would make a merely token defence. This was to say that she would sue him for having falsely boasted of a marriage in such a way as to make people think that such a marriage had taken place, and thereby bring disrepute upon her. The case was heard before the consistory court, she taking the oath that she was not married, and the court accordingly declared her a spinster on 11th February 1769, at the same time imposing silence on Hervey. On 8th March following, Elizabeth Chudleigh became Duchess of Kingston.

Four years later her duke died (on 23rd September 1773) leaving her his real estate for life and his personal possessions in perpetuity, on one condition – that she should remain a widow. This was rendered embarrassingly difficult for her to comply with by virtue of her first marriage, which refused to be swept aside. Hervey wished to reopen the case, and now the Duke of Kingston's family wished to stalk its prey. The Duke's nephew, Mr Evelyn Meadows, charged the Duchess with bigamy, causing a bill of indictment to be drawn up against her. On hearing this she hurred back from Rome (getting some money for the journey at the point of a gun from a terrified bank manager) to prepare her defence. Nothing went right for her. With consummate theatrical timing, the Earl of Bristol then died, and Augustus Hervey succeeded his brother in the title, making Miss Chudleigh a genuine Countess as well as a bogus Duchess. The combination of events drew all eyes upon her, satirists lampooned her, and her trial was awaited with predatory glee by the gossips.

The five-day proceedings began on 15th April 1776, in Westminster Hall before the peers. During the course of a fascinating trial, evidence was given by Anne Craddock, who had for long been in the Duchess's service, by the widow of the Lainston rector who had performed the first marriage service, and various others. Everything was laid bare to public scrutiny, the wedding, the birth and death of a child, the registration of marriage to Hervey, and details of character. Elizabeth came out of the ordeal very badly. The case was clearly proven against her, and was duly found guilty of bigamy by a unanimous verdict of the peers; the scene in which the peers rose from their seats, one after the other, monotonously intoning the one word "Guilty", is justly famous. The spurious Duchess would have had the palm of her hand burnt for the offence, had she not pleaded the privilege of her rank. She was allowed to keep her fortune, the fruit of her duplicity.

Augustus Hervey, Earl of Bristol, died in 1779. The dukedom of Kingston had been extinct since 1773. As for Elizabeth, now legally Countess of Bristol, she went to St Petersburg, where she bought a large estate, which she called "Chudleigh", and later to France. Wherever she wandered, scandal followed in her wake. Her manners remained coarse, her habits disgusting, to the end. She died in Paris in 1788, at the age of sixty-eight. She will always have the distinction of having shocked an unshockable age.

Half a century later, in a less tolerant age, a woman risen "from the ranks" as it were, could not expect to slide so easily into the top drawer. Values were different, and not necessarily better. One such woman was Elizabeth Russell, daughter of a market gardener, Robert Russell, of Burmiston, Yorkshire. She has been described as a washerwoman,[9] with language and manners to match; slang was her only means of intelligible communication. After having been the discarded mistress of the Duke of Bedford, and a mistress of Mr Coutts the banker (Harriot Mellon's first husband), she became Duchess of Cleveland on 27th July 1813, at the age of thirty-six. She was the Duke's second wife; he, incidentally, was Duke of Cleveland of a new creation, vested in the Vane family, but he was related to the wicked Barbara Villiers who bore the same title – she was his great-great-aunt. Contemporaries professed to be astonished that he should choose this infamous title, a bastard descent from an unpleasant adultress, rather than his own ancient and distinguished title of Darlington, in which name he already held an earldom. Anyway, the new Duchess of Cleveland, who addressed her husband as "Niffy-Naffy", and in later years was to refer to her son Lord Harry Vane as "My 'arry", was presented to a dubious world just emerging from the licentious age of the Georgians, dusting their morals and readjusting their values.

Creevey called her a "brazen-faced Pop", and thought the marriage "the wickedest thing I ever heard of", though he confessed she was something of a miracle to have pulled it off.[10] She even managed to retain the allowance from her lover the Duke of Bedford after her wedding. People tolerated her impudence with a stretched smile for the sake of her likeable and generous husband, whose wine-glasses were made without a stem, to oblige you to drink each glass at a throw.

She died a respectable old lady in 1861, in an elegant house in Grosvenor Square. Her husband's three sons each succeeded him in the title, but all died without male issue, so that the title was extinct with the 4th Duke of Cleveland in 1891. The present Lord Barnard is the modern representative of the Vanes, and lives still in their ancestral home, Raby Castle; another branch is represented by Vane-Tempest-Stewart, Marquess of Londonderry, until 1987 at neighbouring Wynyard.

An amusing contrast to the washerwoman Duchess was a later Duchess of Cleveland (1792–1883) who was so intolerant of any departure from etiquette that guests went in fear of saying the wrong thing at the wrong time. She was stiff and precise in her speech, and positively loathed the use of Christian names. Only one person dared to tease her, and that, not surprisingly, was a son of the Duke of Richmond, Lord Henry Lennox. He used to delight in irritating the old woman by using the latest slang, which made her wince with displeasure. "May I enquire, Lord Henry," she said, "whether, when you have completely mastered the language of the servants' hall, you mean to adopt its manners as well?"[11]

There is one dukedom which, though extinct by reason of attainder, is still used by the descendants of the grantee. This is the dukedom of Berwick, bestowed by James II on his illegitimate son by Arabella Churchill – James Fitzjames (1670–1734).

The Duke of Berwick had an extraordinary career. With his grandfather Charles I's handsome features, and the resilience of the Churchills, he was set for a brilliant military career in England. But he fled to France with his father, and in 1691 joined the French Army. (He had, as it happens, been born in France.) By 1693 he had risen as far as lieutenant-general, and in 1703 he became a naturalised Frenchman, in order to be eligible for the ultimate accolade of Marshal of France, which he received in 1706. In all, he served in twenty-nine campaigns, and commanded in fifteen of them, on the opposite side to his uncle, the Duke of Marlborough. He fought one battle, Almanza in 1706, "the only battle recorded in which an English general at the head of a French army defeated an English army commanded by a Frenchman".[12] (The Frenchman was Henri de Ruvigny.)

Berwick's end was ignominious; his head was blown off by a cannon-ball, producing national grief in France, where he was a hero, and relief in England, where he was an embarrassment. His title had already been attainted in 1695, a fact which has in no way deterred his descendants.

His son by the first marriage was made Duke of Liria in Spain, and a son by his second marriage was granted the dukedom of Fitzjames in France. There were descendants of both lines in both countries, but none in England, though the title was originally of English blood royal. The dukedom of Fitzjames has since died out, but the Duke of Liria continues, vested in a Spanish family which prefers to use its superior title of Duke of Alba, and, on occasion, Duke of Berwick. The "Duke of Berwick" in Victoria's time was allowed to use that title on a visit to Windsor, and the late 17th Duke, a personal friend of Winston Churchill, liked to be known as "Duque di Berwick y Alba".

The titles are currently held by Maria Rosario Cayetana Fitzjames

Stuart y Silva, Duchess of Alba, Duchess of Liria and Xerica, Duchess of Montoro, Duchess of Arjona, Duchess of Hijar, Duchess of Olivares, and with no less than forty-three separate other titles, some irresistibly musical, like Marchioness of San Leonardo and La Lota, and Countess of Miranda del Castanor. She lists Duchess of Berwick as her second title, apparently in disregard of its non-existence. Were the attainder ever to be reversed (as it is in the power of the Queen to do), the title would legally go to the *heir male*, Fernando Alfonso Fitzjames Stuart y Saavedra, Duke of Pen-aranda de Bracamonte.

There is even a suspicion that the 1st Duke was never really attainted at all, except verbally, which would not be conclusive; in this case, the claim might well be upheld.[13]

We were reminded how abruptly a title may cease due to failure in the male line with the death in 1963 of John Francis Godolphin Osborne, 11th Duke of Leeds (1901–1963), and the final closing of a story which started with a show of gallantry.

A successful merchant and clothworker called William Hewett had one of the houses on old London Bridge. His infant daughter Anne was being fondled by her nurse, when the careless woman dropped her into the Thames below. A young man was passing, saw what happened, and leapt immediately into the current to save the child. His name was Richard Osborne of Ashford, Kent, and as a result of this gesture, was taken on by Hewett as apprentice clothworker. A working-class lad, he may never have had the opportunity to train for such a position were it not for his impulsive dive. Eventually he married the daughter. As Hewett had no sons, all his ambition was concentrated on his son-in-law, who he intended would one day benefit from his success. The eldest son of Richard Osborne and Anne Hewett was Sir Edward Osborne, Lord Mayor of London in 1583, and two generations later this unknown family had reached the dukedom, with the most famous of the Osbornes, known to history as "Danby".

Danby (1632–1712) was a wily individual, one of those clever politicians England produces from time to time, able to manipulate supporters and seduce objectors. He is generally thought to have been dishonest, in so far as he accepted bribes and indulged in forgery, but such habits did not make him exceptional in Restoration England. From 1673 to 1678 he was Lord High Treasurer of England, and Chief Minister to Charles II, during which time he virtually governed the country single-handed and had to grapple with the balance of payments headaches which have become such a feature of modern political life. Although he was in control, he exercised much diplomatic skill in fostering the impression that the King took all decisions. The events leading up to his impeachment are too complex to warrant examination here, but that he should be charged with treason was manifestly absurd, for he had the King's written approval for his actions. None the less, he languished five years in the Tower, his cleverness for once deserting him, without reaching trial. The impeachment was later reversed, and he returned to the peers. Danby was active in the Revolution, being one of the signatories who invited William of Orange to assume the crown, and was duly rewarded by a grateful William III. The Earl of Danby became Marquess of Carmarthen in 1689 and Duke of Leeds in 1694.

The Osborne descendants never reached the heights of power attained by Danby. The 7th Duke of Leeds has the distinction of being one of the first members of the peerage to choose an American heiress for a wife, as early as 1828, when the United States of America had been in existence barely fifty years. He was then known as Marquess of Carmarthen, and his wife, *née* Louisa Caton, of Maryland, was known as Lady Hervey, by virtue of her first marriage. She was one of three Caton sisters who all married into the English aristocracy, the other two becoming Lady Wellesley and Lady Stafford. Lady Holland's horrified comments are preserved. "The marriage of Lord Carmarthen and Lady Hervey has taken place", she wrote. "The Duke of Leeds bears it quietly on account of the Duchess for whom he dreads agitation. He is, however, deeply mortified; and his friends have no consolation to offer but the improbability of her having any children. The second son is a fine young man, and just what such a father would be proud of; so if these consolations are valid, all will be right. They say Lady Hervey wanted six qualifications, youth, beauty, character, fortune, birth, sense."[14]

The Dukes of Leeds were on the whole good men. At a time when some seats in the House of Commons were still in the gift of the aristocracy, and pressure could be exerted on others, it is unusual to hear said, as the Duke of Leeds said in 1848, "I have particularly assured my tenants that I will not in any way interfere with their opinions in the choice of their representatives."[15]

It is interesting also that the Leeds house was the heirs of line to the dukedom of Marlborough; in the event of the male Spencer line, descended from the Earl of Sunderland who married a Churchill daughter, failing, the title would pass by terms of the patent to the heirs of another daughter, who became Duchess of Leeds.

To such an inheritance John Francis Osborne ("Jack") succeeded in 1927; it was not a spectacular history, but an honourable record of quiet public service and a decent acceptance of the role of landed aristocrats. The family home was Hornby Castle in Yorkshire. Jack was the son of the 10th Duke and Lady Katherine Lambton, was educated at Eton and Jesus College, Cambridge, and moved in literary and theatrical circles. He was a shy man, shunning public attention, and making no capital of his ducal rank. The only occasion when he was pursued by the press was when he sold the Goya portrait of ·Wellington at Sotheby's in 1961, for £140,000.

In 1960 the Duke had suffered the amputation of a leg, made necessary by a disease which attacked the artery. The following year his other leg was removed, and he spent the last months in acute pain. He died on 26th July 1963, leaving a daughter by the second of three marriages, Lady Camilla, the last representative of gallant Richard Osborne and the last person to bear his name. She is now married to the journalist, Nigel Dempster.

The dukedom did in fact pass briefly to a cousin living in Rome, Sir Francis d'Arcy Godolphin Osborne, aged seventy-nine, who for a few months revelled in being a duke, until he too died early in 1964, reducing the number of dukedoms of the realm to the present total of twenty-six disparate individuals, united, in a democratic age, by the one dubious remaining privilege of superior rank.

REFERENCES

1. D.N.B.
2. Timbs, *English Eccentrics and Eccentricities*, Vol. I, p. 111; *Gentleman's Magazine*, 1829, pp. 558–60.
3. Bernard Falk *The Way of the Montagues*, p 151.
4. Ann Hadley to Abigail Harley, 16th March, 1710, in Portland Papers, quoted in E. F. Ward, *Christopher Monck, Duke of Albermarle*, pp. 349–50.
5. Pepys *Diary*, 8th March 1661; 25th February 1666.
6. *ibid.*, 9th December 1665; 4th April 1667.
7. D.N.B.
8. *Complete Peerage.*
9. Augustus Hare, *In My Solitary Life*, p. 149.
10. Creevey *Papers*, pp. 86–7, 92.
11. *Leaves from the Notebooks* of Lady Dorothy Nevill, p. 36.

12. D.N.B.
13. *Complete Peerage*, Vol. XII, Part ii, Appendix H.
14. *Lady Holland to Her Son*, p. 82.
15. F. M. L. Thompson, *English Landed Society in the Nineteenth Century*, p. 201.

Bibliographical notes

A. PEERAGE HISTORY AND GENEALOGY

The Complete Peerage, edited by G. E. Cockayne.
Burke's *Peerage, Baronetage and Knightage*.
Collin's *Peerage*, edited by Brydges.
Debrett's *Peerage*.
Valentine Heywood, *British Titles* (1953).
J. H. Round, *Studies in the Peerage* (1901).

B. HISTORICAL BACKGROUND

Dictionary of National Biography (D.N.B. in reference notes).
Reports of the Historical Manuscripts Commission (*Hist. MSS. Comm.*)
T. B. Macaulay, *History of England* (1906).
G. Burnett, *History of His Own Time* (1897–1900).
H. Walpole, *Memoirs of the Reign of George II* (1846).
H. Walpole, *Memoirs of the Reign of George III* (1845).
Broughton, *Recollections of a Long Life* (1909).
Reresby, *Memoirs* (1735).
C. Greville, *Memoirs*, ed Roger Fulford & Lytton Strachey, 8 Vols., (1938).
Sir N. W. Wraxall, *Historical Memoirs of My Own Time*, 1 vol. (1904).
Sir N. W. Wraxall, *Posthumous Memoirs*, 2 vols. (1836).
J. Bateman, *Great Landowners* (1883).
G. Bebbington, *London Street Names* (1972).
F. M. L. Thomson, *English Landed Society in the Nineteenth Century* (1963).
D. Sutherland, *The Landowners* (1968).
Junius, *Letters*, 2 vols. (1797).
James Pope-Hennessey, *Queen Mary* (1959).
Samuel Pepys, *Diary*, ed. Wheatley (1893–9).

T. Creevey, *Papers*, ed. Maxwell (1903).
T. Creevey, *Life and Times*, ed. Gore (1934).
H. Walpole, *Correspondence*, Yale edition, ed. W. S. Lewis. (Cunningham edition of 1891 is used where specified in notes).
J. Evelyn, *Diary*, ed. E. S. de Beer (1955).

C. OTHER MEMOIRS, ANECDOTES, GOSSIP

Journal of Elizabeth Lady Holland, ed. Earl of Ilchester (1908).
Augustus Hare, *The Years with Mother* (1952).
Augustus Hare, *In My Solitary Life* (1953).
Burke's *Romantic Records of the Aristocracy* (1850).
J. Timbs, *English Eccentrics and Eccentricities* (1866).
W. M. Thackeray, *The Four Georges*.
Anita Leslie, *Edwardians in Love* (1972).
E. F. Benson, *As We Were* (1930).
The Duchess of Bedford and James Frère, *Now the Duchesses* (1964).
Lord Hervey and His Friends, ed. Earl of Ilchester (1950).
Lady Holland to Her Son, ed. Earl of Ilchester (1946).
Leaves from the Notebooks of Lady Dorothy Nevill, ed. R. Nevill (1910).
7th Duke of Manchester, *Court and Society from Elizabeth to Anne* (1864).
9th Duke of Manchester, *My Candid Recollections* (1932).
Lord Ernest Hamilton, *The Halycon Era* (1933).
Chips, the diaries of Sir Henry Channon, ed. R. R. James, (1967).
Sylvester Douglas, Lord Glenbervie, *Diary* (1928).
Emma, Lady Brownlow, *Slight Reminiscences of a Septuagenarian* (1867).
5th Duke of Sutherland, *Looking Back* (1957).
6th Duke of Portland, *Men, Women and Things* (1937).
E. Walford, *Old and New London*, 5 vols. (1908).
Harriette Wilson, *Memoirs* (1924).
Lady Frances Balfour, *Ne Oblifiscaris* (1930).
Frances, Countess of Warwick, *Afterthoughts* (1931).
Consuelo Vanderbilt Balsan, *The Glitter and the Gold* (1953).
Margot Asquith, *Autobiography* (1962).
Thomas Raikes, *Journal* (1856).

D. FAMILY HISTORIES

There are many books not mentioned here which nonetheless find their way into the list of acknowledged references at the end of each chapter. The following is a list of suggested reading for those who wish to delve deeper into individual families.

1. Fitzalan-Howard, Duke of Norfolk
   Neville Williams, *Thomas Howard Fourth Duke of Norfolk* (1964).
   Melvyn Tucker, *The Life of Thomas Howard, Second Duke of Norfolk* (1964).
   A Duke of Norfolk Notebook.

2. Seymour, Duke of Somerset
   Harold St Maur, *Annals of the Seymours* (1902).

3. Montagu-Douglas-Scott, Duke of Buccleuch & Queensbury
   Sir W. Fraser, *The Scotts of Buccleuch* (1878).
   Lord George Scott, *Lucy Walter, Wife or Mistress* (1947).
   Elizabeth d'Oyley, *James Duke of Monmouth* (1938).

4. Gordon-Lennox, Duke of Richmond & Gordon & Lennox
   H. Forneron, *Louise de Kérouaille, Duchess of Portsmouth* (1887).
   Jeanine Delpech, *Duchess of Portsmouth* (1953).
   Earl of March, *A Duke and His Friends* (1911).

5. Beauclerk, Duke of St Albans
   P. Cunningham, *The Story of Nell Gwynn* (1903).
   P. Dewar and D. Adamson, *The House of Nell Gwynn* (1974).

6. FitzRoy, Duke of Grafton
   H. Noel William, *Rival Sultanas* (1915).
   Arthur Bryant, *King Charles II* (1931).
   Osmond Airy, *Charles II* (1904).
   Bernard Falk, *The Royal FitzRoys* (1950).

7. Russell, Duke of Bedford
   J. H. Wiffen, *Memoirs of the House of Russell* (1833).
   Christopher Trent, *The Russells* (1966).
   Gladys Scott Thompson, *The Russells in Bloomsbury* (1940).
   Greater London Council, *Survey of London*, Vols. 35 and 36.
   Georgiana Blakiston, *Lord William Russell and His Wife* (1972).

Lord John Russell, *William, Lord Russell* (1820).
12th Duke of Bedford, *The Years of Transition* (1949).
13th Duke of Bedford, *A Silver-plated Spoon* (1959).
13th Duke of Bedford, *The Flying Duchess* (1968).
Gladys Scott Thompson, *Two Centuries of Family History* (1930).

8. Cavendish, Duke of Devonshire
   Francis Bickley, *The Cavendish Family* (1911).
   Vera Foster, *Two Duchesses* (1898).
   H. Leach, *The 8th Duke of Devonshire* (1904).
   Dorothy Stuart, *Dearest Bess* (1955).
   Georgiana, extracts from Correspondence of Georgiana
   Duchess of Devonshire (1955).

9. Cavendish-Bentinck, Duke of Portland
   A. S. Turberville, *History of Welbeck Abbey* (1939).
   Marion E. Grew, *William Bentinck and William III* (1924).
   Theodore Besterman, *The Druce-Portland Case* (1935).

10. Somerset, Duke of Beaufort
    Horatia Durant, *The Somerset Sequence* (1951).
    Horatio Durant, *Henry 1st Duke of Beaufort and his Duchess Mary* (1953).

11. Spencer-Churchill, Duke of Marlborough
    Winston S. Churchill, *Marlborough* (1933).
    Consuelo Vanderbilt Balsan, *The Glitter and the Gold* (1953).
    Mrs A. Colville, *Duchess Sarah* (1904).

12. Wellesley, Duke of Wellington
    Elizabeth Longford, *Wellington*, 2 vols. (1969, 1972).
    Philip Guedalla, *The Duke* (1931).
    7th Duke of Wellington, *Conversations of the Duke of Wellington with George William Chad* (1956).

13. Percy, Duke of Northumberland
    E. H. de Fonblanque, *Annals of the House of Percy* (1887).
    M. M. Merrick, *Thomas Percy, 7th Earl* (1949).
    Earl Percy, *Letters from Boston and New York* (1902).
    Earl of Northumberland, *Advice to His Son* (1930).
    8th Duke of Northumberland, *The Shadow on the Moor* (1931).

Index